P9-DED-162

Contents

Readings in
Deviant Behavior

Readings in Deviant Behavior

Alex Thio
Thomas C. Calhoun
Ohio University

HarperCollins*CollegePublishers*

Acquisitions Editor: Alan McClare
Project Editor: Ellen MacElree
Design Manager: Lucy Krikorian
Text and Cover Designer: John Callahan
Art Studio: Vantage Art, Inc.
Electronic Production Manager: Su Levine
Desktop Administrator: Laura Leever
Manufacturing Manager: Willie Lane
Electronic Page Makeup: John Callahan
Printer and Binder: R.R. Donnelley & Sons Company
Cover Printer: The Lehigh Press, Inc.

Readings in Deviant Behavior

Library of Congress Cataloging-in-Publication Data

Readings in deviant behavior / [edited by] Alex Thio and Thomas C. Calhoun.
    p.   cm.
  Includes index.
  ISBN 0-673-99261-6
  1. Deviant behavior. I. Thio, Alex.   II. Calhoun, Thomas C.
HM291.R385 1995
302.5'42--dc20

     97 98 9 8 7 6 5 4 3

Preface

This is a comprehensive reader. Unlike other editors, we have shied away from using only one theoretical approach in selecting articles for this anthology. Instead, we have chosen a great variety of readings that represent the full range of deviance sociology. We believe that students should know different, conflicting theories of deviance. They should also know different kinds of data, which are collected with different research methodologies.

This reader covers all the major theories in deviance sociology, from classic ones such as Merton's strain theory and Becker's labeling theory to modern ones such as Braithwaite's shaming theory and Katz's phenomenological theory. In addition, this reader encompasses a wide range of deviant behaviors. There are articles on deviances that have long attracted sociological attention, such as homicide, drug abuse, prostitution, and organized crime. There are also articles on deviances that have only recently leapt into public and sociological consciousness, such as eating disorders, date rape, therapist-client sex, exotic dancing, using the suicide machine, and listening to heavy metal or rap music. Analyses of these subjects rely on data from theory-informed research that runs the gamut from survey to ethnographic studies. All these analyses are multidisciplinary, coming not only from sociologists but also from scholars and researchers in other fields. They all effectively reflect what the sociology of deviance is like today; vibrant, wide-ranging, and stimulating.

This is also a user-friendly reader—it has been put together with student needs in mind. The articles are not only authoritative but are also interesting. Many were chosen from different kinds of books, journals, and magazines. Some were solicited from well-known or well-qualified sociologists and researchers. Most important, all these articles have been carefully edited for clarity and conciseness. Students will therefore find them easy and enjoyable to read.

We would like to thank all the colleagues who specifically wrote for this reader. Our deep gratitude also goes to all those writers whose published works are presented here. Further deserving our thanks are the following reviewers, who have contributed greatly to the development of a truly useful and student-oriented reader: David O. Friedrichs, University of Scranton; Peter B. Morrill, Bronx Community College; John H. Newman, Indiana University Southeast; James Thomas, Northern Illinois University; and Kenrick S. Thompson, Northern Michigan University. We would also like to thank our graduate assistant, Debra Cabrera, for efficiently securing permissions and performing other tasks for the book. Finally, but equally important, numerous undergraduates in our deviance classes have read this anthology, helping to ensure that the selections are both readable and interesting. We want to express our sincere gratitude to all of them, particularly Aaron Fogt, Constance Jones, Douglas Ropp, Sharon Stephan, and Steven Stroud.

Alex Thio
Thomas C. Calhoun

About the Editors

ALEX THIO

Alex Thio is Professor of Sociology at Ohio University. Born of Chinese parentage in Penang, Malaysia, he grew up in a multicultural environment. He acquired fluency in Mandarin (modern standard Chinese), two Chinese dialects (Fukienese and Hakka), Malay, and Indonesian. He also picked up a smattering of English and Dutch.

Professor Thio attended primary school in Malaysia and high school in Indonesia. While in junior high, after two Indonesian soldiers plundered his home and killed his father and sister, he started to think about coming to the United States. After arriving in this country, he first worked his way through Central Methodist College in Missouri. Later he did graduate work in sociology at the State University of New York at Buffalo, where he completed his doctorate while working as a research and teaching assistant.

Dr. Thio regularly teaches courses on introductory sociology, deviance, social problems, and criminology. In addition to teaching, he enjoys writing. He has written many articles and is the author of three popular texts: *Deviant Behavior, Sociology: An Introduction,* and *Sociology: A Brief Introduction,* all published by HarperCollins.

THOMAS C. CALHOUN

Thomas Calhoun is Assistant Professor of Sociology at Ohio University. Born and reared in rural Mississippi, he attended segregated schools and witnessed many civil rights activities of the 1960s. He received his B.A. in sociology from Texas Wesleyan College, M.A. from Texas Tech University, and Ph.D. from the University of Kentucky.

Dr. Calhoun teaches courses in deviant behavior, juvenile delinquency, community-based corrections, and introduction to sociology. He has written a number of articles, which appear in journals such as *Sociological Spectrum* and *Sociological Inquiry.* He also enjoys teaching, having won the University Professor's Award given by students at Ohio University and the Outstanding Teacher Award presented by the University's College of Arts and Sciences.

Introduction

What is deviant behavior? But why ask what it is? Doesn't everybody know it has to do with weirdos and perverts? Not at all. There is, in fact, a great deal of disagreement among people as to what they consider deviant. In a classic study, sociologist Jerry Simmons asked a sample of the general public who they thought was deviant. They mentioned 252 different kinds of people as deviants, including homosexuals, prostitutes, alcoholics, drug addicts, murderers, the mentally ill, communists, atheists, liars, Democrats, reckless drivers, self-pitiers, the retired, career women, divorcees, Christians, suburbanites, movie stars, perpetual bridge players, prudes, pacifists, psychiatrists, priests, liberals, conservatives, junior executives, girls who wear makeup, smart-aleck students, and know-it-all professors. If you are surprised that some of these people are considered deviant, your surprise simply adds to the fact that a good deal of disagreement exists among the public as to the conception of deviant behavior.

There is a similar lack of consensus among sociologists. We could say that the study of deviant behavior is probably the most "deviant" of all the subjects in sociology. Sociologists disagree more over the definition of deviant behavior than they do on any other subject.

CONFLICTING DEFINITIONS

Some sociologists simply say that deviance is a violation of any social rule, but others argue that deviance involves more than rule violation—it also has the quality of provoking disapproval, anger, or indignation. Some advocate a broader definition, arguing that a person can be a deviant *without* violating any rule or doing something that rubs others the wrong way. According to this argument, individuals who are afflicted with some unfortunate condition for which they cannot be held responsible are deviant. Examples include psychotics, paraplegics, the mentally retarded, and other physically or mentally disabled persons. These people are considered deviant because they are disvalued by society. In contrast, some sociologists contend that deviance does not have to be negative. To these sociologists, deviance can be positive, such as being a genius, reformer, creative artist, or glamorous celebrity. But other

1

sociologists disagree, considering "positive deviance" to be an oxymoron, a contradiction in terms.

All these sociologists apparently assume that, whether it is a positive or negative, disturbing or disvalued behavior or condition, deviance is real in and of itself. The logic behind this assumption is that if it is not real in the first place, it cannot be considered positive, negative, disturbing, or disvalued. But other sociologists disagree, arguing that deviance does not have to be a real behavior or condition for it to be labeled deviant. People can be falsely accused of being criminal, erroneously diagnosed as mentally ill, stereotyped as dangerous because of their skin color, and so on. Conversely, committing a deviant act does not necessarily make the person a deviant, especially when the act is kept secret. It is, therefore, the label "deviant"—not the act itself—that makes the individual deviant.

Some sociologists go beyond the notion of labeling to define deviance by stressing the importance of power. They observe that relatively powerful people are capable of avoiding the fate suffered by the powerless—being falsely, erroneously, or unjustly labeled deviant. The key reason is that the powerful, either by themselves or through influencing public opinion or both, hold more power for labeling others' behavior as deviant. Understandably, sociologists who hold this view define deviance as any act considered by the powerful at a given time and place to be a violation of some social rule.

From this welter of conflicting definitions we can nonetheless discern the influence of two opposing perspectives: positivism and humanism. The positivist perspective is associated with the sciences, such as physics, chemistry, or biology. It influences how scientists see and study their subject. On the other hand, the humanist perspective has to do with the humanities, such as art, language, or philosophy. It affects how scholars in these fields see and study their subject. These two perspectives have long been transported into sociology, so that some sociologists are more influenced by the positivist perspective while others the humanist one. Positivist sociologists tend to define deviance in one way, while humanist sociologists pursue another way. The two perspectives further influence the use of certain theory and methodology for producing knowledge about deviant behavior. The conflicting definitions that we have discussed can be couched in terms of these two perspectives. The definitions that focus on deviance as rule-breaking behavior are essentially positivist, whereas those that center on labeling and power are humanist. Let us delve more deeply into the meanings and implications of these two conflicting perspectives.

CONFLICTING PERSPECTIVES

The knowledge about deviance basically consists of answers to three questions. The questions are: (1) What to study? (2) How to study it? (3) What does the result of the study mean? The first question deals with the *subject* of study, the second has to do with the *method* of study, and the third concerns the data-based *theory* about the subject. Positivism and humanism provide conflicting answers to each question.

Subject: What to Study?

Positivism suggests that we study deviance or deviants. The reason has to do with the positivist's absolutist definition of deviance. According to this definition, deviance is absolutely or intrinsically real in that it possesses some qualities that distinguish it from conventionality. Similarly, deviants are thought to have certain attributes that make them different from conventional individuals. By contrast, humanism suggests that we study law enforcers and other such people who label others as deviants, or how the process of labeling takes place and affects the labeled. This is because the humanist assumes the relativist stance in defining deviance as a label imposed on some behavior. Such a definition can be said to be relativist for implying that the deviancy of a behavior is relative to—dependent on—negative societal reaction to the behavior.

Absolutism: Deviance as Absolutely Real   Around the turn of this century, criminologists believed that criminals possessed certain biological traits that were absent in noncriminals. Those biological traits included defective genes, bumps on the head, a long lower jaw, a scanty beard, an unattractive face, and tough body build. Since all these traits are inherited, people were believed to be criminals simply because they were born criminals. If they were born criminals, they would always be criminals. As the saying goes, "If you've had it, you've had it." So, no matter where they might go—they could go anywhere in the world—they would still be criminals.

Then the criminologists shifted their attention from biological to psychological traits. Criminals were thought to have certain mental characteristics that noncriminals did not have. More specifically, criminals were believed to be feeble-minded, psychotic, neurotic, psychopathic, or otherwise mentally disturbed. Like biological traits, these mental characteristics were seen as inherent in individual criminals. And, like biological traits, mental characteristics would stay with the criminals, no matter where they go. Again, because of these psychological traits, criminals would always remain criminals.

Today's positivist sociologists, however, have largely abandoned the use of biological and psychological traits to differentiate criminals from noncriminals. They recognize the important role of social factors in determining a person's status as a criminal. Such status does not remain the same across time and space; instead, it changes in different periods and with different societies. A polygamist may be a criminal in our society but a noncriminal in Moslem countries. A person who sees things invisible to others may be a psychotic in our society but may become a spiritual leader among some South Pacific tribes. Nevertheless, positivist sociologists still regard deviance as intrinsically real. Countering the relativist notion of deviance as basically a *label* imposed on an act, Travis Hirschi argues: "The person may not have committed a 'deviant' act, but he did (in many cases) do *something*. And it is just possible that what he did was a result of things that had happened to him in the past; it is also possible that the past in some inscrutable way remains with him and that if he were left alone he would *do it again.*" Moreover, countering the relativist notion of mental illness as a label imputed to some people's behavior, Gwynn Nettler explicitly voices his absolutist stance: "Some people *are* more crazy than others; we can tell the difference; and calling lunacy a name does not *cause* it." These positivist sociologists seem to say that just as a rose by any other name would smell as sweet, so deviance by any other label is just as real.

Relativism: Deviance as a Label   Humanists hold the relativist view that deviant behavior by itself does not have any intrinsic characteristics unless it is thought to have those characteristics. The so-called intrinsically deviant characteristics do not come from the behavior itself; they come instead from some people's minds. To put it simply, an act appears deviant only because some people think it so. As Howard Becker says, "Deviant behavior is behavior that people so label." So, no deviant label, no deviant behavior. The existence of deviance depends on the label.

Since they effectively consider deviance unreal, humanists understandably stay away from studying it. They are more interested in the questions of whether and why a given act is defined by society as deviant. This leads to studying people who label others as deviants—such as the police and other law-enforcing agents. If humanists study so-called deviants, they do so by focusing on the nature of labeling and its consequences.

In studying law-enforcing agents, humanists have found a huge lack of consensus on whether a certain person should be treated as a criminal. The police often disagree among themselves as to whether a suspect should be arrested, and judges often disagree whether those arrested should be convicted or acquitted. In addition, since laws vary from one state to another, the same type of behavior may be defined as criminal in one state but not so in another. Prostitution, for example, is legal in Nevada but not in other states. There is, then, a *relativity* principle in deviant behavior; behavior gets defined as deviant relative to a given norm, standard of behavior, or the way people react to it. If it is not related to the norm or to the reaction of other people, a given behavior is in itself meaningless—it is impossible to say whether it is deviant or conforming. Humanists strongly emphasize this relativistic view, according to which, deviance, like beauty, is in the eye of the beholder.

Method: How to Study It?

Positivism suggests that we use objective methods such as survey, experiment, or detached observation. The subject is treated like an object, forced, for example, to answer the same questions as presented to everybody else with the same value-free, emotionless demeanor. This is because positivists define deviance as an objective fact, namely, a publicly observable, outward aspect of human behavior. By contrast, humanism suggests that we study individuals with subjective methods such as ethnography, participant observation, or open-ended, in-depth interviews. With these methods, subjects are treated as unique whole persons and encouraged to freely express their feelings in any way they want. This is because humanists define deviance as a personal experience—a hidden, inner aspect of human behavior.

Objectivism: Deviance as an Objective Fact   By focusing on the outward aspect of deviance, positivists assume that sociologists can be as objective in studying deviance as natural scientists can in studying physical phenomena. The trick is to treat deviants as if they were objects, like those studied by natural scientists. Nonetheless, positivist sociologists cannot help being aware of the basic difference between their subject, human beings, and that of natural scientists, inanimate objects. As human beings themselves, positivist sociologists must have certain feelings about their subject. However, they try to control their personal biases by forcing themselves not to pass moral judgment on deviant behavior or share the deviant person's feelings. Instead, they try to concentrate on the subject matter as it outwardly appears. Further, these sociologists have tried hard to follow the scientific rule that all their ideas about deviant behavior should be subject to public scrutiny. This means that other sociologists should be able to check out the ideas to see whether they are supported by facts.

Such a drive to achieve scientific objectivity has produced substantial knowledge about deviant behavior. No longer popular today are such value-loaded and subjective notions as maladjustment, moral failing, debauchery, demoralization, sickness, pathology, and abnormality. Replacing these outdated notions are such value-free and objective concepts as innovation, retreatism, ritualism, rebellion, culture conflict, subcultural behavior, white-collar crime, norm violation, learned behavior, and reinforced behavior.

To demonstrate the objective reality of these concepts, positivist sociologists have used official reports and statistics, clinical reports, surveys of self-reported behavior, and surveys of victimization. Positivists recognize the unfortunate fact that the sample of deviants in the studies—especially in official statistics—does not accurately represent the entire population of deviants. Nevertheless, positivists believe that the quality of information obtained by these methods can be improved and refined. In the meantime, they consider the information, though inadequate, useful for revealing at least some aspect of the totality of deviant behavior.

Subjectivism: Deviance as a Personal Experience   To positivists, the supposedly deviant behavior is a personal experience and the supposedly deviant person is a conscious, feeling, thinking, and reflective subject. Humanists insist that there is a world of difference between humans (as active subjects) and nonhuman beings and things (as passive objects). Humans can feel and reflect, but animals, plants, things, and forces in nature cannot. Humans also have sacred worth and dignity, but the others do not. It is proper and useful for natural scientists to assume and then study nature as an object, because this study can produce objective knowledge for controlling the natural world. It may also be useful for social scientists to assume and then study humans as objects, because it may produce objective knowledge for controlling humans. But this violates humanist values and sensibilities.

Humanist sociologists are opposed to the control of humans; instead, they advocate the protection and expansion of human worth, dignity, and freedom. One result of this humanist ideology is the observation that so-called objective knowledge about human behavior is inevitably superficial whenever it is used for controlling people. In order for a white racist government to control blacks, for example, it needs only the superficial knowledge about blacks being identifiable and separable from whites. Such superficial knowledge has in fact been employed to support the former white racist regime in South Africa. But to achieve the humanist goal of protecting and expanding blacks' human worth, dignity, and freedom, a deeper understanding of blacks is needed. This understanding requires appreciating and empathizing with them, experiencing what they experience as blacks, and see blacks' lives and the world around them from their perspective. We must look at the black experience from the inside as a participant rather than from the outside as a spectator. In a word, we must adopt the internal, subjective view instead of the external, objective one.

The same principle, according to humanist sociologists, should hold for understanding deviants and their deviant behavior. Humanists contrast this subjective approach with the positivists' objective one. To humanists, positivists treat deviance as if it were an immoral, unpleasant, or repulsive phenomenon that should be controlled, corrected, or eliminated. In consequence, positivists have used the objective approach by staying aloof from deviants, studying the external aspects of their deviant behavior, and relying on a set of preconceived ideas for guiding their study. The result is a collection of *surface facts* about deviants, such as their poverty, lack of schooling, poor self-image, and low aspirations. All this may be used for controlling and eliminating deviance, but it does not tell us, in Howard Becker's words, "what a deviant does in his daily round of activity and what he thinks about himself, society, and his activities." To understand the life of a deviant, humanists believe, we need to use the subjective approach, which requires our appreciation for and empathy with the deviant. The aim of this subjective approach, according to David Matza, "is to comprehend and to illuminate the subject's view and to interpret the world *as it appears to him.*"

As a result of their subjective and empathetic approach, humanists often present an image of the deviants as basically the same as conventional people. The deaf, for example, are the same as the nondeaf in being able to communicate and live a normal life. They should therefore be respected rather than pitied. This implies that so-called deviant behavior, because it is like so-called conventional behavior, should not be controlled, cured, or eradicated by society.

Theory: What Does It Mean?

Positivism suggests that we use etiological, causal, or explanatory theories to make sense of what research has found out about deviant behavior. This is because positivists favor the determinist view that deviance is determined by forces beyond the individual's control. By contrast, humanism suggests that we go for noncausal, descriptive, or analytical theories. Such theories provide detailed analyses of the subjective, experiential world of deviance. Humanists feel at home with these analyses because they regard most deviance as a voluntary act, an expression of free will.

Determinism: Deviance as "Determined" Behavior   Overly enthusiastic about the prospect of turning their discipline into a science, early sociologists argued that, like animals, plants, and material objects that natural scientists study, humans do not have any free will. The reason is that acknowledgment of free will would contradict the scientific principle of determinism. If a murderer is thought to will or determine a murderous act, then it does not make sense to say that the murderous act is caused by such other things as the individual's physical characteristics, mental condition, family background, or some social experience. Therefore, in defending their scientific principle of determinism, the early sociologists maintained their denial of free will. However, today's positivist sociologists assume that humans do possess free will. Still, this assumption, they argue, does not undermine the scientific principle of determinism. No matter how much a person exercises free will by making choices and decisions, the choices and decisions do not just happen but are determined by some causes. If a woman chooses to kill her husband rather than continue to live with him, she certainly has free will or freedom of choice so long as nobody forces her to do what she does. Yet some factor may determine the woman's choice of one alternative over another, or the way she exercises her free will. One such factor, as research has suggested, may be a long history of abuse at the hands of her husband. Thus, according to today's positivists, there is no inconsistency between freedom and causality.

Although they allow for human freedom or choice, positivists do not use it to explain why people behave in a certain way. They will not, for example, explain why the woman kills by saying "because she chooses to kill." This is no explanation at all, since the idea of choice can also be used to explain why another woman does not kill her husband—by saying "because she chooses not to." According to positivists, killing and not killing, or, more generally, deviant and conventional behavior, being two contrary phenomena, cannot be explained by the same thing, such as choice. The idea of choice simply cannot explain the difference between deviance and conventionality; it cannot explain why one man chooses to kill while the other chooses not to. Therefore, although positivists do believe in human choice, they will not attribute deviance to human choice. They will instead explain deviance by using such concepts as wife abuse, broken homes, unhappy homes, lower-class background, economic deprivation, social disorganization, rapid social change, differential association, differential reinforcement, and lack of social control. Any one of these causes of deviance can be used to illustrate what positivists consider a real explanation of deviance, because, for example, wife abuse is more likely to cause a woman to kill her husband than not. Etiological theories essentially point out factors like those as the causes of deviance.

Voluntarism: Deviance as a Voluntary Act   To humanists, the supposed-ly deviant behavior is a voluntary act or an expression of human volition, will, or choice. Humanists take this stand because they are disturbed by what they claim to be the dehumanizing implication of the positivist view of deviant behavior. The positivist view is said to imply that the human being is like "a robot, a senseless and purposeless machine reacting to every fortuitous change in the external and internal environment." But humanists emphasize that human beings, because they possess free will and choice-making ability, deter-mine or cause their own behavior.

To support this voluntarist assumption, humanists tend to analyze how social control agencies define some people as deviant and carry out the sanc-tions against them. Such analyses often accent, as Edwin Lemert has observed, "the arbitrariness of official action, stereotyped decision-making in bureau-cratic contexts, bias in the administration of law, and the general preemptive nature of society's controls over deviants." All these convey the strong impres-sion that control agents, being in positions of power, exercise their free will by actively, intentionally, and purposefully controlling the "deviants."

Humanists also analyze people who have been labeled deviant. The "deviants" are not presented as if they were robots, passively and senselessly developing a poor self-image as conventional society expects them to. Instead, they are described as actively seeking positive meanings in their deviant activ-ities. In Jack Katz' analysis, murderers see themselves as morally superior to their victims. The killing is said to give the murderers the self-righteous feel-ing of defending their dignity and respectability because their victims have unjustly humiliated them by taunting or insulting them. Katz also portrays rob-bers as feeling themselves morally superior to their victims—regarding their victims as fools or suckers who deserve to be robbed. If robbers want to rob somebody on the street, they would first ask the potential victim for the time, for directions, for a cigarette light, or for change. Each of these requests is intended to determine whether the person is a fool. The request for the time, for example, gives the robber the opportunity to know whether the prospec-tive victim has an expensive watch. Complying with the request, then, is taken to establish the person as a fool and hence the right victim.

SUMMARY AND CONCLUSION

Each of the positivist and humanist perspectives consists of three related assumptions, and each assumption suggests a strategy for contributing to the sociology of deviance. Of the positivist perspective, the three assumptions are as follows: First is the absolutist assumption that deviant behavior is *absolute-ly real.* This suggests that we study deviance or deviants. Second is the objec-tivist assumption that deviant behavior is an *objective,* publicly observable fact. This suggests that we use objective research methods such as survey, experi-ment, or detached observation. Third is the determinist assumption that deviance is *determined* or *caused* by certain social forces. This suggests that we use causal theories to make sense of the research data. As for the humanist

---

TABLE 1   A Summary of Two Perspectives

Positivist Perspective	*Humanist Perspective*
Absolutism Deviance is absolutely, intrinsically real; hence, deviance or deviants are subject of study.	*Relativism* Deviance is a label, defined as such at a given time and place; hence, labelers, labeling, and impact of labeling are subject of study.
Objectivism Deviance is an objective, observable fact; hence, objective research methods are used.	*Subjectivism* Deviance is a personal experience; hence, subjective research methods are used.
Determinism Deviance is determined behavior, a product of causation; hence, causal, explanatory theory is developed.	*Voluntarism* Deviance is a voluntary act, an expression of free will; hence, noncausal, descriptive theory is developed.

---

perspective, its first assumption is that deviant behavior is basically a *label*. This suggests that we study law enforcers and other labelers, the process of labeling, and the impact of labeling. The second assumption is that the supposedly deviant behavior is a *personal* experience. This suggests that we use objective research methods such as ethnography, participant observation, or open-ended, in-depth interviews. The third assumption is that the so-called deviance is a *voluntary, self-willed* act. This suggests that we develop non-causal, descriptive theories. (See Table 1 for a quick review.)

The diverse definitions, theories, methodologies, and data we have discussed reflect many different aspects of deviant behavior. While they appear to conflict with one another, they actually complement each other. They may be compared to the different views on a house. Looked at from the front, the house has a door, windows, and a chimney on top. From the back, it has a door and a chimney on top but fewer windows. From the side it has no doors, but it has windows and a chimney on top. From the top, it has no doors or windows, but a chimney in the middle. It is the same house, but it looks different, depending on one's standpoint. Taking in the different views on the house ensures a fuller knowledge of what the house actually looks like. Similarly, knowing the different views on deviant behavior ensures a fuller understanding of deviance. This reader is intended to make that possible.

PART 1

Defining Deviance

Charles Farnham is a software writer who has an enormous collection of commercial programs for his Apple Macintosh computer. Like millions of other people, he has not bought most of the programs—he has simply copied them from his friends' software. Federal law prohibits this kind of behavior, but many computer users who would not steal a library book or cheat on a test have no qualms about copying software illegally. Farnham explains that most software is too expensive and that there is nothing wrong with sampling a program before spending $500 or more.[1]

On the other hand, Aleta Walker, an obese 36-year-old woman, has a different kind of experience. Throughout her life she has been ridiculed and abused for her weight. What she suffered during her childhood and adolescence was particularly poignant. Every day, when she walked down the halls at school, boys would step back and yell, "Wide load!" It was worse at lunchtime. As she said, "Every day there was this production of watching me eat lunch." One day, schoolmates threw food at her. Spaghetti splashed on her head and face, and the long greasy strands dripped onto her clothes. "Everyone was laughing and pointing. They were making pig noises. I just sat there," she said.[2]

Is Farnham deviant for copying software illegally? Some people would say yes, but others would say no. Is Walker deviant for being overweight? Again, some people would say yes, but others would say no. In fact, some would claim that it is her tormentors—the so-called normal people—who are deviant because they are grossly insensitive, nasty, or cruel. Given this disagreement, who determines what constitutes deviance? Stephen Pfohl deals with this issue in the first article, "Images of Deviance." In the second reading, "Defining Deviancy Down," Daniel Patrick Moynihan shows how our society today does not define many harmful behaviors as deviant. In Moynihan's words, many people define deviance down by accepting or tolerating a large amount of it as normal, but more conservative Americans define deviance up by demonizing it, condemning it, or advocating harsh penalty for it.

---

[1] John Markoff, "Though Illegal, Copied Software Is Now Common," *New York Times*, July 27, 1992, pp. A1, C4.

[2] Gina Kolata, "The Burdens of Being Overweight: Mistreatment and Misconceptions," *New York Times,* November 22, 1992, pp. 1, 18.

1

Images of Deviance

STEPHEN PFOHL
Boston College

The scene is a crowded church during the American Civil War. "It was a time of great and exalting excitement. The country was up in arms, the war was on, in every breast burned the holy fire of patriotism." So says Mark Twain in his short and searing parable—*The War Prayer.* Amidst the clamor of beating drums, marching bands, and toy pistols popping, Twain describes an emotional church service. A passionate minister stirs the gallant hearts of eager volunteers; bronzed returning heroes; and their families, friends, and neighbors. The inspired congregation await their minister's every word.

> And with one impulse the house rose, with glowing eyes and beating hearts, and poured out that tremendous invocation—
>
>> God the all-terrible!
>> Thou who ordainest,
>> Thunder thy clarion
>> and lightning thy sword!

> Then came the "long" prayer. None could remember the like of it for passionate pleading and moving and beautiful language. The burden of its supplication was that an ever-merciful and benignant Father of us all would watch over our noble young soldiers and aid, comfort, and encourage them in their patriotic work; bless them, shield them in the day of battle and the hour of peril, bear them in His mighty hand, make them strong and confident, invincible in the bloody onset; help them to crush the foe, grant to them and to their flag and country imperishable honor and glory.

Wars come and go. Words vary. Nonetheless, the essential message of this sermon remains alarmingly the same: "God is on our side." Before continuing with Twain's story, I ask you to consider a more contemporary version of this age-old narrative—the 1991 Gulf War between Iraq and the United States-led coalition of "New World Order" forces demanding an Iraqi withdrawal from Kuwait. Claiming it to be its moral imperative to repel an act of international aggression, the United States pictured Iraqi President Saddam Hussein as a

Reprinted with permission of McGraw-Hill from Stephen Pfohl, *Images of Deviance and Social Control*, 2nd ed. (New York: McGraw-Hill, 1994), pp. 1–6.

Hilter-like character bent on world domination. Iraq in turn cited contradictions in the U.S. position (its long-term support for Israeli occupation of Palestinian territories, for example) as evidence of both U.S. hypocrisy and what Iraq alleged to be the true motives for the attack on Iraq—namely, "American" efforts to police the price of oil. Each side in this conflict represented the other as evil, treacherous, and power-mongering. Each side claimed to be righteous and blessed by God. This is typical of societies engaged in war.

Returning to Twain's story, what is untypical about this thoughtful tale is what happens next. It is not only untypical, but "deviant." After the minister completes his moving prayer, an "unnaturally pale," aged stranger enters the church. He is adorned with long hair and dressed in a full-length robe. The stranger motions the startled minister aside and informs the shocked parishioners that he is a messenger from Almighty God. He tells the congregation that God has heard their prayer and will grant it, but only after they consider the full import of their request. In rephrasing the original sermon the mysterious messenger reveals a more troubling side to the congregation's prayer. When they ask blessing for themselves they are, at the same time, praying for the merciless destruction of other humans (their enemies). In direct and graphic language the old man portrays the unspoken implications of their request, as follows:

> help us to tear their soldiers to bloody shreds with our shells;
> help us to cover their smiling fields with the pale forms of their patriotic dead;
> help us to draw the thunder of the guns with shrieks of their wounded, writhing in pain;
> help us to lay waste their humble homes with a hurricane of fire;
> help us to wring the hearts of their unoffending widows to unavailing grief;
> help us to turn them out roofless with their little children to wander unbefriended the wastes of their desolated land.

The strange old man continues—talking about blighting their lives, bringing tears, and staining the snow with blood. He completes his war prayer with a statement about the humble and contrite hearts of those who ask God's blessings. The congregation pauses in silence. He asks if they still desire what they have prayed for. "Ye have prayed it; if ye still desire it, speak! The messenger of the Most High waits." We are now at the final page of Twain's book. The congregation's response is simple and abrupt. As suggested previously, the old stranger was clearly a social deviant. In Twain's words: "It was believed afterward that the man was a lunatic, because there was no sense in what he said."

The stranger in *The War Prayer* directly threatens the normal, healthy, patriotic, and blood-lusting beliefs of the embattled congregation. Yet it is with ease that they contain and control this threat. They do not have to take seriously the chilling implications of his sermon. Their religious and patriotic senses are protected from his disturbing assault. Why? The reason is as simple as their response. They believe that he is a lunatic. They believe that he is a deviant. By classifying the old man as a deviant they need not listen to him. The congregation's beliefs are protected, even strengthened. The lunatic's beliefs are safely controlled. *The War Prayer* is thus a story of how some people imagine other people to be "deviant" and thereby protect or isolate themselves from those whom they fear and from that which challenges the way in which "normal" social life is organized. It is a story of how people convince themselves of what is normal by condemning those who disagree. It is a story of both deviance and social control. . . .

The story of deviance and social control is a battle story. It is a story of the battle to control the ways people think, feel, and behave. It is a story of winners and losers and of the strategies people use in struggles with one another. Winners in the battle to control "deviant acts" are crowned with a halo of goodness, acceptability, normality. Losers are viewed as living outside the boundaries of social life as it ought to be, outside the "common sense" of society itself. They may be seen by others as evil, sleazy, dirty, dangerous, sick, immoral, crazy, or just plain deviant. They may even come to see themselves in such negative imagery, to see themselves as *deviants*.

Deviants are only one part of the story of deviance and social control. Deviants never exist except in relation to those who attempt to control them. Deviants exist only in opposition to those whom they threaten and those who have enough power to control against such threats. The outcome of the battle of deviance and social control is this. Winners obtain the privilege of organizing social life as they see fit. Losers are trapped within the vision of others. They are labeled deviant and subjected to an array of current social control practices. Depending upon the controlling wisdom at a particular moment in history, deviants may be executed, brutally beaten, fined, shamed, incarcerated, drugged, hospitalized, or even treated to heavy doses of tender loving care. But first and foremost they are prohibited from passing as normal women or men. They are branded with the image of being deviant.

When we think of losers in the battle to control acceptable images of social life, it may seem natural to think of juvenile gang members, serial killers, illegal drug users, homosexuals, and burglars. Indeed, common sense may tell us that such people are simply deviant. But where does this common sense come from? How do we come to know that certain actions or certain people are deviant, while others are "normal"? Do people categorized as deviants really behave in a more dangerous fashion than others? Some people think so. Is this true?

Think of the so-called deviants mentioned above. Are their actions truly more harmful than the actions of people not labeled as deviants? In many cases the answer is no. Consider the juvenile gang. In recent years the organized drug dealing and violent activities of gangs have terrorized people living in poverty-stricken and racially segregated urban neighborhoods. Gang-related deviance has also been the focal point for sensational media stories and for social control policies ranging from selective "stop-and-search" police tactics to the building of new prisons and (in Los Angeles) even the criminalization of alleged gang members' parents.

But what about the people most responsible for the oppressive inner-city conditions that lie at the root of many gang-related activities? What about the "gangs" of bankers whose illegal redlining of mortgage loans blocks the investment of money in inner-city neighborhoods? What about the "gangs" of corporate executives whose greed for short-term profits has led to the "offshoring" of industrial jobs to "underdeveloped" countries where labor is cheap and more easily exploitable? Aren't the actions of such respectable people as costly as, if less visible than, the activities of most inner-city gangs? Yet, there is an important difference: unlike gangs of elite deviants, inner-city youths have little or no real access to dominant institutions in which contemporary power is concentrated.

A related question may be posed concerning serial killers. The violence of serial killers haunts our nightly news broadcasts. Indeed, the seemingly random character of serial killings—although they are most commonly directed against women and children—instills a deep and alarming sense of dread within society as a whole. Nevertheless, the sporadic violence of serial murderers, no matter how fearful, is incomparable in terms of both scope and number to the much less publicized "serial killings" perpetrated by U.S.-supported *death squads* in countries such as El Salvador and Guatemala. The targets of such death squads are typically people who dare to speak out in the name of social justice. From 1980 to 1991, for instance, approximately 75,000 Salvadoran civilians were secretly killed or made to "disappear" by paramilitary executioners. Why is it that such systematic murders are rarely acknowledged as true serial killings? Why, moreover, do such cold-blooded killings provoke so little U.S. public outrage in comparison to the attention given to the isolated violence of individual murderers, such as Ted Bundy or Jeffrey Dahmer? Is it because the people who authorize them are respectable persons, sometimes even publicly elected officials? Is it because, though we feel vulnerable to other serial killers, we ourselves—at least those of us who are white, male, North American, and economically privileged to live at a distance from the violence that historically envelops the daily lives of others—feel protected from death squads?

Similar questions might be raised about drug users. When we speak of the abuse of drugs, why do we often think only of the "controlled substances" that some people use as a means of achieving psychic escape, altered consciousness, and/or bodily pleasure? True, we as individuals and as a society may pay a heavy price for the abuse of such drugs as cocaine and heroin. But what about other—legal—substances that many of us are "on" much of the time? Some of these drugs are even more dangerous than their illicit counterparts. In addition to alcohol, tobacco, chemical food additives, and meat from animals that have been fed antibiotics and hormones, our society openly promotes the use of prescription and over-the-counter drugs for everything from losing weight, curing acne, and overcoming anxiety to building strong bodies, fighting depression, and alleviating allergies caused by industrial pollution. Certainly many of these substances have their salutary effects and may help us adjust to the world in which we live. However, even legal substances can be abused; they too can be dangerous. The effects can be direct, jeopardizing an individual's health or fostering addiction, or they can be indirect and more insidious. For example, consider the role drugs play in creating and sustaining our excessively image-conscious, age-conscious environment and in promoting our tendency to avoid dealing with personal conflicts and everyday problems in a thoughtful and responsible manner. Also—not to belabor the issue—just think of what we are doing to our planet, to our future, with our use of pesticides, fertilizers, and other industrial products and by-products. To raise such concerns is not to claim that legal drugs are more dangerous than illegal drugs, but simply to suggest that what is officially labeled illegal or deviant often has more to do with what society economically values than with whether the thing is physically harmful per se.

Further consider the actions of sexist heterosexuals. Such persons may routinely mix various forms of sexual harassment with manipulative patriarchal power and an intolerance of alternative forms of sexual intimacy. Despite the harm these heterosexist individuals cause, they are far less likely to be labeled deviant than are gay, lesbian, or bisexual lovers who caress one another with affection. The same goes for corporate criminals, such as the executives recently implicated in the savings and loan scandal. The stealthy acts of such white-collar criminals have cost the U.S. public as much as $500 billion. Yet the elite deviance of the upper echelon of rule breakers is commonly less feared than are the street crimes of ordinary burglars and robbers.

From the preceding examples it should be evident that many forms of labeled deviance are not more costly to society than the behaviors of people who are less likely to be labeled deviant. Why? The answer . . . is that labeled deviants are viewed as such because they threaten the control of people who have enough power to shape the way society imagines the boundary between good and bad, normal and pathological, acceptable and deviant. This is the crux of the effort to understand the battle between deviance and social control. Deviance is always the flip side of the coin used to maintain social control.

2

Defining Deviancy Down

DANIEL PATRICK MOYNIHAN
U.S. Senate

In one of the founding texts of sociology, *The Rules of Sociological Method* (1895), Emile Durkheim set it down that "crime is normal." "It is," he wrote, "completely impossible for any society entirely free of it to exist." By defining what is deviant, we are enabled to know what is not, and hence to live by shared standards. . . .

The matter was pretty much left at that until seventy years later when, in 1965, Kai T. Erikson published *Wayward Puritans*, a study of "crime rates" in the Massachusetts Bay Colony. The plan behind the book, as Erikson put it, was "to test [Durkheim's] notion that the number of deviant offenders a community can afford to recognize is likely to remain stable over time." The notion proved out very well indeed. Despite occasional crime waves, as when itinerant Quakers refused to take off their hats in the presence of magistrates, the amount of deviance in this corner of seventeenth-century New England fitted nicely with the supply of stocks and whipping posts. Erikson remarks:

> The agencies of control often seem to define their job as that of keeping deviance within bounds rather than that of obliterating it altogether. Many judges, for example, assume that severe punishments are a greater deterrent to crime than moderate ones, and so it is important to note that many of them are apt to impose harder penalties when crime seems to be on the increase and more lenient ones when it does not, almost as if the power of the bench were being used to keep the crime rate from getting out of hand. . . . Hence "the number of deviant offenders a community *can afford* to recognize is likely to remain stable over time. [My emphasis]

Social scientists are said to be on the lookout for poor fellows getting a bum rap. But here is a theory that clearly implies that there are circumstances in which society will choose *not* to notice behavior that would be otherwise controlled, or disapproved, or even punished.

It appears to me that this is in fact what we in the United States have been doing of late. I proffer the thesis that, over the past generation, since the time

Reprinted from *The American Scholar,* Vol. 62, No. 1, Winter 1993. Copyright © 1992 by the author.

Erikson wrote, the amount of deviant behavior in American society has increased beyond the levels the community can "afford to recognize" and that, accordingly, we have been re-defining deviancy so as to exempt much conduct previously stigmatized, and also quietly raising the "normal" level in categories where behavior is now abnormal by any earlier standard. This redefining has evoked fierce resistance from defenders of "old" standards, and accounts for much of the present "cultural war" such as proclaimed by many at the 1992 Republican National Convention. . . .

[In today's normalization of deviance] we are dealing with the popular psychological notion of "denial." In 1965, having reached the conclusion that there would be a dramatic increase in single-parent families, I reached the further conclusion that this would in turn lead to a dramatic increase in crime. In an article in *America,* I wrote:

> From the wild Irish slums of the 19th century Eastern seaboard to the riot-torn suburbs of Los Angeles, there is one unmistakable lesson in American history: a community that allows a large number of young men to grow up in broken families, dominated by women, never acquiring any stable relationship to male authority, never acquiring any set of rational expectations about the future—that community asks for and gets chaos. Crime, violence, unrest, unrestrained lashing out at the whole social structure—that is not only to be expected; it is very near to inevitable.

The inevitable, as we now know, has come to pass, but here again our response is curiously passive. Crime is a more or less continuous subject of political pronouncement, and from time to time it will be at or near the top of opinion polls as a matter of public concern. But it never gets much further than that. In the words spoken from the bench, Judge Edwin Torres of the New York State Supreme Court, Twelfth Judicial District, described how "the slaughter of the innocent marches unabated: subway riders, bodega owners, cab drivers, babies; in laundromats, at cash machines, on elevators, in hallways." In personal communication, he writes: "This numbness, this near narcoleptic state can diminish the human condition to the level of combat infantrymen, who, in protracted campaigns, can eat their battlefield rations seated on the bodies of the fallen, friend and foe alike. A society that loses its sense of outrage is doomed to extinction." There is no expectation that this will change, nor any efficacious public insistence that it do so. The crime level has been *normalized.*

Consider the St. Valentine's Day Massacre. In 1929 in Chicago during Prohibition, four gangsters killed seven gangsters on February 14. The nation was shocked. The event became legend. It merits not one but two entries in the *World Book Encyclopedia.* I leave it to others to judge, but it would appear that the society in the 1920s was simply not willing to put up with this degree of deviancy. In the end, the Constitution was amended, and Prohibition, which lay behind so much gangster violence, ended.

In recent years, again in the context of illegal traffic in controlled substances, this form of murder has returned. But it has done so at a level that induces denial. James Q. Wilson comments that Los Angeles has the equivalent of a St. Valentine's Day Massacre every weekend. Even the most ghastly re-enactments of such human slaughter produce only moderate responses. On the morning after the close of the Democratic National Convention in New York City in July, there was such an account in the second section of the *New York Times*. It was not a big story; bottom of the page, but with a headline that got your attention. "3 Slain in Bronx Apartment, but a Baby is Saved." A sub-head continued: "A mother's last act was to hide her little girl under the bed." The article described a drug execution; the now-routine blindfolds made from duct tape; a man and a woman and a teenager involved. "Each had been shot once in the head." The police had found them a day later. They also found, under a bed, a three-month-old baby, dehydrated but alive. A lieutenant remarked of the mother, "In her last dying act she protected her baby. She probably knew she was going to die, so she stuffed the baby where she knew it would be safe." But the matter was left there. The police would do their best. But the event passed quickly; forgotten by the next day, it will never make *World Book*.

Nor is it likely that any great heed will be paid to an uncanny reenactment of the Prohibition drama a few months later, also in the Bronx. The *Times* story, page B3, reported:

9 Men Posing as Police Are Indicted in 3 Murders

DRUG DEALERS WERE KIDNAPPED FOR RANSOM

The *Daily News* story, same day, page 17, made it *four* murders, adding nice details about torture techniques. The gang members posed as federal Drug Enforcement Administration agents, real badges and all. The victims were drug dealers, whose families were uneasy about calling the police. Ransom seems generally to have been set in the $650,000 range. Some paid. Some got it in the back of the head. So it goes.

Yet, violent killings, often random, go on unabated. Peaks continue to attract some notice. But these are peaks above "average" levels that thirty years ago would have been thought epidemic. . . . A Kai Erikson of the future will surely need to know that the Department of Justice in 1990 found that Americans reported only about 38 percent of all crimes and 48 percent of violent crimes. This, too, can be seen as a means of *normalizing* crime. In much the same way, the vocabulary of crime reporting can be seen to move toward the normal-seeming. A teacher is shot on her way to class. The *Times* subhead reads: "Struck in the Shoulder in the Year's First Shooting Inside a School." First of the season. . . .

The hope—if there be such—of this essay has been twofold. It is, first, to suggest that the Durkheim constant, as I put it, is maintained by a dynamic process which adjusts upwards and *downwards*. Liberals have traditionally been alert for upward redefining that does injustice to individuals. Conservatives have been correspondingly sensitive to downward redefining that weakens societal standards. Might it not help if we could all agree that there is a dynamic at work here? It is not revealed truth, nor yet a scientifically derived formula. It is simply a pattern we observe in ourselves. Nor is it rigid. There may once have been an unchanging supply of jail cells which more or less determined the number of prisoners. No longer. We are building new prisons at a prodigious rate. Similarly, the executioner is back. There is something of a competition in Congress to think up new offenses for which the death penalty is seen the only available deterrent. Possibly also modes of execution, as in "fry the kingpins." Even so, we are getting used to a lot of behavior that is not good for us.

As noted earlier, Durkheim states that there is "nothing desirable" about pain. . . . Pain, even so, is an indispensable warning signal. But societies under stress, much like individuals, will turn to pain killers of various kinds that end up concealing real damage. There is surely nothing desirable about *this*. If our analysis wins general acceptance, if, for example, more of us came to share Judge Torres's genuine alarm at "the trivialization of the lunatic crime rate" in his city (and mine), we might surprise ourselves how well we respond to the manifest decline of the American civic order. Might.

P A R T 2

Positivist Theories: Explaining Deviance

Recently, in a poor neighborhood of Deerfield Beach, Florida, a 16-year-old boy wanted to buy two cigarettes at a corner grocery. He had known that they cost a quarter, but he had only 20 cents in his pocket. So, on his way to the store, he stopped in front of a boardinghouse and asked a neighbor, a 13-year-old pregnant girl, for a nickel. She said she did not have the money. "Give it to me," he shouted. She refused. He pulled out a revolver from his belt, and shot point-blank at her large belly. She staggered into the room that she shared with her mother and four siblings in the boardinghouse. As she fell on a bed, the boy took a nickel from her room. Then, calmly, he walked to the store and bought the cigarettes. Later, the victim's baby was delivered by emergency caesarean. The infant died, though the mother survived. When he returned home, the young killer was persuaded by his father to turn himself in. He was tried as an adult for third-degree murder and aggravated battery, and sentenced to four years in a medium-security prison for juvenile offenders.[1]

Murders committed by young boys such as this one have become much more common. Since the mid-1980s, the number of murders by boys under 18 has soared while the number of murders by adults has declined. Why are young teenagers more trigger-happy today than before? Faced with this question, positivist sociologists would seek the answer from some general theories about deviance. In the first article, Robert Merton explains how the lack of opportunity for achieving success pressures individuals toward deviance. In the second selection, Edwin Sutherland and Donald Cressey attribute deviance to an excess of deviant associations over conventional associations. In the third reading, Travis Hirschi blames deviance on the lack of control in the individual's life. In the final piece, John Braithwaite shows how the lack of (reintegrative) shaming causes deviance to flourish. Using these theories, we may say that the recent increase in teen killing can be attributed to the increasing lack of success opportunity in teen life; excess of association with criminal peers and gangs in poor neighborhoods; lack of control by parents, schools, and law enforcers; and lack of shaming in the underclass culture.

---

[1] Nancy Traver, "Children Without Pity," *Time,* October 26, 1992, p. 46.

3

Strain Theory

ROBERT K. MERTON
Columbia University

The framework set out in this essay is designed to provide one systematic approach to the analysis of social and cultural sources of deviant behavior. Our primary aim is to discover how some *social structures exert a definite pressure upon certain persons in the society to engage in nonconforming rather than conforming conduct.* If we can locate groups peculiarly subject to such pressures, we should expect to find fairly high rates of deviant behavior in these groups, not because the human beings comprising them are compounded of distinctive biological tendencies but because they are responding normally to the social situation in which they find themselves. Our perspective is sociological. We look at variations in the *rates* of deviant behavior, not at its incidence. Should our quest be at all successful, some forms of deviant behavior will be found to be as psychologically normal as conformist behavior, and the equation of deviation and psychological abnormality will be put in question.

PATTERNS OF CULTURAL GOALS AND INSTITUTIONAL NORMS

Among the several elements of social and cultural structures, two are of immediate importance. These are analytically separable although they merge in concrete situations. The first consists of culturally defined goals, purposes and interests, held out as legitimate objectives for all or for diversely located members of the society. The goals are more or less integrated—the degree is a question of empirical fact—and roughly ordered in some hierarchy of value. Involving various degrees of sentiment and significance, the prevailing goals comprise a frame of aspirational reference. They are the things "worth striving for." They are a basic, though not the exclusive, component of what Linton has called "designs for group living." And though some, not all, of these cultural goals are directly related to the biological drives of man, they are not determined by them.

A second element of the cultural structure defines, regulates, and controls the acceptable modes of reaching out for these goals. Every social group invariably couples its cultural objectives with regulations, rooted in the mores or institutions, of allowable procedures for moving toward these objectives. These regulatory norms are not necessarily identical with technical or efficiency norms. Many procedures which from the standpoint of particular individuals would be most efficient in securing desired values—the exercise of force, fraud, power—are ruled out of the institutional area of permitted conduct. At times, the disallowed procedures include some which would be efficient for the group itself—for example, historic taboos on vivisection, on medical experimentation, on the sociological analysis of "sacred" norms—since the criterion of acceptability is not technical efficiency but value-laden sentiments (supported by most members of the group or by those able to promote these sentiments through the composite use of power and propaganda). In all instances, the choice of expedients for striving toward cultural goals is limited by institutionalized norms.

We shall be primarily concerned with the first—a society in which there is an exceptionally strong emphasis upon specific goals without a corresponding emphasis upon institutional procedures. If it is not to be misunderstood, this statement must be elaborated. No society lacks norms governing conduct. But societies do differ in the degree to which the folkways, mores and institutional controls are effectively integrated with the goals which stand high in the hierarchy of cultural values. The culture may be such as to lead individuals to center their emotional convictions upon the complex of culturally acclaimed ends, with far less emotional support for prescribed methods of reaching out for these ends. With such differential emphases upon goals and institutional procedures, the latter may be so vitiated by the stress on goals as to have the behavior of many individuals limited only by considerations of technical expediency. In this context, the sole significant question becomes: Which of the available procedures is most efficient in netting the culturally approved value? The technically most effective procedure, whether culturally legitimate or not, becomes typically preferred to institutionally prescribed conduct. As this process of attenuation continues, the society becomes unstable and there develops what Durkheim called "anomie" (or normlessness).

The working of this process eventuating in anomie can be easily glimpsed in a series of familiar and instructive, though perhaps trivial, episodes. Thus, in competitive athletics, when the aim of victory is shorn of its institutional trappings and success becomes construed as "winning the game" rather than "winning under the rules of the game," a premium is implicitly set upon the use of illegitimate but technically efficient means. The star of the opposing football team is surreptitiously slugged; the wrestler incapacitates his opponent through ingenious but illicit techniques; university alumni covertly subsidize "students" whose talents are confined to the athletic field. The emphasis on the goal has so attenuated the satisfactions deriving from sheer participation in the competitive activity that only a successful outcome provides gratification. Through the same process, tension generated by the desire to win in a poker game is relieved by successfully dealing one's self four aces or, when the cult of success has truly flowered, by sagaciously shuffling the cards in a game of solitaire. The faint twinge of uneasiness in the last instance and the surreptitious nature of public delicts indicate clearly that the institutional rules of the game are *known* to those who evade them. But cultural (or idiosyncratic) exaggeration of the success-goal leads men to withdraw emotional support from the rules.

This process is of course not restricted to the realm of competitive sport, which has simply provided us with microcosmic images of the social macrocosm. The process whereby exaltation of the end generates a literal *demoralization*, that is, a de-institutionalization, of the means occurs in many groups where the two components of the social structure are not highly integrated.

Contemporary American culture appears to approximate the polar type in which great emphasis upon certain success-goals occurs without equivalent emphasis upon institutional means. It would of course be fanciful to assert that accumulated wealth stands alone as a symbol of success just as it would be fanciful to deny that Americans assign it a place high in their scale of values. In some large measure, money has been consecrated as a value in itself, over and above its expenditure for articles of consumption or its use for the enhancement of power. "Money" is peculiarly well adapted to become a symbol of prestige. As Simmel emphasized, money is highly abstract and impersonal. However acquired, fraudulently or institutionally, it can be used to purchase the same goods and services. The anonymity of an urban society, in conjunction with these peculiarities of money, permits wealth, the sources of which may be unknown to the community in which the plutocrat lives or, if known, to become purified in the course of time, to serve as a symbol of high status. Moreover, in the American Dream there is no final stopping point. The measure of "monetary success" is conveniently indefinite and relative. At each income level, as H. F. Clark found, Americans want just about 25 percent more (but of course this "just a bit more" continues to operate once it is obtained). In this flux of shifting standards, there is no stable resting point, or rather, it is the point which manages always to be "just ahead." An observer of a community in which annual salaries in six figures are not uncommon reports the anguished words of one victim of the American Dream: "In this town, I'm snubbed socially because I only get a thousand a week. That hurts."

To say that the goal of monetary success is entrenched in American culture is only to say that Americans are bombarded on every side by precepts which affirm the right or, often, the duty of retaining the goal even in the face of repeated frustration. Prestigeful representatives of the society reinforce the cultural emphasis. The family, the school and the workplace—the major agencies shaping the personality structure and goal formation of Americans—join to provide the intensive disciplining required if an individual is to retain intact a goal that remains elusively beyond reach, if he is to be motivated by the promise of a gratification which is not redeemed. As we shall presently see, parents serve as a transmission belt for the values and goals of the groups of which they are a part—above all, of their social class or of the class with which they identify themselves. And the schools are of course the official agency for the passing on of the prevailing values, with a large proportion of the textbooks used in city schools implying or stating explicitly "that education leads to intelligence and consequently to job and money success." Central to this process of disciplining people to maintain their unfulfilled aspirations are the cultural prototypes of success, the living documents testifying that the American Dream can be realized if one but has the requisite abilities.

Coupled with this positive emphasis upon the obligation to maintain lofty goals is a correlative emphasis upon the penalizing of those who draw in their ambitions. Americans are admonished "not to be a quitter" for in the dictionary of American culture, as in the lexicon of youth, "there is no such word as 'fail.'" The cultural manifesto is clear: one must not quit, must not cease striving, must not lessen his goals, for "not failure, but low aim, is crime."

Thus the culture enjoins the acceptance of three cultural axioms: First, all should strive for the same lofty goals since these are open to all; second, present seeming failure is but a way-station to ultimate success; and third, genuine failure consists only in the lessening or withdrawal of ambition.

In rough psychological paraphrase, these axioms represent, first a symbolic secondary reinforcement of incentive; second, curbing the threatened extinction of a response through an associated stimulus; third, increasing the motive-strength to evoke continued responses despite the continued absence of reward.

In sociological paraphrase, these axioms represent, first, the deflection of criticism of the social structure onto one's self among those so situated in the society that they do not have full and equal access to opportunity; second, the preservation of a structure of social power by having individuals in the lower social strata identify themselves, not with their compeers, but with those at the top (whom they will ultimately join); and third, providing pressures for conformity with the cultural dictates of unslackened ambition by the threat of less than full membership in the society for those who fail to conform.

It is in these terms and through these processes that contemporary American culture continues to be characterized by a heavy emphasis on wealth as a basic symbol of success, without a corresponding emphasis upon the legitimate avenues on which to march toward this goal. How do individuals living in this cultural context respond? And how do our observations bear upon the doctrine that deviant behavior typically derives from biological impulses breaking through the restraints imposed by culture? What, in short, are the consequences for the behavior of people variously situated in a social structure of a culture in which the emphasis on dominant success-goals has become increasingly separated from an equivalent emphasis on institutionalized procedures for seeking these goals?

TYPES OF INDIVIDUAL ADAPTATION

Turning from these culture patterns, we now examine types of adaptation by individuals within the culture-bearing society. Though our focus is still the cultural and social genesis of varying rates and types of deviant behavior, our perspective shifts from the plane of patterns of cultural values to the plane of types of adaptation to these values among those occupying different positions in the social structure.

We here consider five types of adaptation, as these as schematically set out in the following table, where (+) signifies "acceptance," (−) signifies "rejection," and (±) signifies "rejection of prevailing values and substitution of new values."

A Typology of Modes of Individual Adaptation

Modes of Adaptation	Culture Goals	Institutionalized Means
I. Conformity	+	+
II. Innovation	+	−
III. Ritualism	−	+
IV. Retreatism	−	−
V. Rebellion	±	±

I. Conformity

To the extent that a society is stable, adaptation type I—conformity to both cultural goals and institutionalized means—is the most common and widely diffused. Were this not so, the stability and continuity of the society could not be maintained. . . .

II. Innovation

Great cultural emphasis upon the success-goal invites this mode of adaptation through the use of institutionally proscribed but often effective means of attaining at least the simulacrum of success—wealth and power. This response occurs when the individual has assimilated the cultural emphasis upon the goal without equally internalizing the institutional norms governing ways and means for its attainment. . . .

It appears from our analysis that the greatest pressures toward deviation are exerted upon the lower strata. Cases in point permit us to detect the sociological mechanisms involved in producing these pressures. Several researches have shown that specialized areas of vice and crime constitute a "normal" response to a situation where the cultural emphasis upon pecuniary success has been absorbed, but where there is little access to conventional and legitimate means for becoming successful. The occupational opportunities of people in these areas are largely confined to manual labor and the lesser white-collar jobs. Given the American stigmatization of manual labor *which has been found to hold rather uniformly in all social classes,* and the absence of realistic opportunities for advancement beyond this level, the result is a marked tendency toward deviant behavior. The status of unskilled labor and the consequent low income cannot readily compete *in terms of established standards of worth* with the promises of power and high income from organized vice, rackets and crime.

For our purposes, these situations exhibit two salient features. First, incentives for success are provided by the established values of the culture *and* second, the avenues available for moving toward this goal are largely limited by the class structure to those of deviant behavior. It is the *combination* of the cultural emphasis and the social structure which produces intense pressure for deviation. . . .

III. Ritualism

The ritualistic type of adaptation can be readily identified. It involves the abandoning or scaling down of the lofty cultural goals of great pecuniary success and rapid social mobility to the point where one's aspirations can be satisfied. But though one rejects the cultural obligation to attempt "to get ahead in the world," though one draws in one's horizons, one continues to abide almost compulsively by institutional norms. . . .

We should expect this type of adaptation to be fairly frequent in a society which makes one's social status largely dependent upon one's achievements. For, as has so often been observed, this ceaseless competitive struggle produces acute status anxiety. One device for allaying these anxieties is to lower one's level of aspiration—permanently. Fear produces inaction, or, more accurately, routinized action.

The syndrome of the social ritualist is both familiar and instructive. His implicit life-philosophy finds expression in a series of cultural clichés: "I'm not sticking *my* neck out," "I'm playing safe," "I'm satisfied with what I've got," "Don't aim high and you won't be disappointed." The theme threaded through these attitudes is that high ambitions invite frustration and danger whereas lower aspirations produce satisfaction and security. It is the perspective of the frightened employee, the zealously conformist bureaucrat in the teller's cage of the private banking enterprise or in the front office of the public works enterprise.

IV. Retreatism

Just as Adaptation I (conformity) remains the most frequent, Adaptation IV (the rejection of cultural goals and institutional means) is probably the least common). People who adapt (or maladapt) in this fashion are, strictly speaking, *in* the society but not *of* it. Sociologically these constitute the true aliens. Not sharing the common frame of values, they can be included as members of the *society* (in distinction from the *population*) only in a fictional sense.

In this category fall some of the adaptive activities of psychotics, autists, pariahs, outcasts, vagrants, vagabonds, tramps, chronic drunkards and drug addicts. They have relinquished culturally prescribed goals and their behavior does not accord with institutional norms. The competitive order is maintained but the frustrated and handicapped individual who cannot cope with this order drops out. Defeatism, quietism and resignation are manifested in escape mechanisms which ultimately lead him to "escape" from the requirements of the society. It is thus an expedient which arises from continued failure to near the goal by legitimate measures and from an inability to use the illegitimate route because of internalized prohibitions.

V. Rebellion

This adaptation leads men outside the environing social structure to envisage and seek to bring into being a new, that is to say, a greatly modified social structure. It presupposes alienation from reigning goals and standards. These come to be regarded as purely arbitrary. And the arbitrary is precisely that which can neither exact allegiance nor possess legitimacy, for it might as well be otherwise. In our society, organized movements for rebellion apparently aim to introduce a social structure in which the cultural standards of success would be sharply modified and provision would be made for a closer correspondence between merit, effort and reward.

THE STRAIN TOWARD ANOMIE

The social structure we have examined produces a strain toward anomie and deviant behavior. The pressure of such a social order is upon outdoing one's competitors. So long as the sentiments supporting this competitive system are distributed throughout the entire range of activities and are not confined to the final result of "success," the choice of means will remain largely within the ambit of institutional control. When, however, the cultural emphasis shifts from the satisfactions deriving from competition itself to almost exclusive concern with the outcome, the resultant stress makes for the breakdown of the regulatory structure.

4

Differential Association Theory

EDWIN H. SUTHERLAND AND DONALD R. CRESSEY

The following statements refer to the process by which a particular person comes to engage in criminal behavior.

1. *Criminal behavior is learned.* Negatively, this means that criminal behavior is not inherited, as such; also, the person who is not already trained in crime does not invent criminal behavior, just as a person does not make mechanical inventions unless he has had training in mechanics.

2. *Criminal behavior is learned in interaction with other persons in a process of communication.* This communication is verbal in many respects but includes also "the communication of gestures."

3. *The principal part of the learning of criminal behavior occurs within intimate personal groups.* Negatively, this means that the impersonal agencies of communication, such as movies and newspapers, play a relatively unimportant part in the genesis of criminal behavior.

4. *When criminal behavior is learned, the learned includes (a) techniques of committing the crime, which are sometimes very complicated, sometimes very simple; (b) the specific direction of motives, drives, rationalizations, and attitudes.*

5. *The specific direction of motives and drives is learned from definitions of the legal codes as favorable or unfavorable.* In some societies an individual is surrounded by persons who invariably define the legal codes as rules to be observed, while in others he is surrounded by persons whose definitions are favorable to the violation of the legal codes. In our American society these definitions are almost always mixed, with the consequence that we have culture conflict in relation to the legal codes.

6. *A person becomes delinquent because of an excess of definitions favorable to violation of law over definitions unfavorable to violation of law.* This is the principle of differential association. It refers to both criminal and anti-

Reprinted from the authors' book, *Criminology,* 9th ed. (Philadelphia: Lippincott, 1974), pp. 75–77.

criminal associations and has to do with counteracting forces. When persons become criminal, they do so because of contacts with criminal patterns and also because of isolation from anticriminal patterns. Any person inevitably assimilates the surrounding culture unless other patterns are in conflict; a southerner does not pronounce *r* because other southerners do not pronounce *r*. Negatively, this proposition of differential association means that associations which are neutral so far as crime is concerned have little or no effect on the genesis of criminal behavior. Much of the experience of a person is neutral in this sense, for example, learning to brush one's teeth. This behavior has no negative or positive effect on criminal behavior except as it may be related to associations which are concerned with the legal codes. This neutral behavior is important especially as an occupier of the time of a child so that he is not in contact with criminal behavior during the time he is so engaged in the neutral behavior.

7. *Differential associations may vary in frequency, duration, priority, and intensity.* This means that associations with criminal behavior and also associations with anticriminal behavior vary in those respects. "Frequency" and "duration" as modalities of associations are obvious and need no explanation. "Priority" is assumed to be important in the sense that lawful behavior developed in early childhood may persist throughout life, and also that delinquent behavior developed in early childhood may persist throughout life. This tendency, however, has not been adequately demonstrated, and priority seems to be important principally through its selective influence. "Intensity" is not precisely defined, but it has to do with such things as the prestige of the source of a criminal or anticriminal pattern and with emotional reactions related to the associations. In a precise description of the criminal behavior of a person, these modalities would be rated in quantitative form and a mathematical ratio reached. A formula in this sense has not been developed, and the development of such a formula would be extremely difficult.

8. *The process of learning criminal behavior by association with criminal and anticriminal patterns involves all of the mechanisms that are involved in any other learning.* Negatively, this means that the learning of criminal behavior is not restricted to the process of imitation. A person who is seduced, for instance, learns criminal behavior by association, but this process would not ordinarily be described as imitation.

9. *While criminal behavior is an expression of general needs and values, it is not explained by those general needs and values, since noncriminal behavior is an expression of the same needs and values.* Thieves generally steal in order to secure money, but likewise honest laborers work in order to secure money. The attempts by many scholars to explain criminal behavior by general drives and values, such as the happiness principle, striving for social status, the money motive, or frustration, have been, and must continue to be, futile, since they explain lawful behavior as completely as they explain criminal behavior. They are similar to respiration, which is necessary for any behavior, but which does not differentiate criminal from noncriminal behavior.

It is not necessary, at this level of explanation, to explain why a person has the associations he has; this certainly involves a complex of many things. In an area where the delinquency rate is high, a boy who is sociable, gregarious, active, and athletic is very likely to come in contact with the other boys in the neighborhood, learn delinquent behavior patterns from them, and become a criminal; in the same neighborhood the psychopathic boy who is isolated, introverted, and inert may remain at home, not become acquainted with the other boys in the neighborhood, and not become delinquent. In another situation, the sociable, athletic, aggressive boy may become a member of a scout troop and not become involved in delinquent behavior. The person's associations are determined in a general context of social organization. A child is ordinarily reared in a family; the place of residence of the family is determined largely by family income; and the delinquency rate is in many respects related to the rental value of the houses. Many other aspects of social organization affect the kinds of associations a person has.

The preceding explanation of criminal behavior purports to explain the criminal and noncriminal behavior of individual persons. It is possible to state sociological theories of criminal behavior which explain the criminality of a community, nation, or other group. The problem, when thus stated, is to account for variations in crime rates and involves a comparison of the crime rates of various groups or the crime rates of a particular group at different times. The explanation of a crime rate must be consistent with the explanation of the criminal behavior of the person, since the crime rate is a summary statement of the number of persons in the group who commit crimes and the frequency with which they commit crimes. One of the best explanations of crime rates from this point of view is that a high crime rate is due to social disorganization. The term *social disorganization* is not entirely satisfactory, and it seems preferable to substitute for it the term *differential social organization.* The postulate on which this theory is based, regardless of the name, is that crime is rooted in the social organization and is an expression of that social organization. A group may be organized for criminal behavior or organized against criminal behavior. Most communities are organized for both criminal and anticriminal behavior, and, in that sense the crime rate is an expression of the differential group organization. Differential group organization as an explanation of variations in crime rates is consistent with the differential association theory of the processes by which persons become criminals.

5

Control Theory

TRAVIS HIRSCHI
University of Arizona

Control theories assume that delinquent acts result when an individual's bond to society is weak or broken . . . [Elements of the bond are as follows].

ATTACHMENT

It can be argued that all of the characteristics attributed to the psychopath follow from, are effects of, his lack of attachment to others. To say that to lack attachment to others is to be free from moral restraints is to use lack of attachment to explain the guiltlessness of the psychopath, the fact that he apparently has no conscience or superego. In this view, lack of attachment to others is not merely a symptom of psychopathy, it *is* psychopathy; lack of conscience is just another way of saying the same thing; and the violation of norms is (or may be) a consequence.

For that matter, given that man is an animal, "impulsivity" and "aggressiveness" can also be seen as natural consequences of freedom from moral restraints. However, since the view of man as endowed with natural propensities and capacities like other animals is peculiarly unpalatable to sociologists, we need not fall back on such a view to explain the amoral man's aggressiveness. The process of becoming alienated from others often involves or is based on active interpersonal conflict. Such conflict could easily supply a reservoir of *socially derived* hostility sufficient to account for the aggressiveness of those whose attachments to others have been weakened.

Durkheim said it many years ago: "We are moral beings to the extent that we are social beings." This may be interpreted to mean that we are moral beings to the extent that we have "internalized the norms" of society. But what does it mean to say that a person has internalized the norms of society? The norms of society are by definition shared by the members of society. To violate a norm is, therefore, to act contrary to the wishes and expectations of other people. If a person does not care about the wishes and expectations of other people—that is, if he is insensitive to the opinion of others—then he is to that extent not bound by the norms. He is free to deviate.

Reprinted from the author's book, *Causes of Delinquency* (Berkeley: University of California Press, 1969), pp. 16–26.

The essence of internalization of norms, conscience, or superego thus lies in the attachment of the individual to others. This view has several advantages over the concept of internalization. For one, explanations of deviant behavior based on attachment do not beg the question, since the extent to which a person is attached to others can be measured independently of his deviant behavior. Furthermore, change or variation in behavior is explainable in a way that it is not when notions of internalization or superego are used. For example, the divorced man is more likely after divorce to commit a number of deviant acts, such as suicide or forgery. If we explain these acts by reference to the superego (or internal control), we are forced to say that the man "lost his conscience" when he got a divorce; and, of course, if he remarries, we have to conclude that he gets his conscience back. . . .

COMMITMENT

"Of all passions, that which inclineth men least to break the laws, is fear. Nay, excepting some generous natures, it is the only thing, when there is the appearance of profit or pleasure by breaking the laws, that makes men keep them." Few would deny that men on occasion obey the rules simply from fear of the consequences. This rational component in conformity we label commitment. What does it mean to say that a person is committed to conformity?. . . [It means] that the person invests time, energy, himself, in a certain line of activity—say, getting an education, building up a business, acquiring a reputation for virtue. When or whenever he considers deviant behavior, he must consider the costs of this deviant behavior, the risk he runs of losing the investment he has made in conventional behavior.

If attachment to others is the sociological counterpart of the superego or conscience, commitment is the counterpart of the ego or common sense. To the person committed to conventional lines of action, risking one to ten years in prison for a ten-dollar holdup is stupidity, because to the committed person the costs and risks obviously exceed ten dollars in value. (To the psychoanalyst, such an act exhibits failure to be governed by the "reality-principle.") In the sociological control theory, it can be and is generally assumed that the decision to commit a criminal act may well be rationally determined—that the actor's decision was not irrational given the risks and costs he faces. . . .

INVOLVEMENT

Many persons undoubtedly owe a life of virtue to a lack of opportunity to do otherwise. Time and energy are inherently limited: "Not that I would not, if I could, be both handsome and fat and well dressed, and a great athlete, and make a million a year, be a wit, a bon vivant, and a lady killer, as well as a philosopher, a philanthropist, a statesman, warrior, and African explorer, as well as a 'tone-poet' and saint. But the thing is simply impossible." The things that William James here says he would like to be or do are all, I suppose, within the realm of conventionality, but if he were to include illicit actions he would still have to eliminate some of them as simply impossible.

Involvement or engrossment in conventional activities is thus often part of a control theory. The assumption, widely shared, is that a person may be simply too busy doing conventional things to find time to engage in deviant behavior. The person involved in conventional activities is tied to appointments, deadlines, working hours, plans, and the like, so the opportunity to commit deviant acts rarely arises. To the extent that he is engrossed in conventional activities, he cannot even think about deviant acts, let alone act out his inclinations. . . .

BELIEF

The control theory assumes the existence of a common value system within the society or group whose norms are being violated. If the deviant is committed to a value system different from that of conventional society, there is, within the context of the theory, nothing to explain. The question is, "Why does a man violate the rules in which he believes?" It is not, "Why do men differ in their beliefs about what constitutes good and desirable conduct?" The person is assumed to have been socialized (perhaps imperfectly) into the group whose rules he is violating; deviance is not a question of one group imposing its rules on the members of another group. In other words, we not only assume the deviant *has* believed the rules, we assume he believes the rules even as he violates them.

How can a person believe it is wrong to steal at the same time he is stealing? In the strain theory, this is not a difficult problem. (In fact, the strain theory was devised specifically to deal with this question.) The motivation to deviance adduced by the strain theorist is so strong that we can well understand the deviant act even assuming the deviator believes strongly that it is wrong. However, given the control theory's assumptions about motivation, if both the deviant and the nondeviant believe the deviant act is wrong, how do we account for the fact that one commits it and the other does not?

Control theories have taken two approaches to this problem. In one approach, beliefs are treated as mere words that mean little or nothing. . . . The second approach argues that the deviant rationalizes his behavior so that he can at once violate the rule and maintain his belief in it. . . . We assume, however, that there is *variation* in the extent to which people believe they should obey the rules of society, and, furthermore, that the less a person believes he should obey the rules, the more likely he is to violate them.

6

Shaming Theory

JOHN BRAITHWAITE
Australia National University

Cultural commitments to shaming are the key to controlling all types of crime. However, for all types of crime, shaming runs the risk of counterproductivity when it shades into stigmatization.

The crucial distinction is between shaming that is reintegrative and shaming that is disintegrative (stigmatization). Reintegrative shaming means that expressions of community disapproval, which may range from mild rebuke to degradation ceremonies, are followed by gestures of reacceptance into the community of law-abiding citizens. These gestures of reacceptance will vary from a simple smile expressing forgiveness and love to quite formal ceremonies to decertify the offender as deviant. Disintegrative shaming (stigmatization), in contrast, divides the community by creating a class of outcasts. Much effort is directed at labeling deviance, while little attention is paid to delabeling, to signifying forgiveness and reintegration, to ensuring that the deviance label is applied to the behavior rather than the person, and that this is done under the assumption that the disapproved behavior is transient, performed by an essentially good person. . . .

The best place to see reintegrative shaming at work is in loving families. . . . Family life teaches us that shaming and punishment are possible while maintaining bonds of respect. Two hypotheses are suggested: first, families are the most effective agents of social control in most societies partly because of this characteristic; second, those families that are disintegrative rather than reintegrative in their punishment processes, that have not learnt the trick of punishing within a continuum of love, are the families that fail at socializing their children

KEY CONCEPTS

Interdependency is a condition of individuals. It means the extent to which individuals participate in networks wherein they are dependent on others to achieve valued ends and others are dependent on them. We could describe an

From the author's book, *Crime, Shame and Reintegration* (Cambridge: Cambridge University Press, 1989), pp. 55–56, 98–102. Reprinted with the permission of Cambridge University Press.

individual as in a state of interdependency even if the individuals who are dependent on him are different from the individuals on whom he is dependent. Interdependency is approximately equivalent to the social bonding, attachment and commitment of control theory.

Communitarianism is a condition of societies. In communitarian societies individuals are densely enmeshed in interdependencies which have the special qualities of mutual help and trust. The interdependencies have symbolic significance in the culture of group loyalties which take precedence over individual interests. The interdependencies also have symbolic significance as attachments which invoke personal obligation to others in a community of concern, rather than simply interdependencies of convenience as between a bank and a small depositor. A communitarian culture rejects any pejorative connotation of dependency as threatening individual autonomy. Communitarian cultures resist interpretations of dependency as weakness and emphasize the need for mutuality of obligation in interdependency (to be both dependent and dependable). The Japanese are said to be socialized not only to *amaeru* (to be succored by others) but also to *amayakasu* (to be nurturing to others).

Shaming means all social processes of expressing disapproval which have the intention or effect of invoking remorse in the person being shamed and/or condemnation by others who become aware of the shaming. When associated with appropriate symbols, formal punishment often shames. But societies vary enormously in the extent to which formal punishment is associated with shaming or in the extent to which the social meaning of punishment is no more than to inflict pain to tip reward-cost calculations in favor of certain outcomes. Shaming, unlike purely deterrent punishment, sets out to moralize with the offender to communicate reasons for the evil of her actions. Most shaming is neither associated with formal punishment nor perpetrated by the state, though both shaming by the state and shaming with punishment are important types of shaming. Most shaming is by individuals within interdependent communities of concern.

Reintegrative shaming is shaming which is followed by efforts to reintegrate the offender back into the community of law-abiding or respectable citizens through words or gestures of forgiveness or ceremonies to decertify the offender as deviant. Shaming and reintegration do not occur simultaneously but sequentially, with reintegration occurring before deviance becomes a master status. It is shaming which labels the act as evil while striving to preserve the identity of the offender as essentially good. It is directed at signifying evil deeds rather than evil persons in the Christian tradition of "hate the sin and love the sinner." Specific disapproval is expressed within relationships characterized by general social approval; shaming criminal behavior is complemented by ongoing social rewarding of alternative behavior patterns. Reintegrative shaming is not necessarily weak; it can be cruel, even vicious. It is not distinguished from stigmatization by its potency, but by (a) a finite rather than open-ended duration which is terminated by forgiveness; and by

(b) efforts to maintain bonds of love or respect throughout the finite period of suffering shame.

Stigmatization is disintegrative shaming in which no effort is made to reconcile the offender with the community. The offender is outcast, her deviance is allowed to become a master status, degradation ceremonies are not followed by ceremonies to decertify deviance.

Criminal subcultures are sets of rationalizations and conduct norms which cluster together to support criminal behavior. The clustering is usually facilitated by subcultural groups which provide systematic social support for crime in any of a number of ways—supplying members with criminal opportunities, criminal values, attitudes which weaken conventional values of law-abidingness, or techniques of neutralizing conventional values.

SHORT SUMMARY OF THE THEORY

The following might serve as the briefest possible summary of the theory. A variety of life circumstances increase the chances that individuals will be in situations of greater interdependency, the most important being age (under 15 and over 25), being married, female, employed, and having high employment and educational aspirations. Interdependent persons are more susceptible to shaming. More important, societies in which individuals are subject to extensive interdependencies are more likely to be communitarian, and shaming is much more widespread and potent in communitarian societies. Urbanization and high residential mobility are societal characteristics which undermine communitarianism.

The shaming produced by interdependency and communitarianism can be either of two types—shaming that becomes stigmatization or shaming that is followed by reintegration. The shaming engendered is more likely to become reintegrative in societies that are communitarian. In societies where shaming does become reintegrative, low crime rates are the result because disapproval is dispensed without eliciting a rejection of the disapprovers, so that the potentialities for future disapproval are not dismantled. . . .

Shaming that is stigmatizing, in contrast, makes criminal subcultures more attractive because these are in some sense subcultures which reject the rejectors. Thus, when shaming is allowed to become stigmatization for want of reintegrative gestures or ceremonies which decertify deviance, the deviant is both attracted to criminal subcultures and cut off from other interdependencies (with family, neighbors, church, etc.). Participation in subcultural groups supplies criminal role models, training in techniques of crime and techniques of neutralizing crime (or other forms of social support) that make choices to engage in crime more attractive. Thus, to the extent that shaming is of the stigmatizing rather than the reintegrative sort, and that criminal subcultures are widespread and accessible in the society, higher crime rates will be the result. While societies characterized by high levels of stigmatization will have higher crime rates than societies characterized by reintegrative shaming, the former will have higher or lower crime rates than societies with little shaming at all depending largely on the availability of criminal subcultures.

Yet a high level of stigmatization in the society is one of the very factors that encourages criminal subculture formation by creating populations of outcasts with no stake in conformity, no chance of self-esteem within the terms of conventional society—individuals in search of an alternative culture that allows them self-esteem. A communitarian culture, on the other hand, nurtures deviants within a network of attachments to conventional society, thus inhibiting the widespread outcasting that is the stuff of subculture formation.

PART 3

Humanist Theories: Understanding Deviance

Given the same problem of soaring teen violence, humanist sociologists go beyond what their positivist colleagues do. The positivists merely focus on the external causes of teen violence, as we have seen in Part Two. By contrast, the humanists enter into the internal experiences of violent teens, trying to understand their violence from their own perspective. This requires the use of a subjectivist method of investigation such as ethnography, which involves the humanist making friends or even living with the subjects in order to get intimate knowledge of their feelings and thoughts. Consider an ethnographic study by sociologist Elijah Anderson. After living in an extremely poor and high-crime neighborhood, Anderson could easily see that abject poverty was a major cause of mounting teen violence. But, more important, Anderson further discovered that many poor youth see violence as an important way for gaining respect. This positive meaning of violence often comes from parents and friends: "Watch your back. If somebody messes with you, you got to pay them back. If someone disses you, you got to straighten them out." The principle of respect is so important to the youth that "the clear risk of violent death may be preferable to being 'dissed' by another."[1] Since respect is not easily available to them without any jobs, the youth can be expected to kill to get it.

Ideas such as those discovered by Anderson are the stuff of humanist theories. Unlike positivist theories, which focus on the causes of deviance, humanist theories concentrate on the meanings of deviance as well as on how individuals behave in keeping with those meanings. In the first article, "Labeling Theory," Howard Becker shows how the meaning of deviance does not derive from the act a person commits but from society's labeling of the act as deviant. In the second selection, "Phenomenological Theory," Jack Katz provides a tour into the experiential world of deviants, showing how they feel about their so-called deviant activities. In the third reading, "Conflict Theory," Richard Quinney describes what he calls "the social reality of crime." The reality consists of the meanings of such things as criminal laws, enforcement of these

---

[1] Elijah Anderson, "The Code of the Streets," The Atlantic Monthly, May 1994, p. 86.

laws, their violations by relatively powerless people, and the dominant class' crime ideology about the enforcement of laws against lower-class criminals. In the fourth article, "Feminist Theory," Jody Miller exposes male bias in the sociology of deviance and then presents the feminist understanding of deviance.

7

Labeling Theory

HOWARD S. BECKER
Northwestern University

A sociological view . . . defines deviance as the infraction of some agreed-upon rule. It then goes on to ask who breaks rules, and to search for the factors in their personalities and life situations that might account for the infractions. This assumes that those who have broken a rule constitute a homogeneous category, because they have committed the same deviant act.

Such an assumption seems to me to ignore the central fact about deviance: it is created by society. I do not mean this in the way it is ordinarily understood, in which the causes of deviance are located in the social situation of the deviant or in "social factors" which prompt his action. I mean, rather, that *social groups create deviance by making the rules whose infraction constitutes deviance, and by applying those rules to particular people and labeling them as outsiders.* From this point of view, deviance is *not* a quality of the act the person commits, but rather a consequence of the application by others of rules and sanctions to an "offender." The deviant is one to whom that label has successfully been applied; deviant behavior is behavior that people so label.

Since deviance is, among other things, a consequence of the responses of others to a person's act, students of deviance cannot assume that they are dealing with a homogeneous category when they study people who have been labeled deviant. That is, they cannot assume that these people have actually committed a deviant act or broken some rule, because the process of labeling may not be infallible; some people may be labeled deviant who in fact have not broken a rule. Furthermore, they cannot assume that the category of those labeled deviant will contain all those who actually have broken a rule, for many offenders may escape apprehension and thus fail to be included in the population of "deviants" they study. Insofar as the category lacks homogeneity and fails to include all the cases that belong in it, one cannot reasonably expect to find common factors of personality or life situation that will account for the supposed deviance.

What, then, do people who have been labeled deviant have in common? At the least, they share the label and the experience of being labeled as outsiders.

Edited and reprinted with the permission of The Free Press, an imprint of Simon & Schuster, from *Outsiders: Studies in the Sociology of Deviance*, by Howard S. Becker. Copyright © 1963 by The Free Press.

I will begin my analysis with this basic similarity and view deviance as the product of a transaction that takes place between some social group and one who is viewed by that group as a rule-breaker. I will be less concerned with the personal and social characteristics of deviants than with the process by which they come to be thought of as outsiders and their reactions to that judgment.

The point is that the response of other people has to be regarded as problematic. Just because one has committed an infraction of a rule does not mean that others will respond as though this had happened. (Conversely, just because one has not violated a rule does not mean that he may not be treated, in some circumstances, as though he had.)

The degree to which other people will respond to a given act as deviant varies greatly. Several kinds of variation seem worth noting. First of all, there is variation over time. A person believed to have committed a given "deviant" act may at one time be responded to much more leniently than he would be at some other time. The occurrence of "drives" against various kinds of deviance illustrates this clearly. At various times, enforcement officials may decide to make an all-out attack on some particular kind of deviance, such as gambling, drug addiction, or homosexuality. It is obviously much more dangerous to engage in one of these activities when a drive is on than at any other time. (In a very interesting study of crime news in Colorado newspapers, Davis found that the amount of crime reported in Colorado newspapers showed very little association with actual changes in the amount of crime taking place in Colorado. And, further, that peoples' estimate of how much increase there had been in crime in Colorado was associated with the increase in the amount of crime news but not with any increase in the amount of crime.)

The degree to which an act will be treated as deviant depends also on who commits the act and who feels he has been harmed by it. Rules tend to be applied more to some persons than others. Studies of juvenile delinquency make the point clearly. Boys from middle-class areas do not get as far in the legal process when they are apprehended as do boys from slum areas. The middle-class boy is less likely, when picked up by the police, to be taken to the station; less likely when taken to the station to be booked; and it is extremely unlikely that he will be convicted and sentenced. This variation occurs even though the original infraction of the rule is the same in the two cases.

Why repeat these commonplace observations? Because, taken together, they support the proposition that deviance is not a simple quality, present in some kinds of behavior and absent in others. Rather, it is the product of a process which involves responses of other people to the behavior. The same behavior may be an infraction of the rules at one time and not at another; may be an infraction when committed by one person, but not when committed by another; some rules are broken with impunity, others are not. In short, whether a given act is deviant or not depends in part on the nature of the act (that is, whether or not it violates some rule) and in part on what other people do about it.

Some people may object that this is merely a terminological quibble, that one can, after all, define terms any way he wants to and that if some people want to speak of rule-breaking behavior as deviant without reference to the reactions of others they are free to do so. This, of course, is true. Yet it might be worthwhile to refer to such behavior as *rule-breaking behavior* and reserve the term *deviant* for those labeled as deviant by some segment of society. I do not insist that this usage be followed. But it should be clear that insofar as a scientist uses "deviant" to refer to any rule-breaking behavior and takes as his subject of study only those who have been *labeled* deviant, he will be hampered by the disparities between the two categories.

If we take as the object of our attention behavior which comes to be labeled as deviant, we must recognize that we cannot know whether a given act will be categorized as deviant until the response of others has occurred. Deviance is not a quality that lies in behavior itself, but in the interaction between the person who commits an act and those who respond to it.

In any case, being caught and branded as deviant has important consequences for one's further social participation and self-image. The most important consequence is a drastic change in the individual's public identity. Committing the improper act and being publicly caught at it place him in a new status. He has been revealed as a different kind of person from the kind he was supposed to be. He is labeled a "fairy," "dope fiend," "nut," or "lunatic," and treated accordingly.

To be labeled a criminal one need only commit a single criminal offense, and this is all the term formally refers to. Yet the word carries a number of connotations specifying auxiliary traits characteristic of anyone bearing the label. A man who has been convicted of housebreaking and thereby labeled criminal is presumed to be a person likely to break into other houses; the police, in rounding up known offenders for investigation after a crime has been committed, operate on this premise. Further, he is considered likely to commit other kinds of crimes as well, because he has shown himself to be a person without "respect for the law." Thus, apprehension for one deviant act exposes a person to the likelihood that he will be regarded as deviant or undesirable in other respects.

Treating a person as though he were generally rather than specifically deviant produces a self-fulfilling prophecy. It sets in motion several mechanisms which conspire to shape the person in the image people have of him. In the first place, one tends to be cut off, after being identified as deviant, from participation in more conventional groups, even though the specific consequences of the particular deviant activity might never of themselves have caused the isolation had there not also been the public knowledge and reaction to it. . . . Though the effects of opiate drugs may not impair one's working ability, to be known as an addict will probably lead to losing one's job. In such cases, the individual finds it difficult to conform to other rules which he had no intention or desire to break, and perforce finds himself deviant in these areas as well. The drug addict finds himself forced into other illegitimate kinds of activity, such as robbery and theft, by the refusal of respectable employers to have him around.

When the deviant is caught, he is treated in accordance with the popular diagnosis of why he is that way, and the treatment itself may likewise produce increasing deviance. The drug addict, popularly considered to be a weak-willed individual who cannot forego the indecent pleasures afforded him by opiates, is treated repressively. He is forbidden to use drugs. Since he cannot get drugs legally, he must get them illegally. This forces the market underground and pushes the price of drugs up far beyond the current legitimate market price into a bracket that few can afford on an ordinary salary. Hence the treatment of the addict's deviance places him in a position where it will probably be necessary to resort to deceit and crime in order to support his habit. The behavior is a consequence of the public reaction to the deviance rather than a consequence of the inherent qualities of the deviant act.

8

Phenomenological Theory

JACK KATZ
University of California, Los Angeles

The study of crime has been preoccupied with a search for background forces, usually defects in the offenders' psychological backgrounds or social environments, to the neglect of the positive, often wonderful attractions within the lived experience of criminality. The novelty of this [theory] is its focus on the seductive qualities of crimes: those aspects in the foreground of criminality that make its various forms sensible, even sensually compelling, ways of being.

The social science literature contains only scattered evidence of what it means, feels, sounds, tastes, or looks like to commit a particular crime. Readers of research on homicide and assault do not hear the slaps and curses, see the pushes and shoves, or feel the humiliation and rage that may build toward the attack, sometimes persisting after the victim's death. How adolescents manage to make the shoplifting or vandalism of cheap and commonplace things a thrilling experience has not been intriguing to many students of delinquency. Researchers of adolescent gangs have never grasped why their subjects so often stubbornly refuse to accept the outsider's insistence that they wear the "gang" label. The description of "cold-blooded, senseless murders" has been left to writers outside the social sciences. Neither academic methods nor academic theories seem to be able to grasp why such killers may have been courteous to their victims just moments before the killing, why they often wait until they have dominated victims in sealed-off environments before coldly executing them, or how it makes sense to them to kill when only petty cash is at stake. Sociological and psychological studies of robbery rarely focus on the *distinctive* attractions of robbery, even though research has now clearly documented that alternative forms of criminality are available and familiar to many career robbers. In sum, only rarely have sociologists taken up the challenge of explaining the qualities of deviant experience.

From *Seductions of Crime* by Jack Katz. Copyright © 1988 by Jack Katz. Reprinted by permission of Basic Books, a division of HarperCollins Publishers, Inc.

The statistical and correlational findings of positivist criminology provide the following irritations to inquiry: (1) whatever the validity of the hereditary, psychological, and social-ecological conditions of crime, many of those in the supposedly causal categories do not commit the crime at issue, (2) many who do commit the crime do not fit the causal categories, and (3) and what is most provocative, many who do fit the background categories and later commit the predicted crime go for long stretches without committing the crimes to which theory directs them. Why are people who were not determined to commit a crime one moment determined to do so the next?

I propose that empirical research turn the direction of inquiry around to focus initially on the foreground, rather than the background of crime. Let us for once make it our first priority to understand the qualities of experience that distinguish different forms of criminality. . . .

A sense of being determined by the environment, of being pushed away from one line of action and pulled toward another, is natural to everyday, routine human experience. We are always moving away from and toward different objects of consciousness, taking account of this and ignoring that, and moving in one direction or the other between the extremes of involvement and boredom. In this constant movement of consciousness, we do not perceive that we are controlling the movement. Instead, to one degree or another, we are always being seduced and repelled by the world. "This *is* fascinating (interesting, beautiful, sexy, dull, ugly, disgusting)," we know (without having to say), as if the thing itself possessed the designated quality independent of us and somehow controlled our understanding of it. Indeed, the very nature of mundane being is emotional; attention is feeling, and consciousness is sensual.

Only rarely do we actually experience ourselves as subjects directing our conduct. How often, when you speak, do you actually sense that you are choosing the words you utter? As the words come out, they reveal the thought behind them even to the speaker whose lips gave them shape. Similarly, we talk, walk, and write in a sense of natural competence governed by moods of determinism. We rest our subjectivity on rhythmic sensibilities, feelings for directions, and visions of unfolding patterns, allowing esthetics to guide us. Self-reflexive postures, in which one creates a distance between the self and the world and pointedly directs the self into the world, occur typically in an exceptional mood of recognizing a malapropism, after a misstep, or at the slip of the pen. With a slight shock, we recognize that it was not the things in themselves but our perspective that temporarily gave things outside of us the power to seduce or repel.

Among the forms of crime, the range of sensual dynamics runs from enticements that may draw a person into shoplifting to furies that can compel him to murder. If, as social researchers, we are to be able to explain more variation in criminality than background correlations allow, it appears that we must respect these sensual dynamics and honor them as authentic. . . .

Approaching criminality from the inside, social research takes as its subject the morally exceptional conduct that the persons themselves regard as criminally sanctionable in official eyes. Since there is an enormous variety of criminal phenomena, how can one demarcate and set up for explanation a limited number of subjectively homogeneous offenses? I suggest that a seemingly simple question be asked persistently in detailed application to the facts of criminal experience: What are people trying to do when they commit a crime?

The resulting topics will not necessarily follow official crime categories. Crimes, as defined in statutes, surveys of citizens, and police records, take definitional shape from the interests of victims and from practical problems of detection and punishment, not necessarily from the experience of those committing the crimes. But if one begins with rough conventional or folk categories, such as hot-blooded murder, gang violence, adolescent property crime, commercial robbery, and "senseless" and "cold-blooded" murder, and refines the concepts to fit homogeneous forms of experience, one can arrive at a significant range of criminal projects: committing righteous slaughter, mobilizing the spirit of a street elite, constructing sneaky thrills, persisting in the practice of stickup as a hardman, and embodying primordial evil.

By way of explanation, I will propose for each type of crime a different set of individually necessary and jointly sufficient conditions, each set containing (1) a path of action—distinctive practical requirements for successfully committing the crime, (2) a line of interpretation—unique ways of understanding how one is and will be seen by others, and (3) an emotional process—seductions and compulsions that have special dynamics. Raising the spirit of criminality requires practical attention to a mode of executing action, symbolic creativity in defining the situation, and esthetic finesse in recognizing and elaborating on the sensual possibilities.

Central to all these experiences in deviance is a member of the family of moral emotions: humiliation, righteousness, arrogance, ridicule, cynicism, defilement, and vengeance. In each, the attraction that proves to be most fundamentally compelling is that of overcoming a personal challenge to moral—not to material—existence. For the impassioned killer, the challenge is to escape a situation that has come to seem otherwise inexorably humiliating. Unable to sense how he or she can move with self-respect from the current situation, now, to any mundane-time relationship that might be reengaged, then, the would-be killer leaps at the possibility of embodying, through the practice of "righteous" slaughter, some eternal, universal form of the Good.

For many adolescents, shoplifting and vandalism offer the attractions of a thrilling melodrama about the self as seen from within and from without. Quite apart from what is taken, they may regard "getting away with it" as a thrilling demonstration of personal competence, especially if it is accomplished under the eyes of adults.

Specifically "bad" forms of criminality are essentially addressed to a moral challenge experienced in a spatial metaphor. Whether by intimidating others' efforts to take him into their worlds ("Who you lookin' at?") or by treating artificial geographic boundaries as sacred and defending local "turf" with relentless "heart," "badasses" and *barrio* warriors celebrate an indifference to modern society's expectation that a person should demonstrate a sensibility to reshape himself as he moves from here to there.

To make a habit of doing stickups, I will argue, one must become a "hard-man." It is only smart to avoid injuring victims unnecessarily, but if one becomes too calculating about the application of violence, the inherent uncertainties of face-to-face interaction in robberies will be emotionally forbidding. Beneath the surface, there may be, to paraphrase Nietzsche, a ball of snakes in chaotic struggle. But the stickup man denies any uncertainty and any possibility of change with a personal style that ubiquitously negates social pressures toward a malleable self.

Perhaps the ultimate criminal project is mounted by men who culminate a social life organized around the symbolism of deviance with a cold-blooded, "senseless" murder. Mimicking the ways of primordial gods as they kill, they proudly appear to the world as astonishingly evil. Through a killing only superficially justified by the context of robbery, they emerge from a dizzying alternation between affiliation with the great symbolic powers of deviant identity and a nagging dis-ease that conformity means cowardice.

Overall, my objective is to demonstrate that a theory of moral self-transcendence can make comprehensible the minutia of experiential details in the phenomenal foreground, as well as explain the general conditions that are most commonly found in the social backgrounds of these forms of criminality.

9

Conflict Theory

RICHARD QUINNEY
Northern Illinois University

A theory that helps us begin to examine the legal order critically is the one I call the *social reality of crime*. Applying this theory, we think of crime as it is affected by the dynamics that mold the society's social, economic, and political structure. First, we recognize how criminal law fits into capitalist society. The legal order gives reality to the crime problem in the United States. Everything that makes up crime's social reality, including the application of criminal law, the behavior patterns of those who are defined as criminal, and the construction of an ideology of crime, is related to the established legal order. The social reality of crime is constructed on conflict in our society.

The theory of the social reality of crime is formulated as follows.

> I. THE OFFICIAL DEFINITION OF CRIME: *Crime as a legal definition of human conduct is created by agents of the dominant class in a politically organized society.*

The essential starting point is a definition of crime that itself is based on the legal definition. Crime, as *officially* determined, is a *definition* of behavior that is conferred on some people by those in power. Agents of the law (such as legislators, police, prosecutors, and judges) are responsible for formulating and administering criminal law. Upon *formulation* and *application* of these definitions of crime, persons and behaviors become criminal.

Crime, according to this first proposition, is not inherent in behavior, but is a judgment made by some about the actions and characteristics of others. This proposition allows us to focus on the formulation and administration of the criminal law as it applies to the behaviors that become defined as criminal. Crime is seen as a result of the class-dynamic process that culminate in defining persons and behaviors as criminal. It follows, then, that the greater the number of definitions of crime that are formulated and applied, the greater the amount of crime.

> II. FORMULATING DEFINITIONS OF CRIME: *Definitions of crime are composed of behaviors that conflict with the interests of the dominant class.*

Reprinted from the author's book, *Criminology* (Boston: Little, Brown, 1975), pp. 37–41.

Definitions of crime are formulated according to the interests of those who have the power to translate their interests into public policy. Those definitions are ultimately incorporated into the criminal law. Furthermore, definitions of crime in a society change as the interests of the dominant class change. In other words, those who are able to have their interests represented in public policy regulate the formulation of definitions of crime.

The powerful interests are reflected not only in the definitions of crime and the kinds of penal sanctions attached to them, but also in the *legal policies* on handling those defined as criminals. Procedural rules are created for enforcing and administering the criminal law. Policies are also established on programs for treating and punishing the criminally defined and programs for controlling and preventing crime. From the initial definitions of crime to the subsequent procedures, correctional and penal programs, and policies for controlling and preventing crime, those who have the power regulate the behavior of those without power.

III.   APPLYING DEFINITIONS OF CRIME: *Definitions of crime are applied by the class that has the power to shape the enforcement and administration of criminal law.*

The dominant interests intervene in all the stages at which definitions of crime are created. Because class interests cannot be effectively protected merely by formulating criminal law, the law must be enforced and administered. The interests of the powerful, therefore, also operate where the definitions of crime reach the *application* stage. As Vold has argued, crime is "political behavior and the criminal becomes in fact a member of a 'minority group' without sufficient public support to dominate the control of the police power of the state." Those whose interests conflict with the ones represented in the law must either change their behavior or possibly find it defined as criminal.

The probability that definitions of crime will be applied varies according to how much the behaviors of the powerless conflict with the interests of those in power. Law enforcement efforts and judicial activity are likely to increase when the interests of the dominant class are threatened. Fluctuations and variations in applying definitions of crime reflect shifts in class relations.

Obviously, the criminal law is not applied directly by those in power; its enforcement and administration are delegated to authorized *legal agents*. Because the groups responsible for creating the definitions of crime are physically separated from the groups that have the authority to enforce and administer law, local conditions determine how the definitions will be applied. In particular, communities vary in their expectations of law enforcement and the administration of justice. The application of definitions is also influenced by the visibility of offenses in a community and by the public's norms about reporting possible violations. And especially important in enforcing and administering the criminal law are the legal agents' occupational organization and ideology.

The probability that these definitions will be applied depends on the actions of the legal agents who have the authority to enforce and administer the law.

A definition of crime is applied depending on their evaluation. Turk has argued that during "criminalization," a criminal label may be affixed to people because of real or fancied attributes: "Indeed, a person is evaluated, either favorably or unfavorably, not because he *does* something, or even because he *is* something, but because others react to their perceptions of him as offensive or inoffensive." Evaluation by the definers is affected by the way in which the suspect handles the situation, but ultimately the legal agents' evaluations and subsequent decisions are the crucial factors in determining the criminality of human acts. As legal agents evaluate more behaviors and persons as worthy of being defined as crimes, the probability that definitions of crime will be applied grows.

IV.   HOW BEHAVIOR PATTERNS DEVELOP IN RELATION TO DEFINITIONS OF CRIME: *Behavior patterns are structured in relation to definitions of crime, and within this context people engage in actions that have relative probabilities of being defined as criminal.*

Although behavior varies, all behaviors are similar in that they represent patterns within the society. All persons—whether they create definitions of crime or are the objects of these definitions—act in reference to *normative systems* learned in relative social and cultural settings. Because it is not the quality of the behavior but the action taken against the behavior that gives it the character of criminality, that which is defined as criminal is relative to the behavior patterns of the class that formulates and applies definitions. Consequently, people whose behavior patterns are not represented when the definitions of crime are formulated and applied are more likely to act in ways that will be defined as criminal than those who formulate and apply the definitions.

Once behavior patterns become established with some regularity within the segments of society, individuals have a framework for creating *personal action patterns*. These continually develop for each person as he moves from one experience to another. Specific action patterns give behavior an individual substance in relation to the definitions of crime.

People construct their own patterns of action in participating with others. It follows, then, that the probability that persons will develop action patterns with a high potential for being defined as criminal depends on (1) structured opportunities, (2) learning experiences, (3) interpersonal associations and identifications, and (4) self-conceptions. Throughout the experiences, each person creates a conception of self as a human social being. Thus prepared, he behaves according to the anticipated consequences of his actions.

In the experiences shared by the definers of crime and the criminally defined, personal-action patterns develop among the latter because they are so defined. After they have had continued experience in being defined as criminal, they learn to manipulate the application of criminal definitions.

Furthermore, those who have been defined as criminal begin to conceive of themselves as criminal. As they adjust to the definitions imposed upon them, they learn to play the criminal role. As a result of others' reactions, therefore, people may develop personal-action patterns that increase the likelihood of their being defined as criminal in the future. That is, increased experience with definitions of crime increases the probability of their developing actions that may be subsequently defined as criminal.

Thus, both the definers of crime and the criminally defined are involved in reciprocal action patterns. The personal-action patterns of both the definers and the defined are shaped by their common, continued, and related experiences. The fate of each is bound to that of the other.

> V.   CONSTRUCTING AN IDEOLOGY OF CRIME: *An ideology of crime is constructed and diffused by the dominant class to secure its hegemony.*

This ideology is created in the kinds of ideas people are exposed to, the manner in which they select information to fit the world they are shaping, and their way of interpreting this information. People behave in reference to the *social meanings* they attach to their experiences.

Among the conceptions that develop in a society are those relating to what people regard as crime. The concept of crime must of course be accompanied by ideas about the nature of crime. Images develop about the relevance of crime, the offender's characteristics, the appropriate reaction to crime, and the relation of crime to the social order. These conceptions are constructed by communication, and, in fact, an ideology of crime depends on the portrayal of crime in all personal and mass communication. This ideology is thus diffused throughout the society.

One of the most concrete ways by which an ideology of crime is formed and transmitted is the official investigation of crime. The President's Commission on Law Enforcement and Administration of Justice is the best contemporary example of the state's role in shaping an ideology of crime. Not only are we as citizens more aware of crime today because of the President's Commission, but official policy on crime has been established in a crime bill, the Omnibus Crime Control and Safe Streets Act of 1968. The crime bill, itself a reaction to the growing fears of class conflict in American society, creates an image of a severe crime problem and, in so doing, threatens to negate some of our basic constitutional guarantees in the name of controlling crime.

Consequently, the conceptions that are most critical in actually formulating and applying the definitions of crime are those held by the dominant class. These conceptions are certain to be incorporated into the social reality of crime. The more the government acts in reference to crime, the more probable it is that definitions of crime will be created and that behavior patterns will develop in opposition to those definitions. The formulation of definitions of crime, their application, and the development of behavior patterns in relation to the definitions, are thus joined in full circle by the construction of an ideological hegemony toward crime.

> VI.   CONSTRUCTING THE SOCIAL REALITY OF CRIME: *The social reality of crime is constructed by the formulation and application of definitions of crime, the development of behavior patterns in relation to these definitions, and the construction of an ideology of crime.*

The first five propositions are collected here into a final composition proposition. The theory of the social reality of crime, accordingly, postulates creating a series of phenomena that increase the probability of crime. The result, holistically, is the social reality of crime.

Because the first proposition of the theory is a definition and the sixth is a composite, the body of the theory consists of the four middle propositions. These form a model of crime's social reality. The model, as diagrammed, relates the proposition units into a theoretical system (Figure 9.1). Each unit is related to the others. The theory is thus a system of interacting developmental propositions. The phenomena denoted in the propositions and their relationships culminate in what is regarded as the amount and character of crime at any time—that is, in the social reality of crime.

The theory of the social reality of crime as I have formulated it is inspired by a change that is occurring in our view of the world. This change, pervading all levels of society, pertains to the world that we all construct and from which, at the same time, we pretend to separate ourselves in our human experiences. For the study of crime, a revision in thought has directed attention to the criminal process: All relevant phenomena contribute to creating definitions of crime, development of behaviors by those involved in criminal-defining situations, and constructing an ideology of crime. The result is the social reality of crime that is constantly being constructed in society.

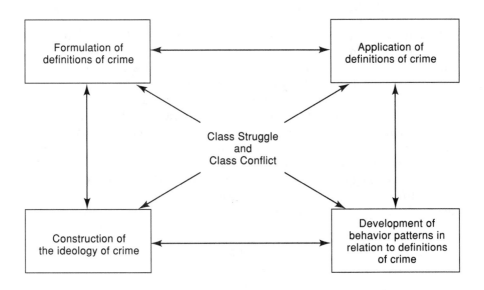

FIGURE 1

The Social Reality of Crime

10

Feminist Theory

Jody Miller
University of Southern California

The study of deviance, like other academic disciplines, is largely a male tradition: Male researchers have mostly focused on male "deviants" and built theories to account for largely male activities. Females have typically been ignored. Since the 1970s, however, feminism has emerged to challenge male bias within the sociology of deviance, while providing alternative perspectives on deviant behavior. Here I will discuss some of the major components of feminist perspectives on deviance. First is a critique of male bias in deviance studies. Second is a focus on female "deviants." Third is an insight into sanctions against deviantized females.* And fourth is a sensitivity to how race, class, and masculinity are implicated in the relationship between gender and deviance.

CRITIQUE OF MALE BIAS

According to feminist theorists, the sociology of deviance has developed to a large extent with an exclusive focus on males; where females enter the discussion it has often only been as sexual objects. The exclusion of women from deviance research has inevitably led to the unwarranted assumption that there is virtually no female participation in deviance, outside of sexual deviance. Thus, for example, researchers have long defined gang involvement as a male phenomenon, even though there has always been evidence of female participation even within the earliest works in the field (see Campbell, 1984). Relatively recent studies have further shown that females are anywhere from 10 to 26 percent of gang members (Campbell, 1984; Chesney-Lind, 1993; Klein, 1971; Miller, 1975), that female gang participation may be increasing (Fagan, 1990; Spergel and Curry, 1993; Taylor, 1993), and that in some urban

---

This article was specifically written for this reader.

* I will use the phrase "deviantized females" rather than "female deviants" throughout this essay to highlight the labeling process by which individuals come to be seen and defined as deviant actors, a process that is not simply a result of individuals' actions, but a political process shaped by gender, race, and class relations in society, among others. For a similar discussion of the reasoning behind the use of the concept "criminalized women" rather than "female offenders," see Bertrand et al., 1992 and Daly, 1992.

areas, upwards of one-fifth of girls report gang affiliations (Bjerregaard and Smith, 1992; Winfree et al., 1992).

When women do appear in deviance research, they are often relegated to the periphery of attention, with men being given center stage. Thus, in studying female participation in gangs, researchers often have sought information from male gang members rather than from the female participants themselves (Campbell, 1990). Not surprisingly, much of the picture of female deviance reflects male bias instead of reality. Short and Strodbeck (1965), for example, suggested that girls are more likely to become involved in gangs if they are physically unattractive and have not developed adequate peer relations. Rice (1963) also described girls in the gang he studied as "exceptionally unattractive" and "dim." These and other researchers routinely describe gang girls as camp followers whose function is to serve the sexual needs of male gang members. Other marginal, subordinate roles that girls are said to play in gangs include carrying weapons, infiltrating rival gangs, instigating or provoking conflict between male gangs, and engaging in cat fights—fighting one another for the attention of male gang members (for a fuller discussion, see Campbell, 1984, 1990). However, recent studies of female gang members by female researchers have shown that female gang participation is more complex than traditional research indicates, both in the roles that girls play in gangs and in the meanings of their gangs for the girls involved (Campbell, 1984; Moore, 1991).

It is true that some studies have focused specifically on female deviance. But such studies were rare. Moreover, they reflect the traditional male bias about female participants in deviance. Such studies typically relate women's deviance to their sexuality, thereby unjustifiably ignoring the social, cultural, and political contexts of their actions (Smart, 1976). Consider Otto Pollack's (1950) highly influential work, *The Criminality of Women*. Pollack theorized that women are just as likely as men to engage in deviant activities but are naturally more able to conceal their deviant acts. Pollack attributed this unusual ability to frequent practice of deceit and manipulation among women, such as hiding their menstrual cycles each month and faking sexual pleasure. Such a condemnatory view of female deviance contrasts sharply with the feminist view.

WOMEN AS DEVIANT ACTORS

While traditional male-biased theory often resorts to biological determinism in explaining women's deviance in terms of their stereotyped sexuality, feminist theorists turn to larger social forces for explanations of female deviance, just as larger social forces have always been used to explain male deviance. In addition, feminists examine gender inequality in society as one of the explanations of female deviance. For illustrations of this point, let us take a look at two feminist analyses, one dealing with female delinquency and the other focusing on female prostitution.

Patterns of Female Delinquency

For the most part, self-report studies indicate that girls participate in various forms of delinquency just as their male counterparts do (Campbell, 1981; Canter, 1982; Chesney-Lind and Shelden, 1992; Empey and Stafford, 1991; Figueira-McDonough, 1985; Sarri, 1983). In a national probability sample of 1725 juveniles, for example, Canter (1982) found that "males and females generally engage in the same delinquent behaviors." However, arrest rates for girls are higher than for boys for sex-related offenses (such as prostitution) and running away, reflecting a sexual bias within the system in the handling of delinquent girls (Chesney-Lind and Shelden, 1992; Steffensmeier and Steffensmeier, 1980).

By contrast, there is evidence of greater male involvement in serious property and violent offenses, as well as in repeated offenses (Canter, 1982). As Canter reports,

> There are significant [gender] differences in the following property items: damaging other property, stealing a motor vehicle, stealing more than $50, evading payment, breaking into a building, and joyriding. . . . Boys are also more involved in the violent crimes of gang fighting, strong-arming students and others, aggravated assault, hitting students, and sexual assault. More generally, the findings point to the substantially greater involvement of males in serious crimes (1982: 337).

The more serious, more violent, and more profitable nature of male delinquency may be attributed to the socialization of boys that encourages them to be more aggressive and masculine than females, in addition to males' greater access to public space resulting from male privilege in patriarchal society.

Even the apparent increase in female deviance over the last two decades reflects the continuing influence of patriarchal society, which places greater limitations on female behavior. For one thing, it is true that female delinquency has increased significantly, but male delinquency has as well. As Canter (1982) reports from studying representative samples of American adolescents, there are "parallel increases" in delinquent involvement among males and females that maintain traditional gender differences in delinquency. It is also true that crime by female adults has increased noticeably, but much of this increase has involved relatively unprofitable, minor crimes such as shoplifting, welfare fraud, and writing bad checks (Steffensmeier, 1981). By all accounts, females are not catching up with males in the commission of traditionally male patterns of violent, masculine, or serious crimes (Chesney-Lind and Shelden, 1992; Empey and Stafford, 1991; Steffensmeier, 1981)

Female Prostitution

For many feminists, female prostitution provides perhaps the clearest example of the oppression of women in patriarchal society. The fact that prostitution flourishes in our culture derives a great deal of support from the sexist view of women as sexual objects that can be sold as commodities for male consumption (Schur, 1988). In addition, economic inequality between women and men leaves prostitution as one of the few viable economic alternatives for some women to earn a decent living. Female prostitutes are subjected to considerable abuse within the male-dominated society.

First, they are stigmatized and punished for breaking the "feminine" norms that prohibit women from having multiple sexual partners. This may explain why Silbert and Pines (1982) found many streetwalkers to be victims of violence: 70 percent of their study sample had been raped by clients, 65 percent reported being beaten by clients, 66 percent were physically abused by pimps, and 73 percent "had experienced rapes totally unrelated to their work as prostitutes."

Second, they suffer abuses in the hands of police officers. These abuses appear in various forms. Most commonly, the women are entrapped by plainclothes police officers or illegally arrested (Carmen and Moody, 1985; James, 1978; Pheterson, 1989). Some police officers use the threat of arrest to get sexual favors from the women (Delecoste and Alexander, 1988). Some officers even arrest the women after having sex with them (James, 1978; Pheterson, 1989).

Many police officers also deny prostitutes their legal rights when victimized by refusing to take any action against the women's attackers (James, et al, 1975; Miller, 1993; Pheterson, 1989). Consider the case of Karen, a street prostitute in Fresno, California. A man held an ice pick to her head, raped her repeatedly for three hours, and walked her to a park where he said he was going to kill her. On the way, a friend spotted her and got her away from the man. Later that day, she saw the man again and several friends cornered him, took away his ice pick, and held him for the police. When the police arrived, they let the man go and instead threatened to arrest Karen and her friend for assault, insisting that Karen as a prostitute could not be raped (Delacoste and Alexander, 1988).

THE TREATMENT OF "DEVIANTIZED" WOMEN

According to feminists, many women are labeled "deviants" simply because they do not conform to the traditional expectation that they be feminine, quiet, passive, and the like. As Schur (1984) has noted, women are informally labeled deviants through the use of labels such as "aggressive," "bitchy," "hysterical," "fat," "homely," "masculine," and "promiscuous." These labels "may not put the presumed 'offender' in jail, but they do typically damage her reputation, induce shame, and lower her 'life chances'" (Schur, 1984). While numerous women face deviant labeling in everyday life, those who commit crimes suffer greater consequences as "double deviants," for not only violating societal norms against criminal conduct, but also for deviating from normative gender expectations for women (Schur, 1984).

Not surprisingly, feminists often find that the justice system deals more harshly with female than male offenders, even when their offenses are less serious than those committed by men. This is particularly true in regard to female delinquents who are sexually active or running away from home. Girls have until recently been routinely arrested for committing these status offenses, but boys were left alone for doing exactly the same thing (Chesney-Lind, 1977). Ironically, the harsher treatment of female delinquents has long been carried out under the guise of judicial paternalism, with the judge acting as the girls' father, trying to "protect" them from "sexual temptation" or "immoral activities."

Today girls are less often sent to detention centers for committing status offenses, but the hidden incarceration of delinquent girls through "voluntary" commitments has increased significantly. Private juvenile placement facilities, where youths, without their consent, can be "voluntarily" committed by their parents, are now estimated to have a clientele that is 60 percent female (Chesney-Lind, 1988; Chesney-Lind and Shelden, 1992). Moreover, delinquent girls continue to receive harsher treatment than delinquent boys in some institutional settings such as training schools, detention centers, and treatment facilities (Chesney-Lind, 1978; Chesney-Lind and Shelden, 1992; Gelsthorpe, 1989; Mann, 1979, 1984). One national study, for example, reported that girls are generally allowed less frequent home visits and fewer visiting hours (Mann, 1984).

NEW TRENDS IN FEMINIST STUDIES OF DEVIANCE

The development of feminist deviance studies has been advanced in recent years by an integrated focus on race, class, and gender, rather than an exclusive focus on gender inequality. In discussing female participation in deviance, feminists have sometimes tended to bring a white, middle-class focus to their studies, instead of being attuned to the complexities caused by the intersection with gender of various social positions, such as class and race. Feminists also tend to focus on female deviance, thereby ignoring male deviance. There are, therefore, some feminists who have recently tried to bring the issues of race and class, as well as male deviance, into feminist perspectives.

Race, Class, and Gender

Many of the feminist assumptions about deviantized females and their treatment by the justice system fail to take into account the impact of race or class. Women of color and poor women are effectively ignored. As African-American feminist theorist Bell Hooks observed, "When black people are talked about, the focus tends to be on black *men,* and when women are talked about, the focus tends to be on *white* women" (Laub and McDermott, 1985). As a consequence, feminist theories may apply to white, middle-class women but not to women of color or poor women. To take a close look at this problem, let us reexamine the treatment of girls within the juvenile justice system.

Feminists have often used the theory of judicial paternalism to explain the treatment of girls within the juvenile justice system. According to this theory, female offenders are treated more severely than male offenders at all levels of the juvenile justice system, not only because they have violated normative gender expectations, but, more important, because the judge assumes the role of father by trying to protect girls from "sexual temptations and immoralities" (Chesney-Lind, 1977, 1978, 1988; Chesney-Lind and Shelden, 1992). The notion of "paternalism," however, may be relevant to white middle-class women but not to poor women or women of color. This is because protection is often extended to middle-class and white women, to the exclusion of poor and working-class women and women of color. Not surprisingly, poor females and females of color are treated more punitively in the justice system.

In her analysis of police-suspect encounters, Visher (1983), for example, found that "young, black, or hostile women receive no preferential treatment, whereas older, white women who are calm and deferential toward the police are granted leniency." In her study of court decisions, Sarri (1983) also found greater discrimination against women of color: African-American females are most likely to be placed on probation, while white females have the best chance of escaping sanctions. Other studies have suggested that African-American and Latina delinquent girls are increasingly more likely to be sent to overcrowded detention centers and training schools, while their white counterparts are more often referred to their parents or to private treatment agencies (Sarri, 1983; Krisberg et al., 1988).

Masculinity and Deviance

The emergence of feminist deviance studies began with a focus on women. Because women have consistently been ignored and stereotyped within the traditions of the field, the primary focus for quite some time was on building a knowledge base for understanding deviantized females and the sanctions and treatment they face. Increasingly, feminist research is expanding, to examine gender not just as it applies to females, but also as it concerns males (Messerschmidt, 1993; Whyte and Dekeseredy, 1992).

Feminists have found a strong link between masculinity and male deviance. Masculinity is a major source of deviance among men and boys, and shapes male participation in crime. According to Messerschmidt (1993), participation in criminal activities is one social resource available for men with which to construct and accomplish masculinity. For example, males who are tough, aggressive, or in possession of other stereotypical masculine traits are more likely to engage in certain violent forms of deviance. This explains why date rape is so common in college fraternities and athletic settings (Martin and Hummer, 1993; Warshaw, 1988).

Race and class shape both masculine ideals and the resources available for constructing masculinity, and these shape the types of deviance males engage in (Messerschmidt, 1993). Participation in street gangs provides an example of how some young men of color from impoverished communities construct a masculine identity. The street gang is especially alluring as a source of masculinity for some young men because they have limited resources available for constructing a masculine identity that fits with the dominant ideal, especially the sense of being able to provide for and take care of their families. The street gang can help them create a masculine identity by offering status, reputation, and self-respect.

Gay-bashing provides another illuminating example of how male deviance involves men seeking masculinity in deviant activities. Gay-bashing is most common among working-class white males. According to Harry (1992), gay-bashing is used to validate the participants' sense of their masculinity, because attacking gay men makes them feel more manly. Gay-bashing can serve this function of validating manliness because patriarchal society associates masculinity with being a male heterosexual. Attacking gay men reaffirms these young mens' sense of themselves as heterosexual.

CONCLUSION

The goal of this essay has been to introduce the reader to feminist perspectives on deviance. It is an expansive and ever-growing field, delving into a wide range of topics, from the critique of mainstream research and theory, to the examination of female participation in deviance, violence against women and children, the treatment of deviantized females, and the ways in which gender is central in any attempt to understand male involvement in deviant behavior. Of course, this brief discussion can in no way cover the full range of topics that feminist perspectives shed light on. Already wide-ranging, the perspective continues to grow rapidly, acquiring many new theories about the relationship between gender and deviance.

References

Bertrand, Marie Andrée, Kathleen Daly, and Dorie Klein, eds. 1992. *Proceedings of the International Conference on Women, Law, and Social Control.* Vancouver: International Centre for Criminal Law Reform and Criminal Justice Policy.

Bjerregaard, Beth and Carolyn Smith. 1992. "Patterns of Male and Female Gang Membership." Working Paper No. 13. Albany: Rochester Youth Development Study.

Campbell, Anne. 1990. "Female Participation in Gangs," pp. 163–182 in *Gangs In America,* edited by C. Ronald Huff. Newbury Park: Sage.

Campbell, Anne. 1984. *The Girls in the Gang.* New York: Basil Blackwell.

Campbell, Anne. 1981. *Girl Delinquents.* New York: St. Martins Press.

Canter, Rachelle J. 1982. "Sex Differences in Self-Report Delinquency." *Criminology* 20: 373–393.

Carmen, Arlene and Howard Moody. 1985. *Working Women: The Subterranean World of Street Prostitution.* New York: Harper & Row.

Chesney-Lind, Meda. 1993. "Girls, Gangs and Violence: Anatomy of a Backlash." *Humanity & Society* 17(3): 321–344.

Chesney-Lind, Meda. 1988. "Girls and Status Offenses: Is Juvenile Justice Still Sexist?" *Criminal Justice Abstracts* 20(1): 144–65.

Chesney-Lind, Meda. 1978. "Young Women in the Arms of the Law," pp. 171–196 in *Women, Crime and the Criminal Justice System,* edited by Lee H. Bowker. Lexington, MA: Lexington Books.

Chesney-Lind, Meda. 1977. "Judicial Paternalism and the Female Status Offender: Training Women to Know Their Place." *Crime & Delinquency* 23: 121–130.

Chesney-Lind, Meda and Randall G. Shelden. 1992. *Girls, Delinquency and Juvenile Justice.* Pacific Grove, CA: Brooks/Cole Publishing Company.

Delacoste, Frédérique and Priscilla Alexander, eds. 1988. *Sex Work.* London: Virago Press.

Daly, Kathleen. 1992. "Women's Pathways to Felony Court: Feminist Theories of Lawbreaking and Problems of Representation." *Review of Law and Women's Studies* 2(1): 11–52.

Empey, LaMar T. and Mark C. Stafford. 1991. *American Delinquency: Its Meaning & Construction.* Belmont, CA: Wadsworth Publishing Company.

Fagan, Jeffrey. 1990. "Social Processes of Delinquency and Drug Use Among Urban Gangs," pp. 183–219 in *Gangs in America,* edited by C. Ronald Huff. Newbury Park: Sage.

Figueira-McDonough, Josephina. 1985. "Are Girls Different? Gender Discrepencies Between Delinquent Behavior and Control." *Child Welfare* 64: 273–289.

Gelsthorpe, Loraine. 1989. *Sexism and the Female Offender: An Organizational Analysis.* Aldershot, England: Gower.

Harry, Joseph. 1992. "Conceptualizing Anti-Gay Violence." *Journal of Interpersonal Violence* 5(3): 350–358.

James, Jennifer, Jean Withers, Marilyn Haft, Sara Theiss, and Mary Owen. 1975. *The Politics of Prostitution.* New York: Social Research Associates.

James, Jennifer. 1978. "The Prostitute as Victim," pp. 175–202 in *The Victimization of Women,* edited by Jane Roberts Chapman and Margaret Gates. Beverly Hills: Sage.

Klein, Malcolm W. 1971. *Street Gangs and Street Workers.* Englewood Cliffs, NJ: Prentice-Hall.

Krisberg, Barry, Ira M. Schwartz, Paul Litsky, and James Austin. 1986. "The Watershed of Juvenile Justice Reform." *Crime & Delinquency* 32: 5–38.

Laub, John H. and M. Joan McDermott. 1985. "An Analysis of Serious Crime by Young Black Women." *Criminology* 23:81–98.

Mann, Coramae Richey. 1984. *Female Crime and Delinquency.* University: University of Alabama Press.

Mann, Coramae Richey. 1979. "Making Jail the Hard Way: Law and the Female Offender." *Corrections Today* 41: 35–41.

Martin, Patricia Yancey and Robert A. Hummer. 1993. "Fraternities and Rape on Campus," pp. 392–401 in *Feminist Frontiers III,* edited by Laurel Richardson and Verta Taylor. New York: McGraw-Hill.

Messerschmidt, James W. 1993. *Masculinities and Crime: Critique and Reconceptualization of Theory.* Lantham, MD: Rowman & Littlefield.

Miller, Jody. 1993. "'Your Life is on the Line Every Night You're on the Streets': Victimization and Resistance among Street Prostitutes." *Humanity & Society* 17(4): 422–446.

Miller, Walter B. 1975. *Violence by Youth Gangs and Youth Groups as a Crime Problem in Major American Cities.* Washington, DC: U.S. Government Printing Office.

Moore, Joan. 1991. *Going Down to the Barrio: Homeboys and Homegirls in Change.* Philadelphia: Temple University Press.

Pheterson, Gail. 1989. *A Vindication of the Rights of Whores.* Seattle: Seal Press.

Pollack, Otto. 1950. *The Criminality of Women.* Philadelphia: University of Pennsylvania Press.

Rice, Robert. 1963. "A Reporter at Large: The Persian Queens." *The New Yorker* 39: 135ff.

Sarri, Rosemary. 1983. "Gender Issues in Juvenile Justice." *Crime & Delinquency* 29: 381–397.

Schur, Edwin M. 1988. *The Americanization of Sex.* Philadelphia: Temple University Press.

Schur, Edwin M. 1984. *Labeling Women Deviant: Gender, Stigma and Social Control.* New York: Random House.

Short, James F. and Fred L. Strodbeck. 1965. *Group Process and Gang Delinquency.* Chicago: University of Chicago Press.

Silbert, Mimi H. and Ayala M. Pines. 1982. "Victimization of Street Prostitutes." *Victimology* 7: 122–133.

Smart, Carol. 1976. *Women, Crime and Criminology: A Feminist Critique.* London: Routledge & Kegan Paul.

Spergel, Irving A. and G. David Curry. 1993. "The National Youth Gang Survey: A Research and Development Process," pp. 359–400 in *The Gang Intervention Handbook,* edited by Arnold P. Goldstein and C. Ronald Huff. Champaign, IL: Research Press.

Steffensmeier, Darrell J. 1981. "Crime and the Contemporary Woman: An Analysis of Changing Levels of Property Crimes, 1960–1975," pp. 39–59 in *Women and Crime in America,* edited by Lee Bowker. New York: Macmillan.

Steffensmeier, Darrell J. and Renee Hoffman Steffensmeier. 1980. "Trends in Female Delinquency: An Examination of Arrest, Juvenile Court, Self-Report, and Field Data." *Criminology* 18: 62–85.

Taylor, Carl. 1993. *Girls, Gangs, Women and Drugs.* East Lansing: Michigan State University Press.

Visher, Christy A. 1983. "Gender, Police Arrest Decisions, and Notions of Chivalry." *Criminology* 21: 5–28.

Warshaw, Robin. 1988. *I Never Called It Rape.* New York: Harper and Row.

Whyte, Donald and Walter DeKeseredy. 1992. "The Homosocial Factor in Male Violence and Masculine Subjectivity." *Men's Studies Review* 9(1): 27–31.

Winfree, L. Thomas Jr., Kathy Fuller, Teresa Vigil, and G. Larry Mays. 1992. "The Definition and Measurement of 'Gang Status': Policy Implications for Juvenile Justice." *Juvenile & Family Court Journal* pp. 29–37.

PART 4

Theoretical Overview and Integration

Twenty or thirty years ago, questions were raised in the sociology of deviance over fundamental issues such as whether deviance really exists. Apparently reflecting the great conflict between liberals and conservatives, between blacks and whites, or between anti-war and pro-war activists in the society of that time, the theoretical debate in the sociology of deviance was largely ideological and negativistic, with humanists charging positivists with supporting the oppressive status quo, and positivists countercharging humanists with distorting reality. Since then both sides have knuckled down to the quiet task of producing theoretical and empirical knowledge about the world of deviance. Now, in the 1990s, some sociologists no longer find any excitement about deviance theories. This is probably because the ideological spark of the earlier decades has dissipated. A more important reason could be the realization that it is useless to develop a general theory to deal with all types of deviance. The enormous diversity of deviance simply makes it impossible to come out with such a theory. It may be more fruitful to develop relatively concrete theories, each applying only to a specific form of deviance, such as those presented in the remainder of this reader.

We may appreciate the need for such theories if we carefully study the first article, "Major Notions and Theories in the Sociology of Deviance," by Jack Gibbs. In this article Gibbs critically and insightfully analyzes a variety of ideas and theories about deviance. He finds all the theories mostly inadequate, because they are too general to be empirically testable. He concludes that it is better to develop more specific, testable theories. But the larger perspectives need not be abandoned. They are still useful for rendering order to an otherwise disorganized mess of seemingly disparate theories. Thus, in the second selection, Ira Reiss shows how positivists (or, to Gibbs, etiological theorists) can enhance their understanding of deviance with humanist consciousness. In the third reading, Alex Thio demonstrates how humanists (or, to Gibbs, reactive theorists) can use positivist theories to explain the influence of power on deviance.

11

Major Notions and Theories in the Sociology of Deviance

JACK P. GIBBS
Vanderbilt University

Despite an enormous surge in the 1960s and 1970s, the sociology of deviance has been declining for several years. The decline is puzzling if only because the field's subject matter encompasses crime and juvenile delinquency in addition to "extralegal" deviance (e.g., mental illness), but criminology has not declined.[1] This brief survey attempts to throw light on the decline, beginning with two observations. First, the link between sociological studies of deviance and mainstream sociology is tenuous—one reason why those studies lack a compelling rationale. Second, there could be at least one compelling rationale: Major socio-cultural changes commence as deviance.

MAJOR NOTIONS IN THE SOCIOLOGY OF DEVIANCE

A notion is scarcely important if it does not enter into theories. So, despite this chapter's division into two parts, notions and theories should be thought of as integrated, though more for some notions than others. As an example, virtually by definition the notion of deviance (including crimes and delinquencies) enters into all of the field's theories; therefore, it is the field's principal notion. Nonetheless, since the early 1960s the field has been haunted by a controversial and difficult question: What is deviant behavior? The controversy centers on two notions that enter into definitions of deviant behavior; hence, they are *major* notions for that reason alone.

The Notion of a Norm

Prior to the 1960s, virtually all definitions went something like this: Deviant behavior is behavior that violates a norm of at least one social unit.[2] That ver-

---

This article was specifically written for this reader.

sion of the *normative* conception of deviant behavior or any other version has a horrendous implication: Problems with the notion of a norm create problems with the notion of deviant behavior.[3] Unfortunately, the notion of a norm is a study in problems, even though most sociologists appear indifferent to those problems.

Consider a very thoughtful definition by George Homans (1961:46): "A *norm* is a statement made by a number of members of a group, not necessarily by all of them, that the members ought to behave in a certain way in certain circumstances." The definition's chief merit is that it forces recognition of problems with the notion of a norm. The most obvious, the "sufficient consensus problem," is introduced by this *corollary question:* What proportion of social unit members must make or subscribe to a statement for that statement to be a norm? The question is suggested by Homans' qualification "not necessarily all." That qualification is needed; without it, norms would be largely peculiar to some families, teams, or cliques, where normative consensus (agreement in evaluations of conduct) is most likely to prevail. But Homans skirted the corollary question, perhaps for a good reason—any answer is bound to be arbitrary or grossly unrealistic if "all members."

Homans' phrase "certain circumstances" raises a question about *normative contingencies.* Exactly what circumstances do the group members have in mind? There are countless possible circumstances pertaining to situations (time and place), the social identity of the actor (e.g., age, race, gender), and the social identity of objects of the act in question (e.g., a crime victim's occupation). So the "normative contingency" problem is perhaps insoluble. Think about responses to this question in an opinion survey: Do you approve or disapprove of abortion? The answer, whether affirmative or negative, depends largely on unstipulated circumstances, or what are technically known as "normative contingencies" (e.g., whether the pregnancy was caused by a rape), all of which influence the responses to such a question substantially.[4] The solution may appear obvious—introduce contingencies when posing normative questions. Unfortunately, it is inconceivable that a normative question can be worded so as to recognize *all* possibly relevant contingencies (e.g., the age of a cigarette smoker), and all the more because what is a relevant contingency for one survey respondent may not be for others.

Finally, Homans' definition creates a problem by focusing on *personal evaluations of conduct*—what the individual making a statement regards as good or bad behavior. That focus becomes suspect in light of this question: Why do sociologists believe that norms are important? Ostensibly because they believe that much of human behavior is governed by norms.[5] If so, however, why limit norms to *personal evaluations* of conduct? After all, our behavior (e.g., locking a parked car) often is determined not by strictly normal evaluations but by *expectations* of consequences. For that matter, our behavior may be dictated not by what we personally believe to be right or wrong but, rather, by our perceptions of the evaluative standards of significant others (parents, friends, etc.). However, once *perceived evaluations* are recognized as relevant in defining a norm, someone is bound to ask: Why not define norms in terms of the frequency with which *types of acts* are punished? After all, punishment clearly signifies disapproval. So, in addition to personal evaluations of conduct, several other normative properties appear relevant; but recognizing them all when defining and identifying norms borders on an impossibility, which is to say that the "multiple normative properties" problem defies a simple solution.

The Notion of Reactions to Deviance

Given the litany of problems with the notion of norms, it should not have come as a surprise in the 1960s when sociologists began to move away from the normative conception of deviance to the "reactive conception."[6] Unfortunately, the reactivists never stated the conception explicitly and clearly, let alone the rationale for it (e.g., perhaps insoluble problems with the notion of a norm). In any case, they appear to prefer (see quotes of Becker, Erickson, and Kitsuse in Gibbs, 1972) a definition something like this: An act is deviant if and only if reacted to distinctively. Surely "distinctively" is vague, but the reactivists would balk—perhaps rightly so—at substituting "punitively." So modified, the latter term would be consistent with the conventional designation of crimes and delinquencies as deviant behavior but inconsistent with the same designation of mental illness, unless one characterizes all psychiatric diagnoses as "punitive." The reactive definition is ambiguous because it does not speak to two questions. First, what kind of reaction to an act identifies the act as deviant? Second, whatever the kind of reaction, who must react? The second question is especially relevant when defining and identifying crimes. Reactivists cannot define a crime as an act prohibited by law, because a law is a type of norm. Nor can they say that an act is a crime if and only if so labeled by a legal official. That statement would be consistent with the reactive conception of deviant behavior, but it does not answer this question: What if legal officials (police, prosecutors, judges, jurors) *disagree* in labeling the same act as criminal or not criminal?

Instead of confronting the problems and issues just raised, reactivists speak of deviant behavior as "behavior so labeled." But when do we know that an act or individual has been labeled deviant? The question is relevant if only because possibly strategic reactors, such as police and psychiatrists, may never use the term "deviant." Consider the suggestion that such words as nut, hooker, crook, queer, and pervert are deviant labels. The objection is not just that the list is bound to be incomplete and peculiar to English-speaking populations; how do we know that such words signify deviance? As the question suggests, the notion of labeling admits norms through the back door.

The reactive conception appears to be fading, but the normative conception has not survived because the issues were resolved. Sociologists evidently came to regard the reactive conception as too radical. Even tacit rejection of the notion of norms make the link between studies of deviance and mainstream sociology all the more tenuous, and the reactive conception makes "secret deviance" a misnomer. What about the great concern of the reactivists (in the tradition of symbolic interactionism) with the actual perceptions of actual people in actual situations? Such "social realism" is commendable (see Thio, 1988:18–20), but imagine a police officer saying to someone, "You have committed a crime because I have arrested you." The point is that reactivists have the cart before the horse. Behavior is not deviant because it is reacted to distinctively; instead, it is reacted to distinctively because it is deviant. Finally, consider the perennial issue of the reliability of official statistics on the incidence of crime. The astonishing implication of the reactive conception as it applies to crime is this: Official statistics are the only possible basis for computing a crime rate. That implication extends even to rejecting *unofficial* surveys of self-reported crimes or victim-reported crimes, with the argument that only a legal official can label acts as crimes.

It may well be that the reactivists put such a subjective if not solipsistic stamp on the sociology of deviance that the field suffered.[7] Even so, the reactive conception has some merits. For one, it extends more readily than the normative conception to a definition of "a deviant": An individual is deviant if and only if he or she is reacted to distinctively.[8] For another, it points the way to circumventing the normative contingencies problem; in reacting to an act, the reactors judge the relevant contingencies.

Prior to the 1960s, sociological studies of deviance were concerned almost exclusively with one of two questions, both etiological. First, why do rates of particular types of deviance (e.g., robbery, suicide) vary among social units and over time? Second, who do only some social unit members commit a particular type of deviant act? Now a third question arises: Why do reactions to deviance vary among social units, over time, and from case to case? The reactivists never explicitly championed the third question, but they did make "reactions to deviance" a major notion in the sociology of deviance. The ultimate possibility—perhaps necessity—is an etiological theory that treats the character of reactions as a major determinant of the official rate of deviance (see Gibbs, 1987:828–831).

Social Differentiation

The concern here is with notions rather than major terms. This distinction is important because sociologists may use different terms in stating a theory, but the terms could actually refer to the same notion. As an example, another major notion in the sociology of deviance—social differentiation—cannot be analyzed fully without using five terms: conflict, inequality, power, social class, and stratification. Each term denotes either a form of social differentiation (inequality, social class, stratification) or something based on social differentiation (conflict and power).

Sociologists commonly explain deviance by referring to social differentiation, even though they may not actually use that term. The practice is illustrated in the subsequent survey of major theories. Here we will simply point out that some explanations of various kinds of deviance (e.g., theft, robbery) attribute them to poverty so as to make inequality the principal etiological factor, but the relevance of social differentiation is not limited to the etiology of deviance. Various explanations of reactions to deviance are couched in terms of power and conflict. Thus, Marxists are prone to describe criminal law as a weapon used by a dominant economic class (capitalist, the nobility, or slave owners) in their conflict with subordinate classes (proletarians, serfs, or slaves).

Control

Most sociological studies of deviance do not seek or prescribe means to prevent deviance (another possible rationale for the studies). Doing so would invite criticism for supporting the *status quo*. In the 1960s and 1970s a definite antiestablishment trend existed in the sociology of deviance, the most conspicuous manifestation being the depiction of deviants as victimized or exploited underdogs.

Today, the antiestablishment orientation is most conspicuous in what Erich Goode (1994:132) identifies as "contrology, the new sociology of deviance." According to Goode, that perspective emerged in the late 1970s, fueled initially by Michael Foucault's books and now promoted by sociologists, such as Stanley Cohen, Nanette Davis, and Andrew Scull (see references in Goode, 1994:132–138).[9] Social control is the perspective's central concern, and it is defined in terms of reactions to deviance, with almost an exclusive focus on state agencies and public institutions, especially prisons and mental hospitals.[10] However, the perspective is barren of anything resembling scientific theories. Instead, "controlologists" make allegations about and offer hostile interpretations of the way that state agents and elites define, identify, and react to deviance. The character of those interpretations is suggested by Goode's statement (1994:137) in connection with Scull: "The purpose of psychiatry is not to heal but to control; the purpose of the welfare system is not to provide a safety net for the poor but to control; the purpose of education is not to teach but to control; the purpose of the mass media is not to inform but to control; and so on." Proponents of such interpretations might well cringe at even the suggestion that control could be sociology's central notion (Gibbs, 1989), but they unwittingly provide support for that argument.

Despite comments about "controlology," sociological studies of deviance do have control implications. Indeed, the most neglected argument in those studies goes something like this: Many types of deviance (e.g., robbery, rape, fraud) cannot be fully explained without recognizing that they are control attempts. Moreover, in recent years a line of sociological studies of deviance does bear directly on crime prevention. Those studies focus on the deterrence doctrine—the argument that crimes can be reduced through certain, swift, and severe legal punishments. That argument is analyzed subsequently, but even at this point it should be recognized now that control is a major notion in the sociology of deviance apart from deterrence.

MAJOR THEORIES IN THE SOCIOLOGY OF DEVIANCE

Although the reactive conception of deviance is fading, interest in reactions to deviance continues to rival interest in the causes of deviance. So there is a rationale for recognizing two broad categories of theories, the etiological and the reactive.

The Etiological: Merton's Anomie Theory

An understanding of the etiological theory is furthered by an answer to this question: Why are few Americans genuinely puzzled by the typical bank robbery? Because recognition of money's desirability makes a bank robber's goal anything but mysterious. However, a prominent surgeon who robs banks would baffle many people. Americans are motivated to acquire money and wealth—both are "cultural goals"—but surgeons surely have greater access to legitimate means to those goals than do the unskilled.

Merton (1957) was primarily concerned with emphasis on cultural goals and differential access to legitimate (institutional) means for realizing those goals (e.g., income from employment), but his neglect of "emphasis on means" is puzzling and unfortunate. Certainly the distinction between access to and emphasis on means is fairly clear. Think about the long prison sentences prescribed in criminal codes for robbery. Such punishments have nothing to do with *access* to legitimate means (e.g., employment) for acquiring money or property, but surely they emphasize those means by threatening the infliction of pain for the use of illegitimate means, robbery being one.

Merton's theory is not limited to crimes. Suppose we hear this conversation concerning a particular student: "Why does he cheat so much? You have no idea how much his parents push him to make high grades!" In terms of Merton's theory, the boy is being pushed to realize a cultural goal. But the illustration has no bearing on differential access to legitimate means, as it would if the boy were described as "scholastically handicapped." Nor does the illustration suggest one of the theory's many debatable features. No one disputes Merton's assumption that social class is a major determinant of access to legitimate means to cultural goals, but he further assumed that *regardless of their class* Americans pursue more or less the same cultural goals. Although the theory is not limited to any particular country, Merton evidently formulated it especially to explain the extremely high official U.S. crime rate. So the theory emphasizes inequality, but it implies that poverty causes a high crime rate only when coupled with differential access to legitimate means to cultural goals. That implication may be one of the theory's merits. Nonetheless, critics question the assumption of shared goals across class lines (specifically, that lower-class children and other children have more or less the same desires and aspirations).

The above discussion leads to this summary of Merton's anomie theory: the greater the disjunction in a social unit between emphasis on culturally shared goals and access to legitimate means to those goals *or* emphasis on those means, the greater the social unit's rate of deviant behavior.[11] That summary ignores the theory's second part, Merton's "modes of adaptation." Other than conformity, each mode is a type of deviance, with each caused by a particular form of disjunction. To illustrate, the "innovation mode" (robbery being one of many instances) stems from a great emphasis on cultural goals but marked inequality in access to legitimate means and/or little emphasis on legitimate means.[12] Unfortunately, the connection between the first and second part of Merton's theory is far from clear (for elaboration, see Gibbs, 1985:44–45), so it is not surprising that many commentaries and purported tests of the theory ignore the second part.

Very little can be said about the theory's validity because purported tests have been indefensible. The basic problem is that the principal variable—the amount of means-goals disjunction—defies measurement even for a very small social unit (e.g., a village). Defensible tests of a theory do not require that all its constituent variables can be measured; but if only some of them can be measured, the theory must be stated such that testable conclusions can be deduced. Like almost all sociological theorists, Merton did not state his theory such that testable conclusions can be deduced from it (for elaboration, see Gibbs, 1985:42–46 and 1987:836–837). To illustrate the problem, suppose that someone purports to deduce this generalization from the theory: the greater a social unit's unemployment rate, the greater its burglary rate. The generalization is testable, and unemployment does tend to reduce access to legitimate means to cultural goals. Nonetheless, even if the generalization could be deduced from Merton's theory, tests of it would be inconclusive, because emphasis on cultural goals and emphasis on means would have been ignored (for that matter, employment is not the only legitimate means to cultural goals).

Now consider a commonly purported test of the theory: an examination of the association among juveniles from lower-class families between their aspirations (e.g., occupations that require university education) and the frequency of their offenses—crimes or delinquencies.[13] Merton's theory is construed as anticipating a positive association between aspirations and deviance frequency, because lower-class individuals with high aspirations lack the opportunities (means) and engage in deviance as a consequence. Even if that association does obtain, as it often has, it is far from conclusive. The very comparisons in question raise doubts about the uniformity of cultural goals. Moreover, one must wonder how vandalism, for example, is the pursuit of a cultural goal by illegitimate means. Then critics allege that Merton incorrectly assumed equal access within and between classes to *illegitimate* means (i.e., opportunities for deviance). Less recognized tests of Merton's theory have ignored *emphasis* on legitimate means.

Although Merton's theory was an enormous advance when first set forth (1938), sociologists should have long since gone far beyond it. Current references to "strain theory" rather than "anomie theory" suggest a difference (i.e., an extension or reformulation of Merton's theory), but it is really cosmetic.

The Etiological: Sutherland's Differential Association Theory

Whereas Merton never made his premises explicit, Edwin Sutherland reduced his theory to nine *numbered* statements. However, only the following two

(Sutherland and Cressey, 1974:75–76) appear absolutely essential: "(6) A person becomes delinquent because of an excess of definitions favorable to violation of law over definitions unfavorable to violation of law."[14] "(7) Differential associations may vary in frequency, duration, priority, and intensity."

Sutherland's arcane terms—"definitions" and "differential associations"—make the theory difficult to understand. But consider two possible reasons why he did not say simply the probability that an individual will commit a particular type of deviant act varies directly with the extent that his or her experiences have predisposed the individual to commit it. First, Sutherland may have feared that such a generalization would prompt critics to dismiss his theory as trite.[15] Second, he may have recognized that independent observers are unlikely to agree when classifying an individual's "experiences" as being conducive to a particular type of deviant behavior, discouraging it, or neither. Even if agreement could be realized, observations on any individual from birth onward are simply not feasible. Such problems are all too real, and Sutherland's arcane terminology does not avoid them.

In tests of Sutherland's theory the researchers have focused on this proposition: the more an individual has associated with criminals or delinquents, the greater the probability that he or she will commit a criminal or delinquent act. The rationale is obvious: Individuals acquire "definitions favorable to violation of law" from associating with violators. Sutherland did emphasize associations as a source of such definitions, but he never identified them as the exclusive source, perhaps because that identification would tax credulity (television and movies are conspicuous alternative sources). So when researchers examine the statistical association among juveniles between the number of self-reported delinquent friends and the number of self-reported delinquencies, their findings could not possibly falsify the theory, because it could be argued that other sources of "definitions" were not taken into account. For that matter, in the typical purported test, definitions *unfavorable* to law violations are not taken into account. So it is no wonder that the number of self-reported delinquent friends (or anything like it) is not highly correlated with the number of self-reported offenses.[16] Finally, the "social learning" version of Sutherland's theory (Akers, et al., 1979) is an advance as far as testability is concerned, but the problems remain far from overcome (see commentary by Gibbs, 1985:40–41).

Two differences between Sutherland's theory and Merton's theory are especially noteworthy for our purposes. First, whereas Merton's theory is most relevant when explaining variation in the rate of deviance, Sutherland's theory is most relevant when explaining individual differences. Second, Merton's theory bears conspicuously on a major notion identified earlier—social differentiation (inequality especially)—but such a connection is less obvious in Sutherland's theory. Nevertheless, the latter can be translated readily as bearing on a property of norms. Briefly, social unit members are unlikely to experience "favorable definitions" of some type of deviance if that type is widely and intensely condemned. That relation suggests a distinct strategy for a testable restatement of Sutherland (see Gibbs, 1987:834–836).

The Etiological: Opportunity Theory

Many criminologists argue that crime requires more than a predisposition (motive); it also requires opportunities. That argument extends to this generalization: the greater the opportunities for a type of crime, the greater the rate for that type. One of many supporting findings is the strong negative association over time between the percent of U.S. homes occupied frequently during the day and the annual residential burglary rate (Cohen and Felson, 1979). The explanation is that an unoccupied house is an attractive target for burglars. Many other associations (e.g., the greater the number of cars per capita, the greater the automobile theft rate) are also readily interpretable in terms of opportunity.

One objection to opportunity theory is that it ignores the kinds of etiological conditions emphasized in contending theories (e.g., Merton's, Sutherland's). But the contenders themselves are open to criticism because they do not emphasize opportunities for deviance. A more defensible objection is that the findings supporting the opportunity theory bear almost exclusively on crime rates; consequently, the theory's relevance in explaining individual differences is debatable.

The theory's most immediate shortcoming is the failure to answer this question: For a given type of deviance, exactly what kinds of conditions are opportunities for it? Without an explicit answer, purported tests of the theory cannot possibly falsify the theory. If the crime rate is not positively or negatively associated with some particular condition, there is always a plausible explanation—other opportunity conditions were ignored. For that matter, many of the findings reported to support the theory can be interpreted as also supporting another theory. Reconsider the negative association between percentage of dwelling places regularly occupied and the burglary rate. That association could be construed as supporting the deterrence theory because it may reflect the deterrent effect of legal punishments (i.e., potential burglars perceive a greater certainty of apprehension if a building is occupied).

None of the criticisms is blunted by an alternative designation of the theory—"routine activities and crime." That alternative merely promotes doubts about the theory. There are myriad routine activities (e.g., dressing, eating a noon meal) that appear unrelated to crime.

Criticisms notwithstanding, opportunity theory is more promising than its rivals when it comes to explaining variation in the probability of criminal victimization (Meier and Miethe, 1993). The theory is also more useful when it comes to feasible means of crime prevention. As an example, West Germany enacted a law that required a steering-wheel lock on all cars, not just new ones; there was a dramatic subsequent decline in car thefts (for a recent survey of such matters, see Felson, 1994: ch. 8). Crime prevention through "reduction-in-opportunities" will become more important if doubts about the effectiveness of legal punishments (especially incarceration and executions) escalate.

The theory's merits justify identification of social differentiation and control as major notions. Insofar as routine activities determine the probability of victimization, social differentiation (through its relation to routine activities) tends to determine variation in that probability among social unit members. As for control, it is not just a matter of crime prevention through reduction of opportunities; it is also a matter of countercontrol by offenders (i.e., reducing the probability of apprehension). Finally and most important, it is difficult to imagine an impressive theory about the etiology of deviance that does not recognize "opportunity" as a major factor.

The Etiological: Social Disorganization Theory

Over recent years Ralph Sampson and several other sociologists have resurrected a theory, one that originated largely from Clifford Shaw and Henry Mckay's delinquency research in Chicago more than 60 years ago (see references in Bursik and Grasmick, 1993). The resurrection did not alter the theory's core generalization: Among communities, the crime or delinquency rate varies directly with the amount of social disorganization. However, the theory has been augmented by an emphasis on a second generalization: Social disorganization reduces the effectiveness of control over deviant behavior in the community.

The augmentation is an improvement. Nonetheless, while the original version was widely criticized because of the vagueness of "social disorganization," the resurrected version scarcely clarifies. Numerous statements in the resurrected version (see Bursik and Grasmick, 1993) suggest this definition: Social disorganization is a decline in the effectiveness of community control. That definition makes the second previous generalization a tautology. The defect is not remedied in the resurrection by an emphasis on still another generalization: Among communities, the amount of residential mobility and sociocultural heterogeneity varies directly with the amount of social disorganization.

Taken together the foregoing generalizations imply (1) a negative association between mobility-heterogeneity and effectiveness of community control and (2) a positive association between mobility-heterogeneity and the crime-delinquency rate. Hence, the notion of social disorganization appears to be inessential. Doubts grow all the more when advocates of the theory purport to show how residential mobility and heterogeneity reduce community control (see references in Bursik and Grasmick, 1993:34–38). For example, it has been argued that both variables make residents less likely to make inquiries about suspicious activities in the community.

Unfortunately, researchers have yet to examine the association (among communities or other territorial units) between actual control effectiveness measures and crime-delinquency rates. Nonetheless, there have been tests of this *implied generalization:* among territorial units, the greater the residential mobility and heterogeneity, the greater the crime rate. The first two variables have a fairly clear meaning, and census data can be used to measure both.

To date, the test findings warrant continuation of research and attempts to improve the theory, but the amount of variation in the crime rate explained by mobility-heterogeneity is not truly impressive (for several references, see Bursik and Grasmick, 1993). Then it remains to be seen whether the theory explains crime-delinquency differences among individuals or even variation in the rate among population divisions (gender and age particularly).

Two merits of the theory warrant special recognition. First, it combines two of the major notions in the sociology of deviance—social differentiation and control. Second, more than contenders, the theory directs attention to the possibility that the etiology of deviance can be analyzed properly only at the community or neighborhood level, which is to say that cities, states, and countries are too large to make population statistics really meaningful.

The Etiological: A Control Theory

Gottfredson and Hirschi's theory of crime (1990) cannot be summarized by quoting premises. Whatever the premises may be, they are implicit; space limitations permit quotes of only three generalizations as suggestive. "We have defined crimes as acts of force or fraud undertaken in pursuit of self-interest" (p. 16). "People vary in their propensity to use force and fraud (criminality)" (p. 4). "The level of self-control, or criminality, distinguishes offenders from nonoffenders" (p. 109).

Because Gottfredson and Hirschi do not identify manifestations of criminality (a propensity) other than crime itself, the asserted positive association between criminality and crime is unfalsifiable. For that matter, they equate a low level of self-control with criminality (see last quote), but elsewhere they depict the former as causing the latter. The suggestion of a tautology is reinforced by Gottfredson and Hirschi's failure to define self-control explicitly, let alone confront conceptual issues and problems. Indeed, they never define the more inclusive notion—control or attempted control; and it is not emphasized in the theory, nor is social control. It is as though being controlled by others or controlling others is irrelevant in the etiology of crime or criminality.

So Gottfredson and Hirschi have contributed to criminology's well-stocked supply of untestable theories (see Barlow's commentary, 1991, esp. pp. 241–242).[17] The immediate reason is that Gottfredson and Hirschi stopped far short of a procedure for measuring either criminality or self-control, and their granting that "opportunity" is relevant (along with self-control) makes defensible tests all the more unlikely. They do identify "ineffective child rearing" as the major cause of low self-control (1990:97), but that identification would be a grossly incomplete step toward tests even if child-rearing effectiveness were the only determinant of self-control.[18] It is difficult to imagine an empirically applicable procedure for measuring the effectiveness of child rearing, and the Gottfredson-Hirschi descriptions (1990, esp. 97–100) of related parental techniques are only illustrative (e.g., prohibiting smoking), incomplete (e.g., the allusion to "minimum conditions"), and far too abstract (e.g., references to punishing children without qualifications as regards severity or consistency).

The Reactive: The Theory of Secondary Deviance

In the minds of many Americans, including legislators, punitive reactions prevent crimes. Paradoxically, however, the theory of secondary deviance

(Lemert, 1972) suggests just the opposite: Punitive reactions to deviance generate more deviance.

Lest the generalization appear absurd, think of repeated failures in an ex-convict's attempt to get a job, all stemming from a prison record. No one is unlikely to deny that possibility, nor the prospect of the ex-convict's return to crime because of sustained unemployment. If recidivism does occur, it would be secondary deviance and consistent with Lemert's theory. However, statements of the theory (including the summary generalization given above) are gross oversimplifications, even if it is understood that deviance prior to reaction is "primary" and that deviance generated by reactions is "secondary." The oversimplification becomes apparent in light of three questions.

First, what kinds of primary deviance can become secondary deviance? If the answer is "any and all kinds," it jeopardizes the theory's credibility, but the answer would not distort because Lemert (1972) did not speak directly to the question.

Second, what kinds of punitive reactions can convert primary deviance into secondary deviance? Most versions of the theory suggest this answer: any kind of punitive reactions. Incredible though the answer may appear, Lemert did not even stipulate that the reaction must be punitive.

Third, is secondary deviance simply *more* deviance caused by reactions to primary deviance? Most versions of the theory answer affirmatively, but that answer is debatable. Although Lemert never denied that secondary deviance may take the form of "more deviance," the issue is not just whether more deviance *of the same kind*. Additionally, so it appears, secondary deviance also may take the form of playing a real or imagined role of a deviant (e.g., dressing and talking like a "tough guy"), which is not necessarily deviant behavior and certainly not a crime. Secondary deviance can then be a purely psychological phenomenon, meaning acceptance of a deviant identification or label. If it appears that the ambiguity of the secondary deviance notion has been exaggerated, Lemert's definitions (1972:48, 63) should be examined carefully.

Extensive clarification of Lemert's theory is necessary for defensible tests of it, but further work would be compatible with the designation of control as a major notion in the sociology of deviance. The designation does not assume that all control attempts are successful, and Lemert's theory suggests that some reactions to deviance are worse than merely failures in control attempts. So the theory has important policy implications for criminal justice.

The Reactive: Societal Reactive Theory

A very important question in the sociology of deviance is this: Why does the character of reactions to deviance vary among social units and over time? For example, in England as of 1688 there were some 50 capital offenses but over 200 as of 1820 (Hay, 1975:18). As the example suggests, reactions to deviance differ most conspicuously in their severity; that variation was once the concern of several theories (see Grabosky's survey, 1984). For obscure reasons, attention has shifted from those theories to this second "reactive" question: What determines the character of reactions to particular instances of deviant behavior or particular deviants? The question shifts the comparisons from social units and historical periods to individual cases in the same social unit, but the focus remains on the severity of reactions to deviance, including "treatment" of those diagnosed as mentally ill.

Only societal reaction theory speaks to the second question, but it is little more than a long line of research. Even if taken as simply a distinct argument about legal reactions to alleged crimes or delinquencies, there are several versions (Gibbs, 1987:822). The most radical version is that reactions depend not on strictly legal factors (including previous criminal history, such as arrests or convictions) but on the extralegal characteristics of (1) the suspect, (2) the situation or circumstances of the alleged crime, (3) the victim or complainant, (4) the legal reactors, and/or (5) the operative rules of the reactors' organization. Even less radical versions also contradict this principle of justice in many countries: The fate of suspects should not depend on extralegal factors (e.g., race or gender).

Any version of societal reaction theory gives rise to this question: Which extralegal factors determine legal reactions to alleged criminality? The power or resources of the accused, as indicated by socioeconomic status (SES) or race, is commonly emphasized. Yet there are reports of instances of *lower* imprisonment rates for women felons and *no* negative association between SES and prison sentences (see, e.g., Wheeler, et al., 1982). Such reports contradict the principal generalization—the most severe legal reactions are the *least* likely for alleged perpetrators who have the most power or resources. Indeed, long ago there was growing evidence that the legal characteristics of an alleged crime (e.g., the use or threat of force, the offender's previous convictions) are the primary determinants of sentences. There is also growing evidence that the importance of extralegal characteristics, such as gender of the alleged offender, depends on the legal nature of the crime in question and also on the stage in the reaction process, such as arrest or sentencing (Curran, 1983). Then the importance of any particular extralegal characteristic evidently varies over time (Krohn, et al., 1983). So there no immediate prospect of a defensible societal reaction theory, and currently the only dramatic evidence is a series of findings indicating that, regardless of the offender's race, a death sentence for murder is most likely in cases of white victims (especially Baldus, 1986).

The need for a sophisticated societal reaction theory cannot be exaggerated, and the rationale is not just that reactions to deviance make the notion of control all the more important. Virtually everything conventionally interpreted as a cause of deviance can be *reinterpreted* as stemming from reactions to behavior. One example must suffice. Time and again, the official suicide rate has been reported as higher for the unemployed. That difference certainly suggests that unemployment is somehow a causal factor in suicide, but the proper classification of many deaths (homicide, suicide, accidental) is debatable. Now consider this possibility: On learning that the deceased was unemployed, the investigating official (coroner or otherwise) is more predisposed to classify the death as a suicide.

What has been said about the importance of societal reaction theory does not extend to the labeling perspective or labeling theory. When someone uses either term, they may mean the reactive conception of deviance, the theory of secondary deviance, or societal reaction theory. That ambiguity is the reason why the term has not been used in this survey. Ambiguity is also the reason for excluding the Marxist or conflict theory of crime. It is not that the theory is untestable; rather, it is not even clear what the theory purports to explain (criminal law, reactions to crime, causes of crime, etc.). The "functional approach to deviance" (see Goode's commentary, 1994:93–96) has also been excluded because of the same ambiguity.

The Reactive: Deterrence Theory

Some forty years ago, following a number of death penalty studies, many criminologists concluded that legal punishments do not deter crimes. Then, about fifteen years later, some social scientists renewed deterrence research, convinced that the earlier studies were badly flawed. The renewed research was more defensible; but a sophisticated deterrence theory is still lacking, and some horrendous evidential problems remain unsolved.

The immediate problem is the common practice of reducing the deterrence doctrine to this generalization: Certain, swift, and severe legal punishments deter crime. Any such statement grossly oversimplifies.

The first step in avoiding oversimplifications must be a definition that distinguishes deterrence from other ways that legal punishments may prevent crime, one being "incapacitation" (e.g., imprisonment makes certain types of crimes difficult if not impossible). This definition is a step in that direction: Deterrence occurs when and only when an individual contemplates what would be criminal activity but curtails that activity or refrains entirely because the individual (1) perceives the threat of a some kind of legal punishment for acting otherwise and (2) fears that punishment.

As for types of deterrence, the most conventional distinction is between *general* deterrence (the deterrent impact of a punishment threat on those who have not been punished) and *specific* deterrence (the deterrent impact of an actual punishment on whomever it is inflicted). A less conventional and almost totally ignored distinction in research is that between *absolute* deterrence (when an individual has contemplated a crime more than once but refrained entirely because of fear of punishment) and *restrictive* deterrence (an individual curtails his or her criminal activity with a view to reducing the risk of apprehension or the severity of punishment if apprehended).

A separate theory about each type of deterrence may be needed because evidence that bears on one has no necessary bearing on the others. Thus, evidence that felons are more predisposed to criminality on leaving prison than when entering would suggest that imprisonment does not result in specific deterrence, but that evidence would not reveal anything about general deterrence. Also, it may well be that the greatest amount of deterrence is realized among habitual felons but virtually all as *restrictive* deterrence (hardcore offenders scarcely refrain from frequent crimes because of conscience). Such considerations should sober critics who declare confidently that "legal punishments do not deter" without considering types of deterrence.

Space limitations permit observations on only two kinds of research on general deterrence (for a much more elaborate survey, see Gibbs, 1986, and Chamlin, et al., 1992): (1) comparisons of the crime rates of territorial units, (e.g., states, cities); and (2) comparisons of individuals. Since the revival of deterrence research, comparisons of territorial units have been less defective than they were in the early death penalty studies. The vast majority of those studies compared the homicide rates of death penalty states and states not having execution as a statutory penalty, with the unexpressed assumption that potential killers perceive execution as more severe than a long prison sentence, perhaps life. So one defect of the early studies was the exclusion of various properties of legal punishments, such as the objective certainty of execution and imprisonment.[19] Such defects undermine the conclusion that the death penalty does not deter more than does imprisonment, but in recent years more adequate research suggests the same conclusion.

Territorial units continued to be compared in the revival of deterrence research, but the concern shifted from statutory penalties to the objective certainty of imprisonment or arrest for some type of crime (e.g., robbery, burglary) and the severity of imprisonment (average or median time actually served) for instances of that type. Consistent with the deterrence argument, researchers have reported for each of several types of crime a moderate *negative* association between the objective certainty of punishment and the crime rate. However, contrary to the deterrence argument, researchers reported very few even moderate negative associations between the length of prison sentences served for a type of crime and the rate for that type. Unfortunately, such findings did not influence American legislators. They appear preoccupied with increasing the severity of punishment but not its objective certainty.

The most conspicuous defect of the territorial comparisons has been the exclusion of perceptual variables, especially perceived certainty (the risk of punishment as estimated by potential offenders). That exclusion is understandable, for the requisite data can be gathered only through very costly surveys. Nonetheless, data on perceptual variables are crucial, because legal punishments deter (if at all) only to the extent that potential offenders perceive them as certain and severe. Recognition of perception's importance has increasingly led deterrence investigators to compare individuals (all too often students). In such research, it is feasible to compute three values for each individual: (1) the frequency of self-reported offenses, (2) the perceived certainty of some stipulated kind of punishment for the kind of offense in question (e.g., shoplifting), and (3) the perceived severity of such punishments. On the whole, the anticipated negative association with offense frequency holds much more for perceived certainty than for perceived severity; indeed, most findings suggest that perceived severity is irrelevant. But even perceived certainty's importance is debatable, especially when investigators examine the association between it and the frequency of offenses during a subsequent period rather than during a previous period (see Chamlin, et al., 1992).

Both principal kinds of research on general deterrence—territorial and individual comparisons—are confronted with the same difficult evidential problem. Obviously, properties of legal punishments are not the sole determinants of crime, and *extralegal* determinants (e.g., perhaps unemployment or the effectiveness of parental control) may be of greater importance. The problem is that no etiological theory enables deterrence researchers to (1) identify extralegal determinants with confidence and (2) take them into account when examining the association between legal punishment and offenses.

There has been considerable research on specific deterrence, and the findings have been predominantly negative. Most researchers have compared the recidivism rate of two or more populations of offenders, with the populations differentiated by the severity of the punishment received for the last offense (e.g., two sets of juvenile offenders, one of which was incarcerated for at least a week, and the other released to parents or surrogates without detention). Time after time, the recidivism rates of the two populations did not differ significantly or the population punished more severely actually came to have the greater recidivism rate.

Almost all research on specific deterrence has been badly flawed, apart from questions about the use of official recidivism rates (i.e., rearrests or reconvictions). Among adults or juveniles apprehended for the same type of offense, those having several previous arrests or court appearances are the most likely to receive a severe sentence. So offenders who receive the most severe punishments are the very ones most likely to commit a subsequent offense, because the subsequent offense is simply another manifestation of a predisposition to criminality. The solution may appear obvious—randomize the punishment of offenders such that there is no significant association between the severity of the sentence and an offender's previous criminal record. However, judges are understandably reluctant to randomize punishments.

The failure to randomize punishments is only one of several defects of research on specific deterrence. Investigators have considered only the severity of punishments and ignored perceptual variables. It is as though they never thought of this question: Why expect that punishing an individual for an act reduces the probability of the individual's repeating that act? From the deterrence viewpoint there can be only one answer: A punitive reaction increases the actor's perception of punishment certainty, the actor's perception of punishment severity, or both perceptions. Yet research on specific deterrence has not really focused on change in the perceptions of offenders (i.e., before and after punishment). That research will be difficult and costly, but it is essential for justifiable conclusions.

Whatever conclusions are eventually reached about deterrence, they will not undercut the argument that control is a major notion in the sociology of deviance. After all, any attempt to deter someone, successful or not, is an attempt to control behavior.

A Fundamental Issue Concerning All of the Theories

Whether etiological or reactive, each major theory is based on the assumption that the theory applies to all types of deviance, or at least to all types of crimes and delinquencies. The assumption is dubious in the extreme. The argument is not that each theory applies more to some types of deviance than others; it is more likely that each theory does not apply at all to several types.

The assumption is remarkable for at least two reasons, the first having to do with evidence. It taxes credulity not only because there is no systematic supporting evidence but also because there is systematic contrary evidence. At one time many criminologists examined the statistical association among territorial units (census tracts, cities, states, etc.) between rates for different types of crimes (see some illustrative references in Gibbons, 1982:29). In one study after another the association between at least two of the rates (e.g., robbery and homicide) was found to be negligible if not negative. So there are two questions. First, in light of such findings, how can the various types of crimes have the same causes? Second, if two types of deviance have different causes, why try to explain them in one theory?

The assumption's other remarkable feature is the obvious character of an alternative. Instead of pursuing a theory that purports to explain all types of deviance, limit the theory to one particular type. The strategy would not preclude the eventual synthesis of special theories into a *general* etiological or reactive theory, but each synthesis would have to be something more than an uncritical assumption.[20] Unfortunately, in the sociology of deviance only one special theory has received sustained attention, that being Durkheim's theory of suicide (1951 [1897]).

CONCLUSION

Each of the major theories, etiological or reactive, illustrates the importance of one or more of four major notions in the sociology of deviance—norms, reactions to deviance, social differentiation, and control. Yet no theory bears on all those notions, even though no one in the sociology of deviance is likely to belittle the importance of any of them.

The suggestion is not that a general theory of deviance—one that purports to explain all types—will be defensible if it emphasizes all four notions. To the contrary, the pursuit of general theories is a blind alley in the sociology of deviance. Nor is the suggestion that recognition of all the major notions in each special theory (one limited to a particular type of deviance) would ensure progress in the sociology of deviance. It is far more important to state theories in such a way that they are amenable to systematic tests. Without such theories, there can be no real progress.

Notes

1. Judgments of decline are based on the number of textbooks published and articles in major sociology journals.

2. The term "social unit" is used here as a generic designation of all socially recognized populations (e.g., tribes, organizations, age groups), including those that have a spatial boundary (e.g., cities, countries).

3. Note the difference between the meaning of "deviance" and "deviant behavior." The first term is used to denote both behavior and individuals identified as deviant. That syntax avoids confusion, but the problems in defining "a deviant" are not the same as those in defining "deviant behavior."

4. Opinion surveys are relevant because there is only one obvious procedure for identifying norms systematically—solicit answers from social unit members to normative (i.e., evaluative) questions. Of course, a procedure is not needed if one assumes that norms are simply out there, like fireplugs, and need not be identified by a systematic method. That assumption encourages indifference to conceptual problems.

5. That belief alone precludes a strictly statistical definition. If a norm is defined in terms of the frequency of acts (i.e., average or typical behavior) in a social unit, a normative explanation of differences in those frequencies is pointless. Thus, if incest is judged contrary to a norm because instances of it are rare, then it is logomachy to say that incest is rare because contrary to a norm.

6. The leaders in this movement were Howard Becker, Kai Erickson, and John Kitsuse. See Gibbs (1966, 1972, 1981) for some strategic quotes and references to relevant publications.

7. Savor Jack Douglas' argument (1967: 196): "since there exists great disagreement between interested parties in the categorization of real-world cases, 'suicides' can generally be said to exist and not to exist at the same time."

8. The definition suffers from all the defects of the reactive conception of deviant behavior, but a normative definition can be little more than this: An individual is deviant if and only if he or she has acted contrary to a norm of some designated social unit. The immediate objection is that such a definition makes almost everyone deviant, and modifications of it to avoid that objection are likely to reek with arbitrariness.

9. Actually, the literature antedates Foucault (e.g., Piven and Cloward, 1971).

10. For criticism of this purely "formal" conception of social control, see Goode (1994:46–49, 134–138); and for criticism of the counteraction-of-deviance conception of social control and an alternative to it, see Gibbs (1994:ch.2).

11. Merton defined "anomie" in terms of such disjunction.

12. Although "innovation" cannot be equated with invention, only Merton's theory has real implications concerning the argument that major sociocultural changes commence as deviance.

13. The offenses are self-reported by the juveniles in the questionnaire used to gather information on their aspirations. Such self-reported deviance led critics to question the higher *official* rate of offenses (based on arrest statistics) for lower socioeconomic divisions of the population, a difference that Merton assumed to be both reliable and explicable by his theory. Subsequently, research on self-reported offenses led many criminologist to conclude that the class difference is due largely if not entirely to a greater official apprehension rate (arrest, juvenile court appearance) for lower-class individuals, meaning that the difference is a *reactive* phenomenon.

14. It is clear that Sutherland's theory (like Merton's) applies not only to crimes and delinquencies but also to deviant behavior in general.

15. Yet the generalization would not be a tautology, especially if one believes that deviance is genetically determined, a common belief when Sutherland stated his theory *more than fifty years ago* and even now hardly extinct.

16. The reason has nothing to do with the duration, priority, and intensity of differential associations. Those variables have been excluded from virtually all purported tests of the theory; but their exclusion is hardly surprising, given that their meaning is so obscure.

17. The theory's unfalsifiable character is all the more puzzling because it evidently supplants Hirschi's earlier theory (1969), one that offers much more in the way of testability. True, the Gottfredson-Hirschi theory appears to be more general, but sacrificing testability is a high price to pay.

18. For that matter, the identification undercuts their emphasis on self-control rather than attempts to control human behavior in general. After all, child rearing is a series of attempts to control the behavior of someone else, not self-control.

19. Objective certainty is simply the proportion of crimes over some period that resulted the in the kind of punishment in question (arrest, execution, fine, etc.). For an elaborate treatment of the subject, see Gibbs, 1986.

20. Long ago, Henry and Short's work (1954) on homicide and suicide pointed the way to a synthesis of theories, but their lead has not been followed.

References

Akers, Ronald L., et al. 1979. "Social Learning and Deviant Behavior." *American Sociological Review* 44:636–655.

Baldus, David C., et al. 1986. "Arbitrariness and Discrimination in the Administration of the Death Penalty." *Stetson Law Review* 15:133–261.

Barlow, Hugh D. 1991. "Gottfredson and Hirschi." *Journal of Criminal Law and Criminology* 82:229–242.

Bursik, Robert J. and Harold G. Grasmick. 1993. *Neighborhoods and Crime.* New York: Lexington Books.

Chamlin, Mitchell B., et al. 1992. "Time Aggregation and Time Lag in Macro-Level Deterrence Research." *Criminology* 30:377–395.

Cohen, Lawrence E. and Marcus Felson. 1979. "Social Change and Crime Rate Trends." *American Sociological Review* 44:588–608.

Curran, Debra A. 1983. "Judicial Discretion and Defendant's Sex." *Criminology* 21:41–58.

Douglas, Jack D. 1967. *The Social Meanings of Suicide.* Princeton, NJ: Princeton University Press.

Durkheim, Emile. 1951 [1897]. *Suicide.* New York: Free Press.

Felson, Marcus. 1994. *Crime and Everyday Life.* Thousand Oaks, CA: Pine Forge Press.

Gibbons, Don C. 1982. *Society, Crime, and Criminal Behavior,* 4th ed. Englewood Cliffs, NJ: Prentice-Hall.

Gibbs, Jack P. 1966. "Conceptions of Deviant Behavior." *Pacific Sociological Review* 9:9–14.

Gibbs, Jack P. 1972. "Issues in Defining Deviant Behavior," pp. 39–68 in *Theoretical Perspectives on Deviance,* edited by Robert A. Scott and Jack D. Douglas. New York: Basic Books.

Gibbs, Jack P. 1981. *Norms, Deviance, and Social Control.* New York: Elsevier North Holland.

Gibbs, Jack P. 1985. "The Methodology of Theory Construction in Criminology," pp. 23–50 in *Theoretical Methods in Criminology,* edited by Robert F. Meier. Beverly Hills, CA: Sage.

Gibbs, Jack P. 1986. "Deterrence Theory and Research," pp. 87–130 in *The Law as a Behavioral Instrument,* edited by Gary B. Melton. Lincoln: University of Nebraska Press.

Gibbs, Jack P. 1987. "The State of Criminological Theory." *Criminology* 25:821–840.

Gibbs, Jack P. 1989. *Control.* Urbana: University of Illinois Press.

Gibbs, Jack P. 1994 (forthcoming). *A Theory About Control.* Boulder, CO: Westview Press.

Goode, Erich. 1994. *Deviant Behavior,* 4th ed. Englewood Cliffs, NJ: Prentice-Hall.

Gottfredson, Michael and Travis Hirschi. 1990. *A General Theory of Crime.* Stanford, CA: Stanford University Press.

Grabosky, Peter N. 1984. "The Variability of Punishment," pp. 163–189 in *Toward a General Theory of Social Control,* Vol. 1, edited by Donald Black. New York: Academic Press.

Hay, Douglas. 1975. "Property, Authority, and Criminal Law." pp. 17–63 in *Albion's Fatal Tree,* Douglas Hay, et al. (contributors). New York: Pantheon Books.

Henry, Andrew F. and James F. Short, Jr. 1954. *Suicide and Homicide.* New York: Free Press.

Hirschi, Travis. 1969. *Causes of Delinquency.* Berkeley: University of California Press.

Homans, George C. 1961. *Social Behavior.* New York: Harcourt, Brace and World.

Krohn, Marvin D., et al. 1983. "Is Chivalry Dead?" *Criminology* 21:417–437.

Lemert, Edwin M. 1972. *Human Deviance, Social Problems, and Social Control,* 2nd ed. Englewood Cliffs, NJ: Prentice-Hall.

Meier, Robert F. and Terance D. Miethe. 1993. "Understanding Theories of Criminal Victimization." *Crime and Justice* 17:459–499.

Merton, Robert K. 1957. *Social Theory and Social Structure.* New York: Free Press.

Piven, Frances F. and Richard A. Cloward. 1971. *Regulating the Poor.* New York: Pantheon Books.

Sutherland, Edwin H. and Donald R. Cressey. 1974. *Criminology,* 9th ed. Philadelphia: Lippincott.

Thio, Alex. 1988. *Deviant Behavior,* 3rd ed. New York: Harper and Row.

Wheeler, Stanton, et al. 1982. "Sentencing the White-Collar Offender." *American Sociological Review* 47:641–659.

12

A Postpositivist Perspective

IRA L. REISS
University of Minnesota

Most of the scientifically oriented sociologists today disavow membership in the traditional positivistic group. But denial notwithstanding, there is clear evidence that much of the older positivistic separation of fact and value, and the view of scientific knowledge as sovereign truth, still survives. Among deviance and other social science researchers, many could be called "recovering positivists." They say that they reject positivistic dogma, but they cannot seem to move beyond the beliefs constituting positivism. But change is possible if they take advantage of the new "postpositivism" that is increasingly dominating scientific work (Alexander, 1982, 1990).

My goal here is to clarify the nature of this new, emerging conception of science and show its great significance for all social science research. I strongly believe that this new meaning is one around which deviance researchers of various theoretical persuasions can be unified. Further, I believe this new postpositivistic meaning of science can greatly enhance our understanding of deviance.

THE IMPORTANCE OF PRESUPPOSITIONS

In 1962 Thomas Kuhn published a momentous book, *The Structure of Scientific Revolutions*. In it he demonstrates with great clarity that the empirical data that scientists gather represent a selective perspective and are not a precise representation of the "true external reality" of the world. According to Kuhn, to see the world we must make some basic assumptions, what I am calling presuppositions, about how the world operates. We need some presuppositional lenses through which to see the world, or we are blind. Our basic assumptions, or presuppositions, lead us into a theory about how the world operates. What we call empirical data or "facts" are shaped by these prior

Adapted from the author's article, "The Future of Sex Research and the Meaning of Science," *Journal of Sex Research*, Vol. 30 (February 1993), pp. 3–11.

views of reality. Facts are not just there to be discovered. Rather, as I will shortly illustrate, we begin to observe a selective set of "facts" only after we start to view the world through the lenses prescribed by our presuppositions.

Presuppositions, as I am using the term, are the general assumptions we make about how the world operates, including moral assumptions about how it should operate. An example would be the assumption that humans are rational creatures using the most efficient means to the ends that they pursue. With this presupposition we can then start to observe the "facts" of our rational behavior. Until we make some such set of assumptions about the world, we are unable to comprehend the "booming, buzzing, confusion" that comprises our world. But after we assume a particular set of presuppositions and related theories, we then have a particular set of lenses that will enable us to understand that world—but always only in terms of what views those lenses permit to enter. In short, the insight we gain by our presuppositions is bought at the price of partial blindness to other ways of understanding the reality that is "out there."

A classic playing-card experiment demonstrated how, on a personal level, our presuppositions and theories determine what registers in our minds (Hanson, 1958). A deck of playing cards was shown to research volunteers. Inserted among the otherwise typical deck were anomalous cards such as a black four of hearts and a red six of spades. Those cards often went unnoticed because the volunteers' "lenses" limited their expectations of what could be seen in a deck of cards. In short, they saw the cards through the presuppositions of what a deck of cards should be, not in line with what the cards "really" were.

Presuppositions not only shape the researcher's initial hypotheses, as traditional positivists assume, they can also influence the very conclusion one can draw from the data, as postpositivists find. This can be seen in the current debate over whether homosexuality is inherited or learned. Simon LeVay (1991), Laura Allen and Roger Gorski (1992), and Dean Hammer et al. (1993) have each presented some preliminary data suggesting that there are genetically programmed causes of homosexuality. Scientists responded quite differently to these reports. Some, particularly biologists, argued that the data support the view that homosexuality is innate. But those social scientists who favor learning as the explanation minimized the importance of the findings. These researchers contend that sexual orientation has a powerful learned dimension because it varies so greatly in different times and in different societies (Reiss, 1986).

Actually, those two different interpretations of the same data reflect the presuppositions about the relative importance of inheritance versus learning. There are also ideological reasons for taking one position or another. Some scientists believe that prejudice would be lessened if homosexuality were found to be genetically induced. Others, also concerned with equality, note that women are seen as biologically different and this does not seem to have helped in their quest for equality.

USING PRESUPPOSITIONS TO ADVANCE SCIENCE

To raise our consciousness about our presuppositions does not mean that we give up our goals of fair and accurate gathering of evidence in terms of what models we do adopt. In fact, this new awareness makes scientists more likely to search themselves and others for bias resulting from their favoring one model over another. This may create a much more realistic and cautious scientific stance when compared with the old positivistic assumption that scientific models are chosen simply on the basis of empirical factual evidence.

I believe that many scientists are uneasy today. The fact that presuppositions play such an important role in scientific work makes them feel uncomfortable. But what is the alternative? Can a human being really have a view about the world that does not reflect some set of basic presuppositions about that world? Is there a scientific "view from nowhere" that assumes nothing about the world? We cannot study everything from every possible perspective. Each scientific project must assume something about how the world works, so we always have a "view from somewhere."

The very language through which we express our thoughts reflects a particular perspective on the world. Languages vary in what words there are for describing different colors, different values, different realities. And so the impossibility of having a scientific "view from nowhere"—a view that makes no such assumptions about reality—should be apparent. To say your perspective is the one true one is to play what Donna Haraway (1988) calls "the God trick," and that surely is an inappropriate position for a scientist to assume.

But, if my reasoning is sound, how do we avoid becoming extreme relativists and asserting that all viewpoints in science are just subjective meanings and cannot serve as the basis for any empirical generalizations or any notion of "objective" knowledge? The relativist position is endorsed by many who call themselves "postmodernists." In opposition to this I take a postpositivist position. Extreme relativism is not acceptable to postpositivists because it eliminates the possibility of gathering fair scientific evidence in accord with the norms of science. Furthermore, if all views are relative, then there is no way to justify the effectiveness of one social or personal change over another. I will illustrate this precise point very shortly. The postpositivist admits the impossibility of knowledge free from presuppositions but this awareness does not lead to despair and the cessation of the search for scientifically "objective" knowledge.

To believe in "objective" knowledge is to assert that knowledge does not solely depend on our personal view of the world. But first we must admit that we can never be certain in science about what we say is objective knowledge. Helen Longino (1990) suggested that we look at scientific work as the product of a community of interacting scientists, not as a product of one individual scientist. That community of scholars negotiates in various ways to arrive at a consensus about what is the "objective" knowledge of that time. The norms of science do say to publish one's results so they may be evaluated by other scientists and we do have many journals that perform precisely that service. In this sense the decision as to what scientists will call objective knowledge is surely a negotiated and in part adversarial process. The product of this process, then, is not totally objective knowledge as traditional positivists believe. It is instead a negotiated, "objective" knowledge.

So we can define objectivity in science as those views of the world that come to be agreed on by the scientific community at any one point in time. This is not a view from nowhere about absolute reality, nor is it a privileged insight into reality. Instead, this perspective affords us a means by which we can put forth our best scientific evidence about what the world is like in the area of our research, but still recognize that in time this scientific understanding will change. In this postpositivist fashion we affirm our belief in objective reality at the same time that we affirm our inability ever to be able to conceptualize fully that reality. To follow through on this belief, we must first make explicit the presuppositions we accept and the values incorporated in them so as to put other scientists on guard against those presuppositions that may pressure us to unfairly examine the evidence. Researchers should not enter into a project without being aware of what presuppositions they accept, whether they be pro, con, or indifferent to the social issues raised by that research.

To illustrate how the postpositivist approach can be used for producing "objective" knowledge, I would like to discuss a research study on the prevention of HIV infection. In 1989 together with Robert Leik, a methodologist and statistician from the Department of Sociology at the University of Minnesota, I published an article evaluating the relative risk of two strategies aimed at lowering an individual's chance of becoming infected with HIV, the virus that causes AIDS (Reiss and Leik, 1989; Reiss, 1990). One strategy was to reduce the number of partners, and the second strategy was to use condoms with all partners. We designed a probability model to compare the changes in risk of HIV infection of these two strategies.

Now, let me be explicit about presuppositions: I started this research with the following presuppositions about the sexual world that we were examining: (1) That sexuality in all its freely chosen forms can and usually is pleasurable and good; (2) That people can and should learn to avoid, for themselves and their partners, the unwanted outcomes of sexuality such as disease, pregnancy, and psychological distress; and (3) That the basis for judging sexual morality should be the amount of honesty, equality, and responsibility in a relationship and not the number of such relationships a person has. Notice that my presuppositions refer to both factual and value assumptions about the world. The tendency is for most of us humans not to state just what the world is like, but also to evaluate that aspect of the world.

Given my presuppositions, it was logical to favor condom use as a strategy to avoid HIV infection because I valued sexuality and believed it could be morally practiced and controlled. But I wanted to fairly and scientifically test whether condom use was indeed the safer strategy. The probability model showed that not using condoms and having only one or two partners was far riskier than using condoms and having 20 partners, even when assuming a condom failure rate of 10 to 25 percent. Our conclusion then was that the evidence supported the greater effectiveness of condom use over partner reduction as a strategy for reducing the risk of HIV infection. This appeared to be good advice to give to people who were deciding between these two strategies. But we discovered that people with different presuppositions would interpret our probability findings very differently.

The vast majority of responses to our published study were very supportive, and I believe this was so at least partly because my three presuppositions about sexuality were shared by many other sexual scientists. But, as I've noted, not all readers were so supportive. One critical response came from a person working in the Centers for Disease Control. He was primarily interested in the very highest HIV prevalence areas where even careful condom use contained a risk of HIV infection that he believed was "too high." This person said that although the risk is clearly far lower with condom use, it still was "too high" in his judgment, and so sex outside of very long-term relationships should be avoided in these high-risk areas. In fact, even in areas where HIV prevalence was low, he would still promote having one very long-term partner because he felt that "casual" sex was not worth even a small increased risk.

Clearly, this critic rejected all three of my presuppositions about sexuality. He did not share my presuppositions about the value of sexuality of various types, or our ability to control disease outcomes, and he did believe that having multiple partners was unacceptable. With those different presuppositions, his interpretation of the evidence and his conclusions about a recommended choice of strategies were radically different. So much for the evidence speaking for itself.

We received another type of response that also challenged the validity of our "clear evidence" for the superiority of the condom use strategy. This response came from two sexologists who counseled young people with sexual problems. They said that they did not believe that very many people would carefully use condoms and that if people did use more condoms, they would likely greatly increase the number of sex partners and be more careless with some of them. So they questioned the relevance of our evidence and arrived at different strategy recommendations than we did. The reason, once again, I believe, was that they did not accept my three presuppositions, particularly not my second presupposition that asserted that people could learn to control the negative outcomes of sexuality. We need to keep in mind that we would not have tested this model if we did not believe people would use condoms.

Nevertheless, judging by the vast number of supportive responses, the scientific community did share our presuppositions and arrive at a consensus supporting our evaluation of the evidence. Such a negotiated position constitutes what I have called the objective conclusion of science today. It is important that we listen to scientists with different presuppositions because it broadens our vision of the world and makes us more aware of the type of prescriptive lenses we are wearing. Now, when we choose one set of presuppositions, we at least will be more aware that we are indeed making a choice about what research model is worth examining and what evidence is a sound knowledge basis for policy recommendations.

I have so far discussed how the presuppositions I share with numerous other—though definitely not all—scientists led to the "objective" knowledge that condom use is more effective than partner reduction in preventing HIV infection. Similar studies can be carried out on the prevention of many other forms of behavior society is trying to control such as rape, teenage pregnancy, and child sexual abuse. Our presuppositions will determine what we will investigate as a possible solution and also how we will react to our findings. Such research can greatly broaden and deepen our understanding of deviant or unwanted behavior if the postpositivist perspective is used to arrive at a negotiated, "objective" knowledge of the subject.

CONCLUSION

The postpositivist perspective makes us aware that within any scientific discipline there is an adversarial dimension. Scientists compete with each other in the marketplace of presenting explanations of events—as I tried to show in my study of HIV/AIDS risk taking and also on the issue of studying homosexuality. Related to this is the element of scientific recognition that goes to those who are judged to be the first and best in some area. The "pursuit of excellence" can promote competition and adversarial relationships. To be sure, science also has a strong cooperative dimension, but we should not allow that characteristic to blind us to the adversarial component that is also an inevitable part of any presuppositional science. Not surprisingly, in the sociology of deviance and all current social science areas, the positivists are at loggerheads with the humanists on issues such as the relative importance of objectivity and subjectivity in understanding deviant behavior.

But the interpretive emphasis on empathy and understanding of the feelings and thoughts of individuals, both conformists and deviants, is fully acceptable to the postpositivist perspective on deviance, which affirms the relevance of subjective assumptions about the nature of the deviant and nondeviant world. There is, though, a very important caveat: Supporters of interpretive perspectives need to be able to accept the legitimacy of the scientific endeavor. Postpositivists aim to strengthen, broaden, and clarify science, not eliminate it. They seek to move beyond the traditionally narrow confines of positivistic science, but they also aim to nourish and sustain postpositivist science.

References

Alexander, J. C. 1982. *Theoretical Logic in Sociology: Volume One: Positivism, Presuppositions, and Current Controversies.* Berkeley: University of California Press.

Alexander, J. C. 1990. "Beyond the Epistemological Dilemma: General Theory in a Postpositivist Mode." *Sociological Forum* 5: 531–544.

Allen, L. S., and Gorski, R. A. 1992. "Sexual Orientation and the Size of the Anterior Commissure in the Human Brain." *Procedures of the National Academy of Science USA* 89: 7199.

Hammer, D., et al. 1993. "A Linage Between DNA Markers on the X Chromosome and Male

Sexual Orientation." *Science* 261 (July 16): 321–327.

Hanson, N. R. 1958. *Patterns of Discovery.* Cambridge, England: Cambridge University Press.

Haraway, D. 1988. "Situated Knowledges: The Science Question in Feminism and the Privilege of Partial Perspective." *Feminist Studies* 14: 575–599.

LeVay, S. 1991. "A Difference in Hypothalamic Structure of Heterosexual and Homosexual Men." *Science* 253: 1036.

Longino, H. 1990. *Science as Social Knowledge: Values and Objectivity in Scientific Inquiry.* Princeton, NJ: Princeton University Press.

Reiss, I. L. 1986. *Journey into Sexuality: An Exploratory Voyage.* Englewood Cliffs, NJ: Prentice-Hall.

Reiss, I. L. 1990. *An End to Shame: Shaping Our Next Sexual Revolution.* Buffalo, NY: Prometheus Books.

Reiss, I. L., and Leik, R. K. 1989. "Evaluating Strategies to Avoid AIDS: Number of Partners vs. Use of Condoms." *The Journal of Sex Research* 26: 411–433.

13

A Posthumanist Perspective

ALEX THIO
Ohio University

A key assumption of the humanist perspective is voluntarism. It holds that a supposedly deviant behavior is a voluntary act—an expression of human volition, will, or choice. Humanists take such a stand because they are disturbed by what they claim is the dehumanizing implication of the positivist view of deviant behavior. The positivist view implies that a human being is like "a robot, a senseless and purposeless machine reacting to every fortuitous change in the external and internal environment."[1] Instead, humanists believe that, unlike machines, people participate in *meaningful activity,* creating their reality and that of the world around them, actively and strenuously.[2] That's why humanists emphasize the importance of delving into the subjective experiences of deviants. But, in doing so, humanists effectively shut themselves out from the positivist enterprise of using determinism to explain causes of deviance, particularly deviance of the powerful, which is a major concern of humanists.

Thus, I will here illustrate an attempt to go beyond the humanist's traditional opposition to positivist determinism by developing a deviance theory with ideas from positivist as well as humanist theories. I will first use conflict theory to suggest that social inequality determines the types of deviance likely to be committed by the powerful and the powerless, and that the powerful are more prone to deviance than the powerless. Then I will use mostly positivist theories to explain why the powerful are more likely to commit deviant acts.

POWER AS A DIFFERENTIATOR OF DEVIANCE

It is a truism that social inequality exists in all societies, all over the world. There may be less social inequality in some societies than in others, but it is never completely absent in any society. Various people may define social

Excerpted from the author's book, *Deviant Behavior,* 4th ed. (New York: HarperCollins, 1995).

inequality by different criteria, but it seems best to define it by power. As political scientist Andrew Hacker says,

> We know America has classes, and that they are more than temporary way stations. No matter how we divide up Americans according to culture, career, even income, *power is at the heart of the question.* Some people have more freedom, more independence, than others. Some are buffeted about from birth to death, never in a position to bend events or answer back to authority. Class may confer power over others; in personal life it affects how you can make the world work on your behalf.[3]

But the concept of social inequality need not be applied to the inequality between upper and lower classes alone. It can also be applied to the inequality between upper and middle classes or between middle and lower classes. It can even be applied to the inequality between whites and blacks, between men and women, between parents and children, between judges and defendants, between psychiatrists and patients, and so on. This is because any two groups can be considered unequal insofar as one is, on the whole, more powerful than the other. For the sake of simplicity and convenience, let us refer to one group as *the powerful* and the other as *the powerless.*

It seems obvious that power inequality affects the quality of people's lives in general, as Hacker suggests. We can easily see that the powerful live better than the powerless, that the powerful reside in bigger and more comfortable homes, eat better food, drive more expensive cars, take longer vacations, get higher-quality medical care, and send their children to better schools and colleges. Similarly, power inequality affects the quality of *deviant* activities likely to be engaged in by people. It is obvious that the rich are more likely than the poor to carry out corporate crimes such as fraudulent advertising, commercial bribery, and tax evasion, which are highly profitable. By contrast, the poor are more likely to commit street crimes such as robbery, mugging, and assault, which are less profitable than corporate crimes. Substantial data support this simple impressionistic observation. As John Braithwaite puts it,

> The conclusion is therefore inescapable from the voluminous, though not always satisfactory, evidence available at this time that lower class people do commit those directly interpersonal types of crimes (murder, rape, robbery, and assault) which are normally handled by the police at a higher rate than middle class people. If, however, we are talking about those less directly interpersonal forms of crimes which involve the abuse of power inherent in occupational roles (and which are normally policed by social regulators of commerce), then, of course, the reverse is true.[4]

In short, power differentiates people into two groups according to the type of deviance each is likely to commit. Thus, we may state the first proposition of our power theory as follows: *The powerful are more likely to commit lower-consensus deviance*—the act that relatively few people consider to be deviant, namely, "less serious," more profitable, or more sophisticated type of deviance, *whereas the powerless are more likely to perpetrate higher-consensus deviance*—the act that numerous people consider to be deviant, namely, the "more serious," less profitable, or less sophisticated form of deviance.

POWER AS A CAUSE OF DEVIANCE

The general public and even many sociologists still hold the traditional view that the poor are more criminal than the rich—that the poor are more likely than the rich to commit crime. As a sociologist observes, "The relationship [between class and crime] tends to be astonishingly linear—the worse the deprivation, the worse the crime."[5] This is correct only if the word *crime* refers largely to street crime. It is obviously incorrect if the word refers to corporate crime, simply because poor people cannot commit such crime. Apparently, the word is meant to refer to "crime in general" or "crime as a whole," which is supposed to include *all* kinds of crime. If that is the case, nobody knows whether class and crime are related, because nobody has been foolhardy enough to conduct an incredibly ambitious, impossible study that samples the entire gamut of crimes including all kinds of corporate crime, official crime, political crime, street crime, and so on. Thus, it is misleading to use the word crime to imply that it means "crime as a whole" while it actually refers to street crime only.

Similarly, other sociologists have misused the word crime to argue that the class-crime relationship is a myth—the research literature fails to show that lower classes are more likely than higher classes to commit crime.[6] In using the word crime, these sociologists apparently wanted their readers to think of crime as a whole, but in reality they referred mostly to juvenile delinquency. Juvenile delinquency makes up only a small portion of the entire crime problem. It can hardly represent crime as a whole. If those sociologists included corporate crime in their definition of crime, they would have had a hard time maintaining that there is no class difference in crime.

However, by analyzing a biased sample of crime studies, which deal mostly with juvenile delinquency, they did find that lower-status youths do not commit more delinquency than higher-status youths. This is not surprising, though, because (1) the difference in social experience between "lower status" and "higher status" adolescents is too small to constitute a real class difference and (2) the "delinquency" in question includes both major and minor types of offenses. If the difference in class is clearly established and the type of delinquency is clearly specified (as either major or minor offense), as has been done by John Hagan and his colleagues,[7] then we are likely to see a class difference in delinquency—upper-class youths committing more minor offenses and fewer major offenses than their lower-class peers. It should also be noted that upper-class children are more likely to learn the sophisticated ways of committing deviance. In their study of elite boarding-school children, Peter Cookson and Caroline Persell found that "in the course of a prep school career, most students will learn to work the system, if not by breaking the rules then by learning to bend them. [Therefore,] getting 'wasted' on liquor or high on drugs is a kind of game, the object of which is not to get caught."[8] When they go on to elite colleges, they are likely to continue sharpening their skills in breaking or bending rules so that they would be able to become "tomorrow's corrupt government officials, tax cheats, toxic waste polluters, medicare defrauders, corporate price-fixers, fraudulent advertisers, and other myriad forms of white-collar criminals."[9] Obviously, lower-class children are less likely to learn how to become such sophisticated criminals.

In short, there is a class difference in the commission of a certain *type* of deviance. It is useless, therefore, to argue about which class is more deviant without initially determining what type of deviance is involved. Since classes do differ in the type of deviance committed, as suggested by our first proposition, we should take this into account if we want to speculate about the causal relation between power and deviance. With the first proposition in the back of our minds, then, we may state our second proposition as follows: *the powerful are more likely to engage in lower-consensus deviance such as corporate crime than are the powerless committing higher-consensus deviance such as street crime.* This implies that if the type of deviance is held constant by treating lower-consensus deviance (antitrust offenses and other corporate crimes) and higher-consensus deviance (armed robbery and other street crimes) as though both were the same deviance, the powerful are more prone to deviance than the powerless. In other words, the likelihood of the powerful committing lower-consensus deviance is greater than the likelihood of the powerless perpetrating higher-consensus deviance. This proposition is suggested by the fact that the powerful (1) have a stronger deviant motivation, (2) enjoy greater deviant opportunity, and (3) are subjected to weaker social control.

Stronger Deviant Motivation

As strain theory suggests, relative deprivation—the inability to realize one's aspiration—is a potent motivation of deviant behavior. Relative deprivation exists when people feel that they are not able to get what they want. It is a feeling of the discrepancy between what people expect to have and what they actually have. It has been referred to by Robert Merton as the gap between the goal and the means for achieving it, or the disjunction between aspiration and opportunity.

It seems like a paradox of human life that relative deprivation stems largely from too many opportunities for success. The reason is that too many opportunities tend to raise one's aspirations so high that they cannot be easily realized. If aspirations cannot be easily realized, one is motivated to resort to some illegitimate means of actualizing the aspirations. This, then, is tantamount to the perpetration of deviant acts.[10]

People who enjoy too many opportunities and consequently suffer great relative deprivation are more likely to be the powerful members of society. This is essentially because, when compared with the powerless, the powerful are more heavily influenced by the pervasive ideology of success to entertain very high success goals. In fact, the powerful have long—since infancy—been conditioned to strive for great success in their lives. "From the cradle, most prep school students," for example, "are told to 'be somebody'; few are told 'just be yourself'. Pressure on these students is relentless."[11] Such pressure for success tends more to generate frustration in powerful persons because their goal is too high for them to achieve. As Merton writes, "An observer of a community in which annual salaries in six figures are not uncommon, reports the anguished words of one victim of the American Dream: 'In this town, I'm snubbed socially because I only get a thousand a week. That hurts.'"[12] Therefore, though far from being *objectively* deprived as the powerless are, the powerful are *relatively* deprived, feeling like failures as a result of comparing themselves with others. They, in effect, feel that what they now have falls short of what others have, which is the same thing as what they themselves want to have. On the other hand, objective deprivation tends to suppress the aspirations of the powerless so that they experience less relative deprivation. All this has been explained by Durkheim many years ago:

> Poverty protects against . . . [relative deprivation] because it is a restraint in itself. No matter how one acts, desires have to depend upon resources to some extent; actual possessions are partly the criterion of those aspired to. So the less one has the less he is tempted to extend the range of his needs indefinitely. Lack of power, compelling moderation, accustoms men to it. . . . Wealth, on the other hand, by the power it bestows, deceives us into believing that we depend on ourselves only. Reducing the resistance we encounter from objects, it suggests the possibility of unlimited success against them. The less limited one feels, the more intolerable all limitation appears.[13]

In brief, the more power one has, the higher one's aspirations are, and the greater one's relative deprivation is. As has been suggested in many studies, relative deprivation is positively related to deviant behavior. Now, since the powerful are more likely than the powerless to experience relative deprivation, the powerful can be said to be more motivated to deviant action.[14] But relative deprivation does not necessarily lead to deviance; it merely serves as a predisposition to it. Powerful people with this predisposition are more likely to commit a deviant act if they have the opportunity to do so. And they seem to enjoy more deviant opportunities than the powerless.

Greater Deviant Opportunity

Once again, it seems like a paradox of human life that the more *legitimate* opportunities there are for an individual to attain success, the more *deviant* opportunities there are to do so. This is primarily because, as Albert Cohen has observed, "There are *not* some things that are legitimate opportunities and *other* things that are illegitimate opportunities, but . . . the *same* things are typically, and perhaps always, both."[15] Thus, since they have more legitimate opportunities than the powerless do, the powerful also have more (illegitimate) opportunities for deviant activities.

It is obvious, for example, that the powerful have far greater opportunities for getting a good education, a well-paying job, social influence and prestige, and other amenities of life. But, at the same time, if they want to commit some deviant acts, they will enjoy far more and better (illegitimate) opportunities to do so than the powerless. Suppose a rich banker and a poor worker want to acquire a huge sum of money illegitimately. The banker has access to more and better opportunities than the worker. The rich banker can easily defraud the Internal Revenue Service as well as her many customers. The banker also has a good chance of getting away with it because the skill for pulling off the crime is simply the skill required for holding the bank position in the first place.[16] In contrast, the poor worker would find his illegitimate opportunity limited to a crude robbery of the banker—such an illegitimate opportunity being further limited by his good chance of getting arrested, convicted, or imprisoned. Suppose the worker chooses instead to steal the money from the company that employs him. The opportunity for doing so is also limited because his lowly position, unlike the banker's high position, generally requires supervision by some higher-up. The differential opportunity can further be demonstrated by the fact that a rich person can commit such lower-class crimes as murder and robbery but a poor person cannot perpetrate such white-collar crimes as price fixing and commercial bribery.

Therefore, given their greater deviant opportunity, the powerful can be said to be more likely to engage in deviant activities. But their likelihood of deviant involvement may increase if an inadequate amount of social control is imposed on them.

Weaker Social Control

Given both their access to greater deviant opportunity and their experience of stronger motivation toward deviance resulting from their greater relative deprivation, the powerful are indeed more prone to deviant action than the powerless. Logically—in the interest of preventing deviance—society should exercise stronger control over the powerful. But, once again, it seems ironical that society does just the opposite—exercising less control over the powerful. The irony of this irony is that compared with lower-class criminals, white-collar offenders are more easily deterred by legal punishment.[17] Since they are aware of the lesser control imposed on them, the powerful, already prone to deviance through their greater deviant motivation and opportunity, are even more inclined to engage in deviant activities.

The source of the irony is the condition of social inequality. Thanks to this condition, the powerful have more influence in the making of laws and their enforcement. It is no wonder that the laws against higher-status criminals are relatively lenient and seldom enforced, but those against lower-status criminals are harsher and more often enforced. Not a single corporate criminal, for example, has ever been sentenced to death for marketing some untested drug that "cleanly" kills many people, but there have been many lower-class criminals sentenced to death for "messily" killing a person.

Given the lesser control imposed on them, the powerful may feel encouraged to resort to some deviant means for amassing their fortunes and power. It is not surprising, that there appear to be more illegal banking practices than armed robberies against banks. As one economist observes, "There is a market for stories about people violently robbing banks, less of one for stories about banks peacefully robbing people. Yet contemplation of banking practices would lead one to suppose the latter to be the more thriving and popular of the two industries."[18]

CONCLUSION

To sum up the whole discussion of power as a cause of deviance: Because of social inequality, the powerful are likely to have a stronger deviant motivation, enjoy greater deviant opportunity, and encounter weaker social control, as compared with the powerless. As a consequence, the powerful are said to be more likely to participate in deviant activities: The probability of powerful persons committing lower-consensus deviance such as corporate crime is greater than the probability of powerless individuals committing higher-consensus deviance such as street crime.

While all this may make sense on theoretical grounds, is there any evidence to underpin it? Are the powerful *really* more likely to commit corporate crime than the powerless committing street crime? It is impossible to find a study that focuses directly on this issue. The reason is that sociologists have long asked the wrong question of whether class is related to deviance *without* taking into account the class difference in *types* of deviance likely to be committed (for example, "Are the rich more likely than the poor to commit deviant acts?"). Sociologists have not come around to asking the kind of question that we have asked here ("Are the rich more likely to commit corporate crime than the poor to commit armed robbery?"). But bits and pieces of evidence can be found to suggest the connection between power and deviance. In the United States, for example, there are about six industrial deaths caused by corporate violation of safety regulations for every one homicide committed by a poor person. In Great Britain the ratio of industrial deaths to homicides is seven to one.[19] In fact, the ratio is substantially higher if we take into account the numerous deaths caused by corporations' untested drugs, unsafe cars and other products, environmental pollution, and so on. Moreover, there is evidence to suggest that the frequency of property crimes (such as consumer fraud, price fixing, and false advertising) typically committed by the powerful is greater than the frequency of property crimes (robbery, theft, and larceny) perpetrated by the powerless.[20] As British sociologist Steven Box says, "Whether we are consumers or citizens, we stand more chance of being robbed by persons who roam corporate suites than we do by those who roam public streets."[21]

Notes

1. I. E. Farber, "Personality and Behavioral Science," in May Brodbeck, ed., *Readings in the Philosophy of the Social Sciences* (New York: Macmillan, 1968), p. 149.

2. David Matza, *Becoming Deviant* (Englewood Cliffs, NJ: Prentice-Hall, 1969), pp. 7, 8.

3. Andrew Hacker, "Who Rules America?" *New York Review of Books,* May 1, 1975, p. 9; emphasis added.

4. John Braithwaite, "The Myth of Social Class and Criminality Reconsidered." *American*

Sociological Review, Vol. 46 (1981), p. 49.

5. Elliott Currie, *Confronting Crime: An American Challenge* (New York: Pantheon Books, 1985), p. 146.

6. See, for example, Charles R. Tittle, Wayne J. Villemez, and Douglas A. Smith, "The Myth of Social Class and Criminality: An Assessment of the Empirical Evidence," *American Sociological Review,* Vol. 43 (1978), pp. 643–656.

7. John Hagan, A. R. Gillis, and John Simpson, "The Class Structure of Gender and Delinquency: Toward a Power-Control Theory of Common Delinquent Behavior," *American Journal of Sociology,* Vol. 90 (1985), pp. 1151–1175.

8. Peter W. Cookson, Jr., and Caroline Hodges Persell, *Preparing for Power: America's Elite Boarding Schools* (New York: Basic Books, 1985), p. 161.

9. Stuart L. Hills, "Crime and Deviance on a College Campus: The Privilege of Class," *Humanity and Society,* Vol. 6 (1982), p. 266.

10. For data supporting this and the following view, see the relevant studies cited in Alex Thio, "A Critical Look at Merton's Anomie Theory," *Pacific Sociological Review,* Vol. 18 (1975), pp. 139–158.

11. Cookson and Persell, *Preparing for Power,* p. 20.

12. Robert K. Merton, *Social Theory and Social Structure,* rev. ed. (New York: Free Press, 1957), p. 136.

13. Emile Durkheim, *Suicide* (New York: Free Press, 1951), p. 254.

14. For a similar explanation of how men, being more powerful than women, generally experience greater relative deprivation and hence have higher crime rates than women, see Joseph Harry and Mary C. Sengstock, "Attribution, Goals, and Deviance," *American Sociological Review,* Vol. 43 (1978), pp. 278–280.

15. Albert K. Cohen, *Deviance and Control* (Englewood Cliffs, NJ: Prentice-Hall, 1966), p. 110.

16. Diane Vaughan, *Controlling Unlawful Organizational Behavior: Social Structure and Corporate Misconduct* (Chicago: University of Chicago Press, 1983), p. 85.

17. John Braithwaite, "White Collar Crime," *Annual Review of Sociology,* Vol. 11 (1985), p. 16.

18. Alexander Cockburn, "Million Dollar Yeggs," *New York Review of Books,* March 20, 1975, p. 21.

19. Steven Box, *Power, Crime, and Mystification* (London: Tavistock, 1983), p. 26.

20. See, for example, Marshall B. Clinard and Peter C. Yeager, *Corporate Crime* (New York: Free Press, 1980); and David R. Simon and D. Stanley Eitzen, *Elite Deviance,* 4th ed. (Boston: Allyn and Bacon, 1993), pp. 91–116.

21. Box, *Power, Crime, and Mystification,* p. 31.

PART 5
Physical Violence

Despite the great increase in teen killing, murder is still a relatively rare form of crime. As government statistics have consistently shown, the murder rate is the lowest among major crimes in the United States. We are even less likely to be murdered by others than to kill ourselves. But murder remains the most serious offense. Its cost to the victim is forever irreparable and its cost to the victim's surviving loved ones is incalculably high. Perhaps because of its seriousness, murder fascinates many of us. Thanks to a legion of novelists as well as television and movie producers, we often seek entertainment from a murder mystery, trying excitedly to figure out "who done it?" But our experiences with many manufactured murders may have led some of us to a distorted view of the real crime. We may fear strangers as our potential murderers, while in reality most killings are done not by people unknown to us but by our acquaintances, friends, lovers, or relatives. We may also imagine that most murders are intriguing mysteries, while in real life they are no mysteries at all—the police can easily find out from the people at the murder scene who the culprit is. Here we will look into some other realities of physical violence.

One commonly observed fact in the United States is that men are more homicidal than women, presumably because men are far more concerned about defending their manhood. Most killings occur between men only, with males killing males. If a man and a woman are caught up in a homicidal interaction, he is more likely to be the offender and she the victim. The men kill their wives or girlfriends mostly because they have persistently tried to keep their victims in an abusive relationship. Such killing, then, is the culmination of a long series of physical violence perpetrated by the men against the women. Moreover, men tend to kill in response to their wives' infidelity. In the fewer cases where women kill, they differ from their male counterparts in the choice of victims. Unlike male offenders, who are more likely to kill others of the *same* sex, female offenders are more likely to kill members of the *opposite* sex. In these opposite-sex killings, the female and male murderers commit the crime for different reasons. The women rarely kill in response to their husbands' infidelity even if their husbands are extremely adulterous. They usually send their husbands to the hereafter as a desperate attempt to get out of a relationship in which they have long been abused. The women basically kill for self-preservation or in self-defense. Violence by women, consequently, is primarily defensive, in contrast to violence by men being offensive.[1] What about the killing in other societies? Are foreign men also more homicidal than women? The answer is provided in the first article, "Men and Violence: Is the Pattern Universal?" by Dane Archer and Patricia McDaniel.

The soaring incidence of teen violence in recent years has prompted a search for explanations. We have observed from Anderson's analysis that the desire for respect among poor youth plays a key role in teen killing. Here, in the second article, "Kids, Guns, and Killing Fields," James Wright and other researchers explain why young criminals and students carry guns and commit violence. In the third reading, "Megamurders," R. J. Rummel puts killing in a larger perspective by showing why states commit more violence than individuals. In the last selection, "Crime, Race, and Values," James Wilson proposes some solutions to the high rate of violence in inner cities.

---

[1] Margo I. Wilson and Martin Daly, "Who Kills Whom in Spouse Killings? On the Exceptional Sex Ratio of Spousal Homicides in the United States," *Criminology,* Vol. 30 (1992), p. 208.

14

Men and Violence: Is the Pattern Universal?

DANE ARCHER AND PATRICIA MCDANIEL
University of California, Santa Cruz

Men are more likely than women to commit virtually all types of violent crimes in the United States. This male-female difference is one of the best-known findings in American criminology. On closer inspection, however, this apparently "obvious" finding turns out to be poorly understood. Is the link between gender and violence strictly an American phenomenon, or is the pattern also found in other, very different societies? Also, how well do we understand the *reasons* for the maleness-violence link—does this pattern reflect socialization patterns, cultural factors, or biological differences between the sexes?

Questions about violence have a special urgency in American society. While violence and aggression are considered important social problems in many societies, the United States leads the industrial world in lethal violence. In any given year, out of every hundred thousand Americans, ten will die from homicide. This homicide rate is 50 times as high as the rate in New Zealand, 30 times as high as the rate in Great Britain, and 10 times as high as the rate in France (Archer and Gartner, 1984). In fact, the American homicide rate is grossly higher than the rate in *any* other industrial nation. This difference is so large that even societies undergoing civil wars—like the periodic factional strife in Northern Ireland—do not reach the normal, everyday, *average* homicide rate of the United States. Clearly, then, violence constitutes an urgent social agenda for American society.

THEORIES ABOUT GENDER AND VIOLENCE

It is a relatively simple matter to illustrate rival theories about the causes of violence in general, and about gender differences in particular. It is far more difficult to arrive at a conclusive test of which theories are valid. This is because violence, like all complex human behaviors, is undoubtedly determined by a confluence of different factors acting either in concert or contradiction.

This article was specifically written for this reader. The research was supported by a grant from the H. F. Guggenheim Foundation and by the University of California.

Even if researchers were able to establish that a human hormone (e.g., testosterone) was linked to violent behavior, one would still be unable to answer some of the most important questions about *variance* in violence rates. For example, why did the American homicide rate double in the 1960s? Why do Southern states in the U.S. have homicide rates twice as high as the national average and ten times as high as the rates in New England or North Central states? Why is the U.S. homicide rate as much as 50 times higher than the rates found in other industrial nations (Archer and Gartner, 1984).

None of these differences can be explained by a human hormone, which presumably remains constant over time, North and South, and across international boundaries. Satisfactory explanations about the causes of violence need to be able to account for the extreme variance that characterizes rates of homicide and other violent crimes. Accounting for variations in violence is thus the "acid test" for any theories about the origins of violence and, if strictly applied, it is a test that few theories have been able to pass.

The research literature on violence and aggression is enormous. Any exhaustive review requires a book-length treatment (e.g., Goldstein, 1986), and thus will not be attempted here. Instead, exemplars of different theoretical traditions will be used to contrast the very different perspectives embedded in research on biological, social, and cultural factors that may cause violence and aggression.

Biological theories have provided intriguing but inconclusive findings. For example, Christiansen and Knussman (1987) compared self-ratings of aggressiveness in 117 individuals with actual levels of serum testosterone. The researchers found a positive correlation—that is, individuals with higher self-ratings tended to have higher levels of serum testosterone—but the relationship was not strong. Rada, Laws, and Kellner (1976) compared 52 men imprisoned for rape with a control group of 12 nonviolent prisoners. In general, the two groups did not differ in testosterone levels, but the most violent rapists (those who committed additional, brutal violence during the rape) did have significantly higher testosterone levels.

Other biology-based research has involved animals, using an at best debatable assumption that the complexities of human behavior can be understood by research on creatures that do not use alcohol, shoot firearms, become disgruntled ex-employees, or do any of 1000 other "human" acts that seem to figure prominently in the commission of violent acts. Nonetheless, researchers studying male rats have found that castration at birth reduces the adult aggressiveness of the rats (Connor and Levine, 1969).

Even in animal communities, however, differential parenting may be at least partially responsible for the gender differences one observes in adult creatures. For example, Mitchell and Brandt (1970) studied 16 female rhesus monkeys and their infants. They found that the mothers of males threatened and bit their offspring more than did the mothers of females. Interestingly, the researchers also concluded that the mothers of female monkeys restrained and protected their infants, while the mothers of males seemed to prompt greater independence and activity in their offspring.

Unsurprisingly, research on social factors has taken a road quite unlike that traveled by most biological researchers. Nearly a half-century ago, researchers began reporting that parental socialization tended to foster greater levels of aggression in boys (Sears, Maccoby, and Levin, 1957). Parents are more likely to encourage boys to fight back if they are challenged and—at least in American society—this encouragement reflects a widespread parental belief that some aggression is a natural, even desirable aspect of masculinity. The picture is quite different for girls. Parents tend to discourage female aggression, or they simply ignore it. In either case, the net effect is the same: female aggression is simply not reinforced. Research by Bardwick (1971) suggested, though, that while being socialized away from using direct physical aggression (the province of boys), girls were socialized *toward* other forms of aggression: verbal aggression, subtle interpersonal rejection, manipulation, and so on. Still, it is precisely *physical* aggression that has become urgently problematic. After all, physical aggression—homicide, assault, or rape—wreaks a much greater toll than verbal unpleasantness.

Much of the research sketched thus far reflects American society or, only slightly less narrowly, industrial societies. It is obviously critical to include in our discussion *cultural* factors by asking how aggression and the male-violence link differ across societies. Clearly, there are vast societal differences, including the provocative finding that lethal violence is pandemic in some societies but relatively unknown in others (Archer and Gartner, 1984). Much of the research on cultural differences derives from anthropology. For example, Rohner (1976) coded published ethnographic accounts of children's behavior in 14 traditional societies. He found large intersocietal differences in fostering aggressive behavior among children—for some societies, high levels of aggression were the norm; for others, aggression was relatively unacceptable.

The question of the link between maleness and violence also has cultural implications. It may be that boys and girls are socialized for different adult roles—that is, a sexual division of labor. Perhaps many societies socialize boys for adult roles that require greater levels of aggression, such as hunting or intergroup conflict. This "differential gender socialization" hypothesis has been invoked to account for the higher levels of male aggression observed in many societies studied by anthropologists (Tieger, 1980; Segall, 1983).

The differential socialization hypothesis is not, however, without its detractors. Most notably, Maccoby and Jacklin (1974) have argued that male-female differences in aggression are too consistent to be the result of the highly variable socialization patterns present in different societies. They further argued that male-female differences are observed as early as age two—too early to be explained by slow, cumulative socialization processes. This argument remains highly controversial, largely because it implies that the maleness-violence link may result, at least in part, from male-female differences that are universal and, perhaps, innate.

NEW CROSS-CULTURAL RESEARCH

During the past six years, we have begun a program of work to try to illuminate cultural aspects of violence. The catalyst for this work was the finding by Archer and Gartner (1984) of large, problematic, and intriguing differences in the levels of violence across societies. This new work complements their use of aggregate statistics on national rates of violent crime by examining social psychological differences across cultures. The basic method used in this new research presents individuals aged 16 to 18 with a series of twelve standardized "problem-solving" tasks. Each task involves a different conflict or problem (an unfaithful spouse, a romantic triangle, disciplining a child, a public dispute, a rejected lover, conflict at work, a quarrel between two nations, etc.). The individual is asked to write an imaginative story about how characters in these situations will respond to the conflict.

In each case, potential solutions range from nonviolent to violent. The research focus is on the *quantities and qualities of violence in the stories as a reflection of attitudes toward, expectations about, and justifications for violence as a means of solving conflicts.* The approach can be illustrated here with a conflict situation involving a woman (Mary) and her unfaithful husband (William). The problem is presented to participants who are asked to write a story about how Mary would respond:

> William and Mary have been married for two years. They both leave the house during the day, but they have different schedules. A friend of Mary's tells her that her husband has been seen with another woman while Mary is away from the house. Mary decides to see for herself. After pretending to leave the house as usual, Mary parks her car half a block from her house. Twenty minutes later, Mary sees a woman drive up to the house. Mary sees William come out of the house. He gives the woman a long, intimate kiss, and they go inside the house together. What will Mary do?

The twelve problem-solving situations used in the study are:

Unfaithful Mary—a husband discovers his wife is unfaithful
Unfaithful William—a wife discovers her husband is unfaithful
Unhappy Ann—a depressed young woman confronts school failure
Demonstrators—an extended protest occurs at a factory

Catherine Leaves James—a young woman tells boyfriend she loves another
James Leaves Catherine—a young man tells girlfriend he loves another
Co-Worker Dispute—a person steals work and credit from a co-worker
Mark the Policeman—a policeman confronts two thieves

Roger and His Son—a father disciplines five-year-old son
Big and Small Nation—two nations are in conflict
Mary Denies Richard—a woman refuses the sexual advances of male friend
John in the Pub—a man is confronted by an aggressive drunk

For each of three of these twelve conflicts (four different test booklets are used, each containing three problems), participants in the study generate an imaginative story about how the characters will respond to or attempt to solve the conflict described. In every case, the problem can be solved by either non-violent or violent means. For example, the previous problem ("Unfaithful William") generates a wide variety of solutions, including the two examples given here. The first was written by a Swedish high school student; the second by an American high school student.

SWEDISH EXAMPLE (Female Subject, 23095): Mary runs into the house and catches them red-handed. Mary is very unhappy. She yells at William and runs out of the house. William runs after her. Mary calms down. They decide to talk about it in peace and quiet. The other woman drives home. William and Mary take a seat on the sofa. William explains that he loves the other woman and wants a divorce. Mary says that she agrees. She will not live with a man who does not love her.

AMERICAN EXAMPLE (Male Subject, 01128): Mary feels a sudden surge of anger deep from within her inner-most self. Mary vows revenge. She slams the car into gear and races out to the hardware store where she purchases a 33-inch McCulloch chainsaw. When she arrives at the house most of the lights are out, so she creeps around back only to discover that William and his mistress are in back on the deck, dining with fine food over candlelight. Seeing this, Mary pulls the rip cord on her chainsaw. The chainsaw whines to life as William jumps up and screams, "What the fuck is going on?" Mary springs up on to the deck and buries the chainsaw deep into the other woman's head. Her body convulses as blood, flesh, gray matter, and bone fragments fly everywhere. William screams with terror as Mary cuts the motor and pulls the chainsaw out of the shaking lump of flesh which used to be a human. William is cornered as Mary fires up the saw. "Don't Mary, I can explain, please wait, don't!" Mary's eyes are glazed over and she seems possessed. She screams, "Rot in hell you stinking motherfucker!," as she slams the roaring chainsaw into William's mouth.

By themselves, of course, two isolated stories tell us little. The important questions involve the possibility of *general* and *systematic* differences in large samples obtained from different societies. Stories written in response to the twelve problem-solving stimuli were obtained from secondary-level schools in several societies. Data were collected from eleven nations. These nations vary with respect to the prevalence of violence—with some characterized by low rates of violent crime and others by high rates.

Within each of the societies included in the study, efforts were made to identify secondary schools diverse in parental social class, academic ability, and probable educational future. Secondary schools were chosen, rather than colleges and universities, because secondary schools are much more likely to be representative of all levels of class and ability. In most societies, tertiary education is highly stratified, drawing overwhelmingly from the highest financial and ability strata. In each case, a knowledgable local scholar was asked to identify schools that were likely to draw from populations diverse in social class. In each national sample, approximately 600 to 750 stories were obtained from 200 to 250 individuals—that is, each individual wrote three stories. The general instructions were as follows:

SOLVING PROBLEMS. In each of the following situations, a specific problem is described. After reading each description, make up a *detailed* story about how the characters in the story will try to solve this problem. In your story, describe *what* the characters do and *what happens* as a result. PLEASE MAKE YOUR STORIES AS *DETAILED* AS POSSIBLE.

A "Violence Code" was created using the method of content analysis to summarize the quantities of violence in the stories from each national sample. While the Violence Code permits the systematic enumeration of the *quantities* of violence in the stories, qualitative differences between the national samples are also extremely important, since these differences are often subtle and elude simple tabulation. The two methods, quantitative and qualitative, are complementary rather than redundant since they tap very different facets of the data set.*

RESULTS: QUANTITATIVE DATA

A comparison of eleven national data sets reveals large differences in quantities of violence contained in the stories, and these differences are indicated in Table 14.1. These data are for all twelve problem-solving stories combined. The overall incidence of violence shows low values for the Korean (18.6 percent), Swedish (19.3 percent), and Mexico samples (19.9 percent); much higher values for the New Zealand (38.7 percent), Australian (37.7 percent) and American (29.8 percent) samples. Differences among the eleven samples are even larger for several specific forms of violence, and the eleven-sample range for the incidence of each form of violence is shown by the "maximum/minimum" ratio in Table 14.1. For example, homicide is more than four times as common in the New Zealand and Australian sample as it is in the Korean sample; weapon use varies by a factor of six; and the ratio for rape varies by a factor of twelve.

The eleven national samples can be ranked from high to low in the following order on the frequency of any form of violence in the stories: New Zealand, Australia, Northern Ireland, United States, Japan, England, Canada, France, Mexico, Sweden, and Korea. If one ranks the eleven samples on the other outcomes shown in Table 14.1, most of the rankings correspond closely to this same order. There are a few cases, however, where a nation's ranking changes by two or more ranks from the overall violence ranking. For example, this is reflected in relatively low incidences of rape in the Canadian stories; relatively high levels of rape in the Korean stories; relatively low levels of war in the New Zealand and Australian stories; and relatively low levels of firearm use in New Zealand. With these exceptions, rankings of the eleven samples generally persist across the different types of violence indicated in Table 14.1.

---

* The methodology is too briefly presented here; a fully detailed description is available from Professor Dane Archer, Department of Sociology, University of California at Santa Cruz, Santa Cruz, CA 95064.

TABLE 14.1 Levels of Violence in Imaginative Stories from Different Societies

Violence type		National Sample (n)									Max/Min[a]
	Aust. (596)	Can. (767)	Eng. (728)	Fran. (561)	Jap. (693)	Kor. (742)	Mex. (417)	N. Zeal. (489)	N. Ire. (258)	Swe. (729)	U.S. (1728)	
Any Violence	37.8%	27.2%	28.7%	24.2%	29.0%	18.6%	19.9%	38.7%	32.6%	19.3%	30.2%	2.1
Homicide	12.9	5.7	5.9	4.5	4.0	3.1	4.1	14.4	6.2	5.9	8.7	4.6
2 or more dead	4.8	1.1	0.9	0.6	1.4	0.9	1.7	4.8	2.7	1.2	3.3	8.0
Suicide	4.9	4.6	3.4	3.1	3.8	2.5	1.9	5.9	3.9	2.7	4.3	3.1
Rape	3.5	0.3	2.1	0.4	2.8	3.0	1.7	3.2	3.6	1.0	1.7	12.0
War	4.0	4.1	2.5	5.0	4.6	1.9	1.4	2.9	2.3	3.0	4.6	3.6
Weapon present	16.2	7.2	7.3	8.4	2.6	2.7	4.3	16.4	7.5	6.6	12.4	6.3
Firearms	8.7	5.4	3.0	6.6	1.6	2.0	3.3	7.4	2.0	4.2	7.5	5.4
Handgun	1.0	0.1	0.3	0.0	0.1	0.0	0.7	1.2	0.4	0.1	0.6	12.0
Nuclear weapon	1.5	0.3	0.1	0.0	0.3	0.0	0.0	1.2	0.4	0.3	0.8	15.0

[a]The Max/Min index is the simple ratio of the maximum value to the minimum value. When the minimum is zero, a minimum value of 0.1 is used.

GENDER DIFFERENCES

Stories written by men are more likely to contain violence than those written by women. This pattern is consistent (1) across all eleven societies and (2) across all twelve problem-solving situations. These gender differences are shown in Table 14.2. A higher proportion of male stories (35 percent overall) contained violence than did female stories (22.5 percent) for all eleven national samples. This indicates that male stories were 1.56 times as likely to contain violence as female stories.

The differential for stories containing homicides was even greater; compared to women's stories, men's stories were 2.40 times more likely to contain a homicide. The differential for stories containing firearms was roughly 2.13. It should be noted that these male-female differences were not due to only one or two societies. Consistent male-female differences occurred for 35 of the 36 comparisons (97.2 percent), and for 28 of the 28 significant differences (100 percent) shown in Table 14.2. Independent of the nation studied, therefore, men were more likely than women to write violent stories.

RESULTS: QUALITATIVE DATA

The eleven national data sets vary dramatically not only in the frequency of violent acts—something quantification does a reasonable job of summarizing—but also in the nuances that make the eleven data sets so dissimilar. These nuances defy quantification, and they reflect some of the most important qualities that make the Swedish stories unlike the American stories, and that make both unlike the English stories, and so on. Many themes, patterns, and outcomes found frequently in the stories from one nation were infrequent or even unknown in the stories from another society. Quantification therefore leaves unanswered many subtle questions regarding cultural differences, and a close reading of the stories is required.

With so many stories to choose from, it is possible here only to illustrate some of their diversity and cultural uniqueness. The examples are all from the "Unfaithful William" and "Unfaithful Mary" conflicts. In American stories written in response to these two problems, reactions generally involve anger and rage. When violence takes place in these stories, it is frequently fatal, occurs rapidly in hot blood, and often involves firearms. There was a gender difference in the frequency of violence in American stories about "Unfaithful Mary" (36.8 percent of male stories contained violence; 9.6 percent of female stories contained violence) and, to a lesser degree, about "Unfaithful William" (22.6 percent of male stories; 14.6 percent of female stories). The following six examples come from the American sample; the first three were written by men and the next three by women.

> *American Male, 01049:* William waits for three hours. Then finally the man comes out of the house tucking his shirt. By this time, William is outraged so he starts up his car and drives casually over towards the man and parks right in the way of the

TABLE 14.2 Who Writes More Violent Stories, Men or Women? (Percentage of Stories with Specified Content)

Content by gender of author	National Sample (n)											Mean
	Aust. (596)	Can. (767)	Eng. (728)	Fran. (561)	Jap. (693)	Kor. (742)	Mex. (417)	N. Zeal. (489)	N. Ire. (258)	Swe. (729)	U.S. (1728)	
Violence												
Male	47.4	31.8	35.9	34.0	32.8	25.5	23.6	43.4	44.6	27.9	37.8	35.0%
Female	28.3	23.0	20.5	18.5	25.0	11.6	18.3	34.3	28.6	15.3	23.9	22.5%
	***	*	***	***	*	***		*	**	***	***	***
Diff.	19.1	8.8	15.4	15.5	7.8	13.9	5.3	9.1	16.0	12.6	13.9	12.5%
Homicides												
Male	20.8	8.1	7.8	9.9	5.6	4.6	6.3	18.1	7.7	10.2	12.4	10.1%
Female	4.8	3.4	3.6	1.4	2.4	1.6	3.0	11.3	5.5	3.7	5.4	4.2%
	***	**	*	***	*	*		*		***	***	***
Firearms												
Male	11.6	6.8	5.9	7.9	3.1	3.5	4.7	9.6	1.5	8.2	9.3	6.6%
Female	5.9	4.4	0.3	5.4	0.0	0.5	2.4	5.8	1.6	2.4	5.8	3.1%
	*	**	***	***	**	**				***	**	***

*** p < .001 (at least)
** p < .01
* p < .05

man's car. William steps out very casually and reaches under the seat and pulls out his service 45 and chambers a round. In the meantime the man steps out of the car and is walking toward William. William sees him coming towards him so he just points it towards the man and pulls the trigger. The shock of the slug to the man's chest was so great it broke all his ribs and put a hole through him that you could stick a baseball through.

American Male, 03102: First, William hit the dashboard as hard as he could and nearly broke his hand doing so. William starts to get an angry look on his face and all of a sudden, pulls out a .357 Magnum, the most powerful in the world. . . . When William began the third knock, the man answered the door. William asked if Mary was there, the man said that he doesn't know any Mary and so she wasn't there. William then blew off his head and took Mary home and romped on her.

American Male, 12180: William is going to go kick some ass on this dude. First thing William does is wait 15 minutes so he can barge into the house and catch this man fucking the brains out of his wife. Then William fucks this dude up, beats his head in and gets a gun and shoots his ass. Then he goes and fucks Mary's pussy all the rest of the day to make sure she won't want any more Dick for a while.

American Female, 12085: William should talk to Mary about what's going on. He should ask her what kind of problem is going on between them, and ask her if there is a problem (and) why she can't tell him instead of sleeping around with other guys. Maybe they should see a marriage counselor.

American Female, 03106: At the door to the bedroom he stops and listens carefully. His blood is pounding so loudly through his ears that it is hard to hear. Taking a deep breath, he opens the door and stalks into the bedroom. Mary is undressed in bed with a man William has never seen before. She jumps up and the blood rushes from her face. "What the hell is going on here?!," William shouts. Mary breaks down and starts crying as the stranger hurriedly gets dressed and runs out the door. . . . Mary rambles on and on, not seeing what Will is doing, then out of nowhere William pulls out a gun and says, "If I can't have you neither can he!," and with that he proceeds to shoot Mary in the head and, only seconds later, to shoot himself.

American Female, 11012: Mary will probably sit there and think "I want to kill them both." But obviously she won't hurt him. The other woman would yell at him for not getting rid of Mary and the two women will end up fighting and, at the end, the other woman will probably just give up and say something to William like, "You'll be sorry."

The following stories are drawn from some of the other national samples. These examples vary in the quantities and qualities of violence they contain. They also reflect some degree of cultural uniqueness, containing themes and solutions encountered rarely if at all in the American stories.

Swedish Male, 23194: William, a bit sexually frustrated himself, is extremely jealous. He finds however that this jealousy provokes an erotic feeling. His loins tingled as he watched them kiss. His normal uncreative mind starts to burn with new and exciting ideas. He decides to cut loose from his inhibitions and join them. Once in the house, he can hear their laughter in the bathroom. He begins to unbutton his shirt as he approaches the door. As he turns the knob, he can hear the couple gasp. "It's OK," he whispers, "I've come to join you." The couple is noticeably apprehensive but, as he undresses, they begin to relax. Their innovative afternoon has begun.

Swedish Female, 23127: William will go into the house and call for an explanation, (and) ask what the other man is doing in his house with his wife and so on. If it just was a temporary romance, they can be friends again. Or perhaps William will sue for a divorce.

English Female, 28066: After a very hard morning at work, she returns home. William by this time would have gone to work. Mary, in her hunt for evidence, finds an article of the woman's clothing under the bed. Later when her husband returns she confronts him. They don't argue about it but talk sensibly, deciding the best course of action calmly among the two of themselves. Agreeing eventually that she, Mary, is willing to give him a second chance if he gives his word to forget that woman.

English Male, 28015: William sat in his car trying to decide what to do. Should he burst in on them, should he kill them both, should he go to a lawyer or ignore what was happening? William drove up to his house, walked up to the door. He goes inside. Giggles can be heard upstairs. He goes up to the bedroom and Mary and her lover are lying on the bed, semi-naked. Both try to cover themselves up. Mary gets out of bed and tries to calm William down. William pushes her away over a chair. Her lover gets up to defend her and receives a fist in the face. William leaves the house and drives off at high speed to the nearest bar.

Japanese Male, 27007: Mary pretends she knows nothing. Mary then, in the morning and at night, uses these times to see how William feels about her. . . . If William still does not show any affection, Mary will leave the house and will live alone. She will never go out with another man and will never change her feelings about her loving William. In short, she will not revenge, hate or hold a grudge against William loving somebody else. If she ever felt this way, she will condemn her feelings. On the other hand, she will try to understand why men behave in this manner. As a result, they will end in a divorce but she will love William more than she ever had during her marriage.

Japanese Male, 27039: William was angered but, having run to the front of the house, he tiptoed to peek into the window where Mary and the man were. He peeked for a while. Shocked by what Mary and the man were doing, William rushed into the house and shouted at Mary, "Who is this guy?" Mary told excuses but William smacks her. . . .

Australian Female, 26018: Mary is stunned. Slowly she walks to her car and in a daze drives off. Images of the woman kissing her husband flash through her mind. Resolutely, she parks her car near a deserted beach and goes for a walk. She is in a turmoil. Should she confront her husband and demand an explanation or should she bide her time and hope that he tells her himself? Direct confrontation is best, so slowly Mary gets back into her car and drives back home. She is just in time to see the lady leaving. . . . Guilt is written all over William's face as he sees Mary. "It was nothing," he stutters desperately. Mary doesn't say anything. She walks determinedly to their bedroom, pulls out her suitcase and starts packing her belongings. For a moment her eyes fall upon their wedding picture, but she turns away. At the door, she turns one last time to take a look at what was her home and at the man she once loved. Then she turns and purposefully walks towards her car.

Australian Male, 26109: There were noises coming from the bedroom so she moved down the passage slowly and then she peered around the corner. Her friend was right. Then Mary quickly moved to the passage closet and pulled out a handgun. She then returned to the bedroom with the loaded gun, shooting her husband first and then his little playmate. Then turning the gun on herself, after shooting everybody. They had all died instantly.

Korean Female, 25043: Mary investigates their relationship with suspicion. She tries to find out whether their relationship is unclean or just friendship, or has to do with business. If the relationship turns out to be serious (unclean), Mary will suffer deeply from agony and anguish. Since Mary loves William very much, she will leave him for his happiness. Mary's life will be filled with joy thinking that William, the one whom she loves the most, is living a happy life by her sacrifice.

Korean Male, 25149: When William gets home, he asks Mary with a smiling face, "Did you have fun while I was gone?" Mary looks surprised, "How did you know?" If I were William, I'd go to the man and hit him a few times, then give my wife (Mary) to the man.

AN ATTEMPT AT THEORETICAL SYNTHESIS

The large gender differences reported in this paper have implications for three different theoretical explanations that emphasize respectively, biological, social, and cultural factors. Each explanation can be examined in light of the new findings presented here.

First, biology. Given the large and highly consistent gender differences obtained in these data, biological factors cannot in our view be discounted— males wrote more violent stories than women in every national sample, and for almost every conflict. In our view, this cross-national finding is apparently consistent with the proposition that gender differences in violence are influenced by biological factors. In the data reported here, the maleness-violence link is both large and apparently universal.

Second, social factors. In all the societies studied here males are consistently more violent than women, but the specific amount of gender difference in violence varies from one society to another. For example, the male-female difference in violence is greater in the United States than in Canada or Japan (see Table 14.2). Similarly, the amount of male violence per se varies from one society to another. Such societal variations can be attributed to socialization, with some societies being more energetic than others in socializing males toward aggression. Socialization does not operate in a social vacuum, though. It seems to work hand in glove with culture.

Third, cultural factors. Gender differences aside, there are dramatic intersocietal differences. Samples from some societies show much higher levels of overall violence and aggression than do those from other societies. This finding is consistent with the view that differences in violence are culturally constructed, and that this process varies in significant ways across societies. Standing alone, however, cultural factors appear unable to account for the gender differences found. Given the diversity of cultural practices and variation in child rearing in different societies, universal gender differences in violence and aggression are relatively unexpected. Again, however, the large aggregate differences across national samples are perfectly consistent with the notion that different cultures produce aggression and violence in different quantities.

CONCLUSION

As noted earlier, there is evident overlap in the predictions implied by social and cultural theories; these perspectives could be referred to collectively as "social-cultural" explanations. While in this study the surprisingly *consistent* pattern of gender differences (men being more violent than women in all societies) lends apparent credibility to biological explanations, the large *differences* across nations just as strongly support "social-cultural" explanations.

The gender differentials in Table 14.2 are consistent with biological models. Because the pattern of these gender differences is largely the same *within* each of the national data sets, biology—or at least universals that transcend national boundaries—may be implicated. However, the different levels of violence between nations (Table 14.1) are difficult to explain without "social-cultural" models. The enormous differences *between* national data sets in the prevalence of violence in the stories cannot be explained by biological factors and, instead, require consideration of social and cultural variables that vary across these societies. The precise nature of these social and cultural variables remains unknown at this point, but the huge cross-national differences reported here appear to provide a "smoking gun" proving that these variables exist.

The data reported here therefore provide support for the role of very different types of etiological explanations. Both "social-cultural" and biological explanations can claim support in these data since both *differences* (the variation in aggregate violence levels across samples) and *similarities* (the almost universally higher levels of male violence) are found in this cross-cultural comparison.

References

Archer, Dane and Gartner, Rosemary. 1984. *Violence and Crime in Cross-National Perspective.* New Haven: Yale University Press.

Bardwick, Judith. 1971. *The Psychology of Women: A Study of Bio-Cultural Conflicts.* New York: Harper and Row.

Christiansen, Kerrin and Knussman, Rainer. 1987. "Androgen Levels and Components of Aggressive Behavior in Man." *Hormones and Behavior* 21: 170–180.

Connor, Robert and Levine, Seymour. 1969. "Hormonal Influences on Aggressive Behavior," in S. Garattini and E. B. Sigg, eds., *Aggressive Behavior.* New York: John Wiley and Sons.

Goldstein, Jeffrey. 1986. *Aggression and Crimes of Violence.* New York: Oxford University Press.

Maccoby, Eleanor and Jacklin, Carol. 1974. *The Psychology of Sex Differences.* Stanford: Stanford University Press.

Mitchell, G., and Brandt, E. M. 1970. "Behavioral Differences Related to Experience of Mother and Sex of Infant in the Rhesus Monkey." *Developmental Psychiatry* 3: 149.

Rada, Richard, Laws, D., and Kellner, Robert. 1976. "Plasma Testosterone Levels in the Rapist." *Psychosomatic Medicine* 38: 257–268.

Rohner, Ronald P. 1976. "Sex Differences in Aggression: Phylogenetic and Enculturation Perspectives." *Ethos* 4: 57–72.

Sears, Robert, Maccoby, Eleanor and Levin, Harry. 1957. *Patterns of Child Rearing.* Stanford: Stanford University Press, 1957.

Segall, Marshall. 1983. "Aggression in Global Perspective," in Arnold P. Goldstein and Marshall Segall, eds., *Aggression in Global Perspective.* New York: Pergamon Press.

Tieger, Todd. 1980. "On the Biological Bases of Sex Differences in Aggression." *Child Development* 51: 943–963.

15

Kids, Guns, and Killing Fields

JAMES D. WRIGHT, JOSEPH F. SHELEY, AND M. DWAYNE SMITH

Tulane University

A plague of youth violence seems to be sweeping the nation. The number of juveniles, eighteen and under, who are arrested annually for murder increased by nearly a quarter between 1983 and 1988 and then increased again by nearly half between 1988 and 1990. Indeed, homicide is now the leading cause of death for black males aged fourteen to forty-four and the reduction of violence among youths has become a leading public health goal. Incidents that would have seemed shocking and inexplicable just a few years ago—gang warfare, drive-by slayings, wanton brutality, in-school shootings—have somehow become commonplaces of urban existence.

Among the many questions that might be asked about violence committed by and against youths is where and how do these youths obtain firearms? Federal law (the Gun Control Act of 1968) prohibits direct sale of handguns to persons under the age of twenty-one and sale of shoulder weapons to those under eighteen. These provisions have evidently not prevented large numbers of youths from obtaining sophisticated, high-quality guns. How prevalent has gun-carrying become among youths in the central cities? What are the methods and sources by which guns are obtained? Is there anything to be learned about the details of youthful gun acquisition that would be useful in getting them to stop it?

For the past two years, we have been involved in research designed to provide some preliminary answers to these and related questions. We have undertaken extensive surveys concerning firearms and firearms behaviors among two groups of youth: 835 criminally active youth (all males, mostly from large cities) currently serving time in six maximum-security juvenile corrections facilities in four states, and 1653 students (males and females) in ten inner-city public high schools in five large cities near the six correctional facilities.

Reprinted from *Society*, Vol. 30 (November/December 1992), pp. 84–89. Copyright 1992 by Transaction Publishers.

Characteristically, our sample is predominantly nonwhite, poorly educated, average age in the late teens; most respondents are correctly described as inner-city, nonwhite poor. The four states where we did the research were California, Louisiana, Illinois, and New Jersey; the specific cities where we surveyed were large cities with well-publicized youth violence problems.

GUN POSSESSION

Eighty-six percent of incarcerated juveniles owned at least one firearm at some time in their lives; 83 percent owned a gun at the time they were incarcerated. Of those who had ever owned a gun, two-thirds acquired their first firearm by the age of fourteen. A large majority (73 percent) had owned three or more types of guns; nearly two-thirds (65 percent) owned at least three firearms just before being jailed. In short, the tendency is for these young inmates to have owned guns in both quantity and variety. . . .

Similar patterns of ownership, although on a considerably diminished scale, were found for male high school students. (Results presented here from the high school survey are restricted to males only.) Nearly a third (30 percent) of the male students had owned at least one gun in their lives; 22 percent possessed a gun at the time the survey was completed. The most commonly owned weapon was again the revolver (29 percent over the lifetime), followed by the automatic or semi-automatic pistol (27 percent). Fifteen percent owned (or possessed) a revolver and 18 percent an automatic or semi-automatic handgun at the time of the study; 15 percent of the high school males owned three or more guns when they were surveyed. . . .

Carrying a gun was also relatively common among our respondents. Among the inmate sample, 55 percent carried a gun all or most of the time in the year or two before being incarcerated and 84 percent carried a gun at least now and then. Among the male high school sample, carrying a gun at least occasionally was more common than gun ownership. Twenty-two percent of the high school males owned a gun at the time of the survey; 12 percent of them reported currently carrying a gun all or most of the time and another 23 percent did so at least now and then, for a combined percentage of 35 percent carrying firearms regularly or occasionally.

Family members and friends of our respondents were also likely to own and carry firearms. Within the families of the incarcerated juveniles, a third reported siblings who had committed serious crimes; four in ten inmates had siblings who had been jailed; 47 percent had siblings who owned guns. More generally, 79 percent of the inmates came from families where at least some of the males owned guns. Most significant, 62 percent had male family members who carried guns as they went about their daily business, at least from time to time. Thus, most of our inmate respondents grew up in families where firearms were routinely present and where gun carrying was the norm. The pattern was even sharper for the peers of the incarcerated juveniles. Ninety percent of the inmates had at least some friends and associates who owned and carried guns. Thus, in the social environment inhabited by these juvenile offenders, owning and carrying guns were virtually universal behaviors—not an aberration characteristic of only a few but a fairly normative and wide-spread standard.

Among our high school males, 12 percent reported siblings who had committed serious crimes; seven out of ten said there were males in their families who owned guns; handguns were present in 37 percent of the homes. In the nation as a whole, about half of all households possess a firearm of some sort and handguns are present in approximately a quarter. Two-fifths of the students said there were males in their families who carried guns, at least now and then. Gun owning and carrying were also common among the friends and peers of the students. More than half (57 percent) had friends who owned guns; 42 percent had friends who carried guns.

QUALITY OF WEAPONS

Perhaps the most striking feature of our data on juvenile gun ownership is the quality of the firearms they possess. Students and inmates who reported ever owning a handgun were asked to describe the characteristics of the type of handgun they had owned most recently. Among these most recently obtained handguns, automatics and semi-automatics predominated: 57 percent of the inmates' and 49 percent of the students' most recently owned handguns were automatics or semi-automatics. The percentages owning revolvers as their most recent handgun (among those who owned any handgun) were 36 and 42 for inmates and male students respectively, with small proportions (7 and 9 percent) owning other types of handguns. Regardless of type, both inmates and students tended to own large caliber guns. . . . Juvenile criminals and male center-city high school students apparently have little use for or interest in light, small-caliber handguns.

The preferences inferred from patterns of ownership were confirmed in direct questions about desirable handgun features. We asked respondents (both samples) what features they considered important in a handgun; the profile of desirable features was remarkably similar in both groups. Among inmates, the three highest rated traits were firepower, quality of construction, and traceability, followed by being easy to shoot and accurate.

Among male students, quality of construction was the trait most highly rated, followed by ease of shooting, accuracy, traceability, and firepower. Neither inmates nor students indicated much preference for small, cheap guns, nor were they attracted to ephemeral characteristics of weapons such as "scary looking" or "good looking." The preference was clearly for high-firepower hand weapons that are well-made, are accurate, easy to shoot, and not easily traced—in other words, guns suitable for "serious" work against well-armed adversaries.

AVAILABILITY OF GUNS

The number and variety of guns owned by our juveniles suggest that guns are abundant and readily accessible to juveniles in the neighborhoods from which our respondents were drawn. We asked our respondents how difficult it was to obtain a gun. Seventy percent of the inmates and 41 percent of the male students felt that they could get a gun with "no trouble at all"; an additional 17 percent of the inmates and 24 percent of the male students said it would be "only a little trouble." Only 13 percent of the inmates and 35 percent of the male students perceived access to guns as a "lot of trouble" or "nearly impossible."

We also asked both groups how they would go about getting the gun. It is obvious from their answers that family, friends, and street contacts were the main sources of guns for the juveniles we surveyed. Drug dealers and junkies seemed to be the major suppliers after family, friends, and other street sources, this for both inmates and students. Purchasing a gun at a gun shop, or asking someone else to do so, was perceived by 28 percent of the students as a reliable method; only 12 percent of the inmates considered it so, or viewed it as necessary. Theft was twice as likely to be mentioned by the inmates as by the students, although relative to other sources, it was not prominent for either group. Perhaps there was little need to seek guns through theft, or to bother with normal retail outlets, when they were readily available through personal contacts or easily obtained through street sources.

STATUS OR SURVIVAL?

It has been claimed with some frequency that juveniles own and carry guns mainly as a means of achieving or maintaining status among their peers. In this view, the gun is principally a symbol for toughness or machismo and its primary function is to make an impression on one's peers. This theory does not appear to describe our respondents. We asked both inmates and students to agree or disagree, "In my crowd, if you don't have a gun people don't respect you." Eighty-six percent of the inmates and 90 percent of the male students rejected this statement, most of them strongly. We also asked them to agree or disagree, "My friends would look down on me if I did not carry a gun." Eighty-nine percent of the inmates and 91 percent of the students also disagreed with this statement, again most of them strongly.

Inmates who said they carried guns at least occasionally, but not "all of the time," were asked about the circumstances in which they were most likely to carry a gun. The least likely circumstance in which inmates would carry guns was when they were "out raising hell," presumably a peer-linked activity. They were also relatively unlikely to carry guns when they were "hanging out with friends" or when they were with friends who were themselves carrying guns. If it were simply a matter of status or reputation, one would expect these to be the most, not the least, likely circumstances in which they would carry.

Finally, we asked both samples about the reasons why they had purchased their most recent weapons. "To impress people" and "because my friends had one" were among the least important of all the reasons we asked about, regardless of weapon type and for students and inmates equally. Instead, the responses to these various questions were overwhelmingly dominated by themes of self-protection and self-preservation—that is, survival in the urban street environment. The most frequent circumstances in which inmates carried guns were when they were in a strange area (66 percent), when they were out at night (58 percent), and whenever they thought they needed to protect themselves (69 percent); the most important reason for having obtained one's most recent gun (students and inmates alike) was to protect myself. The desire for protection and the need to arm oneself against enemies were the primary reasons to obtain a gun, easily outpacing all other motivations.

Our respondents had plenty to protect themselves against. Substantial numbers of both groups had been shot, shot at, stabbed, or otherwise wounded in their young lives; even more had been threatened with physical violence at one time or other. Everyday life in the social milieu in which our respondents live is clearly fraught with danger. If one's enemies and even perfect strangers possess the weapons and mentality that allow them to take a life quickly and easily from a distance, then it would be the height of folly not to do likewise. Even the perpetrators of violence faced significant risks from their victims and rivals. To illustrate, 70 percent of the inmate sample had been "scared off, shot at, wounded or captured" by an armed victim at least once in their lives. . . .

The evidence we have assembled intimates that juveniles who own and carry guns are strongly motivated to do so. The behavior, it appears, is largely if not strictly utilitarian; the odds of surviving are seen to be better if one is armed than if not. Unfortunately, the implications of this result are not encouraging. The decision that one's very survival depends on being armed makes a weapon a bargain at nearly any cost. . . .

JUVENILE CRIME

Concern about juvenile crime and violence has resurfaced periodically throughout the twentieth century, but still one senses that our situation today is qualitatively different from anything in the past. The juvenile felons we analyzed here were generally better armed, more criminally active, and more violent than the adult felons of a decade ago. Even at that, one is struck less by the armament than by the evident willingness to pull the trigger.

From the viewpoint of public policy, it matters less, perhaps, where these juveniles get their guns than where they get the idea that it is acceptable to kill. It may be convenient to think that the problems of juvenile violence could be magically solved by cracking down or getting tough, but this is unlikely. The problem before us is not so much one of getting guns out of the hands of juveniles as it is reducing the motivations for juveniles to arm themselves in the first place. Convincing inner-city juveniles, or adults, not to own, carry, and use guns requires convincing them that they can survive in their neighborhoods without being armed, that they can come and go in peace, that their unarmed condition will not cause them to be victimized, intimidated, or slain. In brief, it requires a demonstration that the customary agents of social control can be relied upon to provide for personal security. So long as this is believed not to be the case, gun ownership and carrying in the inner city will remain widespread.

This is much easier said than accomplished. Center-city residents who own and carry guns, whether adult or juvenile, do so mainly for personal security. If the inner cities were made safer, then fewer people would be motivated to own and carry guns, and that would make them safer still. Even at that, one must be concerned that gun carrying has become sufficiently well established as a cultural practice, at least among certain groups in the inner city, that the behavior would continue even after conditions themselves dramatically improved. Greater investment in community policing and problem solving would repay itself many times over. Police departments who work closely with the residents of central-city neighborhoods to reduce drug traffic, property crime, gang activity, and acts of violence make themselves a critical part of those communities, increase the perceived sense of security, and directly undercut the otherwise widespread impression among many in the inner city that the police themselves are an alien and hostile force.

Not every neighborhood in every large city is a killing field and not all residents of the center city go about their daily business armed. But the violence and fear of violence that pervade inner-city life, especially in minority and underclass neighborhoods, should not be understated. In the past few years, homicide rates in nearly every major city have reached record-setting highs. Arrests for drug offenses have swollen jail and prison populations well beyond capacity; every city of which we are aware finds itself plagued by increasingly violent youth gangs. Surveys of young children in the inner cities report astonishingly high percentages (nearly half in some cases) who say they have seen someone shot or seen a dead body in the streets. In circumstances such as these, possession of a firearm provides a necessary, if otherwise undesirable, edge against the uncertainty of police protection and the daily threat of intimidation or victimization. When the ability of society to protect people from one another becomes problematic, as it evidently has, then we should not be surprised that people take aggressive measures to protect themselves.

Center-city minority and underclass neighborhoods have become remarkably unsafe because decades of indifference to the social and economic problems of the cities has bred an entire class of people, especially young people, who no longer have much stake in their future. Isolation, hopelessness, and fatalism, coupled with the steady deterioration of stabilizing social institutions in the inner city and the inherent difficulties of maintaining security through normal agents of social control, have fostered an environment where "success" implies predation and survival depends on one's ability to defend against it.

Whether predator or prey, the larger urban environment encourages one to be armed. Widespread joblessness and lack of opportunities for upward mobility seem in most accounts to lie at the very heart of the dilemma. In the end, stricter gun control laws, more aggressive enforcement of existing laws, a crack-down on drug traffic, police task forces directed at juvenile gangs, metal detectors at the doors of schools, periodic searches of lockers and shake-downs of students, and other similar measures do not adequately address the true need, the economic, social and moral resurrection of the inner city. Just how this might be accomplished, and at what cost, remains debatable; the evident need to do so is not.

16

Megamurders

R. J. RUMMEL
University of Hawaii, Manoa

Power kills, absolute Power kills absolutely. This power principle—a variant of Lord Acton's dictum "Power tends to corrupt; absolute power corrupts absolutely"—is the message of my work on the causes of war and current, comparative study of genocide, politicide, and mass murder—what I call democide—in this century. The more power a government has, the more it can act arbitrarily according to the whims and desires of the elite, the more likely will it make war on others and murder its foreign and domestic subjects. As Edmund Burke said in *Vindication of Natural Society*, "Power gradually extirpates for the mind every humane and gentle virtue." The poet Percy Shelley described power as "a desolating pestilence" that "pollutes whate'er it touches."

Power in the sense used here encompasses political power and its holders, as well as the agencies (government departments and bureaucracies) and the instruments (armies, concentration camps, and propaganda) at their disposal. Therefore, the more constrained the Power of governments, the more diffused, checked, and balanced it is, the less will it aggress against others and commit democide. At the extremes of Power, totalitarian communist governments have slaughtered their people by the tens of millions, while many democracies can barely bring themselves to execute even serial murderers.

These assertions may be extreme and categorical, but so is the evidence. Consider first war. There is no case of war involving violent military action between stable democracies, although democracies have fought nondemocracies. The exception may be democratic Finland which joined Nazi Germany in its war against the Soviet Union during the Second World War. Although Great Britain declared war on Finland as a result, no military action took place between the two countries. Most wars have been fought between nondemocracies. This general principle is gaining acceptance among students of international relations and war: democracies do not make war on each other. The less democratic two states are, the more likely they will fight each other.

Reprinted from *Society*, Vol. 29 (September/October 1992), pp. 47–52. Copyright 1992 by Transaction Publishers.

This belligerence of unrestrained Power is not an artifact of either a small number of democracies nor of our era. The number of democracies in the world now number around sixty-five containing about 39 percent of the world's population. Yet we have had no war among them. Nor is there any threat of war. Democracies create an oasis of peace.

This is true historically as well. If one relaxes the definition of democracy to mean simply the restraint on Power by the participation of middle and lower classes in the determinations of Power holders and policy making, then there have been many democracies throughout history. Whether one considers the classical Greek democracies, the democratic forest states of Switzerland, or modern democracies since 1787, one will find that they have not fought each other—depending on how war and democracy is defined, some might prefer to say that they rarely fought each other. Once states that had been mortal enemies and had frequently gone to war (as have France and Germany in recent centuries) became democratic, war ceased between them. Paradigmatic of this is Western Europe since 1945. The cauldron of our most disastrous wars for many centuries, in 1945 one would not find an expert so foolhardy as to predict not only forty-five years of peace, but that at the end of that time there would be a European community with central government institutions, moves toward a joint European military force by France and Germany, and no expectation of violence between any of these formerly hostile states. Yet such has happened. All because they are all democracies. Even among primitive tribes, it seems, where Power is divided and limited, war is less likely.

Were all that could be said about absolute and arbitrary Power that it causes war and the attendant slaughter of the young and most capable of our species, this would be enough. But much worse is that even in the absence of combat, Power massacres in cold blood the helpless people it controls. Several times more of them. The eleven megamurderers of the twentieth century— states that have killed in cold blood, aside from warfare, 1,000,000 or more men, women, and children—have wiped out 142,583,000 people between them. This is almost four times the battle dead in all of this century's international and civil wars. States with absolute Power, that is the former Soviet Union, Communist China, Nazi Germany, Khmer Rouge Cambodia, Communist Vietnam, and Communist Yugoslavia account for 122,535,000 or 86 percent.

Among these megamurderers, by their annual percent democide rates [= 100 × democide/population/(the number of years that the type of regime was in Power)], none comes even close to the lethality of the communist Khmer Rouge in Cambodia during 1975 to 1978. They exterminated near 28 percent of the country's men, women, and children; the odds of any Cambodian surviving these four long years was only 2.5 to 1.

Then there are the kilomurderers, or states that have killed innocent citizens by the tens or hundreds of thousands, such as Communist Afghanistan, Angola, Laos, Ethiopia, North Korea, and Rumania, as well as authoritarian Argentina, Burundi, Chile, Croatia (1941 to 1944), Czechoslovakia (1945 to 1946), Indonesia, Iran, Rwanda, Spain, Sudan, and Uganda. All these, and other kilomurderers, add another 8,361,000 people killed to the democide for this century. The total global democide from 1900 to 1987 probably amounts to 150,944,000 people killed. This figure is the most reasonable and prudent mid-estimate within a low to high range. The overall, absolute highest estimate of democide may be around an almost inconceivable 335,000,000 killed; the absolute low near a hardly less horrible 70,000,000 killed. None of the conclusions would change, however, if we only dealt with the rock-bottom total.

Putting the human cost of war and democide together, Power has killed some 187,797,100 people in this century. If this many people came in one door of a room, walking at three miles per hour across the room with three feet between them, and exit an opposite door, it would take over four years for all to pass, twenty-four hours a day, 365 days a year. If all the dead were lined up they would reach from Honolulu in Hawaii, across the Pacific and then the continental United States to Washington D.C., and then back again.

Democracies too are responsible for some of these democides. Preliminary estimates show that some 1,000,000 foreigners have been killed in cold blood by democracies. This includes those killed in indiscriminate or civilian targeted city bombings, like Germany and Japan in the Second World War. (Deliberate targeting of civilians with explosive and incendiary bombs simply because they happen to be under the command and control of an enemy Power is no better than lining them up and machine gunning them—a clear atrocity.) It also includes large-scale massacres of Filipinos during the American colonization of the Philippines at the beginning of this century, deaths in British concentration camps in South Africa during the Boer War, civilian deaths due to starvation during the British blockade of Germany in and after the First World War, the rape and murder of Chinese in and around Peking in 1900, the atrocities committed by Americans in Vietnam, the murder of Algerians by the French, and the deaths of German prisoners of war in French and American prisoner of war camps after the Second World War.

All these acts of killing by democracies may seem to violate the Power principle, but actually they underline it. For in each case, the killing was carried out in secret, behind a conscious cover of lies and deceit by those agencies and Power holders involved. All were shielded by tight censorship of the press and control of journalists. Even the indiscriminate bombing of German cities was disguised before the British House of Commons and in press releases as attacks on German military targets. That the general strategic bombing policy was to attack workingmen's homes was kept secret still long after the war.

The upshot is that even democracies, where Power can take root in particular institutions, remain unchecked and undisciplined, and hide its activities, are capable of murder en masse. Such Power usually flourishes during wartime, for then the military are often given their head, democratic controls over civilian leaders are weak, and the press labors under strict reigns. Democracies too then become garrison states, Power is freed from many institutional restraints (note how easy it was to put tens of thousands of Japanese Americans in concentration camps during the Second World War for nothing more than their Japanese ancestry), and where it can become absolute, as in the military, it may kill absolutely. Witness Hiroshima and Nagasaki.

Strategic reasons for killing innocent civilians in wartime have been used throughout history. The Japanese bombing of Chinese cities during the Sino-Japanese War was justified as a method to shorten the war. The killing of all inhabitants of a city by the Mongols once its defenses were breached was justified by the terror it would cause among inhabitants of other cities, who would then surrender rather than suffer the same fate. Even the Nazi reprisal murders of ten of thousands of civilians in occupied countries was justified as a way of gaining compliance and protecting German lives.

So Power kills and absolute Power kills absolutely. What then can be said of those alleged causes or factors of war, genocide, and mass murder? What about cultural-ethnic differences, out-group conflict, misperceptions, frustrations and aggression, relative deprivation, ideological imperatives, dehumanization, resource competition, and so on? At one time or another, for one state or another, one or more of these factors play an important role in democide. Some are essential for understanding some genocides, as of the Jews or Armenians; some politicide, as of enemies of the people, bourgeoisie, and clergy; some massacres, as of competing religious-ethnic groups; or some atrocities, as of those committed against poor and helpless villagers by victorious soldiers. But then neighbors in the service of Power have killed neighbors, fathers have killed their sons, faceless and unknown people have been killed by quota. One is hard put to find a race, religion, culture, or distinct ethnic group that has not murdered its own or others.

These factors accelerate the likelihood of war or of democide once some trigger event occurs and absolute or near absolute Power is present. That is to say that Power is a necessary factor for war or democide. When the elite have absolute Power, war or democide follows a common process, which I have called "the conflict helix."

In any society, including the international one, relations between individuals and groups are structured by social contracts determined by previous conflicts, accommodations, and adjustments among them. Social contracts define a structure of expectations that guide and regulate the social order, including Power. This structure is based on a particular balance of Powers (understood as an equation of interests, capabilities, and wills) among individuals and groups. Previous conflict, and possibly violence, determines a balance of Power between competing individuals and groups and a congruent structure of expectations, as, for example, war or revolution ends in a new balance of Powers between nations or groups and an associated peace treaty or constitution. This structure of expectations often consists of new laws and norms defining a social order more consistent with the underlying distribution of relative Power.

However, relative Power never remains constant. It shifts as the interests, capabilities, and will of the parties change. The death of a charismatic leader, the outrage of significant groups, the loss of foreign support by out-groups, the entry into war and the resulting freedom of the elite to use force under the guise of war-time necessity, and so on, can significantly alter the balance of Power between groups. Where such a shift in Power is in favor of the governing elite, Power can achieve its potential. Where elites have built up frustrations regarding those who have lost Power but nonetheless continue to be perceived as a threat, where they see them as outside the moral universe, where they have dehumanized them, where the out-group is culturally or ethnically distinct and the elite perceive them as inferior, or where any other such factors are present, Power will achieve its murderous potential. It simply waits for an excuse, an event of some sort, an assassination, a massacre in a neighboring country, an attempted coup, a famine, or a natural disaster, that will justify beginning the murder en masse.

The result of such violence will be a new balance of Power and attendant social contract. In some cases this may end the democide by the elimination of the "inferior" group—as of the Armenians by the Turks. In many cases, the survivors will be subdued and cowered—like the Ukrainians who lived through Stalin's collectivization campaign and intentional famine. In some cases, this establishes a new balance of Power so skewed toward the elite that they may throughout their reign continue to murder at will. Murder as public policy becomes part of the new structure of expectations, of the new social order. Consider the social orders of Hitler, Stalin, Mao, Pol Pot, and their henchmen.

War and democide can be understood within a common framework as part of a social process, a balancing of Powers, where Power is supreme. It is not clear, however, why among states in which Power is limited and accountable, war and significant democide do not take place. Two concepts explain this: cross pressures and the associated political culture. Where Power is diffuse, checked, and made to be accountable, society is riven by myriad independent groups, disparate institutions, and multiple interests. These forces overlap and contend with each other; they section loyalties and divide desires and wants. Churches, unions, corporations, government bureaucracies, political parties, the media, special interest groups, and such, fight for and protect their interests.

Individuals and elites are pushed and pulled by their membership in several groups and institutions making it difficult for any one driving interest to form. They are divided, weak, ambivalent; they are cross-pressured. For elites to coalesce sufficiently to commit itself to murdering its own citizens, there must be a near fanatical, driving interest. But even if such an interest were present among a few, the diversity of interests across the political elite and associated bureaucracies, the freedom of the media to uncover what is being planned or done, and the ever-present potential leaks and fear of such leaks of disaffected members of the elite to the media brake such tendencies.

As for the possibility of war between democracies, diversity and resulting cross-pressures operate as well. Not only is it very difficult for the elite to unify public interests and opinion sufficiently to make war, but the diverse, economic, social, and political bonds between democracies that tie them together usually prevent the outbreak of violence.

Cross pressures are a social force that operates wherever individual and group freedom predominates. It is natural to a spontaneous social field. But human behavior is not only a matter of social forces, it also depends on meanings, values, and norms—that is, a democratic culture is also essential. When Power is checked and accountable, when cross pressures limit the operation of Power, a particular democratic culture develops. This culture involves debate, demonstrations, protests, but also negotiation, compromise, and tolerance. It involves the art of conflict resolution and the acceptance of democratic procedures at all levels of society. The ballot replaces the bullet, and particularly, people and groups come to accept a loss on this or that interest as only an unfortunate outcome of the way the legitimate game is played. "Lose today, win tomorrow."

That democratic political elites should kill opponents or commit genocide for some public policy is unthinkable—although such may occur in the isolated and secret corners of government where Power can still lurk. Even in modern democracies, public defining and dehumanizing of out-groups has become a social and political evil. Witness the current potency of such allegations as "racism" or "sexism." Of course, the culture of democracy operates between democracies as well. Diplomacy, negotiating a middle way, seeking common interests, is part of the operating medium among democracies. A detailed political history of the growth of the European Community would well display this. Since each democracy takes the legitimacy of the other and their interests for granted, conflict is only a process of nonviolent learning and adjustment. Conferences, not war, should be the instrumentality for settling disputes. . . .

The concepts and views promoted in political science text books are grossly unrealistic. They just do not fit in or explain, and are even contradictory to, the existence of a hell state like Pol Pot's Cambodia, a Gulag state like Stalin's Soviet Union, or a genocide state like Hitler's Germany. One textbook, for instance, spends a chapter on describing the functions of government as law and order, individual security, cultural maintenance, and social welfare. Political scientists are still writing this stuff, when we have numerous examples of governments that kill millions of their own citizens, enslave the rest, and abolish traditional culture. It took only about a year for the Khmer Rouge to completely uproot and extinguish Buddhism, which had been the heart and soul of Cambodian culture. . . .

What is needed is a reconceptualization of government and politics consistent with what we now know about democide and related misery. New concepts have to be invented, old ones realigned to correct our perception of Power. We need to invent concepts for governments that turn their states into concentration camps, purposely starve millions of their citizens, set up quotas for those who should be killed. Although murder by quota was carried out by the Soviets, Chinese communists, and Vietnamese, the general political science literature does not give recognition to this incredible inhumaneness of certain governments. We have no concept for murder as an aim of public policy, determined by discussion among the governing elite in the highest councils and imposed through government bureaucracy. There is virtually no index in any general book on politics and government that makes reference to official genocide and murder, to the number of those killed, executed, or massacred, not even in books on the Soviet Union or China. Most indexes omit references to concentration or labor camps or gulags, even if a book contains a paragraph or two on the subject.

The preeminent fact about government is that some murder millions in cold blood. This is where absolute Power reigns. The second fact is that some, usually the same governments, murder tens of thousands more through foreign aggression and intervention. Absolute Power again. These two facts alone must be the basis of a reconceptualization and of taxonomies of states. These must be based, not only on whether a state is developed or not, third world or not, powerful or not, large or not, but also and more important, on whether Power in a state is absolute and has engaged in genocide, politicide, and mass murder.

The empirical and theoretical conclusion—still more work on comparative democide in this century remains to be done—is this: The way to end war and virtually eliminate the conditions for democide appears to be through restricting and checking Power. This means the fostering of democratic freedom.

17

Crime, Race, and Values

JAMES Q. WILSON
University of California, Los Angeles

Sometimes understanding causes does not help in finding solutions. There is no doubt that black rage at white racism brought scores of blacks onto the streets of Los Angeles after four police officers were acquitted of illegally beating a black man, Rodney King. Some may conclude that if we are to improve the police, reduce the anger, and prevent more riots, we must end racism. Such a conclusion, while not entirely wrong, is misleading and, worse, futile.

In 1965, when riots erupted in the Watts section of Los Angeles, racism by any measure was greater than it is today. Then, most whites knew no blacks and, whether they knew them or not, would speak of them in often contemptuous stereotypical terms. It was almost inconceivable that whites would vote for black candidates or take jobs in places with many black workers. Blacks bold enough to move into white neighborhoods were often met with organized resistance. Racial disturbances almost invariably consisted of whites assaulting blacks.

Today, there is far more contact between the races. Every survey of opinion has shown a sharp decline in racist sentiments among whites. Though it may be objected that these polls only measure what people believe others expect them to say, it is remarkable that these expectations now govern what we say and even what we do. But if racist thinking has declined, why are relations between the races so bad? Why has Los Angeles, like many other cities, become more segregated residentially today than it was in 1965? Why do so many whites who cannot be called racists in any fair meaning of the word so often treat blacks warily or react to their proposals with neglect or unease?

Whites are afraid of young black males—and of young Latino males. It is not racism that keeps whites from exploring black neighborhoods, it is fear. It is not racism that makes whites uneasy about blacks moving into their neighborhoods, it is fear. It is not racism that leads white parents to pull their children out of schools with many black students, it is fear. Fear of crime, of drugs, of gangs, of violence. Fear is not confined to whites. Many black women fear black men as well, and their fear is doubly corrosive because they have fewer

Reprinted from *Society*, Vol. 30 (November/December 1992), pp. 90–93. Copyright 1992 by Transaction Publishers.

avenues of escape and less reason to think the police will help them than do white women.

FEAR AND RACISM

There was fear in 1965, too, but it was more mythic than real. The rate of violent crime was one-third of what it is now, gangs were armed with zip-guns and not Uzis, heroin (a sedative) rather than crack (a stimulant) was the drug of choice, and society faced far fewer legal or political constraints in directing state power against domestic threats.

What the four officers did in subduing Rodney King was wrong. They should be punished. In fact, they were punished. The rookie was summarily dismissed and the three veterans were relieved of their duty without pay, pending the outcome of a Board of Rights hearing. Whether what they did was illegal beyond a reasonable doubt is unclear. The racist bigotry now being directed at the Ventura County jurors by people who did not sit through the trial or read the transcript is appalling. Are those people who explain an unpopular verdict by referring to the race of the jurors prepared to use the same explanation when black jurors vote to acquit a black defendant or convict a white one?

It is not to excuse the officers to suggest that fear explains much, though not all, of the tensions that exist between the police and the citizenry. I have been riding around in squad cars with police officers since the early 1960s. The average big-city cop is much less prejudiced today than he was three decades ago, but he (and now she) is more fearful. When police stop a young black male, they expect defiance rather than submission. When they enter a housing project, they expect taunts, not thanks. When they encounter a gang, they fear a fusillade of bullets instead of just sullen complaints.

Fear can produce behavior that is indistinguishable from racism. Fear, like racism, can make an officer seek to intimidate a suspect or use excessive force to subdue him. Fear creates tensions that lead to the telling of jokes identical to those told by people motivated by pure racism. Responding to the fears of others, police officers are more likely to stop and question black men than white men. Statistically the former are more suspect than the latter, with the result that innocent black men are more likely to be stopped than innocent white men.

Fear is sustained by ignorance. We do not know how to reduce the crime and violence, or break up the gangs. The Great Society produced some good things: Head Start, the Job Corps, various civil-rights laws. But it did nothing about crime, and especially nothing about the predatory behavior of young males who inseminate women, abandon children, join gangs, deal drugs, and shoot innocent people.

SOLUTIONS—OLD AND NEW

We can, of course, try more of the same—more Head Start, more Job Corps. That is probably desirable. We can add to the mix a more community-oriented style of policing. That is happening in Los Angeles and it will continue under the new chief. We can try to think of ways of bringing jobs to unemployed people and training those people for the jobs that exist, but the only big new idea around for doing that—Enterprise Zones—is at best a question mark. I cannot imagine many new factories opening in South Central Los Angeles, even if their owners are given tax breaks. The owners will look at what happened to the Korean merchants who started businesses in black areas without tax breaks—they were bombed, burned, and looted.

We can provide cheaper transportation so that blacks can travel to their jobs, but I doubt that transportation is the key problem. Every day there are thousands of Latino men waiting on street corners twenty miles or more from where they live, hoping to be hired as day laborers by contractors and home owners. Many are hired. They all get to these street corners by bus. There are no black men on these corners.

Reducing poverty, ending racism, creating jobs, and improving schooling are all good things to do, whether or not they prevent crimes or riots. But the problem our big cities face runs far deeper. There is an underclass, and though many races are found among it and it accounts for only a small fraction of the black community, it is perceived to be a black phenomenon. So long as black men commit violent crimes at a rate that is six to eight times higher than the rate found among whites, that perception will persist. And as long as that perception persists, fear will heighten our anxieties and erode our civility.

As we obtain a greater perspective on the events in Los Angeles, it will become clear that much of what happened had nothing to do with protest and everything to do with greed, high times, and the settling of old scores. Of the 5438 people arrested by the Los Angeles Police Department from midnight April 30 until the morning of May 4, 568 were white, hardly any of whom, it seems safe to say, were social activists protesting injustice. Hispanic arrestees outnumbered black ones 2764 to 2022. Anger triggered the riots, but once the mechanisms of social control had been overpowered, rapacity took over.

And consider who was not arrested. No minority in California has been treated worse than Japanese-Americans. They were excluded from juries, prevented from voting, and in 1942 torn from their homes and confined for many years in relocation camps in the desert. They were the objects of racism pure and simple. Of the 5438 people arrested, none was Japanese. One was Chinese. Three were Filipinos.

The best way to reduce racism real or imagined is to reduce the black crime rate to equal the white crime rate, which, God knows, is high enough. (I assume no one favors raising the white crime rate to equal that of blacks.) To do this may require changing, in far more profound and all-encompassing ways than anything we now contemplate, the lives of black infants, especially boys, from birth to age eight or ten. We have not yet begun to think seriously about this, and perhaps never will. Those who must think about it the hardest are those decent black people who must accept, and ideally should develop and run, whatever is done.

TEACHING VALUES

The problems of our inner cities are of two sorts. The first consists of scarce jobs, too little capital formation, badly managed public-housing projects, a perverse welfare program, and an overburdened criminal justice system. These are tangible problems that can be addressed by altering the incentives and resources available to people and agencies. Most public debate is about how to do these things in a cost-effective way.

The second consists of racism, fear, despair, defiance, poor work habits, inadequate skills, and a preference for joining predatory gangs to accepting low-wage jobs. These are intangible problems—problems of "values"—that are hard to address by money alone because they make whites less likely to invest or extend opportunities and blacks less likely to take advantage of opportunities.

If public policy addresses only the tangible problems, we will be disappointed by the results. Many people know this; that is why so few have urged responding to the riots with a "Marshall Plan for the cities." The analogy is exact: The Marshall Plan approach worked well when offered to peoples with a history of enterprise who happened to live in war-shattered economies. It did not work so well when offered to peoples with no history of enterprise living in undeveloped nations.

It is imperative that our policies address both the material and the cultural problems of our inner cities. For the policies to work, they must meet three criteria: (1) they must start early in life when character and expectations are formed; (2) they must focus on young males because they are the source of fear, the perpetrators of crime, the fathers of illegitimate children, and the members of gangs; and (3) they must combine carrots and sticks, otherwise many lawful opportunities will not be pursued if unlawful alternatives seem more attractive.

The effects of Head Start often do not last because no one-shot, part-time program can inoculate a youngster against the burdens of being a latch-key child left alone to contend with absent parents, mean streets, predatory gangs, and cynical peers. Head Start ought to be the entry point for a more comprehensive program that, for the neediest cases, offers an alternative to a nonexistent family life. One approach is to give vouchers to the mothers of at-risk children, enabling them to enroll their offspring in residential schools. Well-to-do parents already send their children to boarding schools, yet few of these children are likely to benefit as much from the steady, structured, and nurturant environment of a well-run residential school as would children from homes with no status, little learning, and impeded moral development.

TEACHING HUMAN SKILLS

Many members of the underclass need not only technical skills but human skills as well. Yet the commitment that is the necessary precondition to acquiring such skills will be hard to make if one lives in a disorganized, drug-infested neighborhood surrounded by friends who taunt you with having sold out to "the man" or forsaken your homeboys.

The only large-scale, full-time program of which I am aware that combined character education, skill development, job experience, and in-group bonding was the Civilian Conservation Corps. It is a model, partially copied by the Job Corps, that combined residential living, vocational training, real work, and earned income. We now have military bases in search of new tenants, a Defense Department in search of new tasks, an infrastructure in need of repair, and an environment in need of care. Surely there is some way to create a program out of these coincident opportunities, one that draws on the military's skills at training men, building morale, and improving character.

Gangs arise for may reasons—pride, territory, security, criminality—and not all gangs are bad. But many gangs are criminal conspiracies that terrorize, corrupt, and impoverish whole communities. Federal, state, and local law enforcement authorities should form task forces that use the conspiracy statutes to prosecute street gangs just as those laws have been used to attack the Mafia. Programs of economic reconstruction will not work so long as these gangs control the streets, and economic reconstruction alone, even if it succeeds, will not be sufficient to dislodge the gangs.

Drug dealing exists because there is a demand for drugs. Drug treatment can work, but its reach is limited both because there are too few treatment slots available (a fact everyone discusses) and because too few people feel that treatment is preferable to indulgence (a fact hardly anyone discusses). There is a way to reduce demand and induce enrollment in treatment programs without infringing upon essential liberties, and that is the mandatory, random testing of probationers and parolees.

The majority of arrestees in most big cities have used drugs within a few days preceding their arrest. Some states require testing as a condition of diversion from the system or release on probation. But hardly anywhere do cities enforce testing requirement rigorously; nor do they penalize failing of a test with immediate sanctions. One of the reasons people get upset with alternatives to imprisonment is that the alternatives so often lack teeth. The best way to give them teeth would be to enforce random drug tests on people already under the authority of the criminal justice system. This will require more drug treatment facilities.

There are, no doubt, difficulties with each of these suggestions. All cost money. None can guarantee success. But unless the national debate is shifted to the problems these suggestions address, we are likely to waste money and effort on the mistaken belief that all that is required is opportunity.

PART 6
Sexual Aggression

Mary had dated John four times. On the last date, he took her out for a lobster dinner and then to his apartment. They drank wine, listened to music, talked, laughed, and kissed. When John suggested they go to his bedroom, Mary nodded in agreement. In the bedroom, they started dancing erotically and kissing passionately. When he began to unbutton her blouse, she asked him to stop. He kissed her gently, continuing to undress her. She begged him to stop. He continued anyway, saying to her, "I know you really want it." She then told him "No!" and said that she was not ready for sex with him. He told her to relax and enjoy it. He even assured her that he loved her. He pushed her down on the bed, pulled up her skirt, and pulled down her panties. Holding both of her arms with one of his hands, he penetrated her.[1]

Some people may not consider John a criminal. But he is, because he has committed forcible rape, a crime that involves having sexual intercourse against the victim's will or without the woman's consent. The rape that John committed is called acquaintance or date rape. It is the most common type of rape, far more prevalent than the rape committed by a stranger. Still, acquaintance rape is rarely reported to the police. It is therefore not surprising that every year the number of rapes reported in government statistics such as the FBI's *Uniform Crime Reports* is considerably lower than the number found in unofficial studies. According to the latest FBI's statistics, there are about 106,590 rapes in a year. But unofficial data suggest that the real number is much higher, from two to four times the FBI figure. This is because most victims do not report the crime to the police.

In the first article, "Date Rape on College Campuses," Martin Schwartz discusses the incidence of campus rape, campus reaction to rape, and reasons for sexual violence against college women. In a similar article, "Fraternities and Rape on Campus," Patricia Martin and Robert Hummer zero in on fraternities to explain why they are a major source of campus rape. In the third reading, "The Contribution of Sex-Role Socialization to Acquaintance Rape," Robin Warshaw and Andrea Parrot discuss another major source of rapes, the socialization agents of society such as family, peers, and the media. In the fourth selection, "Young People's Attitudes Toward Acquaintance Rape,"

---

[1] Laurie Bechhofer and Andrea Parrot, "What Is Acquaintance Rape?" in Andrea Parrot and Laurie Bechhofer, *Acquaintance Rape: The Hidden Crime* (New York: John Wiley & Sons, 1991), p. 9.

Jacquelyn White and John Humphrey discuss yet another important source of rapes, the popular belief among the youth that there is nothing wrong with forced sex if it occurs between acquaintances and intimates.

The last two articles caution us not to exaggerate the problem of sexual aggression. In "Realities and Mythologies of Rape," Neil Gilbert shows how several well-known studies on rape are far from objective, blowing the frequency of rape out of proportion to reality. In "Bared Buttocks and Federal Cases," Ellen Frankel Paul suggests that sexual harassment would appear more prevalent than it actually is if it is loosely defined to include simply being morally offensive rather than causing serious harm.

18

Date Rape on College Campuses

Martin D. Schwartz
Ohio University

College and university campuses have long been a breeding ground for virtually an epidemic level of felony crime (Hills, 1984; Thorne-Finch, 1992). Over 150 years ago Harvard University was already complaining that students frequently committed "crimes worthy of the penitentiary" (Shenkman, 1989: 135). During all these years, because universities have been for the most part reserved for middle- and upper-class white America, campus crime has rarely become a target of the "wars on crime." Concern about crime tends to be reserved for the actions of the working class. In recent years, however, a new form of campus crime has created a great deal of publicity. It is date rape, sometimes called "courtship violence."

INCIDENCE

Given their differences in methodology and sampling procedures, various studies on date rape have produced rather different results (Johnson and Ferraro, 1988). The conclusion is nonetheless inescapable that a substantial minority of women on American college campuses have experienced an event that would fit most states' definitions of felony rape or sexual assault (Koss, Gidycz, and Wisniewski, 1987).

Eugene Kanin (1957) first reported over thirty-five years ago that more than 20 percent of college women had been victims of rape or attempted rape. More recently, Levine and Kanin (1987) found that rates of rape on college campuses have risen substantially since those days. In a survey of sorority members, Rivera and Regoli (1987) found 17 percent of them to have been victims of completed rape, but in a survey of over 2000 students at seven colleges, Makepeace (1986) discovered a significantly higher percentage (23.6 percent) to have been victims of forced sex. In the largest U.S. study, Mary

---

This article was specifically written for this reader, though partially based on the author's "Humanist Sociology and Date Rape on the College Campus," *Humanity & Society* 15 (1991):304–316.

Koss (Koss et al., 1987) distributed a self-report questionnaire to 6159 students in thirty-two institutions of all types of higher education across the country. Over 15 percent of the women reported that their most serious sexual victimization had been a completed rape, while another 12.1 percent said that their most serious victimization was attempted but uncompleted forced intercourse. In a similar Canadian study of a national random sample of 3142 women students in forty-four university and community colleges, about 10 percent reported sexual penetration under physical force or threat of force since leaving high school, with about 14 percent reporting attempted sexual intercourse by force or threat (DeKeseredy and Kelly, 1993).

REACTION

How can an injurious act like date rape be so widespread and at the same time be of so little concern to most students, faculty, and administrators? If 15 percent of faculty offices were burglarized, certainly the uproar would be deafening. If 25 percent of college students were the victims of robbery or attempted robbery during their college careers, certainly no campus could avoid massive and high-profile prevention campaigns.

One reason can be found in the enormous feminist literature on rape (e.g., Buchwald, Fletcher, and Roth, 1993; Bart and Moran, 1993). According to these feminist studies, sexism as an ideology encourages men to devalue women and see them as objects to be conquered or used. This sexist ideology, when blended with the catalyst of the American violence ethic, produces at least at the attitudinal level a violent reaction to victims of rape. Thus, we feel that some women, such as flirtatious ones, "deserve" to be the victims of violent sexual crimes, in the same way as annoying people "deserve" to be beaten up or in the same way as countries we don't like "deserve" to be "bombed back into the stone age."

This feminist literature for the most part, though, deals with stranger rape. What about the rape of dates or persons well known to the offender? There are few important differences between stranger rapists and date rapists (Belknap, 1989). Most important is that the stranger rapist knows his action to be criminal, and makes some effort to hide his identity. But the date rapist acts "in public," against someone he knows and may personally like. Thus, the victim of date rape knows the offender. Why, then, are most of the date rapists not brought to the attention of the criminal justice or campus authorities? The answer is that most of the victims do not report the crime. In fact, only 5 percent ever report it to the police, and 42 percent never even mention what has happened to anyone at all (Koss et al., 1987).

Why don't the victims report their awful experience? The answer can be found in the studies by Pitts and Schwartz (1993) and Koss et al. (1987), both of which identify certain women as rape victims in strict accordance with the Ohio Penal Code definition of the crime. Each study discovers that only 27 percent of the women identified as rape victims defined what had happened to themselves as rape. This reluctance to define rape as a crime can be traced to the same popular sexist belief that a woman can be seen as having "deserved" to be the victim of violent sexual attacks and that a woman should bear the brunt of blame for being in the wrong place at the wrong time. But there may possibly be an additional reason for many women's reluctance to see *date* rape as a crime. That is, many women, including college students, are unsure of the difference between rape and just a horrible thing that happened on a date. This has recently caused some observers to argue that if women are confused about what happened to them, perhaps what happened to them wasn't all that bad after all (Gilbert, 1991; Roiphe, 1993). Whether the women are confused or not may depend on what kind of friends they have. As the data in Pitts and Schwartz' survey (1993) suggest, college women whose friends blame them for the sexual assault (being in the wrong place, for example) tend to say that they were not victims of rape, even though the facts of the incident show otherwise. But those who have supportive friends tend to define their experience as rape.

EXPLANATIONS

We live in a society that can accurately be termed a "rape culture" (Buchwald et al., 1993), where no man can avoid exposure to sexist and pro-rape attitudes. But some men seem to respond to these pressures more than others. Men who have strong ties to sexist groups seem particularly amenable to peer pressure. This may explain why in a study by Ageton (1983) over 40 percent of the perpetrators of adolescent sexual assaults had friends who knew about their behavior and virtually all these friends approved of it or at least expressed indifference. It is true that some researchers such as Heilbrun and Loftus (1986) found that college men who enjoyed sadistic sexual practices were loners and hence unlikely to be swayed by peer pressure. However, most date rapists do not seek sexual sadism at all. They are far more interested in sexual domination, where the object is "conquest" through obtaining as much sex with as many women as possible. In fact, Kanin (1985) found that date rapists are *not* loners—men who shun campus social activities as well as fail at locating voluntary sexual partners. Instead, date rapists are mostly men who are highly sociable as well as sexually active. Still, their goal is to "score" as often as possible. Moreover, they expect to have so much sex that they often feel frustrated even while engaging in more sex than is typical for the average male student. All this, according to Kanin, can be attributed to a male hypererotic culture, which, through friends' approval and encouragement, pressures members to have sex with as many women as possible, even with the use of force against at least some women.

The hypererotic culture, however, derives much of its support from the widespread sexist attitudes toward women. Otherwise, the hypereroticism of the culture cannot by itself cause woman abuse such as date rape. It is the *sexism* of the culture that contributes to rape. This seems to occur in two ways. First, sexist attitudes fuel the moral ambiguity about whether rape is really a crime or only normal male aggression. Such ambiguity helps neutralize the criminality of rape by making people wonder whether a crime has been committed when a man forces sex on a woman (Fenstermaker, 1989). Such neutralization, which discourages many women from reporting, provides the moral elbow room the date rapist needs to carry out the act. Second, sexist attitudes feed the social support network by convincing its members that sexual aggression against women to the point of using force is acceptable. Thus, men who are part of this sexist network tend to commit date rape.

Such a network seems to characterize many fraternities on college campuses. Not surprisingly, fraternities have been the setting for most known acquaintance gang rapes (Sanday, 1990; Ehrhart and Sandler, 1985). On many campuses with an active Greek life, it is easy to find through the student grapevine at least one recent example of a fraternity where students engaged in "pulling train" or a "gang bang" (Warshaw, 1988). Given the atmosphere of the sexist moral ambiguity on many campuses, however, not only fraternity men or other college men, but also women students tend to hold the victim responsible in some way. Even faculty and administrators who have been appointed to oversee fraternities tend to see a lot of "boys will be boys" in forcible rape. They would likely be shocked by the idea that those fraternity goings-on could be a serious crime rather than just another rules violation. Such attitude in turn reinforces the sexist moral ambiguity that is conducive to rape on the campus.

There seems to be something more than the moral ambiguity, sexist attitudes toward women, and the hypererotic culture that encourage campus rapes. Researchers have tried to look for that something else. Many feel that sexist men join fraternities, rather than being *made* so by fraternities. But some researchers have found that fraternities "provide a subculture that insulates their members from the on-going campus climate" (Bohrnstedt, 1969; Wilder et al., 1986). Other researchers have found fraternities to be great promoters of conformity (Hughes and Winston, 1987). Still others have found fraternities causing their members to have less moral concern about social injustice (Miller, 1973). Some researchers observe that the highly masculinist, homophobic views promoted by fraternities, along with their preoccupation with loyalty, the use of alcohol and physical force as weapons for acquiring social domination, the obsession with competition, aggression, superiority, and dominance, encourage the sexual violation of women (Martin and Hummer, 1993).

Several scholars have recently argued that sexual aggression against women offers an important meaning for some fraternities. Sanday (1990), for example, finds that fraternity rituals provide an important mechanism for eliminating the feelings of dependency on women, which presumably have been inculcated into men through socialization by their mothers. The rituals serve to give fraternity brothers a new readymade self that includes sexist and homophobic attitudes designed for showing virility and dominance over women to cope with feelings of powerlessness. Such attitudes are sometimes effectively proclaimed to the public. Some fraternities would confront Take Back the Night marchers by loudly chanting pro-rape slogans. At Queens University in Ontario, for example, an anti-rape march with the slogan "No Means No" was countered with large banners reading "No Means Now" and "No Means Kick Her in the Teeth" (Thorne-Finch, 1992). Unfortunately, on some campuses the fraternities that, under the advice of their national office, support Take Back the Night marches most strongly are often rumored in the sorority grapevine to have the most actively sexually coercive members.

CONCLUSION

Many scholars talk mainly about athletic teams and fraternities as the organizations that promote attitudes that foster sexual assaults on women, and it is true that some teams and some fraternities do seem to be the locations of an extraordinary amount of problems. Yet others do not. Perhaps the critics are also correct in suggesting that sexually coercive men join with similar men to get approval for their views, picking out the fraternities and sports teams where they would best fit in. If these groups actively promote moral ambiguity toward rape with men already predisposed toward that view, it is easy to see how problems arise.

Further, there are many men who are sexually predatory but are not members of fraternities or athletic teams. An analysis that is limited to these areas is very incomplete. Sexist values as discussed here, friends supportive of taking advantage of women, and attitudes blaming the victim for her own victimization, are all spread throughout society.

References

Ageton, Suzanne. 1983. *Sexual Assaults Among Adolescents.* Lexington, MA: Lexington Books.

Bart, Pauline B. and Eileen Geil Moran, eds. 1993. *Violence Against Women: The Bloody Footprints.* Newbury Park, CA: Sage.

Belknap, Joanne. 1989. "The Sexual Victimization of Unmarried Women by Nonrelative Acquaintances," pp. 205–218 in Maureen A. Pirog-Good and Jan E. Stets, eds., *Violence in Dating Relationships: Emerging Social Issues.* New York: Praeger.

Bohrnstedt, George W. 1969. "Conservatism, Authoritarianism and Religiosity of Fraternity Pledges." *Journal of College Student Personnel* 10:36–43.

Buchwald, Emilie, Patricia Fletcher and Martha Roth, eds. 1993. *Transforming a Rape Culture.* Minneapolis: Milkweed Editions.

DeKeseredy, Walter S. and Katharine Kelly. 1993. "The Incidence and Prevalence of Woman Abuse in Canadian University and College Dating Relationships." *Canadian Journal of Sociology* 18(2):137–159.

Ehrhart, Julie K. and Bernice R. Sandler. 1985. *Campus Gang Rape: Party Games.* Washington, D.C.: Project on the Status and Education of Women, Association of American Colleges.

Fenstermaker, Sarah. 1989. "Acquaintance Rape on Campus: Responsibility and Attributions of Crime," pp. 257–273 in Maureen A. Pirog-Good and Jan E. Stets, eds., *Violence in Dating Relationships: Emerging Social Issues.* New York: Praeger.

Gilbert, Neil. 1991. "The Phantom Epidemic of Sexual Assault." *The Public Interest* 103:54–65.

Heilbrun, Alfred B. Jr. and Maria P. Loftus. 1986. "The Role of Sadism and Peer Pressure in the Sexual Aggression of Male College Students," *Journal of Sex Research* 22(3):320–332.

Hills, Stuart. 1984. "Crime and Deviance on a College Campus: The Privilege of Class," pp. 60–69 in Martin D. Schwartz and David O. Friedrichs, eds. *Humanistic Perspectives on Crime and Justice.* Hebron, CT: Practitioner Press.

Hughes, Michael J. and Roger B. Winston, Jr. 1987. "Effects of Fraternity Membership on Interpersonal Values." *Journal of College Student Personnel* 28(5):405–411.

Johnson, John M. and Kathleen J. Ferraro. 1988. "Courtship Violence: Survey vs. Empathic Understandings of Abusive Conduct," pp. 175–186 in Norman Denzin, ed., *Studies in Symbolic Interaction,* Vol. 9. Greenwich, CT: JAI Press.

Kanin, Eugene J. 1957. "Male Aggression in Dating-Courtship Relations." *American Journal of Sociology* 63:197–204.

Kanin, Eugene J. 1985. "Date Rapists: Differential Sexual Socialization and Relative Deprivation," *Archives of Sexual Behavior* 14(3):219–231.

Koss, Mary P., Christine A. Gidycz and Nadine Wisniewski. 1987. "The Scope of Rape: Incidence and Prevalence of Sexual Aggression and Victimization in a National Sample of Higher Education Students," *Journal of Counseling and Clinical Psychology* 55(2):162–170.

Levine, Edward M. and Eugene J. Kanin. 1987. "Sexual Violence Among Dates and Acquaintances: Trends and Their Implications for Marriage and Family," *Journal of Family Violence* 2(1):55–65.

Makepeace, James M. 1986. "Gender Differences in Courtship Violence Victimization." *Family Relations* 35(3):383–388.

Martin, Patricia Yancey and Robert A. Hummer. 1993. "Fraternities and Rape on Campus," pp. 114–131 in Pauline B. Bart and Eileen Geil Moran, eds. *Violence Against Women: The Bloody Footprints.* Newbury Park, CA: Sage.

Miller, Leonard D. 1973. "Distinctive Characteristics of Fraternity Members." *Journal of College Student Personnel* 14(3):126–129.

Pitts, Victoria L. and Martin Schwartz. 1993. "Promoting Self-Blame in Hidden Rape Cases." *Humanity & Society* 17(4):383–398.

Rivera, George F. Jr. and Robert M. Regoli. 1987. "Sexual Victimization Experiences of Sorority Women," *Sociology and Social Research* 72(1):39–42.

Roiphe, Katie. 1993. *The Morning After.* New York: Little, Brown.

Sanday, Peggy Reeves. 1990. *Fraternity Gang Rape.* New York: New York University Press.

Shenkman, Richard. 1989. *Legends, Lies & Cherished Myths of American History.* New York: Harper & Row.

Thorne-Finch, Ron. 1992. *Ending the Silence: The Origins and Treatment of Male Violence Against Women.* Toronto: University of Toronto Press.

Warshaw, Robin. 1988. *I Never Called It Rape.* New York: Perennial Library.

Wilder, David H., Arlyne E. Hoyt, Beth Shuster Surbeck, Janet C. Wilder and Patricia Imperatrice Carney. 1986. "Greek Affiliation and Attitude Change in College Students." *Journal of College Student Personnel* 27:510–519.

19

Fraternities and Rape on Campus

PATRICIA YANCEY MARTIN
Florida State University

ROBERT A. HUMMER
East Carolina University

Many rapes, far more than come to the public's attention, occur in fraternity houses on college and university campuses, yet little research has analyzed fraternities at American colleges and universities as rape-prone contexts (cf. Ehrhart and Sandler, 1985). . . . Gary Tash, writing as an alumnus and trial attorney in his fraternity's magazine, claims that over 90 percent of all gang rapes on college campuses involve fraternity men (1988, p. 2). Tash provides no evidence to substantiate this claim, but students of violence against women have been concerned with fraternity men's frequently reported involvement in rape episodes (Adams and Abarbanel, 1988). Ehrhart and Sandler (1985) identify over 50 cases of gang rapes on campus perpetrated by fraternity men, and their analysis points to many of the conditions that we discuss here. Their analysis is unique in focusing on conditions in fraternities that make gang rapes of women by fraternity men both feasible and probable. They identify excessive alcohol use, isolation from external monitoring, treatment of women as prey, use of pornography, approval of violence, and excessive concern with competition as precipitating conditions to gang rape.

The study reported here confirmed and complemented these findings by focusing on both conditions and processes. We examined dynamics associated with the social construction of fraternity life, with a focus on processes that foster the use of coercion, including rape, in fraternity men's relations with women. Our examination of men's social fraternities on college and university campuses as groups and organizations led us to conclude that fraternities are a physical and sociocultural context that encourages the sexual coercion of

Patricia Yancey Martin, Robert A. Hummer, "Fraternities and Rape on Campus," *Gender & Society*, Vol. 3, No. 4, December 1989, 457–473 © 1989 Sociologists for Women in Society and reprinted by permission of Sage Publications, Inc.

women. We make no claims that all fraternities are "bad" or that all fraternity men are rapists. Our observations indicated, however, that rape is especially probable in fraternities because of the kinds of organizations they are, the kinds of members they have, the practices their members engage in, and a virtual absence of university or community oversight. Analyses that lay blame for rapes by fraternity men on "peer pressure" are, we feel, overly simplistic. We suggest, rather, that fraternities create a sociocultural context in which the use of coercion in sexual relations with women is normative and in which the mechanisms to keep this pattern of behavior in check are minimal at best and absent at worst. We conclude that unless fraternities change in fundamental ways, little improvement can be expected.

METHODOLOGY

Our goal was to analyze the group and organizational practices and conditions that create in fraternities an abusive social context for women. We developed a conceptual framework from an initial case study of an alleged gang rape at Florida State University that involved four fraternity men and an 18-year-old coed. The group rape took place on the third floor of a fraternity house and ended with the "dumping" of the woman in the hallway of a neighboring fraternity house. According to newspaper accounts, the victim's blood-alcohol concentration, when she was discovered, was .349 percent, more than three times the legal limit for automobile driving and an almost lethal amount. One law enforcement officer reported that sexual intercourse occurred during the time the victim was unconscious: "She was in a life-threatening situation" (*Tallahassee Democrat*, 1988b). When the victim was found, she was comatose and had suffered multiple scratches and abrasions. Crude words and a fraternity symbol had been written on her thighs (*Tampa Tribune*, 1988). When law enforcement officials tried to investigate the case, fraternity members refused to cooperate. This led, eventually, to a five-year ban of the fraternity from campus by the university and by the fraternity's national organization.

In trying to understand how such an event could have occurred, and how a group of over 150 members (exact figures are unknown because the fraternity refused to provide a membership roster) could hold rank, deny knowledge of the event, and allegedly lie to a grand jury, we analyzed newspaper articles about the case and conducted open-ended interviews with a variety of respondents about the case and about fraternities, rapes, alcohol use, gender relations, and sexual activities on campus. Our data included over 100 newspaper articles on the initial gang rape case; open-ended interviews with Greek (social fraternity and sorority) and non-Greek (independent) students ($N = 20$); university administrators ($N = 8$, five men, three women); and alumni advisers to Greek organizations ($N = 6$). Open-ended interviews were held also with judges, public and private defense attorneys, victim advocates, and state prosecutors regarding the processing of sexual assault cases. Data were analyzed using the grounded theory method (Glaser 1978; Martin and Turner 1986). In the following analysis, concepts generated from the data analysis are integrated with the literature on men's social fraternities, sexual coercion, and related issues.

FRATERNITIES AND THE SOCIAL CONSTRUCTION OF MEN AND MASCULINITY

Our research indicated that fraternities are vitally concerned—more than with anything else—with masculinity. They work hard to create a macho image and context and try to avoid any suggestion of "wimpishness," effeminacy, and homosexuality. Valued members display, or are willing to go along with, a narrow conception of masculinity that stresses competition, athleticism, dominance, winning, conflict, wealth, material possessions, willingness to drink alcohol, and sexual prowess vis-à-vis women.

Valued Qualities of Members

When fraternity members talked about the kind of pledges they prefer, a litany of stereotypical and narrowly masculine attributes and behaviors was recited and feminine or woman-associated qualities and behaviors were expressly denounced. Fraternities seek men who are "athletic," "big guys," good in intramural competition, "who can talk college sports." Males "who are willing to drink alcohol," "who drink socially," or "who can hold their liquor" are sought. Alcohol and activities associated with the recreational use of alcohol are cornerstones of fraternity social life. Nondrinkers are viewed with skepticism and rarely selected for membership.

Fraternities try to avoid "geeks," nerds, and men said to give the fraternity a "wimpy" or "gay" reputation. Art, music, and humanities majors, majors in traditional women's fields (nursing, home economics, social work, education), men with long hair, and those whose appearance or dress violate current norms are rejected. Clean-cut, handsome men who dress well (are clean, neat, conforming, fashionable) are preferred. One sorority woman commented that "the top ranking fraternities have the best looking guys."

One fraternity man, a senior, said his fraternity recruited "some big guys, very athletic" over a two-year period to help overcome its image of wimpiness. His fraternity had won the interfraternity competition for highest grade-point average several years running but was looked down on as "wimpy, dancy, even gay." With their bigger, more athletic recruits, "our reputation improved; we're a much more recognized fraternity now." Thus, a fraternity's reputation and status depends on members' possession of stereotypically masculine qualities. Good grades, campus leadership, and community service are "nice" but masculinity dominance—for example, in athletic events, physical size of members, athleticism of members—counts most. . . .

The Status and Norms of Pledgeship

A pledge (sometimes called an associate member) is a new recruit who occupies a trial membership status for a specific period of time. The pledge period (typically ranging from 10 to 15 weeks) gives fraternity brothers an opportunity to assess and socialize new recruits. Pledges evaluate the fraternity also and decide if they want to become brothers. The socialization experience is structured partly through assignment of a Big Brother to each pledge. Big Brothers are expected to teach pledges how to become a brother and to support them as they progress through the trial membership period. Some pledges are repelled by the pledging experience, which can entail physical abuse; harsh discipline; and demands to be subordinate, follow orders, and engage in demeaning routines and activities, similar to those used by the military to "make men out of boys' during boot camp.

Characteristics of the pledge experience are rationalized by fraternity members as necessary to help pledges unite into a group, rely on each other, and join together against outsiders. The process is highly masculinist in execution as well as conception. A willingness to submit to authority, follow orders, and do as one is told is viewed as a sign of loyalty, togetherness, and unity. . . .

Fraternities' emphasis on toughness, withstanding pain and humiliation, obedience to superiors, and using physical force to obtain compliance contributes to an interpersonal style that de-emphasizes caring and sensitivity but fosters intragroup trust and loyalty. If the least macho or most critical pledges drop out, those who remain may be more receptive to, and influenced by, masculinist values and practices that encourage the use of force in sexual relations with women and the covering up of such behavior.

Norms and Dynamics of Brotherhood

Brother is the status occupied by fraternity men to indicate their relations to each other and their membership in a particular fraternity organization or group. Brother is a male-specific status; only males can become brothers, although women can become "Little Sisters," a form of pseudomembership. "Becoming a brother" is a rite of passage that follows the consistent and often lengthy display by pledges of appropriately masculine qualities and behaviors. Brothers have a quasi-familial relationship with each other, are normatively said to share bonds of closeness and support, and are sharply set off from nonmembers. Brotherhood is a loosely defined term used to represent the bonds that develop among fraternity members and the obligations and expectations incumbent upon them.

Some of our respondents talked about brotherhood in almost reverential terms, viewing it as the most valuable benefit of fraternity membership. One senior, a business-school major who had been affiliated with a fairly high-status fraternity throughout four years on campus said:

> Brotherhood spurs friendship for life, which I consider its best aspect, although I didn't see it that way when I joined. Brotherhood bonds and unites. It instills values of caring about one another, caring about community, caring about ourselves. The values and bonds [of brotherhood] continually develop over the four years [in college] while normal friendships come and go.

Despite this idealization, most aspects of fraternity practice and conception are more mundane. Brotherhood often plays itself out as an overriding concern with masculinity and, by extension, femininity. As a consequence, fraternities comprise collectivities of highly masculinized men with attitudinal qualities and behavioral norms that predispose them to sexual coercion of women. The norms of masculinity are complemented by conceptions of women and femininity that are equally distorted and stereotyped and that may enhance the probability of women's exploitation.

Practices of Brotherhood

Practices associated with fraternity brotherhood that contribute to the sexual coercion of women include a preoccupation with loyalty, group protection and secrecy, use of alcohol as a weapon, [and] involvement in violence and physical force.

Loyalty, Group Protection, and Secrecy.   Loyalty is a fraternity preoccupation. Members are reminded constantly to be loyal to the fraternity and to their brothers. Among other ways, loyalty is played out in the practices of group protection and secrecy. The fraternity must be shielded from criticism. . . . Fraternities try to protect themselves from close scrutiny and criticism by the Interfraternity Council (a quasi-governing body composed of representatives from all social fraternities on campus), their fraternity's national office, university officials, law enforcement, the media, and the public. Group protection was observed in the alleged gang rape case with which we began our study. Except for one brother, a rapist who turned state's evidence, the entire remaining fraternity membership was accused by university and criminal justice officials of lying to protect the fraternity. Members consistently failed to cooperate even though the alleged crimes were felonies, involved only four men (two of whom were not even members of the local chapter), and the victim of the crime nearly died. According to a grand jury's findings, fraternity officers repeatedly broke appointments with law enforcement officials, refused to provide police with a list of members, and refused to cooperate with police and prosecutors investigating the case (*Florida Flambeau*, 1988).

Secrecy is a priority value and practice in fraternities, partly because full-fledged membership is premised on it (for confirmation, see Ehrhart and Sandler, 1985; Longino and Kart, 1973; Roark, 1987). Secrecy is also a boundary-maintaining mechanism, demarcating in-group from out-group, us from them. Secret rituals, handshakes, and mottoes are revealed to pledge brothers as they are initiated into full brotherhood. Since only brothers are supposed to know a fraternity's secrets, such knowledge affirms membership in the fraternity and separates a brother from others. Extending secrecy tactics from protection of private knowledge to protection of the fraternity from criticism is a predictable development. Our interviews indicated that individual members knew the difference between right and wrong, but fraternity norms that emphasize loyalty, group protection, and secrecy often overrode standards of ethical correctness.

Alcohol as Weapon.   Alcohol use by fraternity men is normative. They use it on weekdays to relax after class and on weekends to "get drunk," "get crazy," and "get laid." The use of alcohol to obtain sex from women is pervasive—in other words, it is used as a weapon against sexual reluctance. According to several fraternity men whom we interviewed, alcohol is the major tool used to gain sexual mastery over women. One fraternity man, a 21-year-old senior, described alcohol use to gain sex as follows: "There are girls that you know will fuck, then some you have to put some effort into it. . . . You have to buy them drinks or find out if she's drunk enough." A similar strategy is used collectively. A fraternity man said that at parties with Little Sisters: "We provide them with 'hunch punch' and things get wild. We get them drunk and most of the guys end up with one." "'Hunch punch,'" he said, "is a girls' drink made up of overproof alcohol and powdered Kool-Aid, no water or anything, just ice. It's very strong. Two cups will do a number on a female.". . .

In the gang rape case, our sources said that many fraternity men on campus believed the victim had a drinking problem and was thus an "easy make." According to newspaper accounts, she had been drinking alcohol on the evening she was raped; the lead assailant is alleged to have given her a bottle of wine after she arrived at his fraternity house. Portions of the rape occurred in a shower, and the victim was reportedly so drunk that her assailants had difficulty holding her in a standing position (*Tallahassee Democrat*, 1988a). While raping her, her assailants repeatedly told her they were members of another fraternity under the apparent belief that she was too drunk to know the difference. Of course, if she was too drunk to know who they were, she was too drunk to consent to sex. . . .

Violence and Physical Force.   Fraternity men have a history of violence (Ehrhart and Sandler, 1985; Roark, 1987). Their record of hazing, fighting, property destruction, and rape has caused them problems with insurance companies (Bradford, 1986; Pressley, 1987). Two university officials told us that fraternities "are the third riskiest property to insure behind toxic waste dumps and amusement parks." Fraternities are increasingly defendants in legal actions brought by pledges subjected to hazing (Meyer, 1986; Pressley, 1987) and by women who were raped by one or more members. In a recent alleged gang rape incident at another Florida university, prosecutors failed to file charges but the victim filed a civil suit against the fraternity nevertheless (*Tallahassee Democrat*, 1989).. . .

FRATERNITIES' COMMODIFICATION OF WOMEN

In claiming that women are treated by fraternities as commodities, we mean that fraternities knowingly, and intentionally, *use* women for their benefit. Fraternities use women as bait for new members, as servers of brothers' needs, and as sexual prey.

Women as Bait.   Fashionably attractive women help a fraternity attract new members. As one fraternity man, a junior, said, "They are good bait." Beautiful, sociable women are believed to impress the right kind of pledges and give the impression that the fraternity can deliver this type of woman to its members.

Photographs of shapely, attractive coeds are printed in fraternity brochures and videotapes that are distributed and shown to potential pledges. The women pictured are often dressed in bikinis, at the beach, and are pictured hugging the brothers of the fraternity. One university official says such recruitment materials give the message: "Hey, they're here for you, you can have whatever you want," and, "We have the best looking women. Join us and you can have them too." Another commented: "Something's wrong when males join an all-male organization as the best place to meet women. It's so illogical."

Fraternities compete in promising access to beautiful women. One fraternity man, a senior, commented that "the attraction of girls [i.e., a fraternity's success in attracting women] is a big status symbol for fraternities." One university official commented that the use of women as a recruiting tool is so well entrenched that fraternities that might be willing to forego it say they cannot afford to unless other fraternities do so as well. One fraternity man said, "Look, if we don't have Little Sisters, the fraternities that do will get all the good pledges." Another said, "We won't have as good a rush [the period during which new members are assessed and selected] if we don't have these women around."

In displaying good-looking, attractive, skimpily dressed, nubile women to potential members, fraternities implicitly, and sometimes explicitly, promise sexual access to women. One fraternity man commented that "part of what being in a fraternity is all about is the sex" and explained how his fraternity uses Little Sisters to recruit new members:

> We'll tell the sweetheart [the fraternity's term for Little Sister], "You're gorgeous; you can get him." We'll tell her to fake a scam and she'll go hang all over him during a rush party, kiss him, and he thinks he's done wonderful and wants to join. The girls think it's great too. It's flattering for them.

Women as Servers.   The use of women as servers is exemplified in the Little Sister program. Little Sisters are undergraduate women who are rushed and selected in a manner parallel to the recruitment of fraternity men. They are affiliated with the fraternity in a formal but unofficial way and are able, indeed required, to wear the fraternity's Greek letters. Little Sisters are not full-fledged fraternity members, however; and fraternity national offices and most universities do not register or regulate them. Each fraternity has an officer called Little Sister Chairman who oversees their organization and activities. The Little Sisters elect officers among themselves, pay monthly dues to the fraternity, and have well-defined roles. Their dues are used to pay for the fraternity's social events, and Little Sisters are expected to attend and hostess fraternity parties and hang around the house to make it a "nice place to be." One fraternity man, a senior, described Little Sisters this way: "They are very social girls, willing to join in, be affiliated with the group, devoted to the fraternity." Another member, a sophomore, said: "Their sole purpose is social—attend parties, attract new members, and 'take care' of the guys."

Our observations and interviews suggested that women selected by fraternities as Little Sisters are physically attractive, possess good social skills, and are willing to devote time and energy to the fraternity and its members. One undergraduate woman gave the following job description for Little Sisters to a campus newspaper:

> It's not just making appearances at all the parties but entails many more responsibilities. You're going to be expected to go to all the intramural games to cheer the brothers on, support and encourage the pledges, and just be around to bring some extra life to the house. [As a Little Sister] you have to agree to take on a new responsibility other than studying to maintain your grades and managing to keep your checkbook from bouncing. You have to make time to be a part of the fraternity and support the brothers in all they do. (*The Tomahawk*, 1988)

The title of Little Sister reflects women's subordinate status; fraternity men in a parallel role are called Big Brothers. Big Brothers assist a sorority primarily with the physical work of sorority rushes, which, compared to fraternity rushes, are more formal, structured, and intensive. Sorority rushes take place in the daytime and fraternity rushes at night so fraternity men are free to help. According to one fraternity member, Little Sister status is a benefit to women because it gives them a social outlet and "the protection of the brothers." The gender-stereotypic conceptions and obligations of these Little Sister and Big Brother statuses indicate that fraternities and sororities promote a gender hierarchy on campus that fosters subordination and dependence in women, thus encouraging sexual exploitation and the belief that it is acceptable.

Women as Sexual Prey.   Little Sisters are a sexual utility. Many Little Sisters do not belong to sororities and lack peer support for refraining from unwanted sexual relations. One fraternity man (whose fraternity has 65 members and 85 Little Sisters) told us they had recruited "wholesale" in the prior year to "get lots of new women." The structural access to women that the Little Sister program provides and the absence of normative supports for refusing fraternity members' sexual advances may make women in this program particularly susceptible to coerced sexual encounters with fraternity men.

Access to women for sexual gratification is a presumed benefit of fraternity membership, promised in recruitment materials and strategies and through brothers' conversations with new recruits. One fraternity man said: "We always tell the guys that you get sex all the time, there's always new girls. . . . After I became a Greek, I found out I could be with females at will." A university official told us that, based on his observations, "no one [i.e., fraternity men] on this campus wants to have 'relationships.' They just want to have fun [i.e., sex]." Fraternity men plan and execute strategies aimed at obtaining sexual gratification, and this occurs at both individual and collective levels.

Individual strategies include getting a woman drunk and spending a great deal of money on her. As for collective strategies, most of our undergraduate interviewees agreed that fraternity parties often culminate in sex and that this outcome is planned. One fraternity man said fraternity parties often involve sex and nudity and can "turn into orgies." Orgies may be planned in advance, such as the Bowery Ball party held by one fraternity. A former fraternity member said of this party:

The entire idea behind this is sex. Both men and women come to the party wearing little or nothing. There are pornographic pinups on the walls and usually porno movies playing on the TV. The music carries sexual overtones. . . . They just get schnockered [drunk] and, in most cases, they also get laid.

When asked about the women who come to such a party, he said: "Some Little Sisters just won't go. . . . The girls who do are looking for a good time, girls who don't know what it is, things like that."

Other respondents denied that fraternity parties are orgies but said that sex is always talked about among the brothers and they all know "who each other is doing it with." One member said that most of the time, guys have sex with their girlfriends "but with socials, girlfriends aren't allowed to come and it's their [members'] big chance [to have sex with other women]." The use of alcohol to help them get women into bed is a routine strategy at fraternity parties.

CONCLUSIONS

In general, our research indicated that the organization and membership of fraternities contribute heavily to coercive and often violent sex. Fraternity houses are occupied by same-sex (all men) and same-age (late teens, early twenties) peers whose maturity and judgment is often less than ideal. Yet fraternity houses are private dwellings that are mostly off-limits to, and away from scrutiny of, university and community representatives, with the result that fraternity house events seldom come to the attention of outsiders. Practices associated with the social construction of fraternity brotherhood emphasize a macho conception of men and masculinity, a narrow, stereotyped conception of women and femininity, and the treatment of women as commodities. Other practices contributing to coercive sexual relations and the cover-up of rapes include excessive alcohol use, competitiveness, and normative support for deviance and secrecy.

Some fraternity practices exacerbate others. Brotherhood norms require "sticking together" regardless of right or wrong; thus rape episodes are unlikely to be stopped or reported to outsiders, even when witnesses disapprove. The ability to use alcohol without scrutiny by authorities and alcohol's frequent association with violence, including sexual coercion, facilitates rape in fraternity houses. Fraternity norms that emphasize the value of maleness and masculinity over femaleness and femininity and that elevate the status of men and lower the status of women in members' eyes undermine perceptions and treatment of women as persons who deserve consideration and care. . . . Masculinity of a narrow and stereotypical type helps create attitudes, norms, and practices that predispose fraternity men to coerce women sexually, both individually and collectively (Allgeier, 1986; Hood, 1989; Sanday, 1981, 1986).

Research into the social contexts in which rape crimes occur and the social constructions associated with these contexts illumine rape dynamics on campus. Blanchard (1959) found that group rapes almost always have a leader who pushes others into the crime. He also found that the leader's latent homosexuality, desire to show off to his peers, or fear of failing to prove himself a man are frequently an impetus. Fraternity norms and practices contribute to the approval and use of sexual coercion as an accepted tactic in relations with women. Alcohol-induced compliance is normative . . . because the woman who "drinks too much" is viewed as "causing her own rape."

Our research led us to conclude that fraternity norms and practices influence members to view the sexual coercion of women, which is a felony crime, as sport, a contest, or a game. This sport is played not between men and women but between men and men. Women are the pawns or prey in the interfraternity rivalry game; they prove that a fraternity is successful or prestigious. The use of women in this way encourages fraternity men to see women as objects and sexual coercion as sport. Today's societal norms support young women's right to engage in sex at their discretion, and coercion is unnecessary in a mutually desired encounter. However, nubile young women say they prefer to be "in a relationship" to have sex while young men say they prefer to "get laid" without a commitment (Muehlenhard and Linton, 1987). These differences may reflect, in part, American puritanism and men's fears of sexual intimacy or perhaps intimacy of any kind. In a fraternity context, getting sex without giving emotionally demonstrates "cool" masculinity. . . . Drinking large quantities of alcohol before having sex suggests that "scoring" rather than intrinsic sexual pleasure is a primary concern of fraternity men.

References

Allgeier, Elizabeth. 1986. "Coercive Versus Consensual Sexual Interactions." G. Stanley Hall Lecture to American Psychological Association Annual Meeting, Washington, DC, August.

Adams, Aileen and Gail Abarbanel. 1988. *Sexual Assault on Campus: What Colleges Can Do.* Santa Monica, CA: Rape Treatment Center.

Blanchard, W. H. 1959. "The Group Process in Gang Rape." *Journal of Social Psychology* 49:259–266.

Bradford, Michael. 1986. "Tight Market Dries Up Nightlife at University." *Business Insurance* (March 2): 2, 6.

Ehrhart, Julie K. and Bernice R. Sandler. 1985. *Campus Gang Rape: Party Games?* Washington, DC: Association of American Colleges.

Florida Flambeau. 1988. "Pike Members Indicted in Rape." (May 19):1, 5.

Glaser, Barney G. 1978. *Theoretical Sensitivity: Advances in the Methodology of Grounded Theory.* Mill Valley, CA: Sociology Press.

Hood, Jane. 1989. "Why Our Society Is Rape-Prone." *New York Times,* May 16.

Hughes, Michael J. and Roger B. Winston, Jr. 1987. "Effects of Fraternity Membership on Interpersonal Values." *Journal of College Student Personnel* 45:405–411.

Longino, Charles F., Jr., and Cary S. Kart. 1973. "The College Fraternity: An Assessment of Theory and Research." *Journal of College Student Personnel* 31:118–125.

Martin, Patricia Yancey and Barry A. Turner. 1986. "Grounded Theory and Organizational Research." *Journal of Applied Behavioral Science* 22:141–157.

Meyer, T. J. 1986. "Fight Against Hazing Rituals Rages on Campuses." *Chronicle of Higher Education* (March 12):34–36.

Muehlenhard, Charlene L. and Melaney A. Linton. 1987. "Date Rape and Sexual Aggression in Dating Situations: Incidence and Risk Factors." *Journal of Counseling Psychology* 34:186–196.

Pressley, Sue Anne. 1987. "Fraternity Hell Night Still Endures." *Washington Post* (August 11):B1.

Roark, Mary L. 1987. "Preventing Violence on College Campuses." *Journal of Counseling and Development* 65:367–370.

Sanday, Peggy Reeves. 1981. "The Socio-Cultural Context of Rape: A Cross-Cultural Study." *Journal of Social Issues* 37:5–27.

Sanday, Peggy Reeves. 1986. "Rape and the Silencing of the Feminine." Pp. 84–101 in *Rape*, edited by S. Tomaselli and R. Porter. Oxford: Basil Blackwell.

St. Petersburg Times. 1988. "A Greek Tragedy." (May 29):1F, 6F.

Tallahassee Democrat. 1988a. "FSU Fraternity Brothers Charged" (April 27):1A, 12A.

Sanday, Peggy Reeves. 1988b. "FSU Interviewing Students About Alleged Rape" (April 24):1D.

Sanday, Peggy Reeves. 1989. "Woman Sues Stetson in Alleged Rape" (March 19):3B.

Tampa Tribune. 1988. "Fraternity Brothers Charged in Sexual Assault of FSU Coed." (April 27):6B.

Tash, Gary B. 1988. "Date Rape." *The Emerald of Sigma Pi Fraternity* 75(4):1–2.

The Tomahawk. 1988. "A Look Back at Rush, A Mixture of Hard Work and Fun" (April/May):3D.

20

The Contribution of Sex–Role Socialization to Acquaintance Rape

ROBIN WARSHAW AND ANDREA PARROT
Cornell University

From the moment children are born in the United States, their sex becomes an important factor in their social growth. In hospital nurseries, infants who are otherwise indistinguishable from each other are placed in cribs marked with pink or blue name tags so visitors will know which ones are girls and which are boys. What sex they are makes no difference to the newborns; their cribs are color-coded because the adults in their world consider that information significant.

As these babies become toddlers and then preschoolers, they are deluged with direct and indirect messages about how they are to behave based solely on their sex. These messages come from parents and relatives, other adults, siblings, and friends and from cultural media such as movies, television, books, and song lyrics. Even the most egalitarian parents cannot fully insulate their daughters or sons from being affected by many of the gender-linked roles society expects them to adopt.

For example, girls learn, early on, that they should be "sugar and spice and everything nice" while boys learn that they should be "snips and snails and puppy dogs' tails." The girls' labels sound sweet and passive. The boys' labels sound daring and active.

From such social imprints, many girls proceed along a "niceness" track. They learn that they are supposed to be friendly and to yield to others' needs and wants even if it means sacrificing their own. They may develop a sense of physical and intellectual helplessness in areas deemed unsuitable for females, such as physical achievement and mechanical ability. As girls grow into young womanhood, they often are discouraged from becoming self-reliant and inde-

From Andrea Parrot and Laurie Bechhofer (eds.), *Acquaintance Rape: The Hidden Crime* (New York: John Wiley & Sons, 1991), pp. 73–82. Copyright © 1991 by John Wiley & Sons. Reprinted by permission of John Wiley & Sons, Inc.

pendent. They learn to defer to men, to rely on men to provide them with social status, protection, and, ultimately, a secure future. Many of our society's rape-supportive attitudes and myths about rape are rooted in beliefs about appropriate behavior for women.

For example, if a woman is too friendly, men are likely to perceive her behavior as seduction (Abbey, 1982). If a woman gets drunk and goes back to a man's apartment after a party or a date, many people would say she deserves to be raped, because "nice" girls are not supposed to do those things and in a "just world" she is getting what she deserves. However, if a man gets drunk and forces himself sexually on a woman, his behavior is likely to be excused, because "he couldn't help himself."

Many boys are steered onto an "aggression" track that guides them toward a self-centered view of their place in society. They learn to set aside the needs of others, to use physical responses to beat an opponent when faced with conflict, and to equate showing empathy with being weak and "girlish." This training often leads to beliefs in sexual entitlement and social superiority over women. The result is a string of myths that boys and men are expected to live up to.

Given these divergent social development patterns, some of the travelers on the "niceness" track and some of those on the "aggression" track are on a collision course with each other. They may collide as preteens or teenagers in junior high and high schools or at after-school jobs; as young single adults in college or the workplace; or as marriage partners, dates, or friends in later years.

Whenever it happens, aggressive or assaultive behavior between people who know each other is not an isolated or even an unusual event in society at large. Koss (1988) reported that fewer than half of the undergraduate women she surveyed had *never had* an unwanted sexual aggression committed against them. Makepeace (1981) reported in his study of dating college-age students, that 14 percent had been pushed by a date or did the pushing, 13 percent were slapped by a date or did the slapping, and 4 percent were involved in punching incidents on dates.

Historically, sexual assault is not a new problem. Kirkpatrick and Kanin (1957) reported that more than half of the college women they studied had been sexually "offended" within the past year. Kanin (1967) also found that 25 percent of male college students reported having been sexually aggressive since the beginning of college. In 1980, Malamuth and Check reported that 17 percent of the males they sampled indicated some likelihood that they would rape a female, but 69 percent reported some likelihood that they would rape a female if they could be assured of not being punished.

The continuum of aggression escalates to produce victims and perpetrators in acquaintance rapes and date rapes. As pointed out by Weis and Borges (1973), dating brings together two people who may have firmly socialized roles regarding sex and social behavior—including expectations for the outcome of the date—that may be in opposition with each other. Such roles and expectations, coupled with the ambiguity of a dating relationship and the privacy in which it generally takes place, mean that dating can easily lead to rape. Koss (1988), in a survey of college women, learned that 84 percent of the rape victims knew the men who attacked them; 57 percent of the assaults happened on dates. Russell (1984) studied a random sample of women in San Francisco and found that 88 percent of the rape victims knew their attackers.

THE BATTLE OF THE SEXES

For many men and women, "the battle of the sexes" may be just that. From their socialization in childhood and adolescence, they developed different goals related to sexuality—goals that set them up as adversaries. Both groups learned that women, to maintain their own "worth," are supposed to control men's sexuality and that men are supposed to singlemindedly go after sexual intercourse with a female, regardless of how they do it. Both groups were influenced by traditional stereotypic sexual scripts: men should use any strategy to get women to have sexual intercourse and women should passively acquiesce or use any strategy to try to avoid sexual intercourse (LaPlante, McCormick, and Brannigan, 1980). Even if these patterns are known to be dysfunctional or dangerous by the actors, it is often easier and more comfortable for them to repeat familiar patterns than to counteract them (Burnstein, 1975).

Many men have stereotypic sexual scripts that are tempered by other moral and ethical influences, but a significant number do not. Kanin (1984) called these men, who are products of a hypermasculine, hypererotic peer group culture, "sexually predatory."

By the reasoning of this socialization, if intercourse happens, the woman has "let" the man do something to her. He has won and she has lost. No wonder that in his 1984 study of self-disclosed date rapists, Kanin found that two-thirds of the subjects felt the fault for the incident rested with the woman.

Koss (1988) and others have found that opportunity is the best predictor of who will be raped but that a strong belief in macho attitudes is an important indicator of who will rape. Because the male sex role formed by socialization attitudes pushes boys toward goals of power, success, and aggression (Gross, 1978), it is not surprising that college males show a stronger belief in rape-supportive and sexist attitudes than do their female counterparts (Barnett and Feild, 1977).

Rape myth acceptance is associated with kissing a woman without her consent on a first date, in long-term dating, and within marriage (Margolin, Miller, and Moran, 1989). Disregarding a woman's feelings is usually the first step toward rape. Margolin et al. (1989) believed that the process of rape-supportive attitudes which leads to expressions of male sexual dominance usually occurs on an unconscious level. Unwanted intercourse usually results from four societal norms: male supremacy, male initiative, the expectation that women should not be sexually experienced, and the "stroking norm" for women (Lewin, 1985). The stroking norm results from the notion that women should put their man's needs before their own.

Men's social training tells them that they must initiate sexual activity and that women who say "no" don't really mean it. In fact, Muehlenhard and

Hollabaugh (1988), in a study of 610 undergraduate women, discovered that 39 percent had engaged in "token resistance" (saying "no" when they did not mean it) at least once. These women believed that token resistance was common, that male/female relationships were adversarial, that it was acceptable for men to use physical force in male/female relationships, and that women enjoy it when men use force. These beliefs all relate to traditional sexual scripts in which women should exhibit an insincere display of resistance and men should be sexually aggressive and overcome the women's token resistance (Muehlenhard and Hollabaugh, 1988). When those factors combine with the commonly held belief that sex is a biological need for males but not for females (Peplau, Rubin, and Hill, 1977), some men develop feelings of entitlement to force sex (Rapaport and Burkhart, 1984).

Many men have been socialized to be deaf to women's objections to unwanted sexual aggression, even when women physically resist. Koss (1988) reported that 70 percent of the college women she surveyed (most raped by men they knew) physically fought with their attackers, but only 12 percent of the men who committed rape (nearly all against women they knew) said their victims had physically struggled.

Mahoney, Shively, and Traw (1986) believed that traditional male learning provides attitudes, beliefs, and motivations that make sexual assault possible. In addition, personal characteristics—such as lack of social conscience, irresponsibility, and attitudinal acceptance of sexual aggression—and/or situational characteristics—such as heavy alcohol consumption at a party, or peer pressure—lessen learned inhibitions against sexual assault (Mahoney et al., 1986).

Studies with children show that boys and girls expect different outcomes for aggressive behavior, and these expectations may color what happens in an acquaintance rape. Perry, Perry, and Weiss (1989) reported that girls expect to feel guilty and upset after being aggressive but boys believe aggression increases their self-esteem. The boys they studied said that aggression against a girl would win less disapproval from their male peers than aggression against a boy. Mahoney et al. (1986) found that the basis for sexual assault is rooted in normal aspects of traditional male learning, and the most important factors related to whether a woman will be sexually assaulted are the number of men a woman has had sexual intercourse with and the degree of her attraction to macho males.

In any battle, the outcome usually depends on which side has better fighting skills. Many women learn, through direct social messages as well as media images, that they are unable to physically protect themselves in the event of a rape attack. Young girls generally do not have opportunities (as boys do on the football field, for example) to learn that they can withstand a physical thrashing and still survive. Indeed, for years, many police departments have advocated that women simply give up in rape situations. The fear created by that often misguided advice is frequently enough to debilitate a woman from taking action that might prevent her from being raped. Running away, yelling, and kicking the man have all been shown to be among the most effective rape-thwarting strategies (Bart and O'Brien, 1985).

When faced with acquaintance rape, many women are disabled further by socially ingrained beliefs: A friend wouldn't hurt you; rapists are crazy strangers, not people you know; and so on. Sexual abuse is more common among people who believe rape myths, who don't believe that sexual assault is a problem, and who hold traditional views of women's role in American society (Peterson and Franzese, 1987). Women mistakenly believe that since the threat is coming from a man they know, they can reason or argue him out of it. Instead, talking or quarreling have been shown to more likely end in rape, with either strangers or acquaintances (Levine-MacCombie and Koss, 1986). Some women who would be willing to physically strike a stranger who is attacking them often hesitate to hurt someone they know.

The actual battle between the sexes may be encouraged by movies, television scripts, books, and magazines that depict women as really liking it when men are physically rough with them. That theme was clearly portrayed in *Gone with the Wind,* when Rhett Butler and Scarlett O'Hara fought and he forcibly carried her upstairs against her will. The next morning, Scarlett was humming and smiling, presumably because she enjoyed being forced to have sex. Thousands of film and TV scripts have repeated that message since the landmark movie's release in 1939, and pornographic magazines and books have reiterated it in more explicit terms. On "General Hospital," for example, Luke raped Laura and she subsequently married him.

Men get these messages from childhood on and some turn them into action. Greendlinger and Byrne (1987) found among college men the likelihood to rape was correlated with coercive sexual fantasies in addition to rape-myth acceptance and aggressive tendencies. Abbey, Cozzarelli, McLaughlin, and Harnish (1987) found that the more revealing a woman's dress is, the more attractive and sexually desirable she is considered to be, but she is not regarded as "nice." In addition, males are likely to believe that females are more sexual than the women actually are and to overestimate the sexual intent of a woman they have contact with or merely observe (Abbey et al., 1987). Again, the pattern may be set early in their life. Eron and Huesmann (1984) reported that children who preferred watching violent television in elementary school took part in more violent behavior as adults than did those who had not had that preference when they were children.

Heilbrun and Loftus (1986) looked at this behavior in its extreme. They examined sexual sadism—in which the violence committed on the woman is itself sexually arousing to the man—among college males and found that "serious phenomena" of this kind were occurring among 30 percent of their subjects. Significantly, 60 percent of the men identified as attracted to sexual sadism had repeated episodes of unwanted sexual aggression.

A TYPICAL ACQUAINTANCE RAPE

In the course of researching *I Never Called It Rape,* Warshaw (1988) interviewed a woman whose story exemplifies how sex-role socialization contributes to rape between people who know each other. To protect their identities, the woman will be called Lori and the man who raped her, Eric. What follows is a narrative of her story, with some of her comments:

> Lori was 19 at the time of her rape; one year later, she talked with me about it. She knew Eric, who was in his mid-20s, because he was a customer at the restaurant where she worked. Eric's best friend wanted to date a friend of Lori's, but the young woman felt shy about dating alone and convinced Lori to join them and be Eric's date. Lori agreed.
>
> Unknown to Lori, her friend canceled the date the day before it was supposed to happen. Eric knew but didn't tell Lori. Instead he called her several times to make—and then change—their plans. Each time, he told her what they were going to do. Each time Lori agreed with his decision. Finally, he told her he was inviting some friends over to his house for a barbecue party. Again, she agreed with the plan.
>
> When they arrived at Eric's house, Lori asked about her friend and Eric's friend. Eric still didn't tell her they had canceled their date. "He kind of threw it off," Lori said of her attempt to bring up the subject of her friend's whereabouts. But that didn't raise her suspicions. "I didn't think anything of it," she said. "Not in my wildest dreams would I have thought he was plotting something."
>
> The party broke up early. Lori thought that was odd, but she discounted her feelings of misgiving. "I've been known to overreact to things," she said, "so I ignored it." Even when Eric started to kiss her as they sat on his couch, she didn't think anything was wrong. In fact, she liked kissing him.
>
> Then the telephone rang and Eric answered it in another room. When he returned, Lori was standing up. He grabbed her from behind, put his hands across her eyes, and without saying a word, started walking her through his house. She didn't know what was happening. Moments later, he laid her down on what she discovered—as soon as he took his hands off her eyes—was a bed.
>
> "He starts taking off my clothes and I said, 'Wait—time out! This is not what I want.'" Eric told her that this was what she owed him because he made her dinner. Lori said, "This is wrong. Don't do this. I didn't go out with you with this intent."
>
> To which Eric said, "What do you call that on the couch?"
>
> "I call it a kiss, period," Lori replied.
>
> And Eric answered back, "Well, I don't."

Lori as a child was trained to be nice and to fulfill others' needs, so she had agreed to go out with Eric in order to help her friend. When Eric learned that Lori's friend had canceled her half of the double date, he decided not to tell Lori. He felt entitled to hide that information from her in order to get what he wanted—the date and sex. Eric also assumed that he was in charge of deciding where they would go and what they would do. Lori went along, thereby reinforcing Eric's belief in his right to control her. Eric ignored Lori's question. (Women's questions are unimportant to men, especially when they could create conflict with what men want.) Lori believed that men, especially men she dated or knew, were there to protect her. Like many women, Lori had learned to discount her own opinion and believed it's not nice to have misgivings about another person. Eric didn't ask Lori if she wanted to play this "game"; he was using his physical strength to take control. Lori didn't put up a fight. She didn't know what was happening, but it still didn't occur to her that the situation could be threatening. Eric felt entitled to take off Lori's clothes without her permission. He ignored Lori's clear statement that she didn't want him to undress her. Eric believed that since Lori kissed him she was agreeing to have intercourse. He rejected Lori's opinion again.

> Soon things escalated even more. The two struggled a little and Lori managed to get free. She went into the bathroom.
>
> "The whole time I'm thinking, 'I don't believe this is happening to me,'" she said. She walked out of the bathroom intending to ask Eric to take her home. Instead, he grabbed her, pushed her onto the bed, and started taking her clothes off again. Lori yelled, hit him, and tried to push him off her. Eric said, "I know you must like this because a lot of women like this kind of thing." Then he added, "This is the adult world. Maybe you ought to grow up some." Eric then raped her.
>
> Afterward, he said, "Don't tell me you didn't like that." Lori said, "No."
>
> She recalled, "By this time I'm crying because I don't know what else to do. I never heard of anybody having that happen to them." In the car headed back toward Lori's house, Eric asked her to go out with him again. When she stared at him in disbelief, he laughed.
>
> For the next two weeks, Lori could barely function. She told no one about what happened because she blamed herself. Eric appeared in her restaurant one day and tried to hug her. When she pulled away, he said, "Oh, I guess you didn't get enough." Eventually Lori told her mother, decided not to press criminal charges against Eric, and moved several hundred miles away in order to avoid any further encounters with him.

In the second part of the narrative, Lori's sex-role socialization continued to affect the outcome of the incident. Despite all evidence, Lori still could not believe that the date was about to turn into a rape. Lori expected Eric to take care of her, even though she had just been physically struggling with him. Eric proved that Lori's wishes carried no weight with him. Eric believed that women always say "no" when they mean "yes" and that even physical resistance on the part of a woman is just part of the game women play. Lori was raised to trust men like Eric. She believed that only armed strangers commit rape. As far as Eric was concerned, Lori got what she deserved. "Nice" women don't get raped, Lori knew, so she must have somehow caused this thing to happen. It didn't occur to her to lay the blame where it belonged—with Eric. In Eric's mind, all he did was give Lori what *he* "knew she wanted." He also appeared to enjoy making degrading comments to her about their sexual relations. Lori felt powerless after the rape, especially because Eric remained in the community. Like most other acquaintance rape victims, she decided not to prosecute.

CONCLUSION

Messages we receive from family, the media, and peers socialize us to believe rape myths. Perhaps we can minimize acquaintance rape incidence by changing these socialization messages. Parent education on the dysfunction of current socialization and on how to socialize children in an egalitarian way is the first step. Letters to any television network, magazine, or paper that perpetuates these dysfunctional, rape-conducive myths and attitudes can express our disapproval. If the letters don't produce results, we can boycott the products that advertise in those media or boycott the media themselves.

Men and women are socialized to believe different messages. Men are socialized to think that they are supposed to have unquenchable sexual appetites, that they have a right to sex, and that women do not mean "no" when they say "no." A woman is socialized to think that nice men do not rape (and because she only dates nice men, she doesn't believe she will be raped); that if a woman is raped, it is her fault and she must have done something to bring it on; and that no one will believe her if she tells them that she was raped by someone she knows. Therefore, women are not likely to report an acquaintance rape—they think their assailant will not be arrested, will probably brag about the rape to his friends, and will probably rape other women—and the problem will continue. We need to create a society in which the sexual double standard is passé, men believe what women say, women say what they mean, women feel free to initiate sexually, and men are permitted to say "no" to sex without feeling that they have shirked their male duty and role. Only then will we stand a chance to reduce the incidence of acquaintance rape.

References

Abbey, A. 1982. "Sex Differences in Attributions for Friendly Behavior: Do Males Misperceive Females' Friendliness?" *Journal of Personality and Social Psychology* 42, 830–838.

Abbey, A., Cozzarelli, C., McLaughlin, K., and Harnish, R. 1987. "The Effects of Clothing and Dyad Composition on Perceptions of Sexual Intent: Do Women and Men Evaluate These Cues Differently?" *Journal of Applied Social Psychology* 17, 108–126.

Barnett, N. J., and Feild, H. S. 1977. "Sex Differences in University Students' Attitudes Toward Rape." *Journal of College Student Personnel,* 18, 93–96.

Bart, P. B., and O'Brien, P. H. 1985. *Stopping Rape: Successful Survival Strategies.* Elmsford, NY: Pergamon.

Burnstein, B. 1975, April. *Life History and Current Values as Predictors of Sexual Behaviors and Satisfaction in College Women.* Paper presented at the meeting of the Western Psychological Association, Sacramento, CA.

Eron, L. D., and Huesmann, L. R. 1984. "The Control of Aggressive Behavior by Changes in Attitudes, Values, and the Conditions of Learning," pp. 139–171 in R. Blanchard and C. Blanchard (eds.), *Advances in Aggression Research,* Vol. 1. New York: Academic Press.

Greendlinger, V., and Byrne, D. 1987. "Coercive Sexual Fantasies of College Men as Predictors of Self-Reported Likelihood to Rape and Overt Sexual Aggression." *Journal of Sex Research,* 23, 1–11.

Gross, A. E. 1978. "The Male Role and Heterosexual Behavior." *Journal of Social Issues,* 34, 87–107.

Heilbrun, Jr., A. B., and Loftus, M. P. 1986. "The Role of Sadism and Peer Pressure in the Sexual Aggression of Male College Students." *Journal of Sex Research,* 22, 320–332.

Kanin, E. 1967. "An Examination of Sexual Aggression as a Response to Sexual Frustration." *Journal of Marriage and the Family,* 29, 428–433.

Kanin, E. J. 1984. "Date Rape: Unofficial Criminals and Victims." *Victimology,* 9, 95–108.

Kirkpatrick, C., and Kanin, E. 1957. "Male Sexual Aggression on a University Campus." *American Sociological Review*, 22, 52–58.

Koss, M. P. 1988. "Hidden Rape: Incidence, Prevalence, and Descriptive Characteristics of Sexual Aggression and Victimization in a National Sample of College Students," pp. 3–25 in A. W. Burgess (ed.), *Sexual Assault*, Vol. II. New York: Garland.

LaPlante, M. N., McCormick, N., and Brannigan, G. G. 1980. "Living the Sexual Script: College Students' Views of Influence in Sexual Encounters." *Journal of Sex Research*, 16, 338–355.

Levine-MacCombie, J., and Koss, M. P. 1986. "Acquaintance Rape: Effective Avoidance Strategies." *Psychology of Women Quarterly*, 10, 311–320.

Lewin, M. 1985. "Unwanted Intercourse: The Difficulty of Saying No." *Psychology of Women Quarterly*, 9, 184–192.

Mahoney, E. R., Shively, M. D., and Traw, M. 1986. "Sexual Coercion and Assault: Male Socialization and Female Risk." *Sexual Coercion & Assault*, 1, 2–8.

Makepeace, J. M. 1981. "Courtship Violence Among College Students." *Family Relations*, 30, 97–102.

Malamuth, N. M., and Check, J. V. P. 1980. "Penile Tumescence and Perceptual Responses to Rape as a Function of Victim's Perceived Reactions." *Journal of Applied Social Psychology*, 10, 528–547.

Margolin, L., Miller, M., and Moran, P. B. 1989. "When a Kiss Is Not Just a Kiss: Relating Violations of Consent in Kissing to Rape Myth Acceptance." *Sex Roles*, 20, 231–243.

Muehlenhard, C. L., and Hollabaugh, L. C. 1988. "Do Women Sometimes Say No When They Mean Yes? The Prevalence and Correlates of Women's Token Resistance to Sex." *Journal of Personality and Social Psychology*, 54, 872–879.

Peplau, L. A., Rubin, Z., and Hill, C. T. 1977. "Sexual Intimacy in Dating Relationships." *Journal of Social Issues*, 33, 86–109.

Perry, D. G., Perry, L. C., and Weiss, R. J. 1989. "Sex Differences in the Consequences That Children Anticipate for Aggression." *Developmental Psychology*, 25, 1–8.

Peterson, S. A., and Franzese, B. 1987. "Correlates of College Men's Sexual Abuse of Women." *Journal of College Student Personnel*, 28, 223–228.

Rapaport, K., and Burkhart, B. R. 1984. "Personality and Attitudinal Characteristics of Sexually Coercive College Males." *Journal of Abnormal Psychology*, 93, 216–221.

Russell, D. E. H. 1984. *Sexual Exploitation*. Beverly Hills, CA: Sage.

Warshaw, R. 1988. *I Never Called It Rape: The Ms. Report on Recognizing, Fighting, and Surviving Date and Acquaintance Rape*. New York: Harper & Row.

Weis, K., & Borges, S. 1973. "Victimology and Rape: The Case of the Legitimate Victim." *Issues in Criminology*, 8, 71–115.

21

Young People's Attitudes Toward Acquaintance Rape

JACQUELYN W. WHITE AND JOHN A. HUMPHREY
University of North Carolina, Greensboro

There was a part of me back then that thought that is the way "it" was done. Guys pounced on you, you struggled, then forgot about the whole thing . . . I never told anyone I was raped. I would not have thought that was what it was. It was unwilling sex. I just didn't want to and he did. Today, at 29, I know it was rape.

(statement from a rape victim; Warshaw, 1988, pp. 119–120)

I know you must like this because a lot of women like this kind of thing. . . . [later] Can I call you tomorrow? Can I see you next week-end? . . . [after several weeks of trying to see his victim again, and she avoiding him] Oh, I guess you didn't get enough.

(an acquaintance rapist's statement; Warshaw, 1988, pp. 16–17)

An apparent paradox exists among American young people with regard to rape. On the one hand, rape is consensually viewed as an abhorrent form of interpersonal violence. On the other hand, many young people do not believe that forced sex between acquaintances and intimates is particularly wrong or problematic and they do not think that there is such a thing as rape between acquaintances and intimates.

The purpose of this chapter is to explore the social context of this contradiction. We do this by addressing the conflicting attitudes, beliefs, and norms about male–female roles and sexual relationships that legitimate sexual violence in a dating situation and result in reluctance to label its expression criminal. The chapter examines the content of these attitudes, where they come from, and how they are perpetuated.

The study of attitudes provides insight into the contemporary social norms governing sexual behavior in dating situations. Attitudes about male–female relationships, and about sexual interactions specifically, give young people a frame of reference for understanding their own and others' behaviors, allow them to choose behaviors that will be acceptable to others, and serve as a basis for justifying their actions ("It's okay; everyone does it").

The establishment of meaningful relationships with members of the opposite sex occurs during adolescence, usually in the dating context (Conger and Petersen, 1984; Rice, 1984). Yet, little attention has been given to issues related to adolescent sexual socialization. Goodchilds, Zellman, Johnson, and Giarusso (1988) defined adolescent sexual socialization as

> the sets of attitudes and expectations about the sexually intimate relationship which evolve and coalesce as the individual becomes sexually mature and sexually active.

Since forced sexual encounters most often occur among acquaintances, typically in a dating situation (Ageton, 1983; Koss, 1985), an understanding of adolescents' sexually assaultive experiences and their attitudes about these experiences are crucial to rape prevention.

A SOCIOCULTURAL OVERVIEW

Sociocultural considerations are central to explanations of rape-supportive attitudes and sexual assault. American culture influences the ongoing sex-role socialization of the young, attitudes toward rape, and sexually aggressive behavior (Weis and Borges, 1973). Furthermore, rape reflects the power differential between women and men. Rose (1979) noted:

> From the feminist perspective, rape is a direct result of our culture's differential sex role socialization and stratification . . . the association of dominance with the male sex role and submission with the female sex role is viewed as a significant factor in the persistence of rape as a serious social problem.

Brownmiller (1975), in her landmark book *Against Our Will: Men, Women, and Rape,* described society as not only tolerating but ideologically encouraging sexual hostility toward women. Other investigations confirmed Brownmiller's assertion that rape is a manifestation of a social ideology of male domination over women (Burt, 1980; Costin and Schwarz, 1987; Feild, 1978; Sanday, 1981; Schwarz and Brand, 1983). The traditional view of women as powerless sex objects, who must exchange sexual favors for male protection and financial and emotional support, inevitably leads to an adversarial relationship between the sexes, characterized by confused sexual expectations and aggression (Weis and Borges, 1973).

The sociocultural environment influences socialization both within the family and within the adolescent subculture. Fagot, Loeber, and Reid (1988) suggested that there are three essential familial determinants of male-to-female aggression: (a) parents who are unable to control their demanding children, for example, children who use coercion to get what they want; (b) female members of the family who become targets for male aggression; and (c) attitudes that devalue women (male dominance is supported and aggression toward women is legitimated).

Parents have been found to socialize daughters to resist sexual advances and sons to initiate sexual activity (Ross, 1977), although fathers' strong disapproval of their sons' sexual activities has been found important in reducing sexual aggression (Kanin, 1985). Adolescent peer groups foster similar expectations for male and female sexual behavior. LaPlante, McCormick, and Brannigan (1980, p. 339) suggested that adolescents learn "sexual scripts." These scripts provide "norms which prescribe that the man should be the initiator of sexual activity while the woman is the 'limit setter.'"

Berger, Searles, Salem, and Pierce (1986, p. 20) argued that the pervasiveness of male sexual aggression is viewed by young women as "an inevitable part of the dating game." Forced sexual activity between acquaintances has become culturally normative behavior (Ageton, 1983). Berger et al. (1986) found that undergraduate women tend to downplay the seriousness of most unwanted sexual contact as harmless, commonplace in bars or at parties, and something that "should" therefore be endured. Such rationalizations provide a basis for tolerance of sexually exploitive behavior. Furthermore, young women are socialized to accept responsibility for controlling sexual interaction on a date and to assume blame for their own sexual victimization. Young men, however, are socialized to view female attempts to resist their sexual advances as a part of the "game" that must be disregarded. Young men commonly believe that when a young woman says "no" she actually means "yes" or that if a young woman consents to any sexual activity, she is willing to have sexual intercourse (Brodyaga, Gates, Singer, Tucker, and White, 1975; Dull and Giacopassi, 1987; Kanin, 1969). Misperception of sexual cues becomes the norm in the male–female interactions (Burkhart and Stanton, 1988). Culturally sanctioned sexual scripts are continuously played out in the dating situation. As a consequence, sexual assault perpetrated by an acquaintance is rarely reported to the police. Only rape committed by a stranger is viewed as real rape (Check and Malamuth, 1983; Estrich, 1987; Johnson and Jackson, 1988; Klemmack and Klemmack, 1976; Tetreault and Barnett, 1987; Williams, 1984). Thus, sexual scripts promote a conspiracy of silence among the victim, perpetrator, and larger society. Acquaintance rape is implicitly fostered.

THE STRUCTURE OF STUDENTS' BELIEFS ABOUT DATE RAPE

The general consensus among American students from junior high school through college is that forced sexual intercourse on a date rarely constitutes rape. A large-scale survey of Los Angeles teenagers, a group that might be expected to hold egalitarian sex-role values, revealed some startling results. Though these teenagers understood the difference between consensual and nonconsensual sex, they were frequently reluctant to apply the label "rape" to the examples of forced sexual relations described in the survey (Goodchilds et al., 1988). Two factors affected the likelihood that nonconsensual sex would be labeled rape: the amount of force used and the type of relationship. The greater the force used by the man to obtain intercourse, the more likely the act was labeled rape, but the label rape was used less frequently if the couple had been dating for a while than if they had just met. Goodchilds and her colleagues (1988) concluded that:

> in fact they [adolescents] were pretty unsure about whether rape occurred between dating partners. . . . Adolescents appear reluctant to label nonconsensual sex within a dating relationship as rape, even when the guy slugs the girl.

Surveys by Goodchilds and her colleagues (1988) and others (Fischer, 1986a, b, 1987; Muehlenhard, Friedman, and Thomas, 1985) identified other factors that affect whether forced sex will be justified or labeled rape: the woman's type of dress, location of the date, use of drugs and/or alcohol, the woman's and man's reputations, how much money the man spends, the man's level of sexual arousal, and the level of previous sexual intimacy, that is, the amount of petting and whether intercourse had previously occurred. However, there were marked gender differences in the meaning imparted to the various circumstances surrounding forced sex. In general, there was a consistent tendency for the girls to view certain circumstances and behaviors in a less sexualized way. These gender differences help us to understand the various ways in which young women and young men may misinterpret what is going on during a date.

To elaborate, adolescent girls were more likely to mention personality and sensitivity as desirable attributes in a date, whereas boys were more likely to mention physical appearance. Girls were less likely than boys to see clothing of any type (low-cut top, shorts, tight jeans, see-through clothes) worn by either sex as a signal for the female's interest in sexual activity. Girls were less likely than boys to see any particular location or activity as a signal for sex, but both girls and boys judged "going to the guy's house alone when there is nobody home" as most indicative of the female's willingness for sex. Girls were less likely than boys to feel that a female who accepts a date with a guy with a bad reputation has agreed to sex but were more likely than boys to feel that a male has a right to expect sex from his date if she has a "tarnished" reputation.

Further gender differences were observed in perceptions of circumstances that might signal that the girl has forfeited her right to say no to sexual intercourse. Significantly more girls (44 percent) than boys (24 percent) indicated there are *no* circumstances under which it is "OK for a guy to hold a girl down and force her to have sexual intercourse." This means that 56 percent of the girls and 76 percent of the boys believed forced sex is acceptable under at least some circumstances. The largest differences between girls and boys were for the situations in which "he spends a lot of money on her" (61 percent of the males and 88 percent of the females said forced sex was not acceptable) and "she's led him on" (46 percent of the males and 73 percent of the females: not acceptable); the smallest difference was for "she gets him sexually excited" (49 percent of the males and 58 percent of the females: not acceptable). Goodchilds and her colleagues (1988) concluded that otherwise innocent female behaviors may be construed by a male to have sexual meaning.

Findings consistent with Goodchilds et al. (1988) have been reported for a younger group of adolescents. A survey of 1700 11 to 14 year olds conducted by the Rhode Island Rape Crisis Center (1988) found that 51 percent of the boys and 41 percent of the girls believed that a man has a right to force a woman to kiss him if he had "spent a lot of money" on her; 31 percent of the boys and 32 percent of the girls said it is not improper for a man to rape a woman who had past sexual experiences; 87 percent of the boys and 79 percent of the girls said rape is OK if a man and woman are married; and 65 percent of the boys and 47 percent of all of these seventh to ninth graders said it is OK for a man to rape a woman he has been dating for more than six months.

Other studies have confirmed that sex role stereotyping, acceptance of rape myths, and adversarial sex beliefs are related to college students' judgments that acquaintance rape is within the realm of normative acts (Check and Malamuth, 1983; Jenkins and Dambrot, 1987). However, undergraduate women and men typically perceive sexual aggression differently (Barnett and Feild, 1977). Studies suggest a consistent tendency for college women to judge rape more seriously than do college men (Costin, 1985; Costin and Schwarz, 1987; L'Armand and Pepitone, 1982) and to blame the victim less (Jenkins and Dambrot, 1987; Thornton, Robbins, and Johnson, 1981). For example, Tieger (1981), in a study of junior college students, found that male students were more likely than female students to: (a) perceive that rape victims failed to adequately resist the assault; (b) consider the offense less serious, more normative behavior; and (c) view the victim as seductive and taking pleasure in being raped. . . .

CONCLUSIONS

Our examination of the literature on young people's attitudes toward rape made three points clear. First, acquaintance rape is viewed differently and less seriously than stranger rape. It is less often judged "real" rape, which results in a contradiction: The crime for which young women are most vulnerable, and the one "normal" young men are likely to perpetrate, is the one least likely to be labeled criminal. Second, various cultural norms, and sexual scripts in particular, mitigate efforts to label forced sex as real rape under a variety of circumstances: how long the couple has dated, prior level of sexual intimacy, who initiates the date, who pays, where the couple goes, how the woman dresses, use of alcohol or drugs, the man's and woman's reputations, and the man's level of sexual arousal. Third, various rape-supportive beliefs and adversarial attitudes toward women predict sexually aggressive behavior in men, and competencies such as empathy, emotional expressiveness, and femininity reduce the likelihood of sexually aggressive behavior.

We conclude that the cultural conception of *consent* lies at the core of understanding this problem. (See Berger et al., 1986; Burt and Albin, 1981, for further discussions of consent.) Cultural support for the notion that the presence of certain circumstances means a woman has forfeited her right to refuse sexual intercourse leads to the conclusion that she consented and a crime did not occur. Acceptance of this premise legitimates a man's entitlement to sex under these circumstances. The logic is that a woman's earlier actions (accepting the date, going to isolated locations, choosing certain clothing, engaging in any action that sexually arouses the man, and so on) negate the legitimacy of any subsequent refusal to have further sexual interaction. Her resistance, seen as either token or inappropriate, must be overcome (Lakoff and Johnson, 1987). Forced sex is justified and ceases to be labeled a crime, either by young people or by the law (MacKinnon, 1983). "If the man believed that the woman's resistance was not genuine—and he has probably been socialized to believe this—it becomes difficult to define the act legally as a crime" (Berger et al., 1986, p. 5). Furthermore, as the review of the literature strongly indicated, young women and men frequently perceive the same dating circumstances differently. Misunderstanding and conflict result, and the woman has difficulty communicating her unwillingness (Lewin, 1985). Thus, current cultural norms dictate that the woman who wants to resist must go "beyond what is normally expected of women who want intercourse but wish to maintain a 'moral' appearance" (Weis and Borges, 1973, p. 92).

All of this points to the necessity of changing attitudes and beliefs about acquaintance rape. Young people must learn to define all instances of forced sexual contact as criminal. Furthermore, young men need to feel good about themselves even when their sexual desires go unfulfilled. They need to learn that having a woman say "no" to sex is okay and that part of their male integrity is the ability to respect the woman's decision.

A rape-supportive culture and concomitant social organization are socially constructed realities and, as such, are subject to change. To the extent that attitudes, beliefs, and social norms conducive to sexual assault are scientifically scrutinized and publicly confronted, relations between the sexes can be markedly altered. Forced sexual activity between acquaintances will become socially unacceptable.

References

Ageton, S. S. 1983. *Sexual Assault Among Adolescents.* Lexington, MA: Heath.

Barnett, N., and Feild, H. 1977. "Sex Differences in University Students' Attitudes Toward Rape." *Journal of College Student Personnel,* 2, 93–96.

Berger, R. J., Searles, P., Salem, R. G., and Pierce, B. A. 1986. "Sexual Assault in a College Community." *Sociological Focus,* 19, 1–26.

Brodyaga, L., Gates, M., Singer, S., Tucker, M., and White, R. 1975. *Rape and Its Victims: A Report for Citizens, Health Facilities, and Criminal Justice Agencies.* Washington, DC: U.S. Government Printing Office, J 1. 8/3: R18.

Brownmiller, S. 1975. *Against Our Will: Men, Women, and Rape.* New York: Simon and Schuster.

Burkhart, B. R., and Stanton, A. L. 1988. "Sexual Aggression in Acquaintance Relationships," pp. 43–45 in G. W. Russell (ed.), *Violence in Intimate Relationships.* New York: PMA Publishing Corp.

Burt, M. 1980. "Cultural Myths and Supports for Rape." *Journal of Personality and Social Psychology,* 38, 217–230.

Burt, M. R., and Albin, R. S. 1981. "Rape Myths, Rape Definitions, and Probability of Conviction." *Journal of Applied Social Psychology,* 11, 212–230.

Check, J. V. P., and Malamuth, N. M. 1983. "Sex Role Stereotyping and Reactions to Depictions of Stranger Versus Acquaintance Rape." *Journal of Personality and Social Psychology*, 45, 344–356.

Conger, J. J., and Petersen, A. D. 1984. *Adolescence and Youth: Psychological Development in a Changing World* (3rd ed.). New York: Harper and Row.

Costin, F. 1985. "Beliefs About Rape and Women's Social Roles." *Archives of Sexual Behavior*, 14, 319–325.

Costin, F., and Schwarz, N. 1987. "Beliefs About Rape and Women's Roles: A Four-Nation Study." *Journal of Interpersonal Violence*, 2, 46–56.

Dull, R. T., and Giacopassi, D. J. 1987. "Demographic Correlates of Sexual and Dating Attitudes." *Criminal Justice and Behavior*, 14, 175–193.

Estrich, S. 1987. "Real Rape: How the Legal System Victimizes Women Who Say No." Cambridge, MA: Harvard University Press.

Fagot, B. I., Loeber, R., and Reid, J. B. 1988. "Developmental Determinants of Male-to-Female Aggression," pp. 91–105, in G. W. Russell (ed.), *Violence in Intimate Relationships.* New York: PMA Publishing Corp.

Feild, H. S. 1978. "Attitudes Toward Rape: A Comparative Analysis of Police, Rapists, Crisis Counselors, and Citizens." *Journal of Personality and Social Psychology*, 36, 156–179.

Fischer, G. J. 1986a. "College Student Attitudes Toward Forcible Date Rape: Change After Taking a Human Sexuality Course." *Journal of Sex Education and Therapy*, 12, 42–46.

Fischer, G. J. 1986b. "College Student Attitudes Toward Forcible Date Rape: I. Cognitive Predictors." *Archives of Sexual Behavior*, 15, 457–466.

Fischer, G. J. 1987. "Hispanic and Majority Student Attitudes Toward Forcible Date Rape as a Function of Differences in Attitudes Toward Women." *Sex Roles*, 17, 93–101.

Goodchilds, J., Zellman, G., Johnson, P., and Giarusso, R. 1988. "Adolescents and Their Perceptions of Sexual Interactions," pp. 245–270 in A. W. Burgess (ed.), *Rape and Sexual Assault,* Vol. II, New York: Garland.

Jenkins, M. J., and Dambrot, F. H. 1987. "The Attribution of Date Rape: Observer's Attitudes and Sexual Experiences and the Dating Situation." *Journal of Applied Social Psychology*, 17, 875–895.

Johnson, J. D., and Jackson, L. A. 1988. "Assessing the Effects of Factors That Might Underlie the Differential Perception of Acquaintance and Stranger Rape." *Sex Roles*, 19, 37–44.

Kanin, E. J. 1969. "Selected Dyadic Aspects of Males' Sex Aggression." *Journal of Sex Research*, 5, 12–28.

Kanin, E. J. 1985. "Date Rapists: Differential Sexual Socialization and Relative Deprivation." *Archives of Sexual Behavior*, 14, 219–231.

Klemmack, S. H., and Klemmack, D. L. 1976. "The Social Definition of Rape," pp. 135–147 in M. Walker and S. Brodsky (eds.), *Sexual Assault.* Lexington, MA: Lexington Books.

Koss, M. P. 1985. "The Hidden Rape Victim: Personality, Attitudinal, and Situational Characteristics." *Psychology of Women Quarterly*, 9, 193–212.

L'Armand, K., and Pepitone, A. 1982. "Judgments of Victim-Rapist Relationship and Victim Sexual History." *Personality and Social Psychology Bulletin*, 8, 134–139.

Lakoff, G., and Johnson, M. 1987. "The Metaphorical Logic of Rape." *Metaphor and Symbolic Activity*, 2, 73–79.

LaPlante, M. N., McCormick, N., and Brannigan, G. G. 1980. "Living the Sexual Script: College Students' Views of Influence in Sexual Encounters." *Journal of Sex Research*, 16, 338–355.

Lewin, M. 1985. "Unwanted Intercourse: The Difficulty of Saying No." *Psychology of Women Quarterly,* 9, 184–192.

MacKinnon, C. A. 1983. "Feminism, Marxism, Method and the State: Toward Feminist Jurisprudence." *Signs: A Journal of Women in Culture,* 8, 635–658.

Muehlenhard, C. L., Friedman, D. E., and Thomas, C. M. 1985. "Is Date Rape Justifiable? The Effects of Dating Activity, Who Initiated, Who Paid, and Men's Attitudes Toward Women." *Psychology of Women Quarterly,* 9, 297–310.

Rhode Island Rape Crisis Center. 1988. *The Question of Rape.* Providence, RI: Author.

Rice, F. P. 1984. *The Adolescent: Development, Relations, and Culture.* Boston: Allyn & Bacon.

Rose, S. 1979. *The Youth Values Project.* Washington, DC: The Population Institute.

Ross, V. M. 1977. "Rape as a Social Problem: A Byproduct of the Feminist Movement." *Social Problems,* 25, 75–89.

Sanday, P. R. 1981. "The Socio-cultural Context of Rape: A Cross-cultural Study." *Journal of Social Issues,* 37, 5–27.

Schwarz, N., and Brand, J. F. 1983. "Effects of Salience of Rape on Sex Role Attitudes, Trust, and Self-esteem in Non-raped Women." *European Journal of Social Psychology,* 13, 71–76.

Tetreault, P. A., and Barnett, M. A. 1987. "Reactions to Stranger and Acquaintance Rape." *Psychology of Women Quarterly,* 11, 353–358.

Thornton, B., Robbins, M. A., and Johnson, J. A. 1981. "Social Perception of the Rape Victim's Culpability: The Influence of Respondent's Personal-Environmental Causal Attribution Tendencies." *Human Relations,* 34, 225–237.

Tieger, T. 1981. "Self-rated Likelihood of Raping and the Social Perception of Rape." *Journal of Research in Personality,* 15, 147–158.

Warshaw, R. 1988. *I Never Called It Rape: The Ms. Report on Recognizing, Fighting, and Surviving Date and Acquaintance Rape.* New York: Harper & Row.

Weis, K., and Borges, S. 1973. "Victimology and Rape: The Case of the Legitimate Victim." *Issues in Criminology,* 8, 71–115.

Williams, L. S. 1984. "The Classic Rape: When Do Victims Report?" *Social Problems,* 31, 459–467.

22

Realities and Mythologies of Rape

Neil Gilbert
University of California, Berkeley

According to the alarming accounts of sexual assault by certain feminist groups, about one out of every two women will be a victim of rape or attempted rape an average of twice in her life, one-third will have been sexually abused as children, and many more will suffer other forms of sexual molestation. These claims are based on figures from several studies, among which the *Ms.* Magazine Campus Project on Sexual Assault, directed by Mary Koss, and Diana Russell's survey of sexual exploitation are the most extensive, most widely disseminated, and most frequently cited.

Both studies were funded by the National Institute of Mental Health, giving them the imprimatur of endorsement by a respected federal agency. Often quoted in newspapers and journals, on television, and during the 1991 Senate hearings on sexual assault, the findings from these studies have gained a certain degree of authority by process of repetition. Most of the time, however, those who cite the research findings take them at face value without an understanding of where the numbers come from or what they represent.

Prefaced by sophisticated discussions of the intricate research methods employed, the findings are presented in a blizzard of data, supported by a few convincing cases and numerous references to lesser known studies. But footnotes do not a scholar make, and the value of quantitative findings depends upon how accurately the research variables are measured, how well the sample is drawn, and the analysis of the data. Despite the respected funding source, frequent media acknowledgment, and an aura of scientific respectability, a close examination of the two most prominent studies on rape reveals serious flaws that cast grave doubt on their credibility.

Reprinted from *Society*, Vol. 29 (May/June 1992), pp. 4–10. Copyright © 1992 by Transaction Publishers.

THE KOSS STUDY

The *Ms.* study directed by Koss surveyed 6159 students at thirty-two colleges. As Koss operationally defines the problem, 27 percent of the female college students in her study had been victims of rape (15 percent) or attempted rape (12 percent) an average of two times between the ages of fourteen and twenty-one. Using the same survey questions, which she claims represent a strict legal description of the crime, Koss calculates that during a twelve-month period 16.6 percent of all college women were victims of rape or attempted rape and that more than one-half of these victims were assaulted twice. If victimization continued at this annual rate over four years, one would expect well over half of all college women to suffer an incident of rape or attempted rape during that period, and more than one-quarter of them to be victimized twice.

There are several reasons for serious researchers to question the magnitude of sexual assault conveyed by the *Ms.* findings. To begin with, a notable discrepancy exists between Koss's definition of rape and the way most women she labeled as victims interpreted their experiences. When asked directly, 73 percent of the students whom Koss categorized as victims of rape did not think that they had been raped. This discrepancy is underscored by the subsequent behavior of a high proportion of identified victims, forty-two percent of whom had sex again with the man who supposedly raped them. Of those categorized as victims of attempted rape, 35 percent later had sex with their purported offender.

Rape and attempted rape were operationally defined in the *Ms.* study by five questions, three of which referred to the threat or use of "some degree of physical force." The other two questions, however, asked: "Have you had a man attempt sexual intercourse (get on top of you, attempt to insert his penis) when you didn't want to by giving you alcohol or drugs, but intercourse did not occur? Have you had sexual intercourse when you didn't want to because a man gave you alcohol or drugs?" Forty-four percent of all the women identified as victims of rape and attempted rape in the previous year were so labeled because they responded positively to these awkward and vaguely worded questions. What does having sex "because" a man gives you drugs or alcohol signify? A positive response does not indicate whether duress, intoxication, force, or the threat of force were present; whether the woman's judgment or control were substantially impaired; or whether the man purposely got the woman drunk to prevent her from resisting his sexual advances. It could mean that a woman was trading sex for drugs or that a few drinks lowered the respondent's inhibitions and she consented to an act she later regretted. Koss assumes that a positive answer signifies the respondent engaged in sexual intercourse against her will because she was intoxicated to the point of being unable to deny consent (and that the man had administered the alcohol for this purpose). While the item could have been clearly worded to denote "intentional incapacitation of the victim," as the question stands it would require a mind reader to detect whether an affirmative response corresponds to a legal definition of rape.

Finally, a vast disparity exists between the *Ms.* study findings and the rates of rape and attempted rape that come to the attention of various authorities on college campuses. The number of rapes formally reported to the police on major college campuses is remarkably low—two to five incidents a year in schools with thousands of women. It is generally agreed that many rape victims do not report their ordeal because of the embarrassment and frequently callous treatment at the hands of the police. Over the last decade, however, rape crisis counseling and supportive services have been established on most major campuses. Highly sensitive to the social and psychological violations of rape, these services offer a sympathetic environment in which victims may obtain assistance without having to make official a report to the police. While these services usually minister to more victims than report to the local police, the numbers remain conspicuously low compared to the incidence of rape and attempted rape on college campuses as Koss defines the problem.

Applying Koss's finding of an annual incidence rate of 166 in 1000 women (each victimized an average of 1.5 times) to the population of 14,000 female students at the University of California at Berkeley in 1990, for example, one would expect about 2000 women to have experienced 3000 rapes or attempted rapes in that year. On the Berkeley campus, two rapes were reported to the police in 1990, and between forty and eighty students sought assistance from the campus rape counseling service. While this represents a serious problem, its dimensions (three to six cases in 1000) are a fraction of those (166 cases in 1000) claimed by the *Ms.* study.

What accounts for these discrepancies? Koss offers several explanations, some of which appear to derive from new data or additional analysis. Therefore it is important to distinguish between the data originally reported in 1987 and 1988 and later versions of the findings. The findings from the *Ms.* study were originally described in three articles, one by Koss and two co-authors in a 1987 issue of the *Journal of Consulting and Clinical Psychology,* the second (an expanded version of this article) authored by Koss as a chapter in the 1988 book *Rape and Sexual Assault* (edited by Ann Burgess), and the third by Koss and three co-authors in a 1988 issue of the *Psychology of Women Quarterly.* Also published in 1988, was Robin Warshaw's book, *I Never Called It Rape: The Ms. Report on Recognizing, Fighting, and Surviving Date and Acquaintance Rape,* with an afterward by Koss describing the research methods used in the *Ms.* project on which the book was based.

Two articles reported that only 27 percent of the students whom Koss classified as rape victims believed they had been raped. The third article in the *Psychology of Women Quarterly* (1988) provided additional data on how all these supposed victims labeled their experience. The findings reported here indicated that: (1) 11 percent of the students said they "don't feel victimized"; (2) 49 percent labeled the experience "miscommunication"; (3) 14 percent labeled it, "crime, but not rape"; and (4) 27 percent said it was "rape."

Although there was no indication that other data might have been available on this question, three years later a surprisingly different distribution of responses is put forth. In answer to questions raised about the fact that most victims did not think they had been raped, Koss reported in the *Los Angeles Daily Journal* (July 17, 1991) that the students labeled as victims viewed the incident as follows: "One-quarter thought it was rape, one-quarter thought it was some kind of crime but did not believe it qualified as rape, one-quarter thought it was sexual abuse but did not think it qualified as a crime, and one-quarter did not feel victimized."

In a later paper, "Rape on Campus: Facing the Facts," the gist of these new findings was revised, with Koss recounting: "One-quarter thought it was some kind of crime, but did not realize it qualified as rape; one-quarter thought it was serious sexual abuse, but did not know it qualified as a crime."

These inconsistencies in the reported findings aside, the additional data are difficult to interpret. If one-quarter thought their incidents involved a crime, but not rape, what kind of crime did they have in mind? Were they referring to illegal activity at the time such as drinking under age or taking drugs? Despite Koss's elaboration on the data originally reported, at least one version of the findings reveal that 60 percent of the students either did not feel victimized or thought the incident was a case of miscommunication. Although in the second version many more students assessed the sexual encounter in negative terms, the fact remains that 73 percent did not think they were raped.

Concerning the 42 percent of purported victims who had sex afterwards with their supposed assailants, again new data appear to have surfaced. Describing these findings in her chapter in *Rape and Sexual Assault,* Koss notes: "Surprisingly, 42 percent of the women indicated that they had sex again with the offender on a later occasion, but it is not known if this was forced or voluntary; most relationships (87 percent) did eventually break up subsequent to the victimization." Three years later, in a letter to the *Wall Street Journal* (July 25, 1991), Koss is no longer surprised by this finding and evidently has new information revealing that when the students had sex again with the offenders on a later occasion they were raped a second time and that the relationship broke up not "eventually" (as do most college relationships), but immediately after the second rape.

Referring to this group's behavior, Koss explains: "Many victims reacted to the first rape with self-blame and thought that if they tried harder to be clear they could influence the man's behavior. Only after the second rape did they realize the problem was the man, not themselves. Afterwards, 87 percent of the women ended the relationship with the man who raped them." Koss also suggests that since many students were sexually inexperienced, they "lacked familiarity with what consensual intercourse should be like."

These explanations are not entirely convincing. It is hard to imagine that many twenty-one year old college women, even if sexually inexperienced, are unable to judge if a sexual encounter is consensual. As for the victims blaming themselves and believing they might influence the man's behavior if they tried harder the second time, Koss offers no data from her survey to substantiate this reasoning. Although research indicates that victims of rape tend to blame themselves, there is no evidence that this induces them to have sex again with their assailant. One might note that there are cases of battered wives who stay on with their husbands under insufferable circumstances. But it is not apparent that the battered wife syndrome applies to a large proportion of female college students.

With regard to the operational definition of rape used in the *Ms.* study and described in the earlier reports, Koss continues to claim that the study measures the act of "rape legally defined as penetration against consent through the use of force, or when the victim was purposely incapacitated with alcohol or other drugs." No explanation is offered for how the researcher detects the "intentional incapacitation of the victim" from affirmative answers to questions such as: "Did you have unwanted sex because a man gave you alcohol?" Although these responses account for about 40 percent of the incidents classified as rape and attempted rape, when describing the study to the Senate Judiciary Committee and in other writings, Koss's examples of typical items used to define rape do not include these questions.

Reviewing the research methodology for the *Ms.* survey in *Rape and Sexual Assault* (1988) and the *Journal of Consulting and Clinical Psychology* (1987), Koss explains that reliability and validity studies conducted in 1985 on the ten-item Sexual Experience Survey (SES) instrument showed that few of the female respondents misinterpreted the questions on rape. A serious question arises, however, whether the validity study cited by Koss was conducted on the version of the SES instrument that was actually used in the *Ms.* survey or on the original version of this instrument, which differed significantly from the one the *Ms.* findings are based on. The Sexual Experience Survey instrument originally designed by Koss and Oros, and reported on in a 1982 issue of the *Journal of Consulting and Clinical Psychology* contained none of the questions dealing with rape or attempted rape "because a man gave you alcohol or drugs."

In 1985, Koss and Gidycz reported (again in *Consulting and Clinical Psychology*) on the assessment of this instrument's validity, which they said indicates that: "To explore the veracity of the self-reported sexual experiences, the Sexual Experiences Survey (original wording) was administered to approximately 4000 students." Although Koss cites this report as evidence of the *Ms.* study instrument's validity, if the SES as originally worded was used, it is not at all clear that the assessment of validity included the vague items on "intentional incapacitation," which were absent from the original version of the SES instrument.

Finally, the vast discrepancy between *Ms.* study figures and the number of students who generally seek rape counselling or report incidents of rape to authorities on college campuses is accounted for by the assertion that most college women who are sexually violated by an acquaintance do not recognize themselves as victims of rape. According to Koss, "many people do not realize that legal definitions of rape make no distinctions about the relationship between victim and offender." Findings from the Bureau of Justice Statistics suggest that the crime of being raped by an acquaintance may not be all that difficult to comprehend; in recent years 33 to 45 percent of the women who said they were raped identified their assailant as an acquaintance.

In support of the *Ms.* project findings, Koss invokes additional studies as sources of independent verification. Some of these use different definitions of forced sexual behavior (including verbal persuasion and psychological coercion) and involve samples too small or nonrepresentative for serious estimates of the size of the problem. Others are referred to without explanation or critical examination. For example, Koss cites Yegidis's findings in the *Journal of Sex Education and Therapy* (1986), which show a prevalence rate of rape for college students in the range reported by the *Ms.* study, as supportive evidence. But Yegidis defined rape as forced oral sex or intercourse, where the use of "force" included verbal persuasion. As she explains: "This study showed that most of the sexual encounters were forced through verbal persuasion-protestations by the male to 'go further' because of sexual need, arousal, or love." According to this definition, the conventional script of nagging and pleading "everyone does it," "if you really loved me, you'd do it," "I need it," "you will like it," is transformed into a version of rape.

Claiming that the *Ms.* survey's estimates of rape prevalence "are well-replicated in other studies," Koss refers to Craig's discerning review of the literature to confirm the consistency of prevalence data on college students. This is a curious citation, since Craig in fact is of a different opinion. Analyzing the problems of definition in *Clinical Psychology Review* (1990), she notes that they "vary from use of force to threat of force, to use of manipulative tactics such as falsely professing love, threatening to leave the woman stranded, or attempting to intoxicate the woman." Even when studies use the same general definitions, their authors often develop idiosyncratic measures to operationalize the terms. All of this leads Craig to conclude "that this lack of consistency limits the comparability of studies and makes replication of results difficult."

THE RUSSELL STUDY

Moving beyond the experiences of college students, Diana Russell's study is another major source often quoted as evidence that rape has reached, as she describes it, "epidemic proportions throughout society." Reported in several books, including *Rape in Marriage* (1982) and *Sexual Exploitation* (1984), Russell's findings indicate that 38 to 54 percent of the women sampled were sexually abused as children, 44 percent were victims of rape (26 percent) or attempted rape (18 percent) an average of twice in their lives, and many other women suffered experiences in marriage that, if not rape, were very close to it.

As for the latter, if mutually desired intercourse and rape are placed at either end of a continuum, Russell explains, "our study suggests that a considerable amount of marital sex is probably closer to the rape end of the continuum." Indeed, beyond marital sex, Russell suggests that according to this view "much of what passes for normal heterosexual intercourse would be seen as close to rape." Although this analysis of sex relations is not as censorious as Andrea Dworkin's, for whom all heterosexual sex is rape, it would seem to lean in that direction.

There are several fundamental problems with Russell's survey, which is based on interviews with a group of women in San Francisco. Although serious efforts were made to achieve a random sample of participants, the researchers were able to complete their interviews with only 930 people out of an original sample of 2000. Thirty-six percent of the people contacted refused outright to participate in the study.

As for the other nonparticipants, Russell offers two somewhat different accounts for their inaccessibility. In *Rape in Marriage* she explains: "Because of a high incidence of not-at-homes during the summer months when the interviews were conducted, and because of an unexpectedly large number of households in which no eligible women resided, the original sample of two thousand drawn by the methods described proved insufficient for obtaining one thousand completed interviews." Later, it appears Russell really did not know the number of households ("unexpectedly large") in which no eligible women resided. As she describes the sampling difficulties in *Sexual Exploitation:* "Many of the households that were inaccessible or where no one was at home might have been households without eligible women—there are a large number of all-male households in San Francisco."

In any event, for whatever reasons more than 50 percent of the sample did not participate in the interview survey. The standard textbook criterion recommends that properly executed interview surveys should achieve a completion rate of 80 to 85 percent, which is the range usually required of surveys by Federal agencies. It is highly doubtful that the 930 participants who agreed to be interviewed for Russell's study should be considered a representative random sample of the women in San Francisco.

A more basic problem, however, is that starting with a questionable sample, Russell goes on to claim that her respondents' sexual experiences reflect not only those of all women in San Francisco, but are representative of the entire female population of the United States. A brief disclaimer to the effect that generalizing from the San Francisco sample "would be highly speculative," is quickly forgotten as, after adjusting her findings for age-specific probabilities, Russell concludes: "It is indeed shocking that 46 percent of American women are likely to be victims of attempted rape or completed rape sometimes in their lives."

This conclusion she continues to share with the media. She also notes that these victims are likely to be attacked an average of two times. The fact that only 31 percent of the women in Russell's sample were married compared to a 63 percent marital rate nationally is one of many reasons why this national estimate drawn from the sexual experiences of the San Francisco sample is not only highly speculative, but scientifically groundless. Russell offers a more detailed analysis using the San Francisco findings to extrapolate, not the lifetime probability, but the national incidence of rape and attempted rape in 1978. As she explains in *Sexual Exploitation:*

> The incidence figure for rape in the Russell survey cited above was 35 per 1000 females. (This includes cases of rape and attempted rape that occurred to residents of San Francisco, both inside and outside the city.) This is *24 times higher* than the 1.71 per 1000 females reported by the Uniform Crime Reports. *(emphasis in original)*

Based on this calculation, the 1978 Uniform Crime Report's figure of 67,131 for all cases of rape and attempted rape in the United States is then multiplied by twenty-four, which yields Russell's national estimate of 1.6 million incidents for that year.

Faulty logic and poor arithmetic invalidate this analysis. First, the initial calculation (ironically italicized) is incorrect. The San Francisco rate of 35 per 1000 is 20.5 times (not 24 times) higher than the Uniform Crime Report's 1.71 per 1000. Ignoring, for a moment, this arithmetical error, the logic of the second calculation assumes a correspondence between the Uniform Crime Report rates for San Francisco and the nation at large. If Russell's sample had an incidence rate twenty-four times higher than the Uniform Crime Report's rate for San Francisco, in that case one need only multiply the Uniform Crime Report's national rate by twenty-four to project the local difference on a national scale. However, those who study this subject know very well that the reported rates of rape are considerably higher for metropolitan areas than for the national population. Indeed, the Uniform Crime Report's total of 67,131 cases of rape and attempted rape in 1978 amounted to a national rate of .6 per 1000 females, which was about one-third the rate of 1.7 per 1000 females it showed for San Francisco. Thus, if we include the initial arithmetic error, Russell's national estimate of the incidence of sexual assault exaggerates by about 350 percent the figure that would result from simply an accurate reading of her own facts.

ADVOCACY RESEARCH

The *Ms.* study by Koss and Russell's survey of sexual exploitation are highly sophisticated examples of advocacy research. Elaborate research methods are employed, under the guise of social science, to persuade the public and policy makers that a problem is vastly larger than commonly recognized. This is done in several ways: (1) by measuring a problem so broadly that it forms a vessel into which almost any human difficulty can be poured; (2) by measuring a group highly impacted with the problem and then projecting the findings to society-at-large; (3) by asserting that a variety of smaller studies and reports with different problems definitions, methodologies of diverse quality, and varying results, form a cumulative block of evidence in support of current findings; and (4) by a combination of the above.

Advocacy research is a phenomenon not unique to feminist studies of rape. It is practiced in a wide variety of substantive problem areas and supported by groups that, as Peter Rossi suggests, share an "ideological imperative," which maintains that findings politically acceptable to the advocacy community are more important than the quality of research from which they are derived. Playing fast and loose with the facts is justifiable in the service of a noble cause, just as is condemning or ignoring data and sentiments that challenge conventional wisdom. Denounced for expressing objectionable sentiments, for example, folk singer Holly Dunn's hit, "Maybe I Mean Yes—When I Say No" was clearly out of tune with the feminist mantra, "no means no." The controversy over these lyrics ignored Muehlenhard and Hollabaugh's inconvenient findings that 39 percent of the 610 college women they surveyed admitted to having said no to sexual advances when they really meant yes and fully intended to have their way.

Although advocacy studies do little to elevate the standards of social science research, they sometimes serve a useful purpose in bringing grave problems to public attention. No matter how it is measured, rape is a serious problem that creates an immense amount of human suffering. One might say that even if the rape research magnifies this problem in order to raise public consciousness, it is being done for a good cause, and in any case the difference is only a matter of degree. So why make an issue of the numbers?

The issue is not that advocacy studies simply overstate the incidence of legally defined rape, but the extent to which this occurs and what it means. After all, the difference between boiling and freezing is "only a matter of degree." The tremendous gap between estimates of rape and attempted rape that emerge from data collected annually by the Bureau of Justice Statistics (BJS) and the figures reported in advocacy studies have a critical bearing on our understanding of the issue at stake.

The BJS surveys, actually conducted by the Census Bureau, interview a random sample of about 62,000 households every six months. The confidentiality of responses is protected by federal law and response rates amount to 96 percent of eligible units. The interview schedule asks a series of screening questions such as: Did anyone threaten to beat you up or threaten you with a knife gun or some other weapon? Did anyone try to attack you in some other way? Did you call the police to report something that happened to you that you thought was a crime? Did anything happen to you which you thought was a crime, but you did not report to the police?

A positive response to any of these screening items is followed up with questions like: What actually happened? How were you threatened? How did the offender attack you? What injuries did you suffer? When, where did it happen, what did you do, and so forth.

As a guide to trends in sexual assault, the BJS data show that rates of rape and attempted rape declined by about 30 percent between 1978 and 1988. As for recent experience, BJS findings reveal that 1.2 women in 1000 over twelve years of age were victims of rape or attempted rape. This amounted to approximately 135,000 female victims in 1989. No trivial number, this annual figure translates into a lifetime prevalence rate of roughly 5 to 7 percent, which suggests that one woman out of fourteen is likely to experience rape or attempted rape sometime in her life. As do other victimization surveys, the BJS studies have problems of subject recall, definition, and measurement, which, as Koss and others have pointed out, lead to underestimation of the amount of sexual assault.

Assuming that the BJS survey underestimated the problem by 50 percent—that is, that it missed one out of every two cases of rape or attempted rape in the sample—the lifetime prevalence rate would rise to approximately 10 to 14 percent. Although an enormous level of sexual assault, at that rate the BJS estimates would still be dwarfed by the findings of Koss and Russell's studies, which suggest that one in two women will be victimized an average of twice in their life.

This brings us to the crux of the issue, that is, the huge differences between federal estimates and advocacy research findings have implications that go beyond matters of degree in measuring the size of the problem. If almost half of all women will suffer an average of two incidents of rape or attempted rape sometime in their lives, one is ineluctably driven to conclude that most men are rapists. "The truth that must be faced," according to Russell, "is that this culture's notion of masculinity—particularly as it is applied to male sexuality—predisposes men to violence, to rape, to sexually harass, and to sexually abuse children."

In a similar vein, Koss claims that her findings support the view that sexual violence against women "rests squarely in the middle of what our culture defines as 'normal' interaction between men and women." Catherine MacKinnon, one of the leading feminists in the rape crisis movement, offers a vivid rendition of the theme that rape is a social disease afflicting most men. Writing in the *New York Times* (December 15, 1991), she advises that when men charged with the crime of rape come to trial, the court should ask "did this member of a group sexually trained to woman-hating aggression commit this particular act of woman-hating sexual aggression?"

Advocacy research not only promulgates the idea that most men are rapists, it provides a form of "scientific" legitimacy for promoting social programs and individual behaviors that act on this idea. When asked if college women should view every man they see as a potential rapist, a spokeswoman for the student health services at the University of California, Berkeley told the *Oakland Tribune* (May 30, 1991), "I'm not sure that would be a negative thing." This echoes the instruction supplied in one of the most popular college guidebooks on how to prevent acquaintance rape. "Since you can't tell who has the potential for rape by simply looking," the manual warns, "be on your guard with every man."

These experts on date rape advise college women to take their own cars on dates or to have a back-up network of friends ready to pick them up, to stay sober, to go only to public places, to be assertive, to inform the man in advance what the sexual limits will be that evening, and to prepare for the worst by taking a course in self-defense beforehand. Separately, some of the instructions, such as staying sober, are certainly well advised. Collectively, however, this bundle of cautions transmits the unspoken message that dating men is a very dangerous undertaking.

Beyond seeking courses in self-defense, the implications drawn from advocacy research sometimes recommend more extreme measures. Last year, at a public lecture on "The Epidemic of Sexual Violence Against Women," Diana Russell was asked by a member of her largely feminist audience whether, in light of the ever-present danger, women should start carrying guns to protect themselves against men. Stating that personal armament was a good idea, but that women should probably take lessons to learn how to hit their target, Russell's response was greeted with loud applause.

Not all feminists, or members of the rape crisis movement, agree with the view that all men are predisposed to be rapists. Gillian Greensite, founder of the Rape Prevention Education program at the University of California, Santa Cruz, writes that the seriousness of this crime "is being undermined by the growing tendency of some feminists to label all heterosexual miscommunication and insensitivity as acquaintance rape." (One is reminded that 50 percent of the students whom Koss defined as victims of rape labeled their experience as "miscommunication.") This tendency, Greensite observes, "is already creating a climate of fear on campuses, straining relations between males and females."

Heightened confusion and strained relations between men and women are not the only dysfunctional consequences of advocacy research that inflates the incidence of rape to a level that indicts most men. According to Koss's data, rape is an act that most educated women do not recognize as such when it has happened to them, and after which almost half of the victims go back for more. To characterize this type of sexual encounter as rape trivializes the trauma and pain suffered by the many women who are true victims of this crime, and may ultimately make it more difficult to convict their assailants. By exaggerating the statistics on rape, advocacy research conveys an interpretation of the problem that advances neither mutual respect between the sexes nor reasonable dialogue about assaultive sexual behavior.

CONCLUSION

It is difficult to criticize advocacy research without giving the impression of caring less about the problem than those engaged in magnifying its size. But one may be deeply concerned about the problem of rape and still wish to see a fair and objective analysis of its dimensions. Advocacy studies have, in their fashion, rung the alarm. Before the rush to arms, a more precise reading of the data is required to draw an accurate bead on this problem and attack it successfully.

23

Bared Buttocks and Federal Cases

ELLEN FRANKEL PAUL
Bowling Green State University

Women in American society are victims of sexual harassment in alarming proportions. Sexual harassment is an inevitable corollary to class exploitation; as capitalists exploit their female subordinates. Male professors, supervisors, and apartment managers in ever increasing numbers take advantage of the financial dependence and vulnerability of women to extract sexual concessions.

These are the assertions that commonly begin discussions of sexual harassment. For reasons that will be adumbrated below, dissent from the prevailing view is long overdue. Three recent episodes will serve to frame this disagreement.

Valerie Craig, an employee of Y & Y Snacks, Inc., joined several co-workers and her supervisor for drinks after work one day in July 1978. Her supervisor drove her home and proposed that they become more intimately acquainted. She refused his invitation for sexual relations, whereupon he said that he would "get even" with her. Ten days after the incident she was fired from her job. She soon filed a complaint of sexual harassment with the Equal Employment Opportunity Commission (EEOC), and the case wound its way through the courts. Craig prevailed, the company was held liable for damages, and she received back pay, reinstatement, and an order prohibiting Y & Y from taking reprisals against her in the future.

Carol Zabowicz, one of only two female forklift operators in a West Bend Co. warehouse, charged that her co-workers over a four year period from 1978–1982 sexually harassed her by such acts as: asking her whether she was wearing a bra; two of the men exposing their buttocks between ten and twenty times; a male co-worker grabbing his crotch and making obscene suggestions or growling; subjecting her to offensive and abusive language; and exhibiting obscene drawings with her initials on them. Zabowicz began to show symptoms of physical and psychological stress, necessitating several

Reprinted from *Society*, Vol. 28 (May/June 1991), pp. 4–7. Copyright © 1991 by Transaction Publishers.

medical leaves, and she filed a sexual harassment complaint with the EEOC. The district court judge remarked that "the sustained, malicious, and brutal harassment meted out . . . was more than merely unreasonable; it was malevolent and outrageous." The company knew of the harassment and took corrective action only after the employee filed a complaint with the EEOC. The company was, therefore, held liable, and Zabowicz was awarded back pay for the period of her medical absence, and a judgment that her rights were violated under the Civil Rights Act of 1964.

On September 17, 1990, Lisa Olson, a sports reporter for *The Boston Herald,* charged five football players of the just-defeated New England Patriots with sexual harassment for making sexually suggestive and offensive remarks to her when she entered their locker room to conduct a post-game interview. The incident amounted to nothing short of "mind rape," according to Olson. After vociferous lamentations in the media, the National Football League fined the team and its players $25,000 each. The National Organization of Women called for a boycott of Remington electric shavers because the owner of the company, Victor Kiam, also owns the Patriots and who allegedly displayed insufficient sensitivity at the time when the episode occurred.

All these incidents are indisputably disturbing. In an ideal world—one needless to say far different from the one that we inhabit or are ever likely to inhabit—women would not be subjected to such treatment in the course of their work. Women, and men as well, would be accorded respect by co-workers and supervisors, their feelings would be taken into account, and their dignity would be left intact. For women to expect reverential treatment in the workplace is utopian, yet they should not have to tolerate outrageous, offensive sexual overtures and threats as they go about earning a living.

One question that needs to be pondered is: What kinds of undesired sexual behavior women should be protected against by law? That is, what kind of actions are deemed so outrageous and violate a woman's rights to such extent that the law should intervene, and what actions should be considered inconveniences of life, to be morally condemned but not adjudicated? A subsidiary question concerns the type of legal remedy appropriate for the wrongs that do require redress. Before directly addressing these questions, it might be useful to diffuse some of the hyperbole adhering to the sexual harassment issue.

Surveys are one source of this hyperbole. If their results are accepted at face value, they lead to the conclusion that women are disproportionately victims of legions of sexual harassers. A poll by the Albuquerque *Tribune* found that nearly 80 percent of the respondents reported that they or someone they knew had been victims of sexual harassment. The Merit Systems Protection Board determined that 42 percent of the women (and 14 percent of men) working for the federal government had experienced some form of unwanted sexual attention between 1985 and 1987, with unwanted "sexual teasing" identified as the most prevalent form. A Defense Department survey found that 64 percent of women in the military (and 17 percent of the men) suffered "uninvited and unwanted sexual attention" within the previous year. The United Methodist Church established that 77 percent of its clergywomen experienced incidents of sexual harassment, with 41 percent of these naming a pastor or colleague as the perpetrator, and 31 percent mentioning church social functions as the setting.

A few caveats concerning polls in general, and these sorts of polls in particular, are worth considering. Pollsters looking for a particular social ill tend to find it, usually in gargantuan proportions. (What fate would lie in store for a pollster who concluded that child abuse, or wife beating, or mistreatment of the elderly had dwindled to the point of negligibility!) Sexual harassment is a notoriously ill-defined and almost infinitely expandable concept, including everything from rape to unwelcome neck massaging, discomfiture upon witnessing sexual overtures directed at others, yelling at and blowing smoke in the ears of female subordinates, and displays of pornographic pictures in the workplace. Defining sexual harassment, as the United Methodists did, as "any sexually related behavior that is unwelcome, offensive or which fails to respect the rights of others," the concept is broad enough to include everything from "unsolicited suggestive looks or leers [or] pressures for dates" to "actual sexual assaults or rapes." Categorizing everything from rape to "looks" as sexual harassment makes us all victims, a state of affairs satisfying to radical feminists, but not very useful for distinguishing serious injuries from the merely trivial.

Yet, even if the surveys exaggerate the extent of sexual harassment, however defined, what they do reflect is a great deal of tension between the sexes. As women in ever increasing numbers entered the workplace in the last two decades, as the women's movement challenged alleged male hegemony and exploitation with ever greater intemperance, and as women entered previously all-male preserves from the board rooms to the coal pits, it is lamentable, but should not be surprising, that this tension sometimes takes sexual form. Not that sexual harassment on the job, in the university, and in other settings is a trivial or insignificant matter, but a sense of proportion needs to be restored and, even more important, distinctions need to be made. In other words, sexual harassment must be de-ideologized. Statements that paint nearly all women as victims and all men and their patriarchal, capitalist system as perpetrators, are ideological fantasy. Ideology blurs the distinction between being injured—being a genuine victim—and merely being offended. An example is this statement by Catharine A. MacKinnon, a law professor and feminist activist:

> Sexual harassment perpetuates the interlocked structure by which women have been kept sexually in thrall to men and at the bottom of the labor market. Two forces of American society converge: men's control over women's sexuality and capital's control over employees' work lives. Women historically have been required to exchange sexual services for material survival, in one form or another. Prostitution and marriage as well as sexual harassment in different ways institutionalize this arrangement.

Such hyperbole needs to be diffused and distinctions need to be drawn. Rape, a nonconsensual invasion of a person's body, is a crime clear and simple. It is a violation of the right to the physical integrity of the body (the right to life, as John Locke or Thomas Jefferson would have put it). Criminal law should and does prohibit rape. Whether it is useful to call rape "sexual harassment" is doubtful, for it makes the latter concept overly broad while trivializing the former.

Intimidation in the workplace of the kind that befell Valerie Craig—that is, extortion of sexual favors by a supervisor from a subordinate by threatening to penalize, fire, or fail to reward—is what the courts term *quid pro quo* sexual harassment. Since the mid-1970s, the federal courts have treated this type of sexual harassment as a form of sex discrimination in employment proscribed under Title VII of the Civil Rights Act of 1964. A plaintiff who prevails against an employer may receive such equitable remedies as reinstatement and back pay, and the court can order the company to prepare and disseminate a policy against sexual harassment. Current law places principal liability on the company, not the harassing supervisor, even when higher management is unaware of the harassment and, thus, cannot take any steps to prevent it.

Quid pro quo sexual harassment is morally objectionable and analogous to extortion: The harasser extorts property (i.e., use of the woman's body) through the leverage of fear for her job. The victim of such behavior should have legal recourse, but serious reservations can be held about rectifying these injustices through the blunt instrument of Title VII. In egregious cases the victim is left less than whole (for back pay will not compensate her for ancillary losses), and no prospects for punitive damages are offered to deter would-be harassers. Even more distressing about Title VII is the fact that the primary target of litigation is not the actual harasser, but rather the employer. This places a double burden on a company. The employer is swindled by the supervisor because he spent his time pursuing sexual gratification and thereby impairing the efficiency of the workplace by mismanaging his subordinates, and the employer must endure lengthy and expensive litigation, pay damages, and suffer loss to its reputation. It would be fairer to both the company and the victim to treat sexual harassment as a tort—that is, as a private wrong or injury for which the court can assess damages. Employers should be held vicariously liable only when they know of an employee's behavior and do not try to redress it.

As for the workplace harassment endured by Carol Zabowicz—the bared buttocks, obscene portraits, and so on—that too should be legally redressable. Presently, such incidents also fall under the umbrella of Title VII, and are termed hostile environment sexual harassment, a category accepted later than *quid pro quo* and with some judicial reluctance. The main problem with this category is that it has proven too elastic: Cases have reached the courts based on everything from off-color jokes to unwanted, persistent sexual advances by co-workers. A new tort of sexual harassment would handle these cases better. Only instances above a certain threshold of egregiousness or outrageousness would be actionable. In other words, the behavior that the plaintiff found offensive would also have to be offensive to the proverbial "reasonable man" of the tort law. That is, the behavior would have to be objectively injurious rather than merely subjectively offensive. The defendant would be the actual harasser not the company, unless it knew about the problem and failed to act.

Victims of scatological jokes, leers, unwanted offers of dates, and other sexual annoyances would no longer have their day in court.

A distinction must be restored between morally offensive behavior and behavior that causes serious harm. Only the latter should fall under the jurisdiction of criminal or tort law. Do we really want legislators and judges delving into our most intimate private lives, deciding when a look is a leer, and when a leer is a Civil Rights Act offense? Do we really want courts deciding, as one recently did, whether a school principal's disparaging remarks about a female school district administrator was sexual harassment and, hence, a breach of Title VII, or merely the act of a spurned and vengeful lover? Do we want judges settling disputes such as the one that arose at a car dealership after a female employee turned down a male co-worker's offer of a date and his colleagues retaliated by calling her offensive names and embarrassing her in front of customers? Or another case in which a female shipyard worker complained of an "offensive working environment" because of the prevalence of pornographic material on the docks? Do we want the state to prevent or compensate us for any behavior that someone might find offensive? Should people have a legally enforceable right not to be offended by others? At some point, the price for such protection is the loss of both liberty and privacy rights.

Workplaces are breeding grounds of envy, personal grudges, infatuation, and jilted loves, and beneath a fairly high threshold of outrageousness, these travails should be either suffered in silence, complained of to higher management, or left behind as one seeks other employment. No one, female or male, can expect to enjoy a working environment that is perfectly stress-free, or to be treated always and by everyone with kindness and respect. To the extent that sympathetic judges have encouraged women to seek monetary compensation for slights and annoyances, they have not done them a great service. Women need to develop a thick skin in order to survive and prosper in the workforce. It is patronizing to think that they need to be recompensed by male judges for seeing a few pornographic pictures on a wall. By their efforts to extend sexual harassment charges to even the most trivial behavior, the radical feminists send a message that women are not resilient enough to ignore the run-of-the-mill, churlish provocation from male coworkers. It is difficult to imagine a suit by a longshoreman complaining of mental stress due to the display of nude male centerfolds by female co-workers. Women cannot expect to have it both ways: equality where convenient, but special dispensations when the going gets rough. Equality has its price and that price may include unwelcome sexual advances, irritating and even intimidating sexual jests, and lewd and obnoxious colleagues.

Egregious acts—sexual harassment per se—must be legally redressable. Lesser but not trivial offenses, whether at the workplace or in other more social settings, should be considered moral lapses for which the offending party receives opprobrium, disciplinary warnings, or penalties, depending on the setting and the severity. Trivial offenses, dirty jokes, sexual overtures, and sexual innuendoes do make many women feel intensely discomfited, but, unless they become outrageous through persistence or content, these too should be taken as part of life's annoyances. The perpetrators should be either endured, ignored, rebuked, or avoided, as circumstances and personal inclination dictate. Whether Lisa Olson's experience in the locker room of the Boston Patriots falls into the second or third category is debatable. The media circus triggered by the incident was certainly out of proportion to the event.

As the presence of women on road gangs, construction crews, and oil rigs becomes a fact of life, the animosities and tensions of this transition period are likely to abate gradually. Meanwhile, women should "lighten up," and even dispense a few risqué barbs of their own, a sure way of taking the fun out of it for offensive male bores.

PART 7

Economic Deviance

Economic deviance is popularly referred to as "property crime." Four sociologists were invited to analyze for this reader the type of economic deviance they have done research on. But first let us provide you with some background information on each type of economic deviance.

Since the early 1980s, property crimes such as robbery, larceny, or auto theft have increased significantly, but burglary has declined. Nevertheless, the number of break-ins is still great enough to cause concern among many Americans. According to a recent ABC News/*Washington Post* poll, nearly a third of adults surveyed said that they "worry a great deal" about burglary.[1] In the first article, "Burglary: The Offender's Perspective," Paul Cromwell enters the experiential world of his subjects to learn how they execute their crime.

Another economic deviance, shoplifting, is much more prevalent than burglary. To avoid frightening away their customers, who would feel uncomfortable mingling with thieves, store owners euphemistically refer to shoplifting as "shrinkage." Whatever it is called, shoplifting has become a serious problem in the United States—it costs American stores up to $13.5 billion a year. This is roughly equivalent to 2 percent of their total merchandise, compared with 1.5 percent for shops in Canada and less than 1 percent in Japan.[2] These figures may not sound like much, but in the low-profit-margin business of retailing, 4 or 5 percent loss of sales can bankrupt some stores. Shoplifting also exacts a cost on honest customers, who have to pay more for their purchases because prices are routinely raised to reduce the loss from shrinkage. In the second reading, "Understanding Shoplifting," Lloyd Klemke analyzes various aspects of this deviance, offering both objective and subjective data on shoplifters' age, gender, motivations for the offense, and the like.

More fascinating to the general public is organized crime. It is after all a widely popular subject for the press, television, movies, and novels. Unfortunately it is often portrayed unrealistically in the media. On the one hand, organized criminals are sensationalized as the "grim reapers," the "merchants of death," and the "brotherhood of evil." On the other hand, they are romanticized as men of honor, courage, and toughness. Thus, they have

---

[1] Vic Sussman, "To Stop a Thief," *U.S. News & World Report,* March 30, 1992, p. 55.

[2] Lloyd W. Klemke, *The Sociology of Shoplifting: Boosters and Snitches Today* (Westport, CT: Praeger, 1992), p. 9; "Shoplifting in America," *The Economist,* January 19, 1991, p. 65.

become legends in their own land, regarded by the public as simultaneously villains and heroes. Aside from this ambivalence about mobsters, their portrayal as larger than life has led many people to sense that the gangsters are far removed from us. Actually, organized crime originates largely from the same social conditions that shape our lives. It is an American way of life, a way of realizing the American Dream. In the third reading, "Ethnic Succession in American Organized Crime," James O'Kane presents an objective, historical analysis of how organized crime serves as a vehicle of upward mobility for one poor ethnic group after another.

Unlike other economic deviances, white-collar crimes is more difficult to define. Consider, for example, the case of Walter Krug, age 37, who was killed in his 1988 Chevy pickup truck on a highway near Stanton, Texas. When another pickup hit him from the side, the impact ruptured the gas tank of Krug's vehicle, shooting out fuel that exploded into a huge fireball. Krug was one of more than 300 people killed since 1973 in collisions involving exploding gas tanks in similar pickups manufactured by GM. According to GM documents released in November 1992, the automaker had known since 1983 that the fuel tanks could be made much less vulnerable to side-impact collision. But the company's executives had never tried to do anything about it. By 1992 they even refused to recall some 5 million dangerous GM pickups.[3] Obviously, the auto executives did not believe that they had committed any crime. To sociologists, a crime had been committed. But who were the offenders? The executives alone? Could the company, a nonhuman, be the offender? Gilbert Geis discusses these definitional problems, along with theories of white-collar crime, in the fourth article, "White-Collar Crime."

[3] Thomas McCarroll, "Was GM Reckless?" *Time,* November 30, 1992, p. 61; David Margolick, "Verdict Against G.M. Fuels Debate on Huge Punitive Jury Awards," *New York Times,* February 6, 1993, p. 6.

24

Burglary: The Offender's Perspective

PAUL CROMWELL
University of Miami

Burglary is easy, man. I've done about 500 [burglaries] and only been convicted one time.

BILLY, A JUVENILE BURGLAR

Why am I a burglar? It's easy money. . . . Beats working!

ROBERT, A 20-YEAR-OLD BURGLAR

These burglars are essentially correct in their appraisal of the benefits and risks associated with burglary. Burglary constitutes one of the most prevalent predatory crimes, with an estimated 5.1 million burglary offenses committed in 1990, resulting in monetary losses estimated to be over $3.4 billion annually. Yet only about one-half of all burglaries are even reported to the police (Bureau of Justice Statistics, 1991). More alarming still, U.S. Department of Justice statistics reveal that less than 15 percent of all reported burglaries are cleared by arrest (Uniform Crime Reports, 1991). Consequently, burglary has been the subject of a great deal of research in the hope that understanding would lead to the development of effective prevention measures and ultimately to reduction in the incidence of burglary (Lynch, 1990).

THEORETICAL PERSPECTIVE

Here I will report findings from a study of burglars and burglary as seen through the perspective of the offenders themselves. The study addresses several issues critical to the understanding of burglary and to the consequent development of burglary prevention and control strategies. Among these are: (1) How do residential burglars choose targets? and (2) What determines a burglar's perception of a particular site as a vulnerable target?

This article was specifically written for this reader, with portions drawn from Paul Cromwell, James N. Olson, and D'Aunn W. Avary, *Breaking and Entering: An Ethnographic Analysis of Burglary* (Newbury Park, CA: Sage, 1991).

Such issues are based on the theory that the commission of a crime is primarily a product of opportunity. Thus, how burglars choose targets and make other relevant decisions has much to do with the opportunity for carrying out burglary. In fact, several researchers have concluded that the majority of burglaries resulted from exploitation of opportunity rather than careful, rational planning (Scarr, 1973; Rengert and Wasilchick, 1985, 1989; Cromwell, Olson, and Avary, 1991). The assumption is that offenders develop a sensitivity to the opportunities in everyday life for illicit gain, and that burglars see criminal opportunity in situations where others might not. This "alert opportunism" (Shover, 1971) allows them to rapidly recognize and take advantage of potential criminal opportunities. Their unique perspective toward the world results from learning experiences that have sensitized them to events ignored by most. Just as an architect looking at a house notes its functional, technological, and aesthetic qualities, burglars perceive it in terms of its vulnerability to break-in and potential for gain. They do not simply see an open window, but the chance for covert entry and a "fast buck." These perceptual processes are almost automatic and are as much a part of the tools of the burglar as a pry bar or a window jimmy.

METHOD

The Sample

Thirty *active* burglars in an urban area of 250,000 population in a southwestern state were recruited as research subjects (hereinafter referred to as informants) using a snowball sampling procedure. They were promised complete anonymity and a "referral fee" of $50 for each active burglar referred by them and accepted for the study. They were also paid a stipend of $50 for each interview session. The initial three informants were introduced to the researchers by police burglary detectives who had been asked to recommend "burglars who would be candid and cooperate with the study."

The final sample consisted of 27 men and 3 women, of whom 10 were White, 9 Hispanic, and 11 African American. The mean age of these informants was 25 years with the range 16 to 43.

Procedure

The procedure consisted of extensive interviews and "ride alongs" during which informants were asked to reconstruct burglaries they had previously committed and to evaluate sites burglarized by other informants in the study. During these sessions, previously burglarized residences were visited, evaluated, and rated on their attractiveness as burglary targets. Informants were also asked to select sites in the same neighborhood that they considered too risky as targets and to explain why they were less vulnerable than those previously burglarized. At each site informants were asked to rate the "hypothetical" vulnerability of the site to burglary on a scale of 0 to 10. A rating of "0" meant

"Under the circumstances that are present now, I would not burglarize this residence." A rating of "10" meant "This is a very attractive and vulnerable target and I would definitely take steps to burglarize it right now." Informants were told that a rating of "5" was an "average" score. At the conclusion of the study, informants had participated in as many as nine sessions and had evaluated up to thirty previously burglarized and high-risk sites. Four hundred sixty previously burglarized and high-risk sites were evaluated. Each session was tape recorded and verbatim transcripts made.

FINDINGS

Motivation

Almost every informant used some of his or her proceeds from burglary to buy food or clothing and to pay for shelter, transportation, and other licit needs. But the greatest percentage of proceeds went toward the purchase of drugs and alcohol and for the activity the burglars loosely labeled "partying." In fact, most informants stressed their need for money to fulfill these needs as the *primary* motivation for their burglaries. Only one informant reported a primary need for money to purchase something other than alcohol or drugs or for partying.

Second in importance was the need for money to maintain a "fast, expensive life." Keeping up appearances was stressed by many as a critical concern. One young burglar reported:

> The ladies, they like a dude that's got good clothes. You gotta look good and you gotta have bread. Me, I'm always looking good.

Katz (1988) has noted that young people may find certain property crimes (joyriding, vandalism, burglary, shoplifting) appealing, independent of material gain or esteem from peers. He categorized these as "sneaky crimes that frequently thrill their practioneers" (p.53). Similarly, in the present study, almost every informant mentioned excitement and thrills; however, only a few would commit a burglary for that purpose only. Like Reppetto (1974), we concluded that the younger, less experienced burglars were more prone to commit crimes for the thrill and excitement.

Time of Burglary

Rengert and Wasilchick (1985, 1989) found that burglars work during periods when residences are left unguarded. We found the same thing. Our informants stated they preferred to work between 9:00 and 11:00 A.M. and in midafternoon. Most organized their working hours around school hours, particularly during the times when parents (usually mothers) took children to school and picked them up after school. Several told us that they waited "until the wife left to take the kids to school or to shopping." Most stated that they did not do burglaries on Saturday because most people were home then. Only a small number ($n = 3$) of burglars in our study committed burglaries at night. Most preferred to commit their crimes during hours when they expected people to be at work and out of the home. Those who did night-time burglary usually knew the victims and their schedules or took advantage of people being away from home in the evening.

Inside Information

Burglars often work with "inside men" who have access to potential targets and advise the burglar about things to steal. They may also provide such critical information as times when the owner is away and of weaknesses in security. One female burglar reported that she maintained close contact with several women who worked as maids in affluent sections of the community. She would gain the necessary information from these women and later come back and break into the house, often entering by a door or window left open for her by the accomplice. Others gained information from friends and acquaintances who unwittingly revealed information about potential burglary targets. One told us:

> I have friends who mow yards for people and work as maids and stuff. When they talk about the people they work for, I keep my ears open. They give me information without knowing it.

Information about potential targets was frequently gained from "fences." Because many fences have legitimate occupations, they may have knowledge of the existence of valuable property from social or business relationships. They can often provide the burglar with information about the owners' schedules and the security arrangements at the target site.

People involved in a variety of service jobs (repair, carpet cleaning, pizza delivery, lawn maintenance, plumbing, carpentry) enter many homes each day and have the opportunity to assess the quality of potential stolen merchandise and security measures taken by the residents. Burglars will often establish contact with employees of these businesses for purposes of obtaining this "inside" information. One informant said:

> I know this guy who works for [carpet cleaning business]. He sometimes gives me information on a good place to hit and I split with him.

Occupancy Probes

Almost all burglars avoid selecting houses that are occupied as targets. Only two informants stated that they would enter a residence they knew was occupied. Therefore, it is important that the burglar develop techniques for probing the potential target site to determine if anyone is at home. The most common probe used by our informants was to send one of the burglars to the door to knock or ring the doorbell. If someone answered, the prober would ask directions to a nearby address or for a nonexistent person, example, "Is Ray home?" The prospective burglar would apologize and leave when told that he or she had the wrong address. A female informant reported that she carried her two-year-old child to the target residence door, asking for directions to a nearby address. She reported:

> I ask them for a drink [of water] for the baby. Even when they seem suspicious they almost always let me in to get the baby a drink.

Several informants reported obtaining the resident's name from the mailbox or a sign over the door. They would then look up the telephone number and call the residence, leaving the phone ringing while they returned to the target home. If they could still hear the phone ringing when they arrived at the house, they were sure it was unoccupied.

Burglar Alarms

In general, burglars agreed that alarms were a definite deterrent to their activities. Other factors being equal, they preferred to locate a target that did not have an alarm instead of taking the additional risk involved in attempting to burglarize a house with an alarm system. Over 90 percent of the informants reported that they would not choose a target with an alarm system. Most were deterred merely by a sign or window sticker stating that the house was protected by an alarm system. As Richard, an experienced burglar, stated:

> Why take a chance? There's lots of places without alarms. Maybe they're bluffing, maybe they ain't.

Although several informants boasted about disarming alarms, when pressed for details, almost all admitted that they did not know how to accomplish that task. One informant stated that while she could not disarm a burglar alarm, she was not deterred by an alarm. She stated that once the alarm was tripped, she still had time to complete the burglary and escape before police or private security arrived. She explained that she never took more than 10 minutes to enter, search, and exit a house. She advised:

> Police take 15 to 20 minutes to respond to an alarm. Security [private security] sometimes gets there a little faster. I'm gone before any of them gets there.

Locks on Doors and Windows

Past research has been inconsistent regarding the deterrent value of locks on windows and doors. A few studies have reported that burglars consider the type of lock installed at a prospective target site in their target selection decision. Others did not find locks to be a significant factor in the selection process.

The majority of informants in the present study initially stated that locks did not deter them. However, during burglary reconstructions, we discovered that given two potential target sites, all other factors being equal, burglars prefer not to deal with a deadbolt lock. Several told us that they allowed themselves only one or two minutes to effect entry and that a good deadbolt lock slowed them down too much.

The variation in findings regarding security hardware appears related to the burglar's level of expertise and experience. To the extent to which burglars are primarily opportunistic and inexperienced, locks appear to have deterrent value. The opportunistic burglar chooses targets based on their perceived vulnerability to burglary at a given time. Given a large number of potential targets, the burglar tends to select the most vulnerable of the target pool. A target with a good lock and fitted with other security hardware will usually not be perceived to be as vulnerable as one without those items. The professional or "good" burglar chooses targets on the basis of factors other than situational vulnerability and conceives ways in which he or she can overcome impediments to the burglary (such as the target site being fitted with a high-quality deadbolt lock). Thus, to the extent that burglars are skilled and experienced, deadbolt locks have limited utility for crime prevention. However, our findings support the deterrent value of deadbolt locks. Seventy-five percent of the burglaries reconstructed during our research were opportunistic offenses. Many of those burglaries would have been prevented by the presence of a quality deadbolt lock. *It is important to note that nearly one-half of the burglary sites in the present study were entered through open or unlocked windows and doors.*

Dogs

Almost all studies agree that dogs are an effective deterrent to burglary. While there is some individual variation among burglars, the general rule is to bypass a house with a dog—any dog. Large dogs represent a physical threat to the burglar and small ones are often noisy, attracting attention to his or her activities. We found that while many burglars have developed contingency plans to deal with dogs (petting, feeding, or even killing them), most burglars prefer to avoid them. When asked what were considered absolute "no-go" factors, most burglars responded that dogs were second only to occupancy. However, approximately 30 percent of the informants *initially* discounted the presence of dogs as a deterrent. Yet, during "ride alongs," the sight or sound of a dog at a potential target site almost invariably resulted in a "no-go" decision. As Richard said:

> I don't mess with no dogs. If they got dogs I go someplace else.

Debbie reported that she was concerned primarily with small dogs:

> Little dogs "yap" too much. They [neighbors] look to see what they are so excited about. I don't like little yapping dogs.

Opportunity and Burglary

The "professional burglars" among our informants tended to select targets in a purposive manner, analyzing the physical and social characteristics of the environment and choosing targets that they knew from experience to be ideally vulnerable. But by far the greater proportion of the informants were opportunistic. The targets they chose appeared particularly vulnerable *at the time.* Thus, most burglaries in the jurisdiction studies seem to result from the propitious juxtaposition of target, offender, and situation.

Our findings suggest that a burglar's decision to "hit" a target is based primarily on environmental cues that are perceived to have immediate consequences. Most burglars appear to attend only to the present; future events or consequences do not weigh heavily in their risk-versus-gain calculation. Drug-using burglars and juveniles are particularly oriented to this immediate-gain and immediate-risk decision process. Non-drug-using and experienced burglars are probably less likely to attend only to immediate risks and gains. Our informants, though experienced burglars, were all drug users, and tended to have a "here and now" orientation toward the rewards and costs associated with burglary.

Exploiting opportunity characterized the target selection processes in over 75 percent of the burglaries reconstructed during our research. Even professional burglars among our informants often took advantage of opportunities when they arose. Chance opportunities occasionally presented themselves while the professional was "casing" and "probing" potential burglary targets chosen by more rational means. When these opportunities arose, the professional burglar was as likely as other burglars to take advantage of the situation.

IMPLICATIONS FOR CRIME PREVENTION

This study suggests burglars may be much more opportunistic than previously believed. The opportunistic burglar chooses targets based on their perceived vulnerability to burglary at a given time. Given a large number of potential targets, the burglar tends to select the most vulnerable of the target pool. The burglar does not, however, choose targets on the basis of situational vulnerability alone. He also considers how to overcome impediments to the burglary.

Programs designed to prevent burglary must be based on valid assumptions about burglars and burglary. Measures designed to combat the relatively small population of high-incidence "professional" burglars tend to overemphasize the skill and determination of most burglars. These measures are expensive, complex, and require long-term commitment at many levels. But the typical burglar is not a calculating professional against whom complex prevention tactics must be employed. In fact, most burglars are young, unskilled, and opportunistic. This suggests that emphasis should be directed at such factors as surveillability, occupancy, and accessibility. More specifically, dogs, good locks, and alarm systems deter most burglars. Methods that give a residence the "illusion of occupancy" (Cromwell, Olson, and Avary, 1990) deter almost all burglars and are maintained with little effort or cost. Our study suggests that these simple steps may be the most cost-efficient and effective means for residents to insulate themselves from victimization by burglars.

References

Bureau of Justice Statistics. October 1991. *Criminal Victimization 1990. Bulletin.* Washington, DC: U.S. Department of Justice.

Cromwell, Paul, James N. Olson, and D'Aunn Avary. 1991. *Breaking and Entering: An Ethnographic Analysis of Burglary.* Newbury Park, CA: Sage.

Katz, Jack. 1988. *Seductions of Crime.* New York: Basic Books.

Lynch, James P. 1990. Modeling Target Selection in Burglary: Differentiating Substance from Method. Paper presented at the 1990 annual meeting of the American Society of Criminology, Baltimore, Maryland.

Rengert, G. and J. Wasilchick. 1985. *Suburban Burglary: A Time and a Place for Everything.* Springfield, IL: Charles C Thomas.

Rengert, G. and J. Wasilchick. 1989. *Space, Time and Crime: Ethnographic Insights into Residential Burglary.* A report prepared for the National Institute of Justice. (Mimeo).

Reppetto, T. G. 1974. *Residential Crime.* Cambridge, MA: Ballinger.

Scarr, H. A. 1973. *Patterns of Burglary.* Washington, DC: U.S. Government Printing Office.

Shover, Neal. 1971. *Burglary as an Occupation.* Ph.D. Dissertation, University of Illinois. Ann Arbor, MI: University Microfilms, 1975.

25

Understanding Shoplifting

Lloyd W. Klemke
Oregon State University

While you are out shopping for groceries or a new outfit, other "shoppers" may take advantage of the "five finger discount"—shoplifting. Several examples, drawn from my study, provide an introductory glimpse at who such people might be.

> Case 1: Store security detected a middle-aged male stuffing almost $400 worth of camera, film, and razor blades into a plastic bag hidden under his heavy coat jacket. While interviewed, he confessed to being a drug addict, which was confirmed by the needle tracks on his arms.

> Case 2: A troubled recent high school graduate began to shoplift clothes as she tried to support herself on a minimum wage job. During the last few years, a series of crises had thrown her life into turmoil. Her parents had divorced and recently her father had stopped seeing her, she was raped by an acquaintance but did not tell anyone, a favorite aunt was brutally murdered, and her relationship with her mother became strained when her mother remarried and she was not invited to move in with them. Apparently because of all these problems, she had become bulimic and suicidal.

> Case 3: A young male reported shoplifting numerous times over a ten-year period. He came from an affluent family and usually stole food, cigarettes, and beer with his friends, because, as he said, "it was exciting and they wanted to be cool."

These cases reveal the diverse nature of shoplifting, which challenges the resourcefulness of the sociological analyst seeking to understand this kind of deviance. Shoplifting also represents a challenging topic to the student of human behavior for three other reasons. First, it is a type of deviance that most people have committed at some time in their life. Second, a considerable amount of inaccurate information and stereotypes exists about shoplifting and

---

This article was specifically written for this reader.

shoplifters. And, third, even sociologists have paid only minimal attention to the study of shoplifting. Our goal here is to illustrate how a sociological study can provide accurate data on and meaningful explanations for shoplifting.

THE SHOPLIFTING PROBLEM

It is worth exploring the extent of shoplifting first. Data can be obtained from several sources; the most important are: (1) the Federal Bureau of Investigation (FBI), which collects statistics on shoplifting acts reported to police departments, (2) retail stores, which have information on individuals apprehended for shoplifting, and (3) social scientists' self-report studies on shoplifting.

According to the FBI, 1,179,659 incidents of shoplifting were reported to the police in 1991. The average dollar value per incident was $104. Unfortunately, shoplifting, like rape, is greatly underreported. Many shoplifters do not get caught. Many stores do not report all of those they have apprehended; they would report only when expensive merchandise has been taken. The fact is that much more shoplifting occurs—and for less expensive items—than is shown in the FBI data.

Store apprehension statistics provide more descriptive data. The data I obtained from a large multi-state chain of department stores, for example, reveals that most shoplifters are apprehended for taking relatively *inexpensive* merchandise. As shown in Table 25.1, 81 percent of males and 66 percent of females were apprehended for taking things valued under $50. Interestingly, females are nearly twice (34 percent) as likely as males (19 percent) to have been apprehended for taking items valued over $50. Petty shoplifting, then, is the dominant type of shoplifting.

Finally, data from my self-report study of juvenile shoplifting may shed additional light on the prevalence of shoplifting (Klemke, 1982). In this study I asked 1189 high school youths from four small communities about their shoplifting activity. Overall, 63 percent admitted having shoplifted at some point. More specifically, 27.5 percent of the boys and 19.8 percent of the girls admitted shoplifting during the last school year (almost 9 months). From the

TABLE 25.1   Dollar Value of Merchandise Shoplifted from Department Stores: By Gender

| | Males | | Females | |
Dollar Value	Number	Percent	Number	Percent
$1–$10	2223	46	706	27
$11–$50	1697	35	1102	39
$51–$250	784	16	800	30
$251–$1000	83	2	102	4
$1000+	7	1	3	0
Total	4794	100	2623	100

fact that there were about 15 million high school students and 1 out of 4 had shoplifted at least once, we can deduce that high school students commit some 3.75 million acts of shoplifting. But if we conservatively take into account the fact that high school shoplifters average 5 to 6 incidents during a year, the number of shoplifting incidents can be estimated to exceed 20 million a year. This figure greatly exceeds the 1.1 million reported by the FBI even though it represents only a small segment (high school students) of the total U.S. population. These self-report data clearly confirm that shoplifting is a significant form of deviant behavior in our society. While national estimates are very crude, experts agree that shoplifting and sore security programs cost retailers many billions of dollars each year.

AGE AND GENDER

Individuals of all ages and both genders shoplift, but shoplifting is more likely to occur among youth and males. There is a great deal of consensus among researchers that young people report more shoplifting activity than adults (Klemke, 1982; Osgood et al., 1989). In my research, though, more youth (both males and females) reported shoplifting—typically of inexpensive items—before age 11 than after. The number of youth shoplifting declined as individuals advanced through school. For example, 39 percent of freshmen reported shoplifting during the last school year, but only 18 percent of seniors did. Data from the major research project "Monitoring the Future" further shows that shoplifting continues to drop in the early adult years (Osgood et al., 1989). The most recent studies also confirm that shoplifting declines as age increases and that males shoplift more than females (Klemke, 1992). Finally, nearly all studies agree that shoplifting is very low for both elderly men and women.

SOCIAL CLASS, RACE, AND NONRESIDENT STATUS

There has been considerable speculation by store security personnel that lower-class and minority-group members are more likely to be involved in shoplifting (May, 1978; Murphy, 1986). Because store apprehension data tend to reflect store security's biases against the poor and black, it is important to rely on self-report research.

Several self-report studies do reveal that there is slightly more shoplifting among lower-class youth (Klemke, 1982; Bales, 1982). A self-report study of adult shoppers also revealed significantly more shoplifting among lower-class respondents (Ray, 1987). In addition, shoplifting has been reported to occur frequently in economically deprived subcultures of street youth (Hagen and McCarthy, 1992) and street drug addicts (Johnson et al., 1985; Inciardi, 1980; Kowalski and Faupel, 1990).

The variables of race and ethnicity have typically been neglected in shoplifting research. Frequently, store officials will not release this "sensitive" information and few self-report studies have explored those variables. Two recent self-report studies of youth, however, counter the stereotyped belief that racial minorities are more likely to resort to shoplifting. A study of Seattle youth (Hindelang et al., 1981) and the "Monitoring the Future" study of high school seniors (Flanagan and Maguire, 1990) both report very similar rates of shoplifting for black and white respondents.

Finally, a number of researchers have noted that frequently people go outside their immediate residential area to do their shoplifting. Murphy (1986), for example, has pointed out the prevalence of foreign tourists being apprehended for shoplifting in British stores. But much of the evidence is more anecdotal than scientific. A college band from the United States, for example, recently received considerable media attention when many members were implicated in shoplifting electronic equipment valued at about $23,000 while on a concert tour in Japan. Likewise, I have repeatedly heard respondents describing that they were more likely to go to neighboring communities, stores, and malls to shoplift. Sometimes this was done in a quest for quality merchandise, but more often "shoplifting away from home" was viewed as a strategy to give them a feeling of anonymity or to minimize the consequences if they got caught.

ACCOMPLICES AND SIGNIFICANT OTHERS

Since Edwin Sutherland developed his seminal "differential association" theory, sociologists have tried to find out how people are influenced and socialized by the significant others in their social world. In my research I have found that youth who knew their significant others (parents, siblings, or friends) had shoplifted were more likely to engage in the deviant activity themselves. Shoplifting may also involve accomplices. Many professional shoplifters often work together, as do many youthful shoplifters.

Professional shoplifters, also called "boosters," often organize teams and plan routines and strategies to increase the odds of pulling off thefts of large quantities of expensive items. Some are crude "snatch and grab" thieves who blatantly haul off armfuls of merchandise to an accomplice waiting in an escape vehicle. More sophisticated operations are evident in cases of shoplifting troupes. These shoplifters work as a team with each member assigned a specific role to play. Typically, one person distracts the store clerk while another takes the item. Other sophisticated shoplifters may nurture a friendship with a store employee, or even "plant" an employee in a store, who can inform them of security operations or overlook their thefts. In unusual cases, older persons may become modern-day Fagins, recruiting and training teams of youth to shoplift and then keeping most of the proceeds for themselves.

Many youthful shoplifters also operate with accomplices. As shown by many studies, from 50 to 81 percent of youthful shoplifting takes place in the company of others (Klemke, 1992). Usually, these accomplices are peers of the same gender and age. The various roles peers can play in initiating or supporting shoplifting is more diverse for the youth than for the professionals. For example, a youthful group may issue a challenge or dare to take items.

Sometimes, shoplifting becomes a test to initiate new members into a gang or several youths are sent out to commandeer supplies, such as beer and chips, for a party. Many have told me how they needed to be with friends while shoplifting in order to bolster their courage and alleviate their anxieties. Others have shared with me how they rely on a friend who works in a store with attractive merchandise to serve as an accomplice. The "insider" can provide information on security practices and personnel, not ring up merchandise "being purchased," or simply ignore the shoplifting being done by the "outsider." In return, the insider may receive a portion of the items taken or some other favors.

DEVIANT INVOLVEMENT AND PRESSURE TO DEVIATE

Shoplifting represents a type of deviance that is often connected to other types. This connection is most evident in the street drug subculture, as illustrated by "Case 1" at the beginning of this article. Ethnographic studies have documented the reliance of many street drug addicts on shoplifting as their "main hustle"—their most frequently committed offense. For male addicts, shoplifting ranks second only to drug sales, and for female addicts it ranks behind drug sales and prostitution as sources of income for financing their drug habits. Kowalski and Faupel (1990) found that their street addict respondents who claimed shoplifting as their "main hustle" averaged around 100 shoplifting incidents during the previous year. Clearly, many individuals ensnared in the street drug subculture develop extensive shoplifting careers.

The overlap between shoplifting and other types of deviance can also be found in many studies on juvenile delinquency. My own research reinforces the popular conclusion that youth who are actively involved in shoplifting often get into other types of trouble. Thus, juvenile shoplifters are more likely to (1) have problems getting along with parents, (2) experience problems at school, (3) have significant others who are into shoplifting, and (4) have already acquired a reputation as a "trouble maker."

MOTIVATIONS FOR SHOPLIFTING

The question "Why did you shoplift?" may elicit many different responses. One shoplifter claimed to have stolen five copies of the Bible to "give away as gifts"; tennis star Jennifer Capriatti asserted that she had simply "forgotten" to put back a ring she had tried on; another shoplifter claimed that she did it "to get back at" a store that had treated her unfairly when she worked there; one shoplifter even said, "It was raining, and I needed an umbrella." Beyond these varied, idiosyncratic reasons, however, I have found strong evidence that shoplifting springs largely from two main clusters of motivations (Klemke, 1992).

The first encompasses *economic-instrumental motivations*. Simply put, economic motivations are foremost when individuals emphasize the importance of *the merchandise* they are taking for personal use or for converting into money (fencing the items or returning them for cash). It is not surprising that economic motivations play an important role in shoplifting. Our culture is very consumer-materialistic oriented. Status is often symbolized by possessing and displaying the latest styles and brand-name merchandise. It is inevitable that many citizens will not be able to afford all the products that they want to have (Messner and Rosenfeld, 1994). Shoplifting becomes a convenient way for many to get what they desire but cannot afford. This may explain why more shoplifting occurs among lower-class individuals (Ray, 1987), the homeless, runaways, street youth (Hagan and McCarthy, 1992), and those entrenched in street drug subcultures (Kowalski and Faupel, 1990).

Economic motivations alone, however, cannot account for the wide range of shoplifting activities. Security personnel often discover that apprehended shoplifters often have cash, credit cards, and checking accounts that could have been used to pay for the stolen items. This arouses suspicions that more than dollars and cents are at issue. There must be a second type of motivation, which I call *sporting-expressive motivations*. Such motivations have more to do with the attraction of *the act of shoplifting* than with the attraction of the merchandise. The act of shoplifting is found attractive because it is expected to provide a fun, exciting, challenging, or stress-relieving experience. Expressive motivations play an important role in shoplifting by high school students. Many of my respondents have told me how they considered shoplifting a "game." One said that her friends would have shoplifting "contests" to see who could steal the most during the afternoons they ditched school. Others have described how they resorted to shoplifting during stressful or unhappy phases of their life, as illustrated in "Case 2" and "Case 3."

CHANCES OF GETTING CAUGHT

"It is so easy to do." This is one of the most frequently mentioned comments I have received while interviewing shoplifters. Herein lies probably the most important of several reasons why shoplifting is so popular. First, shoplifting requires little skill; virtually anyone (children, the elderly, addicts, and so on) can do it. Second, shoplifting offers the potential of some financial rewards. Finally—perhaps most important—is the perception that shoplifting carries only a minimal risk of getting caught or of receiving serious penalties if caught.

Indeed, many shoplifters I have interviewed have been very active for a long time but have *never* been apprehended. According to estimates by experienced security personnel, the likelihood of getting caught ranges from one out of ten shoplifters being apprehended to one out of two hundred. Inciardi (1980) found in his study of female street heroin addicts that only 47 apprehensions occurred out of 8713 shoplifting episodes. In another study, designed to assess the ability of security personnel to detect shoplifting, even when observers were assigned to watch specific "customers" (research assistants who were sent into the store to shoplift), the observers still failed to detect over half of the "planted shoplifters" (Baumer and Rosenbaum, 1984).

CONCLUDING REMARKS

Shoplifting constitutes a significant and challenging phenomenon to social scientists and the retail community. Both the intellectual challenge and the economic toll from shoplifting makes it an intriguing and compelling subject. This article has highlighted some basic patterns of shoplifting, mostly involving juvenile shoplifters. Although such offenders still pose many mysteries that need to be investigated, adult shoplifters should be made a top-priority subject for future research. Only then can we gain a fuller and deeper insight into the nature of shoplifting.

References

Bales, Kevin B. 1982. "Contrast and Complementarity in Three Theories of Criminal Behavior." *Deviant Behavior* 3 (2): 155–174.

Baumer, Terry L., and Dennis P. Rosenbaum. 1984. *Combatting Retail Theft: Programs and Strategies.* Boston: Butterworth.

Flanagan, Timothy J., and Kathleen Maguire, eds. 1990. *Sourcebook of Criminal Justice Statistics 1989.* Washington, DC: U.S. Government Printing Office.

Hagen, John, and Bill McCarthy. 1992. "Streetlife and Delinquency." *British Journal of Sociology* 43 (4): 533–561.

Hindelang, Michael J., Travis Hirschi, and Joseph G. Weis. 1981. *Measuring Delinquency.* Beverly Hills: Sage.

Inciardi, James A. 1980. "Women, Heroin, and Property Crime," pp. 214–221 in *Women, Crime, and Justice,* edited by Susan K. Datesman and Frank Scarpetti. New York: Oxford University Press.

Johnson, Bruce D. et al. 1985. *Taking Care of Business: The Economics of Crime by Heroin Users.* Lexington, MA: Lexington Books.

Klemke, Lloyd W. 1982. "Exploring Juvenile Shoplifting." *Sociology and Social Research* 67 (October): 59–75.

Klemke, Lloyd. 1992. *The Sociology of Shoplifting: Boosters and Snitches Today.* Westport, CT: Praeger.

Kowalski, Gregory S., and Charles E. Faupel. 1990. "Heroin Use, Crime, and the 'Main Hustle'." *Deviant Behavior* 11 (No. 1): 1–16.

May, David. 1978. "Juvenile Shoplifters and the Organization of Store Security: A Case Study in the Social Construction of Delinquency." *International Journal of Criminology and Penology* 6: 137–160.

Messner, Steven F., and Richard Rosenfeld. 1994. *Crime and the American Dream.* Belmont, CA: Wadsworth.

Murphy, David J. I. 1986. *Customers and Thieves: An Ethnography of Shoplifting.* Aldershot, England: Gower.

Osgood, Wayne D. et al. 1989. "Time Trends and Age Trends in Arrests and Self-Reported Illegal Behavior. *Criminology* 27 (No. 3): 389–415.

Ray, JoAnn. 1987. "Every Twelfth Shopper: Who Shoplifts and Why?" *Social Casework* 68 (April): 234–239.

26

Ethnic Succession in American Organized Crime

JAMES M. O'KANE
Drew University

Ethnic organized crime is a phenomenon often ignored by those seeking to understand the upward mobility of past immigrants and current minority newcomers. Many prefer a romanticized version of their ancestors' struggle, concentrating on the noble aspects of that odyssey and ignoring the distasteful elements of the move from the bottom of the social hierarchy. Our literature thrives on the rags-to-riches success stories of business tycoons, lawyers, movie stars, and Nobel prize laureates while it often ignores the similar meteoric rise of gangsters, con men, Tammany Hall type politicians, gamblers, and rum runners.

A more realistic view of this ascent from poverty to respectability entails the recognition of how much organized crime plays a crucial role in this upward mobility process: Members of ethnic minorities have used and continue to use crime as a vehicle of individual and group upward mobility. Moreover, this criminal road to respectability places ethnic groups in conflict with each other. Throughout American history ethnic newcomers have clashed with the more entrenched groups as they competed for criminal dominance: Irish mobs challenged and overthrew their Anglo-Saxon rivals; Jewish gangsters eliminated the Irish and were in time displaced by Italian criminals; currently African-American, Hispanic, and Asian mobsters are threatening the hegemony of the Italians who are in the rapidly fading twilight of their criminal power. This ever-recurring process helps to explain how ethnic groups in American society actually "make it," how they rise from the bottom and gradually take their place in the American mainstream.

This article was specifically written for this reader.

THE RISE FROM THE BOTTOM

Throughout the nation's history, millions of newcomers have been absorbed into America's mainstream. Regardless of their origins, the vast majority of these newcomers settled at the bottom of the social hierarchy. They arrived impoverished and illiterate, without any basic knowledge of how to function in an urban-industrial setting. Quickly they constituted what became known as the "unwashed masses" of the nineteenth and twentieth centuries, often resented and harassed by the larger American society.

Yet, as the twenty-first century approaches, it should be noted that the descendants of many of these groups have "made it" as they reside in comfortable suburbs, enjoying the fruits of middle-class material well-being, frequently looking down their noses at current lower-income minorities. But how did this phenomenal transition take place? How did entire ethnic groups move from the bottom to the top in the course of two or three generations? How did the American Dream unfold for these millions of newcomers and their descendants? More important, will those groups currently considered lower income (such as African Americans, Hispanics, Asians, and Native Americans) also undergo this same upward mobility odyssey?

If American social history is any guide to these questions, the answers would imply that the current newcomers will also "make it." In reviewing this history, we should emphasize that newcomer ethnic groups did not achieve success in American life by following the script set forth by the country's established elites. This scenario, known as the Horatio Alger scenario, implies that one's determined efforts, coupled with a clean, respectable life style would propel one from rags to riches. This was the formula for success advocated by Alger in his dime novels at the turn of the century. Yet because of poverty and discrimination, this traditional mode of success had little to do with the realities of the newcomers' lives (O'Kane, 1969:303–304). The actual hostility of the established American groups convinced the newcomer immigrant and migrant groups that their own upward mobility could only be achieved by circumventing traditional avenues of success (e.g., literacy, formal education, respectable labor, or clean living) and creating new routes of upward mobility. But what are these routes?

ROUTES OF UPWARD MOBILITY

Historically, each ethnic minority group used at least seven core routes of upward mobility from the lower classes to the middle classes: unskilled and semi-skilled labor; retail small business; the clergy; the professions; entertainment; urban ethnic politics; ethnic organized crime (O'Kane, 1992: 28). The first five routes constitute legitimate means to the American Dream, and the larger American society considers these the "normal" way incoming groups should pursue success. The sixth route—urban ethnic politics—comprises a semi-legitimate route since the larger society is ambivalent about the ethnic politicians and their tactics which involve bloc voting, Tammany Hall-style deals, and the like. The seventh route—ethnic organized crime—is obviously illegitimate. It involves bootlegging, vice, narcotics, gambling, loan sharking, prostitution, racketeering, and so on.

Of the seven routes of upward mobility, the last one—ethnic organized crime—is perhaps the most interesting because it is the most peculiar. Forty years ago Daniel Bell noted this as he referred to crime as a "queer" avenue of success in American life (Bell, 1953). How true, for the ethnic criminal— the gangster—seeks to achieve fame and economic success through means deemed outrageous and illegitimate by the established society. He aimed at personal success and power, and his route to these goals involved crime. In quick ethnic succession, Irish, Jews, Poles, and Italians have engaged in orga- nized crime as a viable vehicle to success in American life, while currently African Americans, Hispanics, and Asians are continuing on this same road (Ianni, 1974).

IRISH-AMERICAN CRIMINALITY

The first important growth in ethnic organized crime begins in the early nine- teenth century. Crime at this time was controlled by Anglo-Saxon Protestants but was small in scope and limited to relatively small gangs of criminals. It grew rapidly with the convergence of two phenomena in the 1840s and 1850s: the massive waves of immigrants and the rapid growth of America's cities. The most notable new immigrants were Irish Catholics who settled in overwhelm- ing numbers in the rapidly growing and industrializing cities of the eastern seaboard (e.g., New York, Boston, Philadelphia, and Baltimore). Some of these Irish got involved in organized crime, and quickly challenged and over- whelmed their Anglo-Saxon counterparts, wresting control of crime from them and remaining unchallenged until the early 1900s (O'Kane, 1992: ch. 3).

In the earlier part of the nineteenth century, Irish crime was largely preda- tory, with its victims overwhelmingly derived from the waves of Irish immi- grants flocking to America's shores. The notorious Irish gangs of cities like New York (The Dead Rabbits, Plug Uglies, Five Pointers, Bowery Boys, etc.) also spent a great deal of time brawling with each other as well as fighting rival nativist Protestant gangs. When the Irish gangs were not battling each other, they often were engaged in extortion and gambling (Asbury, 1929). By the 1850s those gangs had become involved with political organizations and used their muscle to intimidate voters and serve the legal and illegal interests of their political mentors.

The apex of Irish criminal organization occurred during the Civil War, a time when the Irish gangs and gang leaders controlled the important criminal endeavors of the larger American cities, supported by the protection of, and collusion with, the urban political bosses and their machines, and the urban police forces whose ranks were disproportionately Irish. Hugh Barlow sums this as follows: "From loafing and brawling the New York gangs moved into extortion and the instrumental use of force. They soon discovered that money was easily made through the intimidation of brothel owners, gambling proprietors, and others in the business of providing illicit services. More money came, and with it power, when it was discovered that politicians and businessmen would pay for their muscle. Gangs were hired to break up picket lines to intimidate voters, to stuff ballot boxes, and to protect establishments from harassment by other gangs, not to mention the authorities. By the 1890s, the gangs were the muscle behind Tammany Hall, the Democratic headquarters and political heart of the city. With this new power, the gangs were able to open doors that had been closed to their fellow Irish" (Barlow, 1978: 276–277).

By the 1900s the lower classes comprised millions of Jews, Italians, Poles, and Greeks. They also had criminal ambitions, but were relegated by the Irish to the lower echelons of criminal enterprise such as prostitution, usury, petty crime, and low-level gambling. Likewise, these new immigrants were confined almost exclusively to their own neighborhood where the opportunities for large-scale criminal economic success were distinctly limited. Yet the most important of these new gangsters—the Jews and Italians—eventually came to dominance, particularly in New York. Jewish gangs such as the Eastmans, led by Monk Eastman, and Italian gangs such as the Five Points Gang under Paolo "Paul Kelly" Vaccarelli, and Black Hand gangs such as one headed by Ignacio "Lupo the Wolf" Saietta began to exert their power. Many of the more famous gangsters of this century started their careers in the internecine warfare among these groups (e.g., Meyer Lansky, "Little Augie" Orgen, William "Big Jack Zelig" Alberts, Benjamin "Bugsy" Siegel, Johnny Torrio, Al Capone, "Lucky" Luciano, and Frank Costello).

By the 1920s, the Irish could no longer maintain their dominant criminal leadership: New Irish recruits into criminal gangs were harder to find, for opportunities in legitimate endeavors now were available to them. Consequently, Irish criminal leadership increasingly became isolated from the daily realities of Irish-American life, which no longer needed the criminal and no longer bestowed adulation on him. The Irish increasingly were in touch with middle-class propriety and Irish gangsters constituted an embarrassment to the ethnic group as a whole. The older Irish criminal saw the writing on the wall and "retired" from crime, leaving their enterprises to ambitious Jews and Italians. The younger Irish chieftains resisted and consequently had to be removed forcibly from power (e.g., Dion O'Banion, Richard "Peg Leg" Lonergan, Jack "Legs" Diamond, and Vincent "Mad Dog" Coll,). The famous St. Valentine's Day Massacre of 1929 symbolizes this transition, for the remnants of the Irish-Polish Northside Chicago gang of O'Banion, Weiss, and Moran were executed by the Italians under Al Capone (Kobler, 1971). Since then, the Irish faded from organized crime. In their heyday they had become too smug and consequently failed to seek new markets and pioneer new rackets. Contented in their criminal pursuit, they fell prey to those lower-status ethnic gangs of Jews and Italians obsessed with achieving criminal success. Prohibition proved to be the transition point, as Jews and Italians quickly capitalized on the large-scale organizational efforts needed to control bootlegging. The Irish did likewise but by the late 1920s were worn out. They lacked the sufficient manpower, determination, and drive to compete with Jews and Italians.

JEWISH-AMERICAN CRIMINALITY

The decline of the Irish in organized crime created the impetus for Jews and Italians to move into leadership positions, with each group establishing its own dominance in criminal ventures. As Prohibition ended, Jews (e.g., Louis "Lepke" Buchalter, Jacob "Gurrah" Shapiro, Arthur "Dutch Schultz" Flegenheimer, Benjamin "Bugsy" Siegel, Meyer Lansky, Abner "Longy" Zwillman, and Moe Dalitz) and Italians (e.g., Charles "Lucky" Luciano, Vito Genovese, Frank Costello, Thomas "Three-Fingers Brown" Luchese, Al Capone, and Carlo Gambino) pioneered new forms of criminal activity and revitalizing other types of crime (labor racketeering, numbers, gambling, prostitution, narcotics, loan sharking). Jews and Italian gangsters more often than not cooperated with each other, for the internecine gang wars of the bootlegging era clearly showed that open warfare was destructive and counterproductive (O'Kane 1992: 75).

Yet, like the Irish before them, the Jews eventually were dethroned. The decline began with the murder of Arnold Rothstein in 1928 and the assassination of Dutch Schultz in 1935; it reached full fruition in the 1949s with the imprisonment of "Gurrah" Shapiro and Irving "Waxey Gordon" Wexler, the legal execution of "Lepke" Buchalter, the exposure of Murder, Inc., the death (murder? suicide?) of Abe "Kid Twist" Reles, and the assassination of "Bugsy" Siegel. By the 1960s and 1970s only a few prominent Jews remained in organized crime (such as Moe Dalitz and Meyer Lansky) though even they have shifted their operations to legalized casinos in Las Vegas. Indeed, many such individuals had moved into legitimate business simply because they had ample capital to do so. Nobody knows for sure whether they "infiltrated" legitimate business, or simply used criminally gained capital to launch respectable business careers in hotels, resorts, and entertainment. America is often loath to question the source of respectable enterprise capital investment. If it did, the Rockefeller and Vanderbilts might have fared differently in eventual social acceptance.

Achieving middle- and upper-middle-class status, Jews quickly abandoned organized crime that was no longer necessary or important to them. In so doing, Jews ceased to nourish or protect their gangsters, who by the 1990s had become an embarrassment to them. As with the Irish a generation earlier, the Jewish mobster increasingly was cut off from the mainstream of his ethnic group, exposed to the full wrath of established society. His end was near. The Jewish gangster was thus relegated to the footnotes of history, a fascinating endnote in the upward mobility odyssey of Jewish newcomers. The last of the famous Jewish gangsters, Meyer Lansky, illustrates this transition. As Fried states, "Lansky is . . . scarcely more than a lonely isolated old man on the criminal landscape of America. He bears the mark of Cain and knows no peace. Government investigators (and sometimes reporters too) watch and trail him without letup. Nor is he welcome anywhere else on earth. . . . Since no other country would have him he went back to Miami Beach to face—and ultimately survive—a sea of troubles" (Fried, 1980; 281–282). He died of natural causes in 1983.

ITALIAN-AMERCIAN CRIMINALITY

By the late 1950s, Italian gangsters dominated the world of organized crime, moving beyond regional bases, creating a loosely organized national base. The true extent of this dominance is debated by experts. Some argue that there is a hierarchial structure ruthlessly dictated by the Mafia or Cosa Nostra. Others see a loose federation of numerous local and regional criminal gangs and families composed mainly, but not exclusively, of those of Italian backgrounds who periodically assist each other when it is in their interest.

Italians clearly were the beneficiaries of the spoils of organized crime as the Irish and Jews lost criminal power and influence. Italians increasingly took over all the major rackets by the late 1950s. In the 1960s and 1970s, the public viewed organized crime and Italian "mafiosi" as synonymous entities, and congressional committees, law enforcement agencies, and the mass media did everything possible to reinforce this stereotype.

Thus, Carlo Gambino, Vito Genovese, "Crazy Joe" Gallo and the Gallo mob, Joe "Bananas" Bonnano, Frank "The Banker" Costello, Sam "Momo" Giancana, Willie Moretti, Joe Valachi, Raymond Patriarca, Santo Trafficante, Vinnie Teresa, Joe Profaci, Carlos Marcello, Carmine Galante, Vinnie "The Chin" Gigante, Paul Castellano, John Gotti, and dozens of other gangsters captured the attention of the public. They were the successors of the syndicates pioneered by the Jewish and Italian gangs of the post-bootlegging era, and indebted to the organizational genius of those earlier gang leaders, whose ventures exploited new areas of revenue, focusing beyond gambling, vice, and bootlegging, to labor racketeering, casino operations, and, most lucrative of all, narcotics.

By the 1980s these gangs (or crime families) were in serious disarray as a result of numerous factors, foremost of which were the enforcement of the RICO Act (Racketeer Influenced and Corrupt Organization) and the changing ethnic and racial composition of areas historically dominated by Italian criminal factions.

Currently Italians are in the twilight of criminal power. Their concentration at the upper levels of organized crime belies the fact that the lower levels and, in some cities, the middle levels, are occupied by African Americans, Asians, and Hispanics who show every indication of lusting for greater criminal power. As Italians fail to replenish their ranks with other Italians, the ensuing vacuum creates the natural conditions for the ascendancy of ambitious minority groups. Like the Irish and Jews before them, Italians have largely been assimilated into the American middle-class mainstream, and crime no longer constitutes the main upward mobility outlet for young, poor but ambitious Italians (O'Kane 1992: 86–87). Ianni (1972) found that fourth-generation Italians have little desire to follow the criminal careers of their older kinfolk in the crime family he studied. Instead, they are pursuing careers as lawyers, dentists, teachers, and businessmen. He writes, "I discovered that each succeeding generation of the family had been moving quietly but certainly out of crime. I had managed to trace the family history back seventy years through four generations and could see that from the second generation, only four of the twenty-seven males were involved in organized crime" (Ianni, 1974:11).

The Italian gangster's decline clearly follows the pattern set by previous ethnic newcomers. He will either retire, be eliminated by "young turk" African-American, Asian and Hispanic rivals, or move into more lucrative legitimate endeavors. As Ianni states, "The degree and tenure of minority-group involvement in this business enterprise (organized crime) is basically a function of the social and cultural integration of the group into American society. At their first entrance into this society, immigrants and their children grasp at the immediate means of acquiring what the New World has to offer. As they are accelerated, their crimes become more American and in time merge into the arena of marginal legitimate business practice. Where one stops and the other begins is not always easy to see" (Ianni, 1972: 61).

THE NEW ETHNIC CRIMINALS

Waiting in the wings to succeed the Italian mobs are the new ethnic gangsters—the African Americans, the Hispanics, and the Asians. They have taken over many of the criminal rackets and drug enterprises in inner-city areas and are poised to move into the organized crime mainstream. The departure of the Italian gangsters has created a breach in organized crime into which the ethnic newcomers step.

Blacks (American and Caribbean), Hispanics (Cuban, Mexican, Puerto Rican, Colombian, Bolivian, or Venezuelan), Asians (Chinese, Japanese, Vietnamese, Filipinos, or Korean) constitute the largest segments of these new ethnic minorities. Smaller segments also are operative (e.g., Russian Jews, Nigerians, and Ghanians). They have been "waiting their turn" on the ethnic queue, anticipating their rise on the ladder of success.

Many of these minorities are new to the urban-industrial life of America. Which groups make it, both in the conventional world and the criminal realm, depends on the length of time an ethnic group has been exposed to urban-industrial values and life styles (O'Kane, 1992: 141–143). Those ethnic groups that have had the longest exposure to America's cities (e.g., Irish, Jews, Italians) have been placed higher in the status order and historically have commanded the higher positions in organized crime. The pecking order is clear: Irish Catholics came early to America's cities and occupied the key positions until they were displaced by Eastern European Jews who came later. The Jews in turn were displaced by the later-arriving and less urbanized Italians who subsequently have monopolized organized crime for the past forty years. Italian criminals in turn are about to be displaced by the minority newcomers—African Americans, Hispanics, Asians, and other ethnic newcomers—all relatively new to America's urban-industrial centers.

The names of these new ethnic gangsters are relatively unknown outside their own criminal fiefdoms, their national identities yet to be established. Few with the notoriety of a Capone or an O'Banion or a Dutch Schultz have emerged. Early contenders in the 1970s and 1980s have been neutralized, mainly by imprisonment, retirement, or death (e.g., Ellsworth "Bumpy" Johnson, LeRoy "Nicky" Barnes, the Chambers Brothers, Frank Matthews, "Fat Cat" Nichols, "Pappy" Mason among blacks; Johnny Kon [Kon Yu-Leung], Vincent Jew, Eddie Chan [Chan Tse-Chin], and "Uncle Benny" Ong [Fei Lo Chat], among Asians; "Spanish Raymond" Marques, Jaime Herrera, and Raymond "Mundo" Mendoza, among Hispanics). Yet the criminal gangs of ethnic newcomers are ubiquitous in all the nation's major cities. Black gangs such as Chicago's El RUKN Nation and California's Crips and Bloods, Hispanic groups such as the Mexican Mafia (la EME), La Neustra Familia, The Texas Syndicate, and Asian gangs such as United Bamboo, the Ghost Shadows, Flying Dragons, and Born to Kill are operative and not much different from the Irish, Jewish, and Italian gangs of earlier eras when it comes to producing violence and criminal enterprises. Perhaps the current drug wars will create a new core of national leadership among these newcomer gangsters just as the Prohibition beer wars of the 1920s produced a new type of gangster so familiar to anyone acquainted with James Cagney films of the 1930s or contemporary films such as *The Godfather* and *Goodfellas*. Only time will tell.

For ambitious newcomers, then, crime provides a quick means of success. The rewards within their own ethnic community are immense as are the risks, for many of the above criminals forfeited their lives in the violence that often surrounded their endeavors. Yet there are always ambitious men anxious to take their place, oftentimes from their own ethnic group, but increasingly from different ethnic minorities who likewise see their opportunities.

CONCLUSION

Ethnic organized crime has been one of the most enduring institutions in American society. Present from colonial times, predatory crime represented a vehicle for personal success. Yet organized crime as we now know it was pioneered and masterminded by the Irish in the 1850s, imaginatively expanded by the Jews and the Italians in the early twentieth century, and vigorously pursued currently by African Americans, Hispanics, and Asians.

These ethnic organized criminals—gangsters—seek to achieve their goals of fame and success by means deemed illegitimate and outrageous by the established society. They aimed at personal success and power, and they relied on crime to achieve these goals. In historical succession, the Irish, Jews, and

Italians engaged in organized crime as an important avenue to success in American life; current African-American, Hispanic, and Asian newcomers are doing likewise. Furthermore, each ethnic group competes with the others and is replaced eventually by incoming ethnic minorities: The Irish gangsters were eliminated by the Jews, the Jews by the Italians; currently African Americans, Hispanics, and Asians are engaged in overt conflict seeking to inherit the criminal hegemony that Italians are abandoning, as are smaller ethnic groups (e.g., Russian Jews). Thus, ethnic organized crime mirrors the mobility struggle of incoming minorities in the more conventional realms of American society. Ethnic crime consequently should not be viewed as something alien or dysfunctional to the larger process of upward mobility, for it actually constitutes a necessary and important facet of such mobility, both for individuals and entire groups.

This ethnic succession in organized crime constitutes one of the most distinctive facets of American criminality. No ethnic group maintains its hold in organized crime indefinitely since incoming minority newcomers are always challenging the criminal elites, chomping at the bit for their chance at criminal success. Eventually they succeed and become "fat cats," only to be dethroned by later newcomers. The cycle commenced in the early nineteenth century and continues today; only the ethnic background of the major players changes. What could be more American?

References

Asbury, Herbert. 1919. *The Gangs of New York: An Informal History of the Underworld.* New York: Alfred Knopf.

Barlow, Hugh. 1978. *Introduction to Criminology.* Boston: Little, Brown and Company.

Bell, Daniel. 1953. "Crime as an American Way of Life." *Antioch Review* 13: 131–154.

Fried, Albert. 1980. *The Rise and Fall of the Jewish Gangster in America.* New York: Holt, Rinehart and Winston.

Ianni, Francis. 1974. *Black Mafia: Ethnic Succession in Organized Crime.* New York: Simon and Schuster.

Ianni, Francis and Elizabeth Reuss-Ianni. 1972. *A Family Business: Kinship and Social Control in Organized Crime.* New York: Russell Sage Foundation.

Kobler, John. 1971. *Capone: The Life and World of Al Capone.* New York: G.P. Putnam & Sons.

O'Kane, James. 1969. "Ethnic Mobility and the Lower-Income Negro: A Socio-Historical Perspective." *Social Problems* 16, 3:302–311.

O'Kane, James. 1992. *The Crooked Ladder: Gangsters, Ethnicity, and the American Dream.* New Brunswick, NJ: Transaction Publishers.

27

White-Collar Crime

GILBERT GEIS
University of California, Irvine

The category of "white-collar crime" travels under a number of criminological names. Some prefer the term "upperworld crime," "economic crime," "abuse of power," or "crime in the suites." No matter what they are called, the behaviors being classified are essentially the same: matters such as ripoffs in savings and loan institutions; antitrust violations; health-care frauds; bribery to obtain political favors; misrepresentation of financial statements; offenses against health and safety laws; and unnecessary surgeries or bills for services not rendered by physicians. White-collar offenses can be crimes of violence—hundreds of people die each year from illegally unsafe workplace conditions and from surgeries performed only to collect a hefty fee. More commonly, white-collar crimes involve frauds in which unwitting and unwary customers or consumers are cheated.

The designation "white-collar crime" was introduced into the national vocabulary by Edwin H. Sutherland, a 56-year-old sociologist at Indiana University, in his presidential address to the American Sociological Association in 1939. In his speech, Sutherland deplored the fact that criminology had neglected law breaking by people in positions of power. He argued persuasively that standard explanations of criminal behavior—broken homes, defective intelligence, sociopathic conditions, poverty and slum upbringing, immigrant status—all fell apart when they were brought to bear on the personalities and background of white-collar offenders (Sutherland, 1940).

Sutherland's was a monumental criminological contribution. A *Philadelphia Inquirer* reporter portrayed his audience as "astonished" when "Dr. Sutherland figuratively heaved scores of sociological textbooks into a waste basket" ("Poverty Belittled," 1939:17). *The New York Times* noted that Sutherland had "discarded accepted conceptions and explanations of crime." The reporter then repeated two of Sutherland's more striking observations: That a larger amount of important crime news could be found on the financial pages of the newspaper than on the front pages and that white-collar crime in many respects was "like stealing candy from a baby" ("Hits Criminality," 1939:12).

This article was specifically written for this reader.

Sutherland was the first of many writers to point out that the cost of white-collar crime is much greater than that of street offenses. One bank embezzler in a year typically will steal more than the total taken by all the bank robbers during the same period. Estimates today are that the cost of the savings and loan debacle alone will reach an estimated $1.4 trillion when the final tab is settled in another dozen or so years (Pontell and Calavita, 1993). Such white-collar crime scandals as the Watergate affair and the Iran-Contra imbroglio eat away at public confidence in the country's leaders and in the integrity of their government.

THE DEFINITIONAL DILEMMA

Sutherland defined white-collar crime very loosely, and his imprecision has plagued generations of criminologists seeking to pinpoint exactly what the term means. In the *Encyclopedia of Criminology,* Sutherland depicted the white-collar criminal as "a person with high socioeconomic status who violates the laws designed to regulate his [or her] occupation" (Sutherland, 1949:511). In his book-length treatise on white-collar crime, he relegated definitional matters to a footnote: "A white-collar crime," Sutherland wrote, "may be defined approximately as a crime committed by a person of respectability and high social status in the course of his [or her] occupation" (Sutherland, 1949a:9). Most scientists avoid such equivocal terms as "approximately" when they seek to clarify the object of their inquiry. But Sutherland, as we will see, believed he had a theoretical explanation for *all* crime; therefore, sharp definitional distinctions among forms of criminal behavior were unimportant to him.

In addition, Sutherland flopped back and forth in his writings on white-collar crime between a focus on real people and one on corporate entities. Note, for instance, his sarcastic putdown of psychiatric explanations of crime:

> We have no reason to think that General Motors has an inferiority complex or that the Aluminum Company of America has a frustration-aggression complex or that U.S. Steel has an Oedipus complex, or that the Armour Company has a death wish or that the DuPonts desire to return to the womb (Sutherland, 1956:96).

Then Sutherland added, "The assumption that an offender must have some such pathological distortion of the intellect or the emotions seems to me absurd, and if it is absurd regarding the crimes of businessmen, it is equally absurd regarding the crimes of persons in the lower economic class" (Sutherland, 1956:96).

There are a number of problems with both of Sutherland's statements. First, he does not demonstrate that the corporations (presumably, he means their officers) do not have the problems he makes fun of; second, he is picking on a straw target in the sense that few, if any, criminologists would support the claim that he is ridiculing; and, third, he is guilty of *anthropomorphism,* that is, of ascribing human characteristics to nonhuman creations, such as business corporations.

Early disputation regarding definitional matters has given way today to general, though still somewhat unsettled, agreement about the nature of white-collar crime. The first major breakthrough occurred in 1973 when Marshall Clinard and Richard Quinney distinguished between (1) occupational criminal behavior and (2) corporate criminal behavior. They defined occupational criminal behavior as the "violation of the criminal law in the course of an activity or a legitimate occupation." Corporate crime for its part was said to consist of crimes committed by corporate officials for their corporation as well as offenses charged against the corporate entity itself (Clinard and Quinney, 1973: 189). Laura Schrager and James F. Short, Jr. (1977; see also Ermann and Lundman, 1978) gave further body and differentiation to the second element of the Clinard-Quinney dichotomy, defining what they preferred to call "organizational crime" in the following manner:

> The illegal acts of omission or commission of an individual or a group of individuals in a formal organization in accordance with the operative goals of the organization, which have a serious physical or economic impact on employees, customers, or the general public (Schrager and Short, 1977: 408).

Some scholars of white-collar crime, however, take exception to the final phrase of this definition, insisting that the offense need only be against the law; that it is not necessary that it have a "serious" impact. Indeed, they argue that "serious" is a term of art and not of science.

A further distinction among white-collar offenses adds "state-corporate crime" as a separate component of the generic category. Offenses of this nature are defined as follows:

> State-corporate crimes are illegal or socially injurious actions that result from a mutually reinforcing interaction between (1) policies and/or practices in pursuit of the goals of one or more institutions of political governance and (2) policies and/or practices in pursuit of the goals of one or more institutions of economic production and distribution (Aulette and Michalowski, 1993:175).

A 1991 fire at the Imperial Food Products chicken-processing plant in Hamlet, North Carolina, which killed 25 workers and injured another 56, is used to illustrate "state-corporate crime." The state government had encouraged industry to locate in North Carolina by fighting unions with a right-to-work statute and keeping wages low. As one of the pro-business measures, safety inspections were minimized; as a result, no action had been taken to deal with the illegally locked door at the processing plant that prevented the workers' escape when fire broke out.

A fundamental definitional question remains after the breakdown of white-collar crime into the foregoing subcategories: Should it be the nature of the behavior or the position and power of the offender—or both together—that places the illegal act under the heading of white-collar crime?

The classic Sutherland position was adopted by Albert J. Reiss, Jr., and Albert D. Biderman in their inquiry into the possibility of establishing a data-reporting system (such as we have for murder, robbery, and other traditional offenses) for white-collar crime. They defined white-collar crime as "those violations of law to which penalties are attached and that involve the use of a violator's position of significant power, influence, or trust in the legitimate economic or political institutional order for the purpose of illegal gain, or to commit an illegal act for personal or organizational gain" (Reiss and Biderman, 1980:xxiii; see also Geis, 1992).

For Clinard and Quinney, however, position, influence, and significant power are of no concern. If a corporate president fixes prices with competitors or a part-time salesman fudges on his expense account, both are seen as white-collar crimes.

The Clinard and Quinney definitional stance has been adopted in several important studies of the sentencing of white-collar criminals (Benson and Walker, 1988; Hagan, Nagel, and Albonetti, 1980; Wheeler, Weisburd, and Bode, 1982; but see Hagan and Parker, 1985). Because crimes such as fraud and bank embezzlement are included in these studies, as many as half of the violators in some subcategories turn out to be unemployed or to be working in very low-level positions (Daly, 1989), a matter that is a far cry from Sutherland's emphasis on the white-collar offender's high status. Nonetheless, such an approach democratizes the criminological study of white-collar crime by including everybody who violates a particular law rather than only a select portion of that group.

In a major contribution, Susan Shapiro (1990) has sought to "liberate" the concept of white-collar crime from the definitional shackles she believes have "created an imprisoning framework for contemporary scholarship, impoverishing theory, distorting empirical inquiry, oversimplifying policy analysis, inflaming our muckraking instincts, and obscuring fascinating questions about the relationship between social organization and crime" (p. 362). Shapiro believes that the focus ought not to be on the standing of perpetrators but on the essential nature of white-collar crime—its modus operandi. This, she maintains, involves the violation of trust—of norms of disclosure, disinterestedness, and role competence. As a whimsical example of such misrepresentation, Shapiro relates the story of "Zoogate"—that the Houston Zoo advertised live cobras but displayed rubber replicas, since live cobras cannot live under the lights in the area where they would have been kept.

Shapiro grants that her definition would exclude what have been quintessential white-collar offenses such as antitrust violations and violent union-busting. She also admits that it will be difficult to cast aside the Sutherland legacy, which she agrees is "polemically powerful." Whether Shapiro's redefinition of white-collar crime musters adherents undoubtedly will depend on whether it provides more significant understanding of the dynamics of the behavior and if it offers a sounder framework for research probes.

THEORIES OF WHITE-COLLAR CRIME

His theory of differential association, Sutherland (1949) believed, provided the proper schema for understanding white-collar crime. As he saw it, all criminal offenders behaved in an illegal fashion because they had learned from others, largely through close personal relationships, to regard law violation more favorably than conformity to legal demands. The theory of differential association, unfortunately, is so imprecise as to be untestable, and it fails to meet the scientific criterion of being able to predict reasonably well who will and who will not become a criminal. Besides, two major early studies of white-collar crime found differential association inapplicable to their findings. For Cressey (1953), embezzlers did not need to learn from others, but already possessed the knowledge of how to cheat; their motive to do so derived from their personal financial need. For Clinard (1952), black-market violations were best understood in terms of the personality characteristics of the offenders. In addition, Sutherland's theory of differential association has rightly been criticized for focusing exclusively on the social psychological process of individual offending and failing to attend to "the far-reaching perspective of [the] power structure" (Thio, 1973:5).

For thirty years after Sutherland, the study of white-collar crime became essentially an atheoretical enterprise, relying largely on a case-study approach (Geis, 1991). The exceptions were studies that sought to relate corporate conditions—form of management, capitalization, market conditions, competitive situation, and similar considerations—to criminal records (e.g., Elzinga and Breit, 1976; Farberman, 1975; Lane, 1953). These, however, essentially have been correlational efforts with only crude theoretical implications.

Recently, however, important strides have been made toward providing white-collar crime with a theoretical framework or, alternatively, incorporating it into a general theory of criminal behavior. James W. Coleman (1987), for instance, sought to tie the social structure and the culture of capitalism to motivations to commit white-collar offenses, but granted that consideration of the opportunities presented to persons in different social positions also is essential to an adequate understanding of white-collar crime (Coleman, 1987; for a critique see Braithwaite, 1989).

Michael Gottfredson and Travis Hirschi (1990), for their part, have maintained, as did Sutherland, that all crime can be explained by a single theoretical scheme. For them, the key to crime is an absence of self-control in the perpetrator. They insist that lack of self-control accounts not only for crimes—"acts of force or fraud undertaken in the pursuit of self-interest"—but also for accidents, victimizations, truancies, substance abuse, family problems, and disease.

To seek to make their point, Gottfredson and Hirschi single out white-collar crime—the traditional bugaboo for such efforts—for special attention. First, they argue that there is no value in focusing only on the perpetrator's position, asking: "What is the theoretical value in distinguishing a doctor's Medicaid fraud from a patient's Medicaid fraud?" Then they insist that those who commit white-collar crimes, such as frauds, are likely to engage in other forms of law breaking as well, and that the roots of all such activities lie in inadequate self-control.

Gottfredson and Hirschi's position largely is tautological in that they designate acts that by their nature involve absence of self-control and then seek to explain them by this absence. Their attempt to incorporate white-collar crime in their theorizing has been disputed on a number of specific grounds. Steffensmeier (1989), for instance, takes them to task for their focus on fraud and forgery as the basis for their theoretical statement. He observes:

> The evidence is quite conclusive . . . that persons arrested for fraud and forgery do not qualify as white-collar criminals, whether that term is used restrictively to refer to crimes committed by persons of high socioeconomic status in the course of their occupation, or if the term is used broadly to refer to crimes committed by an employee (Steffensmeier, 1989:347).

Most arrests for fraud or for forgery, Steffensmeier notes, are not occupationally related but rather involve passing bad checks, credit-card fraud, theft of services, falsification of identification, defrauding an innkeeper, fraudulent use of public transport, welfare fraud, and small con games. Besides, even if Gottfredson and Hirschi's definition is taken at face value, Steffensmeier insists, data indicate that they are incorrect when they claim that the ages of people who commit white-collar crime are much the same as those for ordinary crime: White-collar offenders are significantly older than street offenders. For Steffensmeier, low self-esteem, inadequate self-control, and weak social bonds constitute only partial determinants of some criminal behaviors. For most scholars who study white-collar crime, the idea that low self-control holds the key to such offenses as antitrust conspiracies seems exceedingly farfetched.

After examining the pre-sentence dossiers of 2462 individuals charged with an array of white-collar offenses (very broadly defined), Michael Benson and Elizabeth Moore (1992) further criticized Gottfredson and Hirschi by maintaining that they largely erred in their conclusion that such offenders are criminally versatile and as prone to deviance as common offenders. They dispute Gottfredson and Hirschi's rejection of motives as important casual forces, and insist that a more complex casual structure is necessary to account for white-collar offenses.

Gottfredson and Hirschi's theorizing flies in the face of the persuasive statement offered by Robert K. Merton, a guru of criminological theory. "The decision to encompass a great variety of behaviors under one heading," Merton wrote, "naturally leads us to assume that it is what these behaviors have in common that is most relevant, and this assumption leads us to look for an all-encompassing set of propositions which will account for the entire range of behavior." "This is not too remote," Merton adds, "from the assumption . . . that there must be a theory of disease, rather than distinct theories of disease—of tuberculosis and of arthritis, of typhoid and syphilis—theories which are diverse rather than single" (Merton, 1956:7).

Merton's viewpoint is seconded by Francis T. Cullen (1983) who believes that criminological theory is notably flawed in its failure to adhere to a "structuring tradition," that is, to seek to attend to why an individual chooses to commit one particular kind of criminal offense rather than another. Similarly, John Braithwaite (1985) has maintained that progress in the construction of theories of occupational crimes probably will have to be confined to specific forms of such offenses, though he believes that more comprehensive interpretive schemes might be useful for understanding corporate crime.

This last category—corporate crime—itself has led to some vigorous recent disputation. In the last piece written before his death, Donald Cressey (1989:32) took criminologists to task for holding to the "erroneous assumption that organizations think and act, thus saddling theoretical criminologists with the impossible task of finding the cause of crime committed by fictitious persons." Corporations do not behave, Cressey insists; their so-called actions are but manifestations of actions by real persons. For Cressey "there can be no social psychology of so-called corporate or organizational crime because corporations have no biological or psychological characteristics" (p. 37).

In rebuttal, Braithwaite and Brent Fisse (1990) maintain that corporations do indeed have distinctive personalities, that they are something other than the sum of the isolated efforts of individuals, and that reasonable theories can be drawn up to explain their illegal actions.

The debate between Cressey and his challengers brought to the surface a related issue that often arises in corporate crime—that of strict liability, where corporate officers are held criminally responsible even though they were not aware that an offense had been committed. Is it possible to explain such actions in theoretical terms? Cressey would say no, Braithwaite and Fisse would say yes (see also Geis, 1994). This recalls the ancient debate over whether it was possible to explain actions that violated the criminal doctrine of deodand. According to this doctrine, animals and inanimate objects, such as trees, were deemed to be criminally responsible for a death if, for example, they fatally attacked or fell onto a person. Deodands were not abolished until 1846.

CONCLUSION

We have seen various conflicting definitions and theories of white-collar crime. Which one makes the most sense? Consider the illustration offered by Oliver Wendell Holmes, Jr., when he was a U.S. Supreme Court justice:

> The old books say that, if a man falls from a ship and is drowned, the motion of the ship must be taken to be the cause of death and the ship is forfeit [subject to confiscation]—provided, however, that this happens in fresh water. For if the death took place on the high seas, that was outside the ordinary jurisdiction (Holmes, 1881:26).

Will any criminological theory possibly help us comprehend this law breaking? Even in the unlikely event we puzzle our way to such a formulation, how do we satisfactorily differentiate the drowning in fresh water from that on the high seas? Perhaps, in the end, the cynical view of Max Planck, a Nobel Prize laureate in physics, prevails. "A new scientific truth does not triumph by convincing its opponents and making them see the light," Planck wrote, "but rather because its opponents eventually die, and a new generation grows up that is familiar with it" (Crichton, 1988:358).

References

Aulette, Judy Root, and Raymond Michalowski. 1993. "Fire in Hamlet: A Case Study of State-Corporate Crime," pp 171–206 in Kenneth D. Tunnell (ed.), *Political Crime in Contemporary America: A Critical Approach.* New York: Garland.

Benson, Michael L., and Elizabeth Moore. 1992. "Are White-Collar and Common Offenders the Same?: An Empirical and Theoretical Critique of a Recently Proposed General Theory of Crime." *Journal of Research in Crime and Delinquency* 29:251–272.

Benson, Michael L., Elizabeth Moore, and Esteban Walker. 1988. "Sentencing the White-Collar Offender." *American Sociological Review* 53:294–302.

Braithwaite, John. 1989. "White-Collar Crime, Competition, and Capitalism: Comment on Coleman." *American Journal of Sociology* 94:628–632.

Braithwaite, John. 1985. "White Collar Crime." *Annual Review of Sociology* 11:1–25.

Braithwaite, John, and Brent Fisse. 1990. "On the Plausibility of Corporate Crime Theory." *Advances in Criminological Theory* 2:15–38.

Clinard, Marshall B. 1952. *The Black Market: A Study of White-Collar Crime.* New York: Holt.

Clinard, Marshall B. and Richard Quinney. 1973. *Criminal Behavior Systems: A Typology,* 2nd ed. pp. 187–223. New York: Holt, Rinehart, and Winston.

Coleman, James W. 1987. "Toward an Integrated Theory of White-Collar Crime." *American Journal of Sociology* 93:406–439.

Cressey, Donald R. 1953. *Other People's Money: The Social Psychology of Embezzlement.* New York: Free Press.

Cressey, Donald R. 1989. "The Poverty of Theory in Corporate Crime Research." *Advances in Criminological Theory* 1:31–56.

Crichton, Michael. 1988. *Travels.* New York: Knopf.

Cullen, Francis T. 1983. *Rethinking Crime and Deviance Theory: The Emergence of a Structuring Tradition.* Totowa, NJ: Rowman & Allanheld.

Daly, Kathleen. 1989. "Gender and Varieties of White-Collar Crime." *Criminology* 27:769–793.

Elzinga, Kenneth, and William Breit. 1976. *The Antitrust Penalties: A Study in Law and Economics.* New Haven: Yale University Press.

Ermann, M. David, and Richard Lundman. 1978. "Deviant Acts by Complex Organizations: Deviance and Social Control at the Organizational Level of Analysis." *Sociological Quarterly* 19:55–67.

Farberman, Harvey A. 1975. "A Criminogenic Market Structure: The Automobile Industry." *Sociological Quarterly* 16:438–457.

Geis, Gilbert. 1991. "The Case Study Method in Sociological Criminology," pp. 220–223 in Joe R. Feagin, Anthony M. Orum, and Gideon Sjoberg (eds.), *A Case for the Case Study.* Chapel Hill: University of North Carolina Press.

Geis, Gilbert. 1992. "White-Collar Crime: What Is It?," pp. 31–52 in Kip Schlegel and David Weisburd (eds.), *White-Collar Crime Reconsidered.* Boston: Northeastern University Press.

Geis, Gilbert. 1994. "A Review, Rebuttal, and Reconciliation of Cressey and Brathwaite and Fisse on Criminological Theory and Corporate Crime." *Advances in Criminological Theory* 6:321–350.

Gottfredson, MIchael R., and Travis Hirschi. 1990. *A General Theory of Crime.* Stanford: Stanford University Press.

Hagan, John, Ilene H. Nagel, and Celesta Albonetti. 1980. "The Differential Sentencing of White-Collar Offenders in Ten Federal District Courts." *American Sociological Review* 43:802–820.

Hoyan, John, Ilene H. Nagel, Celesta Albonetti, and Patricia Parker. 1985. "White-Collar Crime and Punishment: The Class Structure and Legal Sanctioning of Securities Violations." *American Sociological Review* 50:302–315.

"Hits Criminality in White Collars." 1939. *New York Times* December 28, p. 12.

Holmes, Oliver Wendell, Jr. 1881. *The Common Law.* Boston: Little, Brown.

Lane, Robert E. 1953. "Why Businessmen Violate the Law." *Journal of Criminal Law, Criminology, and Police Science* 44:151–165.

Merton, Robert K. 1956. In Helen L. Witmer and Ruth Kotinsky (eds.), *New Perspectives for Research on Juvenile Delinquency.* Children's Bureau Publication No. 356. Washington, DC: Government Publication Office.

Pontell, Henry N., and Kitty Calavita. 1993. "White-Collar Crime in the Savings and Loan Scandal." *Annals of the American Academy of Political and Social Science* 525:31–45.

"Poverty Belittled as Crime Factor." 1939. *Philadelphia Inquirer* December 28, p. 17.

Reiss, Albert J., and Albert D. Biderman. 1980. *Data Sources on White-Collar Law-Breaking.* Washington, DC: U.S. Department of Justice.

Schrager, Laura S., and James F. Short, Jr. 1978. "Toward a Sociology of Organizational Crime." *Social Problems* 25:407–419.

Shapiro, Susan. 1990. "Collaring the Crime, Not the Criminal: Reconsidering the Concept of White-Collar Crime." *American Sociological Review* 55:346–365.

Steffensmeier, Darrell. 1989. "On the Causes of 'White-Collar' Crime: An Assessment of Hirschi and Gottfredson's Claims." *Criminology* 27:345–358.

Sutherland, Edwin H. 1940. "White Collar Criminality." *American Sociological Review* 5:1–12.

Sutherland, Edwin H. 1949a. *White Collar Crime.* New York: Dryden.

Sutherland, Edwin H. 1949b. "The White Collar Criminal," pp. 511–515 in Vernon C. Branham and Samuel B. Kutash (eds.), *The Encyclopedia of Criminology.* New York: Philosophical Library.

Sutherland, Edwin H. 1956. "Crimes of Corporations," pp. 78–96 in Albert K. Cohen, Alfred Lindesmith, and Karl Schuessler (eds.), *The Sutherland Papers.* Bloomington: Indiana University Press.

Thio, Alex. 1973. "Class Bias in the Sociology of Deviance." *American Sociologist* 8 (February):1–12.

Wheeler, Stanton, David Weisburd, and Nancy Bode. 1982. "Sentencing the White-Collar Offender: Rhetoric and Reality." *American Sociological Review* 47:641–649.

P A R T   8

Drug and Alcohol Abuse

The general public is apparently seized with the terrible vision of huge masses of Americans shooting heroin, smoking pot, snorting cocaine, or dropping acid. Illegal drug use is widely seen as a plague sweeping through the whole country. Mathea Falco, former Assistant Secretary of State for international narcotics matters and drug-abuse adviser to Bill Clinton during the presidential campaign, writes:

> The horrors of drug abuse have become depressingly familiar: crack-addicted mothers abandoning their babies; young children dealing drugs instead of going to school; innocent citizens killed in gang shoot-outs; and sports stars dying from overdoses. . . . Drug abuse is at the heart of what many people think has gone wrong with America. It appears as either the cause or the effect of a wide range of problems which seem out of control: urban blight, the destruction of families, the failure of schools, the loss of economic productivity.[1]

Drug abuse does appear to be a widespread problem in the United States. Over 26 million Americans—about 12 percent of the U.S. population aged 12 or older—use illicit drugs every year, and half of them at least once a month. Drug use is even more common among young people: nearly 30 percent of high school seniors use drugs every year, and over half of them at least once a month.[2] Indeed, the United States has the highest rate of drug abuse among the industrial countries of the world. American high school seniors also have the highest rate among their peers in the industrial world.[3]

All this, however, should not be blown out of proportions. It is true that the United States leads the industrial nations in drug abuse. But it is not true that drug abuse is so pervasive that it invades every nook and cranny, enslaving all

---

[1] Mathea Falco, *The Making of a Drug-Free America: Programs That Work* (New York: Times Books, 1992), pp. 3, 4.

[2] Cheryl M. Greenhouse, "Household Survey Shows Few Changes in Americans' Illicit Drug use," *NIDA Notes*, Vol. 7 (March/April 1992), pp. 5–6; Robert Mathias, "Drug Use Among High School Seniors Continues 16-Year Decline," *NIDA Notes*, Vol. 7 (May/June 1992), pp. 12–13.

[3] Elliot Currie, *Reckoning: Drugs, the Cities, and the American Future* (New York: Hill and Wang, 1993), pp. 10–12.

classes of Americans to the same extent. The fact is that most of the drug problems, especially the most serious ones such as drug addiction or death from drug overdose or drug-related homicide, are largely confined to the lower classes, particularly the socially and economically oppressed minorities, as Elliot Currie points out in the first article here, "Drug Crisis: The American Nightmare." Currie further explains why the poor continue to abuse drugs. In the second selection, "Drugs and Free Will," Jeffrey Schaler analyzes various studies and comes to the conclusion that free will, not loss of control, has much to do with abusing drugs. In the third article, "A Career Perspective on Heroin Use and Criminal Behavior," Charles Faupel shows how the life style of a heroin addict is basically similar to a conventional career. However, these analyses should be put in perspective. They are mostly relevant to the poor. Drug use among the non-poor, middle class, or affluent is far less common and compulsive, and has been steadily decreasing since the early 1980s.[4]

But drinking is a different matter. Over the last two decades, binge drinking has greatly increased among college students. In the fourth reading, "The Effects of Raising the Legal Minimum Drinking Age," Stella Hughes and Richard Dodder report how they conducted a series of ten surveys over a six-year period but failed to find significant changes in college students' drinking habits.

---

[4] Ibid., p. 3.

28

Drug Crisis: The American Nightmare

ELLIOTT CURRIE

University of California, Berkeley

To anyone observing the state of America's cities in the 1990s, it seems devastatingly obvious that we have failed to make much headway against the drug crisis. Americans living in the worst-hit neighborhoods still face the reality of dealers on their doorstep and shots in the night; many fear for their lives, or their children's lives, and sense that their communities have slid downward into a permanent state of terror and disintegration. Even those fortunate enough to live in better neighborhoods cannot pick up a newspaper or watch the news without confronting story after story about the toll of drugs and drug-related violence on communities and families. For most of us, the drug plague seems to have settled in, become a routine feature of an increasingly frightening and bewildering urban landscape.

Yet we also hear official reassurances that, despite appearances, we have made great progress in the war on drugs, or even that victory is just around the corner. The assertion that we are winning the war on drugs is designed to vindicate our present policies: to justify pouring ever-greater resources into what we have already tried, and, in a larger sense, to rationalize our current national priorities. But our visceral reactions are correct, and the cheerleading is premature. The American drug problem remains out of control. It vastly outstrips that of any other industrial nation. And it does so despite an orgy of punishment in the name of drug control that also has no counterpart in the rest of the developed world, or in our own history.

The news is not all bad. Middle-class drug use has declined, and the worst fury of the crack epidemic has abated in many cities. But the first happened in spite of the drug war, not because of it. And the second, while a welcome gain in the short term, pales beside the profoundly troubling long-term trend. Twenty years after the drug war began in earnest, we are far worse off than when we started. And the outlook for the future is not encouraging.

INTERNATIONAL COMPARISONS

To appreciate the magnitude of the drug crisis in the United States, we need to compare it to the experience of other advanced industrial countries. Most Americans do not realize how atypical we are—in part because that most basic reality is curiously left out, or downplayed, in our national debate on drug policy. There is much discussion of the meaning of short-range fluctuations in drug use in the United States, but little about why we lead the world in drug abuse. Those who wish to minimize the implications of our unhappy leadership often point out that the drug problem has risen *everywhere*, not just in the United States; and there is an element of truth in that. Few countries have been spared some problem with illegal drugs during the last two decades; in some it is serious and increasing. But that should not blind us to the dramatic differences between the United States and otherwise comparable societies.

A revealing study by the Canadian scholars Reginald Smart and Glenn Murray has shown that if the world's countries are divided into those with high, medium, and low drug problems, the United States is the *only* developed country that falls into the "high" category. The others—thirteen in all—are all developing countries: Afghanistan, Bolivia, Burma, Egypt, Iran, Lebanon, Malaysia, Pakistan, Peru, the Philippines, Singapore, Thailand, and Vietnam. It is sometimes argued that the reason for the peculiar severity of the American drug problem is that we are unusually affluent and excessively tolerant—or as one observer puts it, "richer and more liberal" than other countries with less severe drug problems. But the truth is precisely the opposite; *every* other country with a drug problem on the American scale or greater is a relatively poor country (though not always among the very poorest), and most are also authoritarian and intolerant, often dictatorial. Most are also "source" countries, which grow or manufacture much of the world's supply of heroin and cocaine; in many, the abuse of those drugs has become a crisis of unprecedented proportions, especially among the young. But in the developed world, no other country matches what one British observer has called the "American Nightmare"—or even comes close.

The British, as we will see, have a significant heroin problem which mushroomed in the early 1980s; the German drug problem, which had been relatively stable up through most of the eighties, began to rise again toward the end of the decade; Spain and Italy both have substantial problems with heroin and milder ones with cocaine. Yet none even *begins* to reach our overall levels of drug use; and in only a few developed countries has cocaine in any form, much less crack, made significant inroads.

This is hardly because suppliers are uninterested in the affluent European and Japanese markets; in the late 1980s the American market was so glutted with cocaine that many high-level suppliers began looking to Europe to absorb their surplus product. Yet by the end of the decade there were fewer known cocaine addicts in all of England, for example, than in many urban *neighborhoods* in the United States. There were 677 cocaine-related arrests in France in 1989, and 4900 in the city of Boston. More people died in 1989 of the effects of cocaine abuse alone in Los Angeles than died of *all* drug-related causes in England. As many died from methamphetamine abuse in the city of San Diego as died of *all* drug-related causes in Holland, with fifteen times the population.

Even measured by surveys of high school students—which, as we shall see, *understate* the severity of the American drug problem because they miss our sprawling population of the socially and economically marginal—there are striking differences in the extent of drug abuse between the United States and Europe. Thus, in 1989 something over 10 percent of American high school seniors admitted having tried cocaine—more than five times the proportion turned up by surveys in Germany, Italy, and England (three countries with relatively severe drug problems by European standards) and about *twenty* times the rate in Sweden, Holland, and Norway.

What is true of drug use also holds for its most deadly social and medical consequences. Drug-related violence is by no means absent in European countries, but on the American scale it is simply unknown. There are twice as many drug-related homicides annually in New York City as there are homicides of any kind in all of England, with seven times the population. There were more drug-related killings in the city of Washington, D.C. (population 600,000) in 1988 than there were murders of any type in all of Scandinavia (population eighteen million). No major European city lacks an illegal drug market, but in none of them are entire neighborhoods gripped by Uzi-wielding drug gangs or terrorized by routine drive-by shootings.

The magnitude of the link between drugs and AIDS in the United States is similarly unparalleled in the rest of the industrial world. Nearly 25 percent of the more than 200,000 diagnosed AIDS cases in the United States have intravenous drug use as the only risk factor; another 6 percent involve both IV drug use and homosexuality. The proportion is far higher in some cities—40 percent in New York and 65 percent in Newark, the nation's drugs-AIDS capital. In Sweden, at the end of 1990, there were slightly more than five hundred known AIDS cases, of which only seventeen, or a little over 3 percent, involved IV drugs. In Holland, there were about seventy-five AIDS cases in 1989 in which IV drug use was the only risk factor, or about 7 percent of their total.

Moreover, the American drug crisis, by itself, is responsible for most of the rise in AIDS among *children* in the entire industrial world. In 83 percent of pediatric AIDS cases known by the end of 1990, the children had contracted the disease from their mothers—most of whom had been infected through contacts with IV drug users. Nationally, about 1.5 out of every 1000 babies are now born to mothers with the AIDS virus (as of 1989); in one hospital in Newark, closer to 40 out of 1000. Mother-child transmission of AIDS is a rare event in most other developed countries (though, again, common in parts of the Third World); in 1989, we had 55 times as many cases as West Germany, 65 times as many as the United Kingdom.

In pointing to these striking differences, I do not mean to idealize the European situation. In some European countries drug abuse is a problem of genuinely troubling dimensions, and in some the AIDS-drugs connection is worsening. But in none of those countries have drugs and drug-related crime rocked the foundations of the social order as they have in the United States, or turned the city streets into urban battlegrounds, or triggered a massive explosion of sexually transmitted disease. . . .

AMERICAN DRUG CRISIS

While it is probably true that the epidemic of cocaine has peaked, both cocaine and heroin are now endemic in America at levels that far surpass those before the start of the drug war. While there is credible evidence that rising health consciousness and growing awareness of the adverse effects of drug abuse have altered the drug habits of the more secure strata of American society, no such evidence exists for the bottom quarter of the population.

Even many who support the thrust of our present drug policies would acknowledge that the drug crisis among "hard-core" users in the more marginal populations is understated by the conventional statistics, and that it has proven remarkably resistant to the conventional tools of the drug war. But they would argue that the declines in *middle*-class drug use prove that the drug war is "on the right track," and that if we only redoubled our efforts we could make it work against the admittedly tougher situation in the inner cities as well.

The trouble with that view is that the conventional drug war had virtually nothing to do with the declines in drug use among the better-off, for it was never *fought* against their drug use. Despite occasional bursts of rhetoric about cracking down on "recreational" drug use in the suburbs, so little did that crackdown actually take place even at the height of the drug war in the late eighties and early nineties that when several University of Virginia fraternities were raided in the spring of 1991—netting, to no one's great surprise, nothing more than small amounts of marijuana and LSD—the story was front-page news in the national press for days. In the Virginia case, law-enforcement officials were reported to have "expressed hope" that the raid would send the message that drug seizures and arrests would no longer "be limited mainly to poor neighborhoods." The drug war has been overwhelmingly targeted at the communities of the poor and near-poor, especially the minority poor. It's possible to argue over whether or not that emphasis is justified; it's not possible to deny that it exists.

Nationally, in 1989, about 40 percent of all arrests for all drug violations were of blacks, who are only 12 percent of the population. The proportion of jail inmates charged with a drug offense who were black or Hispanic rose from 55 percent in 1983 to 73 percent in 1989. The disproportion is even greater in areas where hard-drug use is heavily concentrated: In New York State, over 90 percent of those sent to state prison for drug felonies in 1988 were black or Hispanic, and the figure was even higher—about 95 percent—for the lower-level felonies that made up almost three-fifths of prison commitments for drug offenses. "Measured by jail and prison populations," notes a recent report of the New York State Coalition for Criminal Justice, "one can almost say that drug abuse has been legalized for middle-class whites."

In California, only 19 percent of adults and less than 9 percent of juveniles arrested for felony narcotic violations in 1989 were white and non-Hispanic.

According to a report from the National Institute of Justice, the drug war was the main reason why the number of black and Hispanic youth held in short-term juvenile institutions nationwide increased by 30 percent between 1985 and 1987 alone—while detentions of non-Hispanic white youth rose by only 1 percent. Minority youth were more likely to be detained once arrested than whites, both for drug sales and possession. They were also more likely than whites to be referred to courts for drug offenses in the first place. The result was a 71 percent increase in the number of nonwhite youth detained for drug offenses in the space of just two years.

The drug war, in short, has been fought hardest—in some places, almost exclusively—in precisely those communities where drug use remains most severe and most stubborn, barely at all in those where it has fallen. Likewise, it has been fought most fiercely against the *drugs* that remain most stubbornly persistent—heroin and especially cocaine—and barely at all against marijuana, which has undergone the most significant decline and indeed accounts for the bulk of the much trumpeted fall in illicit drug use in the United States. In New York, for example, research shows that the measures taken against crack in the 1980s were far tougher than those for other drugs—including "widespread arrests for sale and possession, more stringent charging decisions, and harsher sentences."

Meanwhile, revealingly, marijuana use declined (according to the self-report surveys) in spite of a very significant *let-up* in the law-enforcement effort against it. Nationally, marijuana possession arrests *dropped* by over 10 percent between 1980 and 1988, while arrests for possession of heroin and cocaine exploded by 600 percent. In California, the pattern was even more extreme: Juvenile felony arrests for marijuana dropped by well over half during the 1980s.

In short, whatever caused the decline in marijuana use among American teenagers in the 1980s, it was certainly not the war on drugs. In most places there *was* no war on marijuana use, and, in some, authorities had officially declared a truce.

What we know from careful analyses of the high-school drug surveys, indeed, is that most of the decline in marijuana use can be attributed to changing perceptions of its dangers to health and well-being—changes which fit well with the long-run trend toward increasing health-consciousness among middle-class Americans, a trend that encompasses declines not only in drug use but in alcohol, smoking, and unhealthy diet, and increased exercise. These changes are all to the good, but they are *not* the result of the war on drugs. (Indeed, to the extent that they are related to specific antidrug strategies at all, they reflect efforts at education and prevention which the last two administrations have systematically slighted.). . .

ROOTS OF THE CRISIS

"The epidemic areas," [researcher Isidor] Chein concluded, "are, on average, areas of relatively concentrated settlement of underprivileged minority groups, of poverty and low economic status." They were also characterized by low educational attainment and large numbers of disrupted families. Importantly, the data made it clear that race itself was not the overriding factor: low incomes and poor jobs explained most of the link between drug use and race in these neighborhoods. It was not so much that the epidemic neighborhoods were *black* neighborhoods, but that black neighborhoods tended to have large concentrations of low-income people in low-status jobs. . . .

Chein attributed the success of the cohesive family in protecting adolescents against heroin use to its "contribution to a sense of mutuality"—a "sense of human solidarity, a feeling of belonging, respect for the integrity and value of the individual human being, and the long-range motivation of things worth living for"—which was disturbingly rare in the areas of concentrated deprivation in American cities. In interviews, the addicts often expressed "profound pessimism and alienation," agreeing that there was "not much chance for a better world," that "most people were better off not born," and that everyone was "really out for himself: nobody cares.". . . Ideally, a strong, supportive family could shield adolescents against the "prevailing atmosphere of degenerated personal relationships" in these deprived neighborhoods. The catch, of course, was that it was precisely in neighborhoods like these that the family itself was especially vulnerable, as was clear from the high proportion of disrupted and pathological families in them.

As this suggests, Chein's picture of the addicts' backgrounds, personalities, and prospects was generally grim. Young heroin addicts were seen as the most extreme product of a chain of pathologies that began with the economic deprivation of the larger community and were exacerbated by the resulting disintegration or demoralization of many urban families. The boys who became addicted—at least in the white and Puerto Rican neighborhoods—were likely to be those who had suffered the most emotional damage from an inadequate and conflictual family life. But the study was equally emphatic that this was more than just a matter of individual psychopathology. The family's problems were rooted in the larger pathologies of the community—the general bleakness of life, the absence of opportunity, and the breakdown of more supportive cultural values in the American urban environment. . . .

For young people, especially, growing up in these communities, drug use performed a variety of functions which, most observers agreed, reflected ordinary human—and specifically adolescent—needs, but ones which were difficult to fulfill in ordinary ways in these distinctly abnormal circumstances. There were differences of emphasis and specifics, but the serious observers of heroin addiction generally agreed that much more important than the physiological effects of the drug were its uses in helping to build an identity, buttress social status and the esteem of peers, and provide alternative and compelling sources of challenge and purposeful activity for people who were deprived of them through normal channels. In the topsy-turvy world of the shattered communities of the inner city, the very dangers and adversities associated with hard-drug use were transformed into appeals. It was precisely the illegality of heroin use, and the very real danger of arrest and jail, that helped provide the intrigue and "elite-group" identity that observers like Finestone found to be central to the "cat" culture: precisely the high risk of illness, pain, and abject enslavement to addiction that drew the "stand-up cat" to test his mettle against the toughest of drugs. . . .

None of this was to deny that many addicts desperately needed help. But it did shift the perspective on what help should *mean,* in two related ways. First, the research on addiction suggested that what many addicts most needed in the long run was changed lives—broader opportunities for good work and respectable incomes, full participation in the surrounding society. Second, while many addicts did need immediate assistance in the short run, they usually needed a wider range of help than traditional medical or psychiatric treatment offered—help that would enable them to cope with the multiple obstacles they faced in the increasingly inhospitable inner cities. Within this framework, some form of individual treatment could have an important place, but only if it shifted focus, away from the medical model of treating the individual in isolation and toward integration with broader efforts to provide better opportunities and better tools for taking advantage of them.

This view was made explicit in Preble and Casey's classic article. "The ultimate solution to the problem" of lower-class heroin addiction, they argued, "as with all the problems which result from social injustice, lies in the creation of legitimate opportunities for a meaningful life for those who want it." In the meantime, "reparative measures" were necessary. But given their emphasis on the lack of opportunities for good, challenging work as the root cause of the spread of addiction in the inner city, the measures Preble and Casey favored leaned heavily toward "educational and vocational training and placement," rather than chemical treatment with substitute drugs or antagonists, traditional psychotherapy, or group therapy. They proposed a model treatment program that would span a full three years: nine months of intensive vocational and educational training coupled with psychological counseling, and twenty-seven months devoted to "aftercare" in the community, which could involve further training and schooling as needed, along with social and psychological counseling—a "comprehensive social reparation" for those addicts not "too severely damaged by society."

29

Drugs and Free Will

Jeffrey A. Schaler
American University

That was the disease talking . . . I was a victim." So declared Marion Barry, 54, mayor of the District of Columbia. Drug addiction is the disease. Fourteen charges were lodged against him by the U.S. attorney's office, including three counts of perjury, a felony offense for lying about drug use before a grand jury; ten counts of cocaine possession, a misdemeanor; and one count of conspiracy to possess cocaine.

Barry [sought] moral sanctuary in what has come to be known as the disease-model defense. He maintained that he "was addicted to alcohol and had a chemical dependency on Valium and Xanax." These are diseases, he asserted, "similar to cancer, heart disease and diabetes." The implication: It is as unfair to hold him responsible for drug-related criminal behavior as it is to hold a diabetic responsible for diabetes.

The suggestion was that his disease of addiction forced him to use drugs, which in turn eroded his volition and judgment. He did not voluntarily break the law. According to Barry, "the best defense to a lie is truth," and the truth, he contended, is that he was powerless in relation to drugs, his life unmanageable and "out of control." His behaviors or acts were purportedly the result, that is, symptomatic, of his disease. And jail, say those who agree with him, is not the answer to the "product of an illness."

This disease alibi has become a popular defense. Baseball's Pete Rose broke through his "denial" to admit he has a "gambling disease." Football's Dexter Manley claimed his drug use was caused by addiction disease. Addiction treatment professionals diagnosed televangelist Jimmy Swaggart as having "lost control" of his behavior and as being "addicted to the chemical released in his brain from orgasm." They assert that Barry, Rose, Manley and Swaggart all need "twelve-step treatment" for addiction, the putative disease that, claims the multimillion-dollar addiction treatment industry, is reaching epidemic proportions and requires medical treatment. To view addiction-related behaviors as a function of free will, they often say, is cruel, stigmatizing and moralistic, an indication that one does not really understand the disease.

Reprinted from *Society*, Vol. 28 (September/October 1991): 42–49.

Others are more reluctant to swallow the disease model. After testing positive for cocaine in 1987, Mets pitcher Dwight Gooden said he could moderate his use of the drug and was not addicted. This is heresy according to disease-model proponents, a sign of denial, the salient symptom of the disease of addiction and considered by some to be a disease itself. There is no such thing as responsible drug taking or controlled drinking for an addict or an alcoholic, they assert.

The tendency to view unusual or questionable behavior as part of a disease process is now being extended, along with the characteristic theory of "loss of control," to include all sorts of "addictive" behaviors. We are currently experiencing the "diseasing of America," as social-clinical psychologist Stanton Peele describes it in his book of the same name (1989). The disease model is being applied to any socially unacceptable behavior as a means of absolving people of responsibility for their actions, criminal or otherwise. The practice is justified on this basis: Drug use constitutes an addiction. Addiction is a disease. Acts stemming from the disease are called symptoms. Since the symptoms of a disease are involuntary, the symptoms of drug addiction disease are likewise involuntary. Addicts are thus not responsible for their actions.

THREE MODELS OF DRUG USE

Etiological paradigms for understanding drug use can be distilled into three models. Aside from the disease model, there are two other ways of looking at drug addiction: the free-will model and the moralistic model. In the free-will model drug use is envisioned as a means of coping with environmental experience, a behavioral choice and a function of psychological and environmental factors combined. The nervous system of the body is conceived of as a lens, modulating experience as self and environment interact. The self is like the film in a camera, where experience is organized and meaning is created. The self is not the brain.

Individual physiological differences affect the experience of self. They do not create it. The quality of a camera lens affects the image of the environment transposed to the film. When the image is unpleasant, drugs are used to modify the lens.

The self is the executor of experience in this model, not the nervous system. Drug use may or may not be an effective means of lens modification. The assessment of drug effectiveness and the price of drug use are viewed as moral, not medical, judgments.

The recommended therapy for the drug user is: (1) a matter of choice; (2) concerned with awareness and responsibility; (3) a process of values clarification; (4) a means of support to achieve specific behavior goals; and (5) an educational process that involves the learning of coping strategies.

The moralistic model harkens back to the days of the temperance movement and is often erroneously equated with the free-will model. Here, addiction is considered to be the result of low moral standards, bad character, and weak will. Treatment consists of punishment for drug-using behavior. The punitive nature of America's current war on drugs with its call for "user accountability" is typical of the moralistic perspective.

Addicts are viewed as bad people who need to be rehabilitated in "boot camps." They are said to be lacking in values. President Bush gave a clear example of this during the televised debates of the 1988 presidential campaign. When asked how to solve the drug problem, he answered, "by instilling values."

The drug user's loss of values is often attributed to the presence of a disease. A "plague" and "epidemic" of drug use are said to be spreading across the land. Since users are sick and supposedly unaware of their disease, many people feel justified in coercing them into treatment, treatment that is primarily religious in nature. Thus, the moralistic model is paternalistic.

In the disease or medical model, addicts are considered to have physiological differences from normal people, differences based in a genetic source or created through the chemical effects of drugs. Instead of focusing on the interaction between the self and the environment, advocates of the disease model view the interaction between physiology and the chemicals in drugs as both the disease and the executor of behavior and experience. In this sense the model is mechanistic. The person is viewed as a machine, a highly complex machine, but a machine nevertheless. The disease of addiction is considered to be incurable. People in treatment can only reach a state of perpetual recovery. Treatment of symptoms involves admitting that one is ill by breaking through denial of the disease and turning over one's life to a "higher power" in a spiritual sense and psychological support to achieve sobriety. Addicts are not bad but sick people. Intervention is required because the machine has broken. Thus, the disease model is both paternalistic and mechanistic.

THE MYTH OF LOSS OF CONTROL

In 1962 British physician and alcohol researcher D. L. Davies rocked the alcoholism field by publishing the results of a long-term follow-up study of patients treated for alcoholism at the Maudsley Hospital in London. Abstinence, long considered the only cure for alcoholism, was seriously questioned as the only form of treatment when seven out of ninety-three male alcoholics studied exhibited a pattern of normal drinking. Physiological differences purportedly present in alcoholics did not seem to affect their ability to control drinking.

Four years later, *The Lancet* published an important study by British psychiatrist Julius Merry that supported Davies's findings. Alcoholics who were unaware they were drinking alcohol did not develop an uncontrollable desire to drink more, undermining the assertion by supporters of the disease model that a small amount of alcohol triggers uncontrollable craving. If alcoholics truly experience loss of control, then the subjects of the study should have reported higher craving whether they believed their beverages contained alcohol or not.

According to the loss-of-control theory, those with the disease of alcoholism cannot plan their drinking especially when going through a period of excessive craving. Yet, psychologist Nancy Mello and physician Jack Mendelson, leading alcoholism researchers and editors of the *Journal of Studies on Alcohol,* reported in 1972 that they found alcoholics bought and stockpiled alcohol to be able to get as drunk as they wanted even while undergoing withdrawal from previous binges. In other words, they could control their drinking for psychological reasons; their drinking behavior was not determined by a physiologically uncontrollable force, sparked by use of alcohol.

As Mello and Mendelson wrote in summary of their study of twenty-three alcoholics published in *Psychosomatic Medicine:* "It is important to emphasize that even in the unrestricted alcohol-access situation, no subject drank all the alcohol available or tried to 'drink to oblivion.' These data are inconsistent with predictions from the craving hypothesis so often invoked to account for an alcoholic's perpetuation of drinking. No empirical support has been provided for the notion of craving by directly observing alcoholic subjects in a situation where they can choose to drink alcohol in any volume at any time by working at a simple task. There has been no confirmation of the notion that once drinking starts, it proceeds autonomously."

A significant experiment conducted by Alan Marlatt of the University of Washington in Seattle and his colleagues in 1973 supported these findings by showing that alcoholics' drinking is correlated with their beliefs about alcohol and drinking. Marlatt successfully disguised beverages containing and not containing alcohol among a randomly assigned group of sixty-four alcoholic and social drinkers (the control group) asked to participate in a "taste-rating task." One group of subjects was given a beverage with alcohol but was told that although it tasted like alcohol it actually contained none. Subjects in another group were given a beverage with no alcohol (tonic) but were told that it did contain alcohol.

As Marlatt and co-authors reported in the *Journal of Abnormal Psychology,* they found "the consumption rates were higher in those conditions in which subjects were led to believe that they would consume alcohol, regardless of the actual beverage administered." The finding was obtained among both alcoholic and social drinker subjects. Marlatt's experiment suggests that according to their findings the ability of alcoholics to stop drinking alcohol is not determined by a physiological reaction to alcohol. A psychological fact—the belief that they were drinking alcohol—was operationally significant, not alcohol itself.

Similar findings have been reported in studies of cocaine addiction. Patricia G. Erickson and her colleagues at the Addiction Research Foundation in Ontario concluded, in their book *The Steel Drug* (1987), after reviewing many studies on cocaine that most social-recreational users are able to maintain a low-to-moderate use pattern without escalating to dependency and that users can essentially "treat themselves." They state, "Many users particularly appreciated that they could benefit from the various appealing effects of cocaine without a feeling of loss of control."

Erickson and co-authors cite in support a study by Spotts and Shontz (1980) that provides "the most indepth profile of intravenous cocaine users to date." They state: "Most users felt a powerful attachment to cocaine, but not to the

extent of absolute necessity. [A]ll agreed that cocaine is not physically addict-
ing . . . [and] many reported temporary tolerance."

In a study by Siegel (1984) of 118 users, 99 of whom were social-recreational
users, described by Erickson et al. as the only longitudinal study of cocaine
users in North America, "all users reported episodes of cocaine abstinence."

These results thus further support the hypothesis that drug use is a function
of psychological, not physiological, variables. Even the use of heroin, long considered "the hardest drug," can be controlled for psychological and environmental reasons that are important to heroin addicts. A notable study of 943
randomly selected Vietnam veterans, 495 of whom "represented a 'drug-posi-
tive' sample whose urine samples had been positive for opiates at the time of
departure" from Vietnam, was commissioned by the U.S. Department of
Defense and led by epidemiologist Lee N. Robins. The study shows that only
14 percent of those who used heroin in Vietnam became re-addicted after
returning to the United States. Her findings, reported in 1975, support the
theory that drug use is a function of environmental stress, which in this example ceased when the veterans left Vietnam. Veterans said they used heroin to
cope with the harrowing experience of war. . . .

With so much evidence to refute it, why is the view of drug addiction as a
disease so prevalent? Incredible as it may seem, because doctors say so. One
leading alcoholism researcher asserts that alcoholism is a disease simply
because people go to doctors for it. Undoubtedly, addicts seek help from doctors for two reasons. Addicts have a significant psychological investment in
maintaining this view, having learned that their sobriety depends on believing
they have a disease. And treatment professionals have a significant economic
investment at stake. The more behaviors are diagnosed as diseases, the more
they will be paid by health insurance companies for treating these diseases.

Most people say we need more treatment for drug addiction. But few people realize how ineffective treatment programs really are. Treatment professionals know this all too well. In fact, the best predictor of treatment success,
says Charles Schuster, director of the National Institute on Drug Abuse, is
whether the addict has a job or not. . . .

CONCLUSION

All of this is not to suggest that the people we call addicts are bad, suffering
from moral weakness and lack of willpower, character, or values. Drug addicts
simply have different values from the norm and often refuse to take responsibility for their actions. Public policy based on the disease model of addiction
enables this avoidance to continue by sanctioning it in the name of helping
people. As a result, criminals are absolved of responsibility for their actions,
drug prevention and treatment programs end up decreasing feelings of personal self-worth and power instead of increasing them, and people who choose
not to use drugs pay higher taxes and health insurance premiums to deal with
the consequences of those who do. . . .

The legal arguments set forth to exculpate criminals because of addiction disease do not seem to be supported by scientific findings. Quite to the contrary, research suggests that drug addiction is far from a real disease. And as long as drug addiction can be blamed on a mythical disease, the real reasons why people use drugs—those related to socioeconomic, existential, and psychological conditions including low self-esteem, self-worth, and self-efficacy—can be ignored.

30

A Career Perspective on Heroin Use and Criminal Behavior

CHARLES E. FAUPEL
Auburn University

The idea of "career" is popularly associated with professions and other middle-class occupations. But sociologists have been using this concept for many years to refer to criminal and deviant activities. The concept was first introduced into the deviance literature by Goffman (1959) in his treatment of the moral career of mental patients, and was later extended by Becker (1963) to deviant careers in general. Since then, career has been used as an interpretive framework for understanding numerous types of deviance, including prostitution and other sexual behaviors, professional crime, fencing, skid-row alcoholism, gambling, and narcotics addiction. Despite the stereotypes associated with them, all these activities can be understood in terms of career. For purposes of this article, we may define career as a series of meaningfully related statuses, roles, and activities around which an individual organizes some aspect of his or her life over a period of time.

I will here analyze heroin use and heroin-related criminal behaviors from the perspective of a career. The research that informs this perspective was conducted in the Wilmington, Delaware, area in 1979 to 1981. A total of thirty hard-core urban street addicts were interviewed for 10 to 25 hours each about all aspects of their drug-using and criminal behavior.

HEROIN USE AS A CAREER

Occupational careers typically begin when individuals choose and enter a career field. They first make some decision about whether or not to go on to college and, if so, what to major in. After graduating from college, they seek

This article was specifically written for this reader, with data from research partly supported by DHEW Grant No. 1 R01 DA01827 from the Division of Research, National Institute on Drug Abuse.

their first job that ideally is related to their field of study. Career heroin users experience a similar phase of initiation. Typically, someone *turns them on* (introduces them) to heroin, though they have experimented with a variety of other drugs. Similarly, all the heroin users that I interviewed engaged in criminal or quasi-criminal activities as a means of supporting their habits. These *hustles* are cultivated and fine tuned over a period of time, often under the tutelage of older, more experienced addicts.

During the course of a career, one encounters obstacles and opportunities, successes and failures, or "ups and downs," that define one's career path. Heroin addicts also encounter these vicissitudes in their career. A typical experience involves *getting hooked* and *jones-ing*—becoming addicted and then suffering periodic withdrawal from heroin when supplies are unavailable. Over time, most addicts develop a *main hustle,* a criminal specialization that provides them with increased income and stature in the subculture of heroin use. But they also suffer setbacks in their careers, as when they get *busted* by the police, either for crime or drug possession.

Finally, people with conventional careers eventually *retire*, or leave one career to begin another. Heroin users refer to this last career phase of theirs as *burning out* or *shaking the monkey.* Like conventional careerists who come back out of retirement, addicts often return to *the life*, becoming involved again in heroin use and criminal activities. Also, like conventional careerists, criminal addicts often make "career shifts" by abandoning old *hustles* to pursue new ones.

CONTINGENCIES OF HEROIN-USING CAREERS

Social and biographical factors profoundly affect the careers of heroin addicts. A major *score* (proceeds from a criminal act) may establish the reputation of an addict as a big-time hustler, thereby launching a new criminal career or enhancing an existing one. Getting *busted,* on the other hand, may force the addict to abandon a particular criminal career, at least temporarily. But such major events in the addict's life do not completely shape the addict's career. Even far less significant occurrences also affect the addict's career. For example, learning how to prepare and self-inject heroin enables the addict to stop depending on others in the subculture to *get off* (shoot heroin). Whether the events are major or minor, they have much to do with at least two important contingencies in the addict's career: whether drug is available and whether the addict's life structure is disrupted.

Drug Availability

Drugs are not always easy to get. Eddie, a white addict in his late twenties reflected, "You might have money in your pocket and you go up there and you wait until five o'clock that afternoon [for a dealer]; or you might go up there and he's sitting there at ten o'clock and you don't have any money. By the time you get money, he's gone." Such difficulties in connecting with a dealer are part of the challenge of the addict life style. But there is more to drug availability than simply finding a dealer. Because heroin is so expensive, even a modest habit for an addict using street dope is extremely costly. Hence, a critical factor in drug availability is affordability. There are two ways of making heroin more affordable.

One way involves *increasing income* through criminal means. Regular heroin users commonly report a heavy reliance on criminal activity to obtain the necessary funds to support their drug habit. This is because using heroin on a regular basis requires substantially more money than most addicts can earn through a conventional job. Sometimes, in order to make more money, addicts would take up a new *hustle* that is more more profitable than the current one. Consequently, they consume more drugs. This career shift is not unique to heroin addicts, though. It occurs in conventional occupations as well. Employees may get promoted within their own companies or with new companies, which offers significantly more income. When this occurs, the individuals usually spend more money by, say, purchasing a new car, in the same way as heroin addicts buy more drugs.

Another way of making heroin more affordable is *lowering its cost*. This often involves purchasing heroin in large quantities, usually by the *bundle* (the equivalent of about 25 bags), which costs much less than if 25 bags are bought individually. Experienced addicts usually buy one or more bundles, sell four or five bags from each, for a large profit, to less experienced users at street prices, and then use that money to *re-up* (buy another bundle). By getting heroin this way, which addicts call *juggling*, they can use more of the drug. There are other methods of reducing the cost of heroin. Women addicts sometimes move in and live with dealer-boyfriends, from whom they can get all the dope they want. Other addicts become *testers* for dealers by injecting into themselves a quantity of a drug to test for its purity. For their service, testers do not have to pay for the test drug and often are remunerated with additional quantities.

Making drugs affordable, either through increased income or lowered cost, is not the only condition that enhances availability. Addicts may acquire a sizable *stash* (supply) of heroin, but if they cannot get it into their bloodstream they have not enhanced availability at all. They must learn to *cook* (prepare) the drug, *tie up* (expose a vein), and *spike* (inject). Until these skills are learned, the novice user is dependent on others in the subculture to *get off*, a favor which is usually done on a fee-for-service basis. Older, experienced, but temporarily down-and-out junkies will offer this service for a share of the dope. This obviously will reduce drug availability for the inexperienced addict. Learning to self-inject, then, makes one's stash available for consumption at all times.

Life Structure

Heroin addicts participate in a myriad of activities in their daily lives. These activities constitute the addict's *life structure*. It involves settling into a daily routine of conventional and criminal activities. The conventional routine may include going to school, going to work, doing household chores, running errands, drinking beer with friends, and so on. The criminal routine involves regularly performing certain acts required by the type of crime to be committed. There are various examples of criminal routine. In burglary, addicts spend time staking out business establishments or residential areas to determine the best locations and times to strike. In shoplifting, they typically establish *runs*, regular sequences of stores from which they *boost* (shoplift), during certain times of the day, while reserving other times to sort and *fence* (sell) what they have stolen. In prostitution, they keep a busy evening and nighttime work schedule, which normally runs from about 7 P.M. to 3 A.M., while sleeping in the morning and discharging domestic responsibilities in the afternoon. It is within this structure of conventional and criminal activities that *copping, juggling,* and *shooting* dope take place.

In conventional society, cigarette smokers and coffee drinkers often consume much more nicotine and caffeine during "off" times, such as when they are at home during the holidays or on vacation. These are the times when they are out of their usual routine—their life structure is in effect disrupted, though temporarily. Similarly, disruption to the heroin addict's life structure can have a profound impact on drug consumption. In fact, during such times, the addict's drug habit often gets out of control. As Old Ray, a veteran addict, explained, "Usually the person that gets involved in drugs is not totally involved in anything else. I was on the street at the time [I started using more]. I just got laid off. . . . I had encountered a situation of economic castration. This made me susceptible to the street."

A TYPOLOGY OF HEROIN-USING CAREERS

Both drug availability and life structure profoundly influence the addict's career phases. As shown in Figure 30.1, there are four possible career phases dependent on whether drug availability is relatively limited or unlimited and whether life structure is relatively stable or unstable.

The Occasional User

The "occasional use" phase, defined by relatively stable life structure and limited drug availability, is typical of addicts very early in their careers. Most heroin users begin their careers quite young, and many are still in school when they first start experimenting with the drug. Those who are beyond school age are often employed or maintain a stable structure of domestic and child-care responsibilities. To cite a few examples: Mario was working as an apprentice for a local optician when he first began using heroin; Eddie was a full-time student at the local university; Bertha worked as a barmaid and cared for an infant son; and Mona was living at home with a stable family and working full-time doing clerical work. Such routines provide insulation from becoming heavily addicted. Further, these conventional routines fail to provide relatively unlimited drug availability that often comes with lucrative criminal routines.

Life Structure

	Stable	Unstable
Availability		
Limited	The Occasional User	The Street Junkie
Unlimited	The Stable Addict	The Free-Wheeling Addict

FIGURE 30.1

A Typology of Heroin-using Career Phases

While most young users have had some criminal experience prior to using heroin, this early criminality is typically sporadic, not sufficient to provide a dependable income.

Occasional users have not yet spent enough time in the drug subculture to be fully cognizant of, much less to have internalized, its normative proscription against turning others on. They have not yet attended the "school of hard knocks." They have not yet *done time* (been jailed or imprisoned) and may have never even been arrested. They are unlikely to have experienced their first *jones* (withdrawal from heroin). Therefore, they tend to do things that more experienced addicts would not do, especially turning neighborhood friends on to heroin. But this is tantamount to sharing with friends the excitement of their first sexual experience. The rather graphic image of the drug peddler as a "merchant of death" seeking to victimize innocent youth, then, is a highly distorted stereotype and, in most cases, simply wrong. The more realistic image of how drug use is spread is a much more innocent one: It consists of young friends sharing drugs in the same way as adolescents sneaking behind the barn to share a cigarette purloined from a father's coat pocket.

This early, occasional phase of heroin-using careers is also a time of experimentation with crime for most users. By the time they have had their first encounter with heroin, most addicts have had some criminal experience. These early criminality is usually less serious and profitable than later criminal activities. Harry's first crime, for example, was stealing a bicycle at age 13. He stole the bike to demonstrate his worthiness for being accepted into a neighborhood street gang. It was not until several years later that he became involved in burglary and drug dealing on a regular basis.

Finally, in this early phase of heroin-using careers, drug use does not lead to criminal activity. The major reason is that occasional users are still far from being heavily involved in heroin, hence they have no need to turn to sustained criminal activity for quick, lucrative income required for heavy drug use.

The Stable Addict

This is a seasoned, mature addict, enjoying relatively unlimited drug availability and stable life structure. The addict can get a constant supply of heroin at reasonable cost. This has much to do with the addict's relatively stable life structure, which is largely supported by criminal routines that regularly or reliably produce the needed income for drug use.

According to popular belief, it is heavy use of drugs that compels the user to commit crime as a way of getting money for the next fix. In other words, drug use is widely assumed to precede criminal activity. But my research shows just the reverse: Criminal activity precedes drug use. This explains why the more profit an addict gets from crime the more drugs he or she consumes. As Stephanie said, "The better I got at crime, the more money I made; the more money I made, the more drugs I used." She went on to explain, "I think that most people that get high, the reason it goes to the extent that it goes . . . is because they make the money like that. I'm saying if the money wasn't available to them like that, they wouldn't be into drugs as deep as they were."

While stable addicts are heavy users of heroin, they do not use too much of it. Instead, they impose a certain limit on their drug use, so that they are unlikely to die from drug overdose. The reason is the relative stability of their life structure, whose criminal and conventional routines regulate drug use. If their life structure is disrupted, the already heavy use of heroin will likely become uncontrollably excessive, as is often found in the next career phase of heroin addiction.

The Free-Wheeling Addict

In this career phase, the addict uses heroin to uncontrolled excess. An important factor is the relatively unlimited availability of the drug. But, as suggested, far more important is the disruption of the addict's life structure, because it often sharply escalates drug use. Loss of a conventional job, forced abandonment of a criminal routine, or some other negative event may disrupt a life structure. But more often it is a highly positive experience, such as an unprecedented success at a criminal enterprise, that disrupts the addict's routine life. When this occurs, the addict is likely to become a free-wheeling one, using heroin with a vengeance.

A typical example is Harry's experience. His main hustle had been burglary, which provided a reliable, though not greatly lucrative, income. One momentous day, his long-time friend Bart offered him an opportunity that he could not turn down. As Harry said, "I got hooked up with these people that Bart was hanging around with, and they were into [armed robbery of grocery stores]. . . . So there was a string of those that went down, and we went hog-wild." After Harry abandoned his burglary routine for this far more profitable venture, his income soared. This sharply increased his drug availability. But, more important, he no longer had to maintain a rigorous routine as a burglar. Now his work in armed robbery was far from routine. It required only two or three hours per day in a three-day work week, and there was too little time for planning and executing the heists. This, then, disrupted Harry's life structure that had been established by his many burglaries. As a result, his heroin use increased dramatically. This free-wheeling, uncontrolled drug use lasted for nearly eight months, after which he ended his armed-robbery binge and returned to his old hustle as a burglar.

The Street Junkie

Like the free-wheeling addict, the street junkie has an unstable life structure. But the junkie's unstable life is a result of problems, difficulties, failures, or some other negative experiences. Such distressing experiences tend to greatly increase the addict's desire for drug consumption. But, unfortunately, by causing addicts' income to plummet, the same negative events in their life severely limit the availability of drugs. Therefore, they become down-and-out junkies desperate for a fix. This desperation often compels the junkies to commit crimes that would have been unthinkable before, such as mugging poor elderly women for their meager money.

SUMMARY

The life styles of heroin addicts parallel professional and other conventional careers in many ways. Like professionals exploring various career options before choosing one they like, heroin addicts experiment with different types of drugs and criminal activities to sustain their drug use before settling into a preferred drug and crime. Heroin addicts also encounter the vicissitudes of upward and downward mobility in their drug-criminal world. Most important, heroin use among addicts is comparable to consumer behavior among conventional careerists, and criminal activities among addicts are analogous to income-producing jobs among conventional careerists.

The connection between drug use and crime in the world of addiction is also similar to the connection between consumer behavior and income-producing activity in the world of professions. More specifically, crime produces income that makes drug use possible in the same way as a profession generates income that makes consumer activity possible. Thus, the more income crime produces, the greater the quantity of heroin is used, just as the more income a profession produces, the greater the quantity of merchandise is purchased. Moreover, when the addict's life routine is disrupted, heroin use increases. This is basically the same as the situation when the professional's life routine is disrupted and consumer activity increases.

References

Becker, Howard S. 1963. *Outsiders: Studies in the Sociology of Deviance.* Glencoe, IL: Free Press.

Goffman, Erving. 1959. "The Moral Career of the Mental Patient." *Psychiatry* 22: 123–142.

31

The Effects of Raising the Legal Minimum Drinking Age

STELLA P. HUGHES
South Dakota School of Mines and Technology

RICHARD A. DODDER
Oklahoma State University

The Twenty-sixth Amendment, ratified in 1971, lowered the voting age to 18. Many Americans then argued that it was not fair to allow young adults to vote and go to war, but not to consume alcoholic beverages. The early 1970s saw a trend toward lowering the minimum legal drinking age, and by 1975 over half the United States and all Canadian provinces had passed legislation allowing young people to drink at an earlier age.

The investigations that followed produced mixed results. Some reported increases in alcoholic beverage sales or in accident rates among young drivers (Smart, 1977; Smart and Goodstadt, 1977; Wagenaar, 1982; Whitehead et al., 1975), but others found no significant changes attributable to a lower legal drinking age (Barsby and Marshall, 1974; Naor and Nashold, 1975; Rooney and Schwartz, 1977; Zylman, 1974).

After alcohol-related accident and arrest rates, particularly among younger drivers, were reported by the media, American legislators began experiencing pressures to raise the minimum drinking age. These pressures produced changes in laws; but the extent to which age was causally involved in alcohol-related accidents may have been over estimated. Higher accident and arrest rates and increased alcoholic beverage sales comprise inferential information, and factors other than younger drinkers (e.g., freedom to drive at an earlier age, changes in the economy, changes in the price of gasoline, or more young people owning automobiles) could account for any increases. A number of

Reprinted with permission from *Journal of Studies on Alcohol*, Vol. 53, pp. 567–575, 1992. Copyright © by Alcohol Research Documentation, Inc., Rutgers Center of Alcohol Studies, Piscataway, NJ 08855.

studies that examined actual drinking concluded that raising the minimum drinking age had little effect on behavior. Engs and Hanson (1986) compared responses of students from states that had enacted a 21-year minimum with students from states allowing drinking at a younger age and found few differences in drinking-related problems. These authors also reported an *increase* in student drinking after July 1987 when the minimum drinking age became 21 in all states, a possible reaction to the legislation (Engs and Hanson, 1989). Research in Florida, where a cut-off date allowed some 19 year olds to drink while others could not, found no differences between the two groups in drinking behavior (Gonzalez, 1989; Lanza-Kaduce and Richards, 1989).

Most of the available studies have not focused on the long-term effects of legislative changes, and none have utilized baseline information. The purpose of this research was to assess the usefulness of legislation to raise the minimum drinking age by looking at behavior over time, both before and after legislative changes.

METHOD

Information for this research was obtained from anonymous, self-administered questionnaires given to students in randomly selected introductory sociology classes at Oklahoma State University. These classes were chosen because introductory sociology was taken by a cross-representation of the university population to fulfill a social science requirement, because they contained a high proportion of the younger students who would be most affected by age limitations on drinking, and because they have been found to have stable compositions over time and hence could be resampled. A more comprehensive description of sampling techniques and justifications can be found in Hughes and Dodder (1986).

Data were gathered in 10 sampling periods from 1981 through 1987 ($N = 4572$). When the first two samples were taken, 18 year olds could legally drink "weak" beer (3.2 percent or less alcohol content by weight) but could not legally drink other alcoholic beverages. Just after the second sampling (September 1983), the state legislature raised the legal minimum drinking age to 21 for all alcoholic beverages, and the remaining samples were obtained on a semester basis under these conditions. . . .

RESULTS

Quantity—Frequency

Both men and women reported drinking more beer and doing so more often than either distilled spirits, the second choice, or wine. Men tended to register higher scores than women for both beer and distilled spirits, but women reported a higher quantity and frequency of wine consumption. Although there were some significant differences between particular samples in quantity and frequency of consumption for men, consistent changes across sampling periods were not apparent. In the second sampling period, just before implementation of the legislation, both quantity and frequency of beer drinking showed a slight increase, with a similar, but significant, decrease in consumption of liquor. With this one exception, it appears that consumption was fairly constant across the 10 sampling periods (see Figures 31.1 and 31.2).

Among female students, quantity and frequency of consumption showed a similar, but more clearly defined, pattern. With the exception of the sampling periods immediately surrounding the legislation, consumption remained fairly constant. . . . It is not known exactly why drinking among women reportedly increased just before the legislation, and then decreased immediately afterward, but it is possible that female students were more cautious about disobeying the law and waited to see what law enforcement practices would be implemented.

Students reported that enforcement appeared rigorous at first, but then declined, possibly due in part to the expense of monitoring drinking establishments. Young drinkers also became more adept at evading arrest and circumventing efforts to keep them out of taverns. Businesses also learned that if they received half or more of their revenue from sales of items other than alcohol, they would not be designated as taverns and those under age 21 could enter. Several establishments began serving meals or selling items such as sweatshirts to increase that portion of their revenue. Once those under 21 gained entry,

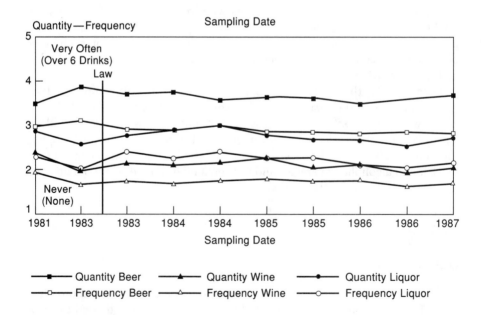

FIGURE 31.1

Alcohol Consumption for Male Students

they could ask older friends to buy beer, and would not be arrested unless the arresting officer saw them actually drinking.

Included were questions about frequency of precollege drinking and how often students had been asked for proof of age. Again, these activities were reported more often by men than by women. Raising the minimum drinking age should, in theory, result in a reduction of younger-age drinking over time but, for both men and women, precollege drinking remained about the same. . . .

Drinking Locations

Among male students, reports of drinking at home or in homes of friends remained quite constant, but drinking in residence halls, fraternities or sororities, bars and restaurants changed significantly. The up-and-down pattern displayed by residence hall drinking may represent a differential enforcement of existing regulations against drinking. Students reported that residence hall counselors (full-time students on each floor whose duties include enforcing the rules) varied considerably in enforcement practices. Thus, changes from year to year could reflect policies of the personnel in charge. On the other hand, there was a trend toward increased drinking in fraternities/sororities. Drinking in both bars and restaurants showed a significant decline across the 10 sampling periods. These findings are consistent with those of Lotterhos et

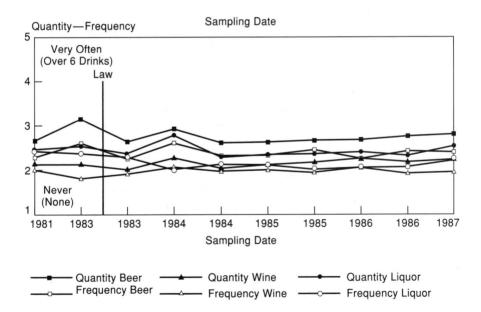

FIGURE 31.2
Alcohol Consumption for Female Students

al. (1988), who reported that only 6 percent of students in their North Carolina sample intended to stop drinking, and 70 percent indicated that they planned to change location of drinking.

Among female students there were some significant differences in drinking locations, but for the most part these did not represent a trend for increased or decreased drinking over time. Reports of drinking in fraternities/sororities did appear to represent a slight trend toward increased consumption. As with male students, fluctuations in enforcement practices may have been responsible for changes in residence hall drinking. Over time, female students reported slightly less drinking in both bars and restaurants.

Both men and women obtained alcoholic beverages primarily from friends who were of age, and this practice increased significantly across the sampling periods. According to these students, parents rarely furnished alcoholic beverages, and the use of false indentification was not common among women. Men reported using false identification more often, and this increased slightly over time. Purchasing alcoholic beverages from store clerks or bartenders who did not check identification decreased significantly over the last four sampling periods. Again, this may be a reflection of enforcement practices.

Problem Drinking

Most of the problems commonly associated with drinking were reported infrequently by the students in this research, and less often by women than by men. The problems most often cited were having a hangover, nausea/vomiting, doing something while drinking that was later regretted, and drinking and driving. Among all students (including those over age 21), reports of being arrested for such activities as drinking and driving ranged from 3.5 percent of the sample (1981) to 7.1 percent (fall of 1983, just before the law change). Reports of being arrested for drinking underage ranged from 2.7 percent (both fall 1983, before the law change, and fall 1985) to 4.7 percent (both fall 1983, after the law change, and spring 1987). These differences, again, could result from different levels of enforcement.

Reports of problem drinking, for both men and women, changed little over the 10 sampling periods. Being arrested and behavior that is illegal (drinking and driving, fighting, damaging property) were cited more often by men than by women. These behaviors showed no significant changes, although drinking and driving on the part of male students tended to decrease somewhat over time. The only significant difference was more frequent reports among male students of being criticized by a date for drinking during the sampling period just prior to the law change.

CONCLUSIONS

The most prevalent observation from analysis of data collected over the 10 sampling periods is that drinking patterns and behaviors exhibited by the students in this research remained roughly constant over time. Only minor changes in drinking patterns were observed, and there were no significant differences in total quantity and frequency of consumption. Some accommodations in drinking locations were apparent, but these seemed to balance out; that is, decreased drinking in one area (e.g., restaurants) was balanced by increased drinking in another (e.g., residence halls). This would seem to indicate that legislation may not have an impact on total drinking behavior to any great extent. After a law is adopted, enforcement agencies frequently find practical difficulties in interpreting or enforcing the law. In addition, businesses and consumers find "loopholes" to allow them to continue behaviors that are targeted by the law.

Not only did the students find different methods for obtaining alcoholic beverages and different places to drink, but taverns seemed to accommodate them as well. Many such establishments changed to a restaurant format during the day in order to remove their tavern status. Most were lax about checking identification, or they used techniques that were easily circumvented (e.g., hand stamping that could be removed). Tavern personnel were responsible legally only for selling to minors; they were not required to monitor those who actually drank (in this case the drinker would be breaking the law). In addition, sales of a nonalcoholic beer, created to look and taste like beer, made the task of monitoring underage drinking even more difficult.

There was little difference in the drinking behavior of those under and those over age 21, and this is also an indication that drinking patterns were not greatly influenced by the legislation. If the legislation and subsequent enforcement had been effective, we would expect to see pronounced differences in the drinking behavior of those who could drink legally and those who could not.

An additional methodological feature of this research may be of importance. Had the baseline data from 1981 not been available, conclusions drawn from the investigation might have been different. Research involving new legislation or changes in current laws often is undertaken after the legislation has been enacted or just before its implementation. In this research, the increase in drinking just before the new legislation could have led to the conclusion that the subsequent lower quantity-frequency mean scores, particularly for beer consumption, were a positive result of changing the minimum drinking age. It is apparent, when including the baseline data, however, that drinking behavior remained fairly constant over time and that changing the minimum drinking age had, at best, only a temporary effect on quantity-frequency of consumption as well as on the other drinking-related variables in the study.

References

Barsby, S. L. and Marshall, G. L. 1974. "Short-Term Consumption Effects of a Lower Minimum Alcohol-Purchasing Age." *J. Stud. Alcohol* 38: 1665–1679.

Engs, R. 1975. Student Alcohol Questionnaire, Bloomington: Indiana University.

Engs, R. C. 1977. "Drinking Patterns and Drinking Problems of College Students." *J. Stud. Alcohol* 38: 2144–2156.

Engs, R. C. and Hanson, D. J. 1986. "Age-specific alcohol Prohibition and College Students' Drinking Problems." *Psychol. Rep.* 59: 979–984.

Engs, R. and Hanson, D. J. 1989. "Reactance Theory: A Test with Collegiate Drinking." *Psychol. Rep.* 64: 1083–1086.

Gonzalez, G. M. 1989. "Effects of Raising the Drinking Age Among College Students in Florida." *College Stud. J.* 23: 67–75.

Hanson, D. J. 1977. "Trends in Drinking Attitudes and Behaviors Among College Students." *J. Alcohol Drug Educ.* 22 (no. 3): 17–22.

Hughes, S. P. and Dodder, R. A. 1986. "Raising the Legal Minimum Drinking Age: Short-term Effects with College Student Samples." *J. Drug Issues* 16: 609–620.

Jessor, R., Graves, T. D., Hanson, R. C. and Jessor, S. L. 1968. Society, Personality, and Deviant Behavior: A study of a Tri-Ethnic Community, New York: Holt, Rinehart & Winston, Inc.

Lanza-Kaduce, L. and Richards, P. 1989. "Raising the Minimum Drinking Age: Some Unintended Consequences of Good Intentions." *Just. Quart.* 6: 247–262.

Lotterhos, J. F., Glover, E. D., Holbert, D. and Barnes, R. C. 1988. "Intentionality of College Students Regarding North Carolina's 21-year Drinking Age Law." *Int. J. Addict.* 23: 629–647.

Naor, E. M. and Nashold, R. D. 1975. "Teenage Driver Fatalities Following Reduction in the Legal Drinking Age." *J. Saf. Res.* 7: 74–79.

Rooney, J. F. and Schwartz, S. M. 1977. "The Effect of Minimum Drinking Age Laws upon Adolescent Alcohol Use and Problems." *Contemp. Drug Probl.* 6: 569–583.

Smart, R. G. 1977. "Changes in Alcoholic Beverage Sales After Reductions in the Legal Drinking Age." *Amer. J. Drug Alcohol Abuse* 4: 101–108.

Smart, R. G. and Goodstadt, M. S. 1977. "Effects of Reducing the Legal Alcohol-purchasing Age on Drinking and Drinking Problems: A Review of Empirical Studies." *J. Stud. Alcohol* 38: 1313–1323.

Straus, R. and Bacon, S. D. 1953. *Drinking in College.* New Haven, CT.: Yale University Press.

Wagenaar, A. C. 1982. "Aggregate Beer and Wine Consumption: Effects of Changes in the Minimum Legal Drinking Age and a Mandatory Beverage Container Deposit Law in Michigan." *J. Stud. Alcohol* 43: 469–487.

Wechsler, H. and McFadden, M. 1979. "Drinking Among College Students in New England: Extent, Social Correlates and Consequences of Alcohol Use." *J. Stud. Alcohol* 40: 969–996.

Whitehead, P. C., Craig, J., Langford, N., MacArthur, C., Stanton, B. and Ferrence, R. G. 1975. "Collision Behavior of Young Drivers: Impact of the Change in the Age of Majority." *J. Stud. Alcohol* 36: 1208–1223.

Zylman, R. 1974. "Fatal Crashes Among Michigan Youth Following Reduction of Legal Drinking Age." *Q. J. Stud. Alcohol* 35: 283–286.

PART 9

Heterosexual Deviance

Is the one-night stand deviant? A single woman recently told a sex researcher what she thought about it:

> It's too demeaning. Making love to someone you don't even know is like Sylvester Stallone punching a piece of meat in his movie *Rocky*. . . . Many of these men like to exaggerate, even lie about, their sexual expertise. Most of the creeps that specialize in one-night stands do so because they lack a great deal in bed. Many of these men are embarrassed to see the same woman again. It may seem cruel, but I once spotted one of these men that had left me high and dry in the same bar, and giving his same spiel to another young woman. I walked up to him, said a loud hello, turned to the young woman and said in an even louder voice, "He's a premature ejaculator!" Sweet revenge was mine.[1]

This woman obviously considers one-night stands deviant. Most Americans (about 57 percent) agree with her. There is, however, a gender difference: more women than men (68 versus 47 percent) find the quickie with a stranger demeaning.[2] Similarly, many other forms of heterosexual acts, including premarital sex as practiced by a majority of young people, elicit different reactions from different sectors of society. Conservative or religious Americans, for example, are more likely than others to regard those sexual practices as deviant. This difference of opinions simply reflects the diverse, pluralistic nature of American society. In the first article, "What Is Sexual Deviance?" Samuel and Cynthia Janus discuss the societal definitions as well as characteristics of various sexual practices.

The next three articles offer a global perspective on prostitution. In "Becoming a Prostitute in Norway," Celilie Hoigard and Liv Finstad present both objective and subjective views of the subject. The objective view focuses on Norwegian prostitutes' social background, entry into prostitution, and reasons for the entry. The subjective view reveals how the prostitutes feel about their first tricks. In "Mother Sold Food, Daughter Sells Her Body," Marjorie

---

[1] Samuel S. Janus and Cynthia L. Janus, *The Janus Report on Sexual Behavior* (New York: John Wiley & Sons, 1993), p. 362.

[2] Ibid., p. 362.

Muecke attributes the prevalence of female prostitution in Thailand to the cultural influence of Buddhism and village morality. But in "Sex Tourism in Asia," Jody Miller portrays female prostitution in Thailand and other Asian countries as gross exploitation and dehumanization of women.

The last two selections bring us back to the United States. In "Does Exotic Dancing Pay Well but Cost Dearly?," Scott Reid and his colleagues show research evidence that the dancers are well paid but do not suffer any damage to their self-image as college students, mothers, or other conventional persons. In "Parade Strippers: Being Naked in Public," Craig Forsyth discusses his research on women exposing their breasts at Mardi Gras parades in New Orleans. Comparable to what Reid and others find, Forsyth's data reveal that the parade strippers do not suffer any negative consequences for exposing their breasts. More important, Forsyth's article highlights informal rules governing the interaction between these women and float riders like any other, more conventional social interactions.

32

What Is Sexual Deviance?

SAMUEL S. JANUS

CYNTHIA L. JANUS

Freud described deviants as "poor devils who have to pay a high price for their limited pleasures," but much of what he considered deviant has become part of the everyday sex lives of many Americans. What is deviance, or *paraphilia*, its new synonym in the professional literature? Most simply, deviance is the violation of society's rules, norms, laws, or customs. Sexual deviance ranges from a personally idiosyncratic routine of having to use a particular perfume or needing to experience the feel of silk, in order to turn on sexually, to the practice of dangerous, life threatening sex preferences, such as simulated (and, on occasion, accidentally completed) asphyxiation by hanging, to become turned on.

Is deviance necessarily bad for the individual or the sex partner, or for society at large? Some types of deviance are obviously criminal, harmful, wrong, and immoral—for example, rape, or the sexual molestation of young children. However, other types of deviance are relatively harmless and almost never impinge on anyone else's rights or liberties—for example, the man who gets some pleasure out of wearing his wife's panties under his three-piece business suit. Kinky, yes! Harmful? Probably not. This chapter examines and discusses the differences between the harmless and the damaging kinds of deviance. Harmless habits that affect one personally, but do not make demands on one's partner, tend to be limited in terms of their impact and potential peril. Sociologists and historians, most notably the classic theorist Emil Durkheim, have told us that, when societies are experiencing rapid change or are in a state of decline or decay, people adhere less and less to the societies' moral norms. Thus, we may infer that, if the rates of deviant acts begin to increase in a society, the increase may reflect, or herald, some major changes in the basic value structure of the society—in some cases, changes of which the society's members may not yet be aware.

Students of sociology and social change are aware of the axiom that today's deviance may well be tomorrow's norm. The present widespread approval of the practice of masturbation and oral sex is an example of a deviance of yesteryear that has changed into a norm. The definitions of what is or is not deviant behavior are established by various legitimate institutions, the most important being government and religion. In a pluralistic society such as ours, however, there are often wide differences between what may be considered deviant by government and what is considered deviant by religion or among different religions. The deeply emotional conflict and debate over abortion illustrate this point. Let us suppose that an adult woman is a devout member of a religion that considers abortion to be a sin or even murder. If she knowingly and willingly participates in an abortion, she may legitimately be described or labeled as a deviant, even though there are no statutes prohibiting abortion. However, if her religion does not define abortion as "abnormal" or "wrong," then she would not be considered deviant. This apparent contradiction comes about because deviance is always defined by the legitimate authorities or institutions. Thus, the definition of an act as deviant should always include the qualifying statement "relative to this or that religion or group or state."

What other legitimate institutions can define deviance? Perhaps the best known is the American Psychiatric Association (APA), which periodically publishes *Diagnostic and Statistical Manual of Mental Disorders* (DSM).[1] How does the DSM determine what is deviant? It depends on the advice of a group of clinicians and scholars who examine different patterns of human behavior that some people have identified as "harmful"—either to oneself or to others. If a behavior pattern regularly consists of specific acts, it is considered an identifiable and definable syndrome and its characteristics are stated in the DSM. Behavior that most people vaguely disapprove of—for example, drinking excessively and habitually to the point of alcohol dependence—becomes categorized as an illness or disease or emotional disorder. For other behaviors, such as cashing a forged-signature check or cheating on our income tax, we do not need the APA to tell us that we have acted deviantly. Criminal codes in the different states, or the Internal Revenue Service, have made it clear that these are deviant and punishable acts. Deviance may be as minor as picking one's nose in a restaurant—which violates only traditional customs—or as emotionally charged and dangerous as treason in wartime.

There is even "good" deviance. When the founding fathers of our country broke many English laws by refusing to obey the orders of the English government and its legitimate designees, they were acting in a criminal manner, just as all revolutionary leaders do; they were "deviants." The great religions of history were founded and nurtured by people acting in defiance of established authority and refusing to obey existing religious or secular law. Similarly, great artistic movements were invariably begun by painters who refused to paint the "right" way and acted on what they believed in. They often were called "weird," "crazy," and even "dangerous."

However, for most people, the term "deviant" seems most closely identified with sexual practices. For sexual norms, Western culture has looked to religion, the institution that has historically considered the regulation of sexual behavior to be its realm. It is the province of Western religion to regulate and interpret the principles and commandments of the Bible and to set up ideals of what is thought to be God's will for human behavior. Government shares religion's concern with sex, but for its own reasons: social order and population expansion. Government sees a need to regulate sexual activity in order to provide economically for the continuity of the family into future generations.

A discussion of the many moral norms relating to sexuality is outside the scope of this book, but we should be aware that they have varied over the centuries and have meant different things in different places. Onanism (the practice of withdrawal before ejaculation) was condemned in the Bible (Genesis 38: 9–10) and punishable by death, as were male homosexual relations (Leviticus 18: 22 and 20: 13). Sexual moral norms are not absolute and constant among the major religions or in the history of religion and theology. The mores, as well as the standards and norms, reflected in the definitions issued by the mental health community have mirrored the enormous flux in the religious community with respect to sexual norms. Perhaps the most illustrative example is masturbation, which, in one generation's lifetime, has moved from being classified as an abnormal behavior that could result in madness, blindness, and impotence, to gradual acceptance as normal for children and teenagers. Today, it is the position of many therapists that masturbation is necessary and healthy for the developing sexual being and may be carried on in the marital relationship as well. Another sexual behavior that was formerly considered an illness is homosexuality. Psychotherapy once tried to "cure" the homosexual individual. However, several years ago, the American Psychiatric Association dropped the listing of homosexuality as an "illness"; it is now generally considered merely a variant of normal sexual behavior.

Regardless of the APA's or the formal institutional churches' classifications, most people have some strong views about what is or is not deviant. By and large, it seems that the commonly held view (rather than the institutionally defined view) is that deviant acts are found to be offensive and are thought to challenge basic established beliefs about sex and religion. People who have strong views about deviance often think that their views are shared by the majority of the population, and, because they view sexual "deviance" to be of such an unusual nature, they may feel compelled to attract attention to the problem. However, attitudes toward sexual practices and beliefs have been changing rapidly in the United States in recent decades, as a result of a broadening of American values and considerations. Because of the rapidity of change of those values, it has been difficult for the mental health profession to keep pace.

Many sexual practices that were once deemed wrong or sick or forbidden appear to be commonplace today. What happens when many people are breaking the traditional rules and restrictions? If "everybody is doing it," or, in statistical terms, if the majority of people are engaging in a particular behavior, does that mean that the norm is changing and the behavior will now be considered "normal" and permissible? That cannot be answered easily. If we use lying as an example, we know that just about everybody will lie on occasion, but that does not mean that lying is morally correct and should not be condemned whenever it occurs. Similarly with sexual behavior: whether something is morally right or "normal," in the sense of being healthy or not dangerous, is for the legitimate institutions to determine. In some instances, the determination or consideration of changes in formal definitions reflects changing behavior, so it is very useful to first learn the extent of the behavior. For example, although premarital sex by consenting adults is still a violation of the norm in most religions, the American people seem not to view this practice with the same negativity that was prevalent several decades ago. In a sense, the public acceptance and widespread manifestation of this behavior seem to have reduced the anxiety these couples might have, in an earlier time, felt about their personal sexual normalcy.

Sexual normalcy appears to be a concern of many Americans, and for good reason. Many of us believe that we have moved, as a nation, from a solid, stable, consensual set of sexual norms—those of "the good old days"—to sexual chaos. This view merely romanticizes the past. Doubts about what is sexually normal, and conflicts between behavior and belief, have, as far as we can learn, been present in our history from the days of the Pilgrims. Individuals in government and the churches, past and present, have decided for themselves and for others what is *sexually moral and immoral.* Our intent here is to probe the limits of what is *sexually normal and deviant,* and to determine where one ends and the other begins. . . .

A major consideration in categorizing sex acts is the possibility of either partner's suffering hurt, pain, or danger. If no one is hurt or bothered by a behavior, should we consider it deviant? We reviewed behaviors ranging from the perfectly "normal," socially valued and accepted sexual practices, such as married, heterosexual, male-superior intercourse (the "missionary position," with the male on top) to some of the most extremely disapproved of behaviors, such as necrophilia (sex with dead bodies). In between, we considered various acts of deviance based on their degree of societal and individual disapproval. Practices that may be offensive to some people, but are not harmful unless they are coercive, were included in our review.

We arrived at two categories of deviant acts. The first consists of acts that are frequently disapproved of yet widely practiced: sadomasochism, dominance/bondage, cross dressing, fetishes, and verbal humiliation.

In the second category are acts that few people would openly acknowledge practicing because they are strongly disapproved of by society. These include: golden and brown showers, necrophilia, group sex, and adult sex with children. We must also point out that deviant sex includes anything that is nonconsensual: rape, forcible acts, and abuse of all kinds.

SADOMASOCHISM

There are two roles in this pleasure-in-pain practice: the sadist and the masochist. Individuals who practice sadomasochism generally prefer one role instead of the other, but will often take whatever role is available.

A *sadist* is an individual who inflicts harm and/or pain on another individual in order to gain sexual and/or psychological satisfaction. The word originates from the name of the Marquis de Sade (1740–1814), who was known for the cruelty and brutality he inflicted, especially on women.

The *masochist* achieves sexual gratification by experiencing pain, whether anticipatory, immediately before, or during the sex act. Sometimes, receiving pain is all that is desired, and it takes the place of sexual relationships. The term masochist derives from the name of a nineteenth-century Austrian novelist, Leopold von Sacher-Masoch (d. 1895). If the masochist is a male, there is often a need to undergo the masochistic experience while dressed in women's clothes. The inflicted pain might range from a simple flagellation to a serious beating that leaves marks on the subject's body. There are houses of bondage that have every conceivable type of apparatus for delivering "discipline." Not only does the masochist have to receive the precise type of punishment he seeks, but he also must be able to tolerate the pain and wring pleasure from the humiliation related to the pain. There have been reported cases of older men, or men with heart trouble, who have died during their requested physical torment and humiliation.

Love bites, more commonly known as "hickeys," are believed by many therapists to be a mild and innocent form of sadomasochism. Other therapists see them as expressions of deeply rooted unconscious drives that relate pain to pleasure.

DOMINANCE/BONDAGE

Dominance can sometimes be only symbolic, but most often it is physically acted out as a sexual performance in which one partner has total physical and emotional control of the other. Suppliers of apparatus, and magazines catering to dominance/bondage (D/B) aficionados, claim that approximately 8 percent to 10 percent of American households have some D/B apparatus, in its simplest form (ropes, to tie the husband or wife to the bed), and practice some of the many varieties of play acting that offer dominant and submissive experiences.

Dominants are the people who place much emphasis on or have a need for the practice of dominance and bondage, and who play the dominant role in the interaction. They often own a great deal of apparatus and know many ritualistic modes of carrying out this sexual practice. Equipment may include masks and ropes or chains, which are used to render the partner helpless. A woman who specializes in this practice is called a dominitrix. The psychological connections between dominance and rape cannot go unnoticed.

Submissives are those who are restrained during the domination act. For some individuals, being tied up is exciting enough to give them spontaneous orgasm. For others, it relieves their guilt feeling about voluntarily performing a sexual act (which, they were taught as children, was "bad" and "dirty"), even with their spouse. Many people who practice D/B consider it an ultimate sexual experience; for others, it is just another variant in a wide repertoire of sexual activity.

CROSS DRESSING

Also known as transvestism, cross dressing is more frequently practiced by males (although this fact is greatly confusing, because women may dress as men in our society without any condemnation or negative connotation). On the streets of big cities, transvestites may be known as "screaming queens." They obtain sexual pleasure by wearing the clothing of the other sex. Some transvestites may masturbate to orgasm while in the garb of the other sex. Young boys who are drawn to transvestism may find that they need to utilize an item of female clothing, such as panties, bras, garters, or stockings, to achieve arousal as they get older. A small but significant minority utilize stockings in near-asphyxiation scenarios involving self-strangulation. They can achieve orgasm only at the height of asphyxiation, and then are able to cut themselves down without succumbing. However, in recent years, in a number of cases, almost all involving teenage boys, the individuals waited too long and died from strangulation during or shortly after orgasm. Their deaths have been termed "autoerotic suicides."

FETISHES

Fetishes are primarily male sexual agendas. A fetishist is quite removed from the person who is the object of his sexual desire. He is interested in the "sexual object" only through a displacement to some item of the person's clothing, such as a shoe, a stocking, or underwear, or to a body part. The most common fetishes are feet, silk, and rubber. There are two major types of fetishists, hard and soft.

The hard fetishist is involved with leather and rubber objects. For the stimulation process to work, the object must be near enough to be touched or the sex partner must wear the object to induce sexual excitement.

The soft fetishist prefers fur, feathers, silk, and similar objects and materials.

Fetishists often have a need to obtain the desired objects by stealing, whether from a family member or a store. Usually, a fetishist becomes attached to an object, such as his mother's panties, that is taboo, which helps to further enhance his sense of excitement. Unlike the transvestite, the fetishist does not need to wear the clothes or other object; rather, he craves any sensory perception of the object. Touching, holding, seeing, or smelling it are enough.

VERBAL HUMILIATION

An individual who derives pleasure from this behavior is given a very abusive, crude, and thorough tongue lashing by his or her partner. Verbal humiliation can accompany other behaviors, and is often a component of sadomasochism. Some individuals—and some prostitutes—specialize in this area. Two, or more, parties who know each other in detail may be involved. To be effective, the humiliator must know the submissive well enough that the invective can be accurate, and therefore hurtful. A frequent theme is to condemn the submissive for wanting the forbidden sex in the first place, and to make very accurate references to the forbidden—but lusted for—person whom the submissive covets. Several madams whom we interviewed, who operate houses of bondage, indicated that they never perform humiliation until they have had some discussions with the "John," so that they know how to be most effective. In those instances when a dominant does not humiliate intensely enough, the submissive may become enraged and humiliate the dominant instead, hoping thereby to infuriate the dominant to the point of heavy retribution.

From the viewpoint of psychoanalysis, those who find verbal humiliation a must are carrying a huge burden of guilt. The struggle to successfully function sexually requires that the guilt be addressed each time there is a potential sexual interaction. Because the forbidden thoughts, or prior experiences, hamper any kind of effective or gratifying sex functioning, they must be dealt with before any sexual action can begin. Therefore, the verbal humiliation marks the beginning of the sexual interaction, almost as an integral part of the sex act. Verbal humiliation serves as a symbolic punishment that cleanses the individual of the guilt; having paid the price with the humiliation, he or she can then indulge sexually. For many submissives, the discussion of the guilt is in itself an obsessive turn-on that colors the whole sex act.

GOLDEN SHOWERS

The medical term for golden showers is urolagnia. In advertisements that practitioners of deviant sex place to find each other, it is colloquially called "the waterworks." In this practice, individuals achieve orgasm while being urinated on. Usually, men are the recipients in the interaction. Because few men can persuade their wives or girlfriends to accommodate them, most seekers of golden showers must go to a callgirl they can count on. Their excitement has two sources: the sound of the woman's voiding and the sight of the yellow stream of urine. A good deal of preparation must be done beforehand by the donor. When a regular customer (these clients remain as regular customers) calls, one to two hours ahead, the prostitute quickly drinks as much as eight to ten beers, or the equivalent, and retains the fluid until the customer arrives and the elaborate ritual action takes place. A woman needs a healthy, strong bladder to succeed in this practice.

BROWN SHOWERS

The scientific term for brown showers is coprolagnia; those involved in this deviance, which is almost exclusively favored by men, achieve orgasm by being defecated on. There are psychoanalytic theories that this form of gratification has much to do with the time when, as a child, the individual was learning to control his sphincter muscles. Of all the perversions, this is probably one that is least openly discussed. Many men may brag about their sexual prowess and tastes, but few will announce a preference for brown showers. Most ordinary houses of prostitution do not accommodate this deviance because of the special equipment and people needed.

NECROPHILIA

In this perversion, an individual becomes sexually aroused by corpses. This socially repugnant practice is rarely acknowledged openly as a sexual stimulus. Some sex killers are also necrophiliacs. A variant of this deviance is seen in a genre of pornographic films called "snuff" films. In this type of film, the woman dies or is killed at the conclusion, after or during sexual intercourse. The action of killing the woman is a grossly fascinating perversion for a surprising number of men. These films, in which deaths were simulated, were gaining popularity until a film of an alleged actual death was shown in New York, commanding a $50 admission fee. This film received such massive condemnation that "snuff" returned to its under-the-counter status.

GROUP SEX

Group sex involves a number of people having sexual relations together, with several individuals, at the same time and place. Both single and married persons may be involved. In addition to the physical interaction with new partners, this practice has a strong voyeuristic and exhibitionistic appeal. There are publications and organizations that list individuals and couples around the country who are looking for new partners to engage in group sex.

ADULT SEX WITH CHILDREN

The practice of adult sex with children is called incest if it involves blood relatives too close to marry, or child sexual molestation if it involves more distant relatives, or strangers. Statistics show that 80 percent to 85 percent of sexual attacks on children are not by strangers, but by relatives or acquaintances who have access to and are in a trust position with children, such as teachers, scout leaders, clergy, and counselors. The typical incest victim is under 10 years of age. Below that age, it is as likely that the victim is a boy as it is a girl.[2] Unlike a one-time rape, child sexual molestation is ongoing and frequently continues for years.

Notes

1. American Psychiatric Association. 1980. *Diagnostic and Statistical Manual of Mental Disorders,* 3rd ed. Rev. (DSM-III-R). Washington, DC: Author, 1987. See also 2nd Ed. (DSM-II), 1986, and 3rd Ed. (DSM-III), 1980.

2. S. Janus. 1981. *The Death of Innocence.* New York: William Morrow & Co., p. 17.

33

Becoming a Prostitute in Norway

CECILIE HOIGARD AND LIV FINSTAD
Institute of Criminology and Criminal Law, Oslo, Norway

Among those we interviewed, the average age for the woman's first trick was 15½. The oldest was 23; the youngest 13.

Fifteen year olds. We know several 15 year olds. They struggle with their German lessons, have crushes on David Bowie and on boys in the class above; they've just started experimenting with mascara and they read teen magazines. Not children, and not adults. Some have begun to have sex, even though according to Norwegian law they're under the age of consent.

How can 15 year olds be so different? Or more accurately, how can 15 year olds live such dissimilar lives?

SOCIAL BACKGROUND OF THE WOMEN

Prostitution researchers have attached a great deal of importance to describing the social background of prostitutes. The picture is relatively unambiguous. It is women from the working class and the lumpenproletariat who are recruited into prostitution. Their backgrounds are also marked by irregular home lives and adjustment difficulties in school and in their working lives. This is established knowledge in prostitution research. We have not placed a particular emphasis on rechecking this, and our own data are not particularly illuminating on this point. The social background of the 664 women registered by the police is not systematically documented. The women from the Oslo Project have the same background patterns as international literature describes. The 26 prostitutes we interviewed also fit this pattern.

The most startling aspect of the social background of those we interviewed is their extensive experience of institutionalization. Of the 26 women only three had not been institutionalized at all. Orphanages, women's homes, reform schools, child and adolescent psychiatric institutions, alcohol and drug rehabilitation clinics, prisons—the whole of institutional Norway is richly represented. And most have a history of *many* institutional stays. Anita, for instance, had the following institutional career: raised in a children's home in western Norway until the age of 14. Then placed in a foster home. Ran away after two months. Placed in a group home in Oslo. Left on her own for a group home in the country near the Swedish border. Ended up at a psychiatric clinic in Oslo. Afterwards at a mental hospital in Oslo, then another mental hospital, and then back to the psychiatric clinic again. Now she is in a mental hospital just outside of Oslo, and says she's been in five times in the last nine months. Anita is 20. She has been institutionalized 12 times. There are few months in her life when she has not been in an institution. There are several other women who have institutional careers like Anita's. The women's narratives contain few praises of these institutions; the stories of neglect and unhappiness are many.

They are young when they turn their first trick. Nonetheless, 15 of the 26 had been institutionalized before that first trick.

This is an important discovery—not only because these figures tell of young women who are already rejected by normal society *before* they become prostitutes, but also because institutions are revealed to be important training grounds for prostitutes. In institutions many young people in trouble are stowed together like surplus wreckage. They often run away together, without money. What could be more natural than that they exchange knowledge about ways to survive?

THE FIRST TRICK

Kari: "It started at the Salvation Army school. That's where I got to know Aina. I got to be good friends with her. She'd learned to smoke hash in Copenhagen, it was in Christiania. She'd been on the street there too. So she knew what it was all about. The first time we knocked back a few beers and then did a trick together."

Knowing what it is all about. The women don't learn much in the way of concrete details before their first trick. Where you should go is important. All of the 26 woman interviewed turned their first trick at well-known prostitution sites. One had her debut at The Rainbow restaurant. The others began on the street. This emphasizes the significance of a known, visible prostitution market.

The other thing you have to know is how much to ask for different tricks. Anita: "Birgit and I became friends at the group home. We really hit it off. We used to get dressed up. I had a devil's cape and looked like Alice Cooper. But we didn't start then. It was later in 1977 when we both didn't have any money. Birgit was together with Georg then, I was on Psilocybin [a psychoactive drug like LSD]. Georg said he could show us where we should go and how to act. He said we should walk calmly back and forth until a car came. Then we should take 300 crowns. I got a john who was 70 years old. I went with him to his office. It was totally disgusting. But I didn't think about it too much. I'd done so many weird things, I'd been doing group sex since I was a little kid. My sex life was already screwed up. I didn't tell the old man it was my first trick. After that Birgit and I worked every day."

Inga didn't know much beforehand either. "I didn't know anything except where they were, that they were at the Bank Square. I'd asked around a little before. I'd heard a little about what to do from hanging out at Egertorvet too. They said you should go up to a car and ask if he wanted a trick."

Most tricks are performed by just one woman. It is only on occasion that they work in pairs: it is harder to get work for two. But the first trick is different. Half of the women worked together with a girlfriend their first time. Often the girlfriend has worked before and knows what it is all about. In this way an important part of the training is a form of participatory observation.

A GRADUAL PROCESS

Not much concrete knowledge is demanded for starting in prostitution. That does not mean that "just anyone" can come out of nowhere and start tricking. It is a marked characteristic that most of the girls associate with other street kids for quite a while before they turn their first trick. (This is also emphasized in American studies.) Here is where self-image is molded, norms for behavior are learned: what counts and does not count, what it is to be a woman or a man.

The *social* learning is extensive. The seeds are often planted early, long before the girls become a part of the group of street kids.

In *Hard Asphalt,* Ida summarizes it like this: "As the years went on prostitution got closer and closer. It was still unthinkable, but not so unthinkable. My best friends were on the street. The alchy friends of my dad always talked about how he could earn good money off me and Berit. Later on, in the crowd I hung out with, it was drummed into us over and over that a woman's body was her most important asset. I saw it every day."

Ida's description shows how the image of women prevalent in her environment ate away at her and how she eventually to some extent incorporated that image into her view of herself. This process represents an essential and necessary self-transformation a woman undergoes before she begins to prostitute herself. Women who can rest secure in their own worth as individual people and who have a view of their body and sexuality as sources of personal pleasure will have a solid defense against prostitution. But how many woman have solid defenses of this type? Different images of women exist side-by-side in our society. We believe that all women in our society have at some time, most likely many times, come up against the notion that our greatest asset is our body. It is one of the more common images of women which makes prostitution possible.

Not all women become prostitutes. The presence in society of this image of the body as an asset is obviously not the only factor responsible for some women prostituting themselves. But in addition to the well-known factors of social class, economics, and the degree of involvement in traditional society, the degree to which a woman adopts this female image as an image of herself is crucial.

Ida travelled in circles where this image of women was almost absolute. The lack of competing female images enabled the image of a woman's body as potential capital to assume enormous proportions; it was readily available as a model for Ida's behavior.

Learned self-image and a learned attitude to one's own sexuality are central elements in the process towards prostitution. At times learning can take place under very dramatic and painful circumstances, as in the sexual abuse of children. Neither we nor Swedish prostitution researchers have systematically asked about the incidence of incest among women. In retrospect it is easy to see that we should have. A number of foreign studies seem to indicate a close correlation between being an incest survivor and being a prostitute, though the results are not definitive. The quality of these studies varies, and they also give very different answers as to how strong the connection is. Several of the Norwegian aid projects for prostitutes emphasize the connection between incest and prostitution.

Male images are not necessarily defined in relation to female images; but female images will often also define male images—as to what men can and cannot do with women. After her interview was finished, Jane said to me, "Make sure to say that lots of women are prostitutes because they've lost respect for men. Like me with my dad. I saw how he treated women. He played around with other women behind Mama's back the whole time. And all the whippings he gave me. If things had been OK I never would have started. Lots of women feel like me. They don't respect men."

The road to prostitution is a process in which the women's experiences cause a breakdown in their respect for themselves, for other women, and also for men. Such individual experiences are seldom sufficient reason for prostitution. It is only when the experiences are translated and incorporated into the collective experience which the girls share with other youths that prostitution becomes a viable alternative.

Peer-group significance is effectively summarized by Anna's account of her first trick. "I was part of the Stener Street gang then. It started with us hanging out at the amusement park in town. Old guys asked if we'd go behind the fence with them or if we would jerk them off. They gave us money to see our underwear—it was insane. It was really fun too—we were really disgusting towards them. Like we'd run away after we'd gotten the money. One time a girl had sandpaper in her hand when she went to jerk some guy off. The whole thing was just a game. But I felt pressured by the others. In the beginning I used to ride along with the other girls when they did tricks. That was before I started. It was too gross. The old geezers were often really stingy with the paint thinner or with the money. The creeps started nagging at me; they wanted to have me 'cause I was younger. Totally disgusting."

After a while her girlfriends also started to nag at Anna. Anna felt it was leeching not to turn tricks. She did have less money than the others then. Often they shared their paint thinner with her. But sometimes they wouldn't share. "You can turn tricks too, you know—go behind the fence and get some cash," they'd reply. She remembers her first trick as if it were yesterday. "I was

14 years old. It was totally disgusting. I thought the devil was gonna come and get me. I'd been living it up on the thinner then suddenly the can was empty. God, what do I do now? I asked myself. I went with an old goat who was 190 years old. His dick was *so* little. [Indicates a couple of centimeters between her thumb and index finger.] I was completely high. I thought he'd been sent by the cops to make a fool out of me with that little dick. I thought that cops were fucked when they'd do something like that. But that I was even more fucked to be going along with it. Afterwards I felt like everything was shit, and I was a goddamned whore. That's just what you are."

Your gang and your girlfriends. These are the important socialization factors before the first trick is turned. Several others besides Anna describe a subculture of sharing, in which prostitution is an act of solidarity, and abstention is sponging. One should share both the good and the bad, contribute a share to the household accounts. This picture differs from the one that occasionally appears in newspapers and in fiction. Here the image of the sleazy pimp who lures or threatens unwitting young women into service predominates. This is wrong. Of the 26 women interviewed, 24 mention other girlfriends or the crowd they hung out with in answering how they found out about prostitution and who told them how they should behave. In 13 of these cases it was, as we've already mentioned, a girlfriend who went along on the first trick.

There are two responses that deviate from this pattern. One has a number of similarities with the notion of men as villains of the drama. Lisa: "It was the summer I turned 17. I had moved away from home. I got to know three boys and they seemed all right. One evening all four of us went out drinking as usual. I got pretty drunk. 'Now you do this and that,' the boys said. They forced me to go through with it. They stood, one in each corner, and made sure I didn't take off. Afterwards we went right down to a nightclub and drank up the money there. It went on that way. They took everything I earned. They hung out with a psychopath who got a share of the money. He bought a Corvette, a two-seater, real American."

Cecilie: "Could you get rid of them?"

Lisa: "It wasn't that I was in love. But I was completely car-crazy. And I got a few black eyes when I didn't feel like working. But the most important thing was that I was car-crazy."

In the second instance it was also a man who was the instigator. Fredrik and Eva had a child when they were both 18 years old. They had a very meager income. Fredrik and Eva's story is atypical. They had no contact with fringe groups or street kids beforehand. Fredrik: "We were in a desperate situation. My pay just didn't do it. We had almost no money. Then I read in the newspaper about a prostitution trial. It made big headlines. It was about a woman who claimed she made 300 crowns per trick for performing sexual services for men in cars. It was right there in print. We discussed it a little, talked about how much you could earn if you had so-and-so many tricks. We couldn't really understand how you could earn so much. We didn't know a single person who did that kind of thing and in terms of background we had no connection to this at all, apart from my experiences at sea. Eva was hesitant to start; she was afraid it would have consequences for our relationship. I reassured her that my love for her would grow when she also earned money for our mutual benefit. There were so many things we needed money for. After a lot of talk back and forth over several weeks, we decided that she'd try it. We agreed that she would only accept 300 crowns, because that was the price we'd read in the paper. The first evening she tried the street, she talked with a lot of people and asked for 300 crowns. But she didn't get any tricks. The price was much too high. The usual price at that time was 100 crowns for a quick one in a car. It was just some damned nonsense in the newspaper about 300 crowns a shot. But OK, 100 crowns was a lot of money too, and as soon as you started doing tricks the money piled up pretty quickly."

For her part Eva believes that they needed money, but that money isn't the only explanation. "At that time we really needed money, but that doesn't actually explain why, because there were thousands in the same position as we were. I can't understand why we started. We were total novices; we didn't have any idea about it. If I'd known what I know today, I'd never have started. It was definitely a gamble."

The whole panorama is represented. At the one extreme, several boys getting together to threaten and pressure a girl into prostitution; at the other end, women who eventually come to see prostitution as a gradual consequence of belonging to a fringe group and of the example set by girlfriends. Numerically, the second group predominates. Their situation is typical. It is also the situation we recognize from the women we got to know in the Oslo Project. The man as "villian" exists only as the exception which proves the rule. The fact that he exists at all allows the stereotype to survive.

REACTIONS TO THE FIRST TRICK

A few of the women describe their first trick with words like "disgusting," "totally fucked," and similar expressions. The customers suffer under the names "creeps," "dirty old geezers," and other choice insults.

Almost all the women describe their subsequent tricks and their customers in this way. But in terms of the first prostitution experience there are many who were surprised that the whole thing went as painlessly as it did. Ida: "God, is it so easy to fuck your way to money? Here I'd been going around worrying for the longest time and it was just . . . just child's play . . . I was 23 years when I actually crossed the line. A grandmother's age to be starting. It was simple and undramatic. I didn't become another person, like I'd thought. It was easy-earned money."

Many women think like Ida. Jane, for example: "God yes, I remember my first trick all right. It was four years ago. I was out partying a fair amount then. I got drunk and hung out at low-life restaurants. I was never an easy lay. I wasn't the kind to trade myself for a glass of beer. My girlfriend and I were out. We were pretty pissed and didn't have any more money. My girlfriend had a regular customer. But then she was sick. We looked him up. I wasn't nervous, but, like, excited-nervous. I thought it was kinda fun and exciting. He said I should touch him. I had to turn my face away when I did it. Then he said I should get undressed. Of course when I'd done it I had to go out and pee. He barely stuck it in, then he came. I got 250 crowns for it. He was happy, because it was my virgin trick. When I came back to my friend I said I wanted to do another trick right away. It was easy money, I thought. My head was totally empty."

The majority of customers probably react like Jane's. It's an extra refinement when a girl has her virgin trick. Many women tell of how they later pretended it was their virgin trick. Then they could get a little extra money. "New women getting tricks fastest" is an expression of the same. The women tell of how some customers preach morality to them and warn them against starting with prostitution *after* they have gotten their paid-for ejaculation. This type of moralizing isn't popular.

However, there are honorable exceptions. Inga: "I remember my first trick very well. It was because the john was so great. I'll tell you, there are lot of nice johns too. Like this guy. He figured out that it was my first time. It was because I didn't know the places you're supposed to go to. I said to him, 'Well, you already know where we can go.' Then he understood. He talked with me instead. He asked if I really knew what I was getting into. He said it was a hard life and that I had to be careful of drugs. He said that I seemed honest and nice and that I shouldn't start. Afterwards he wanted to pay me. I didn't want to take the money since I hadn't done anything for it. But he said I'd deserved it. So I took it."

A few women dreaded their first trick for a long time, like Ida did. Then they find out it's not so bad after all and that there is lots of money in prostitution. It is easy to continue then. The real shit comes later.

34

Mother Sold Food, Daughter Sells Her Body: The Cultural Continuity of Prostitution

Marjorie A. Muecke
University of Washington

... I am concerned with the question, "Why is the rapid growth of female prostitution not culturally problematic for the Thai?" I argue that beliefs that Thai laity tend to associate with Buddhism and village morality paradoxically support the practice of prostitution in their society. The beliefs provide an ideology that justifies parental and village complicity in and denial of the prostitution of their daughters. . . .

I suggest that the economic rewards of contemporary prostitution have enabled young women to support not only the urban-based profiteers who control prostitution, but more important from a cultural perspective, to remit funds home to their families and villages of origin. Prostitution today is accomplishing what food vending did for the young women's mothers: both of these otherwise disparate endeavors have the effect of conserving norms by which women support the family, village, and other basic institutions of Thai society. The cultural consequences of prostitution for women who do not suceed in it are also examined. I suggest that they, too, conserve traditional norms, in this case, the norm associated with the Buddhist ideology of suffering and with the common interpretation that women are fated to suffer more than men, as demonstrated in their bodily sacrifices for their children in pregnancy, childbirth, and breastfeeding. The young female body is thus paradoxically the cynosure of beauty and suffering.

Reprinted with permission from *Social Science and Medicine*, Vol. 35. Majorie A. Muecke, "Mother Sold Food, Daughter Sells Her Body: The Cultural Continuity of Prostitution" (1992), Elsevier Science Ltd., Pergamon Imprint, Oxford, England.

The data for this analysis derive from field research, predominantly in Northern Thailand, where I have conducted 5 years of fieldwork in three segments since 1972. Some of the case descriptions are of women who have participated in my longitudinal anthropological study of some 400 urban Chiang Mai families,[1] and others are of women known through the course of related research and scholarly activities in the country. . . .

HISTORICAL BACKGROUND

Thai scholars ascribe the origins of prostitution in Thailand to the early Ayudthia period, which, in the fifteenth century, codified laws that structured society hierarchically and vested authority over women to men, and required men to leave home for extended periods to serve their lords. From the fifteenth century to the late nineteenth century, prostitutes serviced Siamese peasant men when they left their homes for their obligatory annual corvée labor in the service of the king or nobility.[2] Prostitutes also serviced Chinese men who immigrated to Ayudthia as laborers in the seventeenth and eighteenth centuries.[3] The prostitutes were women who had been sold into prostitution by their parents or husbands. Until the late nineteenth century, it was legal for a man to sell or give away his wife or daughter without her consent, as a present to his superior or in payment of his debts; men could also purchase slave women as their lesser wives, and gain Buddhist merit for their generosity in doing so. Thailand is not unique in this history. China and Japan supplied a "vigorous market for prostitutes" with their daughters of poverty in the colonial port towns of Southeast Asia.[4] Although laws have changed, the historical practice of selling women provides important precedent for the current practice whereby adults, predominantly men, sell family members, particularly daughters, for economic gain.[5]

After World War II, prostitution developed more obviously in cities than in rural areas. The first massage parlor, an imitation of the Japanese steam bath, is reported to have appeared in the Patpong area of Bangkok in 1951.[6] Patpong is now Bangkok's sex entertainment center for international tourists. Although prostitution was outlawed in 1960, massage parlors were legalized in 1966. They quickly became one of the major cover-ups for prostitution in the country. Prostitutes prefer them as worksites over brothels because of their higher class (higher paying) clientele and greater job security.[7]

In the 1980s, prostitution of Thai women mushroomed into an industry of extensive national and international proportions.[8] Its growth parallels that of the economy which has boomed so strongly since 1985 that economists expect Thailand to be "the next Newly Industrialized Country" (NIC). Foreign investments have increased dramatically since 1987, with the bulk of foreign exchange resources being dedicated to the urban infrastructure. This growth has been accompanied by a burgeoning of the middle class of urban consumers, and rural to urban migration of young adults in search of jobs. Meanwhile, the share of agriculture in the economy has fallen from 32.2 percent in 1970 to 24.9 percent in 1980, to 22.3 percent in 1986. In consequence, the income differentials between Bangkok and the rest of the country are increasing: In Bangkok the average annual per capita income in 1988 was estimated as U.S. $2300, in contrast to U.S. $300 for other parts of Thailand, with some areas as low as U.S. $100.[9] The increasing poverty of rural areas relative to urban places contributes to the urban migration of young women to work in the service sector.

Current estimates are that in the Thai population of some 55 million, there are 80,000 to one million women working as prostitutes, plus perhaps some 20,000 girls under the age of 15.[10] An unknown number of Thai women work abroad as prostitutes; estimates for Japan alone are some 10,000.[11] A decade ago, it was estimated that, on a *per capita* basis, twice as many women were prostitutes as men were monks.[12] For Thai Buddhists, this ratio starkly juxtaposes daughters and sons as moral opposites, daughters being of the flesh and "this-worldly," and sons, detached from corporeal desire, so closer to the Buddhist ideal of "otherworldliness."

As large as the above estimates of the number of prostitutes are, they are probably underestimates for several reasons. First, prostitution services are commonly camouflaged in the guise of massage parlors, escort agencies, restaurants, bars, and nightclubs.[13] This is because prostitution is illegal, but creating a site where it is available is not. The figures also minimize the prevalence of prostitution because they exclude both men and women who formerly were involved in the sex trade. Others who profit from prostitution include pimps; procurers; owners (at least some of whom may be highly placed officials or their agents) of massage parlors, escort agencies, bars, and brothels; police and government officials who are given pay-offs to avoid arrest of prostitute employees; and taxi drivers. The figures on prostitution are further biased by the Thai tendency to tolerate polygyny in the form of minor wives (*mia nǫi*).[14] There is little difference between short-term minor wives and prostitutes: "Today's system of prostitution is how traditional polygyny has survived: both provide a man access to the services of more than one woman."[15]

PROSTITUTION IN THE CONTEXT OF CONTEMPORARY BUDDHISM

Theravada Buddhism provides a cultural core for lowland Thai society. As such it shapes the meaning of prostitution and of being a prostitute. Buddhism is linked to prostitution through the concepts of karma (*kam*) and meritmaking (*kaan tham bun*). According to the "law of karma," good actions earn moral merit (*bun*), and wrong actions, demerit (*baap*). The amount of merit and demerit that an individual has earned in past and present incarnations is that person's karma, and determines how much or little suffering that person has in this life. Individuals can change their karma by purposefully making merit. The most common ways to make merit are to give gifts to monks and temples, and to sponsor an ordination of a monk. . . .

Suffering

My Chiang Mai female informants consistently said that the lot of the Buddhist woman is to suffer more because of her greater worldly attachment than man's. . . . The suffering of a prostitute may take a variety of forms, including loneliness, physical abuse and pain, verbal abuse, deception, illness, exhaustion, rejection, uncaring, unsafe abortions, sexually transmitted disease, and the stigma and lethality of HIV infection. Typically, the prostitute's choice was to stay in the suffering of a difficult family or poverty, or to live in the suffering of loneliness, alienation and personal abuse that goes with being a prostitute. . . .

Women informants who were not prostitutes generally believed that prostitutes suffer because they are mistreated, abused, and exploited, not only by their "agents," "owners" and clients, but even by parents. A recent university graduate told the story of her friend Noi (pseudonym). Noi's family was poor. She went to Japan to work as a prostitute because she thought she could make more money there than in Thailand. She stayed there for years, working until she saved one million Baht (U.S. $40,600)! Then when she was 25 and getting too old for prostitution, she came home and gave it all to her parents. They took it, took it all, and wouldn't give her one Baht of it. She was very angry. They used it all up on gambling, Noi got none of it. She was so angry she "went crazy." My informant explained that Noi lost not only her money, but also her parents for whose sake she had sold her body for all the years of her life that she could do so profitably. Their keeping the money and using it on gambling rendered the highly moral purpose to which she had dedicated her life immoral. She lost her earnings, her parents, and her morality in one swift swoop; then she lost her sanity.

Merit Making

The Buddhist way to alleviate suffering, either in this or a future life, is to make merit. Monks present themselves as a field of merit for laypersons. By receiving all gifts as if they were given with the intention of making merit, regardless of who contributes them or how they were obtained, the Sanga (Buddhist order of monks) provides a culturally and morally acceptable means for "laundering" of monies that may have been earned through prostitution or other disreputable means.[16] Women in Thai society engage in meritmaking behavior much more regularly than men; they provide food for monks on a daily basis, and frequent the temples on holy days. The work of a prostitute precludes these types of meritmaking, but allows meritmaking that involves money. When making merit, she avoids presenting herself as a prostitute. Merit making is perceived by her and by folk and doctrinal Buddhism as an independent activity in which she is being a good Buddhist.

Prostitutes who work in massage parlors and hotels commonly make merit by inviting friends and clients to participate in a *thɔɔt phaa paa* ritual, an excursion (usually overnight) to a village temple for the purpose of giving money and gifts as a group to the temple.[17] Some prostitutes indicate that they make merit to compensate for the demerit of their stigmatized career and hope it will prevent them from being a prostitute in their next incarnation. Although not so publicized, their donations contribute to building new temple buildings, a major visible impact on poor villages. There is one temple in Bangkok, however, that is named after a woman donor who is widely known to have been a prostitute, Wat Khanikaphol.

Prostitutes generally report feeling pleased that they are able to send remittences home and to make merit at temple ceremonies. . . .

PROSTITUTION AS ECONOMIC AND CULTURAL SURVIVAL

Contrary to belief common in Thailand (and among foreign customers), prostitutes do not cite sexual satisfaction as a major reason for entering or remaining in their jobs. Chief among their reasons are extricating themselves from poverty or from a difficult home life, and earning enough to help the family of origin out of poverty or to build a foundation for their own futures.[18] These reasons reflect failure of the traditional support system of the self-subsistent landed household-family. And they reflect the young women's craving for security, both economic and domestic.

Prostitutes earn different amounts of money depending upon where they work. Those working in unmarked backstreet whorehouses that are heavily patronized by local lower and middle-class men often earn as little as 15 Baht (U.S. $0.60) a trick (with perhaps half going to the house), and typically service at least 10 customers a day/night. In contrast, women factory and construction workers generally earn much less, some 700–1500 Baht (U.S. $28–$60) a month. Prostitutes working in neon-bedazzled massage parlors, nightclubs, or bars earn much more and have fewer customers a night. The most highly paid are those working in restaurants "with special services" or with elite escort services.

After deducting living and job-related expenses (the latter include payments to agents, procurers, and police, and purchase of clothes and cosmetics), it appears that most prostitutes remit funds home to help their families and to make Buddhist merit. A new and substantial house for parents tops the list of purchases, followed by rice fields and electrical appliances: thus, houses and televisions are exchanged for women's bodies.

But the purchases represent more than material goods. They are one of the very few means women have for fulfilling cultural obligations to repay their parents. One 24 year old described her co-workers:

> Most have worked some 5–10 years, but they don't have the money they've earned because they sent it home. They sent it home as a way to give the family status (*mii naa mii taa*). Their parents built one house after another (*pluuk baan pen lang lang*). It wasn't just for themselves that the girls worked.

Many prostitutes pay for younger siblings' education—often to prevent a sister from having to resort to prostitution—others, for parents' medical bills, and some, for a brother's ordination as a monk through which the mother and family can make Buddhist merit and gain in social status. In Northern villages, remittances from prostitutes often mean that parents and siblings do not have to work in the dry season, and have to plant only one rice crop a year. The labor of a daughter-sister who prostitutes herself can spare her family from work as well as provide them with otherwise unattainable consumer goods. Thus, prostitutes invest heavily in the conservation of their families and homes. In doing so, they carry out traditional obligations of women to take care of aging parents and younger siblings.

Thai women have long been responsible for economic maintenance of the household and have held the family's purse-strings. In the middle and upper classes, women are also well represented among owners of large businesses and corporations. Whereas mothers of lower socioeconomic sector families have traditionally sold food to meet their family's subsistence needs, daughters now can sell their bodies to meet the same needs, but, the parents hope and fantasize, on a gratifying grander, almost grandiose, scale. Today's prostitute is upholding the same value her mother did, but constrained to seek more lucrative ways of doing so.

Some prostitutes also conserve family ties by recruiting sisters and cousins to work with them. This mechanism is a major reason that some villages have many of their daughters "working in Bangkok" while others have none. It also reflects the young women's need for the security of social support against the alienation and abuse of their trade. The latter can involve molesting by violent customers, unintended pregnancies and aseptic illegal abortions, drugs to escape the indecencies of the moment ("How else could I get up there all but nude in front of all those strangers and perform in front of them?!" one asked), HIV and other sexually transmitted diseases, and exhaustion from as many as 20 customers a day. Money and sister-cousins as co-workers make it more bearable to be a prostitute.

CONCLUSION

Beliefs that boys are mischievous and men irresponsible, whereas girls are dutiful and women, loyal, run deep in Thai society. Such gender differences are assumed to be innate. But child socialization teaches a double standard: Children are raised with the expectation that real men need sex, and good girls control their sexuality so as not to overcome men with temptation.[19]

The double standard has long stigmatized the female prostitute. Until now. Now a new common sense allows a double standard within the double standard. Although not explicitly labeled as such, there are not only good and bad girls/women but "justified" and "unjustified" prostitutes as well. Those who are "justified" make money, and largely because of their outstanding beauty, make lots of it.[20] In the streetperson's view, they earn it from foreign clients and send it home to parents and village temples.[21] Remittances and donations tacitly earn them the privilege of hiding their identity as prostitutes from their families and villages.[22] The "blind eye" of the support system back home sanctions the girls' continuing to work as prostitutes. By removing the stigma of prostitution from village daughters in the village, it maintains the bond of security between the young women and those whom tradition and human psychology dictate count most in life. Prostitutes who fulfill the cultural mandate for proper daughters are considered justified. They take care of parents and younger siblings financially, they return home at traditional new years (Songkran) with gifts to receive the blessings of their elders, and they fulfill the Buddhist expectation that women support the Sanga [Buddhist monks] by donating to temples and sponsoring ordinations of their brothers. . . .

Notes

1. Muecke M. A. "Reproductive success" among the urban poor: a micro-level study of infant survival and child growth in Northern Thailand, Ph.D. dissertation, University Washington, Seattle, WA, 1976; Muecke M. A. "Thai Conjugal Family Relationships and the Hsu Hypothesis." *J. Siam Society* 73, 25–41, 1983; Muecke M. A. "Make Money Not Babies: Changing Status Markers of Northern Thai Women." *Asian Survey* 24, 459–470, 1984.

2. Skrobanek S. *The Trannational Sex-exploitation of Thai Women.* M.S. thesis. Institute of Social Studies, The Hague, 1983; Skrobanek S. "Strategies Against Prostitution in Thailand." In *Third World—Second Sex*, Vol. 2 (Edited by Davies M.). Zed Books, NJ, 1987.

3. La Loubere. A New Historical Relation of the Kingdom of Siam. London, 1963 (reprint).

4. Warren J. F. "Prostitution and the Politics of Venereal Disease: Singapore, 1870–98." *J. Southeast Asian Stud.* XXI, 360–383, 1990; Eng L. A. *Peasants, Proletarians and Prostitutes: A Preliminary Investigation into the Work of Chinese Women in Colonial Malaya.* ISEAS, Singapore, 1986.

5. The current prevalence of this practice is, however, unstudied. It is rare enough to be reportable in Thai newspapers, but sufficiently routine to be part of street knowledge.

6. Wiboon Nakornjarupong. "Patronage and the Night Queens." *Business in Thailand,* pp. 40–52, 1981.

7. Suliman Narumon. Krabuan kaanklaai pen mǫǫ nuat: kǫranii sǝksaa yingbǫrikaan nai sathaan bǫrikaan aab ob nuat [The process of becoming a masseuse: a study of service girls in massage parlors]. Master's thesis, Faculty of Sociology and Anthropology, Thammasat University, Bangkok, 1987; Sulimon Narumon. Krabuan kaanklaai pen phanakhngaan aab ob nuat [The process of becoming a massage parlor staff member]. Paper presented at Chiang Mai University, Chiang Mai, 22 July 1988.

8. Ekachai S. "The Operations of the International Sex Trade Rings." *Bangkok Post Outlook* 44, 261, 1989; Enloe C. *Bananas, Beaches and Bases: Making Feminist Sense of International Politics.* University of California Press, Berkeley, 1990.

9. Pasuk P. Thailand: Miss Universe 1988, in *Southeast Asian Affairs 1989* (Edited by Ng Chee Yuen), pp. 337, 348. Institute of Southeast Asian Studies, Singapore, 1989.

10. The Ministry of Public Health recently estimated there are 80,000 prostitutes in the country, but "the police reckon there are at least eight times that number." AIDS? What AIDS? *The Economist,* p. 36, 24 March 1990; Sittitrai W. "Commercial Sex in Thai Society." In *Proceedings of the First National Seminar on AIDS in Thailand.* 1991; Thongpao T. "New Types of Slavery in Thai Society." *Bangkok World* p. 6, 8 October 1986.

11. Haruhi T. "The Japanese Sex Industry: A Heightening Appetite for Asian Women." *AMPO Japan-Asia Q. Rev.* 18, 2–3, 70–76, 1986.

12. Mulder N. *Everyday Life in Thailand: An Interpretation.* Duang Kamol, Bangkok, 1979.

13. "In 1980 Bangkok had 117 massage parlors which means approximately 20,000–25,000 masseuses. However, masseuses form only a minority of women engaged in prostitution. In addition Bangkok had 94 nightclubs and bars, 269 short-term (that is prostitution-oriented) hotels, 123 second-class hotels where prostitutes are commonly available, and 51 tea houses clustered around the Chinatown area. Besides, a number of whore-houses were believed to operate in moderate or high secrecy, either because they provided virgins who were mostly deceived or forced to receive customers, or because the women were high-class and occasional prostitutes." Hantrakul, Sukanya. Prostitution in Thailand. In *Development and Displacement: Women in Southeast Asia,* p. 20. Monash Papers on southeast Asia, No. 18. Monash University, Clayton, 1988.

14. A Norwegian natural scientist who traveled in what is now Laos and Northern Thailand in the 1880s reported that "princes and officials who can afford to do so have a number of concubines who can be sold or otherwise disposed of when they are tired of them." Bock C. *Temples and Elephants,* p. 186. White Orchid Press, Bangkok, 1985. (Originally published London 1884).

15. Khin T. *Providence and Prostitution: Image and Reality for Women in Buddhist Thailand,* p. 23. Change International Reports, London, 1980.

16. "Laundering" occurs to the extent that merit accumulated through meritmaking activities balances out the demerit accrued from acts of prostitution. According to both folk and doctrinal Buddhism, wrong actions such as prostitution can be compensated for but not be erased.

17. Praphot S. *Meesaa kamsaruan khabuankann ɲng nɲa khɲn thin* [The orchids of the north go home]. *Matichon* 8, 16–17, 1985.

18. Foundation for women. *Khamlaa,* 2nd ed. Bangkok, 1988. (In Thai.).

19. See note 1.

20. Narumon reports prostitutes saying that it's better to give up virginity for money than to a boyfriend who drops you anyway and pays nothing.

21. Renu Atthameetr. Women . . . tools of ideals. *Conference on Results of Research of Women in Northern Thailand,* Chiang Mai, 24 August 1988.

22. Mandersen discusses the importance of the daughter-based remittance economy as a strategy of the extended family in island Southeast Asia. Manderson L. (Ed.) *Women's Work and Women's Roles: Economics and Everyday Life in Indonesia, Malaysia and Singapore.* The Australian National University, Canberra, 1983.

35

Sex Tourism in Southeast Asia

JODY MILLER
University of Southern California

The imperialist West has a long history of exploiting non-Western countries. A traditional form of exploitation involves using people as cheap labor for profit. A new form of exploitation, however, calls for using women as sex slaves for pleasure. This comes in the guise of sex tourism, providing foreign tourists with local prostitutes. Sex tourism is most prevalent in Southeast Asia, especially Thailand.

SEX TOURISM AS A DEVELOPMENTAL STRATEGY

Sex tourism flourishes through the support of developmental policies in Southeast Asia and through the representation of Asian women as sexually exotic. In this article I will focus largely on Thailand. The U.S. military presence abroad has helped stimulate tourism in the Third World. But, far more important, Western developmental policies, with the backing of multinational corporations, have cultivated tourism as a strategy for building the economy of the Third World countries. The promotion of tourism first got its impetus from the United Nations declaration of 1967 as "The Year of the Tourist." Subsequently, international aid programs such as the World Bank, the IMF, and US AID, as well as multinational corporations have invested in the development of tourist industries in the Third World.

Multinational corporations in particular have found in tourism a lucrative venture through investment in a variety of industries, such as airlines, hotels, tour operations, and travel agencies (Mies, 1986; Truong, 1990). This has created "a division of labor according to which Third World countries, with few exceptions, merely provide the social infrastructure and facilities with little or no control over the process of production and distribution of the tourist-related services at an international level" (Truong, 1990). As a result, the tourist

---

This article was specifically written for this reader.

industry greatly benefits multinational corporations, local elites, and international tourists but does little to improve the standard of living or availability of services for the majority of the people living in these regions.

In Thailand, the tourist industry has been a priority within the government's economic plans despite the social inequalities it exacerbates. Thai sex tourism got its boost from U.S. militarization. Although prostitution has a long history in Thailand and other Asian countries, "Southeast Asian women were first turned into prostitutes on a mass scale in the context of the Vietnam war and the establishment of American air and navy bases in the Pacific region" (Mies, 1986). All this began to occur in Thailand in 1967, when the Thai government and the U.S. military signed a treaty to allow U.S. soldiers stationed in Vietnam to come on "Rest and Recreation" leave in Thailand. The immediate consequence was a boom in local and foreign investment in hotels and entertainment establishments (Truong, 1990). When the U.S. military withdrew from Vietnam in the 1970s, there was still considerable incentive for investors to turn to tourism, which had become extremely important in sustaining the Thai economy. By the late 1980s, tourism was "the country's major earner of foreign currency" (Cohen, 1988). In 1986, "Thailand earned more foreign currency from tourism . . . than it did from any other economic activity including its traditional export leader, rice" (Enloe, 1989).

The sex trade is at the heart of this tourism. In the early 1980s, for example, "Bangkok had 119 massage parlors, 119 barbershop-cum-massage parlors and teahouses, 97 nightclubs, 248 disguised brothels and 394 disco-restaurants, all of which sold sexual companionship to male customers" (Enloe, 1989). In addition, hotels participate directly or indirectly in sex tourism. It has been estimated that "between 70 and 80 percent of male tourists who travel from Japan, the United States, Australia, and Western Europe to Asia do so solely for the purpose of sexual entertainment" (Gay, 1985). To meet all this demand, numerous Thai women are forced in one way or another to become prostitutes. The Thai police have estimated their number to be 700,000, "about 10 percent of all Thai women between the ages of fifteen and thirty" (Gay, 1985). Many prostitutes are under age 14, representing some 20 percent of the workers in the Thai sex industry (Ong, 1985).

The majority of those women and girls have migrated from rural areas. A large percentage come from the North and Northeast, the two poorest regions of the country. By not investing in those agricultural regions, Thailand's development policies have worsened the poverty of its rural people. This has forced many poor rural families to rely on individual family members migrating to urban areas as a means of survival. Many of these migrants are young daughters ending up in Bangkok's sex trade.

Sex tourism is an extremely exploitive industry in Thailand. It provides huge profits to tourist businesses and the Thai government. Even the laws that prohibit prostitution are used to control female workers in the industry rather than the owners and managers (Cohen, 1982; Truong, 1990). Since their work is illegal, they are stigmatized and must constantly interact with men "who consider it their right . . . to buy themselves exotic women" (Mies, 1986). They receive only a small percentage of the money they earn, and attempts to unionize have been unsuccessful (Prostitution in Southeast Asia, 1987). One woman sums up what it is like to be a sex worker: "Believe me, if it was not necessary, no one would ever want to work like this. . . . But we have no choice. We must persevere, since we have only ourselves to rely on" (Ekachel, 1987).

THE PROMOTION OF SEX TOURISM

The continuing prevalence of sex tourism depends most heavily on its promotion to Western men. This largely involves presenting Asian women and sex tourism as follows:

1. Asian women are naturally submissive, passive, and willing to cater to men's sexual needs.

2. Asian women have a uniquely "Oriental" sexuality—more intense, sensual, and erotic than Western sexuality, while more animalistic, overt, and indiscriminating.

3. Sex tourism in Southeast Asia is a "fun-filled" form of entertainment, neither exploitive nor inappropriate.

4. Sex tourism in Southeast Asia is a legitimate commodity like any other service in the market economy.

Asian Women as Submissive

Part of Western men's attraction to Asian women springs from the popular assumption that Asian women are more subservient and passive than their Western counterparts. The tourism industry often depicts Asian women as docile and submissive by nature, willing to put male needs ahead of their own. One brochure, for example, describes Thai women as "little slaves who give real Thai warmth" (Kanita Kamha in Truong, 1990). Tourist ads routinely emphasize how easy it is for Western men to find willing and enthusiastic Thai girls in bars and coffee shops.

Moreover, to make Asian women appear sexually desireable, the tourist literature often contrasts their submissiveness with the emancipation of Western women. Bangkok's sex workers are described as "without desire for emancipation," only interested in providing men with their "warm sensuality and the softness of velvet" (in Lenze, 1980). Because their submissiveness is assumed to be sexually desirable, the Asian girls are touted as "mostly young, pretty, gay and a welcome change from the hard-faced crones found in the West" (Thitsa, 1980).

Asian Women's Uniquely "Oriental" Sexuality

When their sexuality is presented to Western men as uniquely "Oriental," Asian women are stereotyped in at least three ways. First, they are said to be unusually adept in sex. Thai women are described in one tourist brocure as the "masters of the art of making love by nature, an art that we Europeans do not know" (Life Travel in Truong, 1990). This image not only appears frequently in tourism materials, it most often occurs in pornographic videos about "Oriental" sex. Such videos highlight "the sexual and exotic characteristics of [Asian] cultures, showing how foreign visitors to these countries can enjoy uninhibited sex" (Truong, 1990). One example is *Live from Bangkok,* an adult video that is presented in documentary style. It shows scenes from massage parlors, dance bars, and sex shows. Viewers are encouraged "to see the stimulating erotic night clubs of Bangkok. The women are beautiful, the sex is extraordinary! It's all here and more. You won't believe your eyes." Similar videos show how Asian women are capable of creating "the most fantastic sensations" for their sex partners.

Another representation of Asian women's supposedly unique sexuality involves portraying them as promiscuous and sexually uninhibited. This is suggested in a Thai business magazine, stating that "Everyone who has ever travelled widely in Thailand knows that indiscriminate love-making goes on in every hotel in the land" (*Business in Thailand* in Truong, 1990). In the *All Asia Guide* (1980), sex shows are described as "action of astounding dexterity culminat[ing] in a display of sexual gymnastics." In the video *Live from Bangkok,* a woman is shown dancing in a go-go bar, and going into a bedroom to have sex with one, then later two, men. The voiceover explains, "after a long night of dancing, performers must wind down by letting loose their extra energy."

Asian women's unique "Oriental" sexuality is also presented in terms of their sexual anatomy. Adult videos often refer to Asian women's vaginas as being tighter than Western women's. Examples of such references include advertisements of Asian girls' legendary "tight pussies," "super tight clits," "super tight snatch," and "Oriental pussies tightly awaiting your cumming attractions."

Sex Tourism as Fun-filled Adventure

Sex tourism in Southeast Asia is projected as harmless, exciting entertainment. The imagery is devoid of any recognition of exploitation; the language is that of fun, games, and adventure. Sex tourism, Western men are told, must be experienced. "Bangkok is a captivating city, active, even at night . . . and the publicity about the famous massage parlours can only be tried out" (Truong, 1990). Massage parlors are not the only place where Western male tourists can engage in wild, uninhibited sex. Bars also abound where there is "no trouble in going in for a drink, coming out with a gal" (Jacobs and Jacobs, 1979). In some bars, male tourists seated at a table can have bargirls perform oral sex on them. *Playboy* magazine tells its male readers what they can do in such a bar:

> Step into the corner with your buddies, sit down at the famous table for a game of smiles. Drop trousers as you sit. Movement under the table, a girl or two up to no good. And the game of smiles begins. The last one to smile wins (Kluge, 1986).

Numerous prostitutes can be found not only in brothels but also in hotels. Virtually all male tourists are encouraged to participate in sexual adventure, as suggested by the following anecdote described in a travel guide:

> On arrival at an Asian hotel, an official of the World Council of Churches was asked, as men often are, if he wished female companionship for the night. He declined, but the hotel porter persisted in his persuasions, finally asked why he wasn't interested in one of his beautiful young women. "Because I'm a minister of a Christian church," was the reply. The porter left abruptly. Soon came a knock on the clergyman's door. Enter smiling porter. "Evelything okey–dokey now. Christian woman, she be here soon" (Jacobs and Jacobs, 1979).

Sex Tourism as a Legitimate Commodity in the Market Economy

Sex tourism is regarded as a legitimate commodity because it is part of the market economy where, if there is a need, somebody will always emerge to satisfy it. The sexual commodity in Southeast Asia is easily available for a low price. As a tourist ad says, getting a girl "is as easy as buying a package of cigarettes" (Truong, 1990). According to an American naval officer in the Philippines, "you can fuck a woman up the ass for two apples and a candy bar. . . . I would go get a blow job with the same casualness with which I'd buy a six-pack of beer, and for the same money" (Kluge, 1986). Many Western male tourists do not feel guilty for taking advantage of the girls. Instead, they tend to feel that they are doing a favor to the girls and their country by contributing to their economy. The tourist literature plays a role here. As the voiceover in a promotional video explains,

> [The girls] come from poor families in country areas to work as sex performers or prostitutes or both. These are not bad girls; in Thailand the whore is as respected as the secretary. Sex is an honorable business, necessary to the economy. The girls send most of their money home to support their families. Some work a few years 'til they've saved enough to go home and open a small business of their own.

THEORETICAL IMPLICATIONS

In short, sex tourism flourishes through the support of developmental policies in Southeast Asia as well as through the representation of Asian women as sexually exotic and through the justification of sex tourism as socially and economically beneficial. All this suggests extreme exploitation of Asian women, without which sex tourism cannot exist, let alone flourish. The exploitation of Asian women as poorly paid sex workers brings substantial profits to business elites in the tourist industry, widening in the process the gap between rich and poor in those Third World countries.

Sex tourism further dehumanizes Asian women, allowing Westerners to see Asian women as less than human. As the wife of an American navel officer in the Philippines says:

I told my husband that as long as he doesn't bring back any diseases, if he goes out there for relief while I'm away in the States, it's all right. If he were with a pretty American girl, or an ugly American girl with brains, I'd be worried. But I've been there, and I know the girls. L.B.F.M.s—little brown fucking machines (Kluge, 1986).

But the dehumanization of Asian women does not appear as such to many Westerners, especially male tourists. This is because, as we have seen, the tourist literature often depicts Asian women as cheerfully submissive.

References

All Asia Guide. 1980. Hong Kong: Far Eastern Economic Review, Ltd.

Cohen, Erik. 1982. "Thai Girls and Farang Men: The Edge of Ambiguity." *Annals of Tourism Research,* 9(3): 403–428.

Cohen, Erik. 1988. "Tourism and AIDS in Thailand." *Annals of Tourism Research,* 15(4); 467–486.

Ekachel, Sanitsuda. 1987, December. "A Caberet of Dreams for Bad Girls of Patpong." *ISIS Women's World,* 16:5–6.

Enloe, Cynthia. 1989. *Bananas, Beaches & Bases: Making Feminist Sense of International Politics.* Berkeley: University of California Press.

Gay, Jill. 1985, February. "The 'Patriotic' Prostitute." *The Progressive,* pp. 34–36.

Jacobs, Charles and Babette Jacobs. 1979. *Far East Travel Digest,* 3rd ed. Palm Desert, CA: Paul, Richmond & Co.

Kluge, P.F. 1986, September. "Why They *Love* Us in the Philippines." *Playboy,* pp. 88–90, 162–164.

Lenze, Ilse. 1980. Tourism Prostitution in Asia. *ISIS International Bulletin,* 13:6–8.

Mies, Maria. 1986. *Patriarchy and Accumulation on a World Scale: Women in the International Division of Labor.* London: Zed Books.

Ong, Aihwa. 1985, January. "Industrialization and Prostitution in Southeast Asia." *Southeast Asia Chronicle,* 96:2–6.

Prostitution in Southeast Asia. 1987, January. *Off our backs,* 17 (1):1–2, 7.

Thitsa, Khin. 1980. *Providence and Prostitution: Image and Reality for Women in Buddhist Thailand.* London: Change International Reports.

Truong, Thanh-Dam. 1990. *Sex, Money and Morality: Prostitution and Tourism in Southeast Asia.* London: Zed Books.

36

Does Exotic Dancing Pay Well But Cost Dearly?

SCOTT A. REID, JONATHON S. EPSTEIN,
AND D. E. BENSON
Kent State University

The term "exotic dancer" has a multitude of synonyms including "stripper," "stripteaser," "table dancer," "go-go dancer," and "adult entertainer." Clubs that specialize in this type of entertainment are fast becoming a common feature of the urban landscape. This is primarily because income from this occupation can reach as high as several hundred thousand dollars a year for those employed in elite "high-dollar gentlemen's clubs." Even in the less expensive blue-collar clubs, an exotic dancer can earn at least $20,000 a year. The income is indeed quite attractive, especially considering the fact that the job is often only part-time and requires little training.

Despite its growing popularity, American culture continues to look on exotic dancing as a deviant, somewhat disreputable occupation. One indication of this attitude is the great amount of negative attention the occupation receives from popular television talk shows such as Phil Donahue, Maury Povich, and Oprah Winfrey. Some audience members sport a "to each his own" philosophy, but most believe the occupation as well as the dancers are deviant and morally corrupt. The dancers are often readily equated with drug addicts, prostitutes, exhibitionists, sex addicts, and "deviants" of all types. Many dancers themselves have held similar views before the occupation, referring to dancers as "sluts," "whores," "sleazes," and "druggies."

As with any occupation that the public regards as deviant, it is possible for the women to have different ways of identifying with their role of being exotic dancers. To some, dancing is nothing more than a means to an end, a way to get money for achieving "higher" goals, such as a college education, independence from parental control, or raising children. Thus, many dancers may not feel that exotic dancing is an important defining characteristic of the self. They would instead look to other more conventional roles (e.g., mother, student, or spouse) as more important to their self-definition. To other dancers, though,

---

This article was specifically written for this reader.

dancing may mean much more than a way to make money. These dancers may regard dancing as indicative of an "elite" person who possesses the proper beauty, talent, skill, and stamina required for success in the occupation. These dancers are more likely to perceive their occupational role as central to their sense of self.

Using identify theory, an offshoot of structural symbolic interactionism (e.g., Burke and Rietzes, 1981; Callero, 1985; Howard and Callero, 1991; Stryker, 1968, 1980, 1987) and building on the work of Reid, Epstein, and Benson (1994), we would like to find out whether the deviant occupation of exotic dancing has any negative identity consequences. More specifically, we will focus on two issues: (1) Do exotic dancers regard their occupational role as an important part of their self-identity—their sense of "who they are"? (2) Do they consider the characteristics associated with the role as reflective of their personal values and beliefs?

METHODOLOGY

To find answers to those questions, we first conducted nine informal interviews with exotic dancers in their occupational setting. These interviews were designed to pre-test questionnaire items, determine the appropriate wording of open-ended questions, and establish dancers' willingness to participate in a research project. The length of the interviews ranged from 30 minutes to 2 hours.

A sample was later taken from twelve "strip clubs" in northeastern Ohio, the same area where Skipper and McCaghy (1970) conducted their ground-breaking research. Two hundred and fifty questionnaires were distributed to the clubs that agreed to participate in the research. Fourteen clubs were visited with only two denying access to the researchers. The questionnaires were distributed through liaison persons in each bar rather than to directly to each dancer. The liaisons were mostly dancers themselves, only one being a bar owner and three being bar managers. This distribution procedure produced a total of 41 usable questionnaires.

RESULTS

The ages of the forty-one dancers in the sample ranged from 18 to 35 with a mean of 23. Most of the dancers were high school graduates or had some college. The majority were single, with only 7 percent being married and 12 percent divorced or separated. Most of the dancers were white, making up 88 percent of the sample. As for religious preferences, 51 percent were Catholics, 20 percent Protestants, 2 percent Jewish, and the rest (24 percent) other faiths. Annual income from exotic dancing ranged from under $10,000 to over $70,000, the most common being $20,000 to $25,000. Most (83 percent) of the subjects described themselves as heterosexual; the rest identified themselves as homosexual, bisexual, or "other."

Research Question 1

The data indicate that the exotic identity is not central to the dancers' self-concept. The respondents in this study often go to great lengths to distance themselves from their deviant occupation in order to "buffer" themselves from its stigmatizing effects. As one respondent says,

> I'm partly doing this as a joke. I'm a bit of a bionic hero and I try to experience all of life's adventures of which this is certainly one. I'm an ultra-feminist, too, which adds to the joke. I'm an outside woman pretending to be a girl (dancer).

Other respondents made similar comments:

> The head games or mental side of dancing gets harder as time goes on. You become immune and strong (within yourself) to your surroundings.

> . . . if you're not sleazy or wild after awhile, you just get so tired of perverts, jerks, and drunks. This is just a job for me to go to school and only work a couple of hours since I'm a single parent.

Research Question 2

We also found that most of the respondents do not perceive the characteristics of their deviant occupation as reflective of their personal values. Their motivation for engaging in the occupation is external rather than internal. They often say that they work as exotic dancers not because they really enjoy it (example of internal motivation) but because they can make "quick money" and then leave to strive for some "higher" goal (external motivation). They also report that many other dancers are in the occupation for the same reason. Here are a sample of what they say:

> It (dancing) gets old . . . I'm just tired of the whole scene, but not the money, so I can't leave.

> I thought it was sleazy and all dancers were conceited and bitches. It was stereotypes, because I was jealous. But since I started dancing, I realize allot (sic) of them are just like me, dropouts or paying for school, making ends meet with dancing.

> Since dancing I have classified dancers as: (1) single parent; (2) putting self through school; (3) supporting an old man (spouse); (4) supporting a drug habit; (5) just trying to make it in life without a trade.

> After almost ten years in this business and working most aspects; waitress, bartender, and back to dancing, I've realized we are all very independent women who are just looking for the opportunity to advance financially and professionally and would like to do it with our own merits.

> I thought they were really gross and immoral (when I first started dancing). Now I think they do it because it's good money but I still think its immoral like.

There are exceptions to the rule, though. A few dancers regard their occupation as highly reflective of their values and beliefs. Unlike others who dance for purely economic reasons, these dancers derive personal, psychological satisfaction from their occupation:

> Before I started dancing, what I had imagined a dancer to be was a mysterious, glamorous, beautiful woman with an exciting lifestyle. Now that I'm a dancer, I feel the same way—but only this time I'm the mysterious, glamorous, beautiful woman. Sometimes my job really gets me down, but most of the time it's very exciting and gratifying.

> It (dancing) *constantly* changes, that's what I love about it. It's so-o-o exciting. You don't know what kind of crowd you've got before your shift. It's fun to get out there and "work" the crowd. Kind of like a challenge to get 'em up and get them clapping.

CONCLUSION

In regard to Question One, our data indicate that most dancers do not see the role identity of exotic dancing as important or central to their sense of self. Why, then, do they enter and continue in the role? Identity theory would suggest that other, more important identities (e.g., college students or mothers) are more influential in the dancers' lives and consequently the benefits of playing the dancer role are put "in service" of the more important roles of, say, being a college student. In other words, the short-term benefits (i.e., money) of occupying the role is used to help fulfill the requirements of more important identities.

As for Question Two, the data indicate that most dancers do not feel that their deviant occupational role reflects their true values and characteristics. As identity theory would say, they do not see their occupational role as authentic. Why, then, do they enter and continue in the role? The reason, according to identity theory, is that the dancers only "play at" the deviant role without letting the unsavory characteristics of the role "contaminate" their true sense of self. The dancers can avoid the contamination because they seek external rewards (primarily money) rather than internal rewards (personal satisfaction) from the deviant occupation.

References

Burke, Peter and D. C. Rietzes. 1981. "The Link Between Identity and Role Performance." *Social Psychology Quarterly* 44: 83–92.

Callero, Peter. 1985. "Role Identity Salience." *Social Psychology Quarterly* 48: 203–215.

Howard, J. and P. Callero. 1991. *The Self-Society Dynamic: Cognition, Emotion and Action.* Cambridge: Cambridge University Press.

Reid, Scott A., Jonathon S. Epstein, and D. E. Benson. 1994. "Role Identity in a Devalued Occupation: The Case of Female Exotic Dancers." In review *Sociological Focus.*

Skipper, James K. Jr. and Charles McCaghy. 1970. "Stripteasers: The Anatomy and Career Contingencies of a Deviant Occupation." *Social Problems* 17: 391–404.

Stryker, Sheldon. 1968. "Identity Salience and Role Performance: The Relevance of Symbolic Interaction Theory for Family Research." *Journal of Marriage and the Family* 30: 558–564.

Stryker, Sheldon. 1980. *Symbolic Interactionism: A Social Structural Version.* Palo Alto:

Benjamin Cummings.

Stryker, Sheldon. 1987. "Identity Theory: Developments and Extensions," pp. 89–104 in K. Yardley and T. Honess (eds.), *Self and Identity: Psychological Perspectives*. New York: Wiley.

37

Parade Strippers: Being Naked in Public

CRAIG J. FORSYTH
University of Southwestern Louisiana

This article is concerned with the practice of exposing the female breasts in exchange for "throws" (trinkets and glass beads thrown from floats) from Mardi Gras parade floats in the New Orleans area. It has become so commonplace that the term "beadwhore" has emerged to describe women who participate in this activity. This phenomenon can be compared to other related practices: nude sunbathing, nudism, mooning, and streaking [which many other researchers have studied].

BEING NAKED IN PUBLIC

As a topic for research, being naked in public can be discussed under the broad umbrella of exhibitionism or within the narrow frame of fads or nudity (Bryant 1977). In general, exhibitionism involves flaunting oneself in order to draw attention. In the field of deviance the term exhibitionism may also refer to behavior involving nudity for which the public shows little tolerance (Bryant 1977, p. 100; Bartol 1991, p. 280). This research, however, focuses on a form of public nudity that has a degree of social acceptance.

An extensive sociological study of public nudity was *The Nude Beach* (Douglas et al. 1977). Weinberg's (1981a, 1981b) study of nudists represents another type and degree of public nakedness. Other research has addressed the topics of streaking (running nude in a public area) (Toolan et al. 1974; Anderson 1977; Bryant 1982) and mooning (the practice of baring one's buttocks and prominently displaying the naked buttocks out of an automobile or a building window or at a public event) (Bryant 1977, 1982). Both streaking and mooning were considered fads. One question considered by sociological research on nakedness is when and why it is permissible, appropriate, or acceptable to be naked in public (Aday 1990). Researchers have also

From *Deviant Behavior*, Vol. 13 (1992), pp. 391–403, Craig J. Forsyth. Washington, D.C.: Taylor & Francis, Inc. Reproduced with permission. All rights reserved.

addressed some possible motivations or rationales for public nudity. Toolan et al. (1974, p. 157), for example, explain motivations for streaking as follows:

> While streaking is not in itself a sex act, it is at least a more-than-subtle assault upon social values. Its defiance serves as a clarion call for others to follow suit, to show "the squares" that their "old hat" conventions, like love, marriage, and the family, are antiquated.

Both Bryant (1982) and Anderson (1977) say that streaking began as a college prank that spread quickly to many campuses. As a fad, it still retained parameters of time and place. Bryant (1982, p. 136) contended that it was one generation flaunting their liberated values in the faces of the older, more conservative generation. Anderson (1977, p. 232) said that it embodied the new morality and thus was "perceived by many to be a challenge to traditional values and laws."

Mooning, like streaking, was considered a prank and an insult to conformity and normative standards of behavior. Neither streaking nor mooning had any erotic value (Bryant 1982). Unlike streaking, mooning is still relatively common on college campuses.

Nudism in nudist camps has had little erotic value. Indeed, nudity at nudist camps has been purposively antierotic. Weinberg (1981b, p. 337) believes that the nudist camp would "anesthetize any relationship between nudity and sexuality." One strategy used by nudist camps to ensure this was to exclude unmarried people.

> Most camps, for example, regard unmarried people, especially single men, as a threat to the nudist morality. They suspect that singles may indeed see nudity as something sexual. Thus, most camps either exclude unmarried people (especially men), or allow only a small quota of them (Weinberg 1981b, p. 337) . . . .

Nude sunbathing incorporates many rationales from voyeurism to lifestyle and in many cases has a degree of erotic value. The sexuality of the nude beach has been evaluated as situational.

> Voyeurism . . . poses a dilemma for the nude beach naturalists, those who share in some vague way the hip or casual vision of the nude beach. . . . voyeurs have become the plague of the nude scene. . . . The abstract casual vision of the beach does not see it as in any way a sex trip, but the casual vision of life in general certainly does not exclude or downgrade sex (Douglas et al. 1977, pp. 126–27).

Similar to the nudist in the nudist camp, nude beachers expressed contempt for the "straight" voyeur.

> Sometimes I really feel hostile to the lookers. Obviously you can't look at people that way even if they are dressed . . . it really depends on your attitude in looking. I've even told a couple of people to fuck off . . . and some people to leave. I was thinking this would be the last time I would come down here . . . there were too many sightseers . . . it sort of wrecks your time to have someone staring at you (Douglas et al. 1977, p. 130) . . . .

[What about parade stripping, the most recent phenomenon of being naked in public, as practiced on Mardi Gras day in New Orleans?]

MARDI GRAS: DEVIANCE BECOMES NORMAL

On Mardi Gras day in New Orleans many things normally forbidden are permitted. People walk around virtually nude, women expose themselves from balconies, and the gay community gives new meaning to the term outrageous. Laws that attempt to legislate morality are informally suspended. It is a sheer numbers game for the police; they do not have the resources to enforce such laws. . . .

The celebration of carnival or Mardi Gras as it occurs in New Orleans and surrounding areas primarily involves balls and parades. These balls and parades are produced by carnival clubs called "krewes." Parades consist of several floats, usually between fifteen and twenty-five, and several marching bands that follow each float. There are riders on the floats. Depending on the size of the float, the number of riders can vary from four to fifteen. The floats roll through the streets of New Orleans on predetermined routes. People line up on both sides of the street on the routes. The float riders and the viewers on the street engage in a sort of game. The riders have bags full of beads or other trinkets that they throw out to the viewers along the route. The crowds scream at the riders to throw them something. Traditionally, the scream has been "throw me something mister." Parents put their children on their shoulders or have ladders with seats constructed on the top in order to gain some advantage in catching some of these throws. These "advantages" have become fixtures, and Mardi Gras ladders are sold at most local hardware stores. It is also advantageous if the viewer knows someone on the float or is physically closer to the float. Another technique is to be located in temporary stands constructed along the parade route that "seat" members of the other carnival krewes in the city or other members of the parading krewe.

In recent years another technique has emerged. Women have started to expose their breasts in exchange for throws. The practice has added another permanent slogan to the parade route. Many float riders carry signs that say "show me your tits"; others merely motion to the women to expose themselves. In some cases, women initiate the encounter by exposing their breasts without any prompting on the part of the float rider.

The author became aware of the term "beadwhore" while viewing a Mardi Gras parade. There were several women exposing their breasts to float riders. I had my 3-year-old son on my shoulders and I was standing in front of the crowd next to the floats. I am also a tall person. All of these factors usually meant that we caught a lot of throws from the float riders, but we caught nothing. Instead, the float riders were rewarding the parade strippers. As we moved away to find a better location, a well-dressed older woman, who had been standing behind the crowd, said to me:

> You can't catch anything with those beadwhores around. Even cute kids on the shoulders of their fathers can't compete with boobs. When the beadwhores are here, you just need to find another spot.

The term was also used by some of the interviewees [in this research].

METHODOLOGY

Data for this research were obtained in two ways: interviews and observations in the field. Interview data were gotten from an available sample of men who ride parade floats ($N = 54$) and from women who expose themselves ($N = 51$). These interviews ranged in length from 15 to 45 minutes. In the interviews with both float riders and parade strippers an interview guide was used to direct the dialogue. The guide was intended to be used as a probing mechanism rather than as a generator of specific responses. Respondents were located first through friendship networks and then by snowballing. Snowball sampling is a method through which the researcher develops an ever-increasing set of observations (Babbie 1992). Respondents in the study were asked to recommend others for interviewing, and each of the subsequently interviewed participants was asked for further recommendations. Additional informal interviews were carried out with other viewers of Mardi Gras.

Observations were made at Mardi Gras parades in the city of New Orleans over two carnival seasons: 1990 and 1991. Altogether, 42 parades were observed. The author assumed the role of "complete observer" for this part of the project (Babbie 1992, p. 289). This strategy allows the researcher to be unobtrusive and not affect what is going on. The author has lived a total of 24 years in New Orleans and has been a complete participant in Mardi Gras many times. Observations were made at several different locations within the city.

FINDINGS

The practice of parade stripping began in the late 1970s but its occurrence sharply increased from 1987 to 1991. During this study, no stripping occurred in the daytime. It always occurred in the dark, at night parades. Strippers were always with males. Those interviewed ranged in age from 21 to 48; the median age was 22. Most of them were college students. Many began stripping during their senior year in high school, particularly if they were from the New Orleans area. If from another area, they usually began in college. All of the strippers interviewed were in one location, a middle-class white area near two universities. Both riders and strippers said it was a New Orleans activity not found in the suburbs, and they said it was restricted to only certain areas of the city. One float rider said:

> In Metairie [the suburbs] they do it rarely if at all, but in New Orleans they have been doing it for the last ten years. Mostly I see it in the university section of the city during the night parades.

Parade strippers often attributed their first performances to alcohol, to the coaxing of the float riders, to other strippers in the group, or to a boyfriend. This is consistent with the opinion of Bryant (1982, pp. 141–42), who contended that when females expose themselves it is usually while drinking. Alcohol also seemed to be involved with the float riders' requests for women to expose themselves. One rider stated:

Depending on how much I have had to drink, yes I will provoke women to expose themselves. Sometimes I use hand signals. Sometimes I carry a sign which says "show me your tits." If I am real drunk I will either stick the sign in their face or just scream at them "show me your tits."

Data gained through both interviews and observation indicated that parade stripping is usually initiated by the float riders. But many of the women indicated that they were always aware of the possibility of stripping at a night parade. Indeed, some females came well prepared for the events. An experienced stripper said:

I wear an elastic top. I practice before I go to the parade. Sometimes I practice between floats at parades. I always try to convince other girls with us to show 'em their tits. I pull up my top with my left hand and catch beads with my right hand. I get on my boyfriend's shoulder. I do it for every float . . . I'll show my breasts longer for more stuff and I'll show both breasts for more stuff.

Other parade strippers gave the following responses when asked, "Why do you expose yourself at parades?"

I'm just a beadwhore. What else can I say?

I expose myself because I'm drunk and I'm encouraged by friends and strangers on the floats.

I get drunk and like to show off my breasts. And yes they are real.

Basically for beads. I do not get any sexual gratification from it.

I only did it once. I did it because a float rider was promising a pair of glass beads.

When I drink too much at a night parade, I turn into a beadwhore.

It's fun.

I exposed myself on a dare. Once I did it, I was embarrassed.

Only one woman admitted that she did it for sexual reasons. At 48, she was the oldest respondent. When asked why she exposed her breasts at parades, she said:

Sexual satisfaction. Makes me feel young and seductive. My breasts are the best feature I have.

One woman who had never exposed herself at parades commented on her husband's efforts to have her participate during the excitement of a parade.

We were watching a parade one night and there were several women exposing their breasts. They were catching a lot of stuff. My husband asked me to show the people on the float my breasts so that we could catch something. He asked me several times. I never did it and we got into an argument. It seemed so unlike him, asking me to do that.

Float riders often look on bead tossing as a reward for a good pair of breasts, as the following comments show:

The best boobs get the best rewards.

Ugly women get nothing.

Large boobs get large rewards.

When parade strippers exposed themselves they were not as visible to people not on the float as one would think. Strippers were usually on the shoulders of their companions and very close to the float. For a bystander to get a "good look" at the breasts of the stripper was not a casual act. A person had to commit a very deliberate act in order to view the event. Those who tried to catch a peek but were either not riding the floats or not among the group of friends at the parade were shown both pity and contempt.

> I hate those fuckers [on the ground] who try to see my boobs. If I'm with some people they can look. That's ok. But those guys who seek a look they are disgusting. I bet they can't get any. They probably go home and jerk off. I guess I feel sorry for them too. But I still don't like them. You know it's so obvious, they get right next to the float and then turn around. Their back is to the float. They are not watching the parade. We tell them to "get the fuck out of here asshole" and they leave.

Like a small minority of nude sunbathers who like to be peeped at (Douglas et al. 1977, p. 128), there are strippers who like the leering of bystanders. Our oldest respondent, mentioned earlier, said she enjoyed it. "I love it when they look. The more they look the more I show them," she remarked.

Parade strippers most often perform in the same areas. Although parade stripping usually involves only exposing breasts, three of the interviewees said they had exposed other parts of their bodies in other public situations.

Strippers and their male companions tried to separate themselves from the crowds; they developed a sense of privacy needed to perform undisturbed (Sommer 1969; Palmer 1977). Uninvited "peepers" disturbed the scene and were usually removed through verbal confrontation.

Most strippers and others in attendance apparently compartmentalized their behavior (Schur 1979, p. 319; Forsyth and Fournet 1987). It seemed to inflict no disfavor on the participants, or if it did they seemed to manage the stigma successfully (Gramling and Forsyth 1987) . . . .

CONCLUSION

Parade stripping seemed to exist because trinkets and beads were given; for those interviewed, there was no apparent sexuality attached except in one case.

Parade stripping is probably best understood as "creative deviance" (Douglas et al. 1977, p. 238), deviance that functions to solve problems or to create pleasure for the individual. Many forms of deviance, however, do not work in such simplistic ways.

Most people who go to a nude beach, or commit any other serious rule violation, do not find that it *works* [emphasis added] for them. They discover they are too ashamed of themselves or that the risk of shaming by others is too great, so they do not continue. Other people find it hurts them more (or threatens them) or, at the very least, does not do anything good for them. So most forms of deviance do not spread (Douglas et al. 1977, p. 239).

Some forms of deviance apparently do "work," and parade stripping is one of them. The beadwhore engages in a playful form of exhibitionism. She and the float rider both flirt with norm violation. The stripper gets beads and trinkets and the float rider gets to see naked breasts. Both receive pleasure in the party atmosphere of Mardi Gras, and neither suffers the condemnation of less creative and less esoteric deviants.

References

Aday, David P. 1990. *Social Control at the Margins.* Belmont, CA: Wadsworth.

Anderson, William A. 1977. "The Social Organizations and Social Control of a Fad." *Urban Life* 6:221–40.

Babbie, Earl. 1992. *The Practice of Social Research.* Belmont, CA: Wadsworth.

Bartol, Curt R. 1991. *Criminal Behavior: A Psychosocial Approach.* Englewood Cliffs, NJ: Prentice-Hall.

Bryant, Clifton D. 1977. *Sexual Deviancy in Social Context.* New York: New Viewpoints.

Bryant, Clifton D. 1982. *Sexual Deviancy and Social Proscription: The Social Context of Carnal Behavior.* New York: Human Sciences Press.

Douglas, Jack D., Paul K. Rasmussen, and Carol A. Flanagan. 1977. *The Nude Beach.* Beverly Hills, CA: Sage.

Forsyth, Craig J., and Lee Fournet. 1987. "A Typology of Office Harlots: Party Girls, Mistresses and Career Climbers." *Deviant Behavior* 8:319–328.

Gramling, Robert, and Craig J. Forsyth. 1987. "Exploiting Stigma." *Sociological Forum* 2:401–415.

Palmer, C. Eddie. 1977. "Microecology and Labeling Theory: A Proposed Merger," pp. 12–17 in *Sociological Stuff,* edited by H. Paul Chalfant, Evans W. Curry, and C. Eddie Palmer. Dubuque, IA: Kendall/Hunt.

Schur, Edwin M. 1979. *Interpreting Deviance.* New York: Harper & Row.

Sommer, Robert. 1969. *Personal Space.* Englewood Cliffs, NJ: Prentice-Hall.

Toolan, James M., Murray Elkins, and Paul D'Encarnacao. 1974. "The Significance of Streaking." *Medical Aspects of Human Sexuality* 8:152–165.

Weinberg, Martin S. 1981a. "Becoming a Nudist," pp. 291–304 in *Deviance: An Interactionist Perspective,* edited by Earl Rubington and Martin S. Weinberg. New York: Macmillan.

Weinberg, Martin S. 1981b. "The Nudist Management of Respectability," pp. 336–345 in *Deviance: An Interactionist Perspective,* edited by Earl Rubington and Martin S. Weinberg. New York: Macmillan.

PART 10

Homosexuality

In his 1948 and 1953 surveys of Americans, Alfred Kinsey found that although about 10 percent were predominantly—more or less exclusively—homosexual, only 2.5 percent were *exclusively* homosexual. Today, many surveys, such as the widely publicized study by the Battelle Human Affairs Research Center in 1993, have found about the same incidence of homosexuality—from 1 to 3 percent of Americans are said to be exclusively homosexual.[1] However, the real incidence may be much higher. The problem is that Kinsey and other researchers have focused on the objective, overt, or physical aspect of homosexuality, namely, the fact of having sex with members of the same sex. The researchers have ignored the other—subjective, covert, or unconscious—aspect of homosexuality. This includes the erotic feeling, desire, fantasy, or attraction for members of the same sex.

Suppose we use the same approach to find out how many teenagers in a traditional Asian society that strongly condemns premarital sex are *heterosexual*. We are bound to find only a small minority who are "exclusively heterosexual"—who have had sex exclusively with members of the opposite sex. But we will find a large majority to be exclusively heterosexual *if* we take into account those teenagers who are attracted to members of the opposite sex but afraid to engage in sex before marriage. Given the much stronger condemnation of homosexuality in our society, many who are attracted to members of the same sex may not act on their homosexual feelings. Some would even marry members of the opposite sex. Others, particularly adolescents, would not even know they are homosexual because the predominantly heterosexual society has forced them to repress or deny their homosexual desires. Having failed to take all this into account, virtually all the surveys on homosexuality have underestimated the prevalence of that sexual orientation in the United States. It is, therefore, safe to conclude that much more than 1 to 3 percent of Americans are exclusively homosexual.

The relatively large size of the homosexual population may partly explain why there are so many studies on same-sex orientation. Only a few are presented here. In the first selection, "Rejecting 'Femininity,'" Margaret Cooper discusses how the lesbians she interviewed had rejected traditional femininity

Patrick Rogers, "How Many Gays Are There?" *Newsweek*, February 15, 1993, p. 46; "Realities and Fallacies of Homosexuality," *Society*, July/August 1993, pp. 2–3.

in their childhood. In the second selection, "Radical Gay Activism," homosexual writer Bruce Bawer argues that gay radicalism, as demonstrated on the Gay Pride Day march, ironically reinforces the antigay stereotypes held by heterosexuals. In the third reading, "Homosexuals in Western Armed Forces," David Segal and his fellow researchers discuss how the policies and practices concerning homosexuals in the military are comparable to the heterosexual norms and treatment of gays in the larger society. In the fourth article, "Male Street Hustling," Thomas Calhoun presents an ethnographic analysis of how young men become prostitutes and seek to avoid the stigma associated with this kind of work.

38

Rejecting "Femininity": Gender Identity Development in Lesbians

MARGARET COOPER
Western Kentucky University

The majority of social science research on homosexuality has been on men (see Oberstone and Sukoneck, 1976). Most nonfeminist work on lesbians has been of a quantitative nature, attempting to study the issue of lesbianism numerically. It has not allowed the women's experience to be quoted directly but to be interpreted solely for the reader by the researcher.

This study allows women to speak about their own gender identity development. The difference between "sex" and "gender" should be emphasized since it is a crucial distinction made in this article. Kate Millett (1970, p. 39) wrote of the "overwhelmingly *cultural* character of gender." She, along with others (Stoller, 1968), was active in distinguishing gender from the term "sex," which refers to one's anatomy and physiology. Robert Stoller (1968, pp. viii–ix) wrote that

> gender is a term that has psychological or cultural rather than biological connotations. If the proper terms for sex are "male" and "female," the corresponding terms for gender are "masculine" and "feminine"; these latter may be quite independent of sex.

METHODS AND SAMPLE

Martin and Lyon (1972) felt surveys may not even be likely to include the respondents' true feelings, thereby forcing the respondent to fit into a catego-

From *Deviant Behavior,* Vol. 11 (1990), pp. 371–380, Margaret Cooper. Washington, D.C.: Taylor & Francis, Inc. Reproduced with permission. All rights reserved.

ry she or he might not otherwise. They were critical of quantitative methods in the study of lesbianism when they wrote:

> Experience indicates that the questions are made up generally by heterosexuals and asked of homosexuals who very often find them irrelevant to their particular lifestyle. The questions, for the most part, are un-answerable by the required "yes" or "no" or multiple choice, and their only virtue is that they are easily computerized into instant (misleading) statistics. (p. 2)

With feminist criticism of such studies in mind, a qualitative method, in-depth interviews, was chosen for this article. It allows for respondents to create their own categories rather than merely try to fit into those preconceived by a researcher. The validity of the qualitative method relates directly to the validity of the women's experiences.

Lesbians were identified and contacted through friendship associations. Fifteen women agreed to participate. All respondents were assured confidentiality and assigned pseudonyms. The interviews were conducted and analyzed according to the procedure suggested by Schwartz and Jacobs (1979) and Lofland and Lofland (1984). Rather than utilizing the statistical analyses of quantitative methods, the interview data were examined for emergent patterns of responses and descriptions.

The ages of the respondents ranged from 19 to 38, with the average age of 25.3 years. All of the women were born and reared in small towns and cities in the South and Midwest. All of them currently live in and around cities with a population of 50,000 or less in various towns in the central region of the United States.

Four of the women considered themselves to be feminists. The rest did not. One other woman had recently become involved with the gay rights movement. A few others expressed interest in the gay rights and feminist movements, but not from the standpoint of a participant.

Since the sample size of this study is small, no attempt will be made to say that this sample is reflective of all lesbians. However, this article is an honest account of the experience of the women who did take part in this study.

RESULTS

All of the women interviewed indicated a rejection of traditional femininity. Even as children, some even before they were consciously aware of same-sex attractions, had difficulty fitting into what they saw as the traditional female role. Apparently, even though these women might not have known what they wanted, they knew what they did *not* want. For them, it appears that the female gender role represented more than femaleness. It also represented heterosexuality:

> That role is all sex-oriented. It's the dumb housewife image. If you really look at it, that's just the way it is. (Pat)

> I remember as a very young child not identifying with the female role because it seemed like, and this was growing up in the sixties, that the female role was

strongly attached to your role as a wife and mother and I knew I couldn't do that. So I felt more identified with the male role. When I was a kid, I would play the boy when we played house. And I wanted my mom to buy me "boy clothes". (Kate)

For Kate, this role rejection was directly linked, in her view, to her attraction to other girls. She was aware of this attraction at a very young age and she reported that she developed quite a "macho" image of herself by age seven. She explained it this way:

I used to think, as a kid, that you had to be masculine to get a woman. That women liked masculinity and men liked femininity. So I tried to convince every girl on the block that I was a boy. I even took a male name. And of course, it made perfect sense to me. I never understood when people's parents were flipping out.

The other women's responses fell into three categories: (1) taking the male role (like Kate's example), (2) being a "tomboy" and (3) rejecting items of dress and play associated with female children. These responses overlapped in all of the interviews.

Taking the male role was seen in both play and fantasy. Cindy said, "Kids would play house; and I was the one, when my cousins would come over, I'd play the boy. I'd always do the boy parts." This led her to believe that she might be gay. This also "concerned" her cousins, one of whom later said to her, "We was all worried about you, wondering about you because you always wanted to play the guy." Cindy said she wanted to respond by merely saying, "Take a hint." Anita's childhood fantasies often involved taking the male role. She described them by saying:

I might not have known what it was called when I was real young, I can remember going to see "James Bond" and like when . . . my imagination would run wild or I would have some kind of fantasy, I'd never fantasize as being one of the women. I was always "James Bond" . . . "Matt Dillon," you know.

Wolff (1971) found that many lesbians, as children, desired to be boys. She found lesbians were five times more likely to have expressed this desire than were heterosexual women. In a study by Fleener and reported by Lewis (1979), 82 percent of lesbians sampled had gone through a tomboy phase. In the sample for this article, all fifteen women told of their "tomboy" experiences as children. Not only did they engage in sports, tree-climbing, etc., many of them chose to play with boys. Robin said, "I was the only girl in my neighborhood my age when we moved here, so that was a lot of fun to hang around with the boys . . . I used to be a tomboy really bad." Barbara enjoyed "getting out and playing baseball with my brothers or basketball, things like that." This led her to conclude after some period of time, "I knew I was different. I just couldn't put my finger on it.". . .

Lewis (1979, p. 23) called the "rebellion against what is seen as being female and restrictive" that coincides with the desire for "those elements of male identity that carry independence . . . the first rite of passage into lesbian selfhood." The third set of responses involved this "rebellion against what is seen as being female." Carole said that she would "rather take a beating than put a dress on." Barbara not only disliked the frilly dresses her mother bought for her, she also hated the Barbie dolls. "I wanted to burn the Barbie dolls!" she laughed.

During the childhood years, the rejection of the female role is relatively risk-free. This begins to change in adolescence. The world again becomes the dichotomized place of girl/femininity and boy/masculinity, now with an additional imperative: heterosexuality, complete with its emphasis, for girls, on attracting the boy who will become their future protectors of social responsibility (Lewis, 1979). Lewis found that girls then began to lose their desire to be boys. Only 2 percent of her subjects wished to be boys after puberty. Most accepted female identities. However, most did not succumb to tradition, but sought to personally redefine what it meant to be female. As teenagers, sports became an outlet for many of them. Nine of the fifteen women in this study played in sports. This was enough to cause rumors to start. Two women explained it this way:

> I played basketball and stuff, and you know, when you're an athlete and a woman, there's a lot of stereotypes. You know, "she's real bullish!" Or "she can really shoot that hard for a woman." People would say something and my sister heard about it and she'd go home and tell my mom. She would say, "I heard Stella's gay." (Stella)

> If you were in athletics at that point in time when I was in high school, you were automatically stereotyped that you were gay because you were a big athlete. . . . You were automatically labeled. (Carole)

For Stella, these rumors were instigators of problems at home. The mere label of "lesbian" proved to be a threat to women. It was a warning that they were stepping outside the lines of acceptable gender behavior. Carole felt a lot of pressure from peers to disprove the rumors. She said, "It bothered me to a degree . . . it did put a little more pressure on me as to trying to prove myself not being that way as far as dating and stuff like that."

As teenagers, and for some even into adulthood, a rejection of feminine clothing was also a pattern. This rejection ranged from not wearing overtly feminine apparel to dressing in a way that was considered to be "mannish."

> I went through that stage when I had to play a Dyke. Yeah, I had to ride a motorcycle and wear men's pants, men's clothes and I didn't wear women's stuff at all. Men's underwear even, you know. You go through this phase and it's one of those things. (Pat)

> I don't know why I'm so butch, why I wear men's clothes. It's not that I want to be a man, because I don't. Because God knows, if I were a man, I wouldn't have been with some of the women that I've been with. (Anita)

For Pat, as with the rest of the women with the exception of Anita and Jennifer, it was just, as she said, a phase. Whether as a child, teenager, or adult, it did seem to serve, as previously stated by Lewis, as a "rite of passage." It is crucial to consider, as Anita articulated, that gay women do *not* want to be men. Instead, they had desired male privilege and access to women. They desired the freedom that men had; and *every* woman in the sample, whether or not she considered herself a feminist, found the female role restrictive.

Since adolescents undergo so much pressure concerning gender conformity, lesbian adolescents might experience confusion, frustration, and ridicule. Sasha Lewis (1979, p. 24) wrote, "The young lesbian realizes that she cannot be a boy, yet she realizes that she cannot be like her female peers and in many cases she feels a sense of intense isolation." Not understanding why such pressure to conform even exists, lesbians then must determine their own paths. For many, as Pat and Kate explained, the lack of role models dramatically increased their problems. The problem was not merely finding good or even adequate role models. It was finding *any* role models. The lack of visibility on the part of lesbians reinforced their fears of being "freaks."

In what they perceived as a way to escape the constraints of female roles, two of the women had expressed a youthful intention to enter the military. Two more eventually did. Although the army did not satisfy either in her search for identity, both felt their reason for joining involved this rejection of traditional roles. Pat explained:

> Why did I join the army? Because it was not a female role. To prove that I was just as good as they (men) were. That I could do anything they could do. . . .

CONCLUSION

While the issue of gender identity in lesbians calls for further research, this study does reveal some important points. Even at an early age, the women in this study were rebels where gender behavior was concerned. Many of them described experiences as "tomboys." They, as children, indicated they had no problem with this behavior but were forced by others to "wear dresses" or "play with dolls." Some did these willingly but rejected traditional femininity when they saw it as representing heterosexuality. Most rejected the traditional female role, because even as children, they could not foresee themselves in the future portraying a heterosexual role. Some, in childhood fantasies, already perceived themselves in lives with women. Many of them saw a need to take the "male role" to achieve the relation to women that they desire. At the onset of adolescence, much more pressure existed from both peers and adults to abandon "tomboyish" behaviors. . . .

It should be reiterated that the women in this study found the traditional female role to be restrictive and constraining. Beginning as children, they began a journey of self-discovery usually without the assistance of role models or appropriate guidance from those they considered authorities. As adults, each reached her own conclusion on what it meant to be a woman and what it meant to be a lesbian. Risking the labels of "deviants" or worse, these women have chosen roles for which there were no scripts. Consequently, many feminists would consider their androgynous approach to selfhood to be much more well-rounded than those straining to conform to rigidly limited roles. In their paper on the psychological adjustment of lesbians and heterosexual women, Oberstone and Sukoneck (1976) concluded their analysis on gay women with the following:

> Are they really more "masculine" in their behavior than their "normal" heterosexual counterparts, or are they more free to develop both their feminine and masculine and, in fact, their human potential? It is possible that, rather than being "masculine," the lesbian woman, by virtue of being an outlaw, has had to develop personality qualities that have been traditionally the domain of the male, such as independence, self-determination, competence, and aggression (p. 185).

References

Lewis, Sasha G. 1979. *Sunday's Women: Lesbian Life Today.* Boston: Beacon.

Lofland, John and Lyn H. Lofland. 1984. *Analyzing Social Settings: A Guide to Qualitative Observation and Analysis.* Belmont, CA: Wadsworth.

Martin, Del and Phyllis Lyon. 1972. *Lesbian/Woman.* New York: Bantam.

Millett, Kate. 1970. *Sexual Politics.* New York: Ballantine.

Oberstone, Andrea and Harriet Sukoneck. 1976. "Psychological Adjustment and Life Style of Single Lesbians and Single Heterosexual Women." *Psychology of Women Quarterly,* I(no. 2): 172–188.

Schwartz, Howard and Jerry Jacobs. 1979. *Qualitative Sociology: A Method to the Madness.* New York: Free Press.

Stoller, Robert J. 1968. *Sex and Gender.* New York: Science House.

Wolff, Charlotte. 1971. *Love Between Women.* New York: St. Martin's.

39

Radical Gay Activism: A Critical Gay's View

BRUCE BAWER

"The only time I ever feel ashamed of being gay," says a friend of mine, "is on Gay Pride Day."

I know what he means, though my own emotions on that day are, at worst, closer to dismay than to shame. Every June, on the appointed Sunday, I stand on the sidewalk somewhere along Fifth Avenue in midtown Manhattan, sometimes alone and sometimes with friends, and watch the march file past, each group behind its identifying banner: the gay senior citizens, the separatist lesbians, the Dykes on Bikes, the People With AIDS coalition, the recovering alcoholics who call themselves Clean and Sober, the interracial couples who call themselves Men of All Colors Together (formerly Black and White Men Together), the gay and lesbian student organizations from various colleges and universities, the local chapters of direct-action groups like ACT UP and Queer Nation, the disco-blaring floats advertising various bars and dance clubs, the volunteers from Gay Men's Health Crisis and God's Love We Deliver, the Parents and Friends of Lesbians and Gays, the gay Catholics, the gay Episcopalians, the gay Jews, the Gay Fathers, the gays in leather, the gay swimmers. . . .

My feelings are always mixed. There's a certain comfort in being among so many people who have all experienced self-discoveries similar to one's own, and who have all had to deal with the same slights and cruelties that homosexuals have to put up with from people who want to inflict pain or who don't care or who just don't know any better. The march also provides safety in numbers: no danger of gay-bashing here. And it affords a spectacle of quiet heroism: many of the marchers are dying. (In some cases you can tell, in some you can't.) Watching them file past, I know that I'm looking at thousands of untold stories of extraordinary courage.

Yet on that appointed Sunday in June there is always for me, as well, a certain disquiet. Year by year, I find myself increasingly vexed by certain aspects of the march. Part of me doesn't want to attend it. If at its best the event hints

Reprinted from the author's book, *A Place at the Table: The Gay Individual in American Society* (New York: Poseidon Press, 1993), pp. 153–161. Copyright © 1993 by Bruce Bawer. Reprinted by permission of Pocket Books, a division of Simon & Schuster, Inc.

at the diversity of the gay population in America, altogether too much of it is silly, sleazy, and sex-centered, a reflection of the narrow, contorted definition of homosexuality that marks some sectors of the gay subculture. On Gay Pride Day in 1991, for instance, I was perplexed to see that among the handful of V.I.P.s on the reviewing stand at Forty-first Street was Robin Byrd, an X-rated movie actress who generally appears in public wearing a string mesh bikini. Byrd's weekly public-access TV program showcases the talents of youngsters, some of them teenage runaways, who work in Times Square strip clubs. Did the organizers of the march, I wondered, really want the world to think that *this* was what being gay was all about?

Byrd may also have been on the reviewing stand a year later, but I didn't see her. On Gay Pride Day 1992 I positioned myself a half-mile or so north of the reviewing stand, near the corner of Fifth Avenue and Fifty-fourth Street. This intersection is three blocks north of Saint Patrick's Cathedral, opposite which a few dozen protesters traditionally congregate behind blue police lines, yelling anti-gay epithets and waving homemade signs on which they have scrawled the usual scriptural quotations. It is customary for marchers passing this group to chant, with rather dignified restraint, "Shame! Shame! Shame!" For some reason, on Gay Pride Day 1992 a group of protesters left their assigned spot while the march was still going by. As they headed up the Fifth Avenue sidewalk past me, toting signs that read "Jesus Forever—Repent," the Queer Nation contingent was about to reach Fifty-fourth Street. The two groups clashed near the northeast corner. "Shame! Shame! Shame!" the Queer Nation members chanted, breaking ranks and heading for the sidewalk as a dozen or so policemen moved quickly to form a human barricade. The Queer Nation marchers and the anti-gay protesters exchanged verbal abuse for a few moments; then the protesters resumed walking up the sidewalk and the Queer Nation contingent peeled away to continue marching down the avenue. Everything seemed in order until one Queer Nation member, a short leather-clad young man with a bushy mustache who was at the moment no more than six or eight feet from me, suddenly stopped and turned around to shriek happily, at the top of his lungs, at the departing protesters: *"Jesus was a faggot!"*

I shook my head in disappointment. Now what, I wondered, was the point of *that?*

Apart from that episode, there were the usual sights. Bearded men in dresses. Young men masquerading as Marilyn Monroe, Mae West, Barbara Bush, Joan Collins. Fat men in bathing trunks. Two friends, one dressed as a priest and the other as Jesus. A couple of dozen young fellows in a truck that displayed two banners, one reading "Gay Whores" and the other "Legalize Prostitution." (I recognized one of the young men from my health club, where he always swims in the fast lane.) There was a float blaring dance music and bearing the name of the radical New Alliance Party, some of whose members marched behind and alongside the float, chanting threateningly with raised fists: "N.A.P.! We got to build a New Alliance Movement!" And there were three—count 'em, three—middle-aged members of NAMBLA, the North American Man-Boy Love Association, two of whom carried the organization's banner while the third held up a sign proclaiming the joys of pederasty.

It must be emphasized that most of the marchers were not at all shocking. There were several times more Gay Catholics than Gay Whores, more men in tennis shorts than in underpants. And NAMBLA was the tiniest group of all. Yet there was plenty to make John Q. Public do a double take—plenty, indeed, that appeared to have been designed to accomplish precisely that. It seemed as if people who wore suits and ties on the 364 other days of the year had, on this particular morning, ransacked their closets for their tackiest, skimpiest, most revealing items of clothing. There were hundreds of bare chests, bare bottoms, mesh pants, nipple rings, leather shorts, and tight designer briefs without anything covering them. Couples who almost certainly didn't go in for public displays of affection on an ordinary Sunday made sure to pause every block or so during their progress down Fifth Avenue to kiss or grab each other's crotches or rub their bodies together in a simulation of sex. There was more sashaying and queeny posing in a couple of hours than one could expect to see in a solid month of gay bar-hopping. Smart, talented people who held down respectable jobs in the corporate world or the fashion industry, on Wall Street or Publishers' Row, seemed to have done their best on this special day to look like tawdry bimbos, bar boys, and beach bums. Time and again, glimpsing this or that unconventionally attired or coiffed or made-up marcher, I found myself feeling momentarily as if I'd stumbled into a private costume party and seen something I wasn't supposed to see. Unfortunately, however, this wasn't a private party; it was a public spectacle.

And therein lay its illogic. The signs that some of the participants carried—signs demanding equal rights, more money for AIDS research, and so on—suggested that the march was intended, at least in part, to be a political statement directed at the heterosexual population. But if this was the case, what could explain the grotesque appearance and vulgar behavior of so many marchers, who were, quite frankly, a public-relations nightmare? The facts of the matter, after all, seemed obvious: The Gay Pride Day march provided a first-class opportunity to exhibit the real face of gay America, to demonstrate that the gay population is in every way a cross-section of the country—black and white, rural and urban, rich and poor. If the gay population put that real face forward on Gay Pride Day, it wouldn't look alien to anyone. But instead, the march represented gay America by means of what seems at times to be a veritable circus parade, a parade that too often underlined the sexual aspect of gay life—and underlined the most sordid elements of that sexual aspect. It presented homosexuals less as human beings than as *sexual* beings.

That, indeed, is the hallmark of the gay subculture: The notion that life, for homosexuals, naturally revolves around sex more than it does for heterosexuals. This notion is hardly surprising, given that this particular subculture is the creation of people who are united not by ethnicity, religion, or profession but by sexual orientation; yet one of this notion's unfortunate consequences is an annual march that, instead of giving the world a representative picture of gay life, offers a strange and demeaning caricature thereof. Looking at some of those marchers, I couldn't help thinking that the subculture mentality had worked upon them in such a way that they virtually considered it their responsibility as gay people to reduce themselves to stereotypes every Gay Pride Day;

however much they might or might not have to do the rest of the year with the subculture and its ethos, however far they may have grown away from it and into themselves, it was clear from their dress and deportment that, on some level, they had never rejected completely the subculture's definition of what it meant to be gay—and today, apparently, was their Holy Day of Obligation, their day to be as gay as they could possibly be.

Most homosexuals in the New York area, of course, weren't anywhere near the march. Most hadn't even considered coming; they *never* came. Where were they? Well, some were doubtless enjoying a leisurely brunch; some were spending Sunday with their families; some were puttering around the house, or walking in the park, or taking in a movie. I'd seen at least two dozen gay men at church that morning, every last one of them elegantly turned out in suit and tie and polished black shoes, and would be astonished, to say the least, to see any of them in the march. I hadn't mentioned the march to any of them, but I'd talked about it enough with gay friends to have a pretty good idea how they'd react: with a wince, a grimace, a rhetorical question or two: "Who'd want to be part of that tacky display? Why should I participate in something whose sole purpose is to make a dirty joke out of who I am?"

I can't say I felt very differently. I could never bring myself to take part fully in a march that included the likes of NAMBLA. Yet most years I did go so far as to include myself in the ranks of the thousands of spectators who, after the last marchers had passed, tagged along at the end all the way down to Greenwich Village. For I felt that if the image of homosexuals that the march projected was ever to be set right, those of us who were displeased with it in its present form couldn't keep away entirely. We had to do *something*.

That day, as on every previous Gay Pride Day, I found myself reflecting on the march's ramifications. In the evening, people in New York and around the country would turn on their local news and see a few seconds of this or some other gay march. I'd watched enough of those reports to have a pretty good idea what the producers would choose to show: some leathermen, maybe the Barbara Bush and Marilyn Monroe impersonators, almost certainly the young man dressed as Jesus. In the succeeding weeks and months, moreover, long after the young stockbrokers and magazine editors had stowed away their flamboyant Gay Pride Day accoutrements for another year and slipped back into their everyday Brooks Brothers togs, anti-gay propagandists would put together videotapes showing these young professionals looking very, shall we say, unprofessional. These videotapes, featuring the most outrageous parts of this and other recent gay marches, would be advertised in right-wing political magazines and various church publications and would be sold and shipped to purchasers around the country. These purchasers, in turn, would make copies for friends and relatives or show them at neighborhood get-togethers, at church socials, at P.T.A. meetings. From Maine to California, men and women would watch these videotapes and shake their heads in disgust, not only at the individuals portrayed in them but at what they presumably represented. To those men and women, this was the face of homosexuality.

Standing there as the march went by, I didn't have to imagine the reactions of small-town middle Americans to the Gay Pride Day march. This was, after all, a Sunday in June in midtown Manhattan, and there were tourists all over the place. From my spot on the Fifth Avenue curb, I watched one out-of-town family after another hurry across the avenue or up the sidewalk, maps and cameras and shopping bags in hand, on their way from one metropolitan attraction to another. It was clear that the Gay Pride Day march did not figure on these people's sightseeing itineraries but had, rather, taken them by surprise. In every instance, I saw nothing on their faces but shock, revulsion, and a desperate desire to get away from Fifth Avenue as quickly as possible.

One family in particular stands out in my memory: a husband and wife and their tall, gangly, shy-looking son, who was about thirteen and who, it occurred to me, might well wake up one morning four or five years hence and realize he was gay. It distressed me to think that this march would probably shape that family's most vivid image of homosexuality. If the boy did eventually prove to be gay, the memory of this day could only make it harder for him to recognize and come to terms with his homosexuality and for his parents to understand and accept the truth about him. That shouldn't be the way things worked. If the march had any legitimate purpose, it was to make things easier, not harder, for young gay people and their families. Things would be hard enough for them as it was.

That afternoon, on a float for a drinking establishment called the Crowbar, I noticed a sign: "Greetings from the Planet Gay!" The sign, I felt, summed up the whole day: too many of the people involved in the march *did* think of themselves as living on another planet—or, at least, thought of their sexual identity as being something from another planet. They had been provided here with an extraordinary opportunity to educate the heterosexual population about homosexuality, to destroy backward myths, to win friends and supporters for the cause of gay equality; instead, much of the march simply served to reinforce myths, to confirm prejudices, and to make new enemies for homosexuals. If Jerry Falwell or Pat Robertson had wanted to orchestrate an annual spectacle designed to increase hostility toward gays, I reflected, they could hardly have done a better job than this.

It seemed to me, indeed, that the sort of pride on display in the Gay Pride Day march was, in many cases, not so much pride in the sense of "self-respect" or "dignity" than pride in the sense of "arrogance," "conceit," "hubris." Real pride, after all, is a hard-won individual attribute. It doesn't come from being gay, or from belonging to *any* group. It can come, however, from dealing with the fact of your homosexuality in a responsible and mature manner, from not using it as a club to beat other people with or as an excuse to behave irresponsibly or unseriously. The more loudly someone declares his pride, the more it should be suspected; for real pride is not shrill and insistent but quiet and strong. . . .

The marchers who make the Gay Pride Day march embarrassing to many homosexuals and disgusting to people . . . represent the same small but vocal minority of the gay population that has, for a generation, played no small part in shaping and sustaining most heterosexuals' notions of what it means to be homosexual. I've noted that many heterosexuals speak of the "gay lifestyle" as if there were only one way to be gay; but it must also be said that some gays, encouraged by the subculture to think that they are obliged as homosexuals to adopt certain ways and views and tastes, themselves speak of the "gay lifestyle." I've remarked that many heterosexuals think of homosexuality in terms of "practice" or "activity"; but this is at least partly because subculture-oriented gays center their lives on their sexual orientation and because a generation of gay activists have made the right to engage with abandon in certain kinds of sexual activity their principal cause. One day in December 1992, I walked past Saint Patrick's Cathedral in New York during an ACT UP protest presumably connected to the Roman Catholic Church's opposition to pro-tolerance curricula in the public schools. "Teach gay sex!" the signs read—as if fostering young people's tolerance of homosexuality, or informing them of the existence of gay parents, necessarily involved teaching about bedroom matters. Nothing could be more emblematic of the subculture's view of homosexuality than this reduction of gay identity, gay life, and gay culture to gay sex. I've said that being gay isn't a matter of what one does, in bed or anywhere else, but of what one *is;* too often, alas, the gay subculture acts as if what one does in bed is the *quintessence* of what one is.

40

Homosexuals in Western Armed Forces

DAVID R. SEGAL
University of Maryland

PAUL A. GADE
U.S. Army Research Institute

EDGAR M. JOHNSON
U.S. Army Research Institute

Homosexuality is not a uniquely American phenomenon, although current media attention might lead one to believe it to be. Nor is the policy regarding the integration of homosexuals into the military a uniquely American issue. In recent years there has been both growing awareness and growing tolerance of homosexuality in Western industrial democratic societies. This has been reflected in decisions by medical and psychological associations to cease classifying homosexuality as a mental illness and, in some jurisdictions, in decriminalization of homosexual acts between consenting adults and in making homosexuals legally eligible for "partnership" benefits that previously were restricted to legally married heterosexual couples.

Policies regarding homosexuals in the military seem to reflect, but lag behind the policies in their host societies. However, the social sciences have neither a long research tradition nor a rich data base on the policies and practices that exist cross-nationally that might be used to inform the policy debate.

Social scientists have recently begun to turn their attention to this issue and have presented the results of their work describing policies and practices in individual nations at international professional conferences. We draw on the data presented at two recent conferences in an attempt to begin to define the range and the most common patterns found in the Western nations. The first of these conferences was organized by Charles Moskos of Northwestern University and John A. Williams of Loyola University of Chicago in Baltimore, Maryland, in October 1991, under the auspices of the Inter-University

Reprinted from *Society*, Vol. 31 (November/December 1993): 37–42.

Seminar on Armed Forces and Society and the Olin Foundation. The conference focused broadly on the nature of the armed forces in the post-cold war world. One of the dimensions identified for discussion was the role of homosexuals in the military. The second conference was organized by Gwyn Harries-Jenkins of the University of Hull in Beverly, United Kingdom, in April 1993, under the auspices of the Army Research Institute for the Behavioral and Social Sciences, and dealt more directly with the experience of European nations with homosexuality as a military personnel issue.

ANGLO-AMERICAN NATIONS

The Anglo-American nations—among them the United States, Great Britain, Canada, Australia, New Zealand, and Northern Ireland—comprise a major group of nations where the issue of homosexuals in the military has become of concern in recent history. These nations share a more or less common cultural heritage.

Reporting on Australia and New Zealand at the 1991 conference in Baltimore, Cathy Downes, an analyst in the Office of the Chief of Defense Staff of New Zealand, reported:

> Arguments challenging the exclusion of homosexuals from armed forces have been raised. These flow from changes in the parent societies of these armed forces. For example, the change between early and late cold war periods is also the time period in which there is a significant shift in societal attitudes toward tolerance of homosexuality. . . . If the relationship between social change and military response holds true, the gradual normalization of homosexuality in larger societies, which is a 1980s phenomenon, is likely to be increasingly refracted in military forces of the 1990s.

Downes was president. Late last year, Australia set aside its exclusion. New Zealand began to move toward a policy change after our presidential election, but seems to have delayed further consideration until the direction that the United States will take is clear. At the same conference, Colonel Franklin Pinch, who holds a Ph.D. in sociology and who at the time was the ranking behavioral scientist in the Canadian Forces, reported:

> The Canadian Forces are preparing a defense involving homosexuality which is before the courts. While these outcomes cannot be prejudged, two points are relevant: first, the tribunal on the employment of women did not accept the argument that cohesion and morale would be impaired by the introduction of women, since it was based largely on "customer preference" (that is, men would not accept women), and it is unlikely to be accepted for other issues; second, the Canadian public, and especially opinion leaders, are generally not supportive of such exclusions . . . [homo- and hetero-] sexual behavior that is disruptive may well supplant concerns regarding sexual orientation.

Again, the statement was prescient. Canada has set aside its exclusion, as one part of a more general human rights movement. Pinch is now retired from the Canadian forces and is doing research on the repercussions of this policy change. He recently indicated that in the few months since the change, no adverse effect on recruitment or retention has been noted, nor have there been incidents of harassment of homosexuals. Homosexuals, for their part, have not made declarations of their sexual orientations. The Australian experience is reported to have been similar.

The United Kingdom is a particularly interesting case, because it highlights the direction of social change, reflects a frequently found divergence between official policy and actual practice, and exemplifies a common pattern: one of limited tolerance. In terms of official policy, when most homosexual acts were decriminalized in the 1967 Sexual Offenses Act, the British military was exempted from decriminalization. In May 1991, a parliamentary Select Committee on the Armed Forces recommended decriminalization in the armed forces as well, and in June 1992 the government accepted this recommendation.

Although it has been decriminalized, homosexuality is still regarded as incompatible with military service and is grounds for denial of enlistment or instant dismissal. Thus, the official policy is one of exclusion. However, military personnel are not asked about their sexual orientation. The practice is not to act unless homosexuals call attention to themselves. Indeed, if their orientation becomes known but they are not openly engaged in homosexual behavior, they might be counselled and warned against misconduct, rather than discharged.

EUROPEAN NATIONS

Most of NATO countries do not exclude homosexuals as a matter of policy. The exceptions are Turkey, Greece, where homosexuality is regarded as a mental illness, and Italy. While the latter country has exclusionary policies similar to Great Britain, it does not seem to be completely exclusionary in practice. Turkey does not ask about sexual orientation at entry.

Germany is an especially interesting case because it too manifests major differences between policy and practice—though in the opposite direction of Great Britain—and because it lies at one end of the range of patterns. In practice, it is the most exclusionary country we have studied.

In principle Germany currently does not regard sexual orientation a relevant criterion for determining eligibility for military service. However, in practice very few homosexuals seem to serve. Unlike most nations, German doctors ask conscripts and volunteers about their sexual orientation during the accession process. Many homosexual young men appear to opt for alternative civilian service rather than serving conscripted military service. Conscripts who reveal a homosexual orientation during in-processing are likely to be rejected as "mentally unfit for service," thereby avoiding both military service and alternative civilian service. Official policy states that regular servicemen and volunteers are not rendered unfit for military service by homosexuality, nor can they be discharged for a homosexual orientation. If they are discovered to be homosexual and have served for more than four years, they are not discharged before their term of service is completed.

However, in practice, if their orientation becomes known, homosexuals are allowed neither to assume supervisory positions nor to serve as instructors.

They may be restricted from high-security assignments as well. Junior officers identified as homosexual within three years after commissioning may be discharged on grounds that they are unfit for the career of an officer. Homosexuality has been decriminalized in German society, and homosexual behavior by military personnel off-duty is not prosecuted. However, the German courts have affirmed the right of the *Bundeswehr* to prosecute soldiers for homosexual acts while on duty. Molesting a subordinate is grounds for discharge. Less serious offenses may be punished by demotion, ban on promotions, and salary cuts.

A more common pattern in Europe might be labelled laissez-faire. Spain, for example, decriminalized homosexuality in the military in 1984, making sexual orientation simply a matter of personal choice. France takes a similar position. Two of France's foremost military sociologists, Bernard Boene, head of the sociology program at the French Military Academy, and Michel Martin, of the University of Toulouse, reported at the 1991 Baltimore conference:

> As [a] Catholic [country, France] . . . tolerated deviant behavior . . . because the possibility of forgiveness is current. This explains why one finds great military figures with known homosexual tendencies, or why homosexuality was proverbial among colonial troops. . . . Today the issue is rarely mentioned in the military, though the recognition of homosexuality in the civilian sphere has become a fact. In the military, it is shrouded in a kind of silence that does not express embarrassment, but a complete lack of interest. The clue may be that most homosexuals are screened out or self-selected out. It should be noted that in France, the gay movement as well as the feminist movement, from the 1960s until today has had a strong antimilitarist tradition.

Belgium likewise holds to a laissez-faire position. There are no laws, rules, or regulations discriminating against homosexuals in the military, as long as they separate their personal and professional lives. In the past, they were not allowed to serve in the para-commando regiment, but this seems to have been a function of the commander's preference rather than service policy. Soldiers whose sexual behavior is abusive of peers, that is, harassment, or disruptive of the unit are subject to reassignment or medical discharge.

A similar lack of interest is noted in Switzerland, which is not a member of NATO. Sociologist Karl Haltiner reported in 1991:

> Homosexuality itself has never been a reason for military exclusion. If, as a result of homosexual behavior, social or psychological problems occur, an inspection for leave in the psychiatric-medical manner is possible but not compulsory. The highest [Swiss] military lawyer laconically remarked in 1985: "The problem of homosexuality does not exist in the Swiss army."

Laissez-faire was characteristic of at least one of the countries of the old Warsaw Pact as well. Jerzy Wiatr, the foremost Polish military sociologist, and now a member of parliament, reported in 1991:

> In the Polish armed forces there are no laws discriminating against homosexuals. I have also not found instances of extra-legal discrimination. . . . In Poland, because of

the intensity of conformity in publicly accepted norms of sexual behavior, homosexuality remains taboo. People do not reveal their homosexuality, not because of laws, but because of informal social control. . . . The fact that the armed forces do not discriminate against homosexuals does not mean that they are accepted. Rather it can be said that as far as the military structure is concerned, they simply do not exist.

Some nations, like Germany, have policies of equality but practices of exclusion. Others, like England, have policies of exclusion but practice limited tolerance of homosexuals in the military. Still others, like France and Belgium, have laissez-faire practices of benign neglect. However, a few nations treat homosexuals as a privileged minority, at least in the military accession process. In the Scandinavian countries, for example, up until the late 1970s draftees were asked about their sexual orientation, and homosexuals were registered and in some cases forced out. Draftees are no longer asked about sexual orientation nor are homosexuals registered. However, homosexual draftees can avoid military service, with varying degrees of difficulty among countries, by claiming that their sexual orientation is psychologically incompatible with military service. Thus, control over whether the homosexual draftee serves is in his hands.

The Netherlands probably represents the most tolerant position regarding homosexuals in the military. Dutch sociologist Jan van der Meulen reported at the 1991 conference:

The acceptance and integration of women, ethnic minorities, and homosexuals in the armed forces was initiated as principle and policy before the end of the Cold War. . . .This does not mean that women, ethnic minorities, and homosexuals nowadays meet no discrimination any longer, nor that all three integration processes are concurrent.

Because the Netherlands is among the most open and tolerant of nations with regard to homosexuality in the military, it has been in a position to conduct research and undertake policy initiatives to make integration work. In a major survey of military personnel in 1991, a very small proportion of personnel reported themselves to be homosexual or lesbian (about 1 percent of men, 3.5 percent of women). Most heterosexual military personnel expressed tolerance for the rights of homosexuals, but 30 percent of male respondents indicated that they would respond in a hostile or aggressive manner if a colleague turned out to be homosexual, and about 60 percent of all survey respondents said that they preferred to maintain social distance from homosexuals. Known homosexuals are effectively excluded from social activities. Not surprisingly, most homosexuals in the service seem to prefer not to declare their sexual orientation.

The Dutch defense minister has established a commission for advice and coordination on homosexuality in the armed forces, and homosexuals in the service have their own union, which is financially supported in part by the defense ministry. The approach in the Netherlands is to avoid blaming homosexuals for reactions to them, and to sensitize the heterosexual majority to the rights of homosexuals through training and counselling. However, the effectiveness of these programs in overcoming the reticence of heterosexuals to socially interact with homosexuals must await the results of the research currently being conducted in the Netherlands.

GENERAL PATTERNS

Regardless of national policy, some individuals with a homosexual orientation have always managed to serve undetected in the military forces of their countries. Most homosexuals in the military do not "come out," and prefer to keep their sexual orientation private. Even where policy and practice allow homosexuals to serve, very few soldiers openly declare themselves to be homosexual. Even in the most liberal societies, a stigma is still attached to homosexuality and open declarations may entail career costs. Thus, the number of military personnel in Western nations who publicly identify themselves as homosexual appears to be very small. Even in countries with non-exclusionary policies, open homosexuals may find themselves referred to psychiatric counseling, and may be excluded from combat units and certain other assignments.

The social-historical context of a country's military service is very important in determining its policies and practices toward homosexuals. The more liberal countries seem to have had a long history of grappling with homosexual issues and the liberalization of attitudes toward homosexuals in the military has evolved slowly, lagging behind more general social attitudes. Gay and lesbian activist groups, although they are usually anti-military, have often served as the catalyst for changing policies and practices concerning homosexuals in the military services of more tolerant countries.

Most countries seem to be more conservative in practice than they are in policy. Even in countries where no questions are asked about sexual orientation at accession or during military service, the practice of not asking may be more an act of active evasion of potentially more complex issues, such as "partnership" benefits, than passive acceptance of homosexuality. Potential issues are thus "silenced" by not asking about sexual orientation. In fact, the most common pattern cross-nationally seems to be that military forces do not ask about sexual orientation, even when they have exclusionary policies.

Policies and practices concerning homosexuals in the military seem to follow national social norms. Heterosexuality is clearly the dominant norm in Western societies. Even in the most liberal societies, homosexuals in the military do not flaunt their lifestyle; in fact they often choose not to identify themselves as homosexuals at all.

Perhaps because heterosexuality is the dominant norm, few data are available on homosexuals. No country, no matter how liberal, seems to have data on the precise percentage of its military personnel that is homosexual. Estimates range from less than 1 percent to as high as 10 percent. Neither does it seem known in any of the countries studied what percentage of the general population is homosexual. Again, estimates range from far less than 1 percent to as high as 10 percent.

INTEGRATION AND LIBERALIZATION

What do these generalizations imply for the inclusion of homosexuals in the United States military services? First, based on the trends observed in the countries we reviewed, it seems likely that the integration of homosexuals into the U.S. military services will lag behind the liberalization of attitudes toward homosexuals in American society. For example, the equivalent of a "Don't ask, Don't tell" policy, observed in the early stages of integrating homosexuals into the military services of other nations, is the policy that has initially prevailed in this country as well.

Second, because countries almost always behave more conservatively than their policies indicate, the practices of the military services can be expected to be somewhat more exclusionary with regard to homosexuals than are the official policies. Therefore, gay and lesbian activist groups will continue to press for, and gradually achieve, more liberal treatment of homosexuals in the military services.

Third, even if government policy or the courts compel the military to become more liberal in their policies and practices toward homosexuals, most heterosexuals will still socially shun homosexuals and the threat of violence against homosexuals is likely to remain a problem as well. As a result, few homosexual service members will choose to "come out" even if the policies and practices of the military services become more liberalized.

Finally, the exclusion of sexuality and gender altogether from the workplace are emerging norms in Western societies that will, in all likelihood, eventually serve to regulate homosexual as well as heterosexual behavior in the United States military services. However, the process is far from complete and, based on the social histories of other Western nations, the path to resolution is likely to be a long and difficult one.

41

Male Street Hustling: Introduction Processes and Stigma Containment

Thomas C. Calhoun
Ohio University

In recent years social scientists, journalists, television talk show hosts, and others have become increasingly interested in male street hustlers—young males who provide sexual services to other males. This interest corresponds with our increased awareness about child exploitation associated with running away, the reality of AIDS, and the increased national interest in drug abuse.

The male street hustler is the most visible of prostitutes because he often operates on street corners, out of bus terminals, or in hotel lobbies (Butts, 1947; Reiss, 1961; Weisberg, 1984). Unlike the *call boy*, who either operates alone by advertising in an underground newspaper or works with a pimp, the street hustler neither advertises (excluding the signs conveyed by dress or physical demeanor) nor works for anyone else (Caukins and Coombs, 1976). It is difficult to gather data on *kept boys* because they generally have relationships with only one other individual who meets most of their needs. Since street hustlers operate in the open, they are more accessible to the researcher.

Given society's negative views toward those who engage in homosexual activity, a hustler usually prevents others from learning of his participation. Should his homosexual activities become known, the hustler risks others important to him redefining him negatively. He may face social and familial ostracism. As Goffman (1963) states: "Discovery prejudices not only the current social situation, but established relationships as well . . . not only appearances, but also reputations" (p. 65).

The street hustler engages in highly visible illegal behavior—not only illegal, but also discrediting. The label "homosexual prostitute" may have severe consequences for the individual's self-concept. The old self that the individual

From *Sociological Spectrum*, Vol. 12 (1992), pp. 35–52, Thomas C. Calhoun, Washington, D.C.: Taylor & Francisco, Inc. Reproduced with permission. All rights reserved.

has projected to others now becomes suspect. Goffman (1963) states: "When the discreditable fact is part of current life, then he must guard against more than relayed information; he must guard against getting caught directly in the act" (p. 77). Should the hustler be caught in the act and processed by social control agents, he becomes a discredited person. He takes on new statuses— that of homosexual and prostitute. The hustler must exercise extreme caution to avoid this negative stigmatization and to protect his personal identity. As Churchill (1967) states: "There is really more fear of being considered a 'homosexual' or 'queer' by oneself and others, than there is fear of sexual relationships per se between like-sexed partners" (p. 159).

This article discusses the process used by male street hustlers as they attempt to negotiate a sexual transaction with their customers. The focus is on the nuances and subtleties in the interaction between hustler and would-be-customer, which are designed to prevent others from learning about their discrediting behavior. . . .

METHODS AND SAMPLE

The data were obtained from interviews with 18 young male prostitutes over the course of 3 months in 1984; all subjects were from a southern community with a population of just more than 200,000. In addition to the formal interviews, information was also obtained from other hustlers through informal conversations and by systematic observations.

The subjects were between the ages of 13 and 22 years. The average age is 17.6 years and the modal age is also 17. Of the 18 subjects, 15 are white and the remaining three are black. The family size of these subjects ranged from a low of three members to a high of 10. The average family size was 5.66 members; however, at the time of the interview, 13 of the 18 respondents lived in families that contained 4 to 6 members, with 5 members being the modal size—clearly larger than the typical American family. The overall education level of the street hustlers in this sample is low. Half of the 18 subjects were currently not attending school, 7 of these dropped out before obtaining a high school diploma, and the other 2 subjects completed high school. The average education level of those still in school was 9.75 years. Sixteen of the 18 subjects were single and living at home with a parent or adult guardian. The remaining 2 subjects were married and had established independent households.

In this community, only one part of town was used by male prostitutes to arrange for sexual encounters with other males—the downtown area behind a gay bar. Female street walkers operated in another section of town, approximately five blocks away.

Entrance into the "subculture" of male prostitution is difficult because many young male prostitutes are mistrustful and suspicious of outsiders, especially those seeking information about street prostitution and their involvement in it. Meeting the principal informant occurred quite by accident. While observing informally one evening, Tony approached me as I sat in the parking lot directly across from a popular pickup spot. Because Tony was interested in "turning a trick," I could only identify myself as a researcher and state my purpose.

Each time following our first encounter, when Tony would come on "the block," he would come over and talk with me. As time passed, a mutual trust developed between us. After we became friends, he helped introduce me to other hustlers. The recorded interviews took place at locations convenient to both the hustler and myself; some lasted only 30 minutes, whereas others lasted more than 2 hours.

ENTRY

Before we can appreciate the intricacies of hustlers' defense processes, we need to focus first on (1) how they learn about street hustling; (2) what instructions, if any, they are provided; and (3) then move to the process used by hustlers to negotiate a sexual transaction.

The data indicate two major pathways leading young males to street prostitution: peer introduction, including friends, siblings, and/or relatives; and situational discovery, including those situations in which a young person learns about male prostitution without conscious effort.

The data indicate that the majority of these hustlers learn about street hustling from their friends who are participants. From these interactions the new recruit is given (in varying degrees) instructions, motives, and techniques for carrying out this deviant activity (Sutherland and Cressey, 1978). In rare instances some hustlers stumble on this activity and subsequently become participants, lending credence to Matza's (1964) notion of "drift."

Peer Introduction

Research on teenage male prostitution has demonstrated that the majority of juveniles are introduced to street prostitution through their associations and interactions with significant others (Allen, 1980; Butts, 1947; Ginsburg, 1967; James, 1982; Jersild, 1956; Raven, 1963; Reiss, 1961; Ross, 1959; Weisberg, 1984). Most of the subjects in this study confirm this finding. Fourteen of the 18 respondents indicated that they were introduced to street hustling by a friend. In discussing how he became involved in male prostitution, Mike "C" said:

> This dude told me about it. I went with him behind 'The Bar' and he kept talking about it. It seemed like he didn't want to tell me. He just wanted me to be there and watch or something. I was standing there just freaking out on all of it. He went across the street and talked to somebody. He said 'Mike, this dude will give you 50 dollars to do so and so. . . .' I said, "no," cause I was freaking out . . .

Some juveniles who have friends that are prostitutes will indicate a need for money, and the friends may then offer a way to eliminate the financial hardship (Allen, 1980; Butts, 1947; Caukins and Coombs, 1976; Raven, 1963; Reiss, 1961). Bill said:

I know this friend. I said "Damn, I need some money." He said, "I know how to git it." He showed me the tricks so that I would know what to do. So I tried it and the guy gave me the money.

Although friends constitute the largest group of people who introduce others to prostitution, siblings and/or other relatives are also influential (Reiss, 1961). Of the 14 subjects who were introduced to hustling by another person, 2 were introduced by a sibling or other relative. Boo said:

I followed my brothers down there. I said, "What are y'all doing there?" They said "hustling." I said, "What do you do?" They said "Just go up to one of these cars and just make sure it ain't no cop—ask if they're a cop first. Then you can name your price." . . .

Situational Discovery

Although 14 teenagers were introduced to street hustling by a significant other (i.e., family member or friend), the remaining 4 subjects learned about street prostitution by chance. In the literature about street male prostitutes there is limited reference to this method of introduction (Allen, 1980; Butts, 1947; Caukins and Coombs, 1976; Craft, 1966; Ginsburg, 1967; MacNamara, 1965). Kenny stated:

I was out riding around on my bike, and I seen a man sitting. I stopped and talked to him for a while and I said, "What are you doing down here?" He says, "I'm making money." I said, "How?" He said "Letting these queers suck my dick." I said, "What do you mean?" He says, "Fags, you know what fags are, don't you?" I said, "Yeah, I've heard of them." "Well, I'm letting them suck my dick." I said, "Is that how you're making money?" He said, "Yeah you should try it." So that night, that same night that he told me about it, I took my bike and I hid it. I came back down here. I was scared 'cause it was the first time I had ever done something like that. And I went out with this dude. He gave me 30 dollars to go out with him. Me and him went out, and he sucked my dick. Ever since then I've been down there.

The male prostitute Kenny spoke with provided him incentives for participating in this activity—money and sex—and, by implication, conveyed a dislike for homosexuals. During their conversation, participation in prostitution was portrayed as "no big deal." Also the tone of the conversation implies that one can participate in hustling and maintain a sense of masculinity. The usage of terms such as "fags" and "queers" suggest that men who buy sexual services from other males are not "normal." In this sense, the prostitute is able to separate his sense of self from his perception of homosexuals (Goffman, 1963; Warren, 1972).

PEER SOCIALIZATION

The literature on male prostitution does not give specific information concerning what young males are told by their introducer as they begin hustling. In his now classic study, Reiss (1961) identifies norms that govern the interactions between hustlers and their tricks, such as: the interaction must be for monetary gains and sexual gratification must not be sought; the sexual encounter must be restricted to mouth-genital fellation; the participants must remain affectively neutral during the sexual encounter; and violence can only be used when the shared expectations between the participants is violated. Raven (1963) states, "if someone they know tells them about it, first of painting the affair in general and congenial colors, later explaining the elementary points of application and procedure" (p. 286).

Each subject was asked what instructions, if any, were provided by the person who introduced them to street prostitution. The most common instruction given the soon-to-be hustlers by their mentors were: the location of the prostitution area; which acts a hustler should perform and an idea of the cost for performing these acts; assessment of the potential customer as a law enforcement agent; and something about customer behavior. Ron reported the greatest number of instructions during the interview. He said he was told:

> Let them give me head $20 and nothing else. Be careful about some of the motherfuckers . . . not to let 'em fuck you in the ass, not to give them no head . . . be careful about the police, they'll stop and ask you a bunch of shit.

The hustling instructions given to Ron contain at least three themes: (1) he was told what sex acts were acceptable; (2) he was given some idea about how much to charge for the specific type of sex; and (3) he was warned about law enforcement.

Although some hustlers reported receiving extensive instructions, others were given few. They had to learn on their own. David said:

> He didn't know how it was going on or anything but he did tell me one thing, 'Make sure that you'd ask if they was a cop.' Other than that he really didn't tell me a whole lot about it.

THE NEGOTIATION PROCESS

During informal conversations, interviews, and observations with street hustlers, the following sequence appears as the typical order in which sexual interaction occurs; however, not all interactions pass through each stage as presented. Some stages may be skipped. The stages to be discussed are: initial contact; confirmation; negotiation of the sexual act and fees; and negotiation of location. For analytical purposes, the initial contact stage, the confirmation stage, and the negotiation of location stage are used to illustrate how these hustlers manage the threat of stigma (i.e., arrest and subsequent labeling as a homosexual prostitute). The negotiation of acts/fees stage of the process is used primarily in managing an identity as nonhomosexual.

Initial Contact

For the trick and hustler to reach a mutually acceptable agreement about the buying and/or selling of sexual favors they must be able to talk with each other.

Although the hustler and potential customer may occupy the same physical space, there is no guarantee their copresence indicates desire or availability for sex. Hustlers must develop strategies for identifying potential tricks and strategies for making the initial contact once a potential trick has been identified.

One method of identifying a potential trick is *cruising*. Mink, a 20-year-old hustler, with typical views about the subtleties and intricacies of this process, stated:

> They circle around the block, and they'd look at you, and they'd circle the block again. They'd pull over and stop. And so you are thinking to yourself, in your mind, "This guy is wanting me. I'm gonna go up and see what he wants."

In this case, the hustler is aware of the fact that perhaps the individual who is cruising the block might be a potential customer; however, he does not commit himself initially to being recognizable as a male prostitute.

Once a potential customer has been identified, the hustler may "nod his head or wave" at the trick. This gesture can signal a willingness by the hustler to enter into conversation with the potential trick, which may result in a sexual transaction. As the customer is cruising the block trying to determine if the young male is a hustler, he generally uses gestures to communicate his interest. One respondent told me:

> When somebody's trying to pick you up, they're staring at you. They wave at you, they nod their head for you to walk on down the street so they can talk to you.

Although an initial gesture has been offered, neither the sender of the message nor the hustler is sure that the other is the kind of person he seeks. The hustler may not respond to the gestures for a number of reasons, such as prior knowledge about the trick; the hustler may be waiting for a specific individual; he may have to be home early; or he may be just "hanging out" and is not interested in pursuing a sexual encounter. Assuming the hustler has identified a potential trick, additional efforts may be made to further verify the assessment.

The hustler initially does not commit himself, and his message may be vague and structured so as to force the potential trick to state his purpose. One respondent said after he makes contact with the potential customer: "I'm gonna ask him for a cigarette or I'm going to ask him for a light, and then you tell him, 'Hey man, look you doing anything tonight.'" In other situations, the hustler disguises his purpose from the customer by making reference to a need for employment. One hustler said:

> I go up and say, "Hey man do you know where I can get a job?" He'll say, "I might." Then I say, "Where? Do you care if I get in and sit down a minute." He says, "O.K." And I get in there and sit down, and they drive, and then we start talking about it.

Structuring the interaction in this manner, the hustler is using disidentifiers by not linking himself initially to prostitution. He only tries to verify if the individual is a potential trick. Before the interaction proceeds any further, the hustler needs to know that the person to whom he is talking is not someone (i.e., the police) who could officially sanction his behavior by arresting him and attaching the label "deviant" to him.

Confirmation

If the hustler is satisfied with his assessment of the potential trick, then he will generally ask if the potential trick is a policeman before discussing negotiating sexual favors. Bill said:

> I talk to him, I say, "Hi, my name is Bill, how are you doing." Then I ask them if they are the police or anything to do with the police. And sometimes, if they got an antenna or two on the car, I don't get in. Then I ask them what they looking for tonight.

Hustlers believe that if a potential trick is a police officer he must say so, for failure to do so constitutes entrapment. According to Mitch, "It's a law that requires that he cannot say he is not a policeman if he is." James, in discussing an encounter he had with a potential trick and how he deals with them if he thinks they are the police, said:

> "Are you a cop?" That's the first question I ask and if they say yes—you run like hell. If they are a cop, they have to tell you; if they don't they can't arrest you.

Asking the potential trick if he is a cop then serves two functions. First, hustlers believe if the potential customer does not answer the question truthfully the court case will be dismissed should he be arrested for prostitution. Second, if a policeman informs the hustler of his identity, the hustler can terminate the conversation without telling the policeman he is a prostitute. The cruise site is located in an area that allows easy escape should the person approached indicate he is associated with law enforcement.

The hustlers' understanding of this law is incorrect; however, whether or not hustlers are correct in their interpretation, they make a concerted effort to avoid arrest in an attempt to prevent significant others from learning about their involvement in this type of deviant behavior.

Negotiation of Sexual Act

If the hustler finds the potential trick acceptable, the conversation moves to a more intimate level—sexual negotiation. These negotiations first center around the specific act to be performed followed by a negotiation of the fee.

Negotiating the Act The potential trick may tell the hustler the sexual activity he desires. At this point the hustler and trick attempt to reach an agreement. If an agreement cannot be reached, the interaction ceases. As one hustler stated: "If I don't like it, I don't go. If he asks me to suck his dick, I say no I don't do that." If the initial offer is rejected, the hustler may make a counteroffer. Bill, when discussing the negotiation process stated: "There is a couple of things that I don't do. I tell them, and if they still want to do something then they tell me. If it's alright with me then we do it." In some situations the hustler can be rather adamant about which sexual acts he will perform. Mink illustrated this when he said:

I always told them that all I wanted was to get sucked off, and that was it. If they'd ask me, do you do more than that, I'd tell them, "No that's all I do." You give me head, that's it.

A trick may want the hustler to provide other sexual services, but the hustler generally holds his ground about what he is willing to do. If the trick accepts the counteroffer, the conversation continues; if it is rejected, the trick or hustler may make another offer or terminate the conversation. As previously discussed the hustlers in the Reiss (1961) study constituted a unique subculture whose members specified the type of acceptable sexual behavior that should take place between the hustler and trick; however, such a subculture was not found in this study. Most of these hustlers turn tricks by themselves and as a consequence peer-group influence is not as stringent.

The negotiations between the trick and hustler are complex. The hustler generally enjoys a dominant position in these encounters because he has the option of deciding whether or not he will engage in the requested sexual activity. Male prostitutes, as a category, will not perform any and all sexual acts.

Negotiating the Fee   When the hustler and trick have agreed on the act or acts to be performed, the hustler must decide how much to charge, and the trick must decide if he will pay the price. Many factors influence the cost: the nature of the act being requested; the perception of the trick; and other situational factors, such as a need to be home early or an inability to get picked up.

Nature of Act

The number of acts requested are diverse, but the acts hustlers say they are willing to provide is limited. David best reflects the importance of the act when he stated:

If they just want to suck my dick that's fine. He'll suck you off. Suck each other off for a reasonable price. But after that I'd ask for more. If somebody's going to fuck me they have to look decently—really appealing to me. I don't let anybody that don't look appealing fuck me or vice versa. But even if he was appealing there's going to be a jacked up price, about $60.

At least three themes are evident in this quote: (1) David is aware that tricks may request a number of sex acts; (2) the sexual act requested influences the cost (e.g., anal sex more than oral sex); and (3) participation in some acts (anal sex) is influenced by his perception of the customer. Generally, the more atypical the act requested the more the hustler will charge.

Perception of Trick

If the hustler suspects the trick is under the influence of alcohol or drugs, he will try to extract more money. Asking Mitch why he charged one customer $15 and the other $75 to perform the same act, he said: "Well, the one that I would be charging $75, he would be tore up on drugs, and I would be taking advantage of the situation." Aside from attempting to take advantage of the trick's condition, one respondent said that "if I think he is rich I charge him high." Believing a trick is rich is based on dress, the presence of jewelry, or the automobile driven.

Other Constraints

Most hustlers in this study live at home, and their parents expect them home by a certain time. If the hustler is pressed for time, the price he normally would charge may be lowered. Reflecting on time restrictions, Glenn stated he lowered his price "lots of times on nights when I had to be home early and couldn't make a trick." Two conditions are operating in Glenn's case: (1) time and (2) the difficulty in getting picked up. This young male, like other hustlers, may have difficulty in being picked up for several reasons: the number of available tricks may be limited; tricks may be available but they may not want this hustler for a variety of reasons; and the number of hustlers on the street may exceed the number of available tricks. These conditions may force the hustler to lower his price.

Negotiation of Location

If the hustler and trick have agreed to the act(s) to be performed and the price, one final decision must be made: where to consummate the deal. The 18 hustlers in this study reported having sex with tricks in three locations: 16 in apartment/houses; 11 in cars in parking lots; and 8 in motels or hotels.

The trick is given some latitude in choosing where the sexual transaction is to take place; however, a major concern of the hustler is how best to protect his privacy. Although information was obtained only from hustlers, it is also reasonable to assume that privacy is also a concern of the customer, since arrest could lead to loss of family, friends, and perhaps his job. One hustler said:

> Sometimes you might go to a hotel that they have already rented or you might go to their houses, you might even stay in the car, but you would go away from society. You would go where you wouldn't have any attention.

Despite the variety of locations, it is not clear from the data if hustlers have a preference as to where the sexual encounter should take place. Again, privacy is a common concern. Performing these acts in public increases the probability of detection by law enforcement, and to be caught in the act is the easiest way for one's cover to be blown (Goffman, 1963).

The sexual act can influence the location, since some activities cannot easily be accomplished in a car (i.e., anal intercourse). Some activities require the trick to either take the hustler to his house, with an attendant risk of discovery should a family member come home unexpectedly, or to rent a room in a motel where the risk of discovery is minimal. The latter, however, would require additional expenditures, therefore, the sexual desires of the trick must also be balanced with practical considerations.

Once the act is completed, the trick will return the hustler to the downtown area or take him to another location. Most hustlers in this study did not return to the prostitution site but were dropped off at other locations—a strategy used to avoid detection. If the hustler has been successful in negotiating and completing the sexual transaction, he can continue to engage in this discrediting behavior without being publicly labeled and identified as a discredited person.

SUMMARY

The majority of these hustlers became involved in male prostitution as a result of peer introduction. Their friends provided them with the necessary instructions, motives, and techniques for carrying out this deviant activity. As presented here, one of the key instructions given these hustlers by their introducers was the type of sexual acts they should engage in with their tricks. Other instructions included the location of the prostitution area, how to minimize police detection, and ideas about customer behavior.

The data presented demonstrate that these street hustlers are concerned that significant others or law enforcement officers might learn about their involvement in prostitution. In the negotiation process between hustlers and customers, several techniques were highlighted that help these hustlers avoid arrest and the subsequent label of homosexual prostitute. Particular emphasis is placed on three stages of the negotiation process: initial contact, confirmation, and location of the sexual act. In each of these stages, hustlers made every attempt to prevent others, particularly those with official sanctioning powers, from learning about their involvement in street prostitution. Of those strategies identified, making sure the individual who is cruising is a would-be customer; ascertaining if the customer is connected with law enforcement; and carrying out the sexual transaction out of the public's view are all designed to avoid arrest. . . .

References

Allen, Donald M. 1980. "Young Male Prostitutes: Psychosocial Study." *Archives of Sexual Behavior* 9:399–425.

Butts, William Marlin. 1947. "Boy Prostitutes of the Metropolis." *Journal of Clinical Psychopathy* 8:673–681.

Caukins, Sivan E. and Neil R. Coombs. 1976. "The Psychodynamics of Male Prostitution." *American Journal of Psychotherapy* 30:441–451.

Churchill, Wainwright. 1967. *Homoesexual Behavior Among Males.* New York: Hawthorn Books.

Craft, Michael. 1966. "Boy Prostitutes and Their Fate." *British Journal of Psychiatry* 112: 1111–1114.

Ginsburg, Kenneth N. 1967. "The 'Meat Rack': A Study of the Male Homosexual Prostitute." *American Journal of Psychotherapy* 21:170–184.

James, Jennifer. 1982. "Entrance into Juvenile Male Prostitution." *Final Report*. Washington, DC: Department of Health and Human Services.

Jersild, Jens. 1956. *Boy Prostitution*. Copenhagen: G.E.C. Gad.

MacNamara, Donal E. J. 1965. "Male Prostitution in American Cities: A Socio-economic or Pathological Phenomenon?" *American Journal of Orthopsychiatry* 35:204.

Matza, David. 1964. *Delinquency and Drift*. New York: Wiley.

Raven, Simon. 1963. "Boys Will Be Boys: The Male Prostitute in London," pp. 279–290 in *The Problem of Homosexuality in Modern Society*, edited by Hendrik M. Ruitenbeek. New York: E. P. Dutton & Company.

Reiss, Albert, J., Jr. 1961. "The Social Integration of Queers and Peers." *Social Problems* 9:102–120.

Ross, H. Laurence. 1959. "The 'Hustler' in Chicago." *Journal of Student Research* 1:13–19.

Sutherland, Edwin H. and Donald R. Cressey. 1978. *Criminology* (10th ed). Philadelphia: Lippincott.

Warren, Carole A. B. 1972. *Identity and Community in the Gay World*. New York: Wiley.

Weisberg, D. Kelly. 1984. *Children of the Night: A Study of Adolescent Prostitution*. Lexington, MA: Lexington Books.

PART 11

Academic and Professional Deviance

Traditionally, sociologists have shown little interest in deviance among well-educated people like themselves. They assumed that such deviance is virtually non-existent or too rare to be worth studying. A more likely reason for the lack of interest is the embarrassment that may result from washing the dirty linen in public. In recent years, however, many sociologists have started to study academic and professional deviance.

One form of academic deviance involves cheating by college students. In the first article, "Situational Ethics and College Student Cheating," Emily LaBeff and her co-researchers point to studies that estimate the incidence of student cheating to be as high as 50 percent. The researchers found that the major cause of this widespread deviance is the students' ability to use situational ethics to justify cheating. Another type of academic deviance involves faculty plagiarizing, falsifying data, committing sexual harassment, or engaging in some other unethical conduct. Though far less common than student cheating, faculty deviance is still much more prevalent than popularly assumed. According to a 1994 comprehensive survey, from 6 to 9 percent of professors and graduate students in chemistry, civil engineering, microbiology, and sociology "report that they have direct knowledge of faculty who have plagiarized or falsified data."[1] A systematic classification of this deviance and an explanation for its occurrence are provided in the second article, "Faculty Malfeasance," by John Heeren and David Shichor.

Outside the academic community, deviance by well-educated individuals is also far from rare. As indicated in the third article, "Behind Closed Doors: Therapist-Client Sex," by Carl Sherman, between 7 and 12 percent of psychotherapists—psychiatrists, psychologists, and social workers—have admitted to sexually exploiting their patients. Sherman discusses various aspects of this kind of professional deviance. In the next reading, "Psychotherapists'

---

[1] Marcel C. LaFollette, "Research Misconduct," *Society*, March/April 1994, p. 9.

Accounts of Their Professional Misdeeds," Mark Pogrebin and his colleagues offer data similar to those on student cheating: rationalizing away the deviant nature of professional wrongdoing. There are other forms of professional deviance, including medical misconduct, lawyerly lawlessness, and accounting abuses. Medical misconduct may involve fee splitting (a doctor receiving kickbacks from another for referring patients), unnecessary surgery, or Medicaid or Medicare frauds (claiming payment for unperformed services). Lawyerly lawlessness consists mostly of lawyers' overcharging their clients. Accounting abuses include accountants' preparing phony tax returns for their clients and helping companies make up false financial statements. The professionals themselves, however, perceive much of this deviance as necessary, justifiable, or even legitimate or acceptable. Similar perceptions can be found among the police, which is discussed in last article, "Police Lying," by Tom Barker and David Carter.

42

Situational Ethics and College Student Cheating

EMILY E. LABEFF, ROBERT E. CLARK, VALERIE J. HAINES, AND GEORGE M. DIEKHOFF
Midwestern State University

Studies have shown that cheating in college is epidemic, and some analysts of this problem estimate that 50 percent of college students may engage in such behavior. . . . Such studies have examined demographic and social characteristics of students such as age, sex, academic standing, major, classification, extracurricular activity, level of test anxiety, degree of sanctioned threat, and internal social control. Each of these factors has been found to be related, to some extent, to cheating although the relationship varies considerably from study to study. . . .

In our freshman classes, we often informally ask students to discuss whether they have cheated in college and, if so, how. Some students have almost bragged about which of their methods have proven most effective including writing notes on shoes and caps and on the backs of calculators. Rolling up a tiny cheat sheet into a pen cap was mentioned. And one student said, he had "incredibly gifted eyes" which allowed him to see the answers of a smart student four rows in front of him. One female student talked about rummaging through the dumpsters at night close to final examination time looking for test dittos. She did find at least one examination. A sorority member informed us that two of her term papers in her freshman year were sent from a sister chapter of the sorority at another university, retyped and submitted to the course professor. Further, many of these students saw nothing wrong with what they were doing, although they verbally agreed with the statement that cheating was unethical. . . .

From "Situational Ethics and College Student Cheating" by Emily E. LaBeff, Robert E. Clark, Valerie J. Haines, and George M. Diekhoff, in *Sociological Inquiry*, Vol. 60:2 (Spring 1990), pp. 190–198. By permission of the authors and the University of Texas Press.

The concept of situational ethics might well describe this college cheating in that rules for behavior are not considered rigid but dependent on the circumstances involved (Norris and Dodder 1979, p. 545). Joseph Fletcher, in his well-known philosophical treatise, *Situation Ethics,* defines it as the notion that any action is good or bad depending on the social circumstances. In other words, what is wrong in most situations might be considered right or acceptable. . . . Central to this process is the idea that situations alter cases, thus altering the rules and principles guiding behavior (Edwards 1967).

[Situational ethics seems to be the core of what Sykes and Matza (1957) call "neutralization," the process of justifying violation of accepted rules. Neutralization takes four forms]: denial of responsibility, condemnation of condemners, appeal to higher loyalties, denial of victim, and denial of injury. In each case, individuals profess a conviction about a particular law but argue that special circumstances exist which cause them to violate the rules. . . .

METHODOLOGY

The present analysis is based on a larger project conducted during the 1983–1984 academic year when a 49-item questionnaire about cheating was administered to students at a small southwestern university. The student body (N = 4950) was evenly distributed throughout the university's programs with a disproportionate number (27 percent) majoring in business administration. In order to achieve a representative sample from a cross-section of the university student body, the questionnaire was administered to students enrolled in courses classified as a part of the university's core curriculum. Freshmen and sophomores were overrepresented (84 percent of the sample versus 60 percent of the university population). Females were also overrepresented (62 percent of the sample versus 55 percent of the university population).

There are obvious disadvantages associated with the use of self-administered questionnaires for data-gathering purposes. One problem is the acceptance of student responses without benefit of contest. To maximize the return rate, questionnaires were administered during regularly scheduled class periods. Participation was on a voluntary basis. In order to establish the validity of responses, students were guaranteed anonymity. Students were also instructed to limit their responses regarding whether they had cheated to the current academic year.

Previous analysis (e.g., Haines et al. 1986) focused on the quantitative aspects of the questionnaire. The present analysis is intended to assess the narrative responses to the incidence of cheating in three forms, namely on major examinations, quizzes, and class assignments, as well as the perceptions of and attitudes held by students toward cheating and the effectiveness of deterrents to cheating. Students recorded their experiences in their own words. Most students (87 percent) responded to the open-ended portion of the questionnaire.

RESULTS

Of the 380 undergraduate students who participated in the spring survey, 54 percent indicated they had cheated during the previous six-month period. Students were requested to indicate whether cheating involved examination, weekly quizzes, and/or homework assignments. Much cheating took the form of looking on someone else's paper, copying homework, and either buying term papers or getting friends to write papers for them. Only five of the 205 students who admitted cheating reported being caught by the professor. However, seven percent (n = 27) of the students reported cheating more than five times during the preceding six month period. Twenty percent (n = 76) indicated that most students openly approved of cheating. Only seventeen students reported they would inform the instructor if they saw another student cheating. Many students, especially older students, indicated they felt resentment toward cheaters, but most also noted that they would not do anything about it (i.e., inform the instructor).

To more fully explore the ways in which students neutralize their behavior, narrative data from admitted student cheaters were examined (n = 149). The narrative responses were easily classified into three of the five techniques [of neutralization] described by Sykes and Matza (1957).

Denial of Responsibility

Denial of responsibility was the most often identified response. This technique involves a declaration by the offenders that, in light of circumstances beyond their control, they cannot be held accountable for their actions. Rather than identifying the behavior as "accidental," they attribute wrongdoing to the influence of outside forces. In some instances, students expressed an inability to withstand peer pressure to cheat. Responses show a recognition of cheating as an unacceptable behavior, implying that under different circumstances cheating would not have occurred. One student commented:

> I was working forty plus hours a week and we had a lot to read for that day. I just couldn't get it all in. . . . I'm not saying cheating is okay, sometimes you just have to. . . .

Other responses demonstrate the attempt by students to succeed through legitimate means (e.g., taking notes and studying) only to experience failure. Accordingly, they were left with no alternative but to cheat. One student commented:

> . . . even though I've studied in the past, I've failed the exam so I cheated on my last test hoping to bring a better grade.

Another student explained his behavior in the following manner:

> I studied for the exam and I studied hard but the material on the test was different from what I expected. . . . I had to make a good grade. . . .

In addition, some students reported accidentally seeing other students' test papers. In such instances, the cheaters chastised classmates for not covering up their answer sheets. As one student wrote, such temptation simply cannot be overcome:

> I studied hard for the exam and needed an A. I just happened to look up and there was my neighbor's paper uncovered. I found myself checking my answers against his through the whole test.

Appeal to Higher Loyalties

Conflict also arises between peer group expectations and the normative expectations of the larger society. When this occurs, the individual may choose to sacrifice responsibility, thereby maintaining the interest of peers. Such allegiance allows these individuals to supercede moral obligations when special circumstances arise.

Students who invoke this technique of neutralization frequently described their behavior as an attempt to help another. One student stated:

> I only cheated because my friend had been sick and she needed help. . . . it (cheating) wouldn't have happened any other time.

Another student denied any wrongdoing on her part as the following statement illustrates:

> I personally have never cheated. I've had friends who asked for help so I let them see my test. Maybe some would consider that to be cheating.

These students recognize the act of cheating is wrong. However, their statements also suggest that in some situations cheating can be overlooked. Loyalty to a friend in need takes precedence over honesty in the classroom. Another student described his situation in the following manner:

> I was tutoring this girl but she just couldn't understand the material. . . . I felt I had to help her on the test.

Condemnation of Condemners

Cheaters using this technique of neutralization attempt to shift attention from their own actions to the actions of others, most often authority figures. By criticizing those in authority as being unfair or unethical, the behavior of the offender seems less consequential by comparison. Therefore, dishonest behavior occurs in reaction to the perceived dishonesty of the authority figure. Students who utilize this technique wrote about uncaring, unprofessional instructors with negative attitudes who were negligent in their behavior. These incidents were said to be a precursor to their cheating behavior. The following response illustrates this view:

> The teachers here are boring and I dislike this school. The majority of teachers here don't care about the students and are rude when you ask them for help.

In other instances, students cite unfair teaching practices which they perceive to be the reason for their behavior. One student stated:

> Major exams are very important to your grade and it seems that the majority of instructors make up the exams to try and trick you instead of testing your knowledge.

In this case, the instructor is thought to engage in a deliberate attempt to fail the students by making the examinations difficult. Also within this category were student accounts which frequently express a complaint of being overworked. As one student wrote:

> One instructor assigns more work than anyone could possibly handle . . . at least I know I can't, so sometimes cheating is the answer . . .

Denial of Injury and Denial of the Victim

Denial of injury and denial of the victim do not appear in the student accounts of their cheating. In denial of injury, the wrongdoer states that no one was harmed or implies that accusations of injury are grossly exaggerated. In the second case, denial of the victim, those who violate norms often portray their targets as legitimate. Due to certain factors such as the societal role, personal characteristics, or lifestyle of the victim, the wrongdoer felt the victim "had it coming."

It is unlikely that students will either deny injury or deny the victim since there are no real targets in cheating. However, attempts to deny injury are possible when the one who is cheating argues that cheating is a personal matter rather than a public one. It is also possible that some students are cognizant of the effect their cheating activities have upon the educational system as a whole and, therefore, choose to neutralize their behavior in ways which allow them to focus on the act rather than the consequences of cheating. By observing their actions from a myopic viewpoint, such students avoid the larger issues of morality.

CONCLUSION

The purpose of this report was to analyze student responses to cheating in their college coursework. Using Sykes and Matza's model of neutralization, we found that students rationalized their cheating behavior and do so without challenging the norm of honesty. Student responses fit three of the five techniques of neutralization. The most common technique is a denial of responsibility. Second, students tend to "condemn the condemners," blaming faculty and testing procedures. Finally, students "appeal to higher loyalties" by arguing that it is more important to help a friend than to avoid cheating. The use of these techniques of neutralization conveys the message that students recognize and accept cheating as an undesirable behavior which, nonetheless, can be excused under certain circumstances. Such findings reflect the prevalence of situational ethics.

The situation appears to be one in which students are not caught and disciplined by instructors. Additionally, students who cheat do not concern themselves with overt negative sanctions from other students. In some groups, cheating is planned, expected, and often rewarded in that students may receive better grades. That leaves a student's ethical, internalized control as a barrier to cheating. However, the neutralizing attitude allows students to sidestep issues of ethics and guilt by placing the blame for their behavior elsewhere. Neutralization allows them to state their belief that in general cheating is wrong, but in some special circumstances cheating is acceptable, even necessary. . . .

References

Edwards, Paul. 1967. *The Encyclopedia of Philosophy, #3*, edited by Paul Edwards. New York: Macmillan Company and Free Press.

Fletcher, Joseph. 1966. *Situation Ethics: The New Morality*. Philadelphia: The Westminster Press.

Haines, Valerie J., George Diekhoff, Emily LaBeff, and Robert Clark. 1986. "College Cheating: Immaturity, Lack of Commitment, and the Neutralizing Attitude." *Research in Higher Education* 25:342–354.

Norris, Terry D., and Richard A. Dodder. 1979. "A Behavioral Continuum Synthesizing Neutralization Theory, Situational Ethics and Juvenile Delinquency." *Adolescence* 55:545–555.

Sykes, Gresham, and David Matza. 1957. "Techniques of Neutralization: A Theory of Delinquency." *American Sociological Review* 22:664–670.

43

Faculty Malfeasance: Understanding Academic Deviance

JOHN W. HEEREN AND DAVID SHICHOR
California State University, San Bernardino

If deviance is considered to be "any behavior or attribute for which an individual is regarded as objectionable in a particular social system" (Glaser, 1971, p. 1), then every organization and every occupational context provides opportunities for legal or ethical deviance. Yet, only limited attention has been paid to deviance in the academy. Some analysts (Johnson and Douglas, 1978, p. 227) have suggested this reflects an inclination of social scientists to "protect their own kind," that is, professors. Craig Little (1989, p. 298) makes a similar observation:

> While feeling rather free to debunk those in other professions, college professors have been loath to expose their own deviant ways to the scrutiny of researchers or the public.

Despite this neglect, much has been written about scientific or scholarly deviance (Ben-Yehuda, 1985) and some work has explored the possibilities of deviation with respect to academic teaching and governance (Cahn, 1986). However, these analyses fail to provide any single explanatory scheme which encompasses the diverse components of the professorial role. We attempt such an integrative task in this study by identifying what appear to be the major factors contributing to academic deviance.

ACADEMIC ORGANIZATION AND ROLES

Professors work in institutions of higher education. These institutions developed out of medieval European universities, which were autonomous intel-

From "Faculty Malfeasance: Understanding Academic Deviance," by John W. Heeren and David Shichor, in *Sociological Inquiry*, Vol. 63:1 (Winter 1993), pp. 49–63. By permission of the authors and the University of Texas Press.

lectual communities of scholars and students in larger urban settlements with external support mainly from the endowments of benefactors (Ben-David, 1971). This situation has changed. Instead of existing as an intellectual community in which all of the participants are partners, universities and colleges have become employers and professors have become employees. This change has been accompanied by an increasing portion of governance being taken over by full-time administrators, who act as agents of the employer in managing the institution.

Professors teach, research, and participate in the governance of their academic university (Clark, 1987) whether they are at a major research university or a community college. This does not deny that institutions vary in the emphasis placed on these responsibilities and that professors may carry out one of these tasks to the exclusion of the others. For example, the more prestigious a university, the more likely faculty performance will be evaluated on the basis of publications and the ability of the faculty member to obtain research grants, rather than on the basis of teaching performance.

Some organizational analysts have argued that there is very little integration among the diverse activities that comprise the academic profession (Light, 1974). Other analysts identify common threads and de-emphasize the apparent fragmentation (Clark, 1983; Ruscio, 1987). [Both views seem convincing.] For example, replicability of knowledge is much more important to physics, chemistry, and biology than it is to the humanities and social sciences. However, just as the most well-known research universities set the tone in American higher education and thus are emulated by less prestigious institutions, scientific research has become a model for academic scholarship (Bowen, and Schuster 1986). Disciplinary differences do exist (see Ruscio, 1987), but a common culture loosely unifies the entire university community (Clark, 1983).

One additional consideration involves the adaptation of faculty roles within the academic system. A widely accepted distinction is that between cosmopolitans and locals (Gouldner, 1957; Loether, 1974). Cosmopolitans are faculty members who are highly committed to their professional role and skills, have a moderate level of loyalty to their institutions, and have a reference group comprised of scholars in the discipline. Locals are marginally committed to their professional role but are loyal to their institution. They typically serve on numerous committees, are active in campus politics, and have an inner reference group of other university colleagues, most of whom are also locals. The more prestigious the university, the greater is the likelihood that the faculty will have a cosmopolitan orientation. In less prestigious universities, the local orientation tends to be more prevalent.

Cosmopolitans and locals represent extreme types on a continuum on which two additional types are suggested in Loether (1974): (1) local-cosmopolitans, who balance the purely disciplinary orientation and the home-institution orientation, and (2) indifferents, who are oriented neither toward their academic discipline nor toward their home institution. Often referred to as "dead wood," indifferents have minimal chances for internal and external rewards due to their lack of participation.

TYPOLOGY OF ACADEMIC DEVIANCE

There are various types of deviant behavior in which faculty members may be involved, and two dimensions of activities are useful to describe the nature of academic deviance. First, there is the distinction between occupational and professional types of deviant behavior. The former refers to violations of the general moral and ethical codes prevailing in a society. This type of deviance represents the "normal crimes of normal people in the normal circumstances of their work" (Mars, 1982, p. 1). Professional deviance, on the other hand, involves breaches of the professional norms associated with a specific occupation, and is considered unacceptable by members of the profession. . . .

The second distinction involves academic deviance being directed against property or persons. Many acts of deviance have both property and interpersonal effects, thus leading to some overlap in the categories. Nevertheless, the intersection of these two dimensions yields four basic categories of academic deviance (see Figure 43.1). The first two involve occupational misbehavior which either (1) victimizes persons or (2) misuses resources that do not belong to the perpetrator. The other two categories pertain to professional malfeasance. Again, this can be either (3) interpersonal, resulting in harm to others in academia or (4) fraudulent use of intellectual property. The following discussion analyzes these categories of academic deviance.

Occupational Deviance

The forms of occupational deviance among academics do not differ greatly from those in other occupations. Just as white-collar workers or laborers may pilfer property belonging to the organization which employs them, so also may professors. Another more dramatic example is university misuse of research

| | Norms Violated | |
	Occupational	Professional
Property	Theft or misuse of funds or resources	Plagiarism or falsification of data
Interpersonal	Sexual harassment or exploitation	Misevaluation of others as referee for grants, jobs, articles, etc.

Focus of Deviation

FIGURE 43.1

Dimensions and Types of Academic Deviance

overhead funds. Recently, fifteen universities have been accused of overbilling the federal government for collateral expenses on research grants (Jackson, 1991). . . .

Another example of occupational deviance which has property implications involves conflicts between the professional and the personal interests of academics. Drug-related research might be biased by the researchers' financial interest in the funding provided by pharmaceutical companies (Wheeler, 1990). Similarly, faculty members receive consulting fees or even small grants for applied research from students in their graduate or professional programs who are employed by funding agencies.

Occupational deviance with interpersonal implications includes such behavior as sexual harassment of students or fellow employees. Employees are clearly protected by statute, while students are most often covered by university regulations regarding harassment (Elgart and Schanfield, 1991). Specific behaviors that constitute harassment, such as assault or demand for sexual favors, are easily identified while others are much more subtle and difficult to delineate in abstract legal or ethical terms. Courts are likely to require that the harassment be "unwelcome" and that it cause sufficient harm "to create an abusive working environment" (Elgart and Schanfield, 1991, p. 27). University regulations are much less uniform in their definitions of harassment, with some very restrictive and others quite broad in line with local campus traditions.

Harassment may be commonplace as suggested by Cnudde and Nesvold (1985), who found that 20 to 30 percent of women students felt they had been sexually harassed by male faculty during their college years. Another survey of female members of the American Psychological Association found that 17 percent of the respondents had sexual contact with teachers which they regarded as exploitive and harmful (Glaser and Thorpe, 1986).

Professional Deviance

Professional deviance reflects the distinctive features of university and disciplinary organizations, including their constitutive roles, opportunity structures, and systems of social control. Moreover, the likelihood of any specific deviations will reflect the perpetrator's involvement in one or more of the three main academic roles [involving teaching, research, and service] as well as the cosmopolitan or local adaptation the person has developed.

Professional deviance, such as property offenses, takes the form of misappropriating intellectual property. Two forms of this type of deviance are plagiary and the fabrication or misrepresentation of research findings. Since publication of research findings is modeled after the system of private property, plagiary is equivalent to theft. . . . Collateral forms of deviance include failing to properly reference the works of others, appropriating the ideas of others, and taking credit for the research of graduate students.

While exploitation of students is unacceptable (Cahn, 1986), it is probably widespread among cosmopolitans in major research universities (Hagstrom, 1965). As Ben-Yehuda (1986, p. 11) succinctly states:

Whatever the circumstances may be, if one's name appears as the first (or only) author on a scientific work she/he did not conduct, one is getting credit for something she/he did not do. This is a fraudulent, deviant act which very much contradicts the expressed ethos of science.

This issue is relevant mainly in the case of cosmopolitans, since locals seldom have graduate students conducting publishable research. . . .

[There are other forms of professional property deviation.] Perhaps the most common are the various attempts to stretch the value of academic work by, for example, publishing the same or similar papers in different journals, overfunding a research project by various agencies so that expenses or salary are doubly compensated, padding a curriculum vita, or using a favorable letter written by a journal editor as if it represented a final acceptance of an article for publication. With respect to teaching, a typical offense is the failure of a professor to update course materials to reflect current work in the discipline. While these kinds of activities are probably quite common, they are considered to be mildly deviant and easily detectable with proper oversight in most cases.

Professional deviance that is interpersonal in its object is more subtle. We should begin by noting that a good deal of the work done by academics necessarily involves evaluations of the work of other academics in their roles as scholars, teachers, and colleagues. This is evident in the process of refereeing journal articles and grant proposals, as well as faculty evaluation of colleagues who are candidates for promotion or tenure. Similar kinds of evaluations of junior colleagues take the form of letters of recommendation.

Most published books and articles go through a refereeing system that "involves the systematic use of judges to assess the acceptability of manuscripts submitted for publication" (Zuckerman and Merton, 1971, p. 66). Grant applications go through a similar evaluation process. Since the major attribution of status in academia occurs on the basis of grants and publications, the referee process represents the most significant gatekeeping practice in academia. A faculty member's publication record may affect not only academic status but also material success in the form of tenure and promotion, job offers, book contracts, consultation, and fellowships. Frequently a junior faculty member's tenure may be contingent on favorable decisions in refereeing. The expectation regarding refereeing is that evaluators are to be impartial (Cahn, 1986). Anonymous reviewing is most frequently used as a device to implement this ideal.

Deviance in refereeing involves breaches of impartiality. For example, a reviewer may recognize the author of a manuscript and either give the paper a more favorable review than it deserves or urge its rejection based on personal rather than professional criteria. This kind of partiality can help or cause harm to an individual, a whole school within a discipline, or a particular academic perspective. It is difficult, though, to judge the frequency of this kind of academic deviance, since most evidence is anecdotal (Lipset, 1969). . . .

Letters of recommendation also provide opportunities for deviance. Academicians are often asked to write these letters for colleagues or students. Professional ethics would seem to require a completely honest opinion by the recommender, based solely on the abilities of the person being recommended. Like refereeing, these evaluations play a crucial role in one's advancement on the career ladder, for example, by securing a position or gaining an award or fellowship. Cahn (1986, p. 49) emphasizes the importance and the problematic nature of this issue:

> The wrong approach is to provide a deceitful letter that exaggerates positive traits while disregarding negative ones. Those who engage in such dishonesty may view themselves as merely doing someone a favor with an innocuous fib. . . . As a result of the deception, other applicants may lose out on a vital opportunity. All are victims not of a harmless joke, but of outright dishonesty, the betrayal of a scholar's trust.

If deception is in the opposite direction, that is, writing an inaccurate or negative recommendation, it can be seen as a malicious attempt to block the professional opportunities of a person who placed trust in the good will and objectivity of the academician.

Evaluation also occurs in teaching and the relations of students and professors. While undervaluation of students' work may occur based on a personal dislike of a student, a more recent and common deviation appears to be in the direction of overvaluing the work of students. The basis of this evaluation may be individual traits such as physical attractiveness or importance to the athletic program, thus reflecting the intrusion of particularistic criteria into the grading of academic performance.

Perhaps a more widespread instance of such overevaluation of students is known as grade inflation. Whether grade inflation is meant to attract or retain students in an increasingly competitive environment of enrollment-driven budgets or to improve student evaluations of a faculty member for promotional purposes, it represents deviance insofar as standards are lowered and ulterior reasons are in force (Eckert, 1988). One national survey of college faculty (*Orange County Register* 1989) found that 62 percent of the faculty considered grade inflation to be a problem at their institution. Since teaching is likely to be a more important activity for locals than for cosmopolitans, and the pressure to recruit and retain students is stronger at less prestigous universities, this kind of deviance is more likely to occur at teaching institutions. . . .

SOURCES OF ACADEMIC DEVIANCE

It would appear that the [rewards or] attractions of the *occupational* types of offenses described above are not particularly strong for those who pursue an academic career. If it is accurate to state that academics make career choices in terms of the teaching and learning which are the inherent components of the academic role (Bowen and Schuster, 1986), then such activities as theft of material property or interpersonal violence would seem to be relatively remote from the typical academic life style.

[But the apparent infrequency of this occupational deviance may not be real. It may also reflect underreporting.] Those who might observe, be victimized, or report occupational deviance (such as students, secretaries, janitors, campus police) are likely to have a lower status than the alleged offender. . . . Thus, a status gulf and the fear of possible rataliation may prevent the reporting of suspected deviations, similar to the situation of whistleblowers in government and industry (Glazer and Glazer, 1989). . . .

With regard to professional deviance, the situation is far more complex. The rewards or attractions of these kinds of deviation are more consistent with the values that are central to academic life. Given that academic stratification is based on recognition conducted through a system of peer evaluation (Merton, 1973), it is reasonable to expect that deviations involving intellectual property (e.g., manipulating facts or plagiarizing) or the misuse of authority or prestige for allies or against opponents could easily be seen as accessible avenues to scholarly position. Moreover, the controls on academics are not especially stringent. One of the most widely held values in the academy is academic freedom (Bowen and Schuster, 1986, pp. 53–54). The effect of this freedom is to grant scholars autonomy in their professional roles. A basic investment of trust in faculty members to carry out their responsibilities is one of the hallmarks of academic life (Barber, 1990, pp. 221–239). Beyond the academic freedom to teach, research, and write on virtually any topic, there are other expressions of the trust granted to faculty members. For example, reviews of grant applications and articles for publication are anonymous. Also, letters of recommendation and committee decisions on tenure and promotion operate with a layer of anonymity, justified by the notion of academic freedom (Weeks, 1990) that protects potential deviants. In sum, [rewards and autonomy seem to play a key role in the development of professional deviance]. . . .

CONCLUSION

In this study we have attempted to provide a framework for explaining the kinds of academic deviance that exist in the modern university setting. By looking at two dimensions, types of norms violated (occupational vs. professional) and focus of deviation (property vs. interpersonal), the major ethical problems of the professoriate are delineated and a basis for understanding the relations among these kinds of deviance is established. Although the model does not provide an exhaustive assessment of the causes of academic deviance, it is useful in indicating the . . . rewards which might accrue to academic deviants and the organizational characteristics that allow deviance to occur or hamper its control by professional groups, faculty, or members of society. . . .

References

Barber, Bernard. 1990. *Social Studies of Science.* New Brunswick, NJ: Transaction.

Ben-David, Joseph. 1971. *The Scientist's Role in Society.* Englewood Cliffs, NJ: Prentice-Hall.

Ben-Yehuda, Nachman. 1985. *Deviance and Moral Boundaries.* Chicago: University of Chicago Press.

Barber, Bernard. 1986. "Deviance in Science: Towards the Criminology of Science." *British Journal of Criminology* 26:1–27.

Bowen, Howard R., and Jack H. Schuster. 1986. *American Professors: A National Resource Imperiled.* New York: Oxford University Press.

Cahn, Steven M. 1986. *Saints and Scamps: Ethics in Academia.* Totowa, NJ: Rowman & Littlefield.

Clark, Burton R. 1983. *The Higher Education System: Academic Organization in Cross-National Perspective.* Berkeley: University of California Press.

Clark, Burton R. 1987. *The Academic Life: Small Worlds, Different Worlds.* Princeton, NJ: Carnegie Foundation.

Cnudde, Charles, and Betty A. Nesvold. 1985. "Administrative Risk and Sexual Harassment: Legal and Ethical Responsibilities on Campus." *PS* 18:780–789.

Eckert, Edward K. 1988. "The Day I Realized the Game Was Over." *Chronicle of Higher Education* June 1, 48.

Elgart, Lloyd D., and Lillian Schanfield. 1991. "Sexual Harassment of Students." *Thought and Action* 7:21–42.

Glaser, Daniel. 1971. *Social Deviance.* Chicago: Markham.

Glaser, Robert D., and Joseph S. Thorpe. 1986. "Unethical Intimacy: A Survey of Sexual Contact and Advances Between Psychology Educators and Female Graduate Students." *American Psychologist* 41:43–51.

Glazer, Myron Peretz, and Penina Migdal Glazer. 1989. *The Whistle-Blowers: Exposing Corruption in Government and Industry.* New York: Basic Books.

Gouldner, Alvin. 1957. "Cosmopolitans and Locals: Toward an Analysis of Latent Social Roles." *Administrative Science Quarterly* 2:281–306.

Hagstrom, Warren. 1965. *The Scientific Community.* Carbondale: Southern Illinois University Press.

Jackson, Robert L. 1991. "Audit Ties 15 Universities to Government Overcharges." *Los Angeles Times* May 10, A4.

Johnson, John, and Jack Douglas. 1978. *Crime at the Top.* New York: Lippincott.

Light, Donald. 1974. "The Structure of the Academic Professions." *Sociology of Education* 47:2–28.

Lipset, Seymour Martin. 1969. "Socialism and Sociology." Pp. 143–175 in *Sociological Self-Images.* Edited by Irving Louis Horowitz. Beverly Hills, CA: Sage.

Little, Craig B. 1989. *Deviance and Control.* Itasca, IL: Peacock.

Loether, Herman J. 1974. "Organizational Stress and the Role Orientations of College Professors." In *Varieties of Work.* Edited by Phyllis Stewart and Muriel Cantor. Chicago: Markham.

Mars, Gerald. 1982. *Cheats at Work.* London: Unwin.

Merton, Robert K. 1973. *The Sociology of Science.* Chicago: The University of Chicago Press.

Orange County Register. 1989. "Professors Satisfied with Jobs." November 6, A5.

Ruscio, Kenneth P. 1987. "Many Sectors, Many Professions," pp. in *The Academic Profession.* Edited by Burton Clark. Berkeley, CA: University of California Press.

Weeks, Kent M. 1990. "The Peer Review Process." *Journal of Higher Education* 61:198–219.

Wheeler, David L. 1990. "Two Academic Organizations Offer Their Own Sets of Guidelines to Help Research Units Answer Conflict-of-Interest Questions." *Chronicle of Higher Education* March 7, A21.

Zuckerman, Harriet, and Robert K. Merton. 1971. "Patterns of Evaluation in Science." *Minerva* 9:66–100.

44

Behind Closed Doors: Therapist–Client Sex

Carl Sherman

Suddenly, it seems that psychotherapy has turned into a grotesque distortion of its high-minded healing purpose: headlines and talk shows are full of therapists gratifying their sexual needs at their patients' expense. One national news magazine calls it "a growing crisis of ethical abuse." Has there been a swift, massive breakdown in professional morals?

No, says the evidence. The number of psychiatrists, psychologists, social workers, and other therapists who admit to sexual misconduct—behavior intended to arouse or satisfy their own desire—with past or present patients is indeed alarming: surveys put it between 7 and 12 percent. But there is no indication of any sudden increase; as far back as the 1960s, rates were comparable, and some studies suggest that the number of incidents may have actually declined in recent years. The majority of therapists are still ethical practitioners who respect and protect their clients.

And despite their disproportionate share of publicity, therapists are hardly unique in their libidinous misdeeds. A 1992 survey of family doctors, internists, gynecologists, and surgeons found as many guilty parties—9 percent—as among therapists. Similar rates of sexual misconduct are estimated in the clergy. And recognition of the problem among lawyers and teachers is growing.

What has changed is awareness—a testament, in large part, to the cultural impact of feminist consciousness-raising, so that women are no longer disbelieved when they allege abuse by those entrusted with their care. "The parallels with incest are striking," says Glen O. Gabbard, M.D., director of the famed Menninger Clinic in Topeka, Kansas. "The abuse went on for years, but it didn't come out into the open until the last decade or so. It used to be, when a patient said her therapist had sex with her, we assumed it was a fantasy. The rise of feminism made us all more aware of what is really going on."

Many incidents that swell today's chorus of turpitude actually took place years ago. "I'm seeing women who in the early 1970s tried to make complaints to medical boards, but were dismissed," says Rina Folman, Ph.D., chair of the Massachusetts Psychological Association Committee on Professional Standards. "Some of the same people who were not believed then are believed now." What's more, there's a snowball effect, as patients who hear about the abuses of others feel permission to reveal what shame and fear had long kept buried.

A fuller recognition of its potential destructiveness, including lethality, heightens the outrage about patient-therapist sex. A reported 90 percent of victims are psychologically damaged, many severely. Emotions generated by the intimacy of therapy are intense, and abusive experiences violate taboos as explosively as incest—arousing comparable guilt, shame, anger, and despair. In one survey, 11 percent of sexually exploited patients had been hospitalized as a result of their involvement, and 1 percent committed suicide. "I haven't seen anyone who hasn't had some suicidal thoughts," says Folman, who has treated over 100 victims.

Besides the magnitude of the problem itself, sexual exploitation in therapy ignites impassioned headlines because it taps into a more general societal rage against the abuse of power. "In the last two or three years, we've seen great feelings of anger at and alienation from those in authority who promise the world, take a lot from it, and then screw us over," says Gary Schoener, executive director of the Walk-In Counseling Center of Minneapolis. "What did we hear in the last election but anger at incumbents? 'We trusted you!'"

The river of rage actually began building decades ago, as the civil rights and women's movements brought to the glare of public scrutiny how those with the lion's share of power so often use in selfishly, at the expense of those who have less. Discrimination, poverty, rape, sexual harrassment in school and on the job all have come to be known as the malignant spawn of a power imbalance that cries out for reform.

Recent events have fueled public outrage at those in power: the treatment of Anita Hill during the Clarence Thomas confirmation hearings, the Savings & Loan scandal, the misuse of power by lawmakers such as Senator Bob Packwood and the police who beat Rodney King in Los Angeles, and the unearthing of widespread corruption in politics. The pique seems to be at its peak.

While doctors and lawyers, professors and politicians commit similar misdeeds, the therapist gone wrong seems to symbolize a particularly heinous betrayal. In the closed room of therapy, we are asked to bare not our bodies but our souls, letting down defenses and trusting our most intimate selves to the professional skill and integrity of a stranger.

THE DARK SIDE

Therapists' power to hurt is the dark side of their power to heal. Putting ourselves in their hands with an almost child-like faith that they will help us, we readily bestow on them the same intense affection and urgent need for approval we once felt for our parents. Because (as Freud was the first to recognize) the sex drive begins in childhood, directed toward those who care for us, that affection can have a distinctly sexual tinge. This "transference" into the present of feelings from our early years is seen in many personal and professional relationships, but the emotionally charged conditions of therapy make them especially strong.

Aired and analyzed, these feelings, including erotic ones, can be a potent force for growth and healing change—the intimate relationship with the therapist often makes it possible to come to terms with long-hidden love, shame, anger, and fear. But it is the therapist's highest responsibility to make sure it all remains talk, not action—to keep therapy a safe place where the deepest feelings can be bared without getting out of control.

For this reason, any responsible therapist will scrupulously maintain the businesslike boundaries that separate personal from professional: making sure doctor and patient stay in their respective chairs during the therapy hour and avoiding contact outside the office. Responsible therapists keep their own problems and private life out of the therapeutic relationship.

Not all honor and protect those boundaries, however. A calculating, predatory therapist may violate them deliberately, encouraging a vulnerable patient to act on the strong emotions brought up from the past. He may tell a patient who is confused by the rush of unfamiliar feelings that sex is a legitimate treatment, dismissing her fears and attempts to repel his advances as "resistance" to therapeutic change. A substantial number of sexually exploiting therapists fall into this category, says Gabbard. Many are sociopaths incapable of true remorse or empathy and who may leave a trail of twenty, fifty, or more victims.

But the story isn't always such black and white melodrama. Basically healthy, moral therapists are human, too; in the intimacy of therapy, a patient's powerful needs and affections may call forth intense "countertransference" emotions, awakening strong feelings from the therapist's own past. To feel adored and idealized can be heady stuff even to a professional, particularly one who may be depressed, lonely, in the midst of a personal crisis such as divorce, or just feeling unappreciated at home. Under such circumstances, the best intentions and scruples may be swept away.

Perhaps half of those who engage in sex with patients are what Gabbard calls "lovesick" therapists: they sincerely believe that what's happening to them is true love, not transference. They believe it is a once-in-a-lifetime miracle that obeys no laws but its own, and that they and their patient are "soulmates" to whom ordinary rules do not apply.

To know where transference and countertransference feelings are coming from and how to avoid acting on them should be basic training for all therapists, but in fact it's largely a hit-or-miss affair. Residency training in psychiatry and graduate programs in psychology must include some ethics instruction, but there's no strict requirement that sex issues be treated explicitly or at length. "We've surveyed the field, and there's a range, from excellent to cursory, in teaching about boundary violations and sexual misconduct," says James H. Scully, M.D., deputy medical director of the American Psychiatric Association.

No matter how thorough or lax their education, every psychotherapist in practice today should surely know this: Sex between therapist and patient is ethically wrong, whatever the scenario. Always. Every professional psychotherapy organization—the American Psychological Association, the American Psychiatric Association, the National Association of Social Workers, the American Association for Marriage and Family Therapy—is in unambiguous agreement on that point.

But why, if the patient is willing? Because the feelings unleashed in therapy are so strong, "consent" may have no more meaning than it would with an underaged sex partner. Even when the patient initiates sex—as happens in an estimated 14–25 percent of cases—it is still the therapist who is ethically, and increasingly legally, obligated to make sure it doesn't happen.

"A patient can be seductive, threaten to kill herself if she doesn't get what she wants, or take off her clothes in the session. She has no code to uphold, no standard of behavior to violate," says Thomas Gutheil, M.D., professor of psychiatry at Harvard Medical School. Still, if sex invades therapy, "only the professional can be to blame."

A MALE PRACTICE?

In the majority of cases, the therapist is male and the exploited patient female—a reflection, some say, of power imbalance in a society where men are used to getting what they want and women are conditioned to giving in to them. And so to many, therapy abuse has been reduced to a burning symbol of male oppression, a stark variation on the same theme as the Thomas-Hill hearings.

Some believe, however, this focus has gone too far, transforming a complex issue into a gender-war morality play in which a psychopathic male therapist invariably preys on a passive female patient who has done nothing to elicit such behavior and is always severely traumatized. "Any variation from this rigid formula feels, to some people, as if you excuse the therapist or the sex, or you blame the victim," says Gutheil. In one extreme example, a speaker who chose to illustrate her lecture on sexual misconduct with a case involving a female therapist and male patient was formally accused of sexual harassment by two members of her audience.

Such "politically correct" simplifications stifle vital understanding, Gutheil warns. "Patients, and therapists, come in all flavors," and sexual misconduct is often a complex interaction even if only the therapist can be held responsible. Ignoring the fact that some patients characteristically behave seductively because of their emotional problems—a consequence, for example, of early sexual abuse—can blind therapists to important warning signs that can aid prevention.

In the politically correct scheme of things, "the victim is always severely harmed," adds Gutheil, "and to say anything less is to excuse the crime." But in actuality, while many exploited patients are devastated, others emerge unscathed. And if we truly want to understand the complex dynamics of abuse we should know why.

Paradoxically, the politically correct concept of patient-therapist sex assumes a set of sexual stereotypes—that only men, not women, have sexual feelings, and that men always initiate sexual relationships while women submit to them. That, however, is not the way things really are, Gutheil points out.

The vivid image of predatory male and victimized female is too important to dismiss, insists Peter Rutter, M.D., author of *Sex in the Forbidden Zone*. "I believe it's an accurate perception of the psycho-cultural field in which abuse is happening. We have to keep facing and understanding the image of rapacious, incestuous invasion of masculine energy that our culture has lived by for so long."

But individual cases must be judged on their own merits, he agrees. "Everything about power, trust, and inherent vulnerability is true regardless of gender. The duty to care, potential for tremendous harm, and responsibility are identical."

GENDER COMBOS

In fact, sexual exploitation takes place in all gender combinations, in heterosexual and homosexual variations. In one survey, 7.1 percent of male psychiatrists admitted sexual misconduct—but so did 3.1 percent of female psychiatrists. Another found that while most exploitation (80 percent) involved a male therapist and female client, the second most common scenario—13 percent—involved a female therapist and female patient. The therapist was female and the client male in 2 percent of cases, and both therapist and client male in 5 percent.

Minneapolis psychologist Mindy Benowitz, Ph.D., studied 15 cases of female therapist-female client abuse and found striking similarities to the classic male–female situation: the therapists were older than their patients (an average of 11 years); about half of them were serial offenders; and, like men, they were especially likely to violate the boundaries of therapy when in the midst of personal crisis.

"The dynamics were the same," says Benowitz. "The therapist was meeting her own needs by exploiting the therapy; sometimes, she was fooling herself, too." Half of those who directly broached the subject actually told their patients they were mixing sex and therapy in order to help them—by teaching them how to have a healthy relationship, for example.

Benowitz' study carries a strong lesson about sex, therapy, and power. "Power may typically have to do with gender, but there's also power just in the role of being a therapist, regardless of whether you are male or female," she says. "And being in the client role is inherently vulnerable."

Failing to take seriously the minority of cases in which abusers are female, she says, can turn sexual stereotypes into a dangerous illusion of safety. "It's harder for victims of female therapists to recognize when therapy becomes sexualized, because of the belief that physical contact between women is 'okay.'" One of the patients she interviewed said she'd ignored boundary warning signals because her therapist was a woman. "If it were a man, I would have gotten out after the second session," she said.

Male victims make up a small part—about 7 percent—of the reported total. But this may underrepresent the reality. "Men in this situation rarely view themselves as victims," says Gabbard. "They rarely sue. And usually, if a male patient and female therapist have sex, people blame the patient. Sex-role stereotypes say that men are always the seducers, women the seduced." Like mother–son incest, it was once believed that distasteful as such relationships were, they did not cause much psychological harm. "We know differently now," he says.

Gabbard, who has treated a number of women therapists who have slept with male patients, has repeatedly seen what he calls the "Rowdy Man" scenario: She gets involved with a wild, even criminal, man in the misguided belief that her love can rescue this essentially decent person from his destructive and self-destructive ways.

Such a therapist is buying into a pervasive cultural myth—seen in countless pop novels and such movies as Clint Eastwood's recent *Unforgiven*—that all a "rowdy" young man really needs is a "good woman" to "settle him down." It's a particular risk among women working in prisons and substance-abuse programs.

If offending therapists can't be typecast, neither should exploited patients. Certain persons are clearly at special risk: many who were sexually abused early in life, for example, passively accept exploitative relationships that others would fight against—what one psychiatrist calls the "sitting duck syndrome." And certain personality disorders generate unruly passions that create desperate, eroticized attachments and refusal to accept boundaries.

The exploited, however, include many women who are functioning at a high level. In Benowitz' study, one-third of female patients were themselves training or practicing therapists and came to therapy with relatively minor problems. "We have to get past the belief that those who are well don't let this happen to them," observes Rutter. "The very act of going to a therapist engages that part of oneself that needs to be vulnerable in order to develop."

SYMBOLIC INCEST

Whoever the victim, why is the impact so often so dire? Given the power of feelings aroused by therapy—echoes of the primal feelings first directed toward mother and father—the psychological experience of sex with one's therapist is very much like incest. It is a symbolic incest, and can bring about the same toxic mix of torments, including guilt, shame, a terrible feeling of emptiness, and isolation. Chaotic surges of emotion can be intense and unpredictable. Like the incest victim, the exploited patient is frequently paralyzed by ambivalence, torn between rage at the exploiter and a protective, loyal attachment to him.

A crippled ability to trust is, not surprisingly, a common consequence of exploitation. Adding insult to injury, it often impedes formation of a healing relationship with a future therapist, which is desperately needed to repair the damage. And many victims develop post-traumatic stress disorder (PTSD), with the same pattern of flashbacks and nightmares that inflict agony on combat veterans and victims of crime.

"I developed PTSD, just as strongly as if I had been violently raped," says Barbara Noel, who described her victimization by a prominent psychoanalyst in a recent book, *You Must Be Dreaming* (Poseidon, 1992). Eight years after her therapy ended, she recalls, she fled a restaurant when an older gentleman who resembled the doctor sat at the next table. When she revisited the building where her violation had taken place, "I burst into tears and ran out. I was terrified."

The sexual misconduct needn't be flagrant to do substantial harm. Benowitz found that patients subjected to "covert" exploitation—which might include a therapist's flirting, talking about her own sex life, or pressuring the client to talk about hers, or long full-body hugs—experienced the same intense feelings and suffered the same symptoms as those whose therapists engaged them in real sex acts. "I think covert sexualizing of therapy is a lot more common," she says.

A PROBLEM OF PROFESSIONALS

Although the sexual misdeeds of psychotherapists have reaped the most headlines lately, concern about other professions is also growing. The Hippocratic Oath has unequivocally barred doctor-patient sex for 2400 years, but the American Medical Association didn't add its own explicit ban until 1989. The American Bar Association still doesn't forbid lawyer members to sleep with their clients (such a ruling by the national association would not be legally binding, anyway), although its ethics committee did, for the first time, strongly warn against the practice last summer.

Some state bar associations have passed (California, Oregon) or are considering (Arizona) rules that make such misconduct unethical and subject to disciplinary action. The American Academy of Matrimonial Lawyers added its own ban against client-counsel sex to its Standard of Conduct in 1991.

Perhaps the clearest signs of the times are appearing in the courtroom. "We've just had the first case in the country that held attorney-client sex to be malpractice," says Cambridge, Massachusetts, attorney Linda Jorgensen, who has written extensively on the subject of lawyers' misconduct. "I think we're going to see a surge of cases against attorneys and non-psychiatric physicians who have sex with their clients."

No one knows how many lawyers exploit their clients sexually each year, and statistics about the clergy—another profession whose misconduct has made major headlines of late—are hard to come by (one researcher estimated that, like therapists, the rate runs between 10 and 15 percent). As for physicians, a recent nationwide survey of nearly 2000 family doctors, internists, obstetrician-gynecologists, and surgeons found that 9 percent (10 percent of the men, 4 percent of the women) admitted to sexual contact with patients.

The authors of the study urge that medical education include "comprehensive training on physician-patient sexual contact," teaching doctors-to-be to deal with the strong emotions that arise during treatment, and making sure they understand the legal consequences of misconduct. More than half of the doctors surveyed, however, reported that these issues had never been addressed during training.

THE SAME BREACH OF TRUST

What is also new is the recognition that sexual contact in other professions represents the same abuse of power as in therapy, and can inflict nearly equal damage. Seattle psychologist Shirley Feldman-Summers, Ph.D., contends that like the therapist-patient relationship, these are all "fiduciary" relationships—in which the professional is sworn to act in the client's best interests. Because of the trust the client places in the professional, all such relationships readily give rise to strong feelings similar to those generated by psychotherapy.

As in therapy, when we put ourselves in the knowledgeable hands of anyone who will take care of us, "we transfer to them the feelings we would have for an idealized parent," she says. Such feelings are likely to flare up swiftly and strongly because the client—a woman in the midst of a divorce, for example, or frightened about her health—is so often in a state of heightened emotional vulnerability and need.

The boundless respect, even adoration, that arise are purely situational—we want our doctor or lawyer to be all-knowing because we want to believe he can really help us. But it's easy for the professional to take these feelings personally and respond accordingly. The privacy and confidentiality of the consulting room compound the danger, and a professional who misuses the power given to him by a needy client is unlikely to meet much resistance.

Sexual contact between teachers and students involves the same abuse of power, and many observers say the same boundary standards should apply. Indeed, romancing one's students, once a winked-at professorial perk, has become the subject of harassment suits and ethical censures. Regulations banning such relationships are becoming widespread: Ohio State University, for example, recently forbade them as conflict of interest.

Rarely do academics get any education in the exploitative nature of student-faculty sex, or any training to help them avoid it. The University of Alabama is a notable exception. There Beverly E. Thorn, Ph.D., director of clinical training in psychology and sexual-harassment counselor, gives a two-hour talk on sexual misconduct as part of a week-long training program for graduate teaching assistants. "I stress how a truly 'consensual' relationship cannot occur between faculty and student," she says. "Students see a huge halo over the professor's head. He can exploit that so easily, and some do."

A CRIME?

If the trend in other professions is to see sex with clients as a major ethical violation, in psychotherapy it's fast heading towards a criminal offense. Nine states (Minnesota, Wisconsin, North Dakota, Colorado, California, Maine, Florida, Iowa, and Georgia) now classify it as a felony, with penalties that can include serious prison time. Similar proposals are widely under discussion elsewhere. "It draws a line in the sand," approves Gary Schoener. "We've had some repeat offenders who told us they stopped when it was criminalized."

Lesser penalties—revoking a doctor's or psychologist's license, for example—can't keep the offender from practicing psychotherapy, which requires no license at all in most states. With criminalization, a suspended sentence can be "a club" to get an offender to stop. But not everyone is enthusiastic. "It's killing a fly with a sledge hammer," says Gabbard. "A few of these people—the real predators—should be in jail, but most should not; they need treatment, not prison."

Gutheil observes that complaints in some states dropped after criminalization. "Patients don't want the doctor to go to jail. Lose his license, his money, yes. But jail? People don't want to go that route. It makes them feel sadistic. It's not the coin in which they want to be paid."

Criminalization may also make it more difficult for abused patients to collect compensation for damage from the therapist's malpractice insurance, which generally excludes coverage of criminal activity. And once criminal proceedings begin, control passes from the patient to a prosecutor who may not zealously pursue a crime less blatant than murder or assault. "Think of how prosecutors prosecute date rape. It's not exactly at the top of their agenda," says Feldman-Summers. "Will this be a top priority for prosecutors? I don't think so."

BLAME THE VICTIM?

On a popular talk show last year, two women described sexual betrayal by their therapists. Then the audience had its turn. "She submitted to sex of her own volition. That's not abuse," said one member. "I'm enraged at this woman," said another. "She put herself in that position."

Barbara Noel, one of the women who appeared on the show, wasn't surprised at the reaction. Since she made her victimization public (with the courageous help of advice columnist Ann Landers, to whom she presented the evidence), she has encountered similar hostility—even in rape support groups where she sought help. "People jumped all over me," she recalls. "They'd been raped by strangers and friends. But a therapist? 'How dare you malign these wonderful people, it must be your fault!'"

Such hostility toward victims of therapy abuse, especially from other women, is far from unusual, according to Schoener. Behind it is defensive denial, "a knee-jerk fear response. If the victim caused it, it can't happen to you."

A similar denial leads to the "bad apple" delusion among psychotherapists, that once the sociopathic felons are rounded up and drummed out of the profession, everything will be fine, Schoener notes. "Therapists like to wash their hands of it and say 'It couldn't be me'"—forgetting that perhaps half the offenders are ordinary men and women who would not have crossed the line but for the stress of personal crisis and the spell of intense emotion that comes with the territory of psychotherapy.

"We have to understand that this is a more dangerous line of work than they told us in medical school or graduate school," says Schoener. "We have to come to grips with our own corruptibility.

45

Psychotherapists' Accounts of Their Professional Misdeeds

MARK R. POGREBIN, ERIC D. POOLE,
AND AMOS MARTINEZ
University of Colorado, Denver

Intimate sexual relationships between mental health therapists and their clients have been increasingly reported in recent years (Akamatsu, 1987). In a survey of over 1400 psychiatrists, Gartell, Herman, Olarte, Feldstein, and Localio (1987) found that 65 percent reported having treated a patient who admitted to sexual involvement with a previous therapist. National self-report surveys indicate that approximately 10 percent of psychotherapists admit having had at least one sexual encounter with a client (Gartell, Herman, Olarte, Feldstein, and Localio, 1986; Pope, Keith-Spiegel, and Tabachnick, 1986). It is suggested that these surveys most likely underestimate the extent of actual sexual involvement with clients because some offending psychotherapists either fail to respond to the survey or fail to report their sexual indiscretions (Gartell et al., 1987). Regardless of the true prevalence rates, many mental health professional associations explicitly condemn sexual relations between a therapist and client. Such relationships represent a breach of canons of professional ethics and are subject to disciplinary action by specific licensing or regulatory bodies. . . .

Since 1988 [in Colorado] sexual intimacy between therapists and clients has been explicitly and formally recognized as one of the most serious violations of the professional–client relationship, subject to both regulatory or administrative and criminal penalties. Yet, between August 1, 1988, and June 30, 1990, 10 percent ($n = 33$) of the 324 complaints filed with the State Grievance Board involved allegations of sexual misconduct. Given the impli-

Reprinted from the authors' article, "Accounts of Professional Misdeeds: The Sexual Exploitation of Clients by Psychotherapists," *Deviant Behavior*, Vol. 13 (1992): 229–252. Reproduced with permission. All rights reserved.

cations that these sexual improprieties raise for both the client as victim and the therapist as offender, we wish to examine the written accounts submitted to the board by psychotherapists who have had complaints of sexual misconduct filed against them. . . .

METHOD

To the 33 complaints of sexual misconduct filed from August 1988 through June 1990, 30 written responses from psychotherapists were submitted to the State Grievance Board. Twenty-four therapists admitted to sexual involvement with clients; six denied the allegations. In the present study we examine the statements of the 24 therapists who provided accounts for their sexual relations with clients. Twenty-one therapists are men; three are women.

The analytical method utilized in reviewing therapists' accounts was content analysis, which "translates frequency of occurrence of certain symbols into summary judgments and comparisons of content of the discourse" (Starosta, 1984, p. 185). Content analytical techniques provide the means to document, classify, and interpret the communication of meaning, allowing for inferential judgments from objective identification of the characteristics of messages (Holsti, 1969).

The 24 written responses ranged in length from 2 to 25 pages. Each response was assessed and classified according to the types of explanations invoked by therapists in accounting for their acknowledged sexual relations with clients. We employed Scott and Lyman's (1968) classic formulation of accounts (i.e., excuses and justifications) and Goffman's (1971) notion of the apology as conceptual guides in organizing the vocabularies of motive used by our group of therapists to explain their untoward behavior. . . .

FINDINGS

Accounts are "linguistic device[s] employed whenever an action is subjected to valuative inquiry" (Scott and Lyman, 1968, p. 46). An important function of accounts is to mitigate blameworthiness by representing one's behavior in such a way as to reduce personal accountability. This involves offering accounts aimed at altering the prevailing conception of what the instant activity is, as well as one's role in the activity. Excuses, justifications, and apologies all display a common goal: giving a "good account" of oneself.

Excuses

Appeal of Defeasibility   In an appeal of defeasibility, one accounts for one's behavior by denying any intention to cause the admitted harm or by claiming a failure to foresee the unfortunate consequences of one's act, or both. . . . In the following account, the therapist claims ignorance of professional rules of conduct governing relations with clients:

> I did not know that seeing clients socially outside of therapy violated hospital policy. . . . [I]f I realized it was strictly forbidden, I would have acted differently. . . .

In the following example, a therapist admits that she simply misinterpreted her own feelings and did not consciously intend to become sexually involved with her client:

> It was after a short period of time that I first experienced any sexual feelings toward her. I did excuse the feelings I had as something which I never would act on. Unfortunately, I did not understand what was happening at the time.

Similarly, another therapist seeks to diminish culpability by attributing his sexual indiscretion to a misreading of his client's emotional needs:

> I experienced her expressions of affection as caring gestures of our spiritual bond, not lust. And I had no reason to suspect otherwise from her, since I had been so clear about my aversion to romantic involvement. We had sexual intercourse only once after termination. I am not promiscuous, neither sexually abusive nor seductive. . . .

Scapegoating   Scapegoating involves an attempt to blame others for one's untoward behavior. Scapegoating is available as a form of excuse in the professional-client relationship because of the contextual opportunity for the therapist to shift personal responsibility to the client. The therapist contends that his or her actions were the product of the negative attributes or will of the client, example, deceit, seduction, or manipulation. The therapist in the following example recognizes the wrongfulness of his behavior but deflects responsibility by holding the client culpable for her actions:

> I am not denying that this sexual activity took place, nor am I trying to excuse or justify it. It was wrong. However, the woman who complained about me is a psychologist. She was counseling me as well, on some vocational issues. So if anyone had cause for complaint under the regulations, it seems it would be me.

Another example of an account where the therapist attempts to "blame the victim" for the improper sexual activity reveals the focus on his diminished personal control of the relationship:

> That I became involved in a sexual relationship with her is true. While my actions were reprehensible, both morally and professionally, I did not mislead or seduce her or intend to take advantage of her. My fault, instead, was failing to adequately safeguard myself from her seductiveness, covert and overt.

Here we have a therapist recognizing the impropriety of his actions yet denying personal responsibility because of the client's overpowering charms. The message is that the therapist may be held accountable for an inadequate "self-defense" which left him vulnerable to the client's seductive nature, but that he should not be culpable for the deviant sexual behavior since it was really he who was taken in and thus "victimized." The therapist's account for his predicament presumes a "reasonable person" theory of behavior; that is, given the same set of circumstances, any reasonable person would be expected to succumb to this persuasive client.

Justifications

Sad Tale   The sad tale presents an array of dismal experiences or conditions that are regarded—both collectively and cumulatively—as an explanation and justification for the actor's present untoward behavior. The therapists who presented sad tales invariably focused on their own history of family problems and personal tribulations that brought them to their present state of sexual affairs with clients:

> Ironically, her termination from therapy came at one of the darkest periods of my life. My father had died that year. I had met him for the first time when I was in my twenties. He was an alcoholic. Over the years we had worked hard on our relationship. At the time of his dying, we were at peace with one another. Yet, I still had my grief. At the time I had entered into individual therapy to focus on issues pertaining to my father's alcoholism and co-dependency issues. I then asked my wife to join me for marriage counseling. We were having substantial problems surrounding my powerlessness in our relationship. Therapy failed to address the balance of power. I was in the worst depression I had ever experienced in my entire life when we began our sexual involvement.

Therapists who employ sad tales admit to having sexual relations with their clients, admit that their actions were improper, and admit that ordinarily what they did would be an instance of the general category of the prohibited behavior. They claim, however, that their behavior is a special case because the power of circumstance voids the defining deviant quality of their actions. This type of account is similar to Lofland's (1969, p. 88) "special justification," where the actor views his current act as representative of some category of deviance but does not believe it to be entirely blameworthy because of extenuating circumstances. One therapist outlines the particular contextual factors that help explain his misbehavior:

> The following situations are not represented as an excuse for my actions. There is no excuse for them. They are simply some of what I feel are circumstances that formed the context for what I believe is an incident that will never be repeated.
> (1) Life losses: My mother-in-law who lived with us died. My oldest son and, the next fall, my daughter had left home for college.
> (2) Overscheduling: I dealt with these losses and other concerns in my life by massive overscheduling.

Other therapists offer similar sad tales of tragic events that are seen to diminish their capacity, either physically or mentally, to cope with present circumstances. Two cases illustrate this accounting strategy:

> In the summer of 1988, my wife and I separated with her taking our children to live out-of-state. This was a difficult loss for me. A divorce followed. Soon after I had a bout with phlebitis which hospitalized me for ten days.

> My daughter, who lived far away with my former wife, was diagnosed with leukemia; and my mother had just died. Additional stress was caused by my ex-wife and present wife's embittered interactions. . . .

Sad tales depict individuals acting abnormally in abnormal situations. In short, their instant deviance is neither typical nor characteristic of the type of person they really are, that is, how they would act under normal conditions. They are victims of circumstance, for if it were not for these dismal life events, their sexual improprieties would never have occurred.

Denial of Injury   Denial of injury is premised on a moral assessment of consequences; that is, the individual claims that his or her actions should be judged as wrong on the basis of the harm resulting from those acts. Again, the actor acknowledges that in general the behavior in which he or she has engaged is inappropriate but asserts that in this particular instance no real harm was done. This type of account was prevalent among the therapists who had engaged in sexual relations with clients following the termination of therapy.

> A good therapy termination establishes person-to-person equality between participants. Blanket condemnations of post-therapy relationships also are founded on a belief that such relationships invariably cause harm to the former patient. I defy anyone to meet Gerry, interview her, and then maintain that any harm was done to her by me. . . .

Apology

. . . Two consequences of an accused wrongdoer's action are guilt and shame. If wrongful behavior is based on internal standards, the transgressor feels guilty; if the behavior is judged on external normative comparisons, the person experiences shame. Shame results from being viewed as one who has behaved in a discrediting manner. In the following three cases, each therapist expresses his remorse and laments his moral failure:

> I find myself in the shameful position that I never would have thought possible for me as I violated my own standards of personal and professional conduct.

> I feel very badly for what I have done, ashamed and unprofessional. I feel unworthy of working in the noble profession of counselling.

> I entered into therapy and from the first session disclosed what I had done. I talked about my shame and the devastation I had created for my family and others.

Schlenker and Darby (1981) observe that the apology incorporates not only an expression of regret but also a claim of redemption. An apology permits a transgressor the opportunity to admit guilt while simultaneously seeking forgiveness in order that the offending behavior not be thought of as a representation of what the actor is really like. One therapist expresses concern for his actions and proposes a way to avoid such conduct in the future:

> I continue to feel worry and guilt about the damage that I caused. I have taken steps I felt necessary which has been to decide not to work with any client who

could be very emotionally demanding, such as occurs with people who are border-line or dependent in their functioning.

This account seems to imply that one's remorse and affirmative effort to pre-vent future transgressions are sufficient remedies in themselves, preempting the need for others to impose additional sanctions. . . .

DISCUSSION

The consequences of deviant activity are problematic, often depending on a "definition of the situation." When a particular definition of a specific situation emerges, even though its dominance may be only temporary, individuals must adjust their behavior and views to it. Alternative definitions of problematic sit-uations routinely arise and are usually subject to negotiation. Thus, it is incum-bent upon the accused therapist to have his or her situation defined in ways most favorable to maintaining or advancing his or her own interests. When "transformations of identity" are at stake, such efforts become especially con-sequential (Strauss, 1962). The imputation of a deviant identity implies rami-fications that can vitally affect the individual's personal and professional life. As noted earlier, the negotiation of accounts is a negotiation of identities. The account serves as an impression-management technique, or a "front," that minimizes the threat to identity (Goffman, 1959). If the therapist can provide an acceptable account for his or her sexual impropriety—whether an excuse, justification, or apology—he or she increases the likelihood of restoring a cher-ished identity brought into question by the deviant behavior.

There is a close link between successfully conveying desired images to oth-ers and being able to incorporate them in one's own self-conceptions. When individuals offer accounts for their problematic actions, they are trying to ease their situation in two ways: by convincing others and by convincing them-selves. An important function of accounts is to make one's transgressions not only intelligible to others but intelligible to oneself. Therapists sought to dis-pel the view that their deviation was a defining characteristic of who they real-ly were; or, to put it another way, they attempted to negate the centrality or primacy of a deviant role imputation. The goal was to maintain or restore their own sense of personal and professional worth notwithstanding their sexual deviancy. In a way, laying claim to a favorable image in spite of aberrant behav-ior means voiding the apparent moral reality, that is, the deviance-laden defi-nition of the situation that has been called to the attention of significant oth-ers (Grievance Board) by a victim-accuser (former client).

Goffman (1959, p. 251) maintains that individuals are not concerned with the issue of morality of their behavior as much as they are with the amoral issue of presenting a moral self:

> Our activity, then is largely concerned with moral matters, but as performers we do not have a moral concern with them. As performers we are merchants of morality.

The presentation of a moral self following deviance may be interpreted as an attempt by the individual to reaffirm his commitment to consensual values and goals in order to win the acceptance of others (Tedeschi and Riorden, 1981). The demonstration of shared standards of conduct may also be seen as consistent with the wish to redeem oneself in the eyes of others and to preserve self-respect. The desire for self-validating approval becomes more important when circumstances threaten an individual's identity. In these instances an actor will often make self-presentations for purposes of eliciting desired responses that will restore the perception of self by others that he or she desires. If discredited actors can offer a normal presentation of self in an abnormal situation, they may be successful in having their instant deviant behavior perceived by others as atypical, thus neutralizing a deviant characterization.

Individuals seek a "common ground" in accounts of their deviant behavior, explaining their actions in conventional terms that are acceptable to a particular audience. These accounts should not be viewed as mere rationalizations. They may genuinely be believed in. . . .

Finally, it should be noted that, as retrospective interpretations, accounts may have little to do with the motives that existed at the time the deviance occurred. In this case accounting for one's deviant behavior requires one to dissimulate, that is, to pretend to be what one is not or not to be what one is. As Goffman (1959) asserts, social behavior involves a great deal of deliberate deception in that impressions of selves must be constantly created and managed for various others. Thus, it is not logically necessary that one agree with others' moral judgments in order to employ accounts. Even where no guilt or shame is consciously felt, one may offer accounts in the hope of lessening what could be, nonetheless, attributions of a deviant identity. When used convincingly, accounts blur the distinctions between "appearance and reality, truth and falsity, triviality and importance, accident and essence, coincidence and cause" (Garfinkel, 1956, p. 420). Accounts embody a mixture of fact and fantasy. As shown in the accounts provided by therapists, what is most problematic is determining the mixture best suited for a particular situational context.

References

Akamatsu, J. T. 1987. "Intimate Relationships with Former Clients: National Survey of Attitudes and Behavior Among Practitioners." *Professional Psychology: Research and Practice* 18:454–458.

Garfinkel, H. 1956. "Conditions of Successful Degradation Ceremonies." *American Journal of Sociology* 61:420–424.

Gartell, N., J. Herman, S. Olarte, M. Feldstein, and R. Localio. 1986. "Psychiatrist-Patient Sexual Contact: Results of a National Survey. I: Prevalence." *American Journal of Psychiatry* 143:1126–1131.

Gartell, N., J. Herman, S. Olarte, M. Feldstein, and R. Localio. 1987. "Reporting Practices of Psychiatrists Who Knew of Sexual Misconduct by Colleagues." *American Journal of Orthopsychiatry* 57:287–295.

Goffman, E. 1959. *The Presentation of Self in Everyday Life.* Garden City, NY: Doubleday.

Goffman, E. 1971. *Relations in Public: Microstudies of the Public Order.* New York: Basic Books.

Holsti, O. R. 1969. *Content Analysis for the Social Sciences and Humanities.* Reading, MA: Addison-Wesley.

Lofland, J. 1969. *Deviance and Identity.* Englewood Cliffs, NJ: Prentice-Hall.

Pope, K. S., P. Keith-Spiegel, and B. G. Tabachnick. 1986. "Sexual Attraction to Clients: The Human Therapist and the (Sometimes) Inhuman Training System." *American Psychologist* 41:147–158.

Schlenker, B. R., and B. W. Darby. 1981. "The Use of Apologies in Social Predicaments." *Social Psychology Quarterly* 44:271–278.

Scott, M. B., and S. M. Lyman. 1968. "Accounts." *American Sociological Review* 33:46–62.

Starosta, W. J. 1984. "Qualitative Content Analysis: A Burkean Perspective," pp. 185–194 in *Methods for Intercultural Communication Research,* edited by W. Gudykunst and Y. Y. Kim. Beverly Hills, CA: Sage.

Strauss, A. 1962. "Transformations of Identity," pp. 63–85 in *Human Behavior and Social Processes: An Interactional Approach,* edited by A. M. Rose. Boston: Houghton Mifflin.

Tedeschi, J. T., and C. Riorden. 1981. "Impression Management and Prosocial Behavior Following Transgression," pp. 223–244 in *Impression Management Theory and Social Psychological Research,* edited by J. T. Tedeschi. New York: Academic Press.

46

Police Lying: "Fluffing Up the Evidence and Covering Your Ass"

TOM BARKER
Jacksonville State University

DAVID CARTER
Michigan State University

Lying and other deceptive practices are an integral part of the police officer's working environment. At first blush, you may react to this statement this way: "Police officers should not lie. If you can't trust your local police, who can you trust?" But the matter is not that simple. The police do lie. We will here discuss the patterns of police lying, the circumstances under which it occurs, and its possible consequences.

LEGITIMATE LYING

Certain forms of lying are an accepted part of the police working environment. The lies told are accepted because they fulfil! a defined police purpose. Police administrators and officers believe that certain lies are necessary to control crime and "arrest the guilty." In these instances, the organization will freely admit the intent to lie and define the acts as legitimate policing strategies.

The most apparent patterns of "accepted" lying are the deceptive practices that law enforcement officers believe are necessary to perform undercover operations or detect other forms of secret and consensual crimes. Police officers engaged in these activities must not only conceal their true identity but they must talk, act, and dress out of character, fabricating all kinds of stories in order to perform these duties. One could hardly imagine that FBI Special Agent Joseph Pistone could have operated for six years in

Adapted from the authors' article, "Fluffing Up the Evidence and Covering Your Ass: Some Conceptual Notes on Police Lying," *Deviant Behavior,* Vol. 11 (1990): 61–73. Washington, D.C.: Taylor & Francis, Inc. Reproduced with permission. All rights reserved.

the Mafia without the substantial number of lies he had to tell (Pistone, 1987). However, the overwhelming majority of undercover operations are not as glamorous nor as dangerous as working six years with the Mafia. The most common police undercover operations occur in routine vice operations dealing with prostitution, bootlegging, gambling, narcotics, bribery of public officials, and sting operations.

Much of these undercover operations involves encouraging the target to commit a crime. This may be a legally accepted police practice if the officer acts as a willing victim or the officer's actions facilitate the commission of a crime that was going to be committed in the first place. But this police action can be considered entrapment, which is illegal. According to *Black's Law Dictionary*, entrapment is "the act of officers or agents of the government in inducing a person to commit a crime not contemplated by him, for the purpose of instituting a criminal prosecution against him" (277). It is difficult, though, for individuals with a criminal record to claim that they would not have committed the crime except for the actions of the officer. Nevertheless, the "objective test" of entrapment as advocated by a minority of the Supreme Court focuses on the nature of the police conduct rather than the predisposition of the offender (Stitt and James, 1985). Consider the case of a police organization producing crack for use in undercover drug arrests. According to an Associated Press story, the Broward County Florida Sheriff's Department, not having enough crack to supply undercover officers, has started manufacturing their own. The sheriff's department chemist has made at least $20,000 worth of the illegal stuff. Local defense attorneys have raised the issue of entrapment. As one public defender stated,

> I think there's something sick about this whole system where the police make the product, sell the product, and arrest people for buying the product (*Birmingham Post Herald*, April 19, 1989:B2).

In short, accepted lies are those that the organization views as having a useful role in police operations. The criteria for the lie to be accepted are:

1. It must be in furtherance of a legitimate organizational purpose.

2. There must be a clear relationship between the need to deceive and the accomplishment of an organizational goal.

3. The nature of the deception must be one wherein deception will better serve the public interest than the truth.

ILLEGITIMATE BUT TOLERATED LYING

A second type of police lies includes those recognized as lies by the police but tolerated as "necessary evils." Police administrators will admit to deception or "not exactly telling the whole truth" when confronted with the facts. These situational or "white" lies are truly in the gray area of propriety and the police can provide logical rationales for their use. When viewed from an ethical standpoint, they may be "wrong," but from the police perspective they are necessary (i.e., tolerated) for achieving organizational objectives. The lies are particularly useful for dealing with the basic problems of police work.

The basic problems confronting the police arise from the mythology surrounding their work: statutes usually require, and the public expects, the police to enforce all the laws all the time; the public holds the police responsible for preventing crime and apprehending all criminals; the public views the police as being capable of handling all emergencies, and so on (Goldstein, 1977). But the police do not have the resources, the training, or the authority to do some of those duties. Thus, the police tend to do things contrary to public expectation. One such thing involves discretionary decision making or selective law enforcement. For example, in recent years, many politically active groups such as Mothers Against Drunk Drivers (MADD) have pressured legislators for stronger laws with mandatory enforcement in drunk driving cases. But police officers often make discretionary decisions on D.U.I. offenses even though full enforcement is their department's official policy. One of us (Tom Barker) learned of an individual who had two D.U.I. offenses reduced, and asked a police supervisor about it.

> *Barker:* The chief has said that all D.U.I. suspects are charged and those over the legal blood alcohol level never have the charge reduced. In fact, he said this at a MADD meeting. Yet, I heard that "so-and-so" had two D.U.I. offenses reduced.

> *Supervisor:* That is true, Tom. However, "so-and-so" is helping us with some drug cases. MADD may not understand but they do not have to make drug busts.

In dealing with disorderly or emergency situations, the police often are forced to reach into a bag of tricks. They may tell noisy teenagers to move along or be arrested even though they have neither the intention nor legal basis for an arrest. They may tell complainants that they will follow up on their complaint or turn it over to the proper agency when they have no intention of doing it. They see such lies as a way of handling "nuisance work" that keeps them from doing "real police work" or as a way of dealing with a problem beyond their means. The lies are used as a tool of expediency—arguably an abuse of police discretion but one that is tolerated.

Similarly, in domestic disturbances, police officers may have no legal basis for making an arrest. Frequently, there is a misdemeanor for which the officer does not have a warrant, an offense that has not been committed in the officer's presence, or an incident that occurred in a private residence. However, the officer may feel that something must be done. Thus, the officer may lie and threaten to arrest one or both combatants, or talk them out to the street or the patrol car to discuss the incident and then arrest them for disorderly conduct or public intoxication when they reach public property.

In interrogating the arrested person, the police also often resort to lying. This is not only tolerated but also taught to police officers. The interrogator is told to put forth a facade of sincerity so convincingly that "moisture may actually appear in his eyes." Another recommended technique of deception requires having a *simulated* evidence case folder on hand during the course of the interrogation if an actual case file does not exist. The interrogator may allude to having a large number of investigators working on the case and producing considerable evidence on the suspect's guilt, even though the interrogator is the only person working on the case (Inbau, Reid, and Buckley, 1986).

It is difficult to say whether these tolerated forms of lying are "wrong." Many investigators would argue that they are not really "lies" but good interrogation methods. It could also be argued in their defense that the end justifies the means as long as the officer's actions are not illegal. However, deception in one context may spill over into other contexts. As a veteran police officer told one of us (Barker) while discussing ways to convince a suspect to agree to a consent search,

> *Barker:* That sure sounds like telling a lot of lies.
>
> *Officer:* It is not police lying; it is an art. After all, the criminal has constitutional protection. He can lie through his teeth. Why not us? What is fair is fair.

ILLEGAL LIES

A third type of police lying involves violating a substantive or procedural law or some police department rules and regulations. According to noted defense attorney and legal scholar Alan Dershowitz (1983), this serious illegal form of police lying is well known in the criminal justice system. It is part of the "Rules of the Justice Game," including:

> *Rule IV:* Almost all police lie about whether they violated the Constitution in order to convict guilty defendants.
>
> *Rule V:* All prosecutors, judges, and defense attorneys are aware of Rule IV.
>
> *Rule VI:* Many prosecutors implicitly encourage police to lie about whether they violated the Constitution in order to convict guilty defendants.
>
> *Rule VII:* All judges are aware of Rule VI.
>
> *Rule VIII:* Most trial judges pretend to believe police officers who they know are lying.
>
> *Rule XI:* All appellate judges are aware of Rule VIII, yet many pretend to believe the trial judges who pretend to believe the lying police officers (Dershowitz, 1983:xxi–xxii).

There are studies to support this observation. One study concluded that "the possibility of police perjury is a part of the working reality of criminal defense attorneys" (Kittel, 1986:20). Fifty-seven percent of the 277 attorneys surveyed in this study believed that police perjury occurs "very often" or "often." In another study, police officers themselves reported that they believe their fellow officers would lie in court (Barker, 1978). An English barrister believes that police officers in his country perjure themselves in about three out of ten trials (Wolchover, 1986).

Lying for Legitimate Reasons

Police officers may engage in perjury or other illegal lying for what they perceive to be legitimate reasons. Thus, they lie because they want to "put criminals in jail," prevent crime, or perform various other policing responsibilities. They believe that they know the guilt or innocence of those they arrest because of their unique experiences in dealing with criminals. But they are forced to lie because necessary elements of legal guilt are lacking, such as no probable cause for a "stop," no Miranda warning, or not enough narcotics for a felony offense. Lying, then, constitutes only supplying the missing elements. As one police officer told one of us, it is often necessary to "fluff up the evidence" to get a search warrant or ensure conviction.

The police rationalize that illegal lying is necessary to ensure that criminals do not get off on "technicalities." A deeper reason is officer frustration. The police are frustrated with the criminal justice system because the court cannot handle large caseloads. They are also frustrated with the routine practice of plea negotiations and intricate criminal procedures, which they may not fully understand. They further sympathize with the victims of crime, having difficulty reconciling the harm done to them with the wide array of due process protections given to defendants. They are, in effect, see themselves as doing the "right thing." They cannot see, or could not care less, the fact that their perjury is not only illegal but threatening to civil liberties.

Lying for Illegitimate Reasons

Police officers also often lie for illegitimate reasons, to protect themselves or fellow officers from organizational discipline or civil or criminal liability. Thus, they would lie to cover up their own or others' corruption, an act of police brutality, an injury or death to a suspect, or personal misconduct such as having sex, sleeping, or drinking on duty. Officers may get together to ensure that they tell the same story so as to make the lie look like the truth. This can be illustrated by an experience one of us (David Carter) had. Carter was assisting a police department that was under a federal court injunction related to a long list of civil rights violations involving excessive force and harassment. During one series of inquiries, the following conversation occurred:

Carter: Did you ever talk to other accused officers before giving your deposition in these cases?

Officer: Of course.

Carter: Did you discuss the facts of the allegation?

Officer: Sure. We had to be sure our stories were straight.

Much of the lying does not involve police brutality, though. It has to do with relatively minor violations of departmental rules and regulations. These may include the common practice of eating a free meal, leaving one's beat for personal reasons, not wearing the hat when out of the car, living outside the city limits, and so on. Such violations are extremely common because there are too many rules and regulations, especially in large urban police departments. When a supervisor decides to discipline an officer for violating one of these violations, the officer and fellow officers may resort to lies to protect themselves and each other.

CONCLUSION

Whether police lying is legitimate or illegal, accepted or tolerated, it can have harmful consequences. Lies can and do create distrust within the organization. They encourage police misconduct, including corruption, thereby threatening the department's discipline and viability as a law-enforcement agency. Moreover, when the public learns about police lying, citizen confidence in the police plummets, making it even more difficult for the police to perform their duty. All this inevitably reduces the effectiveness of the criminal justice system as a whole.

References

Barker, T. 1978. "An Empirical Study of Police Deviance Other Than Corruption." *Journal of Police Science and Administration* 6:3:264–272.

Birmingham Post-Herald. 1989. "Sheriff's Chemist Makes Crack," April 19:B2.

Dershowitz, A. M. 1983. *The Best Defense.* New York: Vintage Books.

Goldstein, H. 1977. *Policing a Free Society.* Cambridge, MA: Ballenger.

Inbau, F. E., J. E. Reid, and Joseph P. Buckley. 1986. *Criminal Interrogation and Confessions,* 3rd ed. Baltimore: Williams and Wilkins.

Kittel, N.G. 1986. "Police Perjury: Criminal Defense Attorneys' Perspective." *American Journal of Criminal Justice* 11:1:11–22.

Pistone, J. D. 1987. *Donnie Brasco: My Undercover Life in the Mafia.* New York: Nail Books.

Stitt, B. G. and Gene G. James. 1985. "Entrapment: An Ethical Analysis" in Elliston, F. A. and Michael Feldberg (eds.), *Moral Issues in Police Work.* Totowa, NJ: Rowman and Allanheld.

Wolchover, D. 1986. "Police Perjury in London." *New Law Journal,* February: 180–184.

P A R T 1 2

Physical and Mental Disabilities

Disabilities are far more common than popularly believed. In his well-researched book on the subject, Joseph Shapiro discovers that disabled Americans are the nation's largest minority, numbering from 35 to 43 million, more than three times the size of the African-American population. In fact, as Shapiro further notes, disability "is one minority that anyone can join at any time, as a result of a sudden automobile accident, a fall down a flight of stairs, cancer, or disease. Fewer than 15 percent of disabled Americans were born with their disabilities."[1]

People with disabilities, particularly the deaf, blind, paraplegic, psychotic, or mentally retarded, differ from most other deviances. While they are deviant in the sense of being socially disvalued, the disabled cannot be held responsible for the condition they are in. Humanist sociologists, therefore, do not judge the disabled in the same negative way as the general public does. Also, unlike the public, humanists are able to transcend the negative connotations of the term "disabilities." But positivists tend to be more like the public, taking a less sensitive, more objectivist stance toward the disabled. This entails studying the disabled "from the outside" without any feeling, as opposed to the humanist trying to understand the disabled "from the inside" with empathy. An example of this positivist approach is how Marshall Clinard and Robert Meier analyze disabilities in their deviance textbook. They try to be neutral, claiming "no attempt to 'blame' persons with physical impairments for their condition." But their analysis mostly conveys a negative impression about physical disabilities. It effectively reinforces the popular stereotype of the disabled being sick, weak, inadequate, or pitiable—in essence, inferior to the nondisabled.

As positivists, Clinard and Meier do not seem to realize that persons with disabilities appear inferior only when judged in an unfair, prejudiced way—with the criteria of competence that are *biased in favor of nondisabled people*. Compare, for example, an average blind person with an average sighted person. Who is more competent in walking from one place to another? If we use the criterion of being able to move about with the eyes *open*, of course the

---

[1] Joseph P. Shapiro, *No Pity: People with Disabilities Forging a New Civil Rights Movement* (New York: Times Books, 1993), pp. 6–7.

sighted person is more competent. But if we use the criterion of being able to move about with the eyes *closed,* the blind person is definitely more competent. To humanists, who strongly support human equality, nobody is inferior (or superior) to others unless some biased criteria are used for making the evaluation. In using biased criteria, perhaps as unconsciously as the general public, positivists tend to portray persons with physical disabilities as mostly pitiable—that is, not as competent as positivists themselves. By contrast, humanists tend to respect persons with disabilities, and show that respect by trying to understand their world from their own perspective. This is what Michael Angrosino does in the first article, "How Persons with Mental Retardation See Themselves."

Considerably more common than mental retardation is eating disorder. Most of the victims are young women. This problem has been increasing greatly in the United States and many other societies. In the second selection, "Cross-Cultural Patterns in Eating Disorders," Jennifer Pate and her colleagues review a massive amount of studies, providing a global perspective on anorexia and bulimia. The authors discover, among other things, that eating disorders seem to reflect an attempt to deal with the pressure of growing up in a stressful environment or a young woman's trying to seek control and autonomy over the confusion that results from the conflict between the passing traditional female role expectations and the emerging modern ones. In the next article on the same subject, "Anorexics and Bulimics: Developing Deviant Identities," Penelope McLorg and Diane Taub provide a closer look into the inner, experiential world of mostly female college students with the disorder.

Also more likely to strike relatively young people is mental illness. According to a national survey published in 1994, individuals aged 25 to 34 have the highest rate of mental illness.[2] A 1992 cross-national study also found a significant increase in major depression among the younger generations, especially over the last several decades.[3] In countries as diverse as the United States, Taiwan, Lebanon, and New Zealand, each successive generation has been growing more vulnerable to depressive disorders. In those countries, people born after 1955 are more than three times as likely as their grandparents to come down with a major depression. Among Americans, about 6 percent of those born after 1955 have become severely depressed by age 24, while only 1 percent of those born before 1905 have suffered similar depression by age 75. The increasingly greater prevalence of depression among young people can be attributed to changes in modern society—more specifically, an increase in social stresses and a decrease in social resources for coping with the stress. Most of the stresses come from family problems, such as divorce, child abuse, or parental indifference to children's needs for love and support. And the difficulty in coping with these stresses comes largely from the loss of the

---

[2] Ronald C. Kessler et al., "Lifetime and 12-Month Prevalence of DSM-III-R Psychiatric Disorders in the United States," *Archives of General Psychiatry,* Vol. 51 (1994), p. 13.

[3] Cross-National Collaborative Group, "The Changing Rate of Major Depression: Cross-National Comparisons," *JAMA (Journal of American Medical Association),* Vol. 268 (1992), pp. 3098–3105.

extended family and close-knit, village-like community in modern society. Without taking these social forces into account, it should not be surprising that psychotherapy is relatively ineffective in solving the problem, as shown in the last article, "Oops! A Very Embarrassing Story About Psychotherapy," by Virginia Rutter.

47

How Persons with Mental Retardation See Themselves

MICHAEL V. ANGROSINO
University of South Florida

The study of mentally retarded persons in natural settings (i.e., in the noninstitutional communities in which they live and work) was pioneered by Robert Edgerton and his Socio-Behavioral Group at the University of California at Los Angeles. Their work has demonstrated that the conventional wisdom about adults with mental retardation, based as it was on clinical observations, could be enriched by the application of ethnographic methods, including that of the life history.

The life histories of retarded persons collected in natural settings have been predicated on the assumption that these people are capable of telling us about their experiences and feelings in a coherent fashion. My own research confirms this assumption but in a somewhat different way. I have not been concerned so much with the verifiable truth value of the content of what my informants tell me (some of which has proven, in fact, to be untrue in the strictly literal sense) but with the ways in which our conversations have created interactive communicative contexts in which their views of the world are revealed in spite of the obfuscations (deliberate or not) in the superficial aspects of the narratives. My concern, then, is to contribute to the literature on naturalistic ethnography among stigmatized people by focusing not on what they say but on their ability to create culturally appropriate metaphors by which to convey their sense of identity to others. . . .

METHOD

I conducted my research at an agency called "Opportunity House" (a pseudonym hereafter termed OH) that provided vocational and academic training to

From Michael V. Angrosino, "Metaphors of Stigma: How Deinstitutionalized Mentally Retarded Adults See Themselves," *Journal of Contemporary Ethnography*, Vol. 21 No. 2, July 1992, 171–199 © 1992 Sage Publications. Reproduced by permission of Sage Publications, Inc.

mentally retarded men who also have psychiatric disorders and, in most cases, criminal records. OH provided these services at a residential facility in a suburban community, as well as at a multipurpose center in a nearby large city. I had been involved with OH since 1980 as both a volunteer tutor and an officer of its Board of Trustees.

I found that as friendships with some of the long-term clients deepened, material of a life history nature was emerging. I secured permission from the staff to tape some conversations; four of the clients (who were all legally competent) signed release statements allowing me to cite portions of their interviews as long as names were changed and no privileged clinical information was revealed. The interviews did not have the formalized structure of traditional life history interviews (see, e.g., Dollard, 1935; Kluckhohn, 1945; Langness, 1965), but they did yield much that was revealing about the experiences of people whose lives had been in large measure determined by more powerful "others" and who had been characteristically denied the opportunity to speak for themselves. As one social worker told me, "They can't possibly have anything worth saying!"

My role at OH was one of the participant observer. As I had a set of official functions to perform, I could not be simply a neutral "social scientist." It should be kept in mind, however, that my function, while clear to the staff, was rather hazy as far as clients were concerned. It was apparent to them that I was a teacher of some kind, but because I came and went on an irregular schedule, they knew I was not a member of the staff. Moreover, I tried consistently to be minimally disruptive and always deferred questions about agency policy to the responsible staff members. The clients therefore saw me as one with some sort of prestige, but who declined to exercise authority. I was thus to be treated with respect but not necessarily deference, and after a while, I was seen as a confidante—my tapes of our encounters were explicitly for us alone and not for the official records of the agency.

In most interview sessions, I allowed the clients to set the agenda. They seemed to respond very well to this freedom as they were used to being questioned in very strict, clinical formats that allowed them little room for sorting through their thoughts and finding ways to express their feelings. My role as an interviewer was, in part, to guide the discourse back to topics "relevant" to the subjects' lives, although I tried to let them determine relevance. It was more important to be a good listener, a sympathetic audience to encourage and nurture communication. As a result, the life histories tend to ramble more than might be the case in the ethnography of a set of "normal" informants. But, as will be seen, this extremely loose and open-ended interview style by no means yielded random, meaningless chitchat. Moreover, because the interviews were conducted over a period of several years in most cases, they are documents of ongoing and evolving interactions rather than final, retrospective views of life.

It is also worth noting that the life histories under study here represent the mutual efforts of researcher and subject. I cannot claim that the metaphors of self that my respondents chose to convey to me would be those that they would convey to interviewers who presented them with other kinds of feedback. (I *think* my respondents are consistent in their self-images, but depending on the way they interpret others who talk to them, their narrative means might have to be adjusted to communicate those images.) The life histories are thus multivocalic records of encounters between particular people at particular times in their lives. . . .

Given the special nature of my informants and the very small number of texts under study, I could not possibly make a case for using these narratives as sources for generalization about the culture. But I am reluctant to leave them simply as highly personal records of unique individuals in isolated encounters. I therefore suggest that it is possible to make wider sense of such narratives—to see how otherwise inarticulate, deviant, stigmatized people can create meaningful, "shareable," systematic scenarios through which to convey metaphors of their selfhood—by concentrating on the regularities of their forms rather than on the idiosyncrasies of their contents. I further contend that even the brief narratives of mentally retarded subjects can demonstrate this sort of formal regularity.

LIFE HISTORIES OF MENTALLY RETARDED ADULTS

[There are four life histories in the original article; only two are presented here.]

Tyrell Stokes

Tyrell is now 25 years old. He had been a client at OH for three years and then graduated to full independence in the community. He lived on his own for two years but had recently returned. Tyrell grew up in "the Projects," subsidized low-income housing in the city. He never knew either of his parents, having lived as a child with various relatives, none of whom he cares to talk about. He spent time in a juvenile detention facility for purse snatching. After his release, he lived by his wits on the streets and was ultimately arrested on a weapons charge. He spent a brief time in jail (adult status) before being sent to OH. During all that time, he never received special training, and until he came to OH, he had never heard himself referred to as mentally retarded. He is extremely polished in his social manner and presents a very "cool" face to the world, but he is completely deficient in the most basic academic skills: "I'll tell you how dumb I was. Once I robbed this old lady. She had a bunch of change in her pocketbook. It was a load of pennies—I know that now. But boy! I thought I hit it big! Lookit all that money!" Even after extensive exposure to the OH programs, his academic skills remain marginal. He has also resisted vocational training. Yet he is by far the most articulate of all the clients, the most easily poised in social settings. "Well, you know," he says, "long as I don't have to read and write for nobody they think I'm the baddest dude they ever seen—everybody says I remind them of Eddie Murphy."

Tyrell was eager to graduate. During his first stint at OH, he was openly scornful of the program, although he was grateful for "three hots and a cot." But on his own, he quickly lost his one "honest" job. He fathered a child by the sister of a friend, but he has never assumed a family role, although he still sees the woman and the baby every so often: "Hell, that little baby got enough problems in this world without havin' Tyrell Stokes hangin' around tryin' to be his daddy." He started drinking heavily but always seemed to end up his wanderings in the parking lot of the apartment complex where two other OH graduates were living. They told one of the staffers that Tyrell kept coming around, and she finally convinced him that he had nothing to lose by going back and trying more seriously to learn some real skills.

Since his return, he has stopped drinking but is no more attentive to the training programs. He is terrified at the prospect of going back out on the streets, yet is distressed at the prospect of continuing to rely on OH, where he has to live with "all these weird dudes." He continues to affect a jaunty air, but he is thoroughly frustrated at what his life has become and thoroughly confused about what the future holds.

Tyrell is a classic denier (Zetlin and Turner, 1984). He has only the sketchiest understanding of his handicap and, in any case, will not admit that it has anything to do with his current problems: "I know a whole lotta dudes out on the streets just as stupid as me, but they're all rich. Nice cars, fine women, fancy clothes. It just ain't fair." Tyrell has built this conviction into a consistent philosophy. At first, when I heard him talk about his life and hard times, I assumed that he would be particularly resentful toward White people. I gradually learned, however, that his tormentors were not racially categorized: "Black, White—what the hell? The way I see it, anybody'll get you in the ass if he thinks you can't fight back." I asked him if he thought that I would try to hurt him in some way. "Nah," he said after some reflection. "You're a—what? Teacher? Social worker? Something like that. All you people are losers like me. Never met a 'bad' social worker."

The consistency of this Hobbesian view of society gives Tyrell's autobiography an "oratorical" character (Howarth, 1980). He is always careful to use his reminiscences to prove his central thesis. Despite his casual manner, he rarely says anything off the cuff. He is always trying to make his listeners understand the basic dog-eat-dog nature of the world. Indeed, he began the following story with an explicit instruction to me to make sure that it is accurately recorded:

> You got this story down straight, now? It's like this: Juanita [the girl he got pregnant] never did know nothing about me. How could she know I was poison for her? All she knew was on the surface and that was fine, fine, fine. But I knew what I was, and that's all that mattered. I could tell what she wanted, and I knew she couldn't see me for what I am. So one night I says to her, "Let's go to [the most expensive restaurant in town]." She says, "How on earth?" I says, "Don't worry, baby, you're with Tyrell Stokes now." So she borrows her sister's best dress and fixes her hair and gets done up all like Whitney Houston. I wanted her real bad right then—more than ever. But I had to control it. Me? I show up in cutoffs and some old Nikes I fished out of a dumpster. She didn't say nothing. So we get there and this guy at the

door says, "Can't you read? Jacket and tie required, sir." Sir! I says, "No, *sir*, I *can't* read. I am too fuckin' bad to read your fuckin' sign." He didn't say nothing. "And what's more, *sir*, I don't have no money to pay for your fuckin' food even if you do got the balls to let me in." Poor Juanita was crying. But she didn't say nothing. So I says to the guy, "I'll tell you how bad I am. If I feel like it, I'm gonna take a leak right in that fountain!" And I start to go over, but a couple of waiters ran out and tossed me outside. I guess if they didn't, I'd-a have to take that leak for sure! Juanita didn't say nothing, but she called her brother and asked him to pick her up to drive her home. I stood with her till I seen his car comin', then I took off. I run and run till I just about puked. I didn't even know where I ended up. But she never said a word. But I had to make her see what I was before it was too late.

Although the story itself is wrenchingly emotional, it is introduced with steady calculation. He is also the calculating maker of his own downfall. So eager is he to demonstrate his hypothesis that in this story he deliberately engineers a scenario that could not have ended happily. There is no reason why he could not have taken the young lady on a pleasant, ordinary dinner date, but instead he had to set himself up for a spectacularly humiliating failure lest the poor girl miss the point that things *always* end badly when he is involved.

Tyrell is resignedly tolerant of others, especially OH clients, who do not see life as he does: "They're just dummies, right? What can you expect? I try to tell them the way it is, but it's like nobody's home when you talk to them. Guess they'll have to spend a couple of months in lockup like me before they'll really learn."

Tyrell offers himself as a prototypic victim of an unjust system—despite his good looks and charm, he cannot get anywhere, probably because of the vicious jealousy of the "bad" people out there. Tyrell the paradigmatic martyr is the protagonist in a "self-absolutory" strategy for the mythological rearrangement of his life (Hankiss, 1981). His self-image is negative, but he does not believe that he ever had a chance at something better. He is not speaking specifically of the shortcomings of his own early life; he means more generally the malign nature of society that will always take advantage of a "born loser" like himself.

Nico Petrakis

Nico is 29 years old, although his giggly manner makes him seem more like an adolescent. He was born and raised in a small port town near OH that has long been a center of Greek immigration. Although it has "gone touristy" in the past decade, the town remains a close-knit haven of Greek family, religious, and other cultural values. Nico's retardation was recognized but not given any special emphasis outside school. There were always caring relatives and family friends to help and encourage him, and he was allowed to work in his uncle's dockside café, even earning a small but regular salary there as a cook's helper when he got older. Nico's formal academic skills are good, but he has had a problem matching his behavioral responses to his emotions. He opts to act "silly" rather than try to sort out a more nuanced set of responses to life's challenges.

Nico's particular problem has been dealing with anger. He has decided that it would be "ungrateful" of him ever to admit that things were not to his liking, especially things done by his family. He therefore tended to let his frustrations seethe beneath his giggling exterior. At the flashpoint, he used to retire to his bedroom or to the café storeroom to kick the walls. As he got bigger and stronger, he damaged a fair amount of masonry. His parents were willing to tolerate these outbursts up to the point where they began to threaten the family's very respectable image in the community. They reluctantly agreed to place him in a private supervised boarding home, but after a year's time, they were overcome with remorse and brought him home. Thoroughly confused, Nico got more and more out of control.

Then, after his father heard about OH from a relative who was a high school guidance counselor, he decided that Nico could benefit from the rigorous behavioral training offered there. So Nico was enrolled as a private (i.e., not court adjudicated) client. He spent two years participating in the full program and then graduated to a more lightly supervised apartment program. He is now working at a steady job on the serving line at a busy cafeteria in a big mall. Now that he is "fixed," his family wants him to come back home. Nico does not want to hurt their feelings, but he is afraid that he will relapse if he leaves the care of OH.

Nico is the only one of my main informants with strong and generally positive ties to a community beyond OH, and it is not surprising that he tells much of his story in terms of that community. He is not as adept as the other three in forming coherent narratives, but he leaves no doubt that he is very proud of his heritage and is eager to tell others about it.

Nico does not, however, have a highly visible concept of self. He always deflects discussions of himself onto his family. If asked, for example, what he did at the café, he will instead launch into a disjointed set of anecdotes about his uncle who owned the café. Nico is a fully engaged member of his community. He is simply more comfortable talking about the group than about his special place in it.

Nico copes by means of passing (Zetlin and Turner, 1984). He is well aware of his deficits but tries to put himself in situations where they will not be noticeable. He often asks, "Am I OK? Do I look right?" He winces when he asks such questions: "Don't wanna hurt these guys' feelings," he explains. "I just don't wanna look like a retard." On the other hand, he is not above using his retardation to get himself out of sticky situations. He tells of once encountering an irate customer at the cafeteria. The man wanted to punch him out for some imagined offense. Nico started giggling hysterically until the bully went away: "Better he think I'm a retard than he beat me up!"

Nico savors his past the way that [the other case histories] do not. But it is very difficult for him to reconstruct it in words; despite his superior academic skills, he is far less articulate than they in ordinary conversation. Nico's autobiography exists as a "text" only because I kept asking him prompting questions, as the following excerpt demonstrates:

[Researcher: Tell me about what you did at your uncle's café.]

Yes, Uncle John. He's a great guy. I really love him.

[R: What did you do there?]

He cooks all his own food. Even bakes. Bread, cakes.

[R: Did you help him?]

He opens every day for breakfast and then he stays open until really late. He never likes to turn people away.

[R: Did you help him in the kitchen?]

Oh yeah. I like to help. He's just like my Pop. They always want to help people. That's why he bought the café when he retired. He wanted to help people. People always need good food, he says.

[R: Tell me about Epiphany.]

Yes. It's our great day. Everybody comes to town, even people from very far away who moved away. They all come back. The Archbishop comes to bless the cross. He throws it in the Bay. The boys dive for it. Who gets it gets good luck all year. There's always a party at the café for the winner.

[R: Did any of your brothers ever win?]

No, but my cousin Al came close one year. The year the Garofalous boy won it. But it's OK—he's like family, too.

[R: What happens at the café on Epiphany?]

Big party. All day long. Sometimes even free sandwiches for the people out on the dock. Singing, dancing. Uncle John never closes down at all on Epiphany.

[Did you wait on tables for that big crowd?]

Sure. My brothers and sisters, all my cousins. Everybody helps out. Everybody has something to do. My Mom is a great singer. She sings Greek songs. Italian songs. Even Spanish songs.

[R: Can you sing any Greek songs?]

A little. But my Mom has a beautiful voice. So does my brother Lou. Not my brother Steve. But he's real smart in school, so he don't have to sing, Pop says. He helps out at the café too. He keeps the books for Uncle John. He studies to be a CIA.

[R: Do you mean a CPA, an accountant?]

Yeah, that too. One year he decided he wanted to dive for the cross, but he couldn't swim so good like some of the other guys. He said, "Don't tell Mom." I didn't tell her. He didn't win, but he didn't drown either, so he says it was all worth it.

[R: Did you ever want to dive?]

No. Al's a *really* good swimmer, though. Later he taught Steve to swim better, but Steve said his diving days were over.

Although it may appear that Nico was not able to respond to me very effectively, he was very pleased to participate and was especially delighted to learn that I had come from an ethnic background that, while not Greek, is similar to it in many ways. He felt that I could understand the mixture of affection and bewilderment that he felt about his community, with its promise of security, and all the potential suffocation that went along with it. Nevertheless, his reminiscences do not have a "shape" independent of our interaction. Nico's is the [more] clearly *dialogic* of the [two] autobiographies.

In spite of this drawback, Nico certainly has worked out his own metaphor. His is a "dynastic" story (Hankiss, 1981). He gives the impression of a man with a very positive self-image. He believes that he is making progress in handling himself appropriately, and he knows that in the eyes of society he is now doing well at a real, adult job. On the whole, he thinks of himself as a well-balanced, happy man with decent prospects. There is even a bride in the offing—a girl "from the Other Side" being sent to him by an aunt. He attributes this fortunate status to his upbringing in the bosom of a large, caring family and the sound traditions of the ethnic community.

This metaphor often takes on an aspect of noblesse oblige. Nico's family taught him to work for what he needed and to take pride in honest work; nevertheless, those who were sick or otherwise unfortunate needed to be helped if they were "family." Thus, Nico treats the other OH clients as a surrogate family, and he is always helping them by lending money or giving them his tapes, clothes, or bicycle. He never refuses to help anyone read or tell time or make change. He is not at all supercilious in these ministrations and appears to be genuinely liked and appreciated by all the others.

CONCLUSIONS

In the material discussed, we can see that there is a suggestive associational relationship between the social coping strategies of deinstitutionalized mentally retarded adults (as detailed by Zetlin and Turner, 1984) and the development of consistent self-images. Those self-images are in turn correlated with the adoption of consistent autobiographical forms that convey metaphors of the stigmatized self. Thus, Nico, who has a very positive self-image, chooses to cope by means of strategies that allow him to minimize the effects of his handicap. He has integrated his retardation more or less comfortably into his self-image and so has no need to deny it; in fact, he can use it for strategic defensive purposes when necessary. On the other hand, Tyrell's self-image is very negative, but his feelings about himself are not solely the result of despair over his handicap—indeed, the handicap hardly figures in his worldview of omnipresent oppression. For him, denial is possible because his retardation is the least important burden that he bears in a world of woe. . . .

My autobiographical research demonstrates the ability of mentally retarded people to adopt consistent behavior patterns that enable them to cope in the noninstitutional community. It is therefore a potentially useful addition to the repertoire of ethnographers working among stigmatized and disabled subjects. My contention, however, is that the life history method may not be primarily useful in determining the content of a "culture of deviance," although it can certainly enrich our understanding of what the policy of deinstitutionalization has meant in the lives of its supposed beneficiaries. Rather, it is a way of understanding how deviants manipulate symbolic forms in order to adapt and communicate with the "mainstream" culture in which they must live.

This research reaffirms the implications in the current literature that the adaptive strategies of stigmatized deviants like persons with mental retardation are more than responses of the moment—they reflect a person's preexisting internalized self-image and enhance that image by facilitating social interactions. We may now add that it is possible to encode such self-images in symbolic form, such that when a person tells a life story, meaningful information can be conveyed through the *form* of the story, even when the subject manifests serious linguistic deficits. The autobiography is organized so as to bring to the fore recognizable metaphors of the stigmatized self that resonate with the perceived audience. It is a means to bridge the gap between the "mainstream" and the world of meaning of a heretofore dispossessed and unheard deviant population.

References

Dollard, J. 1935. *Criteria for the Life History.* New York: P. Smith.

Hankiss, A. 1981. "Ontologies of the Self: On the Metaphorical Rearranging of One's Life History," pp. 203–210 in *Biography and Society: The Life History Approach in the Social Sciences,* edited by D. Bertaux. Beverly Hills, CA: Sage.

Howarth, W. L. 1980. "Some Principles of Autobiography," pp. 86–114 in *Autobiography: Essays Theoretical and Critical,* edited by J. Olney. Princeton, NJ: Princeton University Press.

Kluckhohn, C. 1945. "The Personal Document in Anthropological Science," pp. 78–193 in *The Use of Personal Documents in History, Anthropology, and Sociology,* edited by L. Gottschalk, C. Kluckhohn, and R. Angell. New York: Social Science Research Council.

Langness, L. L. 1965. *The Life History in Anthropological Science.* New York: Holt, Rinehart & Winston.

Zetlin, A. G., and J. L. Turner. 1984. Self-Perspectives on Being Handicapped: Stigma and Adjustment, pp. 93–120 in *Lives in Process: Mildly Retarded Adults in a Large City,* edited by R. B. Edgerton. Washington, DC: American Association on Mental Deficiency.

48

Cross–Cultural Patterns in Eating Disorders

JENNIFER E. PATE,
University of Texas

ANDRES J. PUMARIEGA,
University of South Carolina

COLLEEN HESTER,
University of St. Thomas

DAVID M. GARNER,
Beck Institute of Cognitive Therapy and Research

It has been noted that eating disorders (anorexia nervosa, bulimia, and their variants) are unique because they appear to be the only form of psychopathology in which culture appears to play a major role in determining prevalence (Yates, 1990). In the past, it was commonly believed that these disorders were primarily found in young women from achievement-oriented, upper-middle-class families from ethnic backgrounds where food was emphasized as a means of affective expression (Bruch, 1973). For this reason, eating disorders have been considered to be culture-bound syndromes, constellations of symptoms that are restricted to a particular culture or group of cultures (Prince, 1983). However, it appears that the prevalence of these disorders may be increasing dramatically among all social classes and ethnic groups in the United States as well as in a number of other nations with diverse cultures (Jones et al., 1980; Yates, 1989).

Several authors have suggested that changes in cultural values and attitudes may play a significant role in this increase in the development, incidence, and prevalence of eating disorders (Bruch, 1973; Garner and Garfinkel, 1980; Pumariega, 1986). The rise in the prevalence of eating disorders may be a result of the wider adoption of the ideal that thinness has come to symbolize

Reprinted from the authors' article, "Cross-Cultural Patterns in Eating Disorders: A Review," *Journal of American Academy of Child and Adolescent Psychiatry*, 31 (September 1992):802–809.

in Western culture; an ideal symbolizing self-discipline, control, sexual liberation, assertiveness, competitiveness, and affiliation with a higher socioeconomic class, as well as the traditional value of attractiveness (Garner et al., 1983; Nasser, 1988). However, the extent to which this ideal influences the development of eating disorders in non-Western cultures is unclear (Bruch, 1973; Crisp et al., 1976; Nasser, 1988; Prince, 1983). The purpose of the present review of studies from different regions of the United States and other countries is to further clarify possible cultural factors that play a role in the development of eating disorders.

EATING DISORDERS IN DIFFERENT AMERICAN ETHNIC GROUPS

A century ago, Fenwick (1880) observed that anorexia nervosa was more common in the "wealthier classes of society than those who have to procure their bread by daily labor" (p. 107). Bruch (1966) was one of the first modern investigators to suggest a relationship between sociocultural factors and the development of eating disorders. In her series of 43 patients with anorexia nervosa, there were seven Catholics, 11 Protestants, and 25 Jewish individuals. Ten of these individuals came from an upper-class background, 23 from a middle-class background, and six individuals were from a lower-class background. She noted the "conspicuous absence of Negro patients," despite the fact that there were a proportionate number of blacks hospitalized for other problems at the time of her study. She concluded that the main psychological conflicts centered around a struggle for control, a sense of identity, and a sense of effectiveness, with the relentless pursuit of thinness being a final step in this effort. She attributed such attitudes to the strong achievement orientations and psychological insensitivity of the upwardly mobile social and cultural backgrounds of the patients' families.

Rowland (1970), on the other hand, found a high proportion of individuals from lower- and middle-class backgrounds (60 percent and 34 percent, respectively) in his sample. Only 6 percent of his sample was from an upper-class background. Of the 30 patients in his sample, 47 percent were Catholic, 43 percent were Jewish, and only 10 percent were Protestant. Because of the majority of Italian and Jewish individuals (17 of 30) in this study, Rowland (1970) suggested a possible relationship between cultural origin and the importance of food, thus predisposing Jewish, Catholic, and Italian populations to a risk of developing an eating disorder. No black individuals were found in his sample.

Theander (1970) suggested that eating disorders may become more prevalent among all social classes as attitudes about such issues as achievement, appearance, weight, and control become more pervasive throughout all sectors of society.

Although several authors have noted an underrepresentation of black individuals with anorexia nervosa and bulimia in their studies (Garfinkel and Garner, 1982; Gray et al., 1987), there is a growing consensus that the prevalence of anorexia nervosa in the black population is most likely higher than previously thought and is currently on the rise (Hsu, 1987; Pumariega et al., 1984). The reasons for this increase may be attributed to changing referral patterns, greater awareness, and improved case detection, along with increasing use of the health care system by blacks (Crisp et al., 1976; Holden and Robinson, 1988), changing socioeconomic demography with increased exposure to the pressure related to upward social mobility (Andersen and Hay, 1985), and a wider adoption of expectations about body shape and appearance (Hsu, 1987). In other words, it is possible that thinness is becoming as valued by black culture as it is by Caucasian culture (Hsu, 1987). . . .

Very little has been noted about the prevalence and factors associated with eating disorders in Asian-Americans and native Americans. Kope and Sack (1987) described three cases of anorexia nervosa that were documented in Vietnamese refugees. The three individuals came from middle or upper class families that experienced a loss of status concomitant with the Communist takeover that caused them to leave their homeland. Each of these girls had also experienced a major object loss; two of the girls were separated from both parents, and one was separated from her mother.

Yates (1989) has documented cases of anorexia nervosa in adolescent native American girls who have come from the Navajo community in Tucson, Arizona. The author states that in each instance, these individuals were children of families who had moved off the reservation, were high achieving, and expected their children to succeed. "The painful thinness of these anorexic girls seemed to be a repudiation of the image of the traditional woman on the reservation" (Yates, 1989; p. 816). . . .

Van Den Broucke and Vandereycken (1986) studied fourteen European exchange students who were diagnosed with an eating disorder after coming to the United States. The authors suggested that the experience of encountering a culture clash was one of the possible predisposing or precipitating factors that could play a role in the development of an eating disorder. The authors suggest that in addition to the more usual causes of an eating disorder, adolescent exchange students are confronted with a sudden separation from the family of origin, which may create a serious challenge to the individual's autonomy. Furthermore, the adjustment to new social and familial interaction patterns may lead to unique stresses that can potentiate an eating disorder. Particularly, when exchange students come from upper or middle class families with heightened performance expectations, they may be at an increased risk for eating or other adjustment problems.

Few systematic studies have attempted to examine the role of culture and acculturation to American culture in the development and outcome of eating disorders. In a comparative and correlational study of acculturation and eating attitudes in white and Hispanic adolescent girls between the ages of 16 and 18, Pumariega (1986) compared the Eating Attitudes Test (EAT) scores (Garner and Garfinkel, 1979) of Hispanic subjects to those of a group of predominantly white subjects from the southern United States. Although the two groups exhibited similar scores on the EAT, there was a significant correlation between acculturation and higher EAT scores in the Hispanic group. There was also a positive but nonsignificant correlation between socioeconomic status, both current and projected, and higher EAT scores. The author noted that the results supported the hypothesis that cultural factors are related to a higher prevalence of eating disorders. However, he notes that the results fail to fully support a hypothesized relationship between higher socioeconomic status and vulnerability to eating disorders. He suggests that greater adherence to the Western culture may increase an individual's vulnerability toward the development of eating disorders (Pumariega, 1986)

EATING DISORDERS IN CULTURES ABROAD

The psychiatric literature from most countries suggests that anorexia nervosa and bulimia are present but are relatively rare. There is a growing body of literature that indicates at least comparable prevalence in Western-oriented countries and increasing prevalence in developing, Third World nations. The literature from Third World nations does not typically discuss chronic diseases and disorders, because medical professionals are preoccupied with more pressing needs (Dolan, 1991). Nasser (1986) questions the accuracy of Third World findings because of methodological problems, such as the absence of operational criteria to diagnose the syndrome of anorexia nervosa. These disorders have been commonly viewed as manifestations of hysteria or anxiety and not as specific psychiatric entities.

Europe

Several authors have studied anorexia nervosa in European countries, particularly Sweden (Norring and Sohlberg, 1988; Theander, 1970) and Germany (Steinhausen, 1984). Theander (1970) studied 94 individuals in Sweden with anorexia nervosa over a 30-year period. The incidence of this disorder increased throughout the study from 0.24 cases per 100,000 inhabitants during the first decade of the study to 0.45 cases during the last decade of the study (1951 to 1960). . . .

To investigate the incidence of anorexia nervosa over a 20-year period, Willi and Grossmann (1983) reviewed the case histories of females hospitalized in various medical, psychiatric, and pediatric clinics in Zurich, Switzerland during randomly selected 3-year periods. The authors documented an increase in the incidence of this disorder from 0.38 per 100,000 for 1956 to 1958, to 0.55 per 100,000 during 1963 to 1965 to 1.12 per 100,000 during 1973 to 1975. . . .

Lacey and Dolan (1988) presented the first report of nonwhite, normal body weight bulimics in the United Kingdom. Of the five subjects in this study, one was Pakistani, one was Jamaican, and three were from mixed racial backgrounds (two Afro-Caribbean/English, one African/Indian). All of the subjects were from the same catchment area in southwest London. In a comparison with white bulimic patients from the same area, both groups were similar in clinical presentation. However, the nonwhite subjects reported emotional deprivation that was not encountered by the white subjects. This deprivation included family distress, divorce, separation from their parents at an early age, and incestuous abuse. The five nonwhite subjects in this study all showed a poor response to treatment.

Furnham and Alibhai (1983) compared differences in the perception of female body shapes in individuals of Kenyan Asian, Kenyan British, and British origin to test their hypothesis that social and cultural factors play a dominant role in the perception of one's own and other's body shapes. As the authors predicted, the Kenyan Asians tended to perceive thin female shapes slightly more negatively and fat shapes significantly more positively than a comparable British group. It was also noted that the British Kenyans tended to have more similar perceptions to the British than the Kenyan group.

In an epidemiological study of anorexia nervosa comparing Greek adolescents living in Germany with Greek adolescents living in Greece, Fichter et al. (1983) studied three samples of Greek students between the ages of 13 and 19 years of age. Two samples were composed of subjects living in Greek towns, and the third sample represented Greek subjects residing in Munich. In the first part of the study, the authors recorded the subject's height and weight, obtained details of menstrual history, and administered the Anorexia Nervosa Inventory for Self-Rating. In the second stage of the study, subjects who were suspected of having anorexia nervosa participated in a semistructured interview. The authors noted that there was some evidence that the prevalence of anorexia nervosa was higher in the sample of Greek girls in Germany than in the sample of Greek girls who remained in Greece. This finding may be the result of difficulties that individuals in migrant families encounter when attempting to cope with the new social influences that affect family structure, values, and norms. The authors noted that while the idealization of dieting and slimness was strong for both groups, it was more pronounced for the Greek girls in Greece compared with those living in Germany.

Africa and The Middle East

In a study in northern Sudan, El-Sarrag (1968) noted that it is difficult to determine the exact prevalence of anorexia nervosa, as well as other psychiatric disorders, because many patients either do not seek treatment at all or they are treated by native healers or Zar parties. El-Sarrag (1968) noted that anorexia nervosa is uncommon in this area, suggesting that this may be because people are undernourished. Also, obesity in the female is equated with sexual attractiveness and considered a sign of beauty.

Hooper and Garner (1986) utilized the Eating Disorder Inventory to study a group of black, white, and mixed race schoolgirls in Zimbabwe. The authors noted that binge eating was present within all three groups, with the mixed race showing the strongest tendency toward this behavior. Anorexic or anorexic-like behavior was considerably more prevalent among the white and mixed race schoolgirls than among the black schoolgirls.

In a study of psychiatric morbidity among university students in Egypt, Okasha et al. (1977) documented only two cases of anorexia nervosa of the 1,050 cases that were reviewed. They noted that the clinical picture of these cases was somewhat similar to those described in Western literature, but vomiting was more noticeable than food refusal, and response to therapy was better.

Nwaefuna (1981) reported a case of anorexia nervosa in Nigeria. The individual she described was a 22-year-old black woman with a six-year history of anorexia nervosa that had its onset during the course of her first pregnancy. The author notes that the patient had a history of parental and personal marital separation, was living with her mother, and had a history of precocious physical development that had resulted in her being teased by peers during adolescence. Nwaefuna's observations (1981) are consistent with those reported by Pumariega et al. (1984) regarding the pathogenesis of the disorder. . . .

In a comparative study of abnormal eating attitudes among Arab female students of both London and Cairo universities, Nasser (1986) identified six cases of bulimia nervosa in the London sample of 50, as opposed to none in the Cairo sample of 60 subjects. She attributed this difference to the impact of exposure to Western values.

The Far East

In a study examining the frequency of anorexia nervosa in Malaysia, Buhrich (1981) found 28 female and two male cases of a total of 60,000 psychiatric referrals. It was concluded that the disorder was very rare among Malays compared with Chinese and Indians.

Ong et al. (1982) described seven Chinese females with anorexia nervosa referred to a clinical setting in Singapore. The authors concluded that there is a low incidence of this disorder in Singapore, and it appears to present in a less severe manner than is commonly documented in Western countries.

Several authors have reported a marked increase in the prevalence of anorexia nervosa and bulimia nervosa in Japan (Kamata et al., 1987; Nakane and Umino, 1987). Suematsu et al. (1985) noted that the number of patients seeking treatment for anorexia nervosa had doubled between 1976 and 1981. The clinical presentation of this disorder in Japan appears to be similar to that of Western cultures. . . .

IMPORTANT ASSOCIATED FACTORS

There may be certain factors associated with ethnicity that influence the development of eating disorders.

Socioeconomic status has been documented as a factor that correlates positively with the prevalence of anorexia nervosa and bulimia (Anderson and Hay, 1985). Jones et al. (1980), in their epidemiological survey of anorexia nervosa in Monroe County, New York, found that there was little association between social class and the incidence of anorexia nervosa among children 14 years of age or younger. However, a definite association existed with higher social class in females who were 15 years of age or older, along with a higher prevalence rate. Crisp et al. (1976) reported a difference in the prevalence of anorexia nervosa between school girls attending private and public schools. The incidence of this disorder was 1 per 200 in private school girls versus 1 per 330 in public school girls 16 to 18 years of age. . . .

A number of studies have provided some support for the often made clinical observation of a positive relationship between the competitiveness of the environment (i.e., heightened performance demands) and the prevalence of anorexia nervosa (Boskind-White and White, 1983; Garner and Garfinkel, 1980). For example, female medical students were found to have a 15 percent lifetime prevalence of eating disorders (Herzog et al., 1985). There is a five times greater prevalence of bulimia, and substantially more binge eating symptoms, in university women than among working women (Hart and Ollendick, 1985). However, Garner, Olmsted, and Garfinkel (1983) noted that it is important to distinguish between weight preoccupation and actual clinical eating disorders. For example, certain features of anorexia nervosa, such as dieting and attitudes about shape, occur on a continuum and are commonly reported in subjects who are preoccupied with their weight. However, other characteristic features of eating disorders such as ineffectiveness, interoceptive awareness, and interpersonal distrust, as measured by the Eating Disorder Inventory, are less common in nonclinical samples. The symptomatic expression of anorexia nervosa and other eating disorders appears to represent a maladaptive attempt to cope with the pressure of growing up in a stressed environment. Furthermore, individuals at risk for eating disorders appear to rely excessively on the environment for their sense of self-worth, which makes them more vulnerable to cultural pressures to succeed (Garfinkel et al., 1980; Yates, 1989).

It has also been documented that women who serve as physical ideals or physical role models to other women, such as fashion models (Garner and Garfinkel, 1980), ballet dancers (Garner et al., 1987), cheerleaders (Lundholm and Littrell, 1986), and gymnasts (Calabrese, 1985) are more likely to develop an eating disorder (Yates, 1991). In these groups, the competitive values symbolized by their vocation within a cultural context can contribute to vulnerability to these disorders.

As noted earlier by Bruch (1973), Boskind-White and White (1983) suggest that the female adolescent is vulnerable to the development of an eating disorder, because the cultural message to be slim is constantly being transmitted to her through the family, peers, teachers, books, magazines, and television. In an effort to be accepted, she behaves in a way that is consistent with the beliefs and behaviors of people in the groups to which she aspires to belong. Such messages are particularly powerful within the competitive context discussed above. Boskind-White and White (1983) hypothesize that the conflict between the dual messages of conformity and competitiveness being presented to women in Western societies renders them particularly at risk for these disorders.

Although it has been argued that the clinical presentation of eating disorders has changed since the earliest case reported by Morton (1694), asceticism continues to be an important underlying dynamic in some individuals who develop these disorders (Rampling, 1985; Russell, 1985; Yates, 1991). The aims of ascetic practices, such as dietary restriction, have evolved from the pursuit of religious goals to the fulfillment of more narcissistic needs (Rampling, 1985; Yates, 1991). It has been repeatedly suggested that young women from close, competitive families resort to eating disorders such as anorexia nervosa or bulimia as an attempt to establish a sense of control and autonomy as they struggle to resolve their confusion regarding the female's role in society (Bruch, 1973; Turner, 1984). In addition to eating disorders, it is important to note that this asceticism may also be expressed through culturally accepted behaviors such as obligatory running (Yates, 1991). The paradox is that while asceticism may decline in the general population, it may be accentuated in susceptible individuals who are struggling to establish a sense of control in their lives. . . .

DIRECTIONS FOR FUTURE RESEARCH

Several authors have suggested a risk factor model in summarizing the role that culture plays in the development of eating disorders (Garner et al., 1983; Striegel-Moore et al., 1986). As Western society's influence augments the conflicts over issues such as the female's role in society, physical appearance and attractiveness, and impulse gratification and consumption, the impact on biologically or psychologically susceptible individuals potentially increases. Therefore, the susceptible individual will be more likely to express these cultural influences symptomatically through the development of eating disorders. The specific symptomatology that is demonstrated can also be influenced by cultural variables. Anorexia nervosa and bulimia predominate in the context of an ideology of slimness. However, it is also possible that in other cultural contexts other atypical forms of eating disorders may develop.

There is little question of the importance of cultural factors in the development of eating disorders. Even when material well-being is considered, there appears to be variation in the occurrence of these disorders both among American ethnic groups and between different nationalities. However, there is relatively little systematic empirical research on cross-cultural aspects of eating disorders. Furthermore, many of the reviews of the literature on this topic are not comprehensive and are biased by the author's emphasis on his/her country of origin (Dolan, 1991). A review by an author from a non-Western country may be useful for posing future research problems. It may also be important for researchers in non-Western settings to identify and operationalize criteria for subclinical or atypical forms of eating disorders that are unique to their particular culture. . . .

References

Andersen, A. E. and Hay, A. 1985. "Racial and Socioeconomic Influences in Anorexia Nervosa and Bulimia." *The International Journal of Eating Disorders*, 4(4):479–487.

Boskind-White, M. and White, W. C. 1983. *Bulimarexia: The Binge/Purge Cycle,* New York: W. W. Norton.

Bruch, H. 1966. "Anorexia Nervosa and Its Differential Diagnosis." *J. Nerv. Ment. Dis.*, 141(5):555–566.

Bruch, H. 1973. *Eating Disorders: Obesity, Anorexia Nervosa and the Person Within*, New York: Basic Books.

Buhrich, N. 1981. "Frequency of Presentation of Anorexia Nervosa in Malaysia, Australia, and New Zealand." *J. Psychiatry*, 15:153–155.

Calabrese, L. H. 1985. "Nutritional and Medical Aspects of Gymnastics." *Clinical Sports Medicine*, 4:28.

Crisp, A. H., Palmer, R., and Kelney, R. 1976. "How Common Is Anorexia Nervosa: A Prevalence Study." *Br. J. Psychiatry*, 128:549–554.

Dolan, B. 1991. "Cross-Cultural Aspects of Anorexia Nervosa and Bulimia: A Review." *The International Journal of Eating Disorders*, 10(1):67–78.

El-Sarrag, M. E. 1968. "Psychiatry in the Northern Sudan: A Study in Comparative Psychiatry." *Br. J. Psychiatry*, 114:946–948.

Fenwick, S. 1880. *On Atrophy of the Stomach and on the Nervous Affections of the Digestive Organs*, London: Churchill Foster.

Fichter, M. M., Weyerer, S., Sourdi, L., and Sourdi, Z. 1983. The Epidemiology of Anorexia Nervosa: A Comparison of Greek Adolescents Living in Germany and Greek Adolescents Living in Greece, pp. 95–105. In *Anorexia Nervosa: Recent Developments in Research*, eds. P. L. Darby, P. E. Garfinkel, D. M. Garner, and D. V. Coscina, New York: Alan R. Liss.

Furnham, A. and Alibhai, N. 1983. "Cross-Cultural Differences in the Perception of Female Body Shapes." *Psychol. Med.*, 13:829–837.

Garfinkel, P. E. and Garner, D. M. 1982. *Anorexia Nervosa: A Multidimensional Perspective*, New York: Brunner/Mazel.

Garfinkel, P. E. Moldofsky, H., and Garner, D. M. 1980. "The Heterogeneity of Anorexia Nervosa." *Arch. Gen. Psychiatry*, 37:1036–1040.

Garner, D. M. and Garfinkel, P. E. 1979. "The Eating Attitudes Test: An Index of the Symptoms of Anorexia Nervosa." *Psychol. Med.*, 9:273–279.

Garner, D. M., Garfinkel, P. E., 1980. "Socio-Cultural Factors in the Development of Anorexia Nervosa." *Psychol. Med.*, 10:647–656.

Garner, D. M., Garfinkel, P. E., and Olmsted, M. P. 1983. "An Overview of Sociocultural Factors in the Development of Anorexia Nervosa, pp. 65–82. In *Anorexia Nervosa: Recent Developments in Research*, eds. P. L. Darby, P. and D. V. Coscina. New York: Alan R. Liss.

Garner, D. M., Garfinkel, P. E., and Bonato, D. P. 1987. "Body Image Measurement in Eating Disorders." *Ad. Psychosom. Med.*, 17:119–133.

Garner, D. M., Olmsted, M. P., and Garfinkel, P. E. 1983. "Does Anorexia Nervosa Occur on a Continuum?: Subgroups of Weight-Preoccupied Women and Their Relationship to Anorexia Nervosa." *The International Journal of Eating Disorders*, 2(4):11–20.

Garner, D. M., Rockert, W., and Olmstead, M. P. 1987. "A Prospective Study of Eating Disturbances in the Ballet." *Psychotherapy and Psychopharmacology*, 48:170–175.

Gray, J. J., Ford, K., and Kelly, L. M. 1987. "The Prevalence of Bulimia in a Black College Population." *The International Journal of Eating Disorders*, 6(6):733–740.

Hart, K. J. and Ollendick, T. H. 1985. "Prevalence of Bulimia in Working and University Women." *Am. J. Psychiatry*, 142:851–854.

Herzog, D. B., Pepose, M., Norman, D. K., and Rigotti, M. A. 1985. "Eating Disorders and Social Maladjustment in Female Medical Students." *J. Nerv. Ment. Dis.*, 173:734–737.

Holden, N. L. and Robinson, P. H. 1988. "Anorexia Nervosa and Bulimia Nervosa in British Blacks." *Br. J. Psychiatry,* 152:544–549.

Hooper, M. S. H. and Garner, D. M. 1986. "Application of the Eating Disorders Inventory to a Sample of Black, White, and Mixed Race Schoolgirls in Zimbabwe." *The International Journal of Eating Disorders,* 5(1):161–168.

Hsu, L. K. G. 1987. "Are the Eating Disorders Becoming More Common in Blacks." *The International Journal of Eating Disorders,* 6(1):113–124.

Jones, D., Fox, M., Babigian, H. and Hutton, H. 1980. "Epidemiology of Anorexia in Monroe County, New York: 1960–1976." *Psychosom. Med.,* 42:551–558.

Kamata, K., Nogami, Y. and Momma, K. 1987. "Binge-eating Among Female Students." *Jpn. J. Psychiatry Neurol.,* 41(1):151–152.

Kope, T. M. and Sack, W. H. 1987. "Anorexia Nervosa in Southeast Asian Refugees: A Report on Three Cases." *J. Am. Acad. Child Adolesc. Psychiatry,* 26(5):795–797.

Lacey, J. H. and Dolan, B. M. 1988. "Bulimia in British Blacks and Asians: A Catchment Area Study." *Br. J. Psychiatry,* 152:73–79.

Lundholm, J. K. and Littrell, J. M. 1986. "Desire for Thinness Among High School Cheerleaders." *Adolescence,* 21:573–579.

Morton, R. 1694. *Phthisologia: Or a Treatise of Consumptions,* London: Smith and Walford.

Nakane, A. and Umino, M. 1987. "Psychopathology of Anorexia Nervosa in Young Adolescence." *Jpn. J. Psychiatry Neurol.,* 41(1):153.

Nasser, M. 1986. "Comparative Study of the Prevalence of Abnormal Eating Attitudes Among Arab Female Students of Both London and Cairo Universities." *Psychol. Med.,* 16:621–625.

Nasser, M. 1988. "Culture and Weight Consciousness." *J. Psychosom. Res.,* 32(6):573–577.

Norring, C. and Sohlberg, S. 1988. "Eating Disorder Inventory in Sweden: Description, Cross-Cultural Comparison, and Clinical Utility." *Acta. Psychiatr, Scand.,* 78:567–575.

Nwaefuna, A. 1981. "Anorexia Nervosa in a Developing Country." *Br. J. Psychiatry,* 138:270–271.

Okasha, A., Kamel, M., Sadek, A., Lotaif, F. and Bishry, Z. 1977. "Psychiatric Morbidity Among University Students in Egypt." *Br. J. Psychiatry,* 131:149–154.

Ong, Y. L., Tsoi, W. F. and Cheah, J. S. 1982. "A Clinical and Psychosocial Study of Seven Cases of Anorexia Nervosa in Singapore." *Singapore Med. J.,* 23:255–261.

Prince, R. 1983. "Is Anorexia Nervosa a Culture-Bound Syndrome?" *Transcultural Psychiatry Research Review,* 20:299–300.

Pumariega, A. J. 1986. "Acculturation and Eating Attitudes in Adolescent Girls: A Comparative and Correlational Study." *J. Am. Acad. Child Adolesc. Psychiatry,* 25(2):276–279.

Pumariega, A. J., Edwards, P. and Mitchell, C. B. 1984. "Anorexia Nervosa in Black Adolescents." *J. Am. Acad. Child Adolesc. Psychiatry,* 23(1):111–114.

Rampling, D. 1985. "Ascetic Deals and Anorexia Nervosa." *J. Psychiatr. Res.,* 19:89–94.

Rowland, C. 1970. "Anorexia and Obesity." *International Psychiatry Clinics,* 7:37–137.

Russell, G. F. M. 1985. "The Changing Nature of Anorexia Nervosa: An Introduction to the Conference." *J. Psychiatr, Res.,* 19:101–108.

Steinhausen, H. C. 1984. "Transcultural Comparison of Eating Attitudes in Young Females and Anorectic Patients." *Archiv fur Psychiatrie und Nervenkrankheiten,* 234(3):198–201.

Striegel-Moore, R. H., Silberstein, L. R. and Rodin, J. 1986. "Towards an Understanding of Risk Factors of Bulimia." *Am. Psychol.,* 41:246–263.

Suematsu, H., Ishikawa, H. Kuboki, T. and Ito, T. 1985. "Statistical Studies on Anorexia Nervosa in Japan: Detailed Clinical Data on 1011 Patients." *Psychother. Psychosom.*, 43:96–103.

Theander, S. 1970. "Anorexia Nervosa: A Psychiatric Investigation of 94 Female Patients." *Acta. Psychiatr. Scand.*, 214:1–194.

Turner, B. S. 1984. *The Body and Society,* New York: Basil Blackwell.

Van Den Broucke, S. and Vandereycken, W. 1986. "Risk Factors for the Development of Eating Disorders in Adolescent Exchange Students: An Exploratory Survey." *J. Adolesc.*, 9:145–150.

Willi, J. and Grossmann, S. 1983. "Epidemiology of Anorexia Nervosa in a Defined Region of Switzerland." *Am. J. Psychiatry*, 140(5):564–567.

Yates, A. 1989. "Current Perspectives on the Eating Disorders: I. History, Psychological and Biological Aspects." *J. Am. Acad. Child Adolesc. Psychiatry*, 28(6):813–828.

Yates, A. 1990. "Current Perspectives on the Eating Disorders: II. Treatment, Outcome, and Research Directions." *J. Am. Acad. Child Adolesc. Psychiatry*, 29(1):1–9.

Yates, A. 1991. *Compulsive Exercise and the Eating Disorders: Toward and Integrated Theory of Activity.* New York: Brunner/Mazel.

49

Anorexics and Bulimics: Developing Deviant Identities

PENELOPE A. MCLORG AND DIANE E. TAUB
Southern Illinois University, Carbondale

Fear of being overweight—of being visually deviant—often leads to a striving for thinness, especially among women. In the extreme, this avoidance of over-weight engenders eating disorders, which themselves constitute deviance. Anorexia nervosa, or purposeful starvation, embodies visual as well as behav-ioral deviation. Anorexics weigh at least 15 percent less than normal weight standards for their age and height. This visual deviation results from a behav-ioral deviance characterized by self-starvation alone or in combination with excessive exercising, occasional binge-eating, vomiting, or laxative abuse. On the other hand, bulimia nervosa is in most cases only behaviorally deviant. It involves binge eating to be followed by vomiting, laxative abuse, fasting, or vig-orous exercising. Bulimics are not visually deviant because their weight is nor-mal or close to normal (Haller, 1992; Schlundt and Johnson, 1990).

Increasingly prevalent in the past few decades, anorexia and bulimia have emerged as major health problems. Approximately 2.5 percent of college stu-dents are anorexic, while between 4 and 19 percent are bulimic (Schlundt and Johnson, 1990). Six to 20 percent of anorexics die (Haller, 1992), though bulimia is less life-threatening (Giannini et al., 1990).

Eating disorders are most common among young, white, affluent (upper-middle to upper class) women in modern, industrialized countries (Hsu, 1989; Schlundt and Johnson, 1990). Anorexia occurs most often to two age groups: 13 to 14 and 17 to 18. As for bulimia, the usual age of onset is between 16 and 19 (Mitchell and Pyle, 1988).

Eating disorders have mostly been studied from medical and psychiatric perspectives. Such studies are deficient for obscuring the social facets of the disorders and ignoring the individuals' own definitions of their situations.

This article was specifically written for this reader.

Thus, in our research reported here, we focus on those two factors, analyzing how they are interrelated, especially the impact of negative societal reaction on the identities and activities of individuals with eating disorders.

METHODOLOGY

We derive our data from a self-help group called BANISH (Bulimics/Anorexics In Self-Help), which met at a university in an urban center of the mid-South. Founded by one of us (Taub), BANISH was advertised in local newspapers as offering a group experience for individuals who were anorexic or bulimic. Thirty people joined the group.

BANISH's demographic profile typifies what has been found in other studies (Schlundt and Johnson, 1990). Members ranged in ages from 19 to 36, with most being 21. All but one were white females. Most were college students; only 4 were nonstudents, of whom 3 had college degrees. Nearly all came from upper-middle or lower-upper-class households. The duration of eating disorder ranged from three to fifteen years.

The sole male and three of the females were anorexic; the remaining females were bulimic. Far fewer anorexics than bulimics showed up in this sample because in our society anorexia is less prevalent than bulimia (Schlundt and Johnson, 1990) and anorexics are more likely to deny having an eating disorder (Giannini et al., 1990).

We observed the group's weekly 2-hour meetings for two years. During the course of this study, 30 people attended at least one meeting. Attendance varied: 10 individuals came nearly every Sunday; 5 about twice a month; and the remaining 15 once a month or less, often when seeing their eating problems become "more severe" or "bizarre." At most meetings there were 12 members. Modeled after Alcoholics Anonymous, BANISH encouraged participants to discuss their backgrounds and experiences with others. The group constituted the only source of help for many members, who were reluctant to contact health professionals because of shame, embarrassment, or financial difficulties.

After two years of taking notes at the meetings, we conducted informal interviews with 15 members, each lasting from 2 to 4 hours. Chosen for their longer experience with eating disorders, these interviewees were asked to discuss in greater detail their comments made at the meetings. We were most interested in what led to their eating disorders, how others reacted to their actions, and how they interpreted and dealt with those reactions.

Aside from taking notes at group meetings and individual interviews, we were able to learn more about the subjects in other ways. This is because they visited Taub's office, telephoned both of us, and invited us to their homes or out for coffee. Even among the 15 who did not attend the meetings regularly, 10 contacted us once a month. These informal encounters fostered genuine communication and mutual trust, providing us with greater insight into the lives of anorexics and bulimics.

CONFORMITY

The data suggest that, ironically, conformity to conventional values serves as a precondition for becoming deviant. Like most anorexics and bulimics, our subjects started dieting in their teens. They were merely trying to conform to the cultural norm of thinness. In our society, slim bodies are considered most worthy and attractive, while overweight is seen as unhealthy, even offensive or disgusting. This slimness norm is most evident in advertising. Female models in newspaper, magazine, and TV ads are uniformly slender. And ads for diet aids and other similar products suggest that fatness is undesirable (Silverstein et al., 1986). The slimness norm also finds support in the family, where parents socialize children to desiring light body weight and slender shape. According to our subjects, their fathers were preoccupied with exercising and their mothers with food preparation. When those subjects dieted and lost weight, they were enthusiastically praised. Since society emphasizes physical appearance as more important for women than men to have, women feel much more pressured to conform to the slimness norm. Not surprisingly, in one survey, of the 56 percent of all women aged 24 to 54 who dieted, 76 percent did so for cosmetic rather than health reasons.

Among these dieters are some who may develop anorexia or bulimia because of their zealous conformity to the ideal of slimness. This specific conformity seems to be part and parcel of a general, overall pattern of conformity to various conventional values. As our data suggest, before our subjects became anorexic or bulimic, they generally did well in school, joining honor societies or academic clubs. They were also "model children" or "the pride and joy" of their parents, to whom they showed strong emotional attachment.

PRIMARY DEVIANCE

Zealous conformity to the slimness norm does not by itself necessarily lead to anorexia or bulimia. At least two other factors must be at work. One is constant failure to achieve or maintain a desired weight through dieting, exercise, or other means. This repeated failure is likely to compel the individual to resort to extreme, deviant ways of achieving weight loss, such as purposeful starvation or bingeing accompanied by vomiting or other purging methods. Another factor in the development of eating disorders is loss of control triggered by a stressful event, such as entering college, leaving home, or feeling rejected by the opposite sex. The extreme weight-loss efforts serve as coping mechanisms, helping the individual to deal with stress.

Initially, the individual succeeds in maintaining a lowered weight and slim appearance. Moreover, friends and family, unaware of the individual's eating disorders, may compliment the individual for losing weight and looking good. Thus, the individual may not see herself or himself as anorexic or bulimic. Such a person is what Lemert (1951) called a *primary deviant,* whose deviant self-image has not emerged despite the exhibition of deviant behavior such as purposely starving or bingeing and purging.

SECONDARY DEVIANCE

Primary deviance, however, usually leads to *secondary deviance,* in which the individual sees herself or himself as a deviant and this deviant self-image affects the individual's social roles and activities (Lemert, 1967). Anorexics and bulimics may begin to see themselves as deviant when they stop receiving compliments for their slimness or weight loss. This is the time when parents or friends become concerned about the anorexic appearing emaciated. The significant others become increasingly aware of the anorexic's compulsive exercising, preoccupation with preparing food but not consuming it, and ritu-alistic eating patterns (such as cutting food into minute pieces or eating only certain foods at prescribed times). As for bulimics, friends or family members begin to question how they can eat large amounts of food and still stay slim. The significant others may notice telltale marks on the bulimic's hand, which result from repeated inducement of vomiting. Some bulimics may get "caught in the act," bent over the commode.

Given those observations, friends and relatives will likely label the bingeing or purging individual as "anorexic" or "bulimic." Others will label the individ-ual a "starving waif" or "pig." Most significant in this labeling process is soci-ety's tendency to turn the individual's deviant status into the individual's *mas-ter status* (Becker, 1973). Thus, Nicole, a subject of our study, who had been known as the "school's brain," became known as the "school's anorexic."

This negative societal reaction to anorexics and bulimics produces certain consequences. Initially, anorexics tend to vigorously deny the label. Most of the subjects in our research felt that they were not "anorexic enough," not skinny enough. One subject, Robin, did not regard herself as having the "skeletal" appearance she associated with anorexia. These subjects found it difficult to differentiate between socially approved modes of weight loss, eat-ing less and exercising more, and the extremes of these behaviors. In fact, many of their activities—cheerleading, modeling, gymnastics, aerobics—rein-forced their belief that they were normal rather than deviant in trying to be thin. Like other anorexics, Chris felt that she was "ultra-healthy," with "total control" over her body. To Nicole, her anorexic weight was her "true" weight. By rejecting the deviant label, then, anorexics and bulimics remain as prima-ry deviants.

Sooner or later, however, they become secondary deviants by developing a deviant identity, seeing themselves as anorexics or bulimics. Some of our research subjects acknowledged their anorexia after realizing that their eating disorder disrupted their lives. Their inflexible eating patterns unsettled family meals and holiday gatherings. Their regimented life style of compulsively scheduled activities—exercising, school, and meals—precluded any sponta-neous social interactions. Compared with the anorexics, the bulimics were quicker to see themselves as deviant, considering their means of weight loss "abnormal" or "wrong and unhealthy." They further regarded their eating dis-order as indicative of "loss of control," regretting their self-indulgence, "shame," and "wasted time."

People with eating disorders also exhibit what Schur (1971) calls "role engulfment," centering activities on their deviant role so as to downgrade other roles. Among our research subjects, the obligations as students, family members, and friends became subordinate to the eating and weight-control rituals. Socializing, for example, was curtailed because it interfered with compulsive exercising, bingeing, or purging. The role engulfment further affects other aspects of the deviant's life. In a social situation, our research subjects often compared their body shapes and sizes with those of others, and were sensitized to comments about their appearance. They felt self-conscious around people who knew about their eating disorders. Robin, for example, imagined others "watching and whispering" behind her. While hospitalized, Denise felt she had to prove to others she had stopped vomiting, by keeping her bathroom door open. Other bulimics, who lived in dormitories, were reluctant to use the restroom lest several friends be huddling at the door and listening for vomiting.

People with eating disorders also tend to conceal their deviance from others. Thus, the bulimics in our research tried earnestly to hide their bulimia by bingeing and purging in secret. They felt that others regarded bulimia as "gross" and had little sympathy for the sufferer. It is relatively easy to conceal bulimia, because the bulimic's weight is approximately normal. But it is much harder to conceal anorexia because of the emaciated appearance. Some anorexics try to hide their problem by wearing large, padded clothes. Others become reconciled to their stigma. As Brian, one of our research subjects, said, "the stigma of anorexia is better than the stigma of being fat."

Finally, both anorexics and bulimics feel isolated or ostracized by others including some friends and family members. This is because they are often reminded that they are responsible for their eating disorder and that they are able to "get out of it if they try." They further feel discouraged by others' insensitivity to the complexities of eating disorders. In our research, many anorexics reported being told to "just eat more," while bulimics were enjoined to simply "stop eating so much." Not surprisingly, many such deviants find self-help groups like BANISH to be a haven, where they can freely discuss their problems with assurances of mutual understanding, empathy, and support.

SUMMARY

The development of anorexic or bulimic identities involves a sequence of conformity, primary deviance, and secondary deviance. With a background of exceptional conformity to conventional norms, especially the ideal of thinness, individuals subsequently engage in the primary deviance of starving or bingeing and purging. Negative societal reaction, primarily in the form of labeling the individuals as anorexics or bulimics, leads to secondary deviance, wherein they develop the deviant identities with tendencies toward role engulfment, deviance concealment, and feeling isolated.

References

Becker, Howard S. 1973. *Outsiders.* New York: Free Press.

Giannini, A. James, Michael Newman, and Mark Gold. 1990. "Anorexia and Bulimia." *American Family Physician* 41:1169–1176.

Haller, Ellen. 1992. "Eating Disorders: A Review and Update." *Western Journal of Medicine* 157:658–662.

Hsu, L.K.G. 1989. "The Gender Gap in Eating Disorders: Why Are the Eating Disorders More Common Among Women?" *Clinical Psychology Review* 9:393–407.

Lemert, Edwin M. 1951. *Social Psychology.* New York: McGraw-Hill.

Lemert, Edwin M. 1967. *Human Deviance, Social Problems and Social Control.* Englewood Cliffs, NJ: Prentice-Hall.

Mitchell, James E. and Richard L. Pyle. 1988. "The Diagnosis and Clinical Characteristics of Bulimia," pp. 267–273 in *The Eating Disorders: Medical and Psychological Bases of Diagnosis and Treatment*, edited by Barton J. Blinder, Barry F. Chaitlin, and Renee S. Goldstein. New York: PMA.

Schlundt, David G. and William G. Johnson. 1990. *Eating Disorders: Assessment and Treatment.* Boston: Allyn and Bacon.

Schur, Edwin M. 1971. *Labeling Deviant Behavior.* New York: Harper and Row.

Silverstein, Brett, Lauren Perdue, Barbara Peterson, and Eileen Kelly. 1986. "The Role of the Mass Media in Promoting a Thin Standard of Bodily Attractiveness for Women." *Sex Roles* 14:519–532.

50

Oops! A Very Embarrassing Story About Psychotherapy

VIRGINA RUTTER

Does psychotherapy work? Does professional training actually make therapists more effective? These are some of the questions that researchers are currently debating hotly across E-mail networks, at conferences, and, to a lesser extent, in psychotherapy journals.

The matter is scarcely insignificant. Some 16 million people a year use mental-health services such as psychotherapy. And an estimated 24 million more need help, though many of them get it outside the mental-health system.

Now, two heavyweight psychologists have completed a thorough review of the literature. Their findings are eye-opening—though you won't find the mental-health establishment calling a press conference.

The two psychologists report that years of experience, professional education, or lawful credentials do not determine the success of psychotherapy. Never mind that millions of dollars are spent each year on studies comparing the approaches of experienced therapists. Never mind that the more experienced, more educated therapists charge more money for their services. The outcome of therapy is not enhanced by training, education, or years of experience. It may not even matter whether there is a live therapist present!

This is the startling conclusion of Andrew Christensen, Ph.D., and Neil Jacobson, Ph.D. Their study, entitled "Who—Or What—Can Do Psychotherapy?" appeared in the January issue of *Psychological Science*, a publication put out by the politically brave American Psychological Society.

Christensen, professor of psychology at University of California at Los Angeles, and Jacobson, professor of psychology at the University of Washington, contend that no one has made much of an effort to look at therapy delivered by nonprofessionals, despite the fact that it proves just as effective, or more effective, than therapy performed by psychiatrists, psychologists, social workers, and family therapists.

Nor has anyone rushed to fund the study of inexpensive yet promising alternatives such as self-help and support groups led by nonprofessionals, to say nothing of self-administered treatments via self-help books or interactive computer programs—even though the American Psychiatric Association estimates that 15 million people in the United States participate in self-help groups.

"Most studies compare different types of professional treatments," Christensen notes. "It is discouraging, because the most common finding is that there is no difference among treatments. We suggest that more money be allocated to studying nonprofessional treatments—where the results are promising and cost less to achieve."

Comparing professional and nonprofessional treatments tells us more about what actually helps people get better, Christensen insists. He and Jacobson reviewed studies done since 1979 that asked: Are professionally trained therapists more effective than paraprofessional helpers without professional degrees but often with specific training? One study they reviewed showed no differences in the rates of psychological improvement when professional therapists—averaging 23 *years* of experience—were compared with liberal arts college professors having no experience or training. Both were "treating" disturbed college students.

The duo also discussed a 1979 review of 42 studies that compared professional and paraprofessional therapists. Only one component of the study demonstrated superiority of professionals; in 12, paraprofessionals actually helped people more. The remaining 29 found no differences.

Over the years, the data from the troublesome 1979 review have been reanalyzed using more stringent standards; each time the results have come back stronger for paraprofessionals. One study concluded: "Clients who seek help from paraprofessionals are more likely to achieve resolution of their problem than those who consult professionals." *Hmmm.*

"These are provocative findings for the psychotherapy community," note Christensen and Jacobson. "It is hard to imagine a study comparing trained and untrained surgeons, or trained and untrained electricians, for that matter. Dead patients in the first instance or dead trainees in the second could be the unfortunate outcome."

The difference between surgeons and psychotherapists has a lot to do with the difference between surgery and therapy. Across the board, psychotherapy researchers agree that a positive therapist/client relationship is the most important feature of successful treatment.

But get this—the Christensen and Jacobson report questions even the highly touted need for a therapist/client relationship. Self-administered treatments worked *just as well* as those delivered by live therapists, in certain cases. Computerized treatments have been shown to work for obesity, phobias, and depression.

Observes Christensen: "With most professions it is very clear there is a specific skill involved, but in psychotherapy it is not clear that the skills of the therapist are any more helpful than the skills of people with life experience in dealing with a problem."

Despite the solidity of Christensen and Jacobson's findings, a long line of scientists take issue with their conclusions. Psychotherapy researcher Kenneth Howard, professor of psychology at Northwestern University, argues that "it is not possible to test treatment in a lab model." In other words, you can't study psychotherapy in controlled clinical trials the way medical research does. "You or I would never volunteer for a study involving nonprofessionals, so why would anyone else?" Better are naturalistic studies of cases from everyday practice—like one of his own. It shows, he says, that experienced therapists progress more than inexperienced therapists in the first three sessions. But the inexperienced ones catch up by about the sixth session.

Naturalistic research does not necessarily support Howard's optimism for psychotherapy. In a review of child psychotherapy research, John Weisz, professor of psychology at UCLA, found that child psychotherapy actually works *only* in lab settings. When child psychotherapy is studied in "real life" it shows no benefits.

Whether professionals do better than paraprofessionals is irrelevant, Howard insists. He worries that Americans' overall health will be affected by the Clinton health care reform plan, which may limit access to psychotherapy by limiting coverage.

States Christensen, "If you are concerned about access to care, then a crucial question is who can provide the care. If only a small group of people can, then access is going to be limited automatically. But if a much larger group can provide care, then the benefits are much greater."

Wait a minute, says Larry E. Beutler, Ph.D., editor of the *Journal of Consulting and Clinical Psychology*, the leading journal of psychotherapy research. Most psychotherapy research, including the studies cited by Christensen and Jacobson, look at only half the question.

The full answer will come only from asking who is getting the psychotherapy and just what kind of therapy are they getting, Beutler argues. What's needed are "matching" studies that figure out *which* treatments work for *which* clients. Then services can be tailored to people based on the characteristics of clients, not of experts.

Jacobson's concern goes beyond any difference training or matching makes. As a practicing therapist (as is Christensen), he asks whether behavior changes even temporarily. The National Mental Health Association, a mental health lobby, recently reported that mental health professionals have an 80 percent success rate in treating depression.

Jacobson points out that some studies declaring "success" measure how many patients return to a healthy state—that's called clinical significance. Other studies measure only whether improvement has occurred—called statistical significance. At the end of treatment a severely anxious person may be improved—a statistical difference—but still a long way from a functional state—clinical significance.

When he applies the clinical-significance standard, psychotherapy shows disappointingly low success rates—and so does drug therapy—for treating marital distress, agoraphobia, and children's disorders, among others. "All the treatments are pretty weak. Some patients get better without treatment," he explains.

A new study of depression treatment by the National Institute of Mental Health puts the success rate—for drugs or psychotherapy—at 19 to 30 percent. "My mother wonders what I get paid for if this is the best I can do," quips Jacobson.

So how can 40 million Americans get effective help without breaking the public or private bank? The answer lies in examining what makes people get better—not what psychotherapy can do to help. It is indisputable that solving mental health problems—with psychotherapy, computer programs, or help cleaning your house—offers many benefits. It saves employers money by reducing sick days, improves physical health, reduces doctor visits, and reduces violence and abuse.

Sometimes psychotherapy does the trick; sometimes less costly approaches work. It depends on the person and the problem.

However psychotherapy works—whether it heals, or even treats, what ails you—people want it and like it. (There's research that says so.) On the average, psychotherapy offers more benefits than no therapy—it just may be that much simpler interventions yield similar results.

PART 13

Other Deviances

Vincent Foster was a highly successful man. He was deputy White House counsel to President Clinton, his friend since boyhood. He had come to the nation's capital with high expectations, but soon felt overwhelmed by the intensity and relentlessness of the place. After working for slightly over half a year, Foster was having trouble handling the pressure. He couldn't sleep. He felt depressed. He couldn't let go. Finally, at about 1 P.M. on July 21, 1993, he walked out of his office, and drove to a little-visited national park. There, he put the muzzle of a .38 revolver into his mouth and pulled the trigger.[1]

Like Foster, over 30,000 Americans die by their own hands. As a cause of death, suicide ranks eighth among adults and second among adolescents. (Suicide is the second leading cause of death, after accident, among white youths, and the third leading cause, after accident and homicide, among black youths.)[2] There is something ironical about suicide. In a highly individualistic society such as the United States, we are supposed to be more concerned with ourselves than others, to like ourselves more than others. Yet we are more likely to kill ourselves. According to the latest government statistics, the number of suicides in the United States (30,200) in a recent year was significantly higher than the number of homicides (21,505).[3] People in most of the other highly industrialized countries such as France, Germany, Sweden, and Japan are even more likely to take their own lives, as their suicide rates are significantly higher than ours.[4]

Since suicide seems such an unnatural act, many people assume that those who kill themselves must be abnormal, mentally ill. Foster's suicide, for example, is popularly attributed to mental depression. Foster did suffer from occasional depression. But it was not the depression itself that caused his suicide. It was instead his inability to cope effectively with the depression, and this inability had to do with certain social forces in American society. In other words, the overwhelming majority of depressed Americans do not kill themselves. An extremely few who do commit suicide do so usually because they

---

[1] Howard Fineman and Bob Cohn, "The Mystery of the White House Suicide," *Newsweek*, August 2, 1993, p. 16.

[2] *Statistical Abstract of the United States*, 1993, p. 92.

[3] Ibid., pp. 93, 195.

[4] Ibid., p. 848.

have been under the influence of some social forces in their lives. The most important of these forces is probably the lack of social integration or support. The immediate cause of Foster's suicide seemed to be the lack of social support in the form of counseling by a psychiatrist. He had planned to see a psychiatrist, but he eventually did not. This in turn may reflect the influence of a larger social force, the social stigma attached to consulting a psychiatrist, especially in the case of a prominent public official. Other social forces, such as those having to do with his gender, race, and high occupational status, might also have played a role in his suicide.

In the first article, "A Phenomenological Analysis of Suicide," Kimberly Folse and Dennis Peck analyze how the lack of support from significant others, such as relatives and friends, affects the suicides' perception of their failures in life. In the second reading, "'It's a White Thing': An Exploration of Beliefs About Suicide in the African-American Community," Kevin Early and Ronald Akers deal with the race factor in suicide by explaining why African-Americans are much *less* likely than whites to kill themselves. In the third selection, "The Suicide Machine," Norman Denzin argues that many people support Dr. Jack Kevorkian's idea of using a kinder, gentler form of suicide to end pain and miseries.

Ironically, while many adults approve of escaping the miseries of life by using a suicide machine, they disapprove of their youngsters' escaping the miseries by listening to heavy metal and rap music. The condemnation of this music comes through clearly in the media descriptions of how harmful and dangerous the music is. This is the theme of Amy Binder's article, "Media Depictions of Harm in Heavy Metal and Rap Music." But is the music really harmful? The answer is provided in the last selection, "Does Heavy Metal and Rap Music Harm Teenagers?" by Jonathan Epstein and other researchers.

51

A Phenomenological Analysis of Suicide

KIMBERLY A. FOLSE
Southwest Texas State University

DENNIS L. PECK
The University of Alabama

In analyzing various studies on suicide, we discovered perceived failure to be a major factor in suicide. But that failure takes at least three different forms. First is the suicides' perception of their own failure. Second is their perception that significant others fail to provide succor. Three is their perception that significant others also see them as failures. In analyzing a number of suicide cases, we did find one or more of these perceived failures.

PROCEDURE

The data for our analysis came from files of two medical examiner's offices. Some of these files contained suicide notes, which can be used to identify the motives of suicide committers as well as the intrapersonal and interpersonal factors promoting the inclination toward suicide (Farber, 1968; Stephens, 1984). Also available in some files was information obtained from relatives, friends, employers, public officials, or medical staff. Such information is useful for determining the circumstances surrounding the decision to commit suicide. Because of space limitations, we will here present only a few cases for analysis.

CASE ONE

A series of negative events affecting the subject's sense of competence is clearly demonstrated. Experiencing financial difficulty, a 32-year-old married white female embezzled money from her employer to pay family debts. Unsuccessful in an attempt to secure a personal bank loan to repay the stolen money and aware that an arrest warrant had been secured by her employer, she took her life. A note found at the scene stated:

This article was specifically written for this reader.

Steve,

I am so sorry. I love you, Chris and Lee very much, better that anything in the world!

I am so sorry our life together had to end this way.

We got in such a mess financially that I borrowed some money without permission. I was going to pay it back before audit next fall; however Lewis found out about it and wouldn't except (sic) that.

I went to every bank I knew begging so to speak for help. *No one, no one* would help, so I figured out a way to borrow it from work—no one would be hurt. I'd had it paid back before anyone knew about it. Well it didn't work that way.

I am so sorry!

Please raise Chris and Lee with a good life. Daddy, Mimi, Gina, your Mama and Daddy will help you.

I love everyone so much but I can't continue on like this.

My nerves, health are not very good any more.

Please don't tell Chris how this happened until he is grown and maybe can understand better. I love him so much. Just tell him God needed me more, I guess.

Oh, how I wanted a good life.

Oh well. . . .

I love you Steve, Chris and Lee So Very Much

Sissy

I didn't mean to disgrace everyone & myself. Daddy, Mimi, Gina, Yvonne & Vic—I'm sorry but I love you all very much.

Each form of perceived failure can be identified here. The inability to secure financial support from a lending institution exacerbates the individual's sense of failure (Failure I). The statement that "we got into a mess. . . " places the burden on both husband and wife. However, further statements suggest it is the wife who assumed responsibility for resolving the problem. Without support from others, as indicated by the statement, *"No one, no one* would help" (Failure II), the suicide sought to compensate for repeated failure. Aware that the theft had been discovered by her employer, she felt that others saw her as a failure (Failure III). This is discernible in her statement that "I didn't mean to disgrace everyone and myself." It is also detectable in her plea to withhold information concerning the circumstances surrounding her death.

CASE TWO

Similar to the first case, perceived personal failure and an unspecified problem seem to have precipitated the self-inflicted death of a 22-year-old university student. Notes found in the apartment were dated the day of his death.

Note one. A brief note addressed to a brother stated:

Mark

You're the best little brother a guy could have. *Please* do good in college for Mama & Daddy. Do something good with your life, don't do like me.

Get good on the guitar. It's a beautiful instrument.
Please, make our family proud of you. I know you will.

Gary

Note two

Mama & Daddy:

You remember how I was; "Death Before Dishonor" and all that stuff. I was supposed to be the model son, doing the best of everything I did. I'm so sorry I let you down all those times. I've really screwed up now. I can never be your model son again. I know I can't say anything to let you know how bad I feel about all this, but please try to accept this humble apology and realize this is what I thought best. See you in heaven.

Gary

Two types of failure can be identified in these notes. The self's sense of failure comes across in two sentences: In note one, the deceased implores his brother "Do something good with your life, don't do like me," and, in note two, he says, "I've really screwed up now. I can never be your model son again." Moreover, the apologetic tone in the second note reveals his feeling that his parents saw him as a failure.

CASE THREE

A high school senior, described as somewhat impulsive and nervous, but otherwise average, took his life. Despite involvement in many school-related functions, social activities, hobbies, and part-time work, this youth held the belief that his future would be less than desirable.

As reconstructed by investigators, the deceased had previously discussed proving himself a man as well as taking his life. Although specific facts are absent, the tone of this note strongly suggests the subject considered himself a failure as well as a liability to his parents. The content of the suicide note documents the writer's perceived failure and justification for this suicide.

Dear Mom & Dad,

This is your dear deceased son saying a few parting words. I did this because I made a mess of the life I have now ad (sic) it will be worse in the future so I'm bugging out. If anyone even asks you if you had a son tell them no. I wouldn't want to embarrass you. I also have some troubles to cure my mind ad (sic) everyone elses I'm leaving. Cry no tears I'm going to a happier place.

Love, John

This note suggests the decedent considered the present situation hopeless, believing also that the future would be devoid of positive outcomes (Failure I). His assumption that his behavior might prove embarrassing to his parents seems to reveal Failure III.

CASE FOUR

A 22-year-old white married male died after connecting the tailpipe to the cabin of his truck. Separated from his wife, the deceased was depressed because of this separation. Two "missing persons" reports had been filed with the police; one report was filed by the deceased's girlfriend, the other by his wife.

Two notes were found. The first one, unaddressed, contained the following statement:

> Well guys here I am dead. I told you all the weakness was mine. Please take care of alli + Bo. JASC—get a real life. You see where this one goes
>
>   your brother

The second suicide note is addressed, but it is unclear to whom the message is intended:

> Hello Dear!
>
>   Im lying round in my dorm room feeling drained. After I got back here I called home. Steve was the only one home but I told dad anyway. I don't very much see the point of trying to hide it. It's just going to stress me. But tomorrow they're going to get my car. My dad told me that he believes the trip I decided to take with my girlfriend to . . . (city named) was unnecessary.
>
>   I feel so yucky right now. I even took a walk to try and make myself feel better but no dice. I came back and started getting mad at you. (Don't worry I'm not blaming you)

The decedent viewed himself to be weak, incapable, and inadequate (Failure I). Failure II, perceived lack of support, can be inferred from the content of the second note, where reference is made to the father's lack of support for the deceased's judgment. The subject's anger, turned inward through an act of suicide, appears to be directed toward another person. The final paragraph of the second note illustrates this man's sense of failure and the need to express his anger in a physical way.

CONCLUSION

Whether or not a suicide actually takes place depends on many factors. Most of these factors cannot be identified with the kind of data presented here. But suicide notes provide insight into the subjective world of individuals before they end their lives. With its emphasis on the subjectivity of deviant behavior, phenomenological theory assumes that deviant persons' experiences and perceptions are key to deviant reality. Analyzing suicide notes, then, may help us understand how some people decide to kill themselves. The three forms of perceived failure that are often discernible in suicide notes do not necessarily compel a person to commit suicide. But they do enhance the probability of suicide.

Perhaps more important, our analysis has demonstrated perception of failure as part of the *process* that leads to suicide. We have effectively addressed what Robert MacIver said in 1942: "[Suicide] is the end of a process, and the significant object of study is the process that terminates thus" (cited by Wilkins, 1967, p. 295). Our findings may bring us closer to a full understanding of suicide. By shedding light on the subjective side of suicide, they complement data from more positivist, objective studies that focus on such background factors as race, class, or gender as determinants of suicide.

References

Farber, Maurice L. 1968. *Theory of Suicide.* New York: Funk and Wagnall.

Stephens, B. Joyce. 1984. "Vocabularies of Motive and Suicide." *Suicide and Life-Threatening Behavior* 14: 243–253.

Wilkins, James. 1967. "Suicidal Behavior." *American Sociological Review* 32: 286–298.

52

"It's a White Thing": An Exploration of Beliefs About Suicide in the African-American Community

Kevin E. Early
Oakland University

Ronald L. Akers
University of Florida

The low black suicide rate is well documented. There has been an increase in black male suicides in the past two decades, but until the mid-1980s that was matched by an increase in suicides among white males. The differences in suicide between younger black and white males has never been large and may be getting smaller. Nevertheless, overall the white suicide rate is nearly double the black suicide rate. The ratio of white male to black male suicide rates is 1.75: 1, and the suicide rate among white women is more than double the rate for black women (see Department of Health and Human Services, 1992). It is this persistent difference in rates of suicide across racial groups that has been the focus of sociological interest in suicide in the black community. The question raised by this difference is, Why is there relatively little black suicide?. . .

The answer most frequently given in the literature is a general "buffering hypothesis." This hypothesizes that black suicide is lower, in part, because of the role played by religion and the family in the African-American community in ameliorating or buffering social forces that might otherwise promote suicide. Billingsley (1968), Stack (1974), Allen (1978), Martin (1978), and

From Kevin E. Early and Ronald L. Akers, "It's a White Thing: An Exploration of Beliefs About Suicide in the African-American Community," *Deviant Behavior,* Vol. 14 (1993), pp. 277–296. Reproduced with permission. All rights reserved.

McAdoo (1981) all look at the family, church, and social support systems they believe help insulate African Americans from suicide. This perspective is also adopted by Rutter (1985), who used the term protective factors. Woodford (1965) proposed that experiences with urbanization, segregation, and racism have helped to buffer African Americans from suicide by producing adaptability. Davis hypothesized that:

> For blacks, the stresses and anxieties that might lead to suicide have often been offset by strong family and communal ties. Effectively denied all other mechanisms to compensate for rejection and abuse, blacks have in the past used their families, communities, and institutions (i.e., churches, social clubs, fraternal organizations, etc.) to develop positive and functional forms of response to recurrent stressful social situations. The black community, in effect, has functioned as a protective society, providing participation and purpose, a sense of belonging, and the possibility of cooperative and self-help approaches to problems. (Davis, 1980, p. 228)

As stated in the literature the hypothesis remains nonspecific as to just what it is about the church, family, or other institutions in the African-American community that has provided or could provide suicide buffering. We propose that there are both social and cultural dimensions to any suicide buffering effect that may be found. The social dimension relates to the extent to which social relationships and responsiveness to one another provide social support countering suicide situations and motivations. The cultural dimension refers to the normative climate, the values and norms shared by the church, family, and other institutions in the African-American community. Research has not yet identified the empirical content of either of these dimensions.

The purpose of this reading is to report an exploratory, qualitative investigation of the content of the cultural/normative dimension. The study was designed to find what, if any, religious beliefs there are in the African-American community that might serve a suicide-buffering function. Specifically, we report a study of normative views of suicide, contrasted with views of other deviant acts such as drug abuse and crime, reported by religious leaders in one community. The study did not have comparative data from the white community and therefore was not an effort to directly test the buffering hypothesis or to explain differences in white and black suicidal behavior. Rather, the study attempted to identify the content of religiously based antisuicide beliefs to gain a greater understanding of black cultural perceptions of suicide. . . .

METHODOLOGY

The study was conducted in 1991 in a southeastern standard metropolitan statistical area (SMSA) of about 84,000 with 21 percent African Americans. The data were collected by the first author in face-to-face interviews with black pastors. There are a total of 37 black churches located in the area, and 30 pastors agreed to take part in the study. The pastors were interviewed as informants, as persons strategically located in the community to provide information, insight, and contacts within that community. Therefore, they were asked their own opinions and were asked to comment on beliefs about suicide in the general community.

The interviews were loosely structured and undisguised, lasting about 1½ hours each. The interviews were divided into two main sections. The first section covered: (1) The pastor's views as leader of the church and the stated position of his or her church on suicide; (2) The pastor's assessment of the role of the church and religion in the African-American family and community; (3) The extent to which the pastor teaches and preaches on suicide-relevant topics; and (4) The definition and meaning of suicide and its causes and assessment of why there are few suicide deaths in the African American community. The second part of the interview asked the pastors to respond to two vignettes depicting cases of suicide and attempted suicide. . . . Each vignette was succeeded by four to seven follow-up questions that were designed to elicit pastors' judgments and attitudes about several issues related to the nature of suicide depicted in the vignettes and the role that the black church could play or had played in dealing with these social issues.

None of the pastors reported direct experience with cases of suicide, and therefore assessment of actual cases could not be used. The vignettes allowed us to explore what the stated reactions and assessments would have been if the pastors had encountered such cases. . . .

FINDINGS

Not surprisingly, the pastors offer strong support for the contention in the literature iterated above that the church serves unifying and leadership functions in the black community. They point to the black church as an institution that has provided social and cultural integration for black Americans and has interacted with the black family to provide resiliency under stressful conditions. . . .

Beliefs About Suicide

The pastors' perceived significance of the church in the community does not guarantee that its stand on suicide is widely shared in the black culture, and our research did not include a community survey. However, as we have seen, the literature strongly supports this perception, and it seems reasonable to assume that the norms and attitudes expressed by the pastors are reflected to some extent in the larger community. Those norms, as articulated by the pastors in this study, condemn suicide on religious grounds and define it as so alien to the black experience, religious and secular, that willingness to commit suicide runs directly counter to all that is implicit in what it means to be African American. . . .

In the view of the pastors, the black church unequivocally condemns suicide as unforgivable sin. "Man is not the giver of life. Hence, man has not the authority to take life." "The Lord giveth and only the Lord taketh away."

[Interview 08269010] We don't condone suicide. We condemn it to the maximum. We believe that most people that commit suicide never [get the chance before dying] to ask for forgiveness.

[Interview 07289001] God did not put us here to determine our own conclusion of life and taking it upon ourselves to make quick exits. That, Biblically, is not an approved act of God. It's unpardonable sin. One who commits suicide goes to hell and is unpardoned for their sin. . . .

This definition of suicide as a sin that is unpardonable is combined with the view that suicide runs counter to black "soul." The soul represents the gift of life. The soul is tied to the black experience not only spiritually, but has worldly, cultural, and traditional dimensions. If one is to ensure one's soul a proper place in heaven after death, it is important to live life as productively as possible despite life's many obstacles. Obstacles should not be a deterrent to life, but an encouragement to struggle. To struggle with the help of God is believed to enhance the quality of life and to make the individual resilient to pressures that would otherwise cause suicide. The soul belongs to God and is entrusted to the individual who is ultimately held accountable. To the extent that this norm of accountability for one's own life and soul is transmitted in both sacred and secular versions throughout the community, it could act as one of the normative suicide buffers.

Suicide Is a "White Thing"

The pastors were asked directly why they believed that suicide is less of a problem for the African-American community and why suicide occurs infrequently. Their explanations for black suicide are . . . that the person committing suicide has experienced a breakdown in religious and family ties and stress associated with the assimilative effects of racial integration that is seen as undermining the internal integration of the black community. As we have seen, the specifically religious norms on the unexcusable and inexplicable nature of suicide may be one element buffering gainst these suicide-inducing pressures.

But the pastors' responses reflects a fusion of these religious norms with secular norms. The message in their assessments is that suicide, in addition to being unholy and sinful, is almost a complete denial of black identity and culture. It is assumed that suicide is outside the black experience. It is simply not done. In the revealing words of the first pastor interviewed, which inspired the title of this paper, "suicide is a white thing."

Suicide is viewed as a white thing not simply because of its recognized greater statistical frequency among whites. Rather, the phrase captures the idea that suicide is antithetical to black culture. This was communicated to the interviewer and first author, who is black, not only by the first pastor but by several others in subsequent interviews. They insisted that he should not even have to ask questions related to blacks and suicide because suicide is a white thing, not a black thing. "As a rule blacks don't kill themselves . . . you should know this already." "Well, being black you should know that black people want to live." "You should know that suicide is somethin' that occurs over there, on the other side of the tracks." "We want to live, son . . . we want to get there . . . you should know this."

All of the pastors presented the view that there are unique features of black culture that render some of the same difficulties and problems that might lead to suicide by whites less of a suicide threat for African Americans. The belief is that having to deal historically and currently with economic, political, and social deprivation has made black Americans more resilient against these problems. Indeed, one of their worries was that racial integration, in spite of all its other benefits, may break down some of that resiliency because it may foster blacks taking on white culture and attitudes about suicide. . . .

[Interview 09049013] I think in this case it goes back to our culture. We have been taught down through the years that we as a people don't do these kinds of things . . . committing suicide. As a boy growing up I never knew anything about blacks committing suicide until integration came about and I believe black America then began to take on the traits, if you will, of white America.

[Interview 09229020] We as a race have always been used to hardships. We are more used to hardships than whites. Suicide was always more prevalent among whites than it was blacks. I personally believe that if black folks are killin' theyself it's because of the integration. We've gotten where we're communicating closer with whites every day. . . .

The pastors portrayed blacks as being a more religious people than their white counterparts. Additionally, blacks were described as being able to endure more hardships and not succumb to the despair and despondency that leads to suicide. The black experience in America is one of struggle. Survival represents hope and the promise of a better life after death. The church unifies black Americans around a common tradition shaped out of suffering. The church is a source of strength, identity, coping skills, and a reason for living. Thus, the pastors identified secular as well as religious norms forming a cultural buffer against suicide in the black community to keep suicide from having become a black thing. Suicide is excluded as contradictory to what it means to be black. Whites may do it, but blacks do not.

SUMMARY AND CONCLUSIONS

The most common explanation for the relatively little black suicide proposed by scholars is that the black church and family ameliorate social forces that might otherwise lead to suicide. We have referred to this as the buffering hypothesis and noted that it leaves unspecified what it is that does the buffering. The principal goal of this study was to investigate what some of these buffers might be.

Thirty pastors in one community in a southeastern state were interviewed to elicit their observations and views on suicide in the black community. . . . According to the pastors, the church is a refuge, problem-solver, and moral voice of the black community. They describe the church as central to the black experience, which is consistent with what sociologists of race and ethnicity have been saying for a long time. Assuming the importance of the black church in the larger community as asserted by these pastors and as stated in the literature, we have tentatively identified religiously based beliefs with the potential for countering suicide.

The pastors condemned suicide as an unpardonable sin. Theologically, they defined it as an unpardonable sin "against God's perfect will." Suicide does nothing for the "soul" except place it in peril of eternal damnation. The church recognizes no justification for suicide. . . .

Our research has uncovered another dimension of the pastors' beliefs about suicide to which future research should pay particular attention, namely the perception of suicide as inherently contradictory to the black experience and a complete denial of black identity and culture. The pastors reasoned, "Why talk about suicide? [Not concentrating on suicide in sermons] is not an oversight, it just is not a problem." Problems that might lead to suicide by whites do not pose a threat to black Americans. Blacks have developed an apparent resilience to direct self-destructive behavior. To struggle and endure hardships toughens one to withstand sorrows and religious faith offers hope and the promise of a better life. Suicide is seen as peculiar to white America "across the tracks." Black Americans may get involved in crime and drug abuse, but "to our credit at least we don't kill ourselves. That's a white thing." . . .

Other factors in black suicide beyond buffering of moral norms and values are not examined in this study. Therefore, there is no claim to have provided a test of the buffering hypothesis. However, the study has provided evidence of a religiously influenced social meaning of suicide as unacceptable, perhaps even unthinkable, for the vast majority of black Americans. This permits us to go beyond the general hypothesis of the suicide-buffering function of the religious institution in the black community found in the literature to propose the following specific hypothesis: The condemnation of suicide as wrong and as an unthinkable contradiction of black culture is sufficiently pervasive in the black community that it helps to keep the rate of suicide low.

References

Allen, Walter. 1978. "Black Family Research in the United States: A Review, Assessment and Extension." *Journal of Comparative Family Studies* 9:168–189.

Billingsley, Andrew. 1968. *Black Families in White America*. Englewood Cliffs, NJ: Prentice-Hall.

Davis, Robert. 1980. "Suicide Among Young Blacks: Trends and Perspective." *Phylon* 41:223–229.

Department of Health and Human Services. 1992. Statistical Series, annual data, 1990. Series E-21. *Vital Statistics of the United States*, Vol. II, Mortality, Part A. Washington, DC: Public Health Service, National Center for Health Statistics.

Martin, Elmer P. 1978. *The Black Extended Family*. Chicago: University of Chicago Press.

McAdoo, Harriette. 1981. *Black Families.* Beverly Hills: Sage Publications.

Rutter, Michael. 1985. "Resilience in the Face of Adversity." *British Journal of Psychiatry* 147:598–611.

Stack, Carol. 1974. *All Our Kin.* New York: Harper & Row.

Woodford, J. 1965. "Why Negro Suicides Are Increasing." *Ebony* 20:89–100.

53

The Suicide Machine

NORMAN K. DENZIN
University of Illinois

The mercitron, Jack Kevorkian's suicide machine, was invented in 1989 and displayed on television on the *Donahue Show*. The mercitron delivers, on demand (the patient pushes a plunger), a lethal dosage of sodium penthothal and potassium into the veins of the individual hooked up to its valves. On June 4, 1990, Kevorkian announced in the *New York Times* that he helped a woman, Janet Adkin, commit suicide. She had seen his machine work on the *Donahue Show*. Here is how he described her death in *Free Inquiry*:

> I started the intravenous dripper, which released a salt solution through a needle into her vein, and I kept her arm tied down so she wouldn't jerk it. This was difficult as her veins were fragile. And then once she decided she was ready to go, she just hit the switch and the device cut off the saline drip and through the same needle released a solution of thiopental that put her to sleep in ten to fifteen seconds. A minute later, through the same needle flowed a lethal solution of potassium chloride.

Kevorkian calls this planned death, a rational system that honors self-determination. He distinguishes this form of dying from medicide or euthanasia, which are deaths performed by a medical professional. To date at least six chronically ill individuals have died with the help of Kevorkian's machine: 43-year-old Sherry Miller, 58-year-old Marjorie Wantz, 54-year-old Janet Adkins (who had Alzheimer's disease), two women from Oakland, California, and Gary Sloan, 44-year-old terminally ill dentist, who was advised (they exchanged letters) by Kevorkian on how to kill himself with a suicide machine. On February 5, 1991, an Oakland county judge ordered Kevorkian to stop using his suicide machines. In the same week he faced a preliminary hearing in Oakland county on two counts of murder. On February 18, 1992, the *New York Times* reported that Kevorkian was to be tried for murder in the State of Michigan in the assisted deaths of Sherry Miller and Majorie Wantz. An earlier murder charge against the doctor (for the assisted death of Janet Adkins) had been dropped since Michigan does not have a law against suicide assisted deaths.

Reprinted from *Society*, Vol. 29 (July/August 1992): 7–10.

A DEATH CULTURE

The mercitron is the postmodern method of death. Suited for those who have the luxury and the time to seek a kinder form of death, the mercitron is for the middle classes. It is not an option for the walking and wounded members of America's ethnic underclasses, among whom violent deaths are everyday occurrences, and drug addiction and alcoholism are the preferred softer, gentler forms of suicide and self-annihilation. The suicide machine must be located in its historical period. America is a death culture. . . . Kevorkian is not alone in his desire to bring a different form of death and dying into American culture.

In mid-1991 Derek Humphry's book *Final Exit: The Practicalities of Self-Deliverance and Assisted Suicide for the Dying* went to the top of the best-seller lists with sales of over 500,000 for the year. In 1991 membership in the Hemlock Society, a group dedicated to the rights of the terminally ill to choose voluntary euthanasia, climbed to over 38,000 with seventy chapters. By 1992 euthanasia societies in the Netherlands, Britain, France, and the United States were lobbying for legal reforms permitting euthanasia. On December 1, 1991, the Patient Self-Determination Act became law in the United States. Enacted a few short years after the right-to-die celebrity cases involving Nancy Cruzan, Karen Ann Quinlan, and Roswell Gilbert, this law mandates that all health-care providers receiving Medicare or Medicaid inform patients over the age of 18 of their right to plan in advance for their care. The living will has become commonplace in America, and hospitals are now routinely asking patients if they wish to make a death plan.

Right-to-Die groups, influenced by the Hemlock Society, have started to appear in other states besides California, including Oregon and Washington, and New York where the Choice-in-Dying group promotes patients' rights to refuse care. All states, except Nebraska and Pennsylvania, now have laws that honor at least one form of the living will. On average 5,800 Americans die each day. Over 75 percent of these deaths are timed or negotiated.

Middle-class Americans are taking death seriously. The cultural taboos of suicide for reasons of health have been broken. Suicide now ranks as the eighth leading cause of death in the United States (heart diseases are number one). By the year 2000, the largest age group in the United States will be the 65 and over category and suicide by the elderly will continue to be a leading cause of death for this group, as it will also be for the chronically ill, including those dying from AIDS. Active and passive euthanasia will be taken for granted as the dying members of this culture seek their private forms of death. . . .

Medicide, assisted suicides, planned deaths, hospice-managed deaths, and the new medical humanism, are now everywhere present in our culture. Nowadays, to paraphrase C. Wright Mills, Americans are taking death into their own hands. A self-managed death is the only real symbolic violence they can wage against the impersonal, structural violence of the postmodern moment. . . .

The postmodern moment is characterized, as Max Weber and C. Wright Mills predicted, by the irrational rationalization and bureaucratization of everyday life. Large technological structures, including the medical establishment and the health-care industries, exert ever greater control over the human body and its destiny. Throughout this century the medical establishment has wielded power over life and death. This system of control, Arthur Frank observes, has led to the progressive medicalization of everyday life. Today more and more issues, including who can work when and where, are decided by medical opinion. Health, life, and death have become commodities only few can afford, and health-care rationing (who lives and who dies) is now largely a matter of wealth and status.

An increasingly hospital-based medicine has eroded the traditional doctor-patient model of treatment, while clinical judgment has become a matter of laboratory technologies. As Arthur Frank has noted: "My body is decentered in videotapes of angiograms and ultrasounds, in files of CAT scan images, in graphs of blood cell counts, and serum levels. When I am asked how I feel, it is these to which I refer and which refer to me. In the medical simulacrum I lose myself in my image . . . the reality of how I feel passes into signs without feeling."

This regime of power and control is now under attack. Those drawn to the new forms of self-determined death are no longer willing to accept the medical establishment's place in this life and death equation. The growing attraction of the assisted suicide movement reflects the belief that doctors and hospitals have gone too far in their care of the terminally ill. Life at any cost is no longer desirable, especially when the last days of life in an intensive-care unit can cost $100,000 or more. People are seeking a cheaper way to die, while coming to the conclusion that they are no longer willing to prolong the dying process needlessly. They seek other systems of signs and meanings that will give them the illusion of control over their lives. This is where Kevorkian's mercitron again enters the picture.

THE IDEOLOGY BEHIND THE MACHINE

Kevorkian's arguments rest on a new medical humanism that would allow patient and family to determine the moment of death. This he calls a "positive" death. According to Kevorkian, this humanism carries three benefits: a reduction in patient suffering, less psychological pain for family and friends, and a savings in resources that would be spent on prolonged care. The benefits, he argues, do not counterbalance the loss of human life. Hence, he adds one more benefit, of major importance: the ability of the patient who opts for a planned death to save the life of another. Under Kevorkian's system the dying patient is asked how his or her body should be used to save the life of another human being. A patient might, he suggests, decide to donate vital organs, or undergo a critical medical experiment. So in dying the person contributes to science, medicine, society, and the lives of others.

The key to Kevorkian's model lies in the body's uses after death. He thus distinguishes between positive and negative death; negative death being defined as death without positive social, medical, or scientific consequence for society. Medicide produces positive death. All other forms of death our culture sanctions, including obligatory (death row), assisted (euthanasia), and optional suicide (mental illness) produce negative death, a loss without meaning. His is an attempt to turn death into something positive, into both a merciful experience and a process that yields something "of real value to suffering humanity left behind."

SUICIDE CENTERS

From this reasoning derives the mercitron. This machine will be located in suicide centers. In these centers, centralized, rationally organized, well-controlled, merciful, dignified deaths will occur. Ethical and experimental manipulations on the body will also be conducted. Because suicide and euthanasia carry negative connotations, Kevorkian offers the word *obitorium* (from the Latin *obitus,* meaning to go to meet death) for the center. . . .

Obitoria would be staffed by experts who know how to use the mercitron. These medical specialists will consult with other specialists when the time comes to connect an individual to the mercitron. Every community will have a five-member group of obitiatry specialists who will vote on a given instance of medicide. All members of the group must agree before a death can occur. As these decisions are being made, dying individuals will fill out questionnaires concerning their decision to die. Everybody is thereby protected, as this final decision, which is a medical problem, is implemented. It can then be said that the patient died in order to save the lives of others.

Rational death. Science fiction now. Come to the *obitorium* to die. This is altruistic death with a vengeance. It asserts the primacy of the social over the individual, making a distinction between selfish (nongiving) and giving (the good) death. It reduces the existential phenomenon of patient suffering and the psychological pain and guilt for family and friends to minor benefits. These existential realities of death are erased in a single stroke, replaced by a new logic of the social and the scientific. This new logic subordinates the body, its history, and its parts to a higher goal: service to humankind and the perpetuation of human life. . . .

FATAL VISIONS

In the desire to escape an older medical ethic and an Enlightenment set of social ideals, the new medical humanism advocated by Kevorkian ends by embracing what it started out to reject. And it does this with a vengeance. For if, when I die, I must consider what my life means to others, then I have not escaped the social net that had previously prolonged life for me and my fellows. Now I die early for another set of individuals. Who wins?

No longer can we just go gently into that good night. Even if, as the philosopher Martin Heidegger reminds us, we are born dying, our dying now becomes a matter of social planning, social concern, and commitments to higher ideals. Here at the end science fiction meets and even anticipates reality. Death machines, clean, antiseptically sterile obitoria, the new funeral homes, soft organ music playing, obitiatrists in white jackets, rows upon rows of mercitrons plugged into inert bodies, happy family members mingle in joy as their loved ones drift off into death, and behind closed doors their bodies are taken apart to be experimented upon.

Postmodern death has won. . . . [But] it should be possible to imagine a form of dying that does not require the invention of new machines and new medical specialities. After all, it was science, medicine and the new technologies that got us into this mess in the first place. Can we not imagine a new set of ethics that would allow individuals to determine their moment of death without all of the complications that accompany Kevorkian's suicide machine?

54

Media Depictions of Harm in Heavy Metal and Rap Music

Amy Binder
Northwestern University

In September 1985, a group of politically well-connected "Washington Wives" calling themselves the Parents' Music Resource Center (PMRC) was invited to testify before the U.S. Senate Committee on Commerce, Science, and Transportation. Led by Tipper Gore (wife of then Senator Al Gore of Tennessee) and Susan Baker (wife of then Treasury Secretary James Baker), the group's objective was to reveal to committee members the current state of rock music lyrics—particularly the lyrics of heavy metal music. The PMRC and its expert witnesses testified that such music filled youthful ears with pornography and violence, and glorified behaviors ranging from suicide and drug use to occultism and anti-patriotic activities. The mass media covered the hearing in great detail, provoking debate in the national press over the alleged harmfulness of rock music lyrics and whether the proposed labeling of music lyrics constituted censorship.

Almost five years later, another event again focused the nation's attention on music lyrics—the lyrics in rap music. In June 1990, a U.S. District Court judge in Fort Lauderdale, Florida found the 2 Live Crew album *As Nasty as They Wanna Be* to be obscene in the three counties under his jurisdiction. This was the first recording ever declared obscene by a federal court (*New York Times* 17 June, 1990). During the following week, authorities from one of those counties' Sheriff's Department—Broward County—arrested a local record storeowner who had continued to sell the album and took into custody two members of the 2 Live Crew band when they performed material from the album at an adults-only show in the area. The arrests and impending trials again galvanized heated public debate over whether the lyrics in contemporary music harmed listeners and warranted restriction.

Reprinted from the author's article, "Constructing Racial Rhetoric: Media Depictions of Harm in Heavy Metal and Rap Music," *American Sociological Review*, Vol. 58 (December 1993): 753–767.

These two widely publicized debates about contemporary music, both of which concerned "harmful" lyrics and occurred within five years of each other, provide comparative cases for examining how the mass media serve as an ideological vehicle. In both cases, writers in the mainstream press expressed concern about the harm that could result from exposure to lyrics containing sexual and violent themes, and called for action against such content. Despite these similarities, however, the substance of media arguments changed significantly as the controversy shifted from heavy metal music to rap music. Foremost among these differences was the change in emphasis regarding whom the music was harming: the individual listener or society as a whole.

I suggest that two factors drove the changes in the media discourse surrounding the dangers of heavy metal music versus rap music. One factor is the difference in the content of the lyrics themselves. In general, the controversial rap lyrics were more graphic than their heavy metal counterparts, and discussions in the media reflected this variation.

Second, the broad cultural context in which the "white" music and "black" music were being received also significantly affected changes in the discourse. Rather than asserting a simple reflection model (i.e., the media only mirror "what's out there"), I argue that the pronounced shift in the discourse about lyrics cannot be explained by differences in the cultural objects alone. Instead, the shift reflects opinion writers' perceptions of the populations represented by these two musical genres. Writers who were concerned about heavy metal lyrics and rap lyrics did not address the content of the music alone; embedded in their discussions were reactions to differences in the demographic characteristics of the genres' producers and audiences—music made by and for working and middle-class white youth versus music they perceived as predominantly by and for urban black teenagers. In a cultural landscape marked by divergent perceptions of black youths versus white youths, different concerns emerged in the mainstream media about the impact of each group's form of cultural expression. I show that rap music—with its evocation of angry black rappers and equally angry black audiences—was simultaneously perceived as a more authentic and serious art form than was heavy metal music, and as a more frightening and salient threat to society as a whole than the "white" music genre.

METHODOLOGY

I examine the national discourse surrounding the harmfulness of music lyrics by analyzing nationally distributed mainstream publications that target a range of audiences. Demographic profiles as of 1991 provided by these publications show that readerships varied along socioeconomic lines: the *New York Times* and *Time* magazine have the wealthiest and most highly educated readers, *Newsweek* and *U.S. News and World Report* represent an intermediate socioeconomic level, and the readership of the *Reader's Digest* has low levels of annual income and education. The publications also vary politically: the *New*

York Times is considered one of the most liberal large newspapers, the *Reader's Digest* is considered conservative, and the other three publications fall somewhere in between.

For comparison to this mainstream debate, which was written for a "general" (primarily white) American readership, I also examined the discourse in two popular middle-class publications that serve a predominantly black readership: *Ebony* and *Jet* (hereafter referred to as black or African-American magazines). The articles in these African-American magazines were coded to determine if the race of the readership made a difference in how the music genres were framed.

The articles published in the five mainstream publications and the two black magazines were located in the *Reader's Guide to Periodicals* and the Lexis/Nexis data bank. Between 1985 and 1990, these publications printed more than 1000 news and opinion articles that concerned heavy metal music or rap music. Of these, 108 of the mainstream articles and 10 of the black magazines' articles were opinion pieces that specifically addressed the lyric content of the music. . . . In the African-American magazines, all 10 articles were written about rap music. Although all of the roughly 1000 articles were read, for methodological and theoretical reasons I limited coding and analysis to these 118 opinion articles.

The 118 opinion pieces were content-analyzed using coding categories constructed by the author. This first reading generated 68 categories, which were collapsed into nine frames. This set of nine frames accounts for the total discourse surrounding the issue of harm in lyrics in these publications from 1985 to 1990. Each article was then read again to determine which of the nine frames were used in each piece. The mean number of frames per article was 1.6.

Frames are "schemata of interpretation that enable individuals to locate, perceive, identify, and label" events they have experienced directly or indirectly (Snow, Rochford, Worden, and Benford, 1986, p. 464; see also Goffman, 1974, p. 21). Frames help receivers make sense of social occurrences because they organize events into recognizable patterns and help individuals understand what actions they can then take in light of these events. The nine frames that were used in the 118 articles analyzed here to depict heavy metal and rap music are of two types. The "music is harmful" frames include corruption, protection, danger to society, and not censorship. The other, "music is not harmful" frames comprise no harm, threat to authorities, generation gap, and important message/art (see Table 54.1).

HARMFUL OR NOT HARMFUL: FRAMING MUSIC LYRICS

Popular music has always been denigrated by adult society. Musical genres like the blues, jazz, and early rock and roll and dances like the jitterbug, samba, and rhumba provoked complaints from the older generation about the perversion and general corruption of its children (Peterson, 1972; McDonald, 1988; Rosenbaum and Prinsky, 1991). Thus, the controversy that made its way into the limelight in the late 1980s to early 1990s was one episode in an ongoing debate.

TABLE 54.1   Percentage Distribution of Frames by Type of Frame, for Mainstream Publications and African-American Publications and Type of Music, 1985–1990

Type of Publication and Frame	Type of Music		
	Percent Heavy Metal	Percent Rap	Percent Heavy Metal and Rap
Mainstream Publications[a] (Chi-square = 72.1, 16 d.f., p < .01)			
"Music Is Harmful" Frames			
Corruption	34	0	31
Protection	31	14	23
Danger to society	13	64	38
Not censorship	22	21	8
Total	100	100	100
Number of frames	32	14	13
"Music Is Not Harmful" Counterframes			
Freedom of speech	18	14	27
No harm	39	22	16
Threat to authorities	4	1	21
Generation gap	25	3	5
Important message/art	14	60	21
Total	100	100	100
Number of frames	28	65	19
African-American Magazines[b]			
"Music is Harmful" Frames			
Corruption	0	0	0
Protection	0	0	0
Danger to society	0	0	0
Not censorship	0	0	0
Total	0	0	0
Number of frames	0	0	0
"Music Is Not Harmful" Counterframes			
Freedom of speech	0	6	0
No harm	0	24	0
Threat to authorities	0	6	0
Generation gap	0	17	0
Important message/art	0	47	0
Total	0	100	0
Number of frames	0	17	0

[a]The *New York Times, Time* magazine, *Newsweek, U.S. News and World Report,* and *Reader's Digest.*

[b]*Ebony* and *Jet.*

But to understand the specific nature of the controversy surrounding the lyrics in heavy metal music and rap music, it is necessary to examine the two defining events that shaped this media discourse: the Senate hearing in 1985 and the arrests and trials of rap musicians and record storeowners in Florida in 1990. The data in Table 54.1 indicate that these events focused the media discourse first on heavy metal music (in 1985, 13 of 15 mainstream articles addressed heavy metal) and later on rap music (in 1990, 33 of 48 mainstream articles addressed rap). In the intervening years, 1986 to 1989, mainstream media attention was more evenly split between the two music genres.

The Senate Hearing and Its Aftermath

Considered the "hottest ticket in town all year" (Gore, 1987), the 1985 standing-room-only Senate hearing launched a maelstrom of media debate about music lyrics. The competing arguments introduced at the hearing were generally used to discuss heavy metal for the duration of the five-year debate.

One of the most frequent arguments made about heavy metal music throughout the five-year controversy was introduced in 1985 by members of the PMRC and its witnesses. This argument, which I call the *corruption* frame, stated that explicit lyrics—whether glorifying suicide, anti-authority attitudes, or deviant sexual acts—have a negative effect on children's attitudes. This frame emphasized the music's corrupting effect on young listeners rather than on the effects such listeners might have on the society at large. A five-minute speech delivered to the Senate Committee by PMRC witness Joe Steussy illustrates this frame:

> Today's heavy metal music is categorically different from previous forms of popular music. . . . Its principal themes are, as you have already heard, extreme violence, extreme rebellion, substance abuse, sexual promiscuity and perversion, and Satanism. I know personally of no form of popular music before, which has had as one of its central elements the element of hatred. (U.S. Senate Hearing Before the Committee on Commerce, Science, and Transportation 1985, p. 117)

The *corruption* frame also appeared frequently in the national press. In an article titled "How Shock Rock Harms Our Kids," one writer argued, "lyrics glamorize drug and alcohol use, and glorify death and violent rebellion, ranging from hatred of parents and teachers to suicide—the ultimate act of violence to oneself" (*Reader's Digest* July 1988, p. 101). The idea that children's values were corrupted by music received considerable play inside and outside the Capitol.

Like *corruption,* the *protection* frame was also introduced around the time of the Senate hearing and was prominent in references to heavy metal music throughout the five-year debate. Similar to the rhetoric found in *corruption,* this frame argued that parents and other adults must shield America's youth from offensive lyrics. Reflecting on her campaign against graphic lyrics, Tipper Gore (1987) wrote:

> We feel as we do because we know that children are special gifts, and deserve to be treated with love and respect, gentleness and honesty. They deserve security and

guidance about living, loving, and relating to other people. And they deserve vigilant protection from the excesses of adult society. (p. 46)

While opinions varied over how best to protect children from the dangers of lyrics (some thought that lyrics should be labeled, while others thought laws should be enacted against harmful music), the underlying theme infusing this argument invoked adult responsibility, particularly as exercised by caring parents. In his discussion of heavy metal, William Safire wrote:

> I am a libertarian when it comes to the actions of consenting adults, and hoot at busybodies who try to impose bans on what non-violent grown-ups can say or read or do. With complete consistency, I am anti-libertarian when it comes to minors. Kids get special protections in law . . . and deserve protection from porn-rock profiteers. (*New York Times* 10 Oct. 1985, sect. 1, p. 31)

Danger to society was a third theme that emerged around the time of the Senate hearing, although arguments containing this frame were used infrequently in relation to the "white" music genre. In contrast to the *corruption* frame, which warned of harm to the individual, the *danger to society* frame warned that when lyrics glorify violence, all of society is at risk. As applied to heavy metal music, the argument focused largely on the satanic influences inherent in some heavy metal music, and warned that vulnerable youths under the music's spell might wreak havoc on innocent citizens. Paul King, a child and adolescent psychiatrist who testified at the Senate hearing on behalf of the PMRC, stated:

> One of the most pathological forms of evil is in the form of the cult killer or deranged person who believes it is OK to hurt others or to kill. The Son of Sam who killed eight people in New York was allegedly into Black Sabbath's music. . . . Most recently, the individual identified in the newspapers as the Night Stalker has been said to be into hard drugs and the music of the heavy metal band AC/DC. . . . Every teenager who listens to heavy metal certainly does not become a killer. [But] young people who are seeking power over others through identification with the power of evil find a close identification. The lyrics become a philosophy of life. It becomes a religion. (U.S. Senate Hearing Before the Committee on Commerce, Science, and Transportation 1985, p. 130)

In addition to cult-like violence, this frame—when it was used vis-à-vis heavy metal—suggested that violence against parents, teachers, and sometimes women could also result from listening to this music.

Of course, the serious charges brought against music lyrics by the PMRC and supportive media writers did not go unanswered, either at the Senate hearings or in the media. Music industry executives, outraged musicians, and media writers hastened to defend the content of contemporary music and the artistic integrity of its creators. These arguments appeared in the counterframes that were produced in this debate.

Frank Zappa, John Denver, and Dee Snider (of the heavy metal band Twisted Sister) kicked off the attack against PMRC activities and concerns when they served as opposing witnesses at the Senate hearing, where these counterframes first widely appeared. One common argument, termed the *no harm* frame, argued that lyrics were not harmful to young listeners. Covering a variety of ideas around this central theme, this frame claimed that youthful audiences know that the cartoonish lyrics are not meant to be taken seriously, that songs with explicit lyrics represent a small minority of music, that music lyrics are a negligible part of the culture's barrage of sexual and violent images in the media, and that there is no causal connection between music and behavior. This last point was picked up by the media—one writer suggested that "the social impact of a heavy metal concert is belching" (*Time* 30 September 1985, p. 70). The *no harm* frame was often used in this sarcastic manner, where the writer argued that music was safe and belittled the concerns of the opposition.

Opponents of the PMRC also suggested that opposition to heavy metal's lyrics could be explained by the generation gap between Gore and her allies, and the youths they sought to protect. The *generation gap* frame was used at the Senate hearing and subsequently to point out that vulgarity, parental anxiety, and censorship are all perennial concerns, and that outrage expressed about music lyrics bespeaks a generation gap between parents and their children. Although this frame's rhetoric is clearly a subset of the *no harm* frame (e.g., the music isn't harmful, parents just perceive it as harmful), it differs from the *no harm* frame by making explicit the role of parents in the controversy surrounding lyrics. In an article that appeared two weeks after the Senate hearing, Russell Baker picked up the theme of misplaced, but predictable, parental concern:

> Stirred by the [PMRC] alarmed mothers, my mind began playing back the full repertory of bawdy, off-color, and just downright dirty songs it had gathered during years when my mother would have cringed if I let on that I knew a more emphatic way of saying "gosh darn it all to the dickens." (*New York Times* 13 Oct. 1985, sect. 6, p. 22)

The *threat to authorities* frame, which is closely related to the *generation gap* frame, suggested that people in positions of political power felt most threatened by contemporary music. Using this argument to ridicule a competing critic's attack on music, one writer complained:

> [Mr. Goldman, a writer for the *National Review*] hallucinates rather luridly: "You needn't go to a slasher film to see a woman being disemboweled in a satanic ritual—just turn on your local music video station." No example is named. Such notions have been a right-wing staple for decades, and they'd be as risible as Mr. Goldman's article if legislators hadn't begun to take them seriously. (*New York Times* 26 Mar. 1989, sect. 2, p. 24)

Here, the conservative right, which traditionally has caused trouble for youth culture, is blamed for the condemnation of music.

Witnesses at the Senate hearing and media writers frequently disparaged the concerns of the PMRC and its supporters by arguing that they advocated censorship. In one of the most colorful exchanges during the hearing, Frank Zappa charged that "the complete list of PMRC demands reads like an instruction manual for some sinister kind of toilet training program to housebreak all composers and performers because of the lyrics of a few" (U.S. Senate Hearing Before the Committee on Commerce, Science, and Transportation 1985, p. 53). The *freedom of speech* frame maintained that labeling albums, printing lyrics on album covers, and encouraging musicians to use restraint restricted artists' First Amendment right to freedom of speech and created a "chilling effect" on expression. By arguing that "the real danger is presented not by rock music, but by those who want to control what should or should not be heard," this frame minimized the perceived threat of graphic lyrics by focusing on the dangers of abridging musicians' freedom of speech (*New York Times* 8 December 1985, sect. 11, p. 40).

In a vivid example of how this discourse about music was a media dialogue, the *freedom of speech* counterframe spawned a countercounterframe from media supporters of the PMRC, who claimed that they did not favor censorship. Writers sympathetic to the PMRC used the *not censorship* frame to defend their positions against accusations of censorship and presented themselves as providers of consumer information (to parents), not as enemies of free speech. Tipper Gore said:

> We do not and have not advocated restrictions on [freedom of speech]; we have never proposed government action. What we are advocating, and what we have worked hard to encourage, is responsibility. (*Newsweek* 29 May 1989, p. 6)

Rap to the Fore: Framing 2 Live Crew

While most of the frames applied to heavy metal music were also applied to rap music, new concerns emerged as writers turned their attention to the "black" music genre. Some of these concerns were expressed in a frame new to the five-year debate, while others were voiced using frames already developed for heavy metal music.

For example, the *danger to society* frame was frequently used to talk about rap music following the arrests of 2 Live Crew in Florida. However, the concerns about the *types* of danger contained in rap lyrics differed sharply from the concerns about heavy metal. Rather than focusing on the dangers of one-in-a-million devil-worshipping mass killers, the *danger to society* frame as applied to rap much more pointedly emphasized that rap music created legions of misogynistic listeners who posed a danger to women, particularly because rap music depicted rape and other brutality. Providing a short inventory of women-harming abuses, one writer argued, "What we are discussing here is the wild popularity (almost 2 million records sold) of a group that sings about forcing anal sex on a girl and then forcing her to lick excrement. . . . Why are we so sure that tolerance of such attitudes has no consequences?" (*U.S. News and World Report* 2 July 1990, p. 15).

One counterframe that was specifically instituted for rap (although it later was occasionally applied to heavy metal) was the *important message/art* frame, which was used most dramatically around the time of the government actions against rap music in Florida.

The *important message/art* frame, which argued against the "harmful" position, asserted that rap lyrics have serious content. The frame includes statements about the important messages and concerns of rap music, the artistic expression contained in the music, the lyrics as a reflection of urban reality, and the fact that rappers were positive role models for young black listeners. Foreshadowing arguments that appeared four months later in the trial over 2 Live Crew lyrics, one media writer stated:

> In its constantly changing slang and shifting concerns—no other pop has so many anti-drug songs—rap's flood of words presents a fictionalized oral history of a brutalized generation. (*New York Times* 17 June 1990, sect. 4, p. 1)

This frame argued that the music itself is worthy of serious contemplation, and that all people—black, white, young, old—could benefit from its important messages.

With the injection of new concerns in the *danger to society* frame and the emergence of the *important message/art* counterframe largely for rap, the set of frames used to analyze the discourse surrounding these two genres of music in the years 1985 through 1990 is complete.

RACIAL RHETORIC: MAPPING THE SHIFT IN FRAMES

The top half of Table 54.1 presents a percentage distribution of types of frames applied to heavy metal and rap music genres in mainstream publications. Mainstream media writers used certain frames about equally in their discussions of heavy metal and rap, suggesting that some frames were applicable to both genres. The *freedom of speech* and *not censorship* frames, for example, were about equally frequent in the discourse about both music forms. Both frames were used in 1985 in reference to heavy metal and continued to characterize the discourse about rap. Other frames, however, were applied primarily to one genre and not the other.

"Music Is Harmful" Frames

A pronounced shift occurred in the frames used to construct the "harmful" discourse in the mainstream media: Frames that were used most frequently to describe the dangers of heavy metal—*corruption* and *protection*—were rarely used to describe the harmfulness of rap music; conversely, the *danger to society* frame was prominent for rap music but not for heavy metal music. Thus, the frames used most often to decry heavy metal music were less salient for rap music, while the frames used most often to condemn rap music were less relevant for heavy metal music. The arguments represented by these frames may have been based on different referent images, given their disparate concerns.

The *corruption* frame, which accounted for more than one-third of all frames supporting the harmfulness of heavy metal music, concerned the music's effects on young listeners' values and behavior (e.g., the lyrics may lead some listeners to indulge in "self-destructive" activities). A corollary to this frame, the *protection* frame, urged parents and other adults to care enough about society's youth to get involved in activities that would guarantee their children's welfare. The *corruption* and *protection* frames together accounted for two-thirds of all "music-is-harmful" frames used in the mainstream press' discussion of heavy metal music.

The power of these frames derived from the referent images they evoked. Articles in which the *corruption* frame appeared often referred to the writers' own children (or children like theirs) being exposed to this dangerous material and the potential suffering because of it. Writer Kathy Stroud reported:

> My 15-year-old daughter unwittingly alerted me to the increasingly explicit nature of rock music. "You've got to hear this Mom!" she insisted one afternoon . . . , "but don't listen to the words," she added, an instant tip-off to pay attention. The beat was hard and pulsating, the music burlesque in feeling. . . . Unabashedly sexual lyrics like these, augmented by orgasmic moans and howls, compose the musical diet millions of children are now being fed at concerts, on albums, on radio and MTV. (*Newsweek* 6 May 1985, p. 14)

And in another article titled "What Entertainers Are Doing to Your Kids," the following passage was one of many that charged that decent children were being exposed to obscene lyrics so that the music industry could profit:

> President Reagan stepped into the fray in mid-October, venting outrage over music's messages. "I don't believe our Founding Fathers ever intended to create a nation where the rights of pornographers would take precedence over the rights of parents, and the violent and malevolent would be given free rein to prey upon our children," the President told a Republican political meeting. According to growing numbers of critics, irresponsible adults in the entertainment business are bedazzling the vulnerable young with a siren song of the darker sides of life. Violence, the occult, sadomasochism, rebellion, drug abuse, promiscuity, and homosexuality are constant themes. (*U.S. News and World Report* 28 October 1985, p. 46)

The frame's implicit message to the reader was that even privileged children from good homes were at risk from the lyrical content of heavy metal music. These arguments contended that *our own kids* were endangered by this music, a message that was absent from the frames used to discuss rap.

While the *corruption* and *protection* frames clearly emphasized the music's harmful effects on individual listeners, writers using these frames expressed little concern that the lyrics would have an unfortunate effect on other members of society. Except for a few references to satanic murders and abusiveness to women, articles using these two frames rarely mentioned the possibility that young listeners might violently direct their new-found rebellion, anti-authority sentiment, and heightened sexuality on the society at large.

The *danger to society* frame argued that changes in attitudes and behaviors stemming from lyrics endangered society as a whole (i.e., listening to lyrics that extol violence and the brutalization of women and police would lead to rape and murder). Nearly two-thirds of the "harmful" frames applied to rap music were the *danger to society* frame, compared to about one-tenth of the frames applied to heavy metal music.

It might be expected that in turning their attention from heavy metal to rap, media writers would have continued using the *corruption* frame and would have argued that rap lyrics harmed young black listeners by spreading messages that would lead to self-destructive behaviors. Because most writers considered rap lyrics to be even more explicit than the heavy metal messages, rap lyrics should have been framed as even more harmful to their young audience. Yet, rather than warning the American public that a generation of young black children was endangered by musical messages, the writers argued that the American public at large would suffer at the hands of these listeners as a result of rap music. Clearly, the listener's welfare was no longer the focus of concern.

Unlike the referent images of "my daughter" and "our own kids" that appeared in articles about heavy metal, the prominent rap frames referred to a very different young listener: a young, urban, black male, or more often a group of urban, black male youths. George Will, drawing on the same images, invoked in the Summer 1990 trial of the alleged Central Park rapists, wrote:

> Fact: some members of a particular age and social cohort—the one making 2 Live Crew rich—stomped and raped [a] jogger to the razor edge of death, for the fun of it. Certainty: the coarsening of a community, the desensitizing of a society will have behavioral consequences. (*Newsweek* 30 July 1990, p. 64)

An article called "Some Reasons for Wilding," which appeared approximately one year before Will's, used the same referent image of the Central Park rape. In this article, Tipper Gore and Susan Baker stated:

> "Wilding." It's a new word in the vocabulary of teenage violence. The crime that made it the stuff of headlines is so heinous, the details so lurid as to make them almost beyond the understanding of any sane human being. When it was over, a 28-year old woman, an investment banker out for a jog, was left brutally beaten, knifed, and raped by teenagers. . . . "It was fun," one of her suspected teenage attackers told the Manhattan district attorney's office. In the lockup they were nonchalantly whistling at a policewoman and singing a high-on-the-charts rap song about casual sex: "Wild Thing." (*Newsweek* 29 May 1989, p. 6)

In this passage, the teenagers—who from media accounts were known to be black and Hispanic—"nonchalantly" whistle and sing rap lyrics following their alleged crime spree. The image of listeners here (minority, urban youths) differs dramatically from the listeners portrayed in articles about heavy metal (white, middle-class teenagers). Furthermore, the referent images of the threats posed by these two groups of youths also changed. Whereas "our kids" listening to heavy metal lyrics might stray off their expected social tracks because of their incited disrespect for authority or early interest in sex, listeners to rap music were lamented not because their self-destructive activities were of great importance or concern, but because they would probably travel in packs, rape women, and terrorize society.

"Music Is Not Harmful" Counterframes

The arguments proclaiming that music was not harmful also shifted as the discussion turned from heavy metal to rap. While the *freedom of speech* and *threat to authorities* frames were used about equally for heavy metal and rap, the mainstream press used the three remaining frames (*generation gap, no harm,* and *important message/art*) differently for the two genres. The *generation gap* frame, which derided parents for following the age-old tradition of disliking their children's music, made up 25 percent of the "not harmful" frames applied in the discourse about heavy metal, but only 3 percent of the frames used in the discourse about rap. Thus, writers on the "not harmful" side of the debate also detected the *parental* concerns that infused the debate about heavy metal—concerns that were largely absent in the debate about rap. That mainstream writers on the "not harmful" side rarely used the *generation gap* frame to defend rap against parental assaults is another indication of invisibility of "parents" and "our kids" in the discourse about rap music.

Just as the *generation gap* frame was used disproportionately to defend heavy metal, so the *important message/art* frame was used asymmetrically by the mainstream press to defend rap. Led by the *New York Times,* 60 percent of the "not harmful" frames used for the "black" genre were the *important message/art* frame, compared to only 14 percent of the frames used for the "white" music form. Mainstream opinion writers described heavy metal music as exaggerated, cartoonish buffoonery that posed no danger to listeners (the *no harm* frame) while they legitimated rap as an authentic political and artistic communication from the streets (the *important message/art* frame). Variously described in the media as "folk art," a "fresh musical structure," a "cultural barometer," and "a communiqué from the underclass," rap was valorized as a serious cultural form by the *New York Times, Newsweek,* and *Time* (but not *U.S. News and World Report* or *Reader's Digest*). As suggested by other authors (Bourdieu [1979] 1984; Thompson 1990), elites, such as writers and readers of the *New York Times,* seem to have exerted a pervasive effort to adopt rap as an "authentic" cultural form (just as jazz, country music, and comic books had been adopted previously), but to dismiss heavy metal as inconsequential—the politically empty macho posturing of white males.

The *important message/art* frame also received considerable play in the two African-American magazines, *Ebony* and *Jet.* Of the 10 articles published about music lyrics in these magazines from 1985 to 1990, all were about rap (presumably the "white" genre was not of concern to black readers' children), and all argued that music was not harmful to children or society. Eight of the ten articles contained the *important message/art* frame.

Articles in *Ebony* and *Jet* consistently valorized rap music, assessing its lyrics as harmless and containing only positive and important messages from and for black youths. The African-American magazines also argued that the older black generation could learn something from rap: By listening to the lyrics of the music, black adults could comprehend the daily lives of their own children. . . .

CONCLUSION

I argue that media writers use frames selectively to represent the stories they tell. They choose from a set of social-cultural images to make their accounts convincing, compelling, and familiar to themselves and to their audiences. Although there are many different icons and memories that could be used to catch readers' imaginations, writers choose the same cultural images and memories over and over again to relate their concerns about an issue. This repeated use of certain images produces recognizable patterns of frames, which media writers use to comment on socially important issues.

In the discourse surrounding the harmfulness of music lyrics from 1985 to 1990, media writers in the mainstream press invoked different frames to address the "white" genre of heavy metal music than they used to discuss the "black" genre of rap music. They constructed images of race and adolescence to tell separate stories of the dangers lurking in the cultural expressions of the two distinct social groups. In doing so, they called upon memories of historical events and cultural icons to demonstrate the detrimental effects of these objects on their audiences and on society as a whole. These racially charged frames were most powerful when they built on the stated or unstated fears and anxieties of readers and tapped into their audience's understandings of what white youths and black youths were like.

Finally, in using these frames, writers provided audiences with a map for understanding what was wrong with the younger generation—whether it was their "own kids" or urban, poor, black kids. This map portrayed a causal relationship between music and behavior and explained phenomena like teen suicide, sex, and violence as consequences of explicit lyrics. These explanatory frames made no reference to such existential conditions as teens' feelings of hopelessness or powerlessness, or to material concerns like diminishing economic prospects. . . .

References

Bourdieu, Pierre. [1979] 1984. *Distinction: A Social Critique of the Judgement of Taste.* Cambridge, MA: Harvard University Press.

Goffman, Erving. 1974. *Frame Analysis.* Cambridge, MA: Harvard University Press.

Gore, Tipper. 1987. *Raising PG Kids in an X-Rated Society.* Nashville, TN: Abingdon Press.

McDonald, James. 1988. "Censoring Rock Lyrics: A Historical Analysis of the Debate." *Youth and Society* 19:294–313.

Peterson, Richard. 1972. "A Process Model of the Folk, Pop, and Fine Art Phases of Jazz," pp. 135–151 in *American Music: From Storyville to Woodstock,* edited by C. Nanry. New Brunswick, NJ: Transaction Books.

Rosenbaum, Jill Leslie and Lorraine Prinsky. 1991. "The Presumption of Influence: Recent Responses to Popular Music Subcultures." *Crime and Delinquency* 37:528–535.

Snow, David, E. Burke Rochford, Steven Worden, and Robert Benford. 1986. "Frame Alignment Processes, Mobilization, and Movement Participation." *American Sociological Review* 51:464–481.

Thompson, John. 1990. *Ideology and Modern Culture.* Palo Alto, CA: Stanford University Press.

U.S. Senate Hearing Before the Committee on Commerce, Science, and Transportation. 1985. *Contents of Music and the Lyrics of Records.* Washington, D.C.: U.S. Government Printing Office.

55

Does Heavy Metal and Rap Music Harm Teenagers?

JONATHON S. EPSTEIN
Kent State University

DAVID J. PRATTO AND JAMES K. SKIPPER, JR.
University of North Carolina, Greensboro

Since its infancy in the 1950s, rock music has frequently come under attack as being a significant contributor to adolescent behavior problems. To the adult world, rock music has been traditionally viewed as foreign and dangerous symptoms of teenage aggression and nonconformity. . . .

The proposition set forth by most rock music opponents is that rock music often presents opinions, attitudes, values, and lifestyles which are contrary to existing adult standards for teenage behavior. The high status given to rock performers by adolescents (Dotter, 1987) leads to teenagers looking toward these performers in an effort to define themselves and form opinions about the world around them. It is further argued that the ideas expressed in rock music are often contrary to adult values and are therefore unwholesome. Because adolescents use this music to define their social milieu, rock music contributes causally to adolescent behavior which is considered inappropriate by adults.

This argument has been used to explain extreme cases of adolescent deviance and delinquency. A recent court case argued that the suicide of a Nevada youth was the result of his listening to excessive amounts of the British heavy metal band, *Judas Priest* (Billard, 1990). King (1988) maintains that extensive involvement in a sub-genre of rock music called "heavy metal" can contribute directly to the practice of what Baker (1990) refers to as violent satanism. Violent satanism reportedly involves both animal and human sacrifice. Gore and Baker (1989) assert that involvement with rap music contributed to an attack on a jogger in New York's Central Park by a group of inner-city youths. A recent shooting incident in a Greensboro, North Carolina,

From *Deviant Behavior*, Vol. II (1990), pp. 381–394. Washington, D.C.: Taylor & Francis, Inc.

housing project reinforced Gore and Baker's argument when the rifles used by the youths in the incident were found to have the initials of the rap band, *NWA*, "Niggers With Attitude," carved on the rifle stock. NWA has recently gained notoriety for its semi-popular song, "Fuck The Police." Interestingly, the attack in Greensboro was, in fact, on a police officer (Barkley, 1990). What links these individual acts of juvenile crime is the claim that involvement with popular music leads to decisions to commit acts of violence.

The converse argument is that popular music is a reflection of the social environment of its target population, or market. For rock music, this market is usually considered to be the 12–20-year-old population. Popular music does not attempt to change attitudes and values, it simply reinforces what already exists. If it did otherwise, it would not be commercially successful, as the popular music industry is mostly concerned with "what fits." From this point of view, rather than causing specific types of deviant behavior, the production of popular music is influenced by the adolescent social environment (Epstein and Pratto, 1990). The music simply reflects already existing adolescent sentiments back to the youth subculture. From this perspective, popular music recreates and affirms teenage behavior, it does not cause or create it.

Two studies provide support for this converse argument. Miller and Skipper (1968) argue that black youth violence during the civil rights movement in the 1960s was widespread before themes of radical protest were incorporated into the music of black artists, particularly the work of avant garde jazz. The music followed social sentiment; it did not lead. Second, Moore, Willis, and Skipper (1979) found that norms of greater sexual freedom were present before so called "arousal" lyrics appeared in rock music. They argued that rock music could not be held responsible for greater promiscuity among youth. Rock lyrics merely reflected the existing sexual norms of youth, but not that of their parents who were less affected by the change in sexual freedom. The music was the music of youth, not of adults. This particular focus may be part of the reason that the adult population viewed rock music as a cause of sexual promiscuity. . . .

HYPOTHESES

There are essentially three assumptions which can be drawn from the arguments of the rock music detractors. These assumption form testable hypotheses. The first is based on the assumption that adolescent music subcultures are oriented to race. While most of the popular literature does not actually state this, it is implied (cf., King, 1988, and Gore, 1987). Literature on heavy metal subculture is, by implication, about white youth; literature on rap is about black youth. This assumption is reinforced both by common experience and the demographic information available on record sales (Perry, 1988).

The second hypothesis drawn from this literature is that musical preference can be used to predict behavior problems. The underlying assertion is that adolescents who express a preference for heavy metal or rap music are more likely to engage in behaviors considered unacceptable when compared to those who express other preferences.

The third hypothesis is, in effect, an extension of the second. It follows from the second hypothesis that the degree of commitment to heavy metal or rap music should be positively related to the probability of behavior problems. The greater the commitment young people have to heavy metal or rap music, the more likely they are to have behavior problems. . . .

METHODS

[To test those three hypotheses] data were collected from a survey administered to all core and special education classes at an optional middle school located in a middle sized southern [metropolitan area]. Eighty students, out of a total school population of 109 on the day the survey was administered, completed the survey. This school was much like the achievement school described by MacLeod in *Ain't No Makin' It* (1987). It served to meet the needs of students who experienced academic or behavior difficulties in a less structured setting. Despite the school's academic focus, the public perception was that it had the highest percentage of behavior problem students in the school system. In reality, a higher proportion of the students attended the school due to academic, rather than behavioral, difficulties. Most students who attend this school are from working or lower class homes, as indicated by an analysis of zip codes and 1980 census information (Sullivan and Fields, 1990). Most reside in one of the local public housing developments. It is tacitly understood by most of the students, as well as by the school staff, that few of the students will continue their education past high school. A large number of the students who do go on to high school enter a vocational track curriculum.

Data were collected in several ways. We collected information during one and one half academic years using participant observation techniques. Further perspective was gained on the music of adolescents by a careful reading of the 1989 issues of the music magazines *Rip* and *Circus*. We collected all record albums which were positively reviewed, in 1989, in either magazine, in an effort to be fully aware of the music preferred by adolescents. We attended a number of heavy metal concerts in order to learn about the concert experience. While no rap concerts were attended, however, students at the school made a large number of rap tapes available to us and we were able to collect an extensive sample of rap music.

Behavioral and academic records for all of the students who participated in the study were provided by the school. Research findings and statistics, generated by a research team working within the school were used for this analysis (Sullivan and Fields, 1990). These statistics included race, age, other demographic information, and types of behavior problems.

Behavior problems were measured by an examination of school records. If one or more of the behavior problems were recorded in the school records, the student was classified as having behavior problems. These behaviors could range from cursing to assaults on school staff members.

Using a survey distributed in the school, we were able to measure musical preference and commitment to that preference for a sample of the student body. This information was then combined with information provided by the school.

To measure musical preference, students were asked to list their favorite type of music, favorite band, last record or CD purchased, and last concert attended. These survey items were open ended. The items referring to favorite band, record purchases, and concert attendance served as control questions for vague or ambiguous answers to the first item asking about musical preference. This was important because of the confusion similar questions about musical preference have caused in previous studies (cf. Hakanen and Wells, 1990). If, for example, a student gave the response "rock" to the first question and went on to indicate that his or her favorite band was *Guns n' Roses,* the last concert attended was *Metallica,* and the last album purchased was by *Slayer,* it was assumed that their musical preference was, in fact, heavy metal.

To measure commitment to their preferred music, students were asked to indicate how much time they spent each day listening to music. Respondents could choose from one of four answers: none, less than one hour, from one to two hours, and more than two hours.

The musical preference and level of commitment were crosstabulated with behavioral problems and race. Chi-Square, with a significance level of 0.1, was used in order to determine even modest relationships that might be evidenced.

RESULTS

A sample of 80 (75 percent) of the 109 students responded to the survey and it adequately represented the demographic composition of the entire school population. The respondents for the survey were 66 percent black and 34 percent white and 82 percent males and 18 percent female. Ages at the school ranged from 11 to 16 with a modal age of 14.

About 95 percent of the respondents to the survey spent at least one hour per day listening to music with 61 percent listening for two or more hours. Only four students listened to less than one hour of music per day.

Two genres of popular music, heavy metal and rap, accounted for 94 percent of musical preferences. The choices of the remaining 6 percent were various other types of pop music. The results of crosstabulating race by musical preference, reported in Table 55.1, supports the first hypothesis. The analysis

TABLE 55.1 Relationship Between Race and Musical Preference Among Middle School Students*

Preference	Race		
	Black	White	Total
Pop	3 (60%)	2 (40%)	5 (100%)
Rap	**52 (98%)**	1 (2%)	53 (100%)
Heavy Metal	1 (4%)	**23 (96%)**	24 (100%)

*Significant for Chi-square (= 67.50, d.f. = 2) alpha = .0001.

indicates that race is a good indicator of musical preference. About 98 percent of the black respondents indicated that rap was their musical preference. About 96 percent of the white respondents indicated that their musical preference was heavy metal. The preference for pop music was more or less equally divided by race, the n being only five. Because of the exceedingly high correlation between race and musical preference, further analysis which included both race and musical preference was not warranted.

The second hypothesis, that musical preference can predict behavior problems, was not supported by the data. Table 55.2 contains the results of crosstabulating musical preference by behavior problems. [The percentage of *rap* fans with problems (40 percent) is exactly the same as the percentage of *pop* fans. While rap fans appear more likely than heavy metal fans to have problems (40 percent vs. 33 percent),] this difference is not statistically significant.

The third hypothesis, that commitment to music can predict behavior problems, was not supported by the data. The results shown in Table 55.3 indicate that commitment to music measured in hours spent listening has no effect on identification as a behavior problem. [In fact, contrary to the hypothesis, those who spent less time listening to music seemed more likely to be identified as having problems, compared with those who spent more time on music (39 percent vs. 37 percent). This difference is not statistically significant, though.]

CONCLUSION

This study tested three hypotheses drawn from assumptions made by rock music detractors. The first hypothesis, that musical preference was associated with race, was supported by the research. The second and third hypotheses, that musical preference and commitment to music could predict behavior problems were not supported. . . .

Heavy metal and rap music are essentially different expressions of similar adolescent sentiments. Both genres address the alienation and powerlessness that reflect the marginal social position of youth in American society. For the teenagers in this study, both alienation and marginal status are a daily reality as evidenced by their enrollment in the optional school. The simple act of

TABLE 55.2   Relationship Between Musical Preference and Behavioral Problems Among Middle School Students*

Behavioral Problem	Musical Preference		
	Pop	Rap	Heavy Metal
Yes	12 (40%)	21 (40%)	8 (33%)
No	3 (60%)	32 (60%)	16 (67%)
Total	15 (100%)	53 (100%)	24 (100%)

*Not significant using Chi-square (= 2,612, d.f. = 2) alpha = 0.1.

TABLE 55.3   Relationship Between Commitment to Music and Behavior Problems Among Middle School Students*

| | Time Spent Listening to Music | |
Behavioral Problem	Less Than 2 Hours	More Than 2 Hours
Yes	12 (39%)	18 (37%)
No	19 (61%)	31 (63%)
Total	31 (100%)	49 (100%)

*Not significant using Chi-square (= 2,612, d.f. = 2) alpha = 0.1.

being optional middle school students sets these young persons apart; it forces further marginal status on an already marginal population.

Despite their popularity, rap and heavy metal are popularly conceived of as [having such negative themes as] sexual promiscuity, drug use, violence, and satanism. [It is true that negative themes make up a certain percentage of the lyrics. But other, more positive topics appear at least as often, including] environmental issues, the dangers of drug use, social responsibility, and the need for critical thinking and honesty (Epstein and Pratto, 1990). A study by Singletary (1983) found that rock music contained less sexual content than two other music genres, soul and country. Somehow, rock music detractors have failed to acknowledge the inconsistency.

An increasing number of rock musicians heavy metal and rap artists included and the music they create have become responsible both to their audience and to broader social issues (Frith, 1981). It is the way in which this responsibility is expressed, in a music that is historically, and by definition, confrontational, that may be the root of the problem. When *NWA* says "fuck the police" it is because they perceive law enforcement officers as being pawns in the white domination, and oppression, of black culture. It is not because they simply do not like police officers and want to cause trouble. It can be argued that what distinguishes heavy metal and rap music from pop is the stance they take toward the hegemonic culture. [Pop reflects and supports] hegemonic values and culture, [while] heavy metal and rap confront and often reject them. The political complexity of this music is often lost in the rhetoric of fear and misunderstanding on the part of its detractors. It is easier for rock music opponents to address the issue of violence present in these musical genres than to address the basis of the rage and violence.

References

Baker, Kandee S. 1990. The Destructive and Non-destructive Cults of Satanic Worship. Paper presented at the Annual Meeting of the Southern Sociological Society, Louisville, KY.

Barkley, Meredith. 1990. "Gunmen Shoot At Officer, Leave Shotguns Left Behind." *Greensboro News and Record.* May 6, p. C8.

Billard Mary. 1990. "Heavy Metal Goes on Trial." *Rolling Stone.* 582/583 July: 83–87.

Dotter, Daniel. 1987. "Growing Up is Hard To Do: Rock and Roll Performers as Cultural Heroes." *Sociological Spectrum.* 7 (1):25–44.

Epstein, Jonathon S. and David J. Pratto. 1990. "Heavy Metal Rock Music, Juvenile Delinquency and Satanic Identification." *Popular Music and Society.* 14(4):67–76.

Frith, Simon. 1981. *Sound Effects.* New York: Pantheon.

Frith, Simon. 1985. Is Pop Music Culture? Paper presented at the Conference on Music and Society.

Gore, Tipper. 1987. *Raising PG Kids in an X-Rated Society.* Nashville: Abingdon.

Gore, Tipper and Susan Baker. 1989. "Some Reasons for Wilding." *Newsweek* 113: 6–7.

Hakanen, Ernest and Alan Wells. 1990. Adolescent Music Marginals Who Likes Metal, Jazz, Country and Classical. Paper presented at the Annual Meeting of the North Central Sociological Association, Louisville, KY.

King, Paul. 1988. *Sex, Drugs and Rock n' Roll.* Bellevue, WA: Professional Counselor Books.

McLeod, Jay. 1987. *Ain't No Makin' It.* Boulder, CO: Westview.

Miller, Lloyd and James K. Skipper Jr. 1968. "Sounds of Protest Jazz and the Militant Avant Garde," pp. 128–140 in Mark Lefton, James K Skipper Jr. and Charles McCaghy (Eds.), *Approaches to Deviance Theories, Concepts, and Research Findings.* New York: Appleton Century Crofts.

Moore, Mike, Cecil Willis, and James K. Skipper Jr. 1979. "Rock and Roll: Arousal Music as a Reflection of Changing Sexual Mores," pp. 481–485 in Mark Cook and G. Wilson (Eds.), *Studies in Love and Attraction.* London: Pergamon.

Perry, Steve. 1988. "Ain't No Mountain High Enough: The Politics of Cross Over," pp. 51–87 in Simon Frith (Ed.), *Facing the Music.* New York: Pantheon.

Singletary, M. W. 1983. "Some Perceptions of the Lyrics of Three Types of Recorded Music: Rock, Country and Soul." *Popular Music and Society* 9(1):51–63.

Sullivan, Matthew and Larry D. Fields. 1990. The Delineation of Specific Student Characteristics Within an Optionally Placed Middle School. Paper presented at the Fourth Annual Dropout Prevention and Students at Risk Conference, Raleigh, NC.

Index